**CHEFS AND C[...]**
*JOY OF[...]*

measurement
conversion p. 283-287
BK. 2

# VOLUME 1
## MAIN COURSE DISHES

# Joy
## OF
## COOKING

## Irma S. Rombauer
## Marion Rombauer Becker

### Illustrated by Ginnie Hofmann
### and Ikki Matsumoto

## A SIGNET BOOK

SIGNET
Published by the Penguin Group
Penguin Putnam Inc., 375 Hudson Street,
New York, New York 10014, U.S.A.
Penguin Books Ltd, 27 Wrights Lane,
London W8 5TZ, England
Penguin Books Australia Ltd, Ringwood,
Victoria, Australia
Penguin Books Canada Ltd, 10 Alcorn Avenue,
Toronto, Ontario, Canada M4V 3B2
Penguin Books (N.Z.) Ltd, 182–190 Wairau Road,
Auckland 10, New Zealand

Penguin Books Ltd, Registered Offices:
Harmondsworth, Middlesex, England

Published by Signet, an imprint of Dutton Signet,
a member of Penguin Putnam Inc.

Published by arrangement with Scribner, an imprint of Simon & Schuster, Inc.
Originally published by The Bobbs-Merrill Company, Inc.

First Signet Printing, November, 1997
10  9  8  7  6  5  4  3  2  1

To friends of the **Joy** who over the years through their countless letters and words of appreciation have made us feel that our efforts are worthwhile.

*"That which thy fathers have bequeathed to thee,
earn it anew if thou wouldst possess it."*

—GOETHE: *Faust*

# ACKNOWLEDGMENTS

**Joy** has always been a family affair. Written by my mother, Irma Starkloff Rombauer, a St. Louisan, it was tested and illustrated by me, with technical assistance from my mother's secretary, Mary Whyte Hartrich. It was privately printed in 1931 and distributed from the home. The responses **Joy** evoked were collected and published on its thirtieth birthday in a celebratory account entitled *Little Acorn*. Now over forty, **Joy** continues to be a family affair, revealing more than ever the awareness we all share in the growing preciousness of food.

Since his retirement from architectural practice, my husband, John, has given constant and unstinting effort toward **Joy's** enrichment. My sons—Ethan, with his Cordon Bleu and camping experiences, and Mark, with his interest in natural foods—have reinforced **Joy** in many ways, as has my own sensitivity over the years to a oneness with the environment, culminating in the highly satisfying experience of writing *Wild Wealth* with ecologists Frances Jones Poetker and Paul Bigelow Sears.

As the scope of **Joy** has increased, so have other generous sources of proffered knowledge—too many and too specialized to mention in detail. Ever-ready understanding has continued to come from Jane Brueggeman, our valued co-worker for thirty years; from our competent home economics consultants Lolita Harper and Lydia Cooley; from our legal literary aide, Harriet Pilpel; from our guide to the New York cooking world, Cecily Brownstone; and from our kitchen mainstay, Isabell Coleman. More recently we have received thorough testing help from Joan Woerndle Becker, devoted editorial advice from Marian Judell Israel, and perfectionist secretarial assistance from Nancy Swats. Throughout the years Leo Gobin, now president of Bobbs-Merrill, has guarded for us great freedom in our work, and Eugene Rachlis, the editor-in-chief, has lent a sympathetic ear. Thanks also to Gladys Moore, our copy editor, for unending patience; to William Bokermann for the excellent book design; and to John van Biezen for his care in the physical production of this edition. We are sure our readers are as grateful as we are to Ginnie Hofmann and Ikki Matsumoto, whose drawings so skillfully enhance our text.

But **Joy,** we hope, will always remain essentially a family affair, as well as an enterprise in which its authors owe no obligation to anyone but themselves and you.

—MARION ROMBAUER BECKER

# CONTENTS

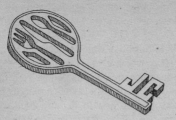

# FOREWORD

We present you first with the front-door key to this book. Whenever we emphasize an important principle, we insert a pointer to success ♦. We use other graphic symbols, too—❋, ▲, ( ), ◗, 人, 目, ★—described on the next page to alert you quickly to foods appropriate for certain occasions or prepared by certain methods. Among the symbols is the parenthesis, which indicates that an ingredient is optional. Its use may enhance, but its omission will not prejudice the success of a recipe. ♦ Note, too, the special meanings of the following terms as we use them. Any meat, fish, or cereal, unless otherwise specified, is raw, not cooked. Eggs are the 2-ounce size; milk means fresh whole milk; butter is sweet and unsalted; chocolate means bitter baking chocolate; flour denotes the unbleached all-purpose variety; spices are ground, not whole; condensed canned soup or milk is to be used undiluted. In response to many requests from users of the **Joy** who ask "What are your favorites?" we have indicated some by adding to a few recipe titles the word "Cockaigne," which in medieval times signified "a mythical land of peace and plenty" and which we chose as the name for our country home. Where a recipe bears a classic title, you can be assured that it contains the essential ingredients or methods that created its name in the first place. And for rapidity of preparation we have grouped in Brunch, Lunch and Supper Dishes many quickly made recipes based on cooked and canned food.

There is a back-door key, too—the Index. This will open up for you and lead you to such action terms as simmer, casserole, braise, and sauté; such descriptive ones as printanière, bonne femme, rémoulade, allemande, and meunière; and to national culinary enthusiasms such as couscous, Devonshire cream, strudel, zabaglione, rijsttafel and gazpacho.

Other features of this book which we ask you to investigate include the chapter on Heat, which gives you many clues to maintaining the nutrients in the food you are cooking. Know Your Ingredients reveal vital characteristics of the materials you commonly combine, how and why they react as they do, how to measure them and, when feasible how to substitute one for another. Then, in the paragraphs marked "About," you will find information relating to those food categories including the amounts to buy.

But, even more important, we hope that in answering your question "What shall we have for dinner?" you will find in Foods We Eat a stimulus to combine foods wisely. Using this information, you may say with Thomas Jefferson, "No knowledge can be more satisfactory to a man than that of his own frame, its parts, their functions and actions." Choose from our offerings what suits your person, your lifestyle, your pleasure; and join us in the joy of cooking.

—M.R.B.

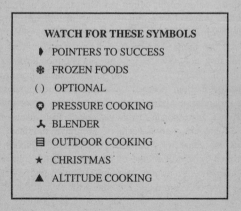

WATCH FOR THESE SYMBOLS
- POINTERS TO SUCCESS
- ✳ FROZEN FOODS
- ( ) OPTIONAL
- PRESSURE COOKING
- BLENDER
- OUTDOOR COOKING
- ★ CHRISTMAS
- ▲ ALTITUDE COOKING

# THE FOODS WE EAT

Put this puzzle together and you will find milk, cheese and eggs, meat, fish, beans and cereals, greens, fruits and root vegetables—foods that contain our essential daily needs.

Exactly how they interlock and in what quantities for the most advantageous results for every one of us is another puzzle we must try to solve for ourselves, keeping in mind our age, body type, activities, the climate in which we live, and the food sources available to us. How we wish someone could present us with hard and fast rules as to how and in what exact quantities to assemble the proteins, fats and carbohydrates as well as the small but no less important enzyme and hormone systems, the vitamins, and the trace minerals these basic foods contain so as best to build body structure, maintain it, and give us an energetic zest for living!

Where to turn? Not to the sensational press releases that follow the discovery of fascinating bits and pieces about human nutrition; nor to the oversimplified and frequently ill-founded dicta of food faddists that can lure us into downright harm. ► First we must search for the widest variety of the best grown unsprayed foods we can find in their freshest condition, and then look for foods with minimal but safe processing and preservatives and without synthetic additives. While great strides have been made in the storage of foods commercially and in the home, ► if fresh foods in good condition are available to you, choose them every time. To compare the nutritive values in frozen, canned and fresh vegetables, (see II, 607–609).

Next we can find in the *U.S. Handbook on the Composition of Foods* some of the known calorie, protein and other values based on the edible portions of common foods. Recent mandatory labeling information, 11–12, is of some help, although the U.S. Recommended Daily Allowances are based on information from a nongovernmental agency, the National Research Council, a source not acceptable to some authorities. But no one chart or group of charts is the definitive answer for most of us, who are simply not equipped to evaluate the complex relationships of these elements, or to adapt them to the practicalities of daily living. Such studies are built up as averages, and thus have greater value in presenting an overall picture than in solving our individual nutrition problems.

Nevertheless, by applying plain common sense to available mass data, we as well as the experts are inclined to agree that many Americans are privileged to enjoy superabundance ▶ and that our nutritional difficulties have to do generally not with under- but with overeating. Statistics on consumption also bear out other trends: first, that we frequently make poor choices and eat too much of the wrong kinds of foods; second, that many of us overconsume drugs as well as foods. Medication, often a lifesaver, may, when used habitually, induce an adverse effect on the body's ability to profit fully from even the best dietary intake.

Individually computerized diagnoses of our lacks may prove a help in adjusting our deficiencies to our needs. But what we all have in our bodies is one of the greatest of marvels: an already computerized but infinitely more complex built-in system that balances and allocates with infallible and almost instant decision what we ingest, sending each substance on its proper course to make the most of what we give it. And since nutrition is concerned not only with food as such but with the substances that food contains, once these essential nutrients are chosen, their presentation in the very best state for the body's absorption is the cook's first and foremost job. Often taste, flavor and color at their best reflect this job well done. Read The Foods We Heal, 91, and follow our pointers to success for effective ways to preserve essential nutrients during cooking. An note at the point of use recommendations for optimum storage and handling conditions, for one must always bear in mind the fragility of food and the many ways contaminants can affect them, and consequently us, when they are carelessly handled or even when such a simple precaution as washing the hands before preparing foods is neglected.

But now let's turn to a more detailed view of nutritional terms: calories, proteins, fats, carbohydrates, accessory factors like vitamins, minerals, enzymatic and hormonal fractions—all of which are needed—and see how they interact to maintain the dietary intake best suited to our individual needs.

## ABOUT CALORIES

A too naïve theory used to prevail for explaining regeneration through food. The human system was thought of as an engine, and you kept it stoked with foods to produce energy. Food can be and still is measured in units of heat, or calories. A **calorie**, sometimes called a kilocalorie or K calorie, is the amount of heat needed to raise one kilogram of water one degree Centigrade. Thus translated into food values, each gram of protein in egg, milk, meat or fish is worth four calories; each gram of carbohydrate in starches and sugars or in vegetables, four calories; and each gram of fat in butters, in vegetable oils and drippings, and in hidden fats, 8, about nine calories. The mere stoking of the body's engine with energy-producing foods may keep life going in emergencies. But to maintain health, food must also have, besides its energy values, the proper proportions of biologic values. Proteins, vitamins, enzymes, hormones, minerals and their regulatory functions are still too complicated to be fully understood. But fortunately for us the body is able to respond to them intuitively.

What we really possess, then, we repeat, is not just a simple stoking mechanism, but a computer system far more elaborate and knowledgeable than anything that man has been able to devise. Our job is to help it along as much as possible, neither stinting it nor overloading it. Depending on age, weight and activity the following is a rough guide to ▶ the favorable division of daily caloric intake: a minimum of 15% for proteins, under 25% for fats, and about 60% for carbohydrates. These percentages are relative: some people with highly efficient absorption and superior metabolism require both lower intake and the lesser amount of protein. No advice for reducing is given here, nor are the vaunted advantages of unusually high protein intake considered—as again such decisions must be highly individual, see About Proteins, 4. In general, and depending also on age, sex, body type and amount of physical activity, adults can use 1700 to 3000 calories a day. Adolescent boys and very active men under fifty-five can utilize close to 3000 calories a day. At the other extreme, women over fifty-five need only about 1700 calories. Women from eighteen to thirty-five need about 2000 calories daily. During pregnancy they can add 200 calories and, during lactation, an extra 1000 calories. Children one to six need from 1100 to 1600. Before a baby's first birthday, his diet should be closely watched, and parents should ask their pediatricians about both the kinds and the amounts of food to give their baby.

Given your present weight, perhaps a more accurate way to calculate your individual calorie requirement is to consider your activity rate. If you use a car to go to work and have a fairly sedentary job, or even if you are a housewife with small children, your rate is probably only 20%; 30% if you are a delivery man or patrolman working out of doors, and 50% if you are a dirt farmer, construction worker or athlete in training. If you multiply your weight by 14 calories, you will get your basal need, that is, the calories you would require if you were completely inactive. When you multiply this amount by your own activity factor and add it to your basal needs, you should get an approximation of your required daily caloric intake. If you reduce your caloric intake much below this approximate norm, you may be lacking in your mineral, vitamin and protein requirements. Whatever your caloric intake, distribute your choices properly among protein, fat and carbohydrate values.

## ABOUT PROTEINS

On our protein intake depends the constant virtual replacement of self. And nowhere in the diet is the relation of quantity to quality greater. The chief components of proteins are 22 amino acids. They form an all-or-nothing team, for food is utilized by the body only in proportion to the presence of the scarcest of them. Fourteen of the 22 aminos are both abundant and versatile. If they are not present when food is ingested, the body is able to synthesize the missing ones from those present. The remaining 8 aminos, however, cannot be synthesized and must be present in the food when ingested. These eight are known as the **essential aminos**. Four of them—leucine, valine, phenylalanine and threonine—are relatively abundant in foods, but the other four—isoleucine, lysine, methionine and tryptophan—are more scarce. And because utilization of protein by the body depends in each instance on the least abundant member of the essential aminos, these latter four are known as the **key aminos**.

Generally speaking, proteins from animal sources like egg, meat, fish, and dairy products are valued because their total protein content is high, and they are referred to as **complete** because they are rich in the essential aminos, and therefore more of the total protein present is utilizable. Those from vegetable sources such as whole grains, nuts, seeds, and legumes—with the exception of soybeans—are less valuable because their total protein content is low. They are referred to as **incomplete** because they are also low in one or more of the eight essential amino acids, meaning that less of their total protein can be utilized by the body. The terms "complete" and "incomplete" are somewhat misleading, however, because of their absolute connotations. It is still possible to fulfill your daily requirements for protein from incomplete vegetable sources, provided you are willing and able to consume large enough quantities of the incomplete protein item in question. But the utilizable protein content of most cereals is so poor that consuming enough to satisfy protein requirements would be a practical impossibility.

Take corn, for example. It has little protein and many starch calories. A diet based exclusively on corn would require consumption of enormous quantities of corn to establish the needed essential aminos. A complete protein source like eggs would therefore be more realistic and desirable in satisfying the same protein requirement with far less caloric intake. In fact, for 10 grams of egg protein at 125 calories, you would have to eat 16.5 grams of corn protein at 500 calories to get an equivalent amount of usable protein. But since no one wants to live on corn or eggs alone, a more reasonable way to approach the problem is to note how complete and incomplete proteins complement each other.

There are various ways of expressing protein values—net protein utilization, or NPU; protein efficiency ratio, or PER; and biologic value, or BV. Another unit of measure used on product labels is protein value in relation to casein, 11. Although these terms are all derived by different methods, they correlate well with each other. Whatever the method of expressing this utilization efficiency, one fact remains: that is, the body requires certain kinds and amounts of essential amino acids which must be supplied each day.

Any excess intake of amino acids not compensated for is metabolized away and thus not used for growth or maintenance of the body. Eggs, with a BV of 94, may be considered the most ideal protein from the point of view of utilization to replace body protein. But we can't survive on one food alone.

If we combine durum wheat, with a BV of 60, and lima beans, with a BV of 50, we get through their complementarity of utilizable protein a score of 60. But a BV of 60 is marginal for body replacement, and so a more complete protein such as that contained in milk or eggs should be added to such a meal. Combine, for instance, 1 tablespoon of peanut butter, with a BV of 43, and one slice of white bread, with a BV of 52. If you add 4 ounces of milk, with a BV of 86, the combination stabilizes at a BV of approximately 80.

In countries dependent mainly on beans and rice or other cereal combinations, the beneficial effects of adding to the diet even small amounts of meat, fish, eggs or dairy products is well recognized. And when various pastas are the staple foods, the inclusion of at least one-third in the form of a complete protein is considered the minimal amount to bring the meal up to acceptable levels. Furthermore, it should be stressed that any meal or snack which fails to include sufficient complete protein, although it may temporarily stay one's hunger, will not replenish all of the metabolic losses of the body.

In regions where only vegetable protein is available, grains combined with pulses such as beans and peas are classic. It has been found that increments of about one-third complete

protein reinforce incomplete protein to form a total that is greater than the sum of its parts.

Even more significant differences are found between processed and unprocessed foods. Brown rice has a BV of 75, as opposed to white rice with a BV of 65. Whole wheat bread has a BV of 67; white bread, 52.

To meet the needs of underdeveloped areas and the threat of worldwide protein shortages, in recent years experiments involving grain, seed and legume combinations, 175, have been undertaken which may one day prove valuable to all of us. Gross nutritional deficiencies are more conspicuous in areas where protein imbalances are drastic and prolonged, and the effects of improved diet are easier to evaluate than in areas like ours, where such deficiencies are less severe and thus harder to detect. Until recently, we have relied on animal experimentation, and although dietary results thus achieved are valuable, they are not always applicable to man, and, for the most reliable results, data must be based on human reactions.

◗ Since vegetable proteins are incomplete except as noted above, it is wise to draw two-thirds of the daily protein intake or 10% of your caloric intake from animal sources. Preferably, meats should be fresh—not pickled, salted or highly processed. ◗ Protein foods when cooked should not be subjected to too high heat, for then they lose some of their nutrients. Familiar danger signals are curdling in milk, "stringiness" in cheese and dryness in meat and fish.

Protein requirements generally are slightly higher in colder climates ◗ but no matter what the climate, growing children, pregnant women and nursing mothers need a larger proportion of protein than the average adult. The elderly, whose total caloric intake often declines with age, should consume a relatively larger percentage of protein to reinforce their body's less efficient protein metabolism. Again, absolute amounts cannot be given, because needs will depend on the efficiency of utilization by your own body. If your protein supply is largely from meats, fish, fowl and dairy products, a useful formula for calculating average daily protein intake is to allow .4 gram of protein per pound of body weight for adults, and for children from one to three years, 1 gram of protein per pound of body weight. In vegetarian diets structured on vegetable sources alone, with no animal by-products such as eggs and milk, careful balancing is needed to ensure enough complete protein. It is also suggested that the protein content of such a diet be upped from .4 to .5 gram per pound of body weight.

Experiments have shown variations in protein utilization between individuals to be as high as two to one. They have also demonstrated that an individual's protein needs may rise by one-third when he is under great physical or emotional stress. A natural luster in hair, firmness of nails, brightness of eyes and speed of healing are superficial indications of a well-being that comes from adequate protein intake. For a listing of approximate protein content—complete, incomplete and mixed—in average servings of individual foods, see 14.

Today, we cannot mention protein and protein sources without looking beyond our own frontiers. With overpopulation a world problem, can we continue our upward trend in meat consumption? Amounts of land required to produce protein increase by a ratio of one to ten as we proceed from the beginning to the end of the food chain: that is, from the growing plant to meat-eating man. To put it another way, the herbivorous animal must consume about 10 pounds of vegetable or cereal matter to turn it into 1 pound of meat. Or, as another example, the same amount of land is required to produce 10 pounds of soybeans as 1 pound of beef. You can readily see that there is protein waste in this type of food production.

As long as chickens scratched more or less on their own; as long as pigs scavenged family wastes; as long as cattle ingested grasses from lands often too rough or too dry for efficient grain harvesting, a something-for-nothing process existed. Today's animal husbandry competes in the main for crops that could also be utilized by humans. Chickens fed in batteries, pigs and cattle concentrated in feed lots need preprocessed foods and drugs to prevent the diseases these abnormal living conditions encourage. And their droppings, once recycled on the land, are too often uselessly burned or channeled into our streams, thus initiating gross pollution of air and water.

But should conditions be changed to allot greater quantities of grains, seeds and pulses to human consumption, we would still be faced with the problem of incomplete vegetable protein. As the growing of soybeans, the only complete-protein plant, is limited to certain climates, other vegetable protein sources must be improved or compensated for by combinations of grains and pulses or by the addition of some complete animal protein.

However, amazing genetic advances have been made in the development of grain hybrids, (II, 213), higher both in protein content and in yield than the older types: short, sturdy, storm-resistant, heavy-headed wheat and rice hybrids, rich in protein and quick-maturing; high-lysine corns; and the intergeneric rye-and-wheat hybrid, triticale, are among the recent developments that promise primary improvements in natural sources of vegetable protein. Vegetable protein mixtures, see 5, combined with dry milk or fish meals, now mainly used for animal feeding, would find greater human acceptance if they were made more palatable, which in turn would guarantee a tremendous advance in protein availability at low cost for all. Protein has also been developed from yeasts, algae, kelp and petroleum products, and there is even the possibility of recycling the proteins in animal wastes; but, again, unpalatability has kept most of these newer protein sources from the table.

It is of the utmost importance that we guard our ecological soundness with all the knowledge we have at hand—knowledge that in some fields is far in advance of our willingness to apply it. It is essential that we consider new methods of utilizing and conserving land, for many of our soils are exploited to the point of depletion and are yielding crops with reduced protein and mineral content. Other soils produce only when saturated with chemical fertilizers and develop an inability to recover crop yields without revitalization through either animal or green manuring.

We must also be on the alert for various air pollutants. Spinach and romaine, for instance, will not grow where the air-sulfur content is high, and acreage yields of grains and other vegetables in such areas are adversely affected as well. Further research is needed to explain why saltwater fish die in waters made up from our formula for seawater but will thrive in natural seawater. Readings of chromatograms of synthetic as opposed to natural vitamins reveal startling differences which are as yet unexplained. These instances would indicate there are present in natural substances certain micronutrients—as yet not completely identified—which an organism needs in order to carry on vital internal chemical processes and which are lacking in engineered or synthetically produced foods, (II, 193).

Further research and development of genetic seedbanks, now in their infancy, are needed to maintain efficient seed strains as the wild areas where natural hybridization has taken place are impinged on. For many of our best strains still come from fortuitous rather than man-induced selection. There is an unfortunate tendency to utilize these new seed strains in all areas before their climatic and soil adaptability has been proved, procedures that make them vulnerable to massive failure.

Again, just as variety in the selection of the foods we eat is necessary for our health, a variety of seed sources is essential to maintain the health of our foods. The breeding of plants resistant to disease, drought and insects, and tolerant of varying climates, is as important as hybridization aimed at protein increase. We like to keep in mind the wise old Indian who, when asked why he continued to grow three strains of corn when only one was his favorite for food, yield and flavor, answered that he was hedging his bets; the other two strains would always protect him against a too dry or too cold season or against insect infestation, while his favorite would succumb unless conditions were ideal.

We cannot leave our ecological

musings without stressing the importance of these fundamental interrelationships, as complex and subtle in the world of edible plants as are those of the protein combinations and their subsequent utilization by the body, as discussed on page 7.

Although most grains are wind-pollinated, few of us realize how large and often unexpected a role insect life plays in pollination, and how insecticides can destroy this vital link in the food chain. The current abundance of fruit and vegetables in America can be traced in large part to the importation of the honeybee. The Indians had an excess of arable land, but for many of their crops they had to rely on much less efficient native pollinators such as noncolonizing bees, wasps and flies. Today, guarding against losing helpful insects is as important as destroying insect enemies—a fact stressed less often than is the need to solve the equally knotty problem of pesticide poisons in the food chain. We can no longer afford to ignore the interrelationships on which global food supplies depend.

## ABOUT FATS

While fats have acquired a bad image of late, we must not forget how essential they are. As part of our body fabric ◗ they act as fuel and insulation against cold, as cushioning for the internal organs, and as lubricants. Without fats there would be no way to utilize fat-soluble vitamins. Furthermore, the fats we eat that are of vegetable origin contain unsaturated fatty acids which harbor necessary growth factors and help with the digestion of other fats. An important consideration in fat intake is the percentage of saturated to unsaturated fats. We hear and read much about cholesterol—that essential constituent of all body cells. It is synthesized, and its production regulated, by the liver. Cholesterol performs a number of indispensable body functions. Up to a limit, the more of it we eat, the less the liver produces. Excess cholesterol intake, however, like other excesses, is to be avoided, since a surplus of cholesterol may have serious consequences. The fatty acids in the **saturated fats,** which are derived from dairy products, animal fats, coconut oil and hydrogenated fats, (II, 202), tend to raise the amount of cholesterol in the blood, while the fatty acids in **polyunsaturated vegetable oils** tend to lower cholesterol levels if taken in double proportion to saturated fats. To differentiate between these types of fat, see (II, 199).

Few of us realize that much of the fat we consume—like the great mass of an iceberg—is hidden. Hamburgers and doughnuts, all-American classics, contain about one-fourth fat; chocolate, egg yolk and most cheeses about a third; bacon and peanut butter, as much as one-half. And in pecans and certain other nuts and

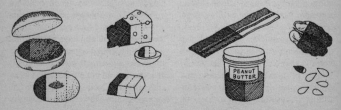

seeds, the fat content can be almost three-fourths! These proportions are graphically suggested on 8.

All fats are sensitive to high temperatures, light and air. For best nutritive values store them carefully; and when cooking with them be sure that you do not let them reach the smoking point, (II, 203). If properly handled they have no adverse effect on normal digestion. Favorable temperatures are indicated in individual recipes. Fats are popular for the flavor they impart to other foods, and for the fact that, being slow to leave the stomach, they give a feeling of satiety.

◗ We suggest, again, the consumption of a variety of fats from animal and vegetable sources, but remind you that fat consumption in the United States has climbed in twenty years from the recommended minimum of 20% to more than 40% today.

## ABOUT CARBOHYDRATES

Carbohydrates, found largely in sugars, fruits, vegetables and cereals, are classed as starches or sugars. The sugars include monosaccharides, such as fruit sugars, (II, 228), and honey, (II, 229), which are sweeter than the disaccharides, such as common table sugar, and the polysaccharides, such as starch. The latter two types must be broken down into simple sugars before they are available for body use. This action is initiated by an enzyme in the saliva, which means that these complex starch carbohydrates should be carefully chewed. So dunking is not only bad manners but bad practice.

The caloric value of fruits and vegetables is frequently lower than that of cereals, while that of all concentrated sweets is higher. Children and athletes can consume larger amounts of

sugars and starches with less harm than can relatively inactive people; but many of us tend to eat a greater amount of carbohydrates than we can handle. Our consumption of sweet and starchy foods, to say nothing of highly sweetened beverages, is frequently excessive. Since the 1900s U.S. sugar consumption has increased by 25%, mainly in foods commercially prepared before they come into the home, making our per capita intake of these empty calories 103 pounds annually. The imbalance that results is acknowledged to be one of the major causes of malnutrition, for the demands excess carbohydrates make on the system may cause, among other dietary disturbances, a deficiency in its supply of the vitamin B complex. For itemized Calorie Values, see 14.

## ACCESSORY FACTORS

Besides those already described, there are some fifty-odd important known nutrients required by the body, including minerals, vitamins, and other accessory factors. The body can store a few of these, such as the fat-soluble vitamins, A, D, E and K, but others, such as the water-soluble vitamins B complex and C, must continually be replaced. The latter occur in those fragile food constituents that are lost through indifferent handling, excessive processing and poor cooking. For instance, ◗ if you fail to utilize vegetable cooking waters, you are throwing out about one-third the minerals and water-soluble vitamins of the vegetable. To retain as much of them as possible, please follow the cooking suggestions given in subsequent chapters, and see About Stocks, (II, 167).

If you maintain an adequate intake in such a way as to achieve the complete-protein and fat and carbo-hydrate balance described on page 9, and if you choose from the following food groups, you will probably in-clude all the necessary accessory fac-tors. So fill your market basket first ♦ so as to assure two 3-ounce servings of complete-protein foods daily—meat, fish, fowl or eggs. Or, if you use combinations of incomplete pro-teins such as cereals and legumes, seeds, peanuts or gelatin, make sure you plan for the inclusion of some complete-protein food at the same meals, see 12–13.

♦ Drink daily or use in cooking 2 cups of fresh milk or reconstituted dry milk, (II, 185), or allow enough of the following milk equivalents: for each 1/2 cup of milk allow 1 cup ice cream, 1/3 cup cottage cheese or one 1-inch cube cheddar-type cheese. If you are one of those persons lacking the ability to digest the lactose in milk, get your major milk require-ments from cheeses, which are low in lactose.

♦ Plan four or more daily servings of starchy foods such as baked goods, cereals or pastas, accenting whole grains. Potatoes are sometimes in-cluded in this group.

♦ Also include daily four or more 1/2- to 3/4-cup servings of fruits and vegetables distributed among citrus fruits or tomatoes and three or more dark green or deep yellow fruits and vegetables, including preferably one raw leafy green vegetable.

♦ Also check the constituents of each meal for the bulk found in vege-tables and fruits to make sure there are more high- than low-residue foods.

Foods abundant in accessory val-ues include: eggs, cheese, butter, whole milk, egg yolks, fish—especially her-ring, salmon, tuna and shellfish; beans, peas, nuts, seeds and whole

grains; red meats and pork, variety meats, 638; fresh vegetables—espe-cially the yellow and leafy green types—including white and sweet potatoes, brown rice and yellow corn; fresh fruits and berries and their juices; tomatoes and tomato juice; cab-bage, spinach and cauliflower, as well as watercress, lettuces and other salad greens, and vegetable oils, (II, 202). Bake with whole grains and flavor with brown sugars, molasses, wheat germ and butter. Don't forget to ingest one of the important accessory values, vitamin D, which you can get through exposure to sunlight, and remember that although outdoor exercise will tone your muscles and increase your oxygen intake—and perhaps your calorie needs—it will not necessarily make greater demands on your store of protein, vitamins or minerals.

If you have chosen wisely from the above substances, you may not need additional vitamin supplements. We all know from practical experience and statistical evidence that a well-nourished body has greater resistance to disease than a poorly nourished one. Recent research tends to support the thesis that adequate intake of accessory factors can contribute not only to disease resistance but also to disease prevention.

Other incidentals to bear in mind are: drink 5 to 7 glasses of fluid a day, including water, and, if you live in a region that calls for it, use iodized salt, see About Salts, (II, 247).

The schedule outlined above is not necessarily a costly one. It is nearly always possible to substitute cheaper but equally nutritious items from the same food groups. Vegetables of simi-lar accessory value, for example, may be differently priced. Seasonal foods, which automatically give us menu variations, are usually higher in food value and lower in cost. You can also profitably grow your own. Whole-grain cereals are no more costly than highly processed ones. Fresh fruits are frequently less expensive than canned fruits, which are often loaded with sugar.

If you are willing to cut down on sugar-laden processed cereals and other sugar items, especially fancy baked goods, bottled drinks, and candies, a higher percentage of the diet dollar will be released for dairy products, vegetables and fruits. ♦ Do not buy more perishable foods than you can properly store. Use leftovers cold, preferably. To reheat them with minimal loss, see 286.

To sum up, our fundamental effort always must be to provide this highly versatile body of ours with those elements it needs for efficient functioning, and to provide them in such proportions as to subject the body to the least possible strain.

However, not realizing the importance of variety in the selection of foods, some people are guided by calorie values alone. For instance, with bread and potatoes, almost equal in carbohydrates, you will find that bread scores higher in protein and fat factors but potatoes are greatly superior in iron, provitamin A, vitamin C and thiamin, all valuable accessory factors. Some help in making choices is available through product labeling. If any prepared and packaged food shipped in interstate commerce makes nutritional claims as to protein, fat, carbohydrate, calories, vitamins, minerals or enrichment, it must have labels declaring certain nutrient contents and giving both serving size and servings per container. The food processor has the option of declaring fatty acid and/or cholesterol content. He may also indicate the sodium content in the food. Because of differences in protein quality, two levels of protein intake are shown according to the protein efficiency ratio, 13, of casein: foods with levels equal to or greater than casein, and foods with less than casein values. ♦ If a food has less than 20% of the PER of casein, its label cannot declare that it is a source of protein. Sometimes labels indicate the percentages of available nitrogen instead of protein. Given the nitrogen percentage, you may approximate the protein content by multiplying the nitrogen figure by six.

Well-grown minimally processed foods are usually our best sources for complete nourishment; and a well-considered choice of them should in most cases meet our dietary needs.

You will find in this book, along with the classic recipes, a number which remain interesting and palatable even though they lack some everyday ingredient such as eggs or flour. These may be used by those people who have allergies. But we do not prescribe corrective diets; we feel that such situations demand special procedures in consultation with one's physician. As to the all-too-prevalent condition of overweight, it is now generally recognized that on-and-off crash diets are dangerous, and that a reeducation in moderate and varied eating habits is the only safe and permanent solution to this problem.

We stress again that the cook who has the responsibility for supplying the family with food will do well to keep alert to advances in the field of nutrition.

Take an active part in working toward consumer protection, for more and more food processors are gaining control over the condition and content of foods as we buy them. Take an interest, too, in legislative changes affecting labeling. The FDA's original intent for foods included under "standards of identity" ensured that terms like "mayonnaise" or "ice cream" would guarantee the same basic ingredients required in the government-established recipe no matter who manufactured it. But since the manufacturer is free to disclose or reveal as it pleases a wide variety of added ingredients, the consumer is at a loss to know just what he is buying. And there is a further, more recent loophole. While formerly the word "imitation" was required on labels for any deviations from the original substance, such as variations in taste, smell, color, texture, melting quality, or method of manufacture, today the term "imitation" may be omitted if the government considers the substitute to be nutritionally equal to the original. This so-called equality of the substitute food may be chemically induced or may be achieved by additives or enrichments. "Buyer, beware!"

But in planning menus and cooking, there are considerations other than mere percentages of intake in relation to fats, carbohydrates, proteins, minerals and vitamins. People have learned over the centuries how to cope with poisonous elements that exist in some of the most basic foods. They know sprouting potatoes are heavy in glycoalkaloids; that cassava must be washed in a complicated fashion to rid it of its hydrocyanic content; that soy products must be either heated or fermented to destroy their trypsin- and urease-inhibiting factors; that cabbage, if it plays a large part in the diet, should be cooked in quantities of water to release its goiterogenic factors even at the expense of vitamin losses, just as wild greens frequently need several blanchings and discardings of the cooking water to rid them of their toxic content, 324. But people have also discovered a twentyfold increase in calcium content in limewater-soaked corn for tortillas; that oatmeal, if left wet and warm overnight, will with subsequent cooking release the phytin which otherwise inhibits the body's calcium absorption from other ingested food. Recently it has been noted that the phytins in soy depress the absorption of zinc. To ensure a control factor against these and various other food pollutants, it would be wise to vary your choice of foods.

So we come back to our puzzle. Unless and until greater and more practical advice about food properties becomes common knowledge, each of us must choose a wide variety from the basic food groups to make us feel well and to furnish our bodies with the components they need for growth and for maintaining stamina.

## APPROXIMATE CALORIE AND PROTEIN VALUES IN AVERAGE SERVINGS

"Personal size and mental sorrow have certainly no necessary proportions. A large, bulky figure has as good a right to be in deep affliction as the most graceful set of limbs in the world. But, fair or not fair, these are unbecoming conjunctions, which reason will patronize in vain—which taste cannot tolerate—which ridicule will seize."—Jane Austen.

We have tried, from data currently furnished by the U.S. Department of Agriculture and other authoritative sources, to give you in the first column of the charts beginning on 14 as accurate a calorie count as possible for the total edible portion of each serving of food as it comes to you at the table. Our soup figures are for canned soups diluted with the same amount of water—or whole milk, in the case of cream soups—unless we specify them as homemade. A cup is the standard 8-ounce measure, and a tablespoon or teaspoon is always a level one. Since we do not expect you to weigh your food at table, this chart should give you a fairly accurate guide to normal servings for a healthy adult. Remember, however, that two martinis before dinner count as much as a generous slice of pie for dessert, and, if you are watching your weight, second thoughts may be better than second helpings.

To use the protein values in the second column on the charts which follow, determine how many grams of protein you require each day, 5. Remember that adequate protein is vital for body maintenance and repairs. Note that with some foods you get too many calories per gram to make that food desirable as a protein source, 4. What is the price in calories you have to pay for a given gram of protein? To find out, divide the number of calories given in a portion of food by the grams of protein in that same portion of food. Foods with less than 35 calories per gram of protein are considered acceptable. Those

with 35 to 70 calories are considered marginal, and those with 70 or more calories per gram are usually considered unacceptable. But it must be pointed out that the above figures apply only to protein values. While the apple, for instance, is clearly unacceptable for its protein value, it is treasured for its vitamins and minerals and its carbohydrates, mainly in the form of natural sugars. Again there must be a balancing of interrelationships in your intake of basic requirements.

In calculating protein content for the foods listed in the following charts, we have followed those values as suggested by government laws on labeling expressed as to whether the Protein Efficiency Ratio is greater or less than that of casein, the chief protein of milk. You will need 45 grams if the PER is equal to or greater than casein, in which case the figure is in bold-face type, and 65 grams of protein if the PER is less than the value of casein, in which case the figure is in light-face type. If the protein has a value of less than 20% of casein, it cannot be considered a significant source of protein and should not be included in your protein calculations. If the figure appears in italics, there is a mixture of foods. A "T" indicates only a trace of protein, and where a dash appears, reliable information on the protein value is not presently available.

| Food | Calories | Protein Grams | Food | Calories | Protein Grams |
|------|---------|---------------|------|---------|---------------|
| Almonds, 1 cup shelled | 850 | 26.0 | Beans, kidney, cooked, ½ cup | 115 | 7.. |
| Apple, 1 raw, 3″ diam. | 117 | .4 | Beans, lima, cooked or canned, ½ cup | 95 | 5. |
| Apple, 1 medium-sized, baked with 2 tablespoons sugar | 200 | .3 | Beans, navy, cooked, ½ cup | 112 | 7.. |
| Apple butter, 1 tablespoon | 37 | .1 | Bean soup, homemade, 1 cup | 170–260 | 7. |
| Apple dumpling, 1 medium-sized | 235 | 3.0 | Bean sprouts, Mung, cooked, ½ cup | 18 | 2. |
| Apple juice, 1 cup | 120 | .3 | Bean sprouts, raw, ½ cup | 10 | 1. |
| Apple pie, ⅙ of 9″ pie | 400 | 3.0 | Beef, corned, cooked, 3 oz., 3 slices, 3″ × 2½″ × ¼″ | 185 | 22. |
| Applesauce, sweetened, ½ cup | 127 | .3 | Beef, corned, hash, 3 oz. | 155 | 7. |
| Applesauce, unsweetened, ½ cup | 50 | .2 | Beef, dried, 2 oz. | 115 | 19. |
| Apricot nectar, canned, ½ cup | 70 | .4 | Beef, 1 filet mignon, 4 oz. | 400 | 63. |
| Apricots, canned, sweetened, 4 halves, 2 tablespoons juice | 80 | .8 | Beef, hamburger, lean to average fat, 1 patty, 3 oz. | 185–245 | 21. |
| Apricots, dried, stewed, sweetened, 4 halves, 2 tablespoons juice | 123 | 1.4 | Beef, rib roast, 3 oz. | 375 | 19. |
| Apricots, 3 whole fresh | 55 | 1.0 | Beef, roast, lean round, 3 oz. | 140 | 23. |
| Artichoke, globe, 1 large, cooked | 51 | 2.8 | Beef heart, 3 oz. | 160 | 21. |
| Artichoke, Jerusalem, 4 small | 70 | — | Beef loaf, 1 slice, 2½″ × 2¼″ × ⅝″ | 115 | 6. |
| Asparagus, 8 stalks | 20 | 2.2 | Beef potpie, 4¼″ diam. | 560 | 23. |
| Asparagus soup, cream of, 1 cup | 160 | 5.9 | Beef soup with meat, 1 cup | 113 | 18. |
| Avocado, ½ medium-sized | 190 | 2.5 | Beef steak, sirloin, lean to average fat, 3 oz. | 172–330 | 20–2 |
| | | | Beef stew, 1 cup | 260 | 18. |
| Bacon, 1 crisp 6″ strip | 45 | 1.8 | Beef tongue, 3 slices, 3″ × 2″ × ⅛″ | 160 | 12. |
| Banana, 1 medium-sized | 100 | 1.3 | Beer, 12 oz. | 150 | 1. |
| Banana cream pie, ⅙ of 9″ pie | 300 | 6.1 | Beet greens, cooked, ½ cup | 12 | 1. |
| Barley, pearled, light, uncooked, 1 cup | 700 | 16.5 | Beets, ½ cup | 30 | 1. |
| Beans, baked, canned, ½ cup | 155 | 8.1 | Berry pie, ⅙ of 9″ pie | 400 | 4. |
| | | | Biscuit, baking powder, 2½″ diam. | 150 | 3. |
| Beans, green or snap, cooked, ½ cup | 15 | 1.0 | Blackberries, fresh, ¾ cup | 62 | 1. |

| Food | Calories | Protein Grams |
|---|---|---|
| Blueberries, fresh, 3/4 cup | 64 | .7 |
| Bologna sausage, 1 slice, 3″ diam. × 1/8″ | 40 | 2.0 |
| Boston cream pie, 1/12 of 8″ diam. | 210 | 3.5 |
| Bouillon, 1 cup | 32 | .8 |
| Bouillon cube, 1 | 5 | .8 |
| Braunschweiger sausage, 1 slice, 2″ diam. × 1/4″ | 33 | 1.5 |
| Brazil nut, 1 shelled | 30 | .7 |
| Bread, commercial, rye, 1 slice, 1/2″ thick | 55 | 2.1 |
| Bread, commercial, white, 1 slice, 1/2″ thick | 60–65 | 2.0 |
| Bread, commercial, whole wheat, 1 slice, 1/2″ thick | 60 | 2.3 |
| Bread, gluten, 1 slice, 4″ × 4″ × 3/8″ | 64 | 7.0 |
| Bread pudding, 1/2 cup | 200 | 6.0 |
| Broccoli, cooked, 1 large stalk or 2/3 cup | 29 | 3.3 |
| Brown Betty, 1/2 cup | 160–250 | 1.7 |
| Brownie with nuts, 1 piece | 95 | 1.3 |
| Brussels sprouts, 1/2 cup, approx. 5 | 30 | 3.0 |
| Butter, 1 square, 1/4″ thick | 70 | .8 |
| Buttermilk, 1 glass, 8 oz. | 90 | 9.0 |
| Cabbage, chopped, raw, 1/2 cup | 10 | .5 |
| Cabbage, cooked, 1/2 cup | 15 | .8 |
| Cake, angel, plain, 3″ slice | 150 | 4.0 |
| Cake, cheese, 2″ wedge | 250 | 25.0 |
| Cake, chocolate layer 2″ square | 356 | 4.1 |
| Cake, coffee, 1 piece, 3″ × 21/2″ × 2″ | 133 | 2.6 |
| Cake, cup, 1 frosted, 21/2″ diam. | 130 | 1.5 |
| Cake, fruit, dark, 1 small slice, 1/2″ thick | 142 | 1.8 |
| Cake, pound, 1 slice | 473 | 5.7 |
| Cake, sponge, 2″ slice | 145 | 3.7 |
| Cake, white, 2-layer, with chocolate icing, 1 slice | 375 | 3.3 |
| Cake, yellow, 2-layer, with chocolate icing, 1 slice | 365 | 4.2 |
| Cantaloupe, 1/2 of 5″ melon | 60 | 1.4 |
| Caramel, 1 medium | 42 | .4 |
| Carbonated water | 0 | 0 |
| Carrots, cooked, 1/2 cup | 25 | .7 |
| Cashew nuts, 11 to 12 | 100 | 3.0 |
| Catsup, 1 tablespoon | 17 | .3 |
| Cauliflower, cooked, 1 cup | 25 | 2.5 |
| Caviar, granular sturgeon, 1 tablespoon | 66 | 6.7 |
| Celeriac, 1 medium-sized | 40 | 1.8 |
| Celery, raw, 3 small inner ribs | 9 | .5 |
| Charlotte Russe, 1 serving | 265 | 5.5 |
| Cheese, American, 1″ cube | 65 | 4.1 |
| Cheese, Camembert, 11/3-oz. wedge | 115 | 7.5 |
| Cheese, cheddar, 1″ cube | 70 | 4.4 |
| Cheese, cottage, creamed, 1/2 cup | 106 | 13.6 |
| Cheese, cottage, plain, 1/2 cup | 86 | 17.0 |
| Cheese, cream, 1/2 3-oz. cake | 160 | 4.0 |
| Cheese, Edam, 1 oz. | 87 | 7.7 |
| Cheese, Liederkranz, 1 oz. | 85 | 4.6 |
| Cheese, Parmesan, 1 tablespoon, grated | 25 | 2.3 |
| Cheese, Roquefort or Blue, 1″ cube | 65 | 3.6 |
| Cheese, Swiss, 1″ cube | 55 | 3.8 |

| Food | Calories | Protein Grams | Food | Calories | Protein Grams |
|------|----------|---------------|------|----------|---------------|
| Cheese soufflé, 1 cup | 238 | 10.8 | Cinnamon bun, | | |
| Cheese straws, 3 | 100 | 2.5 | 1 average | 200 | 3.9 |
| Cherries, canned, | | | Clam chowder, Manhattan, | | |
| sweetened, 1/2 cup | 100 | 1.0 | 1 cup | 87 | 2.4 |
| Cherries, fresh, sweet, | | | Clams, canned, solids and | | |
| 15 large | 61 | 1.1 | liquid, 3 oz. | 45 | 6.8 |
| Chicken, broiler, small | 136 | 23.8 | Clams, raw, 3 oz. | 65 | 11.2 |
| Chicken, canned, boned | | | Cocoa, made with milk and | | |
| meat, 3 oz. | 170 | 18.6 | water, 1 cup | 150 | 7.0 |
| Chicken, fried, 1/2 breast | 155 | 24.7 | Cocoa, made with whole | | |
| Chicken, fried, drumstick | 90 | 12.5 | milk, 1 cup | 245 | 10.0 |
| Chicken, roasted, | | | Coconut, shredded, dried, | | |
| dark meat, 3 1/2 oz. | 184 | 29.3 | firmly packed, 1 cup | 450 | 4.9 |
| Chicken, roasted, light | | | Coconut custard pie, | | |
| meat, 3 1/2 oz. | 182 | 32.3 | 1/6 of 9″ pie | 311 | 7.9 |
| Chicken livers, 1 medium- | | | Codfish, creamed, | | |
| large liver | 74 | 10.3 | 1/2 cup | 200 | 28.5 |
| Chicken pie, 1 individual | | | Codfish balls, | | |
| pie, 4 1/4″ diam. | 535 | 23.0 | 2, 2″ diam. | 200 | 17.1 |
| Chicken salad, 1/2 cup | 200 | 17.4 | Cod liver oil, | | |
| Chicory, or curly endive, | | | 1 tablespoon | 100 | 0 |
| 15 to 20 inner leaves | 10 | .5 | Coffee, clear, 1 cup | 0 | .3 |
| Chocolate, bitter, 1 oz. | 144 | 3.1 | Coffee, with 1 lump | | |
| Chocolate, made with | | | sugar, 1 cup | 27 | .3 |
| milk, 1 cup | 245–277 | 3.6 | Coffee, with 1 tablespoon | | |
| Chocolate, sweet, 1 oz. | 155 | 1.3 | cream, 1 cup | 30 | .6 |
| Chocolate, semisweet, | | | Cola beverages, 1 glass, | | |
| 1 oz. | 147 | 1.2 | 12 oz. | 145 | 0 |
| Chocolate bar, milk, | | | Coleslaw, with mayonnaise, | | |
| 1 oz. | 145 | 1.2 | 1/2 cup | 85 | 2.9 |
| Chocolate creams, | | | Consommé, canned, | | |
| 1 small | 51 | .5 | 1 cup | 35 | 5.2 |
| Chocolate éclair, | | | Cookies, chocolate chip, | | |
| custard filling, | | | 1, 2 1/2″ diam. | 50 | .5 |
| 1 average-sized | 316 | 8.2 | Cookies, sugar, | | |
| Chocolate fudge, 1″ cube | 85 | .8 | 1, 3″ diam. | 64 | .9 |
| Chocolate malted milk, | | | Corn, canned, 1/2 cup | | |
| made with 8 oz. milk | | | drained solids | 70 | 2.2 |
| and ice cream | 502 | 14.1 | Corn bread, 1 square, | | |
| Chocolate milk shake, | | | 2″ × 2″ × 1″ | 139 | 5.6 |
| made with 8 oz. milk | | | Corn on cob, 1 medium, | | |
| and ice cream | 421 | 11.2 | 7″ long | 100 | 3.7 |
| Chocolate soda | 255 | 2.7 | Corn soup, cream, 1/2 cup | 100 | 3.1 |
| Chocolate syrup topping, | | | Corn syrup, 1 tablespoon | 57 | 0 |
| 1 fl. oz. | 90 | 1.0 | Cornflakes, 3/4 cup | 75 | 1.5 |

| Food | Calories | Protein Grams | Food | Calories | Protein Grams |
|---|---|---|---|---|---|
| Cornmeal, cooked, 2/3 cup | 80 | 1.8 | Deviled ham, canned, | | |
| Cornstarch, blancmange, | | | 1 tablespoon | 45 | **1.8** |
| 1/2 cup | 152 | .1 | Divinity, 1 1/2" cube | 102 | — |
| Crab meat, canned, 3 oz. | 85 | **14.8** | Doughnut, cake type, | | |
| Crab meat, fresh, 1/2 cup | 54 | **9.3** | plain, 1, 3 1/4" diam. | 165 | *1.9* |
| Cracker, butter, 1 | 16 | .2 | Doughnut, sugared, 1, | | |
| Cracker, graham, 1, | | | 3 1/4" diam. | 180 | *1.8* |
| 2 1/2" square | 27 | .6 | Doughnut, yeast, plain, | | |
| Cracker, oyster, 12, 1" | 50 | *1.2* | 1, 3 3/4" diam. | 175 | 2.7 |
| Cracker, saltine, 1, | | | Duck, roast, | | |
| 2" square | 17 | .4 | 1 medium piece | 300 | **15.0** |
| Cracker, soda, 1, | | | Dumpling, 1 small | 100 | *1.0* |
| 2 1/2" square | 24 | .5 | | | |
| Cranberry jelly, | | | Egg, boiled or poached, | | |
| 2 tablespoons | 47 | T | 1 whole | 80 | **6.3** |
| Cranberry sauce, | | | Egg, 1 fried with | | |
| 2 tablespoons | 21 | T | 1 teaspoon butter | 105 | **6.7** |
| Cream, coffee, 18.5% fat, | | | Egg, 1 scrambled with | | |
| 1 tablespoon | 30 | .5 | 2 tablespoons milk and | | |
| Cream, half-and-half, | | | 1 teaspoon butter | 110 | **7.1** |
| 1 tablespoon | 20 | .5 | Egg white, 1 raw | 15 | **3.5** |
| Cream, sour, cultured, | | | Egg yolk, 1 raw | 60 | **2.7** |
| 1 tablespoon | 25 | .4 | Eggnog, 1/2 cup | 196 | *10.5* |
| Cream, sour, imitation, | | | Eggplant, breaded and | | |
| 1 tablespoon | 12 | .2 | fried, 2 slices, | | |
| Cream, whipped topping | | | 1/2" thick | 210 | 10.1 |
| of vegetable oil, | | | Farina, cooked, 3/4 cup | 80 | *2.3* |
| 1 tablespoon | 10 | T | Fig, 1 large dried | 55 | .9 |
| Cream, whipping, | | | Fig, 3 small fresh | 95 | 1.4 |
| 1 tablespoon | 45–55 | .4 | Figbars, 1 small | 50 | .5 |
| Cream soups, | | | Fishsticks, breaded, | | |
| canned, 1 cup | 175–250 | 7.0 | cooked, frozen, | | |
| Cream of wheat, | | | 10 sticks or | | |
| cooked, 3/4 cup | 100 | 3.1 | 8-oz. package | 400 | *37.8* |
| Creamers of vegetable | | | Flounder, baked, | | |
| oil, 1 tablespoon | 15 | .3 | average serving | 204 | **30.2** |
| Creamers of vegetable | | | Frankfurter, 1 | 170 | 7.2 |
| oil, powdered, | | | French dressing, | | |
| 1 teaspoon | 2 | T | commercial, | | |
| Cucumber, 12 slices | 10 | .6 | 1 tablespoon | 65 | *.1* |
| Custard, 1/2 cup | 153 | 7.2 | French dressing, home- | | |
| Custard pie, 1/6 of 9" pie | 325 | 9.1 | made, no sugar, | | |
| | | | 1 tablespoon | 86 | *.1* |
| Daiquiri cocktail, 3 oz. | 130 | .1 | French toast, 1 piece | 170 | *5.4* |
| Dates, 3 or 4 | 85 | .7 | | | |

| Food | Calories | Protein Grams | Food | Calories | Protein Grams |
|------|----------|---------------|------|----------|---------------|
| Frog legs, fried, 2 large | 140 | **8.6** | Hard candy, 1 oz. (3 or 4 balls, ¾" diam.) | 110 | 0 |
| Fruit cocktail, canned, drained, ½ cup | 50 | .7 | Hard sauce, 1 tablespoon | 50 | T |
| Fruit cocktail, canned with heavy syrup, ½ cup | 100 | .5 | Herring, fresh, 3 oz. | 128 | **9.1** |
| | | | Herring, pickled Bismarck, 3½" × 1½" × 1¼" | 218 | **19.5** |
| Fruit cocktail, fresh, ½ cup | 50 | .7 | Herring, smoked, 3 oz. | 200 | **21.0** |
| | | | Hickory nuts, about 12 | 100 | 2.1 |
| Gelatin, dry, 1 tablespoon | 25 | 6.4 | Hollandaise sauce, 1 tablespoon | 65 | 1.4 |
| Gelatin dessert, ½ cup | 70 | 1.8 | Honey, 1 tablespoon | 65 | .1 |
| Gin, 1½-oz. jigger | 105 | 0 | Honeydew melon, | | |
| Ginger ale, 12 oz. | 115 | 0 | 1 wedge, 2" × 7" | 50 | 1.2 |
| Gingerbread, 1, 2" square | 170 | 2.0 | Horseradish, grated, | | |
| Gingersnap, 1 | 20 | .3 | 1 tablespoon | 12 | .4 |
| Goose, roast, 3½-oz. serving | 426 | **23.7** | | | |
| Gooseberries, cooked, sweetened, ½ cup | 100 | 2.0 | Ice cream, commercial, plain, ½ cup | 125–165 | **1.9–2.9** |
| Grape juice, 1 glass, 8 oz. | 165 | 1.0 | Ice milk, commercial, plain, ½ cup | 65–100 | **2.0–3.0** |
| Grapefruit, ½ medium | 45 | .7 | Icing, chocolate, with milk and butter, | | |
| Grapefruit juice, unsweetened, 1 cup | 100 | 1.0 | 1 cup | 1,035 | 9.7 |
| Grapes, green seedless, | 66 | .5 | Icing, coconut, boiled, 1 cup | 605 | 3.2 |
| Grapes, Malaga or Tokay, ½ cup | 55 | .5 | Icing, white, boiled, 1 cup | 300 | 1.3 |
| Gravy, thick, 3 tablespoons | 180 | 1.3 | Jam or jelly, | | |
| Green pepper, 1 whole | 20 | 1.0 | 1 tablespoon | 50–60 | .1 |
| Griddle cakes, 2, 4" diam. | 150 | 4.5 | Kale, cooked, 1 cup | 30 | 3.3 |
| Grits, hominy, cooked, ¾ cup | 90 | 2.1 | Kidneys, beef, braised, 3½ oz. | 159 | **20.9** |
| Guavas, 1 medium | 70 | .9 | Kohlrabi, cooked, ½ cup | 23 | 1.6 |
| Gum drop, 1 large | 35 | 0 | Kumquats, 3 | 35 | .5 |
| Haddock, 1 fillet, breaded, fried, 3 oz. | 140 | **16.6** | Ladyfingers, 1 | 37 | .8 |
| Halibut steak, sautéed, 3" × ½" × 1" | 125 | **18.4** | Lamb, roast leg, lean to average fat, 3 oz. | 156–235 | **11.7–22.8** |
| Ham, baked, medium fat, 3 oz. | 245 | **26.3** | Lamb, roast shoulder, lean to average fat | 170–285 | **11.7–15.8** |
| Ham, boiled, 2 oz. | 135 | **14.5** | | | |
| Hamburger—*see* Beef | | | | | |

| Food | Calories | Protein Grams |
| --- | --- | --- |
| Lamb chop, broiled, 4 oz. | 400 | 20.2 |
| Lamb stew with vegetables, 1 cup | 250 | 14.8 |
| Lard, 1 tablespoon | 115 | 0 |
| Leek, 1 | 10 | .5 |
| Lemon, 1 medium-sized | 20 | .8 |
| Lemonade, 1 cup | 88 | .3 |
| Lemon gelatin, 1/2 cup | 100 | 2.0 |
| Lemon ice, 1/2 cup | 116 | 1.0 |
| Lemon juice, 1 tablespoon | 5 | .1 |
| Lemon meringue pie, 1/6 of 9″ pie | 345 | 5.0 |
| Lentil soup, home-made, 1 cup | 150–260 | 5.0 |
| Lettuce, iceberg, 1/4 large head | 18 | 1.2 |
| Lettuce, 6 large leaves | 30 | 2.2 |
| Lime juice, 1 tablespoon | 5 | .1 |
| Liver, beef, fried, 2 oz. | 130 | 13.2 |
| Liver, calf, fried, 2 oz. | 110 | 15.1 |
| Liverwurst or liver sausage, 2 slices, 3″ diam. × 1/4″ | 160 | 8.5 |
| Lobster, 1 cup | 105 | 19.5 |
| Lobster, whole, small, baked or broiled with 2 tablespoons butter | 308 | 10.6 |
| Loganberries, canned, 1/2 cup | 55 | .6 |
| Macaroni, cooked, plain, 1/2 cup | 80 | 2.7 |
| Macaroni and cheese, 1/2 cup | 215 | 8.4 |
| Mackerel, broiled, 3 oz. | 200 | 20.0 |
| Malted milk, 8 oz. | 245 | 11.1 |
| Mangoes, tropical, 1 large | 85 | .9 |
| Manhattan cocktail, 3 oz. | 160 | T |
| Maple syrup, 1 tablespoon | 50 | 0 |
| Margarine, 1 tablespoon | 100 | .1 |

| Food | Calories | Protein Grams |
| --- | --- | --- |
| Marmalade, 2 tablespoons | 120 | .2 |
| Marshmallows, 5 | 125 | .8 |
| Martini cocktail, 3 oz. 3:1 | 145 | .1 |
| Mayonnaise, 1 tablespoon | 65–109 | .2 |
| Meat loaf, beef and pork, 1 slice, 4″ × 3″ × 3/8″ | 264 | 12.2 |
| Melba toast, 1 slice, 4″ × 4″ | 39 | 1.2 |
| Milk, condensed, sweetened, 1/2 cup | 490 | 12.3 |
| Milk, dry, nonfat instant, water added, 1 cup | 82 | 8.2 |
| Milk, evaporated, 1/2 cup | 173 | 8.8 |
| Milk, half-and-half, 1/2 cup | 163 | 3.9 |
| Milk, partly skimmed, 2%, 1 cup | 145 | 14.5 |
| Milk, powdered, whole, 1 tablespoon | 40 | 2.2 |
| Milk, skimmed, 1 cup | 90 | 9.3 |
| Milk, whole fresh, 3.5% fat, 1 cup | 160 | 8.0 |
| Mincemeat pie, 1/6 of 9″ pie | 417 | 3.8 |
| Minestrone, 1 cup | 105 | 5.0 |
| Mints, chocolate cream, 3 small | 100 | .9 |
| Molasses, 1 tablespoon | 55 | — |
| Muffin, 2″ diam. | 55 | 1.6 |
| Muffin, corn, 2 3/8″ diam. | 125 | 2.5 |
| Muffin, English, 1 large | 140 | 3.7 |
| Mushrooms, canned, 1/2 cup | 20 | 2.2 |
| Mushrooms, fresh, 10 small | 16 | 1.5 |
| Mushrooms, sautéed, 7 small | 78 | 1.7 |
| Mustard greens, cooked, 1 cup | 35 | 3.3 |
| Mutton—see Lamb | | |

| Food | Calories | Protein Grams | Food | Calories | Protein Grams |
|------|----------|---------------|------|----------|---------------|
| Nectarine, 1 | 40 | .4 | Peas, dried, cooked, 1/2 cup | 103 | 7.2 |
| Noodles, egg, cooked, 1/2 cup | 100 | 3.3 | Peas, fresh, cooked, 1/2 cup | 56 | 3.8 |
| | | | Pecans, 6 halves | 52 | .7 |
| Oatmeal, cooked, 1/2 cup | 65 | 3.4 | Pepper, green, 1 medium-sized | 15 | .7 |
| Okra, sliced, 1/2 cup | 25 | 1.7 | Perch, breaded and fried, 3 oz. | 195 | 22.5 |
| Old-fashioned cocktail, 1 glass | 185 | 0 | Persimmons, 1 medium-sized | 78 | .7 |
| Olive oil, 1 tablespoon | 124 | 0 | Pickles, cucumber, 1 large dill | 15 | .5 |
| Olives, green, 2 small or 1 large | 8 | .1 | Pickles, cucumber, 1 sweet-sour | 20 | 1.0 |
| Olives, ripe, 2 small or 1 large | 10 | .1 | Pigs' feet, pickled, 1/2 foot | 125 | 10.5 |
| Onion soup, 1 cup | 100 | 8.1 | Pimiento, canned, 1 medium | 10 | .3 |
| Onions, 4 small | 100 | 4.0 | Pineapple, fresh, diced, 1/2 cup | 40 | .3 |
| Onions, creamed, 1/3 cup | 100 | 12.0 | | | |
| Onions, raw, green, 5 medium | 23 | .6 | Pineapple, with syrup, canned, 1 slice | 78 | .3 |
| Orange, 1 average-sized | 65 | 1.1 | Pineapple ice, 1/2 cup | 120 | 1.0 |
| Orange ice, 1/2 cup | 110 | 1.0 | Pineapple juice, 1 cup | 135 | 1.0 |
| Orange juice, 1 cup | 110 | 1.4 | Pizza (cheese), 1/8 of 14" pie | 185 | 9.4 |
| Oxtail soup, 1 cup | 100 | — | Plums, canned, 3 or 4 with syrup | 150 | .7 |
| Oyster stew, with milk, 1 cup | 275 | 15.8 | Plums, fresh, Japanese, 2" diam., 3 or 4 | 100 | 1.0 |
| Oysters, raw, 1 cup | 160 | 21.2 | Popcorn, no butter, 1 cup | 25 | .8 |
| | | | Popover, 1 | 100 | 3.9 |
| Pancake, 1, 4" diam. | 60 | 1.8 | Pork chop, rib, broiled, 3 1/2 oz. | 260 | 21.4 |
| Papaya, 1/2 medium | 72 | 1.1 | Pork roast, 3 oz. | 310 | 18.9 |
| Parsley, chopped, 2 tablespoons | 2 | .1 | Pork tenderloin, 2 oz. | 200 | 12.2 |
| Parsnips, cooked, 1/2 cup | 50 | 1.1 | Potato, baked, 1 medium-sized | 90 | 2.5 |
| Peach, fresh, 1, 2" diam. | 35 | .5 | Potato, boiled, 1 medium-sized | 90 | 2.5 |
| Peaches, canned, 2 halves with 2 tablespoons syrup | 85 | .4 | Potato, sweet, baked, 1 medium-sized | 155 | 1.5 |
| Peanut butter, 2 tablespoons | 190 | 8.5 | Potato, sweet, candied, 1 potato, 3 1/2" × 2 1/4" | 295 | 2.3 |
| Peanuts, 20 to 24 nuts | 100 | 4.5 | | | |
| Pear, fresh, 1, 2 1/2" diam. | 60 | .8 | | | |
| Pears, canned, 2 halves with 2 tablespoons juice | 85 | .2 | | | |
| Pea soup, cream, 1 cup | 270 | 13.3 | | | |
| Peas, canned, 1/2 cup | 65 | 3.7 | | | |

| Food | Calories | Protein Grams | Food | Calories | Protein Grams |
|---|---|---|---|---|---|
| Potato chips, 8 to 10 large | 100 | .9 | Rhubarb, stewed, sweetened, 1/2 cup | 192 | .7 |
| Potato salad, 1/2 cup | 125–180 | 4.9 | Rice, brown, cooked, 1/2 cup | 100 | 2.1 |
| Potatoes, French-fried, 10 pieces | 155 | 2.4 | Rice, white, cooked, 1/2 cup | 100 | 1.8 |
| Potatoes, hash-browned, 1/2 cup | 175 | 2.4 | Rice, wild, cooked, 2/3 cup | 103 | 2.2 |
| Potatoes, mashed, milk and butter added, 1 cup | 185 | 4.1 | Roll, hard, white, 1 average-sized | 155 | 4.9 |
| Potatoes, pan-fried, 1/2 cup | 230 | 3.4 | Roll, Parker House, 1 | 81 | 2.0 |
| Potatoes, scalloped, no cheese, 1/2 cup | 125 | 3.6 | Root beer, 12 oz. | 105 | 0 |
| Praline, 1 | 300 | — | Rum, 1 1/2-oz. jigger | 150 | 0 |
| Preserves, 1 tablespoon | 55–75 | .1 | Rutabagas, cooked, 1/2 cup | 25 | .6 |
| Pretzels, 5 small sticks | 5 | .1 | Salami, dry, 1 oz. | 130 | 6.9 |
| Prune juice, 1 cup | 200 | 1.0 | Salmon, fresh, poached, 3 1/2 oz. | 200 | 29.7 |
| Prunes, dried, cooked, 1/2 cup | 125 | 1.0 | Sardines, canned, in oil, 3 oz. | 175 | 19.6 |
| Prunes, dried, cooked, sweetened, 1/2 cup | 205 | 1.0 | Sauerkraut, 2/3 cup | 27 | 1.5 |
| Prunes, stewed, 4 medium with 2 table-spoons juice | 120 | .6 | Sauerkraut juice, 1/2 cup | 4 | .3 |
| Pudding, chocolate, home recipe, 1 cup | 385 | 8.1 | Sausage, pork link, 2 oz. | 125 | 2.3 |
| Pudding, mix, 4-oz. package | 410 | 3.0 | Scallops, fried, 5 to 6 medium-sized | 427 | 39.5 |
| Pumpkin, 1 cup | 76 | 4.0 | Shad roe, sautéed, average serving | 175 | 32.6 |
| Pumpkin pie, 1/6 of 9" pie | 315 | 6.0 | Sherbet, 1/2 cup | 135 | 1.0 |
| | | | Sherry, dry, 3 oz. | 110 | .3 |
| Rabbit, baked, 3 1/2 oz. | 177 | 22.7 | Sherry, sweet, 3 oz. | 150 | .3 |
| Radishes, 5 medium | 6 | .4 | Shortcake with 1/2 cup berries and cream, 1 medium-sized biscuit | 350 | 4.0 |
| Raisins, seedless, 1/4 cup | 107 | .9 | Shredded wheat biscuit, 1 large | 100 | 2.8 |
| Raspberries, red, fresh, 1/2 cup | 35 | .7 | Shrimp, boiled, 5 large | 70 | 15.5 |
| Raspberries, red, frozen, sweetened, 1/2 cup | 120 | .9 | Shrimp, canned, 3 oz. | 100 | 20.8 |
| Red snapper, baked, 3" × 1/2" × 4" | 183 | 39.0 | Shrimp, fried, 4 large | 259 | 23.5 |
| | | | Smelts, baked or broiled, 4 or 5 medium-sized | 91 | 17.3 |
| Rhubarb, fresh, diced, 1 cup | 20 | .7 | Smelts, fried, 4 to 5 medium-sized | 448 | 17.3 |
| | | | Snow pudding, 2/3 cup | 114 | — |

| Food | Calories | Protein Grams | Food | Calories | Protein Grams |
|------|----------|---------------|------|----------|---------------|
| Soft drinks, fruity, 12 oz. | 140–170 | 0 | Swordfish, broiled in butter, 3 oz. | 150 | 24 |
| Sole, Dover, baked, 3¹/₃ oz. | 202 | 30.0 | Syrup, corn, 1 tablespoon | 57 | |
| Sole, fillet—see Flounder | | | Syrup, sorghum, 1 tablespoon | 55 | |
| Soybeans, dried, cooked, ¹/₂ cup | 120 | 9.9 | | | |
| Spaghetti, plain, cooked, 1 cup | 155 | 5.2 | Tangerine, 1 | 35 | |
| | | | Tangerine juice, ¹/₂ cup | 55 | |
| Spareribs, meat from 6 average-sized ribs | 246 | 14.9 | Tapioca pudding, ¹/₂ cup | 133 | 4 |
| Spinach, cooked and chopped, ¹/₂ cup | 23 | 2.8 | Tartare sauce, 1 tablespoon | 100 | |
| Spinach soup, cream, homemade, 1 cup | 240 | 7.0 | Tea, clear, unsweetened, 1 cup | 0 | |
| Split pea soup, 1 cup | 145 | 9.0 | Thousand Island dressing, 1 tablespoon | 80 | |
| Split peas, dried, cooked, 1 cup | 290 | 19.0 | Tomato, fresh, 1, 3″ diam. | 40 | 2 |
| Squab, 1 whole, unstuffed, 2¹/₂ oz. meat | 149 | 10.0 | Tomato catsup, 1 tablespoon | 17 | |
| | | | Tomato juice, 1 cup | 50 | 2 |
| Squash, Hubbard or winter, cooked, ¹/₂ cup | 65 | 2.3 | Tomato purée, 1 tablespoon | 6 | |
| | | | Tomato soup, clear, 1 cup | 90 | 2 |
| Squash, summer, cooked, ¹/₂ cup | 15 | 1.0 | Tomato soup, cream, homemade, 1 cup | 175–250 | 7 |
| Starch, cornstarch, etc., 1 tablespoon | 29 | T | Tomatoes, canned, 1 cup | 60 | |
| Strawberries, fresh, ¹/₂ cup | 30 | .6 | Tripe, cooked in milk, average serving | 150 | 28 |
| Strawberries, frozen, sweetened, ¹/₂ cup | 120 | .5 | Trout, brook, broiled, 3 oz. | 216 | 19 |
| Strawberry shortcake with cream, average serving | 350 | 3.7 | Trout, lake, broiled, 3 oz. | 290 | 21 |
| Succotash, canned, ¹/₂ cup | 85 | 3.8 | Tuna fish, canned, water-packed, ¹/₂ cup | 165 | 36 |
| Sugar, brown, 1 tablespoon | 50 | 0 | Tuna fish, canned, in oil, 3 oz. | 170 | 25 |
| Sugar, confectioners', 1 tablespoon | 30 | 0 | Turkey, roast, dark meat, 3¹/₂ oz. | 203 | 30 |
| Sugar, granulated, 1 tablespoon | 48 | 0 | Turkey, roast, light meat, 3¹/₂ oz. | 176 | 32 |
| Sweetbreads, broiled, ¹/₂ medium pair | 185 | 15.0 | Turnip greens, cooked, 1 cup | 30 | 3 |
| | | | Turnips, cooked, 1 cup | 40 | 1 |

| Food | Calories | Protein Grams |
|------|----------|---------------|
| Vanilla wafer, 1 | 20 | .2 |
| Veal chop, loin, fried, 1 medium-sized | 186 | 21.0 |
| Veal cutlet, 3 oz. | 185 | 23.0 |
| Veal roast, 3 oz. | 230 | 23.3 |
| Veal stew, 1 cup | 242 | 23.9 |
| Vegetable cooking fats, 1 tablespoon | 110 | 0 |
| Vegetable juice, 1 cup | 48 | 2.5 |
| Vegetable soup, 1 cup | 80–100 | 5.0 |
| Venison, baked, 3 slices, 3½″ × 2½″ × ¼″ | 200 | 34.5 |
| Vienna sausage, canned (7 per 5-oz. can), 1 sausage | 40 | 2.3 |
| Vodka, 1½-oz. jigger | 105 | 0 |
| Waffles, 1, 7″ diam. | 210 | 5.0 |
| Waldorf salad, average serving | 137 | 1.3 |
| Walnuts, English, 4 to 8 halves | 50 | 1.1 |
| Watercress, 10 sprigs | 5 | .6 |
| Watermelon, 1 slice, ¾″ thick, 6″ diam. | 90 | 1.7 |

| Food | Calories | Protein Grams |
|------|----------|---------------|
| Welsh rarebit, 4 tablespoons on 1 slice toast | 200 | 9.1 |
| Wheat germ, 1 tablespoon | 25 | 1.8 |
| Whisky, bourbon, 1½ oz. | 120 | 0 |
| Whisky, Scotch, 1½ oz. | 105 | 0 |
| White sauce, ¼ cup | 106 | 2.6 |
| Whitefish, average serving | 100 | 13.4 |
| Wines, dry, 3 oz. | 65–95 | T |
| Wines, sweet or fortified, 3 oz. | 120–160 | .2 |
| Yams—see Potatoes, sweet | | |
| Yeast, brewer's, 2 teaspoons | 18 | 2.5 |
| Yeast, compressed, 1 cake | 10 | 1.4 |
| Yogurt, fruit-flavored, ½ cup | 130 | 4.4 |
| Yogurt, plain, ½ cup | 65 | 4.4 |
| Yogurt, whole milk, ½ cup | 75 | 3.6 |
| Zucchini, cooked, 1 cup | 40 | 2.8 |
| Zwieback, 1 slice | 35 | .9 |

# BEVERAGES

As our friend the late Edgar Anderson pointed out in his stimulating book, *Plants, Man and Life,* primitive man located the only sources of caffeine known to this day: tea, coffee, cola, cocoa and yerba maté and its relatives. Subsequent generations have adopted social rituals and created special equipment to enhance the cheer and communicativeness that these plants release. Shown here is a massive Russian samovar with its charcoal pipe, the tea essence above, the hot water container below, and a few typical metal-encircled serving glasses: a strong cultural contrast to the Japanese teabowl and whisk nearby. Illustrated, too, is a charming porcelain coffee mill from Central Europe which makes a much coarser grind than does its tall Turkish counterpart. Rounding out the assembly are two examples from south of the border. From Mexico comes a wooden chocolate-stirrer, or molinillo; from South America, carved gourds for yerba maté. The gourd is supported on a silver stand, but after it has been filled with maté leaves and boiling water it becomes a communal cup and is passed from hand to hand, each guest taking a sip through the bombilla, a metal "straw," finely perforated at its bulbous base to strain out the herbs.

Other less rousing brews have been traditionally made from leaves, roots, bark, blossoms and seeds. In France, for example, the tisane mentioned so lovingly by Colette is frequently served as a comforting after-dinner drink, 31. Grow your own herbs, (II, 262), if possible, and use them frequently, fresh or dried, as infusions. If you buy them, you will find them on your grocers' shelves, more and more of them freeze-dried, a process which helps somewhat to preserve essential oils and savor.

The recipes in this chapter are nonlcoholic, except for a few variations under Coffee and Tea and one or two composite party drinks. Even these are very low-power—even lower than the kind of potation that an outrageous punster once declared "took two pints to make one cavort." For alcoholic liquors of all kinds, their preparation and use, see Drinks, (II, 34). Remember that, in any beverage you may brew, the quality of the water greatly affects results.

## ABOUT COFFEE

Coffee has always thrived on adversity—just as people in adversity have thrived on coffee. When this beverage began its highly successful career, Islamic leaders identified it with wine—a new kind of wine which was all the more offensive to Koranic teaching because it did not merely loosen men's tongues but sharpened their critical faculties.

Thanks especially to vacuum-packed cans—with freeze-dried instants running a fairly respectable second among those in pressing need—making good coffee at home has become a surefire delight, although some people still prefer to blend and grind their own for each making in a small mill, a picturesque example of which is shown in the chapter-head illustration.

Of the several ways of preparing this beverage, we prefer the drip method. Vacuum preparation and the percolator have their advocates, too; but we regard them as, respectively, more troublesome and less apt to produce fresh flavor. The steeped-coffee recipe which follows is suggested for campers or others who happen to lack any equipment more specialized than a saucepan. Illustrated on the next page are several devices for making filtered coffee: one type employs a metal or plastic filter; another, which is made of chemical glass, uses a paper filter folded into conical shape. The latter gives a pure essence with no sediment—which a coffee connoisseur demands in a perfect brew. Also sketched is the proper equipment for Caffè Espresso and Turkish coffee.

Whatever device you choose ▶ follow the directions of its manufacturer carefully, especially as to the grind recommended—regular, drip or fine. In each case, to assure a full-bodied brew, ▶ use not less than 2 level tablespoons of coffee to each 3/4 cup of freshly drawn water. Other things to remember are: use soft, not softened or hard, water; when brewing coffee, keep the coffeemaker almost full; time your method consistently; keep the coffeemaker scrupulously clean, rinsing it with water in which a few teaspoons of baking soda have been dissolved and always scalding it before reuse. If cloth filters are required, do not allow them to become dry but keep them immersed in cold water. ▶ Never boil coffee, since boiling brings out the tannic acid in the bean and makes for a bitter as well as a cloudy brew. Remember that any moisture activates coffee; and that water between 200° and 205° is ideal for extracting flavor without drawing acids. Never, of course, reuse coffee grounds.

If coffee is ground in the household, it should be ground in small quantities in a meticulously clean grinder. Open only one can at a time. Store ground coffee in a tightly closed jar in the refrigerator.

For those who love coffee but are highly sensitive to caffeine or in whom it induces insomnia, we suggest the use of a decaffeinized product rather than a coffee substitute. However, tests show that nondecaffeinated instants, due to a processing factor called hydrolization, contain up to 50 percent less caffeine than freshly brewed coffee. It may be helpful to remember also that certain varieties of coffee—such as those grown in Puerto Rico—have a substantially lower caffeine content than the typical Brazilian or Colombian bean.

For those who hanker after coffee like the kind their German grandmother used to make or a brew which reminds them of that little brasserie on the Left Bank, the answer may be to add an ounce of ground chicory— the root of the wild plant, *Cicoria entybus*—to a cup of ground coffee before brewing. ▶ When cream is used in coffee, allow it to reach room temperature beforehand, so as to cool the drink as little as possible. For coffee-chocolate combinations, see About Chocolate, 32, Brazilian Chocolate, 33, and Cocomoka, 40.

## DRIP COFFEE OR CAFÉ FILTRÉ

Place finely ground coffee in a drip filter.
Allow:

**2 tablespoons coffee for each ³/₄ to 1 cup water**

Pour freshly boiled water over the coffee. When the dripping process is complete, serve coffee at once. Dripping coffee more than once through a filter, contrary to popular belief, does not strengthen the brew. Serve with a
**Twist of lemon peel**

## VACUUM-METHOD COFFEE

This needs special equipment.
Allow:

**2 tablespoons regular- or fine-grind coffee for every ³/₄ to 1 cup water**

Measure water into lower bowl. Place on heat. Place a wet filter in upper bowl and add the ground coffee. Insert upper bowl into lower one with a light twist to ensure a tight seal. If your equipment has a vented stem, you may place it, already assembled, on the heat. If it does not have this small hole on the side of the tube above the hot-water line, wait until the water is actively boiling before putting the upper bowl in place. When nearly all the water has risen into the upper bowl—some of it will always remain below—stir the water and coffee thoroughly. In 1 to 3 minutes, the shorter time for the fine grinds, remove from heat.

## PERCOLATED COFFEE

Place in the percolator:

- **³/₄ to 1 cup cold water for every**
- **2 tablespoons regular-grind coffee you have measured into the percolator basket**

When water boils, remove percolator from heat. Put in the basket. Cover percolator, return to heat and percolate slowly 6 to 8 minutes. Remove the coffee basket and serve. ♦ Overpercolating does not make coffee stronger. It impairs its flavor.

## STEEPED COFFEE

Place in a pot:

> 2 tablespoons regular- or fine-grind coffee to each ¾ to 1 cup freshly boiling water

Stir the coffee for at least ½ minute. Let it stand covered in a pan of boiling water 5 to 10 minutes, depending on the grind and the strength of brew desired. Pour the coffee off the grounds through a strainer.

## COFFEE IN QUANTITY

**40 to 50 Servings**

Put in a cheesecloth bag large enough to allow for double expansion:

> 1 lb. medium-grind coffee

Shortly before serving, have ready a kettle holding:

> 5 to 7 quarts water

Bring the water to a boil. Place the coffee-filled bag in it. Let stand in a warm place 7 to 10 minutes. Agitate the bag several times during this period. Remove bag, cover kettle and serve at once.

## INSTANT COFFEE

The polls are against us, but we really can't yet regard the jiffy product as equal to the one that takes a few minutes longer to prepare. Instant coffee, whether regular or freeze-dried, begins to deteriorate in flavor after about 2 weeks' storage. Use for each serving:

> 1 teaspoon instant coffee
> 5½ oz. boiling water

For 6 servings:

> 6 teaspoons instant coffee
> 1 quart boiling water

Add the water to the instant coffee to avoid foaming. A better flavor is obtained by simmering gently about 2 minutes.

## ESPRESSO COFFEE

This Italian specialty, which, of course, is called Caffè Espresso on its home grounds, must be carefully distinguished from any brew made by filtering, no matter how concentrated. The Espresso machine works by an entirely different "steam pressure" principle, uses a very dark, very powdery grind identified as "Espresso" on the package, and delivers a powerful drink with the consistency of light cream. Use the recipe for Espresso which comes with your equipment and serve it after dinner, in a demitasse or Espresso glass, with or without lemon peel. Vary the brew with a dash of Tia Maria, Strega or apricot brandy and a dollop of whipped cream.

## COFFEE CAPPUCCINO

Combine equal parts of:

> Espresso Coffee, above
> Hot milk

with a:

> Dash of cinnamon or cardamom or a grating of nutmeg

## TURKISH COFFEE

As Turkish coffee settles very rapidly, it is made at the table, over an alcohol lamp. The average content of the long-handled metal pot is about

10 ounces of liquid, and it should never be filled to more than two-thirds capacity. The pot is narrowed before it flares at the top, to allow the swishing and swinging of its contents between "frothings"—a procedure which keeps the very finely divided grains in suspension until the liquid is sipped from tiny stemmed cups holding about a tablespoon of fluid. In the Middle East it is considered impolite to drink more than three of these, although more may be served in the United States. The glass of ice water and the Rahat Loukoum candy, (II, 598), served on the side for non-habitués are often welcome additions. The connoisseur adds no sweetening to the brew itself. Serve the coffee so that a little of the lighter frothy top goes into each cup first and is followed on the next round by some of the heavier liquid on the bottom. No commercial grind available in America proves fine enough for Turkish coffee, so take the finest you can get and pulverize it further in an electric blender. For each serving, place in a Turkish coffeemaker:

⅓ cup water
1 teaspoon to 1 tablespoon finely pulverized coffee
(2 teaspoons sugar)

Heat until the coffee rises to a boil. Remove at once from heat but only momentarily. Repeat this process a second and third time. ◗ Never allow the coffee to boil. Serve at once as described above.

## CAFÉ AU LAIT

The milk coffee of France.
Combine equal parts of:

Strong coffee
Hot milk

Add:

(Sugar to taste)

## CAFÉ BRÛLOT, DIABLE OR ROYAL

8 Servings

This festive coffee bowl requires a darkened room.
Prepare:

1 small orange

by studding it with:

20 whole cloves

Place in a deep silver bowl:

Thinly sliced peel of 1 orange
Thinly sliced peel of 1 lemon
2 sticks cinnamon
10 small cubes sugar

Heat but ◗ do not boil, and pour over these ingredients:

¾ cup brandy or ¼ cup Cointreau

Place bowl on a tray and bring bowl, orange and a ladle to the table. Ignite the brandy and ladle the mixture repeatedly over the spices until the sugar melts. Pour into the bowl:

4 cups freshly made coffee

Now fill the ladle with:

¼ cup warm brandy or ¼ cup Cointreau

Tip the orange carefully into the ladle, ignite liquid, and lower the flaming ladle into the bowl, floating the orange as shown on 29. Ladle the café brûlot into demitasse cups. Here are 2 miniature versions: for individual servings put a small cube of sugar in a coffee spoon, saturate it with brandy and ignite it. When sugar is melted, lower spoon into a partially filled demitasse of hot coffee. Add a lemon twist and 1 or 2 cloves, and stir mixture with a cinnamon stick. Also, you may simply stir a teaspoonful of warmed light rum or whisky into a small cup of hot coffee—adding a twist of lemon peel and sweetening to taste. While brandy and Cointreau are the usual fireworks, you may want to try white crême de menthe, curaçao, or kümmel.

## CAFÉ CONTINENTAL

**4 Servings**

Prepare, using 3 tablespoons coffee to 1 cup water, and keep very hot:

    **4 cups Coffee, 26**

Just before serving add:

    **1/2 teaspoon coriander**
    **1 tablespoon sugar**
    **1/2 cup warmed sweet red wine**
    **(1 tablespoon powdered ginger)**

Pour into mugs topped with:

    **A quartered slice of orange**

## IRISH COFFEE

**Individual Serving**

Some people hold that Irish coffee can only be made "proper" with Demerara sugar, (II, 228). It does make a difference.

Heat ▶ but do not boil and place in a prewarmed 7-ounce goblet or coffee cup:

    **1 jigger Irish whisky**
    **1 or 2 teaspoons sugar**

Fill to within 1/2 inch of top with:

    **Freshly made hot coffee**

Stir until sugar is dissolved. Float on top of liquid:

    **Chilled whipped cream**

## ICED COFFEE

Prepare Coffee, 26, any way you wish, using:

    **2 1/2 to 3 tablespoons coffee to 3/4 cup water**

Chill it or pour it hot over cubed ice in tall glasses. You may sweeten the drink with:

    **(Sugar or Sugar Syrup, (II, 35), to taste)**

Stir in:

    **(Cream)**

or top with:

    **(Whipped cream or vanilla ice cream)**

## ICED COFFEE VIENNOISE

**Individual Serving**

Prepare:

    **Iced Coffee, above**

in a tall glass. Add:

    **1 small jigger light rum or brandy**

topping it with:

    **Whipped cream**

## ⚘ BLENDER FROZEN COFFEE

Place in electric blender for each drink:

    **1/4 cup coffee**

prepared as for Iced Coffee, above. Add:

    **1 tablespoon sugar**
    **1/16 teaspoon ground cloves**
    **(1 small jigger medium rum)**

Add not less than:

    **1 cup crushed ice**

Blend thoroughly and serve in chilled tall glasses.

## ABOUT TEA

In one of Lin Yutang's books, he tells of the infinite care with which a certain sage living in the second or Classical period of Chinese tea-making procured from a famous spring, in just the proper sort of earthen pot, sufficient water for a brew with which he intended regaling an honored guest; how, on a clear, calm evening, taking pains to keep the water undisturbed, he sailed with it cautiously across an arm of the sea to his home; and how, before steeping the choice leaves, he brought the water to precisely the critical boil. There were other refinements, too, most of them equally unthinkable in our less leisurely age.

However, no matter how we abridge the tea-making ritual today, it is well to keep in mind the importance of the water we use and its temperature. It should be freshly drawn, soft—not softened and not hard—and heated, if possible, in a glass or enameled vessel. When the leaves are dropped into it, the water should only just have arrived at a brisk rolling boil—so the tea will not have a flat flavor and the leaves will describe a deep wheel-like movement, each one opening up for fullest infusion.

Tea brewers who do not wish to trouble with a strainer and are willing to compromise may use a tea ball. In any case ▶ stirring the brew just before serving in a scalded, preheated pot is imperative, since it circulates through the liquid the essential oils that contribute so much to tea's characteristic flavor.

There is only one tea plant, but there are many commercial varieties of tea, depending on soil, locality, age of leaf, manufacture, grading, blending and the addition of blossoms, zests or spices. The two chief basic types are green and black. The former is dried immediately after plucking; the latter—by all odds the

more favored—is allowed to ferment before further processing. **Oolong,** a semi-fermented leaf, is in a class by itself.

Chinese teas, which less than a century ago dominated the world market, have now largely yielded to the more robustly aromatic varieties of India, Sri Lanka and Southeast Asia. There are also any number of blends in which teas of several regions are mingled. Unfortunately, tea producers have not yet followed the example of coffee manufacturers, by putting up tea in vacuum packages. Therefore, when it reaches your kitchen, we suggest you place it at once in a tightly sealed jar.


## TEA

Place tea leaves in a preheated pot. Allow:

**1 teaspoon tea leaves**
for each:

**5 to 6 oz. water**

Proceed as indicated above, permitting the leaves to steep not less than 3 and not more than 5 minutes. Serve the tea promptly, stirring, for the ultimate touch, with a small bamboo whisk, as shown at the chapter head. Strain. Sugar or lemon? Yes, if you wish—the earliest tea-makers curiously enough, added salt! On a chilly afternoon we sometimes like to put a small decanter of rum or brandy on the tea tray for the cup that cheers. But we draw the line at tea bags and cream. The bag container or the fat in the cream will adulterate the flavor of this subtle beverage. Milk is frequently added in England. Never steep tea leaves more than once.

## SPICED TEA

**8 Servings**

Prepare an infusion by bringing to a boil:

   **½ cup water**
   **¾ cup sugar**

Remove from heat and add:

   **¼ cup strained orange juice**
   **½ cup strained lemon juice**
   **6 cloves**
   **1 stick cinnamon**

Meanwhile, prepare:

   **Tea, 30**

Use, in all, 10 teaspoons tea and 5 cups water—in a regular measuring cup. Put the hot, spiced infusion in a heavy crystal bowl. Pour the steeped tea over the mixture and serve at once in punch or tea cups.

## ICED TEA

We swell with patriotic pride when we recall that this beverage originated in our native town, St. Louis—even though the inventor was actually an Englishman who arrived at the concoction as an act of desperation. The year was 1904; the place, the St. Louis World's Fair; the provocation, the indifference of the general public, in the sweltering midwestern heat, to Richard Blechynden's tea concession. In brewing iced tea, avoid China teas—they lack the requisite "body." Hard water produces murky iced tea due to precipitation. Prepare:

   **Tea, 30**

◗ Use twice the quantity of leaves indicated for making the hot beverage. Stir, strain and pour over cubed ice. Serve with:

   **Lemon slices**
   **(Sprigs of mint)**
   **(Sugar to taste)**

Instant tea is now available, sometimes sweetened with sugar, and lemon-flavored. If speed of preparation is a real factor, it makes a convenient, if not superior, iced tea.

## ICED TEA WITH COLD WATER

This effortless brew has a fine flavor, will keep for several days, and never clouds. Combine in a glass jar:

   **4 teaspoons tea**
   **1 quart water**

Refrigerate covered overnight. Strain out the leaves before serving over ice cubes.

## FLAVORINGS FOR ICED TEA

**I.** Pour hot, steeped tea over:

   **Bruised mint leaves**
   **Lemon rind**

Chill the tea. Remove leaves and rind. Pour the tea into tall glasses. Add ice cubes and:

   **Sugar to taste**
   **(Sprigs of mint)**

**II.** Add to each serving of iced tea:

   **1 teaspoon rum**

Garnish the glasses with:

   **Slices of lemon or lime**
   **(Sprigs of lemon thyme)**

## ABOUT TISANES AND OTHER INFUSIONS

From time immemorial various plants, less stimulating than tea or coffee, have been used the world over as restoratives. An old herbalist recommended them "for wamblings of the stomach." Today, the French often serve them shortly after dinner. They range all the way from such homely makings as rose hips and alfalfa to that Paraguayan tea shrub, maté, the leaves of which are commercially obtainable in some North American localities.

Some of the homegrown herbs which, singly or in combination, may become interesting beverages are the fresh or dried leaves of angelica, bergamot, comfrey, hyssop, lemon verbena, mints, sages, thymes; the blossoms of chamomile, clover, linden, orange, lemon, wintergreen and elderberry; the seeds of anise and fennel. There is a good general rule for quantity per cup of water in preparing these infusions.

For strong herbs, allow:

> 1/2 to 1 tablespoon fresh
> material
> 1/4 to 1/2 teaspoon dried
> material

For mild herbs, allow:

> **Twice the above amounts**

◗ Never use a metal pot. Before straining and serving, steep for 3 to 10 minutes in water brought to a rolling boil. Serve with:

> **(Honey or lemon)**

Habitués say "never use cream." Try one of the following dried herbs, allowing for each cup:

> 1 star anise cluster
> 6 chamomile flowers
> 1/8 teaspoon powdered mint
> 1/4 teaspoon powdered fennel
> 1/2 teaspoon linden blossom
> 1/2 teaspoon verbena

## ABOUT CHOCOLATE AND COCOA BEVERAGES

Chocolate, an Aztec drink, comes to us via Spain with the addition of sugar and spice. It really pains us to speak evil of so distinctively delicious a drink. But chocolate, with its high fat and sugar content, if habitually substituted for milk, may create an imbalance in the diet. In some places, unless you ask for French chocolate, the base will be water and the drink garnished with whipped cream. In France you can count on a milk base and cream incorporated into the drink. In Vienna they add a generous topping of whipped cream. In America you may have to face a marshmallow or a piece of cinnamon-stick candy; in Russia and Brazil, coffee is added; and in modern Mexico we find in it cinnamon and even orange rind and sherry. For more information about chocolates and cocoas, see (II, 242).

Cocoa does not always combine easily with liquid. To remove any lumps before cooking, combine it with the sugar or mix it in the blender with a small quantity of the water called for in the recipe. You may want to keep on hand homemade cocoa or chocolate syrups, below and on 33. ◗ Both cocoa and chocolate scorch easily, so brew them over hot water as suggested below. In Mexico a special wooden stirrer or whipper called molinillo, illustrated at the chapter head, is used to fluff chocolate drinks just before serving. This also inhibits the formation of the cream "skin" which often appears on top. If you want this aerated effect, try a wire whisk or a rotary beater. Serve the hot beverage in a deep narrow chocolate cup so as to retain the heat.

### COCOA

**About 4 Servings**

Combine, stir and boil for 2 minutes in the top of a double boiler over direct but low heat:

> 1 cup boiling water
> 1/4 cup cocoa
> 1/8 teaspoon salt
> 2 to 4 tablespoons sugar

Then add:

> 1/2 teaspoon cinnamon

$^1/_{16}$ teaspoon cloves and/or
nutmeg

Place the top of the boiler ◗ over boiling water. Add:

3 cups scalded milk

Stir and heat the cocoa. Cover and
keep over hot water 10 more minutes. Add:

1 teaspoon vanilla

Beat with a wire whisk before serving.

## CHOCOLATE

**About 6 Servings**

Melt ◗ in the top of a double boiler
until thoroughly dissolved:

1$^1/_2$ to 2 oz. chocolate
$^1/_2$ cup boiling water

Scald:

3$^1/_2$ cups milk

with:

1 vanilla bean, or add just
before serving 1 teaspoon
vanilla

Dissolve in the hot milk:

$^1/_4$ to $^1/_3$ cup sugar
($^1/_8$ teaspoon salt)

If you have used the vanilla bean, remove it. Pour the milk mixture while
hot over the smooth chocolate mixture and beat well with a wire whisk.
In each heated cup, place:

(A stick cinnamon)

Before serving, top each cup with:

1 tablespoon whipped cream
at room temperature

## BRAZILIAN CHOCOLATE

**About 4 Servings**

Melt in a double boiler ◗ over hot
water:

1 oz. chocolate
$^1/_4$ cup sugar
$^1/_8$ teaspoon salt

Add and stir in:

1 cup boiling water

Continue to heat 3 to 5 minutes. Add:

$^1/_2$ cup hot milk
$^1/_2$ cup hot cream
1$^1/_2$ cups freshly made hot
strong coffee

Beat mixture well and add:

1 teaspoon vanilla
(A grating of cinnamon)

## ICED CHOCOLATE

Prepare and then chill:

Chocolate, or Brazilian
Chocolate, above

Serve over crushed ice. Top with:

Whipped cream or coffee
ice cream

Garnish with:

Grated sweet chocolate

## CHOCOLATE OR CHOCOLATE
## MALT SHAKE SYRUP

**About 20 Servings**

First, make the following syrup which
you may keep on hand in the refrigerator about 10 days.

Melt in the top of a double boiler
◗ over hot water:

7 oz. chocolate

Stir slowly into the melted chocolate:

15 oz. sweetened condensed
milk
1 cup boiling water

Stir in until dissolved:

$^1/_2$ cup sugar

Cool and store the syrup.

To make up an individual shake, use:

2 tablespoons chocolate
syrup, above
1 cup chilled milk

Beat the mixture well or blend it. For
increased food value, add:

($^1/_2$ cup milk solids or malt)
(2 teaspoons nutritional yeast)

Serve at once blended with:

A dip of vanilla, chocolate
or mint ice cream

or over:

Cracked ice

## COCOA SHAKE SYRUP

### About 8 Servings

In the top of a double boiler make a lumpless paste of:

**1  cup sugar**
**¹/₂  cup cocoa**
**¹/₄  cup cold water**
**(¹/₂  cup malt)**

Bring this mixture just to a boil over low direct heat, stirring constantly. Then continue to heat ♦ over hot water 3 to 5 minutes. Cool mixture. You may store it covered and refrigerated 2 to 3 weeks.

## HANDY HOT CHOCOLATE OR COCOA

### About 1 Serving

Prepare:

**Chocolate Shake Syrup or Cocoa Shake Syrup, above**

For each 8-ounce cup of cocoa desired, use:

**2  tablespoons syrup**

Stir in slowly:

**³/₄  cup scalding milk**

and heat thoroughly without boiling before serving.

## MILK EGGNOG

### 4 Servings

The following three recipes, as well as the fruit eggnog, 38, can serve as liquid-diet meals. See note on uncooked egg whites, (II, 523).

**I.** Combine in a shaker:

**4  cups chilled milk**
**4  eggs**
**4  tablespoons confectioners' sugar or honey**

**1  teaspoon vanilla, grated orange or lemon rind**
**(¹/₂  cup orange juice)**
**¹/₂  cup cracked ice**

Shake well. Sprinkle the top with:

**Freshly grated nutmeg**

Of course it will do no harm to add a jigger or two of whisky, cognac or rum.

**II.** To enrich or change the flavor of I, above, add one or more of the following:

**Ice cream**
**3  tablespoons carob powder**
**1  tablespoon nonfat milk solids**
**¹/₄  to ¹/₂ cup nutritional yeast**
**1  to 3 teaspoons smooth peanut or other nut butter**

## FRUIT MILK SHAKE

### 4 Servings

Combine in a shaker or blender:

**1¹/₃  cups chilled sweetened apricot, prune, strawberry or raspberry juice**
**2²/₃  cups cold milk**

Serve over cracked ice.

## ABOUT JUICES AND FRUIT BEVERAGES

Fresh herbs and fruits, when available, make attractive garnishes for cold or hot fruit beverages. For examples, see the illustration below: a sprig of mint, intense blue borage blossoms, lemon balm, strawberries, cherries, sweet woodruff or waldmeister, pineapple, apple mint, and fancy-shaped or clove-studded citrus

Another way to heighten the charm of cold beverages is to spruce them up with decorative ice cubes. Fill a freezer tray with water. Place in each section one of the following: a maraschino cherry, a preserved strawberry, a piece of lemon or pineapple, a sprig of mint, etc. You may flavor the cubes, before freezing, with sherry or whisky—using not more than 2 tablespoons per tray.

The short recipes that immediately follow are designed mainly to whet the appetite. They are dedicated to two kinds of people—those who cannot take cocktails because of their alcoholic content and those who like to appear convivial but who are convinced that a stiff alcoholic drink before dinner blunts the flavor of good food. The basic liquid ingredients may, of course, be served without our suggested modifiers. To make rich vegetable juices, blend vegetables, but be sure to cook and strain first any fibrous ones such as celery. Don't forget the convenience of frozen concentrates, especially for strongly flavored, quick-chilling drinks.

## TOMATO JUICE

### I. From Fresh Tomatoes

4 Servings

Simmer 1/2 hour:

    **12 medium-sized raw ripe tomatoes**

with:

    **1/2 cup water**
    **1 slice onion**
    **2 ribs celery with leaves**
    **1/2 bay leaf**
    **3 sprigs parsley**

Strain these ingredients. Season with:

    **1 teaspoon salt**
    **1/4 teaspoon paprika**
    **1/4 teaspoon sugar**

Serve thoroughly chilled.

### II. From Canned Tomatoes

4 Servings

Combine in a shaker:

    **2 1/2 cups tomato juice**
    **1/2 teaspoon grated onion**
    **1 teaspoon grated celery**
    **1/2 teaspoon horseradish**
    **1 1/2 tablespoons lemon juice**
    **A dash of Worcestershire or hot pepper sauce**
    **1/8 teaspoon paprika**
    **3/4 teaspoon salt**
    **1/4 teaspoon sugar**

This juice may be served hot or chilled. Curry powder, a few cloves, a stick of cinnamon, tarragon, parsley or some other herb may be steeped in the cocktail and strained out before it is served.

## CHILLED TOMATO CREAM

4 Servings

Combine in a pitcher:

    **1 1/2 cups chilled tomato juice**
    **3/4 cup chilled cream**
    **1 teaspoon grated onion**
    **1/8 teaspoon salt**
    **1/8 teaspoon celery salt**
    **A few drops hot pepper sauce**
    **A few grains cayenne**
    **1/4 cup finely cracked ice**

## TOMATO JUICE AND CUCUMBER

4 Servings

Combine in a pitcher:

    **2 cups tomato juice**
    **2 tablespoons vegetable oil**
    **1 tablespoon vinegar**
    **1/2 teaspoon salt**
    **1/8 teaspoon paprika**
    **(1/4 teaspoon basil)**
    **1/2 cup cracked ice**

Peel, seed, grate and add:

    **1 cucumber**

## ORANGE AND TOMATO JUICE

**4 Servings**

Combine in a pitcher:

1 1/2 **cups tomato juice**
1 **cup orange juice**
1 **teaspoon sugar**
1 **tablespoon lemon or lime juice**
1/2 **teaspoon salt**
1/2 **cup crushed ice**

## SAUERKRAUT JUICE

**4 Servings**

The straight article is—like brandy— a decoction for heroes; modifications like those which follow will encourage the rest of us.

**I.** Combine and chill:

1 **teaspoon lemon juice**
1/8 **teaspoon paprika**
2 **cups sauerkraut juice**

**II.** Chill, then combine:

1 **cup sauerkraut juice**
1 **cup tomato juice**
(1/2 **teaspoon prepared horseradish**)

## CLAM JUICE

**4 Servings**

Combine:

2 **tablespoons lemon juice**
1 1/2 **tablespoons chili sauce**
2 **cups clam juice**
**A drop hot pepper sauce**
**Salt if needed**
(1/2 **teaspoon grated onion**)
1/4 **teaspoon celery salt**

Chill these ingredients. Strain before serving. This is a tasty combination, but there are many others. Horseradish may be added; so may Worcestershire sauce. The cocktail may be part clam juice and part tomato juice. Serve sprinkled with:

**Freshly ground pepper**

## ORANGE AND LIME JUICE

**4 Servings**

Combine in a pitcher:

2 **cups orange juice**
1 **tablespoon lime juice or**
2 **tablespoons lemon juice**
1/8 **teaspoon salt**
1/2 **cup cracked ice**

## FRESH PINEAPPLE JUICE

**About 1 1/2 Cups of Juice**

A very refreshing drink.
Peel and core, (II, 133):

**A pineapple**

Cut it into cubes. Extract the juice by putting the pineapple through a food grinder or a 🥄 blender. There will be very little pulp. Strain the juice and serve it iced with:

**Sprigs of mint**

## PINEAPPLE AND TOMATO JUICE

**4 Servings**

Combine in a pitcher:

1 **cup pineapple juice**
1 **cup tomato juice**
1/4 **teaspoon salt**
1/2 **cup crushed ice**

## PINEAPPLE AND GRAPEFRUIT JUICE

**4 Servings**

Boil together 3 minutes:

1/3 **cup sugar**
1/3 **cup water**

Add:

1 1/4 **cups grapefruit juice**
2/3 **cup pineapple juice**
1/4 **cup lemon juice**

Serve chilled.

## FRUIT SHRUBS OR VINEGARS

These are most refreshing in hot weather. Try adding rum in the winter. Prepare:

**Fruit juice**

Depending on the sweetness of the juice, simmer until the sugar is dissolved:

**1 cup juice**
**1 to 1½ cups sugar**

For every cup of juice, add:

**¼ cup white wine vinegar**

Use at once or bottle in sterile jars. Serve the shrub over shaved ice.

## CITRUS FRUIT JUICE MEDLEY

**4 Servings**

Combine in a pitcher:

**¾ cup grapefruit juice**
**¼ cup lemon juice**
**½ cup orange juice**
**⅓ to ½ cup sugar**
**1 cup cracked ice**

Pour into glasses and serve garnished with:

**Sprigs of mint**

## ★ HOT OR MULLED CIDER

Great on a frosty night, with canapés or sandwiches. Heat well, but do not boil:

**Apple cider**
**A few cloves or cardamom seeds**
**A stick of cinnamon**

## CRANBERRY JUICE

**4 Servings**

Cook until skins pop open, about 5 minutes:

**1 pint cranberries**
**2 cups water**

Strain through cheesecloth. Bring the juice to a boil and add:

**¼ to ⅓ cup sugar**
**(3 cloves)**

Cook for 2 minutes. Cool. Add:

**¼ cup orange juice or**
**1 tablespoon lemon juice**

Serve thoroughly chilled. Garnish with:

**A slice of lime**

## ★ HOT CRANBERRY JUICE

Heat well, but do not boil:

**Cranberry juice**
**A thin sliced lemon**
**A few cloves**
**A cracked nutmeg**
**(Honey to taste)**

Strain out the spices. Serve in mugs, with cinnamon stick stirrers.

## FRUIT JUICE TWOSOMES

Good combinations are equal parts of:

**Orange juice and pineapple juice**

or:

**Loganberry juice and pineapple juice**

or:

**White grape juice and orange juice**

or:

**Cranberry juice and sweetened lime, pineapple or grapefruit juice**

## ⚘ ABOUT BLENDED JUICES

The blender transforms many kinds of fruit and vegetables into rich and delicious liquid food. The only trouble in using it is that the enthusiast often gets drunk with power and whirls up more and more weird and intricate combinations—some of them quite undrinkable. Resist the temptation to become a sorcerer's apprentice.

Sometimes, too, a gray color results. If so, gradually stir in lemon juice, a little at a time. Serve immediately after adding the lemon juice, as the clear color may not last long. A few suggestions follow. Each recipe yields 2 to 3 cups.

**I.** Combine in a blender:

1 1/2 **cups chilled seeded orange pulp**
1 **cup chilled melon meat: cantaloupe or honeydew**
2 **tablespoons lemon juice**
1/8 **teaspoon salt**
1/2 **cup finely crushed ice**

**II.** Made with fresh fruit, this is almost like a sherbet.
Combine in a blender:

1 1/2 **cups chilled apricot or peach pulp**
1/2 **cup milk**
1/2 **cup cream**
2 **tablespoons sugar**
1/2 **cup finely crushed ice**
(1 **tablespoon lemon juice**)

**III.** Combine in a blender:

1 **cup chilled unsweetened pineapple juice**
1 **cup peeled seeded chilled cucumber**
1/2 **cup watercress**
2 **sprigs parsley**
1/2 **cup finely crushed ice**

**IV.** Combine in a blender:

1 1/2 **cups chilled unsweetened pineapple juice**
1 **ripe banana**
2 **teaspoons honey**
**Juice of** 1/2 **lime**
1/2 **cup finely crushed ice**
Garnish with:

(**Sprigs of mint**)

## PINEAPPLE OR ORANGE EGGNOG

**4 Servings**

For other drinks that serve as liquid meals, see 37. Please see note on uncooked egg whites, (II, 523).
Combine in a shaker or blender:

2 **cups chilled pineapple or orange juice**
1 **tablespoon confectioners' sugar or honey**
1 1/2 **tablespoons lemon juice**
1 **egg or 2 egg yolks**
**A pinch of salt**
1/4 **cup cracked ice**
Shake or blend well.

## ABOUT PARTY BEVERAGES

As with Party Drinks, each of the following recipes, unless otherwise indicated, will yield about 5 quarts and accommodate approximately 20 people. For "ice-bowl" containers and other suggestions for attractively serving large groups of people, see Party Drinks, (II, 56).

## GALA TOMATO PUNCH

For a summer brunch in a shady corner of the patio.
Combine:

4 **quarts tomato juice, (II, 623)**
1 **quart canned beef consommé**
Season to taste with:

**Lemon juice**
(**A chiffonade of herbs**)
Chill and pour into a bowl that has been rubbed with:

(**Garlic**)
Adorn with:

**Decorative ice ring, (II, 57)**
in which has been set:

**An herb bouquet**

## LEMONADE OR LIMEADE

For each cup of water, add:

> 1½ tablespoons lemon or lime
> juice
> 3 to 4 tablespoons sugar
> ⅛ teaspoon salt

The sugar and water need not be boiled, but the quality of the lemonade is improved if they are. Boil the sugar and water for 2 minutes. Chill the syrup and add the fruit juice. Orange, pineapple, raspberry, loganberry, white grape juice and other fruit juices may be combined with lemonade. Chilled tea added to these fruit combinations, about ⅓ cup for every cup of juice, gives lemonades an invigorating lift. Quite acceptable are frozen lemonade and limeade concentrates, diluted a little less than prescribed by the processor.

## LEMONADE FOR 100 PEOPLE

Boil for 10 minutes:

> 4 cups water
> 8 cups sugar

Cool the syrup. Add:

> 7½ cups lemon juice

Stir in the contents of:

> 7 cups crushed pineapple:
> 2 No. 2½ cans, or
> 6 to 8 cans frozen juice
> concentrate: 6-oz. size

Add:

> 8 sliced seeded oranges
> 4 gallons water

Chill. Serve over ice.

## LEMONADE SYRUP

> About 4½ Cups

I. Boil for 5 minutes:

> 2 cups sugar
> 1 cup water
> Rind of 2 lemons, cut into
> thin strips

> ⅛ teaspoon salt

Cool and add:

> Juice of 6 lemons

Strain the syrup. Store in a covered jar. Add:

> 2 tablespoons syrup

to:

> 1 glass ice water or
> carbonated water

II. Add:

> 1 tablespoon syrup, above
> 2 tablespoons orange, apricot
> or pineapple juice

to:

> 1 glass ice water or
> carbonated water

## ORANGEADE

Serve undiluted:

> Orange juice

over:

> Crushed ice

or add to the orange juice, to taste:

> (Water, lemon juice and
> sugar)

## PINEAPPLE PUNCH

Place in a large bowl:

> 2 cups strong tea

Add and stir well:

> ¾ cup lemon juice
> 2 cups orange juice
> 2 tablespoons lime juice
> 1 cup sugar
> Leaves from 12 sprigs mint

Place these ingredients on ice for 2 hours. Shortly before serving, strain the punch and add:

> 8 slices canned pineapple,
> including juice
> 5 pints chilled ginger ale
> 4 pints chilled carbonated
> water
> Crushed ice

## RED RASPBERRY COOLER

Pour:

**3    tablespoons Red Raspberry Vinegar, (II, 179)**

over:

**Crushed ice**

and dilute to taste with water. Or, you may add:

**1    or more tablespoons Red Raspberry Vinegar, (II, 179)**

to:

**Lemonade, 39**

## FRUIT PUNCH

Boil for 10 minutes:

**1¼  cups sugar**
**1¼  cups water**

Add:

**2½  cups strong hot tea**

Cool the mixture. Add:

**1    cup crushed pineapple**
**2½  cups strawberry juice or other noncitrus fruit juice**
**Juice of 6 lemons**
**Juice of 7 oranges**

Chill these ingredients for 1 hour. Add sufficient water to make 4 quarts of liquid. Immediately before serving, add:

**1    quart carbonated water**

Pour over large pieces of ice in punch bowl.

## FRUIT PUNCH FOR 50 PEOPLE

Make a syrup by boiling for 10 minutes:

**1¼  cups water**
**2½  cups sugar**

Reserve ½ cup. Add to the remainder, stir, cover and let stand 30 minutes or more:

**1    cup lemon juice**
**2    cups orange juice**
**1    cup strong tea**
**2    cups white grape juice,**

**grapefruit juice, pineapple juice or crushed pineapple**
**(1  cup maraschino cherries with juice)**
**2    cups fruit syrup**

This last—the fruit syrup—is the key ingredient. It may consist of strawberry or raspberry jam diluted with hot water; or canned berry juice thickened by boiling. Strain the syrup. Add ice water to make about 1½ gallons of liquid. Add at the last minute:

**1    quart carbonated water**

If you find the punch lacking in sugar, add part or all of the reserved sugar syrup.

## STRAWBERRY FRUIT PUNCH

Boil for 5 minutes:

**4    cups water**
**4    cups sugar**

Cool the syrup. Combine:

**2    quarts hulled strawberries**
**1    cup sliced canned or fresh pineapple**
**1    cup mixed fruit juice— pineapple, apricot, raspberry, etc.**
**Juice of 5 large oranges**
**Juice of 5 large lemons**
**(3  sliced bananas)**

Add the syrup, or as much of it as is palatable.

Chill these ingredients. Immediately before serving, add:

**2    quarts carbonated water**
**3    cups or more crushed ice**

The basic mix is a concentrated one, to offset dilution through icing. Water may be added later if desired.

## COCOMOKA HOT

Prepare and combine, using 3 tablespoons coffee to 1 cup water:

**9    cups Coffee, 26**

9 cups Cocoa, 32
Bring to just under the boiling point
and add immediately before serving:

> 3/4 cup warmed rum
> 1 cup warmed crème de
>    cacao
> 4 tablespoons cinnamon or
>    2 tablespoons cardamom
> 2 tablespoons almond extract
> (1/4 cup honey)

Stir, test for desired sweetness, and
pour into hot mugs. Top with:

> Whipped cream

sprinkled with:

> Grated nutmeg or grated
> sweet chocolate

## COCOMOKA COLD

Prepare, then chill well:

> 7 cups freshly made coffee

Whip until stiff:

> 2 cups whipping cream

You may whip an additional 1/2 cup
heavy cream and then reserve it to
garnish the tops. Have in readiness:

> 2 quarts chocolate ice cream

Pour the chilled coffee into a
large chilled bowl. Add 1/2 the ice
cream. Beat until the cream is partly
melted. Add:

> 1/4 cup rum or 1 teaspoon
>    almond extract
> 1/4 teaspoon salt

Fold in the remainder of the ice
cream. Pour into tall glasses. Garnish
the tops with the reserved cream.
Sprinkle with:

> Freshly grated nutmeg or
> grated sweet chocolate

## ABOUT "SOFT DRINKS"

We cannot resist, as a postscript, a
few words of caution regarding the
increased use of certain types of beverages commonly and loosely classi-
fied as "soft drinks." Not the least of
our concern is the hard-core fact that
colas, carbonates and synthetic fruit
concoctions make up a disturbingly
large fraction of the juvenile intake,
and that this fraction almost everywhere stands in inverse proportion to
the size of the household food budget. With cola beverages the family
provider finds himself between the
devil and deep blue sea. The "normal" bottled or canned cola drink is
a blend of caffeine, sugar, flavoring
and water; caloric, unless you use a
sugarless counterpart, both devoid of
nutritional value.

As to canned or bottled "fruit
drinks," the government has seen
fit to identify no less than six categories, ranging from those in which
genuine fruit juice—with certain
preservatives—predominates, to those
in which the product is entirely or almost entirely artificial. Close attention to the list of ingredients printed
on the container—sometimes in very
small lettering—is urgently recommended. Our suggestion is to make a
practice of offering children unsweetened, unadulterated fruit juice, or on
occasion, if the going gets really
rough, sugar-sweetened juice.

# SALADS

We remember the final scene of a Maeterlinck play. The stage is strewn with personages dead and dying. The sweet young heroine whimpers, "I am not happy here." Then the head of the house—or what remains of it—an ancient noble, asks quaveringly, "Will there be a salad for supper?"

With virtually everyone, from the youngest commoner to the most palsied of patricians, salad nowadays has assumed a legitimately high priority, as well as—increasingly—first place on the menu. We are still inclined to prefer it in its traditional location—between entrée and dessert—mainly because a green salad makes a clean break between meat and sweet. But the initial presentation of a light salad at dinner can be a life-saver for a host or hostess whose pièce de résistance has, in fact, resisted and is not so ready as the guests.

All salads were once light salads: the edible parts of various herbs and plants, seasoned solely with salt—from which the word "salad" comes.

In more or less this form they play a cooperative role in reducing diets, always assuming that further sprucing up is limited to a sprinkling of lemon juice, a touch of spiced vinegar, or at most a low-calorie dressing, 417–418.

For those who can be more expansive, salads mean all sorts of combinations of chilled fruit, vegetables, herbs, meat, cheese, fish—even, we acknowledge with less than wholehearted enthusiasm, cereals and pasta served with some kind of moist dressing. At informal luncheons they may not only accompany the entrée but actually stand in for it. However, the chief danger in the present-day embarrassment of salad riches is that in carelessly planned meals the salad often tends to compete with the main dish, whenever or however served.

Keep the rest of the menu well in mind when preparing your salad and its dressing. A rich, heavy entrée demands a tart green salad. Slaws go well with casual meals, cookouts and impromptu suppers at which hearty, uncomplicated foods are served. Elaborate salads beautifully arranged and garnished, brilliant aspics, and decorative chaud-froids all look well on formal buffet tables or at special summer luncheons. In some cases these are served individually rather than as a single glittering showpiece.

We have suggested suitable dressings for the individual salads in this chapter and want you to try some of the variations listed. See also Sauces, Savory Sauces and Salad Dressings, 374–429. Don't go overboard, however; an undiluted heavy dressing will make any lettuce except iceberg collapse just when you want to keep it crisp. Your dressing should enhance the salad by summoning forth its special flavor and texture and by adding a delicate piquancy. Don't overlook, incidentally, the possibility of using a salad such as Celeri-Rave Rémoulade, 57, as an appetizer; and, conversely, an appetizer like Vegetables à la Grecque, 285, as a salad.

## ABOUT CULTIVATED SALAD GREENS

Enjoy the full range of cultivated greens, a number of which are sketched on 44. In successive rows at top, left to right, are crisphead or iceberg lettuce, Boston, bibb, Oakleaf, and Matchless; on the next row, witloof chicory, curly endive, watercress, and corn salad or mâche; at the bottom, Chinese cabbage, celtuce, roquette, escarole, and cos or romaine.

### CRISPHEAD OR ICEBERG LETTUCE

Large firm head, crisp, brittle, tightly packed. Outer leaves medium green, inner pale green and chunky. Can be torn, shredded or sliced like cabbage. Adds "crunch" and does not readily wilt. Improved recent varieties are Imperial, Great Lakes, Vanguard and Western.

### BUTTERHEAD LETTUCE

Smaller, less compact, softer than crisphead. Delicate leaves, of which the outer are dark green, the inner light green to yellowish and "buttery" to the taste. **Boston** and **buttercrunch** are the time-honored cultivars, but the aristocrat of the line is undoubtedly **bibb**. A Hawaiian-bred variety, **Manoa,** holds up in warm weather and is slow to bolt.

### LOOSE-LEAF LETTUCE

Some of these much more fragile, delicious and highly diversified kinds of lettuce can be occasionally and fleetingly bought at market or at roadside stands. If they are not purchasable, they are well worth bringing on early in the spring or fall in the family garden patch. The loose leaves branch from a single stalk, do not bunch, and vary in color. They are frequently used as an undergarnish for molded salads, aspic, or arrangements of salad vegetables and fruits.

Green and bronze **Oakleaf** is one of these types; **Salad Bowl,** which looks like a curly pale-green nosegay, another. **Matchless** is a deer's-tongue variety developed to resist heat and drought. **Prizehead** has a red-pigmented leaf that adds dash to a tossed salad.

### FIELD OR CORN SALAD, LAMB'S LETTUCE OR MÂCHE

Roughly also in the loose-leaf category, these plants, found wild in America, have been extensively cultivated in France and Italy. The clusters are small, made up of smooth green leaves; they may be grown in cold weather with little mulching. Like other varieties of lettuce, they are sometimes used as cooked greens.

### COS OR ROMAINE LETTUCE

Elongated head, with long stiff leaves which are usually medium dark to dark green on the outside and become greenish-white near the center. Its more pungent flavor enlivens a tossed salad.

### STEM LETTUCE

A Chinese variant in which the stem, rather than the leaves, furnishes the edible portion. It is used in Chinese cookery rather like the water chestnut, the taste of which it resembles when raw. Although easy to grow, it is rarely found in this country. Much more familiar to us is a close relative, **celtuce,** which may be eaten uncooked or braised like celery and which has a very high vitamin C content.

### RED-LEAVED CHICORY OR ARUGULA

A lettucelike sparker-up of salads, much favored in northern Italy. Its

spectacular crimson color, much showier than that of Prizehead, 43, i characteristic only of the youn growth that is carefully shielded from sunlight.

### CURLY ENDIVE OR CHICORY

Spiky leafage from a yellow-white stem. It adds a bitter flavor and somewhat prickly texture to a tossed salad. Occasionally used as a garnish

### ESCAROLE OR CHICORY ESCAROLE

Also known as **Batavian endive**. The leaves are broader, paler, less highly crimped than curly endive, above and the taste is less bitter.

### BELGIAN OR FRENCH ENDIVE OR WITLOOF CHICORY

Another bitterish salad component although highly variable: its freshly harvested heads are quite bland in flavor. They look rather like young unshucked corncobs. The outer of the closely packed greenish-white leaves may, like celery ribs, serve as receptacles for hors d'oeuvre.

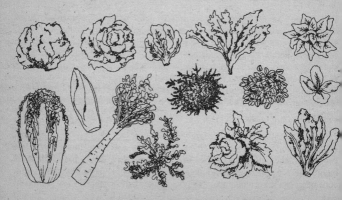

## ROQUETTE

The kind of salad material that sets up a love-hate relationship but which an impassioned minority contends it cannot do without. There are a number of varieties, all coarse-leaved, fuzzy, aggressive in flavor. To avoid a mixed reception, we advise its use only in a mixed salad.

## WATERCRESS

Dime-sized dark green glossy leaves on sprigged stems. The leaves and the tender portions of the stems are spicy and peppery additions to any tossed salad. They contain twice the protein, four times the vitamin C and much more calcium than lettuce.

In France, watercress is the invariable accompaniment to a roast chicken. In America it is one of our most interesting greens, frequently available in the wild. Its consumption, however, is often discouraged, because it may be growing in polluted water. To settle any doubts you may have, soak the cress first in 2 quarts of water in which 1 tablet of water purifier has been dissolved. Then rinse in clear water. Dry and chill before serving.

◗ To store watercress, cut off 1/2 inch of the stems. Loosen the tie and set in a container which does not press it on the sides or top. Fill the container with 1 inch of cold water, cover and set in the refrigerator. Wash thoroughly when ready to use. Cut off the tough ends before tossing.

## SEA KALE

Although this plant grows wild along European coasts, it also flourishes in inland gardens, where its thick, glaucous basal leaves, cropped from February to June, make a nutty-flavored salad component.

## CELERY AND SPINACH

The tender yellow tops of the celery as well as the sectioned ribs lend color and flavor to salads. So do the smaller leaves of spinach.

## CABBAGES

Not all types, of course, are candidates for salad. **Chinese** and **celery cabbage** very definitely are. Coleslaw, 49, it is important to remember, can be made of the **red** and the Chinese variety as well as the conventional "white" cabbage.

## GARDEN CRESS

Do not confuse with watercress. Garden cress has very tiny leaves which are picked 14 days after sowing. In sandwiches and hors d'oeuvre they are frequently combined with baby mustard greens. To grow, see (II, 241).

## WHITE MUSTARD

A European annual, with small tender green leaves, usually cut about a week after the seeds have been sown and used with garden cress in salads or for garnish.

# ABOUT WILD SALAD GREENS

Young **purslane, miner's lettuce, wild mustard, pepper grasses, plantains, dandelion, sorrels, Canadian burnet, winter cress, chickweed** and **spiderwort** may be used raw in salads; and some flower buds, like **hemerocallis,** (II, 155). **Milkweed** buds must be parboiled three times (discard the waters), then simmered

10 minutes before drying and cooling. In using wild greens, it is prudent to add them in relatively small amounts to more conventional greens, because many of them contain oxylates and other substances that may be harmful if ingested in quantity. Be very sure you can identify the greens you propose using, and wash them with great care.

Dandelion, or *Taraxacum officinale,* is easy to find and easy to handle if it is cut off at the root crown so that the leaf cluster holds together. Its slightly acid taste complements that of beetroot. After the plants flower, the leaves become tough and quite bitter. Edible varieties of sorrel are numerous, the best being *Rumex acetosella* and *R. acetosa.* The leaves have a pleasantly sour taste and when cooked make an esteemed garnish for seafood. Winter cress, or *Barbarea vulgaris,* is, as its name implies, highly resistant to cold and is widely distributed. The rosette of smooth dark-green leaves may be gathered as new growth either in early spring or late fall.

## ABOUT TOSSED SALADS

Salad ingredients prepared long in advance suffer a loss of nutritive value and arrive at table looking discouragingly limp. Take care in washing not to bruise them; see that they are well chilled, crisp and—especially—dry. It is usual to tear rather than cut greens, except iceberg lettuce, which, if you desire smaller pieces, can be sliced or shredded.

▶ To prepare lettuce, separate the leaves and wash them thoroughly. With iceberg lettuce this is difficult unless you core the solid part of the stem, either by using a sharp knife or by pounding the bottom of the head

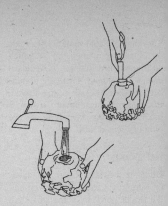

quite hard on a wooden board, when the core will simply fall out. Hold the head upside down under running water. Water pressure pushes the leaves apart without bruising them. Boston and field lettuces must be inspected carefully for grit and sand. Try some of the wild as well as the cultivated salad greens previously listed, for their texture and flavors differ distinctively.

▶ Dry greens by letting them drip in a colander, wrapping them lightly in a soft absorbent towel until dry, and chilling in the refrigerator until crisp and ready to use. Whirling greens in a wire salad basket is often recommended, but a Breton friend observes that, at home, this kind of treatment is contemptuously referred to as "a ride in the jail wagon," because it manhandles the occupants. If you like to whirl, try doing it in a tea towel. To dry such lettuces as bibb, which may be cleaned while still in head form, invert to drain, then place in the refrigerator on a turkish towel, cover with another plain towel and chill for several hours. Gravity and capillary action render them dry and crisp.

Place the greens in an ample bowl

and give them a preliminary light coating of oil. About 1 tablespoon of salad oil will suffice for a medium-sized head of lettuce. Toss repeatedly by lifting the leaves gently with a large fork and spoon until each leaf is completely coated. This conditions the greens against the wilting actions of the vinegar. Follow up with more oil, vinegar—in all, about ¼ the amount of oil—salt to taste, and further tossing. If the salad is mixed on this principle it will stay crisp, although it is usually eaten too quickly to prove it.

Since vinegar and salt release juices and impair vitamin content, add them as close to serving time as possible. ☰ For a picnic or barbecue, prepare the greens, wash and drain them, and put them in a large plastic bag. Take the dressing along in a separate container. Just before serving, pour the dressing into the bag and gently work it until the salad greens are coated. Serve from the bag or turn out into a large bowl.

The choice of salad oil is important. First in order of excellence is virgin-press olive oil, slightly unsaturated, light in color and with a faint aroma. Also available are mixtures of bland polyunsaturated oils, 8, preferred by some for dietetic reasons. You will also encounter an occasional gourmet who uses nothing but sesame oil, or a cholesterol-conscious

person who will eat only oil of safflower. An economical and effective substitute for straight safflower oil is a mixture of 20% safflower and 80% of another polyunsaturated oil such as peanut or cottonseed. If you find the taste of olive oil too strong, try combining it with any one of the blander, more highly polyunsaturated salad oils.

Your choice of a sour ingredient will depend on your own taste, but a good wine vinegar or lemon juice is the usual accompaniment to oil. Various kinds of herb vinegars are frequently chosen, but you may prefer to add these herbs separately later when you add the other seasonings. For a discussion of vinegars, see (II, 177–178). The classic oil-to-vinegar proportions are 3 or 4 to 1. Remember the old admonition: "Let the salad-maker be a spendthrift for oil, a miser for vinegar, a statesman for salt, a madman for mixing." To which we would add: an abolitionist for moisture.

Additional dressings, condiments and trimmings may be added after oil and vinegar to produce that infinite variety in flavor that is one of the chief charms of a tossed salad. Garlic is perhaps the most influential seasoning. There are two ways of giving to a salad a delicate touch of this pungent herb. Split a clove of garlic and rub the inside of the salad bowl with it. Or rub a rather dry crust of bread on all sides with a split clove of garlic; this is called a **chapon**. Place the bread in the bowl with the salad ingredients. Add the dressing and toss the salad lightly to distribute the flavor. Remove the chapon and serve the salad at once. If you wish to have a slightly stronger flavor, you may mash the garlic at the bottom of your salad bowl with other seasonings before adding oil and vinegar. This seems to modify its heavy pungency. ▶ Never leave a whole clove of garlic in any food brought to the table. Salting your salad may be unnecessary. If, after a cautious taste-test, you decide that it will improve your mix, sprinkle it on very sparingly and give the salad a final thorough tossing.

Additions to tossed salads may include sliced hard-cooked eggs, radishes, chopped olives, nut meats, pimiento or green pepper, sardines, anchovy, slivered cheese, julienned ham, chicken, tongue, grated carrots, cubed celery, onions—pickled, grated or as juice—and horseradish. Even a bit of cream or catsup may transfigure an otherwise lackluster mayonnaise, French or boiled dressing. In particular, the use of fresh herbs, (II, 265), may make a salad the high point of a meal. For already made-up dressings suitable for tossed salads, see variations on French Dressings, 415–416, Low-Calorie Dressings, 417–418, and Mayonnaise Dressings, 419–420, 427. The last may be used as indicated or slightly thinned with cream or yogurt.

▶ It is unwise to add cut-up tomatoes to a tossed salad; their juices will thin the dressing. Prepare them separately and use them for garnishing the salad bowl. The French cut tomatoes into vertical slices, 64, since they bleed less this way. Another nice last-minute addition is small hot Croutons, (II, 219), sprinkled over a tossed salad just before serving.

Well-seasoned wooden salad bowls have acquired a sacred untouchability with some gourmets which we think is misplaced. If the surface of a wooden salad bowl is protected by a varnish, as many are nowadays, the flavors of the oil, vinegar and herbs will not penetrate it, and you might just as well wash it in the usual way. An untreated wooden surface will certainly absorb some of the dressing used, but the residue left after wiping the bowl tends to become rancid, since we house our utensils in quarters warmer than they do abroad. This rancidity can noticeably affect the flavor of the salad. We prefer a bowl made of glass, of pottery with a glazed surface, or of hard, dense, greaseproof plastic.

## CAESAR SALAD

**4 Servings**

Steep:

    **1 clove garlic, peeled and sliced**

in:

    **½ cup olive oil: none other**

for 24 hours. Sauté:

    **1 cup cubed French bread**

in 2 tablespoons of the garlic oil, above.

Break up into 2-inch lengths:

    **2 heads washed, dried romaine**

Place the romaine in a salad bowl. Sprinkle over it:

    **1½ teaspoons salt**

    **¼ teaspoon dry mustard**

    **A generous grating of black pepper**

    **(5 fillets of anchovy, cut up small or mashed to a paste, II, 251)**

    **(A few drops of Worcestershire sauce)**

Add:

    **3 tablespoons wine vinegar**

and the remaining 6 tablespoons of garlic oil. Cook gently in simmering water for 1 to 1½ minutes, or use raw, (II, 523):

    **1 egg**

Drop the egg from the shell onto the

ingredients in the bowl. Squeeze over the egg:

**The juice of 1 lemon**

Add the croutons and:

**2 to 3 tablespoons Parmesan cheese**

Toss the salad well. Serve at once.

## WESTERN SALAD

**4 Servings**

Prepare:

**Caesar Salad, 48**

omitting the anchovies and adding:

**2 tablespoons crumbled blue cheese**

## WILTED GREENS

**4 Servings**

Exceptions prove the rule, and we justify the formulas for wilted greens in this section as applying to semi-cooked rather than raw salads—and thus outside our previous insistence on crispness of leaf.

Sauté:

**4 or 5 slices bacon**

Remove from pan, drain on absorbent paper and cut or crumble into small pieces. Heat:

**2 tablespoons melted butter, bacon drippings or oil**

Add:

**1/4 cup mild vinegar**

**(1 teaspoon chopped fresh herbs, II, 265)**

Add the bacon, and also at this time if you choose:

**(1 teaspoon grated onion)**

**(1 teaspoon sugar)**

Pour the dressing while hot over:

**1 head lettuce, separated; shredded cabbage; dandelion, young spinach leaves or other greens**

Serve at once from a warm bowl onto warm plates, garnished with:

**Sliced hard-cooked eggs**

## CHICORY AND BEETROOT SALAD

**4 Servings**

A favorite winter salad in France. Cut in 1/2-inch slices into a salad bowl:

**6 heads Belgian or French endive**

Add:

**2 cups drained sliced canned or cooked beets**

Toss in:

**French Dressing, 413, or Watercress Dressing, 414**

## ORIENTAL BEAN SPROUT SALAD

**6 Servings**

Place in a salad bowl:

**4 cups crisp salad greens**

**1 cup drained bean sprouts**

**1/2 cup thinly sliced water chestnuts**

**1/4 cup toasted slivered almonds**

Toss, just before serving, in:

**1/4 to 1/3 cup Oriental Dip, (II, 103)**

thinned with:

**2 tablespoons cream**

## COLESLAW

**6 Servings**

For those who wonder why cabbage is way out in front as the American vegetable crop, the answer is a rude four-letter word: slaw. Use "white" or red cabbage alone, or combine them for more interesting color. Or substitute Chinese cabbage, or bok choi, 45. Pared and diced pineapple or apple may be added, and bean sprouts are a welcome addition. Remove the outer leaves and the core from:

**A small head of cabbage**

Shred or chop the remainder, cutting

only as much as is needed for immediate use. Chill. Just before serving, moisten with:

> French Dressing, 413, or
> Boiled Dressing, 424, or
> Sour Cream Dressing, 425,
> or equal parts mayonnaise
> and chili sauce, or sweet or
> cultured sour cream

If you choose the cream, be sure to season with a little vinegar, salt and sugar. You may add to any of the above dressings:

> (Dill, caraway or celery
> seed)
> (Chopped parsley, chives or
> other herbs)

## COLESLAW DE LUXE

**8 Servings**

Shortly before serving time, remove the core from:

> A small head of cabbage

Cut it into the thinnest shreds possible. Place in a deep bowl. Add:

> 1 to 2 tablespoons lemon
> juice
> (Fresh herbs: chopped
> parsley, chives, etc.)

Beat until stiff:

> ³/4 cup whipping cream

Fold in:

> ¹/2 teaspoon celery seed
> ¹/2 teaspoon sugar
> ³/4 teaspoon salt
> ¹/4 teaspoon freshly ground
> white pepper
> 1 cup seedless green grapes
> ¹/2 cup finely shredded
> blanched almonds

Pour this mixture over the cabbage. Toss quickly until well coated. Serve at once with:

> Tomatoes, or in an Aspic
> Ring, 76

## ROQUEFORT COLESLAW

**4 Servings**

Based on a recipe from Herman Smith. His engaging little books, *Stina* and *Kitchens Near and Far* have appealed to all lovers of good eating and reading.

Shred finely:

> 1¹/2 cups young white or red
> cabbage

Peel and cut into long, narrow strips:

> 1 cup apples

In order to keep them from discoloring, sprinkle with:

> Lemon juice

Toss salad lightly with:

> Roquefort Sour Cream
> Dressing, 425

Serve at once, garnished with:

> Parsley

## ▤ COLESLAW FOR BARBECUE

**6 Servings**

The tangy dressing in this slaw goes well with meat broiled or barbecued outdoors. If you are cooking farther from home than your own backyard or patio, try the plastic bag method of "tossing" the slaw described on 47.

Combine:

> 1 cup Mayonnaise, 419
> 4 chopped scallions
> 2 teaspoons vinegar
> ¹/8 teaspoon Worcestershire
> sauce
> ¹/4 teaspoon salt
> ¹/8 teaspoon pepper
> ¹/4 teaspoon sugar

Add this mixture to:

> 3 cups shredded cabbage
> 3 cups salad greens
> 1 thinly sliced carrot
> ¹/2 green pepper, cut into
> strips

Toss salad lightly and serve.

## HOT SLAW WITH APPLE

**6 Servings**

Place in a skillet:

**1/2 lb. finely diced salt pork**

Render it slowly, then remove the crisp browned pieces, drain on absorbent paper and reserve. Add to the rendered fat in the skillet:

**3 tablespoons vinegar**
**2 tablespoons water**
**1 tablespoon sugar**
**1 teaspoon caraway or celery seed**
**1 teaspoon salt**

Cook and stir these ingredients over high heat until they boil. ♦ Reduce heat to a simmer. Stir in:

**3 cups shredded cabbage**
**1 large pared, grated apple**

Simmer the slaw about one minute longer and serve garnished with the tiny browned cubes of salt pork.

## ⚘ BLENDER SLAW

**4 Servings**

Quarter and core:

**1 small head of cabbage**

Core, seed and remove membrane of:

**1/2 green pepper**

Peel:

**1/2 medium-sized onion**
**1 carrot**

Chop these vegetables coarsely into the blender container until it is half filled. Add to within 1 inch of the top:

**Cold water**

♦ Cover and blend for 2 seconds—no longer—using the chopping speed. Empty the vegetables into a sieve to drain, and repeat the process until all the vegetables are shredded. Place them in a salad bowl and sprinkle with:

**(1 teaspoon caraway seeds)**

Toss lightly in:

**Mayonnaise, 419, or**

**Sour Cream Dressing, 425**

thinned with:

**2 tablespoons lemon juice**

## GINGHAM SALAD WITH COTTAGE CHEESE

**4 Servings**

Place in a mixing bowl and toss:

**1 1/2 cups coarsely chopped young spinach leaves**
**2 cups shredded red cabbage**
**1/3 teaspoon salt**
**1/4 teaspoon celery seed**
**3 tablespoons chopped olives or chives**
**1 cup cottage cheese**

Place these ingredients on:

**4 large lettuce leaves**

Serve the salad with:

**Mayonnaise, 419, Sour Cream Dressing, 425, or Green Mayonnaise, 420**

## ABOUT TOSSED COMBINATION SALADS

Serve combination salads as a luncheon main dish, accompanied by Toasted Cheese Rolls, (II, 73), or savory sandwiches, 267. Practically every restaurant serves some kind of combination salad, often named after its own inventive chef, but all have the distinction of containing some form of protein such as meat, chicken or cheese in addition to the greens and vegetables. Here are variations:

## COMBINATION SALADS

I. Rub a salad bowl with:

**Garlic**

Place in it:

**Lettuce or spinach leaves**
**Chopped, pitted ripe olives**
**Sliced radishes**

Sliced hard-cooked eggs
Shredded Swiss cheese
(Chopped anchovies or bits
of sautéed bacon or salami)

Toss the salad with:

French Dressing, 413

Garnish it with:

Skinned and quartered
tomatoes

For a **Greek Salad,** add sliced cucumbers, cubes of the crumbly white cheese known as feta, and a sprinkling of oregano.

## II.

About 30 Servings

This makes a showy platter for a luncheon buffet. On an oblong tray, make a base of salad greens:

Lettuce
Endive
Romaine
Watercress

Prepare, but do not overcook:

1　whole cooked cauliflower
3　cups cooked green beans
2　cups cooked beets
4　bunches cooked asparagus
tips

Add:

3　cups bean sprouts
1　cup raw sliced mushrooms
1　cup raw julienned celeriac

Marinate all the above several hours in:

French Dressing, 413, or
Italian Dressing, 416

Use about ¼ cup of dressing to 2 cups of vegetables. Drain well. Arrange the vegetables around the cauliflower center as shown, garnished with:

Deviled Eggs, 220
Radishes
Red pepper lobster cutouts

Other garnishes might include:

(Olives)
(Sardines or anchovies)
(Cherry tomatoes)

## III.

2 Servings

What various chefs call their **Maurice Salad** has spread like a brushfire all over America and abroad. Ours is not the original version, which was put together by a Cincinnatian; but at least the ingredients, except for the optional ones, remain fairly orthodox. Place in each of 2 sizable salad bowls:

A bed of shredded
crisphead lettuce

Divide and arrange on the top of each:

½　cup julienned cooked
chicken
½　cup julienned baked ham
(10　or 12 strips julienned Swiss
cheese)

Add to each bowl:

(1　to 2 chopped anchovies)
(A　few capers)

Garnish with:

2　sections skinned, quartered
tomatoes
2　quarters hard-cooked egg

Toss with a dressing made of:

½　chopped hard-cooked egg
1　teaspoon finely chopped
chives
¾　cup Mayonnaise, 419
1　teaspoon lemon juice

1 teaspoon Worcestershire
sauce
1 tablespoon chopped dill
pickle or pickle relish
(1 pressed clove garlic)

## CUTTING VEGETABLE GARNISHES AND CASES

Use vegetables as cases for piquant fillings as sketched at the top of following page: a hollowed-out pepper which can be lidded with its own handsomely fat stem portion; next, a trimmed cooked artichoke, with core removed to form a cup; an onion sliced to produce rings which will hold vinaigretted asparagus upright—center—on an hors d'oeuvre tray; to right of center, citrus rind rings or green or red pepper rings which can be used in the same manner to support food; onion cups made from raw or slightly blanched onions; a cucumber slashed and hollowed out to hold olives or gherkins; and, last in line, a scored cucumber cup.

Try your hand at carving vegetables and see what fun you can have and how attractive your trays can look with a little effort. Don't force effects. Use them sparingly. Begin with a choice of assorted herbs, 54, from left—thyme, burnet, tarragon, chives and garlic chives, fennel and watercress—carrots cut in scrolls, radishes made into roses, and pickles into fans. Provide geometric accents with hors d'oeuvre cutters and scoops, shown at center left and at the top on the right. Shape flowers and borders of red, yellow or green peppers; olives, at right of center, with twists of cucumber at lower right. Make an ingenuous turnip or egg white and carrot daisy, gay for spinach dishes, or small daffodil blooms of carrots and turnips, shown at center right.

The flowers can have fernlike stems and leaves of chive or other herbs, as you like. Try for some asymmetric drawinglike effects, such as shrimps suggested by thin lines of red pepper. One of the loveliest decorations we've ever seen were 2 small lobsters cut in conventionalized style from red peppers and placed casually on the side and the top of a cream-covered mousse. Seaweed, indicated by fennel leaves, partially crowned the top. See also (II, 252) for varied lemon garnishes.

## ABOUT VEGETABLES FOR SALAD

A welcome summertime alternative to crisp green salads or slaws is a vegetable salad, attractively arranged and dressed. Try the marinated Combination Salad, (version II on 52); simply prepare chilled cooked vegetables and serve them with a light vinaigrette or chiffonade dressing; or use Vegetables à la Grecque, 285, including snow peas. All the vegetables should be lightly cooked so as to retain some "bite."

### GARNISHES FOR SALADS

To garnish salads, use the following:
   Tomato slices dipped in
   finely chopped parsley or
   chives
   Parsley or watercress in
   bunches or chopped lettuce
   leaves, cress, endive or
   romaine
   Heads of lettuce cut into
   slices or wedges
   Lemon slices with pinked
   edges, dipped in chopped
   parsley

Shredded olives or sliced
stuffed olives
Cooked beets cut into
shapes or sticks
Carrots cut into shapes
Pearl onions
Pickles
Capers
Pomegranate seeds
Seedless or seeded table
grapes
Fennel slices
Cucumber or Cucumber
slices, 58
Green and red peppers,
shredded
Pepper slices
Mayonnaise or soft cream
cheese forced through a
decorating tube
Aspic jellies in small molds,
or chopped aspic
Eggs—hard-cooked, sliced,
riced or stuffed
Small-sized tomatoes,
halved, and stuffed with
cottage cheese
Cherry tomatoes
Slices of Spanish or
Bermuda onion
Fresh herbs, sprigs or
chopped

Mint leaves
Nasturtium leaves
Nutmeats
Chopped truffles
Shaped truffles

RUSSIAN SALAD

6 Servings

This recipe can be made quickly with
canned vegetables, although it is not
quite so good. If you wish, you may
marinate your vegetables for 1 hour
in French dressing, then drain and
toss them in the mayonnaise. Prepare
and dice in ¼-inch cubes:

1 cup cooked carrots
1 cup cooked waxy potatoes
1 cup cooked beets
½ cup cooked green beans

Add:

½ cup cooked peas

Toss the vegetables in:

Mayonnaise, 419

Serve in mounds on lettuce leaves
garnished with:

(A few capers)
(Julienned strips of ham)

For a more elegant occasion, after incorporating the mayonnaise—which
should be a stiff one—mold the salad
into a fish shape and cover with thin

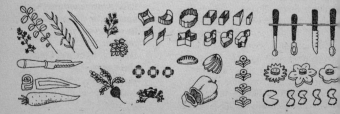

verlapping slices of cucumber, suggesting fish scales.

## TUFFED ARTICHOKE SALAD

### With Seafood

ook:

> Artichokes, 287–288

hill, and remove the inedible choke.

Marinate:

> Shrimp, crab meat, oysters
> or bay scallops

n:

> French Dressing, 413

ill the artichokes with the seafood
nd serve with:

> Mayonnaise, 419

n a bed of:

> Shredded lettuce

### I. With Caviar

ill the artichokes with:

> Cultured sour cream
> Caviar or salmon roe

### II. With Meat

ill with:

> Minced ham, veal, tuna or
> chicken

ombined with:

> Andalouse Sauce, 421

## RTICHOKE HEART SALAD

reshly cooked or canned artichoke
earts are delicious and may be cut
p and added to green salads or as-
ics, or used as the groundwork for
n attractive individual salad plate.
Ve like to pour over them:

> ♪ Blender Anchovy and
> Roquefort Dressing, 415

## SPARAGUS SALAD

ook:

> Asparagus, 290

Drain and chill. Cover the tips with:

> Vinaigrette Dressing, 413,
> or Mayonnaise, 419, or
> Boiled Salad Dressing, 424

thinned with a little:

> Cultured sour cream

Add:

> (Chopped tarragon, parsley
> or chives)

## ASPARAGUS TIP AND GREEN PEPPER SALAD

Drain the contents of a can of:

> Asparagus tips

Place around 4 or 5 tips a ring of:

> Red or green pepper

Place the asparagus in the ring on:

> Shredded lettuce

Serve the salad with:

> French Dressing, 413,
> Italian Dressing, 416, or
> Mayonnaise, 419

## ASPARAGUS AND EGG SALAD

**6 Servings**

Chill in a dish:

> 2 cups well-drained, cooked
> asparagus cut into pieces
> 3 sliced hard-cooked eggs
> 6 sliced stuffed olives

Wash, drain and place in refrigerator
to crisp:

> 1 bunch watercress
> 1 small head of lettuce

When ready to serve, combine:

> 1/2 cup cultured sour cream
> 2 teaspoons grated onion or
> chopped chives
> 2 tablespoons lemon juice,
> caper liquor or vinegar
> 1 teaspoon salt
> 1/4 teaspoon paprika
> 1/16 teaspoon curry powder
> (2 tablespoons capers)

Line a serving dish with the larger
lettuce leaves. Break the rest into
pieces. Add these to the asparagus

mixture. Cut up coarsely and add the watercress. Pour the dressing over these ingredients. Toss lightly. Place them in the serving dish. Serve the salad at once, garnished with:

**Parsley**

## DRIED BEAN SALAD

**4 to 6 Servings**

Lentils, kidney, navy, lima or miniature edible soybeans, cooked or canned, are the basis of these "stick-to-the-ribs" salads. Drain well and chill:

2½ **cups canned or cooked beans**

Combine with:

¼ **cup French Dressing, 413, or Thousand Island Dressing, 421**

**(A pinch of curry powder or ¼ cup chopped gherkins or pearl onions)**

Serve on:

**Lettuce leaves**

Sprinkle with:

**Chopped parsley**
**Chopped chives or grated onion**

## ⊟ GREEN BEAN SALAD

**4 to 6 Servings**

Prepare:

3 **cups cooked Green Beans, 291**

Drain well and toss while warm in:

**French Dressing, 413, or Lorenzo Dressing, 415**

Chill thoroughly, then add:

**Chopped or grated onions, chives or pearl onions**

Serve on:

**Lettuce leaves**

## HOT GREEN BEAN SALAD

**6 Servings**

Prepare:

3 **cups cooked Green Beans, 291**

Drain them. Combine them with the dressing for:

**Wilted Greens, 49**

Season as desired or with:

**(Summer savory)**

Serve from a warm bowl onto warm plates.

## COLD BEET CUPS

Cook:

**Large Beets, 300**

and chill. Hollow out the beets and fill them with:

**Chopped Wilted Cucumbers II, 58, with cultured sour cream, or Russian Salad, 54, Coleslaw, 49, or Deviled Eggs, 220**

Garnish with:

**Curly endive**

## PICKLED BEET SALAD

**5 to 6 Servings**

Drain:

2½ **cups cooked or canned beets**

Reserve the juice. Slice the beets. Place them in a fruit jar. Boil:

½ **cup sharp vinegar**
½ **cup beet juice**

Add and heat to boiling:

2 **tablespoons sugar**
2 **cloves**
½ **teaspoon salt**
3 **peppercorns**
¼ **bay leaf**
(1 **sliced green pepper)**
(1 **sliced small onion)**
(½ **teaspoon horseradish)**

Pour these ingredients over the beets. Cover the jar. Refrigerate at least 12 hours before serving on:

> **Watercress**

with:

> **Quartered hard-cooked eggs**

## CARROT SALAD WITH RAISINS AND NUTS

**4 Servings**

Scrape well:

> **4 large carrots**

Place them on ice for 1 hour. Grate them coarsely into a bowl. Add and mix lightly:

> **1/2 cup raisins**
> **1/2 cup coarsely chopped pecans or peanuts**
> **3/4 teaspoon salt**
> **Freshly ground black pepper**
> **2 teaspoons grated lemon peel**
> **1 tablespoon lemon juice**

Place the salad in a bowl. Pour over it:

> **1 cup or more cultured sour cream, or half sour cream and half mayonnaise**

Toss the salad and serve.

## CELERY CABBAGE SALAD

Use celery cabbage in any recipe for hot or cold slaw, 50–51, or in the following colorful recipe. Wash well, then crisp:

> **1 stalk celery cabbage**

Cut it crosswise into shreds. Serve very cold with:

> **French Dressing, 413**
> **Curry Mayonnaise, 422**

This cabbage combines superbly with:

> **Watercress**

Use any convenient proportion. Garnish the salad with:

> **Pickled Beets, 56**

## COOKED CELERY OR ENDIVE SALAD

**I.** Prepare:

> **Braised Celery or Endive, 312**

and serve cold on:

> **Lettuce leaves**

**II.** Simmer until tender:

> **Trimmed, halved dwarf celery or endive heads**

in a quantity of:

> **Veal or chicken stock**

Drain. Refrigerate the juices for use in sauces. Marinate the vegetable in:

> **French Dressing, 413**

to which you may add:

> **(1 teaspoon anchovy paste)**

Chill and serve on:

> **Lettuce**

## CELERIAC OR CELERY ROOT SALAD

Prepare:

> **Celeriac, 313**

Chill it. Toss it in:

> **Mayonnaise, 419, well seasoned with mustard, or Salsa Verde, 415**

or, best of all, in:

> **French Dressing, 413**

to which you may add:

> **(Minced shallots or chives)**

Serve on:

> **Endive or watercress**

## CELERIAC OR CELERI-RAVE RÉMOULADE

**5 to 6 Servings**

This also makes an interesting hors d'oeuvre. Wash well and pare as for Cooked Turnips, 372, in 1/4-inch rounds:

> **2 celeriac, about 4 inches in diameter**

Blanch, 106, in boiling salted water 3 to 4 minutes. Drain at once. Cool and dry. Cut into a fine julienne, 310. Cover with:

**Rémoulade Sauce, 420**

allowing about ¹/₂ cup sauce for each 2 cups of celeriac strips. Chill well and serve on:

**Watercress**

## TURNIPS RÉMOULADE

**4 Servings**

Wash well, pare, 372, and slice julienned, 280:

**2 cups turnips**

Cover with:

**Rémoulade Sauce, 420**

allowing about ¹/₂ cup sauce for each 2 cups of julienned turnips. Serve chilled on:

**Chicory**

## CUCUMBER SALAD

Be sure to select firm, hard cucumbers. Unless you are dealing with the roundish "apple" cucumber, yellowness is an undesirable trait, as is flabbiness. Both signify age, a pithy interior, and a tough skin. Otherwise the skin is edible, sometimes even by allergics who cannot tolerate the pulp alone. The skin should have a slight sheen; if highly polished, however, it has probably been waxed and should then be discarded. If you wish to make the cucumbers more decorative, leave them unpared and score them with a fork, as sketched, before slicing.

Chill, pare and slice:

**Cucumbers**

Combine them with:

**French Dressing, 413, or**
**Sour Cream Dressing, 425**

to which you may add:

**(Finely minced parsley)**

Serve at once.

## WILTED CUCUMBERS

As with other wilted salad materials, nutritive value declines; but heightened delicacy of flavor and appealingly smooth texture go far to compensate.

**I.** Pare and slice very thin:

**Cucumbers**

A potato peeler, left, does a fine job. Place the slices in a bowl. Salt each layer and place a weighted plate over the whole. Cover and refrigerate 3 to 6 hours. Drain and toss in:

**Cultured sour cream or**
**yogurt**

Garnish with:

**Chopped dill, basil or**
**tarragon**

Serve chilled at once.

**II.**

**3 Servings**

Slice, leaving the skins on if very young and unwaxed:

**1¹/₂ to 2 cups cucumbers**

Salt and weight as above. Refrigerate 2 hours. Rinse in cold water, drain and dry. Place the cucumbers in a bowl and toss them in:

**¹/₄ cup vinegar**

and:

**1 tablespoon sugar**

dissolved in:

**1 tablespoon water**

**Season to taste**

Chill 1 to 2 hours and serve garnished with:

**Chopped dill or burnet or very thinly sliced Bermuda onion rings**

## COLD STUFFED CUCUMBERS

Refreshing on a luncheon plate or as an hors d'oeuvre.

Chill:

**Small, shapely cucumbers**

Pare them. Cut them in halves lengthwise or cut off a slice lengthwise and remove the seeds. The cucumber boats may be wrapped in waxed paper and chilled. Fill with:

**Chicken Salad, 68, a fish salad, 65–67**

or anything suitable that you can think of, such as:

**Nutmeats or green grapes in seasoned cream cheese, minced ham, etc.**

These ingredients may be moistened with or served with:

**Mayonnaise, 419, Anchovy Dressing, 415, or Chutney Dressing, 416**

Serve the cucumbers on:

**Shredded lettuce or watercress**

## LOTUS ROOT SALAD

Peel and slice thin, crosswise:

**1 lb. lotus root**

Soak 10 minutes in:

**Acidulated Water, (II, 167)**

Drain and dip slices into:

**Fresh, boiling acidulated water**

Plunge quickly into:

**Cold water**

and drain again. Combine and heat:

**2 tablespoons sesame oil**
**1 to 2 drops hot pepper sauce**

**1½ tablespoons sugar**
**2½ tablespoons soy sauce**

Pour this sauce over the drained lotus root and let stand about 1 hour. Serve chilled in the sauce.

## OKRA SALAD

A hot-weather salad. The marinated pods are slightly reminiscent of oysters, even more so if white-podded okra is used.

Prepare:

**Stewed Okra, 332**

Drain. Place in a dish and cover with:

**Well-seasoned French Dressing, 413, Horseradish Dressing, 417, or Mayonnaise, 419**

Chill. Serve very cold on:

**Lettuce**

## HEARTS OF PALM SALAD

**I.** Cut into strips lengthwise:

**Chilled canned hearts of palm**

Serve on:

**Romaine**

garnished with:

**Stuffed olive slices**
**Green or red pepper rings**

Sprinkle with:

**Chopped parsley**
**Paprika**

Serve with:

**French Dressing, 413, or Roquefort or Blue Cheese French Dressing, 415, or Mayonnaise, 419**

**II.** If you live in Florida, you can have fresh:

**Hearts of Palm**

but see page 337. Be sure to eat them as soon as peeled, for they discolor quickly. Cut them into dice and sprinkle with:

Lemon juice

and serve with:

French Dressing, 413, made
with lime juice, or
Sauce Louis, 422

Another way to serve them is to treat
the hearts as for Coleslaw, 49–50.

## SALAD NIÇOISE

4 Servings

This recipe from the South of France
is often carried to the point of agreeable anarchy, when it becomes a sal-
magundi, and is apt to include strips
of cooked chicken, seedless grapes or
little onions, and hard-cooked eggs.
In compounding, keep in mind the
law of diminishing returns.

Rub your salad bowl with garlic,
then place in it:

2 skinned and quartered
tomatoes
1 pared and finely cut
cucumber
6 coarsely chopped fillets of
anchovy
12 coarsely chopped pitted
black olives
1 cup bibb lettuce
1 cup romaine

Toss in:

French Dressing, 413, or
Italian Dressing, 416

## PEPPER SLICES WITH FILLINGS

8 to 10 Slices

Highly decorative. These make a pretty
salad and are bracing as canapés on
toast or crackers.

Wash:

2 medium-sized red or green
peppers

Cut a piece from the stem end and
remove the seeds and membranes.
Stuff the peppers with a Cream Cheese
Spread, (II, 71–72), or Ham Salad, 68,

and chill 12 hours. Slice, not too thinly,
with a sharp hot knife and replace on
ice. You may serve the slices on:

Lettuce

with:

French Dressing, 413, or
Mayonnaise, 419, or
Curry Mayonnaise, 422

## ★ FILLED PIMIENTOS OR
CHRISTMAS SALAD

6 Servings

Cheery as Santa's chuckle; but do not
expect the peppers to look like fresh
ones. They are simply a gift-wrap for
the soft filling.

Drain:

6 large canned pimientos

Dice:

2½ cups drained canned
pineapple

Add to it:

1½ cups diced celery
1 tablespoon pickled tiny
pearl onions

Whip until stiff:

¼ cup whipping cream

Combine with:

1 cup Mayonnaise, 419

Fold into these liquid ingredients the
pineapple, celery and onions. Stuff
the pimientos with the mixture. Chill.
Bed on a nest of:

Shredded lettuce

## POTATO SALAD

Potato salad is best prepared from
potatoes cooked in their jackets and
peeled and marinated while still
warm. The small red waxy potatoes
hold their shape and don't crumble
when sliced or diced, but medium-
sized mature Idahos are also entirely
satisfactory. Do not try to make do
with yesterday's cold boiled potatoes; they will have lost much of their

down-to-earth savor. ♦ For hot weather picnics, use an eggless dressing to avoid dangerous spoilage.

## I.

**4 Servings**

Prepare as described above:

    **2 cups sliced boiled potatoes**

Marinate in:

    **½ cup heated French Dressing, 413**

Mix in gently with a wooden spoon, just before serving:

    **1 tablespoon chopped parsley**
    **1 tablespoon chopped chives or 1 tablespoon finely grated onion**

Serve tepid.

## II.

**4 Servings**

Marinate the potatoes well with:

    **½ cup French Dressing, 413, soup stock or canned bouillon**

Chop or slice and add discreetly a mixture of any of the following:

    **Hard-cooked eggs, onions, olives, pickles, celery with leaves, cucumbers, capers**
    **1 to 2 teaspoons salt**
    **Paprika**
    **A few grains cayenne**
    **(2 teaspoons horseradish)**

After one hour or more of refrigeration, add:

    **— Mayonnaise, 419, Boiled Salad Dressing I, 424, or cultured sour cream**

Refrigerate about 1 hour longer. Shortly before serving, you may toss in:

    **(Coarsely chopped watercress)**

## POTATO AND HERRING SALAD

**6 Servings**

Place in a large bowl and toss gently:

    **2 cups diced boiled potatoes**

    **1¼ cups diced marinated or pickled herring fillets**
    **¾ cup chopped celery with leaves**
    **1 tablespoon minced parsley**
    **1 tablespoon minced chives**
    **6 tablespoons cultured sour cream**
    **1½ tablespoons lemon juice**
    **¾ teaspoon paprika**

Served the salad chilled in:

    **Lettuce cups**

## GERMAN HOT POTATO SALAD

**6 Servings**

Cook in their jackets, in a covered saucepan, until tender:

    **6 medium-sized potatoes**

Peel and slice while hot. Heat in a skillet:

    **4 strips bacon, minced, or 2 tablespoons bacon drippings**

reserving bacon. Sauté until golden:

    **¼ cup chopped onion**
    **¼ cup chopped celery**

Add:

    **1 chopped dill pickle**

Heat to the boiling point:

    **¼ cup water or stock**
    **½ cup vinegar**
    **½ teaspoon sugar**
    **½ teaspoon salt**
    **⅛ teaspoon paprika**
    **(¼ teaspoon dry mustard)**

Combine all the ingredients in the skillet, stir gently with the potatoes, and serve at once with chopped parsley or chives. Leftovers are good served cold.

## POTATO SALAD NIÇOISE

**12 Servings**

Cook:

    **3 cups Boiled New Potatoes, 344**

in water to which a clove of garlic has

been added. Peel and slice and, while still warm, sprinkle potatoes with:

> 1/2 **cup heated white wine or**
> 1/4 **cup wine vinegar and**
> 1/4 **cup stock**

Let stand 1 hour at 70°. Have ready:

> 3 **cups chilled cooked green beans**
> 6 **skinned quartered tomatoes**

which have been marinating in:

> **French Dressing, 413**

To serve, mound the potatoes in a volcano shape in the center of a platter garnished with:

> **Salad greens**

Garnish the potatoes with:

> **Capers**
> **Small pitted black olives**
> 1 **dozen anchovy fillets**

Alternate the tomato quarters and small heaps of the green beans around the potatoes.

## RICE SALAD

> **6 Servings**

A variation of this theme with bulgur or cracked wheat as the cereal is called **tabuli.**
Prepare:

> 2 **cups Boiled Rice, 189**

The grains must be dry and fluffy. While the rice is warm, mix in:

> 1/2 to 3/4 **cup Herbed French Dressing, 414**
> 1/4 **cup finely chopped celery**
> (1/4 **cup coarsely chopped green pepper)**
> (10 **black olives, pitted and halved)**
> 1 1/2 **cups chopped Poached Scallops, 449, or 2 cans white tuna: 7 oz. each**

Garnish with:

> **Skinned, quartered tomatoes or strips of red pepper**

in a bowl lined with:

> **Leaf lettuce or watercress**

or in:

> **Halves of avocado**

If the fish is omitted, this dish teams up very successfully with cooked chicken or cooked smoked tongue. Serve tepid.

## ABOUT TOMATOES FOR SALAD

Please read About Tomatoes, 365. In preparing tomatoes for salad, always cut out the stem-end core, which is tough and may be bitter. Good texture is as important as good flavor. Vine-ripened tomatoes are infinitely superior to those picked green and allowed to mature on their way to the supermarket. Use the latter for Stuffed Tomatoes, 63, where they can be somewhat redeemed with a spicy filling. If available, the pear-shaped Italian variety, which has a distinctive mellow flavor, makes an excellent substitute. Another way to cope with this problem is to choose, instead, small cherry tomatoes, which, because of their proportionately large skin area, are pleasantly sharp in flavor. Halved or whole, they also lend themselves to dainty decorative uses.

## FRENCH TOMATO SALAD

Cut into very thin vertical slices, 64:

> 6 **medium-sized unskinned tomatoes**

Place them so that they overlap around a cold platter or across it. Pour over them a dressing made of:

> **French Dressing, 413**
> 1/4 **cup minced parsley**
> 2 **minced shallots or green onions**

## CANNED TOMATO SALAD

Chill the contents of a can of:

**Whole tomatoes**

or use the firm part of any canned tomatoes. Place them in individual dishes. Sprinkle with:

**Celery salt**
**Salt**
**Lemon juice**
**Brown sugar**

or a garnish of your own improvisation. The main thing is to serve them very cold.

## ABOUT COLD STUFFED TOMATOES

A bit of tomato skin was once as much out of place at a dinner table as a bowie knife. The discovery that tomato skins contain highly valued vitamins makes them *salon-fähig*—so whether to serve tomatoes skinned or unskinned rests with the hostess's sense of delicacy or her nutritional single-mindedness.

To skin tomatoes, first wash them, and then use one of the following methods: stroke the skin with the dull edge of a knife blade until the skin wrinkles and can be lifted off; or immerse in boiling water for 1 minute, then immediately in cold water, then drain and skin; or pierce with a fork and rotate over a burner until the skin is tight and shiny, plunge into cold water and peel.

To prepare tomato cases, first skin the tomatoes as described above, then hollow them out. Invert the tomatoes to drain for 20 minutes. Chill them and fill the hollows with one of the fillings suggested below.

Tomatoes cut and stuffed in a variety of attractive ways provide a gay splash of color for buffet salads. If you do not wish to serve large portions, cut the tomatoes into halves or slices. Place on each slice a ring of green pepper 1/2 inch or more thick. Fill the ring.

You may also cut tomatoes crosswise in zigzag fashion, fill them sandwich-style and top them with a mint leaf. Or, fill deeply gashed halves separately. Fill a whole tomato, which can have small or large gashes, and garnish with an olive slice or pimiento star; or cover with a pepper lid. Or, slice horizontally in thirds and fill like a double sandwich. All these cuts are shown below.

### FILLINGS

**I. Pineapple and Nutmeats**
Combine equal parts of:

**Chopped celery**
**Shredded fresh pineapple**
**A few walnut meats**
**Mayonnaise, 419**

**II. Eggs and Anchovies**
Combine:

**Chopped hard-cooked eggs**
**Chopped anchovies or anchovy paste**
**Onion juice or grated onion**
**Chopped parsley or other herb**
**Mayonnaise, 419, or cultured sour cream**

**III. Eggs and Ham**
Combine:

**2 chopped hard-cooked eggs**

1 cup ground or minced ham
1/2 cup chopped celery
12 sliced olives
   Fresh or dried savory
2 chopped sweet pickles
   Sour Cream Dressing, 425,
   or Mayonnaise, 419

## IV. Deviled Eggs
Place in each tomato hollow:
   1/2 Deviled Egg, 220
Serve on:
   Lettuce
with:
   Anchovy Sauce, 386

## V. Aspic
For about 6 tomato cases prepare:
   1 1/2 cups aspic, 76
This may also be an Aspic Salad,
76, to which chopped meat or fish
and vegetables may be added. When
the aspic is about to set, fill the
tomato cases. Chill until firm. Garnish with:
   Olives, parsley, etc.
and serve with:
   Mayonnaise, 419

## VI. Some other good fillings are:
   Wilted Cucumbers I, 58
   Crab Salad, 65, or a Fish
   Salad, 67
   Chicken Salad, 68
   Guacamole I, (II, 91)
   Coleslaw, 49
   Shrimp with Mayonnaise,
   419
   Cottage cheese or soft
   cream cheese mixed with
   Mayonnaise, 419, and
   chopped chives

## TOMATO AND ONION OR CUCUMBER SALAD

Skin and chill:
   Medium-sized tomatoes

Cut 5 or 6 vertical gashes in the tomatoes, equal distances apart. Place
in each cut, as shown below, a thin
slice of:
   Bermuda onion or
   cucumber

Or, cut the slices through, and arrange
them alternately on a so-called bone
plate, shown above. Serve on:
   Lettuce or watercress
with:
   French Dressing, 413, or
   Sour Cream Dressing, 425,
   or Avocado Dressing II, 416

## MOLDED EGG AND CAVIAR SALAD

Also notable as an hors d'oeuvre.
Crush with a fork:
   8 hard-cooked eggs
Stir into them:
   3 tablespoons soft butter
   1/3 teaspoon dry mustard
   2 oz. caviar or salmon roe
   3 tablespoons lemon juice
   1 tablespoon Worcestershire
   sauce
Pack these ingredients into an oiled
tall glass. Chill. Unmold and cut into
1/2- to 1-inch slices. Serve on:
   Skinned thick tomato slices
cut in the French manner, as shown
above, or use to decorate a salad platter. Cover with a dab of:
   Mayonnaise, 419
   (A rolled anchovy)

## STUFFED LETTUCE ROLLS

Add to:

> Creamed cottage cheese

all or some of the following:

> A sprinkling of chives or
> grated onion
> Chopped boiled ham
> Seedless raisins
> Chopped celery
> Chopped green peppers
> Chopped nutmeats

Spread a thick layer of the cheese mixture on:

> Large lettuce leaves

Roll the leaves and secure with toothpicks. Chill. Allow 2 or 3 rolls to a person. When set, remove the toothpicks and serve with:

> Mayonnaise, 419, or
> French Dressing, 413

Garnish with a fancy-cut vegetable as sketched on 54.

## MACARONI OR SPAGHETTI SALAD OR CALICO SALAD

**5 Servings**

Prepare:

> 2 cups cooked elbow
> macaroni, 200

Drain. Beat well:

> 1½ tablespoons lemon juice or
> 2 tablespoons vinegar
> 1 tablespoon salad oil

Combine this with the cooked macaroni. Chill the salad several hours. Toss with it a mixture of:

> 1 teaspoon grated onion or
> 2 tablespoons chopped
> chives
> 1 cup diced celery with leaves
> 1 cup minced parsley
> ½ cup chopped stuffed olives
> ¾ teaspoon salt
> Freshly ground black
> pepper

> 3 tablespoons cultured sour
> cream
> 2 tablespoons chopped
> pimiento

Try substituting for the mixture above:

> Basil Pesto, (II, 251)

Serve on:

> Lettuce

or in:

> A Tomato Aspic Ring, 77

## CRAB OR LOBSTER SALAD

**4 Servings**

Dice:

> 1 cup canned or cooked crab
> or lobster meat

Add:

> (Grated onion)

Marinate in:

> ¼ cup French Dressing, 413

Chill 1 hour. Combine with:

> 1 cup chopped celery

Place on:

> Lettuce

Cover or combine with:

> ½ cup Mayonnaise, 419

to which you may add:

> (2 tablespoons dry sherry)

Garnish with:

> Lobster or crab claws
> Olives and radishes
> Hard-cooked eggs
> Capers and pickles

Or prepare:

> Tomato Aspic, 77

in a ring or in individual molds. Invert the aspic on:

> Lettuce or very tender
> cabbage

Fill the ring or surround the aspics with the shellfish.

## CRAB LOUIS

**4 Servings**

A version from the West Coast, where the magnificent Dungeness or Pacific crab, or the Alaskan King crab is frequently served in this way. Arrange around the inside of a bowl:

**Lettuce leaves**

Place on the bottom:

**¾ cup shredded lettuce leaves**

Heap on these:

**2 cups cooked crab meat**

Pour over the crab:

**1 cup Sauce Louis, 422**

Slice:

**(2 hard-cooked eggs)**

Place them on top of the crab. Sprinkle over them:

**Chopped chives**

## ★ HERRING SALAD

**About 20 Servings**

Herring is traditional for our family at Christmastime. The rich color, thanks to the red beets, and elaborate garnishing make this dish an imposing sight.

Soak in water 12 hours:

**6 milter herring**

Skin and remove the milt and the bones. Rub the milt through a colander with:

**1 cup dry red wine or vinegar**

Cut into ¼-inch cubes the herring and:

**1½ cups cold cooked veal**
**2 hard-cooked eggs**
**1½ cups Pickled Beet Salad, 56**
**½ cup Spanish or Bermuda onions**
**½ cup pickles**
**2 ribs celery**
**½ cup diced cold boiled potatoes**
**3 cups peeled diced apples**
**1 cup blanched, shredded almonds**

Combine the milt mixture with:

**1 cup sugar**
**2 tablespoons horseradish**

**2 tablespoons chopped parsley**

Pour this over the other ingredients. Mix well. Shape the salad into a mound or place it in a bowl. Garnish with:

**Riced hard-cooked eggs**
**Pickles and olives**
**Anchovies and sprigs of parsley**

## ★ VIENNESE BEAN AND HERRING SALAD

**20 Servings**

Drain the juice from:

**2 cups pickled beets:**
**1 lb. jar**

reserving the juice. Dice the beets. Combine and set aside:

**¼ cup beet juice**
**2 tablespoons prepared mustard**
**2 to 4 tablespoons sugar**

Drain the following vegetables and combine them with the beets in a large bowl:

**1 cup baked beans**
**½ cup canned or cooked kidney beans**
**1 cup canned or cooked lima beans: 8½ oz. can**
**1 cup diced boiled potatoes**
**1 cup canned or cooked peas and carrots: 8½ oz. can**
**2 cups diced, peeled and cored tart apples**
**1 cup finely diced sweet gherkins**
**1 large diced, peeled dill pickle**

Drain, dice and add:

**2 cups canned herring in wine sauce**

Toss the salad thoroughly with the sweetened mustard sauce and refrigerate at least 2 hours. Mound onto a large platter of lettuce and surround with:

> Curly endive
> Onion rings

## SHRIMP OR LOBSTER MOLD

**4 Servings**

This makes a lovely center for an hors d'oeuvre tray. Chop and combine:

> 1 lb. cooked shrimp or lobster
> 1 tablespoon capers
> 1/3 small onion

Add and mix well:

> 1/3 cup softened butter
> 3 tablespoons whipping cream
> 2 tablespoons Pernod
> A dash of hot pepper sauce
> 1 teaspoon salt
> 1 teaspoon fresh tarragon

Pack into a mold. Refrigerate 3 to 4 hours before serving. For a special occasion, mold the mixture flat in either individual molds or one large mold.
Cover with a thin icing of:

> Whipped cream

Cut large crescents from pieces of:

> Red peppers

and arrange them on the salads to suggest the tails, claws and antennae of lobster or shrimp. For an added touch of realism, garnish with seaweed made of:

> Wisps of finocchio leaf

and a few:

> Seedless green grapes

## TUNA FISH, SHRIMP OR SHAD ROE SALAD

**4 Servings**

Have ready:

> 1 cup canned fish or canned or cooked roe

Flake it with a fork. Add:

> 1/2 to 1 cup diced celery or cucumber

Make a French dressing using:

> 2 tablespoons olive oil
> 2 tablespoons lemon juice

or use:

> 1/4 cup Mayonnaise, 419

Add:

> (1 tablespoon chopped chives)
> (1 tablespoon chopped parsley)

Serve very cold on:

> Lettuce

## FISHERMAN'S SALAD

**12 Servings**

Have ready raw or unshucked:

> 1 lb. medium-sized shrimp
> 1 1/2 lb. squid
> 24 cherrystone clams
> 3 lb. mussels

To prepare them, rinse shrimp, mussels and clams, scrubbing if necessary to remove weed and scum. If fishmonger has not done so, lift out beak, eyes and backbone of squid; remove ink sac and pull off brown skin, 493.
Simmer uncovered 40 minutes:

> 1 cup sliced onions

in:

> 2 cups Fish Stock, (II, 173)
> 2 cups dry white wine
> 2 cups water
> 1 bay leaf
> 1 rib celery

Add successively to the above the following seafood, first simmering uncovered 7 minutes:

> The shrimp

Remove shrimp, let cool, shell and devein. Add to liquid, simmering uncovered 17 minutes:

> The squid

Remove squid, let cool, and cut into 1/4-inch slices. Add to liquid, simmering uncovered until shells open—about 5 minutes:

### The clams

Remove clams; remove meat, discarding shells; let meat cool. Add to liquid, simmering uncovered until shells open—about 7 minutes:

### The mussels

Remove mussels; remove meat, discarding shells; let meat cool.

Mix in a large bowl:

**3/4 cup olive oil**
**3 tablespoons wine vinegar**
**1½ tablespoons Dijon mustard**
**1 teaspoon crushed garlic**
**1 teaspoon salt**
**1 tablespoon chopped parsley**
**1 tablespoon capers**
**¼ teaspoon white pepper**

Toss this dressing with the fish and let marinate 10 to 12 hours in refrigerator, retossing once or twice. Serve on bed of:

**Curly endive or watercress**

Garnish with:

**Lemon wedges**

## CHICKEN SALAD

**4 Servings**

A traditional party dish, chicken salad should taste of chicken, the other ingredients being present only to enhance flavor and add variety of texture. So always keep the proportions of at least twice as much chicken as the total of your other ingredients. Since the meat is usually combined with mayonnaise, be careful to ♦ refrigerate this salad, particularly if you make it in advance.

Dice:

**2 cups cooked chicken**
**1 cup celery**
**(¼ cup salted almonds)**

Chill these ingredients. They may be marinated lightly with:

**French Dressing, 413**

When ready to serve, combine with:

**1 cup Mayonnaise, 419**

Season the salad to taste with:

**Salt and paprika**

Serve it on:

**Lettuce**

Garnish with:

**Pimiento and olives**
**(Sliced hard-cooked eggs and capers)**

**Quantity note:** Generous main-dish servings for 50 will require:

**1 gal. cooked cubed chicken**

To obtain this amount, you need about 17 pounds ready-to-cook chicken. If you substitute turkey, you need only a boneless 12-pounder.

## CHICKEN SALAD VARIATIONS

Follow the preceding recipe. You may substitute cooked duck, turkey or veal for the chicken, remembering to keep the proportions of 2 of meat or fowl to 1 of the other ingredients.

**Chicken, celery and hard-cooked eggs**
**Chicken, bean sprouts and water chestnuts**
**Chicken, cucumber and English walnut meats**
**Chicken, Boiled Chestnuts, 313, and celery—pimiento may be added**
**Chicken and parboiled oysters**
**Chicken and fruit such as seedless grapes, fresh chopped pineapple and pomegranate seeds**

You may add to the mayonnaise:

**(Chili Sauce, II, 686)**

See also Chicken Mousse, 86.

## HAM, CORNED BEEF, VEAL OR BEEF SALAD

**I.** Let this be largely a matter of inspiration.

Dice:

Cooked ham, corned beef,
veal or beef
Hard-cooked eggs
Celery with the youngest
leaves
(Green peppers or pickles)

Combine these ingredients with:

Tart Mayonnaise, 419, or
French Dressing, 413

Garnish with:

Chopped chives, parsley or
other herbs

Surround the meat with tomatoes,
sliced or whole.

**II.** Serve, garnished as above:

Thinly sliced cooked beef,
veal or ham

covered with:

Sauce Gribiche, 422

## ABOUT FRUIT SALADS

Somehow the contrast between fresh
and canned components seems to
become more pronounced whenever
we address this topic, but perhaps
we have been obliged too often to
confront the syrupy peach-half, the
scoop of cottage cheese, the blob of
mayonnaise and—crown and anticlimax of the whole sorry construction—that maraschino cherry. With
the increasing wealth and diversity
of fresh materials available, and the
scope they afford the designer, fruit
salads can in fact be utterly irresistible and, when skillfully arranged on
a platter, can substitute for flowers as
a buffet centerpiece.

With protein such as chicken, meat,
cheese or fish, fruits make wonderful
summer luncheon dishes. As a general rule, keep the dressings for pre-
dessert fruit salads fairly tart, so that
the appetite is not dulled. As a change
from the usual base of salad greens,
serve them where suitable in baskets,

cups or cases made from fruit as described on (II, 131). In advance preparation, to avoid browning, bananas,
peaches and other fruits that discolor
quickly should be covered during
storage with the acid dressing you
plan on using.

## BIRD OF PARADISE SALAD

This exotic Hawaiian hybrid makes a
festive appearance at a luncheon or
supper table. For two individual servings, split in two lengthwise:

A green-tufted ripe
pineapple

Scoop out the center of each half, discarding the tough pulp; reserve and
chop the remainder, keeping enough
intact to form a bird's head, see illustration below. The birds in the foreground contain either mixed fruits or
a fruited chicken salad. The bird in
the background with the more flam-
boyant tail holds enough pineapple
for 4 servings and is suggested as a
centerpiece for an intimate dinner.
Combine:

1 cup finely diced cooked
chicken

with the pineapple and:

1/2 cup Cream Mayonnaise,
422

Fill the hollow in the bird's back with
the chicken mixture and round it
slightly. Attach the pineapple head
with a countersunk toothpick. Em-
broider the bird's back with a pattern

of halved grapes or pomegranate seeds, using a portion of the garnish on countersunk toothpicks for the bird's eyes. As can be readily imagined, this *rara avis* easily evolves into an all-fruit salad when the major fillers are seedless grapes or pitted Queen Anne cherries and of course pineapple, and when the dressing is hopped up with a liberal dash of fruit liqueur. See About Fruit Salads, 69.

## APPLE, PEAR OR PEACH SALAD

Try this with an omelet, French bread and coffee. Pare, core, slice and sprinkle with lemon juice to keep them from discoloring:

>**Well-flavored apples, pears, or peaches**

Serve on:

>**Lettuce**

with:

>**Yogurt Dressing, 426**
>**or French Dressing, 413**

Garnish the salad with:

>**Vicksburg Cheese, (II, 88),**
>**or Nut Cheese Balls, (II, 88)**

The apples may be cut into rings and the cheese balls placed in the center.

## WALDORF SALAD

**6 Servings**

Prepare:

>1 **cup diced celery**
>1 **cup diced apples**
>(1 **cup Tokay grapes, halved and seeded)**

Combine with:

>1/2 **cup walnut or pecan meats**
>3/4 **cup Mayonnaise, 419,**
>**or Boiled Salad**
>**Dressing III, 425**

## ABOUT AVOCADO SALADS

Please read About Avocados, (II, 119). To prepare avocado cups, cut the fruit in half lengthwise, place between the palms of the hands and gently twist the halves apart. Tap the large seed with the edge of a knife and lift or pry it out, as shown at top, above. ▶ To prevent the fruit from darkening after cutting, sprinkle with lemon juice. ▶ To store a cut avocado, allow the seed to remain embedded, spread the edges with mayonnaise, soft butter or cream, cover well with wax paper or plastic, and refrigerate. Avocado has a soft, buttery texture and taste which combines best with citrus fruits or tomatoes and a sharp or tangy dressing. It also has an unexpected affinity for shrimp, crab or lobster. All of these combinations offer a pleasing contrast of color as well as texture and taste—the hallmark of a delectable salad.

Illustrated center and at bottom in the sketch above are steps in cutting avocado into a charming fan-shape.

Select only ripe fruit; lay the peeled halves cut side down on a flat surface; then, using a sharp knife inserted at a slight angle, and with a slight spiraling motion, slice thinly from one end to about ¾ inch from the other. You will find that the slices may be splayed out in an overlapping pattern. The finished product is shown in the sketch opposite, amplified by the addition of cherry tomatoes and watercress. On the right are variations of avocado and orange or grapefruit slices.

## AVOCADO SLICES

These may also be used as a garnish for meats and fish.
Chill:
> **Avocados**

Pare and slice them. Marinate about 5 minutes in highly seasoned, chilled:
> **French Dressing, 413**

You may also add:
> **(Hot pepper sauce, Chili Sauce, II, 686, or Catsup, II, 686)**

Sprinkle with:
> **Chopped parsley or chopped mint**

Try these avocado slices in:
> **(Tomato Aspic, 77)**

## AVOCADO AND FRUIT SALAD

Pare:
> **Avocados**

Slice them lengthwise and arrange them with skinned sections of:
> **Orange and grapefruit or pineapple slices**

in wheel shape, on:
> **Lettuce**

as shown above, or make a rounded salad by alternating the fruit with the green avocado slices into an approximate half globe on the lettuce as pictured above.
Serve with:

**Celery Seed Dressing, 417, or French Dressing for Fruit Salad, 415**

## AVOCADO SALAD CUPS

Cut into halves and remove the seeds from:
> **Chilled avocados**

You may then fill the hollows with:

**I.** Chili Sauce, (II, 686), seasoned with horseradish

**II.** Marinated seedless grapes, 72
Garnish with:
> **A sprig of parsley, mint or watercress**

**III.** Dress up:
> **Crab meat, chicken or fruit salad**

with:
> **Mayonnaise, 419**

thinned with a little:
> **Lemon or lime juice**

and fill the avocado cup.

**IV.** Fill with a **Tomato Ice** which can be made like:
> **Fruit Ice, (II, 557)**

substituting tomato juice for the fruit juice.

**V.** Scoop the pulp out of the skin instead of paring the avocado. Turn it into:

**Guacamole, (II, 91)**

Put the mixture back in the half shell and garnish with:

**A slice of stuffed olive**

## BANANA, ORANGE AND NUT SALAD

For each serving, peel and split lengthwise:

**1 banana**

Arrange the 2 halves on either side of:

**Skinned orange sections, (II, 125)**

or:

**Dates stuffed with cheese, (II, 127–128)**

Sprinkle with:

**Chopped peanuts or English walnuts**

Garnish with:

**Tender lettuce leaves**

Serve with:

**Honey Dressing, 416**

## CHERRY AND HAZELNUT SALAD

Drain and pit:

**Canned white cherries**

Insert in each cherry:

**A hazelnut meat**

Serve very cold with:

**Cottage cheese Mayonnaise, 419, or Fruit-Salad Mayonnaise, 421**

## ABOUT GRAPE SALADS

Ever peel a grape? Well, it takes time, but what is more luxurious than a lovely mound of peeled, seeded table grapes—seedless green, or Tokay, Malaga, olivette, etc.—lightly tossed in a mild olive oil and vinegar dressing, served in lettuce cups or as the center for a clear gelatin salad ring mold, 76? To make a baroque grape finish on a gelatin top, see II, 234. Or mix seedless grapes with cultured sour cream, yogurt or creamed cottage cheese as a fruit salad garnish.

## CITRUS FRUIT SALAD

### I.

4 Servings

Prepare:

**Sections of 2 grapefruit or 4 oranges, (II, 127 and 125), or a combination of the two**

Arrange them on individual plates on:

**Lettuce, witloof chicory, or watercress**

You may place between alternate sections of the citrus fruit:

**Strawberries or cooked cranberries**

Serve with:

**French Dressing, 413**

**II.** When the entrée is game, prepare the above salad with oranges only and dress with a mixture of:

**2 tablespoons brandy**
**2 tablespoons olive oil**
**1 teaspoon sugar**
**1/4 teaspoon salt**
**A few grains cayenne**

Sprinkle the tops of the fruit with:

**Chopped tarragon**

## MELON SALAD

Prepare:

**Melon Baskets, (II, 131), or Melon Rounds, (II, 131)**

Fill with:

**Hulled berries**
**Diced pineapple or seedless grapes**

Moisten with chilled:

**French Dressing, 413, or Cream Mayonnaise, 422, or cultured sour cream**

## ORANGE AND ONION SALAD

Arrange:

>**Skinned orange sections or peeled, sliced oranges**
>**Thin slices of Bermuda onion**
>**(Pink grapefruit sections)**

on:

>**Lettuce leaves, endive or escarole**

Serve with:

>**Celery Seed Dressing, 417**

An Italian version of this salad adds:

>**Pitted black olives**

## FRESH PEACH AND CHEESE SALAD

**6 Servings**

Cut into 6 parts:

>**3 oz. cream cheese**

Roll the cheese into balls, then in:

>**Chopped nutmeats**

Pare; cut into halves and pit:

>**6 ripe peaches**

Place a ball of cheese between 2 peach halves. Press the peach into shape. Roll it in lemon juice to enhance flavor and prevent discoloration. If the peaches are not to be served at once, chill them in closed containers. Serve on:

>**Watercress**

with:

>**French Dressing for Fruit Salad, 415**

A bit of cress may be placed in the top end of each peach. Decorative—though it may puzzle a horticulturist.

## PEAR SALAD

Chill and pare:

>**Ripe fresh pears or drained canned pears**

Follow the preceding recipe for Peach Salad. Or fill the hollows with:

>**Cream cheese**

combined with:

>**Chopped Candied Ginger, (II, 605)**

Brush the sides of each pear with:

>**Red vegetable coloring**

Insert in the base:

>**A clove**

and at the top, simulate leaves with:

>**A bit of watercress**

Serve with:

>**French Dressing, 413**

## PEAR AND GRAPE SALAD

Pare:

>**Fresh pears**

or drain:

>**Canned pears**

Place half a pear cut side down on a plate. Thin:

>**Cream cheese**

to spreading consistency with:

>**Cream**

Cover each pear half with a coating of cheese. Press into the cheese, close together to look like a bunch of grapes:

>**Stemmed halved seedless grapes**

Add a leaf of some kind, preferably grape.
Serve with:

>**Mayonnaise, 419, or**
>**French Dressing, 413**

## JAPANESE PERSIMMON SALAD

An opportunity for color. If you wish to skin the fruit, rub it first with the blunt side of a knife and peel with the sharp edge.
Chill:

>**Ripe Japanese persimmons**

Leave them whole or cut them lengthwise almost to the base and insert in the slashes:

Slices of peeled orange,
grapefruit and avocado
and serve with:
Boiled Salad
Dressing III, 425

## PINEAPPLE SALAD

Drain:
Slices of canned pineapple
Serve them on:
Lettuce with French
Dressing, 413
Add to the French Dressing:
A little confectioners' sugar
Or cover the slices with:
Riced soft cream cheese
topped with:
A spoonful of currant jelly
Serve the salad with:
French Dressing, 413, or
Mayonnaise, 419

## ABOUT MOLDED SALADS

For utilizing leftovers, an aspic is second only to a soufflé. Any clever person can take a few desolate-looking refrigerator scraps and glorify them into a tempting molded salad or mousse. This kind of dish has two further advantages. One is that it can be prepared a day or so in advance and kept chilled in the refrigerator. The other is built in, so to speak, and has to do with gelatin's properties as a protein-extender, (II, 233). Each of these salads depends on gelatin to

hold its shape, so please read About Gelatin, (II, 233). Molds may be filled dry, but a jellied mixture is more readily removed when the molds have been moistened with water. If the mixture is not a clarified one, you may lightly brush the mold with oil. Be sure to sample your salad before molding and season to taste. ◗ Under-salt if it is to be held 24 hours. ◗ Never freeze gelatin salads.

Many of the recipes that follow may be made either in a large mold or in individual small ones like those shown below. Use ring molds if you wish to fill centers with some other kind of salad, such as chicken, Vegetables à la Grecque, 285, fruit, or a cream cheese mixture, dressed and garnished to your fancy. Fish-shaped molds can make a seafood aspic appear very professional. For large groups, you may even use small paper drinking cups for individual portions: simply tear off the cup when the aspic has congealed, and behold—jiffy jelly! Or use large No. 2½ cans and cut around the bottom of the can when ready to turn out the cylinder. Push the salad out of the can, slice, and serve the rounds on lettuce.

Aspics and other molded salads with a clear body lend themselves to highly decorative treatment, although their preparation can be time-consuming. However, certain ingredients naturally come to rest either at

the top or bottom of a jelling salad, and you can achieve interesting layered effects by manipulating "floaters" and "sinkers." See (II, 235) for a list of the ingredients that can be incorporated into your salad simultaneously and which will more or less automatically layer themselves.

## ABOUT ASPICS

Nothing gives a cooler, lovelier effect on a hot summer night and nothing is easier to prepare than a brilliantly clear aspic. The problem, of course, is to keep the jelly properly chilled when serving. For small groups, chilled plates, individually served, will do if you can control the timing. For large groups, if you want to use a quivery aspic, serve it molded in a crystal-clear glass bowl set in another larger glass bowl with crushed ice between, or on a handsome, well-chilled platter set on ice.

The most delicious aspics of all are reduced chicken and veal stocks, cooked down from the clarified gelatinous portions of these animals, (II, 170). Clarified strong meat, fish and fowl stocks with added gelatin are next in favor—but the average home cook seldom clarifies her own. She depends largely on canned bases for her jellies. ◗ Canned consommés, if over a year old, tend to lose some of their jelling power, so it is wise to refrigerate the can before using to test for texture. The consommé is still good to eat even if it fails to jell fully out of the can, but when used for aspic it will need about 1 teaspoon of gelatin per cup of consommé to firm it. To add gelatin, see (II, 233). If you save vegetable stocks, (II, 167–168), you can add them to meat or fish stocks to modify and enrich the otherwise easily identifiable canned

flavors. It is wise to choose a stock that has the same general base as the food to be molded: fish stock for fish, meat stock for meat. For gelatin salads made with eggs or cream—that is, unclear types—see Mousses, 86.

One package of unflavored gelatin is the equivalent in strength to 1 tablespoon gelatin. To make aspics, allow 1 tablespoon gelatin to 1¾ to 2 cups liquid. Use the lesser amount of liquid if the solids to be incorporated are juicy or watery. ◗ Never reduce aspic made with added gelatin with the idea of thickening it. It only wastes your good stock and never thickens. If you run into trouble, start the gelatin process over again, making a guesstimate as to the added fresh gelatin required.

◗ The addition of wine or liqueur to your aspics can make them something rather special. Don't add too much, ◗ one or two tablespoons per cup of liquid being sufficient to heighten the flavor significantly. Substitute the wine for part of the liquid called for in the recipe ◗ and add it when the gelatin has been dissolved and is beginning to cool. Dry white wine or a dry sherry goes well with savory aspics such as chicken and veal. Sweeter wines, such as sauterne or fruit-flavored liqueurs, are good for molded fruit salads.

Aspic should be made of clarified stocks, (II, 170), unless you want to serve up something that resembles a molded London fog. If you decide to skip this process, be sure to plan to mask your mold, see Mayonnaise Collée, 427, or Sauce Chaud-Froid, 428.

◗ To make decorative molds, see (II, 234). Clear aspic jelly can serve as an attractive garnish for a meat or chicken salad. Chill it in a refrigerator ◗ but do not freeze, and when ready to serve, cut in squares or fancy shapes or chop it rather fine and arrange it around the center.

Many salads can become full-fledged luncheon dishes with the addition of various types of chopped meat, chicken or flaked fish. For other recipes including meat, fish and shellfish and Chicken Mousses see 86–89.

A choice or a combination of the following ingredients may be included in a molded salad, but always keep in mind that fresh or frozen—but not canned—pineapple must be brought to a boil before you use it in a gelatin-based salad.

> **Cooked diced meat or poultry**
> **Cooked flaked fish**
> **Hard-cooked eggs**
> **Cooked sweetbreads**
> **Shredded cabbage**
> **Diced celery**
> **Diced cucumbers**
> **Cooked celeriac**
> **Sliced green peppers**
> **Raw or cooked carrots**
> **Cooked beets**
> **Canned asparagus**
> **Canned drained fruit**
> **Halved cranberries**
> **Seedless grapes**
> **Peeled seeded table grapes: Tokay or Malaga**
> **Skinned grapefruit, orange or tangelo sections**
> **Stuffed ripe or green olives**
> **Pickles**
> **Nutmeats**
> **Chopped parsley, chives or other herbs**

## BASIC ASPIC OR GELATIN SALAD

**5 Servings**

Please read About Gelatin, (II, 233).
Soak:

> **1 tablespoon gelatin**

in:

> **¼ cup cold water**

Dissolve it in:

> **¼ cup boiling stock**

Add this to:

> **1½ cups cold stock or 1¼ cups stock plus ¼ cup tomato juice**
> **2 tablespoons vinegar or 1½ tablespoons lemon juice**
> **Salt and paprika**
> **Celery salt**
> **(1 tablespoon grated onion)**

If the aspic is to cover unseasoned food, make the gelatin mixture more piquant. Chill it, and when it is about to set, combine it with:

> **1½ to 2 cups solid ingredients**

Pour the aspic into a wet mold and chill until firm. Unmold. Surround with:

> **Lettuce leaves**

Serve with or without:

> **Mayonnaise, 419, Sour Cream Horseradish Dressing, 408, or yogurt**

## JELLIED VEAL STOCK

**4 to 6 Servings**

Sometimes it is rewarding—and fun—to make an aspic without added gelatin. Place in a soup kettle:

> **A knuckle of veal**
> **¼ cup cut-up onion**
> **½ carrot**
> **6 ribs celery with leaves**
> **1 teaspoon salt**
> **¼ teaspoon pepper**

Cover the veal with:

> **Boiling water**

Simmer the meat until tender. Strain and reserve the liquid. Remove the veal. When cold, cut the meat into small cubes. After removing the fat, reheat the stock. Add the veal or reserve it for other dishes, and use the stock after clarifying it, (II, 170), to mold other ingredients.

**Season to taste**

Add:

(1 teaspoon dried herbs—
basil, tarragon, etc.)

Rinse a mold in cold water. Pour in the veal mixture. Cover and keep in a cold place to set. Unmold and slice.

## ASPIC GARNISH

Prepare:

**Basic Aspic or Jellied Veal
Stock, 76**

When firm and just before serving, chop the aspic so the light catches its many facets, and use it to garnish salads or meats.

## CUCUMBER ASPIC

**8 Servings**

Fine for a meat platter or a ring mold.
♦ Please read About Gelatin, (II, 233).
Pare and seed:

**Cucumbers**

Grate them. There should be 4 cups of pulp and juice. Soak:

**2 tablespoons gelatin**

in:

½ cup cold water or chicken
stock

Dissolve it in:

¾ cup boiling water or
chicken stock

Add:

6 tablespoons lemon juice
2 teaspoons grated onion

Add the gelatin mixture to the cucumber pulp with:

1 teaspoon sugar
Salt, as needed
¼ teaspoon paprika

Strain the jelly. Place it in small wet molds. When firm invert onto:

**Thick slices skinned
tomatoes**

Garnish the slices with:

**Watercress**

Serve the salad with:

**Mayonnaise, 419**

Or place it in a wet 9-inch ring mold. Chill the jelly. When firm, invert onto a platter. Fill the center with:

**Marinated shrimp**

Garnish the edge with:

**Tomato slices**

Serve the ring with:

**Green Mayonnaise, 420, or
Watercress Dressing, 414**

## TOMATO ASPIC

**8 Servings (without the addition
of solid ingredients)**

I. ♦ Please read About Gelatin, (II, 233).

Simmer 30 minutes, then strain:

3½ cups tomatoes
1 teaspoon salt
½ teaspoon paprika
1½ teaspoons sugar
2 tablespoons lemon juice
3 tablespoons chopped onion
1 bay leaf
4 ribs celery with leaves
(1 teaspoon dried basil or
tarragon)

Soak:

**2 tablespoons gelatin**

in:

½ cup cold water

Dissolve it in the strained hot juice. Add water to make 4 cups of liquid. Chill the aspic. When it is about to set you may add 1 to 2 cups of solid ingredients—a choice or a combination of:

Sliced olives
Chopped celery
Chopped green peppers or
grated carrots
Sliced avocados
Chopped meat

Flaked fish or chopped
shellfish
Well-drained oysters

Chill the aspic until firm. Unmold and serve with:

Mayonnaise, 419, or Boiled
Salad Dressing II, 424

**II.** If you prefer a clear ring, keep the aspic simple and fill the center with:

Coleslaw, marinated
cucumbers or avocados,
chicken or shrimp salad, or
cottage cheese and chives

Serve with:

Chiffonade Dressing, 414

**III.**

8 Servings

Not quite up to the preceding basic recipe in clarity, but delicious, unusual and much simpler.
Soak:

1 tablespoon gelatin

in:

2 tablespoons cold water

Dissolve it in:

2 tablespoons boiling water

Add the contents of:

1 can condensed tomato
soup: 10¹/₂ oz.

Heat:

2 cups tomato juice

Dissolve in it:

1 package lemon- or lime-
flavored gelatin

Combine the two mixtures. Add:

¹/₈ teaspoon salt

Mold and chill the aspic.

CANNED TOMATO OR
VEGETABLE JUICE ASPIC

8 Servings

◗ Please read About Gelatin, (II, 233).
Soak:

2 tablespoons gelatin

in:

¹/₂ cup cold canned tomato
juice

Dissolve it in:

3¹/₂ cups hot tomato juice or
canned tomato and
vegetable juice

Tomato juice varies. It is wise to taste the aspic to see whether additional seasoning is required. Lemon juice is good; so is a teaspoon of chopped or dried herbs, (II, 264), preferably basil. Add, if desired:

(1 or 2 cups solid ingredients)

See Tomato Aspic, 77. Mold, chill, unmold and serve the aspic as directed.

MADRILÈNE RING WITH SHAD
ROE COCKAIGNE

A fine summer dish.
Fill a ring mold with:

Canned Madrilène aspic or
tomato-seasoned meat
stock aspic

Chill. Invert on:

Shredded lettuce

Place in the center:

Chilled canned shad roe

Garnish with:

Mayonnaise, 419, or
Curry Dressing, 425
Lemon wedges or parsley

MOLDED VEGETABLE GELATIN
SALAD

6 Servings

Dissolve the contents of:

1 package lime- or lemon-
flavored gelatin

in:

2 cups hot water

Prepare and add, when the jelly is about to set:

1¹/₂ cups finely diced
vegetables: cucumber,
carrot, celery, sliced

**unpeeled radishes, olive,
pimiento**
**1/2 diced green pepper**
**2 teaspoons grated onion**
**3/4 teaspoon salt**
**1/4 teaspoon paprika**
Place the salad in wet individual ring
molds. Chill thoroughly. Unmold on:
**Lettuce or watercress**
Fill the centers with:
**Boiled Salad
Dressing II, 424**

## GOLDEN GLOW GELATIN SALAD

**8 to 10 Servings**

Good in flavor and lovely in color.
Grate or grind:
**2 cups raw carrots**
Drain, reserving the juice:
**1 cup canned crushed
pineapple**
Heat to the boiling point:
**7/8 cup pineapple juice**
**7/8 cup water**
**1/2 teaspoon salt**
Dissolve in the hot liquid:
**1 package lemon-flavored
gelatin**
Chill, and when the gelatin mixture is
about to set, combine it with the carrots, the pineapple and:
**(1/2 cup chopped pecans)**
Place in a wet mold. Chill until firm.
Unmold on:
**Lettuce**
Serve with:
**Mayonnaise, 419**

## ASPARAGUS AND CELERY ASPIC

**10 Servings**

Another refreshing warm-weather salad.
♦ Please read About Gelatin, (II, 233).
Drain the contents of:
**3 cups canned asparagus tips**

Reserve the liquor. The tips may be
cut in two or they may be used whole
as a garnish around the edge of the
mold. Soak:
**1 tablespoon gelatin**
in:
**3 tablespoons asparagus
liquor**
Heat the remaining asparagus liquor
and dissolve the gelatin in it. Add to
make 2 cups of liquor in all:
**Chicken bouillon or canned
bouillon**
Season these ingredients with:
**Salt and paprika**
Chill them. When they are nearly set,
combine them with:
**2 cups chopped celery**
and the cut asparagus tips in a wet
mold.
Chill the salad until firm. Unmold
and serve with:
**Cream Mayonnaise, 422**

## BEET GELATIN SALAD

**8 Servings**

Wash well, then ♥ pressure-cook:
**8 medium-sized beets, or use
canned beets**
Drain and reserve the beet juice. Peel
the beets and dice them. There should
be about 1 cup. Prepare:
**3/4 cup diced celery**
Dissolve the contents of:
**1 package lemon-flavored
gelatin**
in:
**1 cup boiling water**
Add to it:
**3/4 cup beet juice**
**3 tablespoons vinegar**
**1/2 teaspoon salt**
**2 teaspoons grated onion**
**1 tablespoon prepared
horseradish**
Chill these ingredients until they are
about to set. Fold in beets and celery.

Place the salad in a wet mold. Chill until firm. Unmold on:

**Lettuce or endive**

Serve with:

**Boiled Salad Dressing II,
424, or cultured sour cream**

## JELLIED CLAM RING

**8 Servings**

◗ Please read About Gelatin, (II, 233). Dilute:

**Clam juice or minced clams**

with:

**Water or vegetable juices**

to make a palatable mixture. There should be 4 cups. Season with:

**Lemon juice and paprika
A few drops Worcestershire
sauce**

Soak:

**2 tablespoons gelatin**

in ¹/₂ cup of the liquid.

Heat ◗ just to the boiling point 1 cup of the liquid. Dissolve the soaked gelatin in it. Return it to the remaining liquid with the minced clams, if they were used. Pour into a wet 9-inch ring mold. Chill until firm. Invert the jelly onto a plate. Fill the center with:

**Marinated vegetables**

Surround the ring with:

**Tomato slices**

Serve with:

**Watercress Sauce, 422, or
Chiffonade Dressing, 414**

## JELLIED SEAFOOD MOLD

**6 Servings**

◗ Please read About Gelatin, (II, 233). Prepare:

**Basic Aspic, 76**

using a fish fumet, (II, 173), or light meat stock. Dice:

**Celery**

Pare, seed and dice:

**Cucumbers or green
peppers**

Drain and flake:

**Salmon, crab or tuna fish:
1¹/₂ cups fish and vegetables
in all**

Add:

**(2 chopped hard-cooked eggs)
(Sliced stuffed olives)**

When the jelly is nearly set, combine it with the solid ingredients. Pour it into a wet mold and chill until firm. Unmold and serve on:

**Lettuce**

with:

**Boiled Dressing I or II, 424,
or Green Goddess
Dressing, 420**

## LUNCHEON ASPIC SALAD

**8 Servings**

◗ Please read About Gelatin, (II, 233). Drain, reserving the juices:

**2¹/₂ cups grapefruit sections
¹/₄ cup green or white cooked
asparagus tips
1 cup canned or cooked crab
meat or shrimp**

Cut the asparagus into pieces. Pick over the crab meat or remove the intestinal vein from the shrimp. Add to the juices, to make 2³/₄ cups of liquid:

**Chicken broth, Poultry
Stock, (II, 172), canned
consommé or dissolved
chicken bouillon cubes**

Soak:

**1¹/₂ tablespoons gelatin**

in ¹/₂ cup of this liquid. Dissolve it in 1 cup of hot liquid. Combine the gelatin and the remaining liquid. Season well with:

**Juice of 1 or more lemons
or with ¹/₄ cup dry white
wine**

Add, if needed:

**Salt**

Add:

**(3 or more tablespoons
 capers)**

Chill the gelatin until it begins to
thicken. Have ready a mold which
has been rinsed in cold water. Pour
part of the gelatin into it, sprinkle
some grapefruit, crab meat and asparagus over it, then alternate layers
of gelatin and the other ingredients.
Wind up with gelatin on top. Chill
the aspic until very cold. Serve on:

**Lettuce**

with:

**Green Mayonnaise, 420**

## CHICKEN SALAD IN ASPIC

**6 to 8 Servings**

Soak:

**1 tablespoon gelatin**

in:

**¼ cup cold water**

Dissolve it in:

**2 cups boiling chicken broth
 or stock**

Add:

**Seasoning, if needed**

Chill, and when the gelatin begins to
set, rinse a mold in cold water and fill
it with ½ inch of the jelly. Build up
layers of:

**3 cups cooked diced chicken**

and the jelly. Ornament the layers
with:

**1 cup canned mushroom caps
2 hard-cooked eggs, chopped
 or sliced
12 sliced stuffed olives**

Chill the jelly until firm. Unmold and
serve with or without:

**Mayonnaise, 419, or
Curry Mayonnaise, 422**

## MOLDED EGG RING

**4 Servings**

A one-platter luncheon if the center
of the mold is filled with crab meat or
chicken salad.

Rice:

**8 hard-cooked eggs, 212**

Add:

**1 tablespoon finely chopped
 onion
2 tablespoons finely chopped
 parsley
A dash of hot pepper sauce
½ cup Mayonnaise, 419**

Pack into a 7-inch ring mold and refrigerate until firm. Unmold just before serving and garnish with:

**Tomato quarters and
 artichoke hearts**

or surround the ring with:

**Watercress**

and frost it lightly with:

**Chutney, (II, 685)**

## EGGS IN ASPIC OR OEUFS EN GELÉE

Make:

**Basic Aspic, 76, or Jellied
 Veal Stock, 76, flavored
 with port or brandy**

Have ready:

**Poached Eggs, 213**

Swish cold water in individual molds
until they are cold and wet. Drain but
do not dry. Coat the interior with the
congealing aspic so that it adheres
to the sides. Chill until jelled. Place
an egg in the center of each mold
and fill with more aspic. Chill. Serve
masked with:

**Mayonnaise Collée, 427, or
 cold Mayonnaise, 419**

## EGGS IN ASPIC COCKAIGNE

Molded with one-half hard-cooked or deviled egg, this makes a pleasant hors d'oeuvre. With three halves, it makes enough for a luncheon salad. Prepare:

**Eggs in Aspic, 81**

using rich chicken stock for the aspic base and replacing the poached eggs with:

**Deviled Eggs, 220**

Place the molds on a bed of:

**Watercress**

Mask the eggs with a coating of:

**Cultured sour cream**

Garnish with:

**Finely chopped chives, basil and chervil**
**Red caviar and tomato slices**

"for pretty," as the Pennsylvania Dutch put it.

## BASIC GELATIN FOR FRUIT SALADS

**6 Servings**

♦ Please read About Gelatin, (II, 233). It is well known that fresh or frozen pineapple cannot be added to a gelatin salad without ruining it. This also applies to frozen pineapple juice, alone or combined with other frozen juices such as orange or grapefruit. The pineapple or the juice must be brought to ♦ a boil. Canned pineapple has been cooked and may be used as is. Soak:

**1 tablespoon gelatin**

in:

**1/2 cup cold water**

Dissolve it in:

**1 cup boiling water or fruit juice**

Add:

**4 to 6 tablespoons sugar, less if sweetened fruit juice is used**
**1/8 teaspoon salt**
**1/4 cup lemon juice**

Chill the aspic, and when it is about to set, combine with:

**1 1/2 cups prepared drained fruit**

Place it in a wet mold and chill until firm. Serve with:

**Cream Mayonnaise, 422**

## MINT GELATIN FOR FRUIT SALADS

Pour:

**1 cup boiling water**

over:

**1/4 cup crushed mint leaves**

Let steep 5 minutes. Drain this infusion. Add:

**A few drops of green vegetable coloring**

Prepare, by the recipe, left:

**Basic Gelatin for Fruit Salads**

substituting the mint infusion for the boiling water.

## MOLDED AVOCADO SALAD

**3 to 4 Servings**

♦ Please read About Gelatin, (II, 233). Soak:

**1 tablespoon gelatin**

in:

**2 tablespoons water**

Dissolve it in:

**1 cup boiling water**

When cooled somewhat, add:

**1/4 cup lemon juice**
**1 cup mashed avocado**
**1/4 teaspoon celery salt**
**1 teaspoon salt**
**1/2 teaspoon Worcestershire sauce**
**A few grains cayenne**
**1/4 cup chopped pimiento**

Mold and serve.

## MOLDED CRANBERRY SAUCE

**6 to 8 Servings**

▶ Please read About Gelatin, (II, 233).
Soak:

**1 tablespoon gelatin**

in:

**3 tablespoons water**

Cook until the skins pop:

**2 cups cranberries**

in:

**1 cup boiling water or fruit juice**

Use the cranberries strained or unstrained. If the former, strain them at this time. Add and cook for 5 minutes:

**1/2 cup sugar**
**1/4 teaspoon salt**

Add the soaked gelatin. Chill the jelly. When it is about to set, fold in:

**2/3 cup diced celery**
**(1/2 cup chopped nutmeats)**
**(1 cup drained canned crushed pineapple)**

Place in a wet mold and chill until firm. Serve with:

**Mayonnaise, 419**

## MOLDED CRANBERRY AND APPLE SALAD

**8 to 10 Servings**

▶ Please read About Gelatin, (II, 233).
Put through a food grinder:

**1 lb. cranberries**

Add:

**The grated rind of 1 orange**
**1/2 cup orange juice**
**3 1/2 tablespoons lemon juice**
**1 1/2 cups sugar**

Refrigerate overnight. Soak:

**1 tablespoon gelatin**

in:

**3 tablespoons cold water**

Dissolve:

**1 package lemon-flavored gelatin**

in:

**1 cup boiling water**

Add the soaked gelatin. Stir until dissolved. Combine these ingredients with the cranberry mixture. Pare, then chop and add:

**3 tart apples**

Place the salad in a wet mold. When firm, unmold and serve on:

**Watercress**

with:

**Cream Mayonnaise, 422**

## SEEDLESS GRAPE AND CELERY RING

**8 to 10 Servings**

Prepare:

**1 package lemon- or orange-flavored gelatin or Basic Gelatin for Fruit Salads, 82**

When about to set, add to it:

**3 cups halved seedless grapes and diced celery, combined in any proportion**

Place the jelly in a wet 9-inch mold and chill. Unmold on:

**Lettuce**

Fill the center with:

**Cream Mayonnaise, 422**

## GRAPEFRUIT SHERRY ASPIC

**10 Servings**

▶ Please read About Gelatin, (II, 233).
Soak:

**2 1/2 tablespoons gelatin**

in:

**1/2 cup cold water**

Stir over heat until the sugar is dissolved:

**1/2 cup water**
**1 cup sugar**

Dissolve the gelatin in the hot syrup. Cool. Add:

**2 cups and 6 tablespoons fresh grapefruit juice**
**3 tablespoons lemon juice**
**1/2 cup dry sherry**

1/4 teaspoon salt

Pour these ingredients into a wet 9-inch ring mold. Chill until firm. Turn it out on a platter. Fill the center with:

**Soft cream cheese balls rolled in chopped nuts**

Garnish the outer edge of the platter with:

**Avocado slices**

alternating with skinned:

**Grapefruit or orange sections**

on:

**Watercress or shredded lettuce**

Sprinkle with:

**Pomegranate seeds**

Serve the salad with:

**Mayonnaise, 419, or French Dressing, 413**

## GINGER ALE GELATIN SALAD

**10 Servings**

♦ Please read About Gelatin, (II, 233).
Soak:

2 tablespoons gelatin

in:

1/4 cup cold water

Dissolve it in:

1/2 cup boiling fruit juice

Add:

1/2 cup sugar

1/8 teaspoon salt

2 cups ginger ale

Juice of 1 lemon

Chill these ingredients until nearly set. Combine with:

1/2 lb. skinned, seeded table grapes

1 peeled, sliced orange

1 grapefruit in skinned sections

6 slices drained canned pineapple, cut in pieces

3 teaspoons chopped preserved ginger

Place the salad in a wet 9-inch ring mold. Chill and unmold on:

**Lettuce**

Serve with:

**Cream Mayonnaise, 422**

## FRUIT SALAD MOLDED WITH CHEESE BALLS

**8 Servings**

♦ Please read About Gelatin, (II, 233).
Soak:

2 1/2 tablespoons gelatin

in:

1/2 cup water

Drain and reserve the juice from:

3 1/2 cups canned peaches, apricots or pears

(1 cup seedless grapes)

Combine and boil:

2 cups of the juice

1 1/2 cups sugar

Dissolve the gelatin in it. Add these ingredients to the remaining juice with:

3/4 cup lemon juice

3 tablespoons lime juice

1/4 teaspoon ginger

Add water or other fruit juice to make up 4 cups of liquid in all. Chill the gelatin. Soften:

1 package cream or pimiento cheese: 3 oz.

with a little:

**Mayonnaise, 419**

Roll it into balls. Roll the balls in:

**Chopped nutmeats**

When gelatin is about to set, incorporate the fruit with it; place the cheese balls evenly around the bottom of a ring mold and surround them with the fruit and gelatin mixture. Chill well and invert onto:

**Watercress**

Serve with:

**Mayonnaise, 419**

## CHEESE RING

**8 Servings**

Drain and reserve the liquid from:

 1 can crushed pineapple:
    8¼ oz.

Should there not be enough, add water to make ½ cup of reserved liquid in all.

Soak:

 2 teaspoons gelatin

for 5 minutes in:

 ½ cup cold water

Boil the reserved pineapple juice and water and dissolve the gelatin in it. Cool. Meanwhile mix together:

 2 cups small-curd cottage
    cheese
 8 oz. crumbled blue cheese
 1 finely chopped green
    pepper
 2 teaspoons onion juice
 ½ cup Mayonnaise, 419
 (½ cup blanched almonds)

and the reserved crushed pineapple. When the gelatin is almost set, add the cheese mixture and pack into a ring mold that has been rinsed in cold water. Refrigerate until ready to serve.

## MOLDED PINEAPPLE RING

**8 Servings**

Please read About Gelatin, (II, 233).

Soak:

 2 tablespoons gelatin

in:

 ½ cup cold water

Strain and reserve the juice of:

 2½ cups canned crushed
    pineapple

Add to the juice:

 ½ cup hot water

Bring these ingredients to the boiling point. Stir in the soaked gelatin until dissolved. Add:

 ⅝ cup sugar: ½ cup plus
    2 tablespoons

Cool the mixture. Add the pineapple and:

 (2 cups grated cabbage)
    The grated rind of 1 orange
    or lemon
 ¾ cup orange juice
 5 tablespoons lemon juice

Pour these ingredients into a wet 9-inch ring mold. Chill the gelatin. Unmold on a bed of:

 Lettuce or watercress

Fill the center with:

 Cottage cheese, soft cream
    cheese balls rolled in
    chopped nutmeats, or
    chicken salad

Serve with or without:

 Mayonnaise, 419

## ASPIC-FILLED MELON

**6 Servings**

It is perfectly possible to serve this dish as a dessert; in which case, of course, the lettuce bed and the dressing are omitted. For the latter, try instead a garnish of Cold Sabayon Sauce, (II, 566).

Pare:

 1 large melon

leaving it whole. Cut off enough from one end so you can scrape out the seeds. Reserve the cap. Fill the cavity with water, then pour the water into a measuring cup; this is to guide you for the amount of gelatin you have to prepare. Stand the melon upside down to drain. Then fill, depending on the color of the melon flesh, with:

 Fruit-flavored gelatin
 (Diced or small fruits)

Try a combination of:

 Orange-flavored gelatin,
    canned crushed pineapple,
    canned mandarin oranges
    or sliced bananas

or:

### Raspberry gelatin with
### fresh raspberries

Refrigerate, and after the center is set, replace the cap, toothpicking it in place. Slice the melon horizontally, being careful not to dislodge the gelatin. On individual plates, bed it down on:

**Leaf lettuce**

Top it with a spray of fresh herbs. Keep chilled until ready to serve with:

**Cream Mayonnaise, 422**

## STRAWBERRY AND RHUBARB SALAD MOLDS

**8 to 10 Servings**

Dissolve:

3 packages strawberry-
flavored gelatin

in:

3 cups hot water

Drop in:

2 packages frozen rhubarb:
10 oz. each

Stir to separate the rhubarb. When the jelly begins to set, add:

1 quart sliced fresh
strawberries

Pour into individual wet molds and chill until set. Unmold on:

**Watercress**

Garnish each with:

A fresh whole strawberry

Serve with:

Cream Mayonnaise,
422, or Fruit-Salad
Mayonnaise, 421

## ABOUT SAVORY MOUSSES

This kind of salad gelatin differs from the aspic in its lack of transparency—or, putting it more positively, in its inclusion of two additional ingredients: cream and egg. We qualify the "mousse" with "savory" to distinguish the recipes that follow from the sweet mousses you will find further along under Desserts, (II, 507). A **mousseline** may be either a kind of pastry or, as in this section, a mousse confected with whipped cream.

## JELLIED HAM MOUSSE

**10 Servings**

Soak:

1 tablespoon gelatin

in:

1/4 cup cold water

Dissolve it in:

1 1/2 cups boiling Stock, (II, 171)

Chill the jelly. When it is nearly set, combine it with:

3 cups cooked ground or
chopped ham
1/4 cup chopped celery
1 tablespoon grated onion
1/2 cup Mayonnaise, 419
1/4 cup chopped sour or sweet-
sour pickles

Add, if required:

Worcestershire sauce
Season to taste

Seasonal variation: omit onion and pickles and add:

(1 cup seedless green grapes)

Moisten a mold with cold water. If desired, and if the grapes have been omitted, decorate the sides and bottom with:

Stuffed olives and sliced
hard-cooked eggs

Add the other ingredients. Chill the mousse until firm.

## JELLIED CHICKEN OR VEAL MOUSSE

### I.

**10 Servings**

Use the recipe for Jellied Ham Mousse above. Use chicken stock. Substitute cooked ground chicken or veal for the ham, or use part chicken and part ham.

**8 Servings**

oak:

1½ tablespoons gelatin

¼ cup Chicken Stock, (II, 172)

issolve it in:

½ cup hot stock

eat:

3 egg yolks

dd:

1½ cups milk

ook these ingredients in a double
oiler until they are smooth and fairly
ick. Stir in the dissolved gelatin.
hen the mixture is cool, add:

2 cups cooked minced or
  ground chicken or veal
(½ cup diced seeded
  cucumber)

eason with:

Salt, white pepper and
paprika

hill the jelly. When it is about to set,
old in:

1 cup whipped cream

lace the mousse in a wet mold and
ill it until firm. Unmold it.

## CUCUMBER MOUSSE

**4 Servings**

Please read About Gelatin, (II, 233).
oak:

2 teaspoons gelatin

3 tablespoons cold water

issolve these ingredients over heat.
dd:

2 teaspoons vinegar, or lime
  or lemon juice
1 teaspoon grated onion
¾ teaspoon salt
¼ teaspoon paprika

hill until about to set. Drain well:

1 cup pared, seeded, chopped
  cucumbers

Whip until stiff:

½ cup whipping cream

Beat the gelatin mixture gradually
into the cream, fold in the cucumbers. Rinse individual molds. Fill
them with the mousse. When they are
thoroughly chilled, invert onto a garnished platter.

## II.

**5 to 6 Servings**

Dissolve:

1 package lime-flavored
  gelatin

in:

¾ cup hot water

Add:

¼ cup lemon juice
1 tablespoon grated onion

Chill until about to set, then stir in:

1 cup cultured sour cream
1 cup finely chopped unpared
  cucumber

Pour into 6 small wet molds and chill
until firm.

## SEAFOOD MOUSSE

**6 Servings**

◗ Please read About Gelatin, (II, 233).
Soak:

2 teaspoons gelatin

in:

¼ cup cold water

Dissolve it in:

¼ cup boiling water

Add it to:

¾ cup Mayonnaise, 419

Combine it with:

1 cup flaked crab meat or
  flaked tuna fish
½ cup chopped celery or
  carrots
2 tablespoons chopped
  parsley
½ cup chopped cucumber
2 tablespoons chopped

stuffed or pitted black
olives
1 tablespoon or more lemon
juice
Season to taste

Place these ingredients in an oiled
mold. Chill them until firm. Unmold on:

Cress or shredded lettuce

Serve with:

Cucumbers in sour cream

If you want a mousse based on
whipped cream, see Lobster Mousse,
next.

## LOBSTER MOUSSE

6 Servings

An attractive salad made in a 9-inch
ring mold. ◗ Please read About Gelatin, (II, 233).

Soak:

1 tablespoon gelatin

in:

1/4 cup water

Dissolve it over boiling water. Combine:

3/4 cup minced celery
1 1/2 cups canned or cooked
lobster meat
(2/3 cup minced apple)

Season these ingredients with:

Salt and paprika

Stir the gelatin into:

3/4 cup Mayonnaise, 419
3 tablespoons lemon juice
(1 teaspoon dry mustard)
(1/2 clove garlic, pressed)
(A few drops hot pepper
sauce)

Whip until stiff, then fold in:

1/3 cup whipping cream

Fold this mixture into the other ingredients. Place the mousse in an oiled
9-inch ring mold. Chill thoroughly.
Unmold on a platter, garnished with:

Watercress
Marinated cucumbers

Serve with:

Cold Quick Tomato
Sauce, 400, or
Mayonnaise Collée, 427

## MOLDED CREAMED FISH

### I.

6 Servings

◗ Please read About Gelatin, (II, 233).

Soak:

3/4 tablespoon gelatin

in:

2 tablespoons water

Combine in a double boiler, then stir
constantly ◗ over—not in—boiling
water until thickened:

2 egg yolks
1 1/2 tablespoons soft butter
1/2 tablespoon flour
1 1/2 teaspoons salt
2 teaspoons sugar
1 teaspoon Worcestershire
sauce or 3/4 teaspoon curry
or 1 teaspoon dry mustard
1 teaspoon grated onion
A few grains red pepper
1 tablespoon chopped
pimiento
1/4 cup lemon juice
3/4 cup milk or tomato juice

Add gelatin and stir until dissolved.
Refrigerate. Prepare:

1 1/2 cups seafood: cooked or
canned shrimp, salmon, etc.

Or use part fish and part chopped celery. When the gelatin is nearly set,
place some of it in the bottom of an
oiled ring mold, add some of the fish,
then more gelatin. Repeat this until
all ingredients have been used, finishing with gelatin on top. Chill the
salad until firm. Serve on:

Watercress

Fill the ring with:

Wilted Cucumbers, 58

Surround it with:

Sliced tomatoes

**.**

6 Servings

A quick version of the above.

Soak:

1½ teaspoons gelatin

in:

3 tablespoons cold water

Dissolve it in:

1 can heated condensed
cream of chicken soup:
10¾ oz.

When the gelatin mixture begins to
set, add:

1 teaspoon Worcestershire
sauce

½ cup finely chopped celery

2 tablespoons chopped
parsley

1 tablespoon chopped chives

1 can shredded white meat
tuna fish: 6½ oz.

Chill until set. Serve garnished with:

Halved, cored, very thinly
sliced Cucumbers, 58

which have been marinated briefly in:

Herb vinegar

MOUSSELINE OF SHELLFISH

6 Servings

Line a 1½-quart fish mold with
half-set:

Fish- or chicken-flavored
Basic Aspic, 76

Refrigerate it. Prepare, using a
Rumet, (II, 173):

2 cups Velouté Sauce, 387

to which has been added:

1 tablespoon gelatin

soaked until dissolved in:

¼ cup cold stock or water

Combine the cooled sauce with:

1 lb. chopped cooked
shellfish meat

Add:

½ cup partially whipped
cream
Season to taste

and pour into the fish mold over the
aspic. Chill before unmolding onto a
cold serving platter.

CHILLED FRUIT SALAD
MOUSSE

4 Servings

Dissolve:

1 package lime-flavored
gelatin

in:

1 cup hot water

Add:

½ cup cold water

½ cup Mayonnaise, 419

2 tablespoons lemon juice

¼ teaspoon salt

Whip with a rotary beater until well
blended. Pour into a refrigerator tray
and chill until firm at the edge but
still soft in the center. Turn into a
bowl and whip in the same manner
until fluffy. Fold in:

1 cup peeled and diced
apples

¼ cup chopped pecans

¾ cup seeded Tokay grapes

Pour into a mold and refrigerate until firm.

TWENTY-FOUR-HOUR FRUIT
SALAD WITH CREAM

12 to 14 Servings

Cook in a double boiler ♦ over—not
in—hot water until thickened:

2 egg yolks

¼ cup sugar

¼ cup cream
Juice of 2 lemons

⅛ teaspoon salt

Stir these ingredients constantly.
Chill them and add:

6 diced slices canned
pineapple

2 cups pitted canned Queen
Anne cherries

1 cup shredded blanched
  almonds
1/2 lb. marshmallows, cut in
  pieces
2 cups whipped cream
(1/2 lb. peeled, seeded grapes)

Chill the salad 24 hours. Serve on:
    **Lettuce**
with:
    **Mayonnaise, 419**
or as a dessert, garnished with:
    **Whipped cream**

# THE FOODS WE HEAT

We are told that a hard-boiled professional cook, when asked what she regarded as primary briefing for a beginner, tersely replied: "Stand facing the stove." While our own first cooking lesson would substitute the gradual approach for the frontal assault, it is perfectly true that somewhere along the line, in perhaps ninety-five out of a hundred kitchen sequences, heat will have been applied. This has been so from ages past.

The chapter head illustration shows the contemporary metal counterpart of a clay kebab-roasting pan unearthed from the Palace of Nestor. In an equally time honored tradition is the three-legged cast-iron pot behind it, which has accompanied military campaigns for three millennia, and with its rimmed lid is still in use in Appalachia. On a more sophisticated level is the elegant Chinese fire-pot, primarily intended for the gentle poaching in delicious stocks. The aventador, or fan, right front, encourages a draft; behind it the salamander, when heated, helps to brown omelets and casseroles. Neither, needless to say, is required to operate today's efficient electric skillet, shown left.

Yet from Charles Lamb's legendary Bobo—you will remember him from your high school English classes as the boy who couldn't make roast pig without burning down the house—to the bride described by her matron of honor as incapable of boiling an egg, heating food, despite a wealth of equipment, has often turned into a frustrating, sometimes even disastrous, experience.

It needn't be. We have tried throughout our book, but especially in this chapter, to identify and explain the various types of cooking heat; to tell you simply and clearly how these heats are initiated, controlled and arrested to ensure highest nutritive value and best flavor, texture and color. We have tried also to indicate what processes, when followed, will bring cooked food to the table in that ideal state of readiness the French call **à point.**

Asking a cook why he heats food at all is, of course, like asking an architect why men do not live in caves. The obvious answer is that it usually tastes better that way. There are other reasons, too. Some are prosaic. Cooking destroys unwanted and sometimes unfavorable microorganisms. Contrary to some remarkably persistent notions, it makes many categories of food more digestible, more nutritious, and less—to toss in a stylish term—allergenic.

Cooking, again, can seal up in food most of those natural juices which nourish and delight us. For some kinds of preparation—stocks and soups are examples—the objective is just the reverse. It is true, also, that certain salted and variety meats, as well as a good many vegetables, profit by a precooking or blanching which modifies texture or releases disagreeable odors and off-flavors.

Many cooks, like the rest of humankind, are born innovators, too. And they often introduce stimulating refinements in the heating of food, some of which—like the smoking process—emphasize taste at the expense of nutritional integrity.

## ▲ HIGH-ALTITUDE COOKING

Cooking in the mountainous country is an art all in itself. If high altitudes are new to you, watch for the high-altitude cooking symbol ▲ which will give you formulas for adjusting ingredients or temperatures. Roasting procedures do not differ materially from those at sea level. Adjustments required in using sea-level baking recipes at high altitudes are indicated where necessary for each baking category. Basic cake recipes for high altitudes and their baking temperatures, marked ▲, may be found in Volume II on pages 442–445. But any process involving liquid will be proportionately lengthened as altitude increases: see the chart below showing the boiling point of water at different levels.

|  | F. | C. |
|---|---|---|
| Sea level | 212° | 100° |
| 2,000 ft. | 208° | 98° |
| 5,000 ft. | 203° | 95° |
| 7,500 ft. | 198° | 92° |
| 10,000 ft. | 194° | 90° |
| 15,000 ft. | 185° | 85° |
| 30,000 ft. | 158° | 70° |

If these hints are not sufficiently specialized for your area, write the home economics department of your state college or call on your county home demonstration agent for more information. And if you are doing any pressure cooking, the accuracy of the gauge is vital. These agencies can also tell you where to have gauges tested.

## ABOUT HEATS

Let us consider first how heats are transferred to food, whether in air or in moisture, in fat or through a pan. Results in each case will be quite astonishingly different. Cooking heats are generally known as dry or moist. In the following text, we shall list types of each separately.

## ABOUT DRY HEATS

Truly dry heats are achieved in a number of ways. Grilling over coals is one, broiling or roasting in a ventilated oven another. When we say "barbecue," we may be referring to Pit-Cooking, 109, in which case we refer to a moist-heat process. Or we may mean skewer-cooking with its variants—spit, brochette or rotisserie—which are dry processes and are themselves forms of grilling. Parenthetically, the word "barbecue" has been traced back by some philologists to the Spanish "barbacoa," a raised platform for cooking; but we like to think of it, with other authorities, as originating among the French settlers in Florida, who roasted the native goats whole, *de barbe en queue*—from beard to tail. Some further remarks on barbecuing will be found later in this chapter, see Outdoor Cooking, 108.

Baking is a dry-heat process, too. In addition to the reflected and radiant heat of the oven, heat is transferred from the pan to the food and may be further diffused by the use of paper liners, temporary covers of foil, or a dusting of flour between food and pan-bottom. Since, in baking, moisture is released from the food itself and continues to circulate as warm vapor in the closed oven chamber, this process is less dry than those previously mentioned.

Oddly enough, deep-fat frying is still another kind of dry-heat cooking. Here the heat is transferred not only by the oil or fat used as a cooking medium, but by the moisture in the food itself, some of the steam from the food juices being forced into the fat and then out into the atmosphere. Among dry-heat pan processes, sautéing uses the smallest amount of fat. Pan-broiling and pan-frying are successive steps beyond sautéing and away from the driest heat. In pan-broiling and pan-frying, the food develops a greater amount

of rendered fat than in sautéing and absorbs a larger share of it. In doing so, it gives up proportionately more of its juices. To keep both pan-frying and pan-broiling at their best, excess fat should be poured off during cooking.

Among dry-heat processes which may be described as "partial" are planking and flambéing—or flaming. Either way, the food is heated beforehand, and these processes only give it its finishing touch.

BROILING

Whether you broil on a grill or in a range, the principle is identical. The heat is a radiant glow; and the process differs from roasting or baking in that only one side of the food at a time is exposed to the heating source—unless you happen to use the rather special kind of equipment shown on 483.

However, all three of these types of dry heat depend, for their effectiveness, on proper ventilation. In the great majority of modern ranges, either gas or electric, you are given no selectivity in broiling temperatures. And individual variations in wattage—coil or burner area—as well as venting capacity make it necessary that you become familiar with the special requirements of your own equipment. Some ranges, for example, must be preheated before broiling can begin; in others, broiler heat is almost instantaneous. Likewise, in some electric ranges, broiling takes place with the oven door ajar; in others, the door may, or even must, be kept closed.

When the heat indicator on a household range is turned to a ▶ broil position, the temperature is around 550° or slightly above and should remain constant. If you wonder why you cannot always match the results you admire in some restaurant cookery, remember that commercial installations deliver much higher heats which are quite beyond the reach of home equipment.

Under the limitations of the household range ◗ as much temperature control in broiling is exerted by the placement of the oven rack as by any other means. It is usually adjusted so that there is a 3-inch space between the source of heat and the top of the food. ◗ To lower the broiling heat for browning fragile sauces or delicate dishes like sweetbreads or for cooking very thick meats—where the heat must have time to penetrate deeply without charring—lower the broiling rack to make a 4- to 6-inch space between the food and broiler. Place food on a cold rack to prevent sticking. If the rack is hot, grease it—or grease the food. For details of broiling and pan-broiling meats, see 552; fowl, 113 and 516; fish, 483; vegetables, 246 and 286.

## SKEWER COOKING

From a marshmallow impaled on a stick, to the most delicate bay scallops, skewer-grilled food never seems to lose its charm for young or old. A most important first step is to ◗ choose items that will cook at the same rate of speed, or to make the proper adjustment if they do not. When the meat or fish selected is a quick-cooking one, see that the onions, peppers or other more resistant vegetables which alternate with it are blanched in advance, so that the food will all be done at the same time. Should the meat need relatively longer cooking, skewer delicate alternates like tomatoes and mushrooms

separately and mingle meat and vegetables in serving. Protect delicate meats such as sweetbreads and liver with breading or a wrapping of thinly sliced bacon. Choose skewers whether of metal or wood, that are either square or oval, so that, as the food softens in cooking, it will not slip while revolving. Soak bamboo or wood skewers in water for several hours before using.

If using a grill, grease it and place the skewered food on the grill over medium heat. Turn the skewers often. Food grilled in this way may take anywhere from 6 to 12 minutes. For skewered food combinations, see (II, 87).

If cooking in a range, broil on a greased grill about 3 inches from the source of heat, or adjusted on a pan as shown in the chapter heading. You may, of course, prefer to use the skewer element on your rotisserie. For more details about rotisserie and spit-cooking, see 113–114. Should you decide to precook any sort of skewered food, you may do so on the skewers themselves in a skillet, provided, of course, the skewers are no longer than the pan bottom. Sometimes partially precooked, skewered foods are coated with a sauce or with a bound breading and then cooked to completion in deep fat. When handled in this way, they are called **attereaux.** In flambéing skewered foods, 108, provide some protection for your hand.

## DEEP-FAT FRYING

Deep-fat frying, like a number of other accomplishments in cooking, is an art in itself—an art in which experience is the best teacher. Even a novice, however, who follows our instructions to the letter can succeed in turning out delicious dishes in this ver-popular category—and, what's more, food fried without excessive fat absorption. A serving of French fried potatoes properly cooked may have a lower calorie count than a baked potato served with butter. Remember, too, that fat absorption increases with the length of cooking time and with the amount of surface exposed to the fat.

Equipment such as that shown below need not be elaborate, for equally good French fried potatoes can come out of a black iron kettle as from the latest model electric fryer. This is not to underestimate the value of the fryer, which offers the convenience of a built-in thermostat, but any deep kettle or saucepan, preferably a heavy one, serves nicely for deep frying. Use in a 3- or 4-quart kettle about 3 pounds of fat. It isn't wise to try to skimp on the amount, for there must always be enough to cover the food and to permit it to move freely in the kettle. ♦ There must also be room for the quick bubbling up of the fat which occurs naturally in frying potatoes, onions and other wet items. ♦ Never fill any container more than half full of fat. ♦ Remember also to heat the fat gradually, so that any moisture in it will have evaporated by the time it reaches the required temperature.

The kettle should have a flat bottom, so that it will sit firmly on the heating unit. Keep the handle of the kettle turned inward to avoid knocking against it. A short handle is desirable, to avoid the danger of accidentally overturning the hot fat and causing a small conflagration. In case fat should ever catch fire, have a metal lid handy to drop over the kettle. You may also smother the flame with salt or baking soda. ♦ Never use water, as this will only spread the fire.

For frying certain types of food such as doughnuts and fritters where bubbling is not a problem, a heavy skillet, an electric frypan or a tempura pan is sometimes preferred to a deep kettle because of the wider surface, which allows more pieces to be fried at one time.

A wire basket is practically a necessity for successful results in frying any quantity of small-sized material. The food is raised and lowered more easily and uniform browning is assured.

For judging the temperature of the fat, use a frying thermometer, no other. Have the thermometer ready in a bowl of hot water to lessen the chance of breakage; but ♦ never plunge it into the fat without wiping it very dry. Nothing is more important in frying than proper temperatures. As that wise old gourmet, Alexandre Dumas, so aptly put it, the food must be "surprised" by the hot fat, to give it the crusty, golden coating so characteristic and so desirable. The proper temperature in most instances is 365°, as easy to remember as the number of days in a year.

When no thermometer is available, a simple test for temperature can be made with a small cube of bread about 1 inch square. When you think the fat is hot enough, drop in the bread cube and count slowly to sixty, or use a timer for sixty seconds. If the cube browns in this time, the fat will be around 365°. A few foods—soufflé potatoes, for instance—may require higher or lower temperatures, but these will always be noted in the specific recipes.

Above all, do not wait for the fat to smoke before adding the food. Not only is this hard on the fat, since smoke indicates that it is breaking down and may be spoiled for reuse; but the crust that forms on the food is likely to be overbrowned before the product is cooked through, and the food will be burned on the surface and raw inside. On the other hand, food introduced into fat that isn't hot enough to crust immediately will tend to become grease-soaked.

After frying one batch ◗ let the temperature come up again to the required heat, so that you may continue to "surprise" each additional one. ◗ Skim out bits of food or crumbs frequently as they collect in the fat during frying. If allowed to remain, they induce foaming, discolor the fat, and affect the flavor of the food. Have ready a supply of paper toweling on which to drain the cooked food and so rid it of excess fat before serving.

At the end of the frying, and after the fat has cooled somewhat and become safe to handle, strain it to remove all extraneous particles, then store it well covered and refrigerated for future use. To clarify fats before reusing, see (II, 204). Adding some fresh fat for each new frying materially lengthens the life of the fat. When it becomes dark and thickish-looking, it will no longer be satisfactory for frying. At this stage, the smoking point has dropped too low, the flavor that it contributes to the food will be unpleasant and absorption high. Discard it.

Fats known simply as **shortening** are favorites for deep frying. These include suitable solid fats such as lard and the hydrogenated fats; and the liquid oils, among which corn, cottonseed, safflower, soybean and peanut are most commonly available. Except for lard, which has a characteristic odor and flavor, these fats are bland and very similar in appearance and composition. Most of them are 100% vegetable in origin. These all have smoking points well above those needed for deep frying. For more details, see About Oils, (II, 202).

◗ Butter and margarines, also known as shortenings, and valuable as they are for other purposes, are not considered suitable for deep frying because of their low smoking points.

Various other fats are sometimes used for deep frying. Olive oil is popular where locally produced, and canola and sesame oils are widely used where they are commonly grown and processed.

For special purposes and in certain circumstances, chicken and goose fat are rendered in the home for frying, as are also veal, pork, suet and beef kidney fats. These are inclined to have low smoking points, but when handled with care they can be used to produce acceptable fried foods. If it seems desirable, the smoking point of these animal fats can be brought up to the required limit by blending them with any one of the cooking oils. To render these fats, see (II, 203).

◗ Whenever possible, foods should be at room temperature and as dry as possible when introduced into the kettle. ◗ Always immerse gently with long-handled tongs or a slotted spoon or in a frying basket. ◗ Always dip these utensils into the hot fat first, so that the food will release quickly from them without sticking. And have a pan ready in which to rest the utensils when they come dripping from the fat.

◗ For good results, the food to be fried must be properly prepared. So that they will all cook in the same length of time, pieces should be uniform in size and preferably not thicker than 1½ inches. Small pieces, obviously, will cook through faster than large ones. It is difficult here to give advice about length of cooking. When in doubt, it is wise to remove one piece and try for doneness.

Raw foods, ◗ especially wet ones, should be patted between towels or paper toweling before cooking, to remove excess surface moisture. This reduces the amount of bubbling when the food is introduced into the fat. In adding a batch of raw food, always lower the basket gradually so that you can observe the amount of bubbling and be ready to lift it up if it looks as though the fat might be going over the top. Do not try to put too many pieces into the basket; fry several small batches rather than one large one. The cooked food may be kept hot on a paper-lined pan in an oven set at very low heat.

Certain types of food, such as croquettes, eggplant and fish, need special coating for proper browning and crust formation. For Breading, see (II, 219). The coating may be simply flour, cornmeal or finely crushed dry cereal. Or it may be a Fritter Batter, (II, 153–156), an egg and crumb mixture, or even a pastry envelope. Whatever it is, it should cover the surface evenly.

Foods to be coated with batter—shrimp, for instance, or pineapple slices—should be surface-dried beforehand. Doughnuts, fritters and other batter foods need no extra coating, as the egg-starch mixture browns nicely by itself when lowered into the hot fat. Many cooks do not realize that ◗ the richer a dough or batter mixture, the more fat it will absorb during frying. By adding even a little too much shortening or sugar to the mix, a doughnut may become so rich that it will end up grease-soaked. Or a fritter may simply disintegrate in the hot fat, or a too-rich batter slide off onion rings altogether.

✿ Frozen foods already breaded and deep-fat-fried need only defrosting and reheating in the oven. They should be defrosted outside the package to avoid the formation of surface moisture that would interfere with the crisping of the outer coating. Uncooked frozen foods that have to be coated should be dried on the surface after defrosting, and the coating applied as usual.

▲ In deep-fat frying at high altitudes, you will find that moist foods will require lower fat temperatures because of the lower boiling point of the water within them. For instance, French fries, which call for 365° in their final frying period, might need only a 355° fat temperature at high altitudes.

SAUTÉING OR PAN-FRYING

*Sauter* literally means "to jump," and this is just about what happens to the food you cook by sautéing. The cooking is done in an ◗ open pan which is kept in motion. The process is rapid, the food is usually thin or minced, and the ◗ heat must be kept up from the moment cooking starts until the food is tender.

There are other requirements, too. The pan and the ◗ small quantity of fat used must be hot enough, when the food is added, to sear the food at once, to prevent the loss of juices and to prevent sticking. The food at the start should be 70° or more, cut to a uniform thickness and size, and dry on the surface. If the food is too cold it will lower the heat, and if it is wet it will not brown properly. Worst of all, steam will form and break the seal holding the juices. To ensure a dry surface, food is frequently floured or breaded, see (II, 219). ◗ Steam will also form if the pan is crowded. There must be space between the pieces of food you are sautéing.

For the best sauté, use a Clarified Butter, 396, or a combination of 3 parts butter and 4 parts oil. When the combined fats reach the point of fragrance, add the 70° food, but not so much at a time as to reduce the heat in the pan. To keep the food from browning too quickly, agitate the pan constantly. Too much turning of the food delays the quickness of heating. But food with a bound breading, especially if the coating has not been dried long enough before cooking, may steam. In this case, turning will help to release some of that steam more rapidly. Meat not floured or breaded is browned or cooked on one side until the juice comes up to the surface of the exposed side, then turned and browned on the other side. Proceed in the same way for fish, but the cooking time is apt to be considerably shorter.

To serve sautéed food with a sauce, remove the food from the pan and keep it warm on a hot serving dish. Quickly deglaze the delicious residue in the sauté pan—unless you have been cooking a strongly flavored fish—with stock or wine. Re-duce the sauce and pour it over the sautéed food. ◗ If you heat or keep sautéed food hot in a sauce, you steam it too much.

## SKILLET-PANNING OR SHALLOW- OR STIR-FRYING

If you are an American housewife you may have added to your wanted-for-Christmas list a **wok,** shown with its conical- or round-bottomed pan on 282, and its supporting and heat-concentrating metal ring. Ironically enough, most of the East Asian brides living in our area happily substituted for it some while ago a good old-fashioned skillet with a tight-fitting lid, even though the cooking period involved is slightly longer. With either utensil the vegetables are prepared the same way: that is, subjected to high heat in an open pan at the outset, and steamed, lidded, at the finish. In anywhere from 3 to 8 minutes, depending on the material, you have tender but still crunchy vegetables and thin strips of fresh-tasting meat— all for immediate consumption.

Preparing the food is the slowest part of this procedure. If the meat is cooked along with vegetables— a popular practice—it is uniformly sliced to a thickness of about 1/8 inch and partially cooked first, until red changes to bright pink. Then it is removed from the frypan and reserved for addition later to the half-cooked vegetables for final cooking. For further details about vegetable stir-frying, see 281; for meats, see Suki-yaki, 571.

# ABOUT MOIST HEATS

What a number of processes can be assigned to the moist-heat category! There are complete ones like boiling,

ressure cooking, scalding, simmer-
ng, poaching, stewing, fricassee-
ng, braising, casseroling, cooking in
raps, double-boiler cookery and
teaming. Just as with dry heats,
here are partial moist-heat processes,
ke those in blanching and fireless
ookery. We may as well mention
ere and now—although not on the
ide of simplification—that certain
lassic terms for kinds of moist-heat
ookery are broadly interpreted, even
y the most knowledgeable cooks.
lso a number are neither moist nor
ry, but a combination of both. Some
tews, for example, may be begun in
pan by browning, while others, like
he Irish variety, never see the inside
f a skillet. Similarly, a braise, a fric-
ssee and a "smother" may all, like a
rowned stew, have their origin in
ry-heat sautéing and then are fin-
shed by cooking in a little stock.

### OILING

Discussing this process tempts us to
mention stews again, in connection
with the old adage, "A stew boiled is
stew spoiled." And we may point
ut that the same sentiment can be
applied to almost every other kind of
ood. While recipes often call for
oods to be brought to the boiling
oint—that is, in liquid which has
eached 212° F.—or to be plunged
nto boiling water, they hardly ever
lemand boiling for a protracted pe-
iod. Even "boiled" eggs, so-called,
hould be simmered.

Quick evaporation—seldom advis-
ble except in parboiling—is one of
he few justifications for keeping a
ood at boiling point. When evaporat-
ng, never boil covered, as steam
ondenses on the lid and falls back
nto the pot, reducing the amount of
iquid very little, if at all.

Adding foods to boiling water will
lower the boiling point, unless the
quantity of water is at least three
times as much as will cover the
food—to offset its lower temperature. Such compensation is recommended in Blanching, 106, and in the
cooking of cereals and pasta. When
the pores of food are to be sealed, it
may be plunged into rapidly boiling
liquid, after which the temperature is
usually reduced to a simmer.

### ❂ PRESSURE COOKING

We often wonder what is done with the
moments saved by the purchase and
preparation of "convenience foods."
Something, we assume, of major
importance, to compensate for their
second-hand flavor. For the cook in a
terrible hurry, but who still hankers
after taste and nutritional value, we
offer the pressure pan as a kind of
consolation prize.

No matter how high the heat source,
boiling in water in the presence of air
can never produce a temperature over
212°. But, because in pressure cooking the air in the pan is withdrawn
first, heat as high as 250° can be maintained at a 15-pound gauge reading.
Some home cookers are geared to
a range of from 3¾ to 20 pounds,
although 15 pounds is commonly
used. Cooking at 15 pounds pressure
takes only about one-third the total
time—from the lidding of the pressure cooker through the capping of
the vent and the release of pressure—
that it takes to cook food in conventional ways at boiling temperatures.
In pressure-cooking vegetables over
short periods at these higher temperatures, more than time is saved. Nutrients and flavor are also conserved,
see Pressure-Cooking and Pressure-
Steaming Vegetables, 281.

In the pressure cooking of meats and soups, however, the higher heats involved tend both to toughen the protein and to affect flavor adversely. Therefore, we recommend this method only when time is more important to you than choice results.

In the canning of all nonacid foods, the higher heat of pressure cooking is essential to kill unwanted organisms, see (II, 613).

Pressure cooking of ♦ beans and cereals and dried or puréed fruits, which may sputter and clog the vent, is not recommended.

It is essential in any pressure cooking to know your equipment well. ♦ Follow manufacturer's directions to the letter, observing the following general principles: ♦ Never fill a pressure cooker with more food than half its capacity if there is much liquid, or two-thirds, if the contents are mainly solids. ♦ Be sure the required amount of liquid has been put into the cooker. ♦ Season lightly, as there is less liquid to dilute the flavor than in more traditional types of cooking.

If you have a timer, use it. If not, watch the time carefully, as overcooking results very quickly. As soon as the time is up, to arrest further cooking and reduce the pressure in your cooker instantly, place it in cool water or let cool water run over the sides. Exceptions are steamed puddings, many meats, and soups, which should be allowed to cool gradually.

♦ The cover must not be removed until all the steam is out of the pressure cooker. Here again, handle your particular type of appliance exactly as you are instructed. ♦ When the cover is difficult to remove, do not force it; there is still steam in the container which will be exhausted if you wait a few minutes.

When cooking foods that require different periods of cooking, begin with the ingredient that requires the longest time. Always reduce the pressure, as directed in the manufacturer's booklet, before opening the lid to add the ingredient that requires the shorter period of cooking. Readjust the cover, place the cooker again over high heat and proceed as before. When the desired degree of pressure has been reached, recap the cooker, reduce the heat and begin to count the rest of the cooking time.

Or, when cooking together vegetables that require an unequal period of cooking, equalize them by cutting into small dice those that require the longer period, such as potatoes and turnips.

▲ A general rule for pressure cooking at high altitudes, whether you are cooking at 10, 15 or 20 pounds pressure, is to maintain the same timing as at sea level, but to increase the pressure by $1/2$ pound for every 1,000-foot rise, using a specially calibrated gauge.

For additional details about high-altitude pressure cooking, see Vegetables, 287; Meat, 556; and Canning (II, 616). To use a pressure-cooker as a steamer, see Steamed Puddings, (II, 539).

### SIMMERING

This ranks as one of the most important moist heats. The temperatures range from about 140° to 185°. Simmering protects fragile foods and tenderizes tough ones. The French verb for the slow simmer is *mijoter,* and the French engagingly refer to low simmers—between 130° and 135°—as "making the pot smile." When food is simmering, bubbles come gently to the surface and barely seem to break. It is the heat best used for soups—uncovered; and for stews, braises, pot roasts and fricassees—covered; and for food prepared à l'étouffée, 102—covered.

## POACHING

This kind of moist-heat cooking is one that most people associate only with eggs, but its range is much wider. The principle of poaching never varies. The heat source is a liquid just under the boiling point, and a distinguishing feature of the process is the basting or self-basting which is constant during the cooking period.

When an egg is properly poached, it is floated on simmering water and then either basted with this simmering liquid or covered with a lid, so that steam accumulates to perform a self-basting action. Because the egg cooks in just a few minutes, the lid does not allow the formation of excess steam. In poaching meat or fish, where the cooking period is lengthened, entrapped steam may become too heavy. For these and delicate foods, therefore, a lid is not recommended. Instead, substitute a **poaching paper**, see sketch opposite.

A poaching paper permits excess steam to escape through its small top vent and around the sides. The narrow vent also maintains better color in the food than when air is excluded altogether—as in other more tightly confined moist-heat processes, such as casseroling. ♦ To make a poaching paper, take a piece of square cooking **parchment**, the sides of which are a little larger than the diameter of the pan you wish to cover. Fold it in fourths and roll it diagonally: begin at the folded tip, as sketched. Hold it over the pan to determine the radius. Then snip off the part that projects beyond the edge of the pan. Cut a tiny piece off

the pointed end to form a vent. When you unfold the paper, you will have a circle just the area of your pan, with a perforation at its center. Place it over the food to form a self-baster.

If the cooking process is a short one, or if the food to be cooked is in small units, the liquid may be at simmering point when the food is added. If the food is chunky, like a whole chicken, the water is put on cold, the food added and the water brought to a simmer ♦ uncovered. The liquid may then be skimmed and the poaching paper applied. If the liquid becomes too greatly reduced during the cooking process, it must be replenished. This type of poaching is often miscalled boiling or stewing.

## CASSEROLING

The term casserole has been bandied about so carelessly that it is time we took stock of its meaning—or, rather, all its meanings. In correct parlance, a "casserole" is both a utensil—usually a lidded one—and the process used for cooking a raw food in that utensil. But it has also come to mean a favorite type of self-service dish which graces so many American buffets but is not in the least the real McCoy. This mock casserole is a mixture of several foods, one of which may be a pasta or rice in a sauce. The mixture is often precooked or consists of a combination of precooked and quick-cooking food; and it is served in the baking dish in which it was heated. ◗ Such mock casseroles are usually cooked uncovered in a moderate oven to avoid building up too much steam and breaking down the sauce in which they are served. They often have a gratinéed top to protect the food and absorb excess fat. ◗ It is wise to wipe off the edges and exposed surfaces of these "prefabricated" casserole dishes after filling and before heating, so they will not show any browned spilled-over areas on the outside surfaces when served. Often, for large groups, a rather shallow dish is used, both to ensure its heating through quickly and to provide plenty of gratinéed top for each serving. If topping with biscuit or corn pone, heat in a 375° to 400° oven.

The basic character of the casserole as a utensil has hardly altered since men learned to shape clay into pots. The typical earthenware casserole is squat, with bulging sides, easily grasped round handles and a slightly arched lid. Clays used in some unglazed pots have been found to be heavy in lead and are not recommended. ◗ To season an unglazed casserole and to prevent an "earthy" taste or the subsequent retention of unwanted flavors, rub it well, inside and out, with cut cloves of garlic. Then fill it with boiling water, add onion skins, celery and leek tops, put in a low oven, let the water come to a boil, and simmer covered about 4 hours. Finally, discard the water and wash the dish and lid, after which the casserole is ready for use. ◗ To

avoid cracking, never set a clay casserole directly on a heating element. If your burner is not thermostatically controlled, it is wise to use an asbestos pad or wire trivet.

Today the word casserole is applied to any deepish pot in which cooking actually goes on, or even to pots more rightly called *sautoirs,* or straight-sided deep skillets. ◗ In true casseroling, as distinguished from "mock" casseroling, a tight lid is integral to the process. Generous quantities of butter, fat or oil are added, and sometimes—but not always—a small amount of stock; the stock, as well as the juice from the food, condenses on the lid and supplies a measure of self-basting, although some hand-basting with the pan fats may be necessary. The very slow cooking goes on in about a 300° oven and develops a bare simmer, condensing the food juices into a delicious residue. After the food is removed, the residue, when degreased if necessary and then deglazed, forms the sauce for the dish. This method of cooking, if in a lidded pot, is also called cooking à l'étouffée.

FIRELESS AND OTHER SLOW MOIST-HEAT COOKING PROCESSES

If fuel is scarce and a long heating period is needed in certain foods, there is a possible advantage in using a fireless cooker. This appliance is enclosed on all sides by material that is a nonconductor of heat and is preheated to a desired temperature by an electric coil or by hot stones. Hot food set in it continues to cook without the addition of further heat.

Deep-wells, pots countersunk in range tops, and pots thermostatically controlled for low, slow heat are also favored at times of fuel shortage or when the cook cannot keep check on a stew over a long period. Some models have electric coils built into the sidewalls as well as the base of the container to give a very consistent low heat.

## WRAP COOKERY

Wrapping food before introducing it into direct heat is almost as old as cooking itself. Primitive societies to this day surround pieces of food with various materials to tenderize them and to protect them from burning. In the Caribbean, petate mats serve this tenderizing purpose, just as papaya leaves do in the Pacific islands. One of the most mouth-watering sights we've ever seen was shown in a documentary movie of an Indonesian tribe on the march. When mealtime came, everyone, from oldster to tot, stopped to devise a case for cooking his food in the coals—an intricately folded leaf, a stoppered section of bamboo, a reed basket. You knew at once that in each "case" the steam produced would give special flavor and succulence to the food. Our American Indians baked fish, see 477, small animals, and birds in clay. Drawn but not skinned, the animal was completely packaged in mud and bedded in coals—up to several hours if the size required it. Removal of the clay brought along with it skin and feathers, leaving the skinned game ready to eat.

More sophisticated methods of exploiting the wrap principle are the dough-encased meat pastries of En-

glish kiln workers and the esteemed French en croûte, 556, and en papillote, 105, methods, in which pastry and paper are the respective casings. And one could consider the prized product of a New England clambake, 447—with seaweed the incomparable flavoring agent—as a glorified example of wrap cookery. But in any true wrap cookery, the enclosing material allows some steam to escape. If you use aluminum foil, 104, in indoor or outdoor cooking, remember that the food is actually steamed, and far removed in taste and texture from food cooked either by direct heat or in a less impervious wrapping.

### LEAF-WRAPPINGS

Certain fresh green unblemished leaves such as lettuce, cabbage, grape and papaya give an edible coating to food, while banana skins, palm leaves and corn husks only furnish protection during cooking. Preparation of suitable leaves and the wrapping and timing of the food for cooking are described as follows.

**Cabbage Leaves:** Cut the stem from a head of cabbage deep enough to start a separation of the very outer leaves from the core. Dip the head in boiling water. This will loosen three or four leaves. Dip again and continue to remove the loosened leaves. Blanch, 106, the leaves 2 minutes, drain and plunge into cold water. Wrap a meat mixture in the leaves as shown in the illustration below. Either tie the leaf packet as shown, or

place it, if left untied, seam side down. Cook as follows.

**I.** Melt in a casserole:
   **2 tablespoons butter**
Add:
   **2 cups boiling water or stock**
Put packets in a single layer on bottom of casserole. Place in a heavy plate directly on top of the food as a weight during cooking. If the leaf-filling is uncooked, bake or simmer the packets, ♦ covered, 35 to 40 minutes—longer for pork. If the wrapped filling is precooked, 10 minutes is enough to heat the packet through.

**II.** If packets are tied, they may be dropped into simmering broth and cooked, ♦ covered, gently until done. See timing under I.

**III.** Or, steam the tied packets in a vegetable steamer. See timing under I.

**Lettuce Leaves:** Soak them very briefly in boiling water. Drain, dry and fill. Wrap as for cabbage leaves and cook only as for I or III. The leaves are not strong enough to cook as for II.

**Fresh Grape Leaves:** for Dolmas, 626. Drop young pale-green leaves into boiling water and blanch till color darkens—about 4 to 5 minutes. Remove leaves. Drain them on a rack. Should you have to use large leaves, remove the tough part of the central rib. Place shiny side down on a board. Roll the filling into 3/4-inch balls. If the filling is of rice, use not more than 2 teaspoons, as the rice will swell. Set a ball of stuffing near the broad end of a leaf and fold over the left and right segments, as sketched on 103. Then roll the enclosed ball toward the leaf-tip. Place

the packet loose side down, and cook as directed in I above.

**Canned Grape Leaves:** Place them briefly in hot water to separate, then drain and dry. Fill and cook as above.

**Papaya Leaves:** Cover them with cold water. Bring ♦ just to the boiling point, uncovered, to remove any bitterness. Drain. Plunge into boiling water to cover and ♦ simmer, uncovered, until tender.

**Banana Leaves:** Cut away the central rib and carefully tear sections about 10 inches square by pulling along the veins. Sponge off the leaves on both sides with cold water, always keeping the action along the leaf veins. Dry the leaves gently with paper toweling or a soft cloth. Center the filling as for tamales, illustrated on 103, but fold first against the veining, and then secure the loose ends by folding them up and securing them with a string. When filled, cook as for III, opposite.

**Corn Husks:** Place them in boiling water, remove from heat and allow to stand 30 to 45 minutes before draining. To roll food in them, overlap two or three corn husks. Fold the leaves first lengthwise from one side to slightly past the center and then overlap from the other side, as shown on 103. Fold up the ends so they can be tied with one string. For use in Tamales, see 180.

FOIL COOKERY

Aluminum foil solves many kitchen problems, but if you cook food wrapped in foil, please consider the following: Foil is impervious to air and moisture from the outside. Therefore, it traps within its case all the moisture released from the food during the cooking period. So even if the heat source is dry, like that of an oven, the result will always be a steamed food, never a roasted one. Since the foil also has high insulating qualities, foil-wrapped food will require ♦ longer cooking periods at the same temperatures indicated in non-foil cookery. An exception is poultry, see 515.

You may be willing to pay for both the foil and extra heat needed to enjoy the convenience of, for example, the practically effortless Pot Roast described on 579. If you are cooking outdoors, see Campfire Vegetables, 286, and the comments in Outdoor Cooking, 108.

❀ Frozen food may be cooked in foil by leaving the ends of the foil-wrap open, in which case a four-pound frozen rolled beef roast will require about 3 hours in a 400° oven, a five-pound frozen chicken the same time at 450°, and a three-pound frozen fish more than 1 hour, again at 450°. The foil may then be turned back altogether to brown the food: about 20 minutes for the chicken or roast, 10 for the fish. You may prefer, after opening the foil, to insert a meat thermometer instead, and cook to the recommended internal temperature.

## COOKING EN PAPILLOTE

This is a delightful way to prepare delicate, quick-cooking, partially cooked or sauced foods. The dish, served in the parchment paper in which it was heated, retains the aromas until ready to eat. As the food cooks, some of the unwanted steam it generates evaporates through the paper. Just the same, the paper rises

and puffs as heating progresses, putting considerable strain on the folded seam. So note the following directions and sketches carefully.

To make a papillote: fold in half, crosswise, a piece of cooking parchment, ♦ not foil, of appropriate size. Starting at the folded edge, cut a half-heart shape, so that when the paper is unfolded the full heart shape materializes, as shown below.

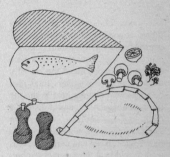

Be generous in cutting, allowing almost twice again as much paper as the size of the object to be enclosed. Place the food near the fold—but not too near. Turn the filled paper with the folded edge toward you. Holding the edges of the paper together, make a fold in a small section of the rim. Crease it with your fingers and fold it over again. Hold down this double fold with the fingers of one hand, and with the other start a slightly overlapping and again another double overlapping fold. Each double fold overlaps the previous one. Repeat this folding, creasing and folding around the entire rim, finishing off at the pointed end of the heart with a tight twist of the parchment—locking the whole in place.

Now butter the paper well. Place the papillote in a buttered ovenproof dish in a 400° preheated oven for 5 to 6 minutes or until the paper puffs. In serving, snip about three-fourths of the paper on the curved edge just next to the fold to reveal the lovely food and release the aroma.

Because of the varied and doubtful chemical composition of the paper, we do not recommend the brown paper bag of the supermarket type as a substitute for the cooking parchment in papillote cookery.

### DOUBLE-BOILER COOKING

For those foods which are quickly ruined beyond hope of resurrection if overheated, even for a short period—especially egg, cream or chocolate dishes—we recommend the use of a double boiler. Sometimes food may be started over direct heat in the top of a double boiler and finished ▶ over—not in—boiling water. For sauces, we like a double boiler that is rather wide. Deep and narrow vessels tend to overheat the sauce at the bottom even when it is stirred—if it is held for any time at all. ▶ The material of which the upper portion of the double boiler is made is very important. When it is too thin, it transmits heat too fast. If it is too thick, it absorbs and retains too much heat.

For years we made magnificent Hollandaise in a stoneware bowl that fit the base of an aluminum double boiler. It was a completely effortless procedure. Then the bowl broke and the magic fled. We found stainless steel and aluminum too quick. A deluxe saucière of stoneware, deep set in a copper base, was too reluctant and, when it finally heated, too retentive of heat. A heat-resistant glass double boiler, 410, has been a reliable substitute for our favorite old makeshift, and it does allow us to keep track easily of the over—not in—boiling water factor.

### STEAMING

For cooking vegetables, steaming is an excellent process. On 281 we describe two methods for this purpose: direct steaming over boiling water and pressure steaming at greater temperatures. Direct steaming is also a good way to plump raisins, to release salt from smoked meats and, more importantly, to cook fish and to prepare delicate vegetables for freezing.

## ABOUT PARTIAL HEAT PROCESSES

Certain processes involve heating but are not in themselves complete methods of cooking. They extend from the driest, like **toasting**, which adds color and flavor, to complete immersion, in **steeping**, which may plump foods or remove unwanted flavors.

### BLANCHING AND PARBOILING

These terms are among the most carelessly used in a cook's vocabulary. To introduce some order into traditional confusion, we describe and differentiate among four different types of blanching.

### BLANCHING I

This means pouring boiling water over food to remove outer coverings, as in loosening the brown hulls of almonds or making the skins of peaches and tomatoes easier to peel off. This process is also used to soften herbs and vegetables for more flexible and longer-lived decoration.

### BLANCHING II OR PARBLANCHING

This involves placing food to be blanched into ▶ a large quantity of cold water, bringing it slowly to a boil, uncovered, and continuing to simmer it for the length of time specified for blanching. Following this hot bath, the food is drained, plunged quickly into cold water to firm it and to arrest further hot-water cooking, and then finished as directed in the recipe. This is the process used to leach excess salt from tongue, cured ham or salt pork and to remove excess blood or strong flavors from variety meats. The cold-water plunge after blanching effectively firms the protein in the more fragile variety meats, like brains and sweetbreads.

### BLANCHING III OR PARBOILING

This means that food is plunged into ♦ a large quantity of rapidly boiling water—a little at a time so as not to disturb the boiling—and then boiled for the blanching period indicated in the recipe. The purpose of this particular kind of blanching or parboiling may be to set color or—by partial dehydration—to help preserve nutrients and to firm the tissues of vegetables. If further cooking follows immediately, the blanched food need not be chilled as above, but merely drained. Should an interval elapse before final cooking and serving, use the cold water plunge, drain and store the food refrigerated. Blanching vegetables in this way preparatory to canning or freezing is described in greater detail in Volume II, 615. Small amounts of the vegetable are plunged into ♦ boiling water just long enough to retard enzymatic action and to shrink the product for more economical packaging. Then the vegetables are drained and quickly plunged into ice water, so that cooking is arrested at once.

### BLANCHING, IV, STEAM-BLANCHING OR PARSTEAMING

Similar to steaming, 106, but of shorter duration. An alternate method for food to be frozen or canned is described in Volume II, 615.

### REDUCING LIQUIDS

This process is used mainly to intensify flavor: a wine, a broth or a sauce is evaporated and condensed over lively heat. A so-called double consommé is made in this way, the final product being half the original in volume. Naturally, reducing applies only to sauces without egg. And those which have a cream or flour base must be watched carefully and stirred often to avoid scorching. For further details, see 378.

### PLANKING

Why bother about planking? One reason is the attractive appearance of a planked meat, surrounded with a decorative band of duchess potatoes beautifully browned on their fluted edges and garnished with colorful vegetables. Another reason is the delicious flavor a hardwood slab can give to meat. Planks are usually 1-inch-thick kiln-dried oak ovals. They often have a tree design cut down their length to drain juices into a shallow depression toward one end.

If all the cooking is done on the plank, the plank will char rapidly. Usually steaks are broiled on an oven grill fully on one side and partially on the other before being planked. To season a new plank, brush it with cooking oil and heat in a 225° oven for at least one hour before using. To protect it when cooking, oil well any exposed part, or cover, as suggested on 107, with a decoration of mashed potatoes or other puréed vegetables.

### FLAMING OR FLAMBÉING

Flaming always comes at a dramatic moment in the meal, sometimes a tragi-comical one if you manage to get only a mere flicker. To avoid anticlimax, remember that ◗ food to be flamed should be warm and that the brandy or liqueur used in flambéing should also be warm—but well under the boiling point. For meat, do not attempt this process with less than one ounce of liquor per serving. For nonsweet food served from a chafing dish or electric skillet, pour the warmed liquor over the surface of the food and ignite by touching the edge of the pan with the flame of a match or taper. For hot desserts in similar appliances, sprinkle the top surface with granulated sugar, add the warm liqueur and ignite as above. Or, ignite brandy-dipped sugar cubes. To flambé fruits, see (II, 112).

### SCALDING

As the term is used in this book, scalding means cooking at a temperature of about 185° or just below boiling. You will find this process discussed in relation to Milk, (II, 184), the food for which it is most frequently used.

## OUTDOOR COOKING

Cooking out of doors may put to use all kinds of heat, but its enthusiasts do best when they stick to simple methods. As soon as cookouts get complicated, the whole party—in our perhaps jaundiced opinion—will do well to move back into the kitchen, where equipment is handy, controls positive, and effects less problematical. We never attend a patio barbecue featuring paper chef's hats, aprons with printed wisecracks, striped asbestos gloves, an infrared broiler on white-walled wheels, and yards and yards of extension cord and culinary red tape without entertaining the possibility of a heavy thunderstorm.

Speaking of easy outdoor cooking devices, we once went on a picnic with some friends in a beech woods. Our host, toward suppertime, made crisscross fires, just big enough for each individual steak. First, he set up log-cabinlike cribs about four layers high with twigs approximately one inch thick. In these he laid a handful of dry leaves and fine brush. On top of the cribs, he continued to build for about three inches an additional structure of pencillike material. When, after firing, the wood had been reduced to a rectangular framework of glowing rods, he unlimbered some thin steaks from a hamper and, to our consternation, laid them calmly and directly on the embers. In a few moments he removed them with tongs, shook off whatever coals had adhered, turned the steaks over and repeated the process on the other side. They were delicious.

There is no law, of course, against availing oneself of ready-made instead of improvised cooking gear, and as much of it as the traffic will bear. There are even available, for the Davy Crocketts of the New Frontier, various solar-heat cookers; but it is suggested that they be given homeside tryouts in advance. Various solid fuels based on hexamethylene tetramine can be purchased in granular form, in bulk, from a chemical supply house, or in tablets at outfitters. This fuel is only adequate for emergencies or when traveling light. For fancy or long-cooking camp foods, gas, either liquid or vapor, is the preferred fuel. Liquid-gas stoves have many adherents but may be a bit cranky. Bottled-gas stoves are easier to use but do not work so well at very low temperatures.

For campers, al fresco cooking is a necessity rather than a pleasant indulgence. But fires in wilderness areas carry for the builder perhaps his greatest responsibility. Before starting your fire, dig or scrape a narrow trench around the area to stop roots under the fire pit from catching fire and smoldering, sometimes for days, then suddenly bursting into flame many yards away. Through the duration of the fire, watch for sparks on surrounding vegetation.

To start a wood fire, collect a few small dead branches with the twigs attached and break up the branches into categories, beginning with matchstick thickness, then pencil thickness, then thumb size and larger. Make a loose untidy pile about 3 or 4 inches high of the smallest size, thrust a burning match into the center, and, as it blazes up, slowly add the next thickness, and then the thumb size. Add fuel on the downwind side of the fire, and remember to let it breathe— air is as important as fuel! Hardwoods smoke less and provide much more heat than do most of the softwoods. Those preferred are oak, beech, maple, ash and then the evergreens. Beech wood will burn green; aspen will not burn at all. If the wood is wet, split it; the interior portions are usually drier, and if a fire is started and is hot, it will use all but soaking-wet wood—albeit with a great deal of smoke. Take a tip from the Indians and keep your fire small: it takes less wood for cooking, it is less bothersome and cozier, and in winter it is easier to cuddle up to for warmth.

◗ Never leave a fire untended. Be sure to watch for overhead branches as fire hazards. When you finally leave a fire, drown it, mix it with mud, stir it into non-vegetation-carrying dirt, stomp on it, mix it with snow or sand, and leave it ◗ dead.

◗ Before bringing any sort of cooking container into close contact with a wood fire, remember to cover the pan's undersurface with a film of soap or detergent. This precaution will greatly facilitate the removal of soot later, when the pan is cleaned.

**Pit-Cooking** is the most glamorous of all primitive types because it is so largely associated with picturesque places, hearty group effort and holiday spirit. Pits may be small holes of just sufficient depth and width to take a bean pot, a three-legged kettle or a true braising pot with a depression on top for coals, as sketched in the chapter heading. Or the pit may be big enough to accommodate all the makings of a king-sized luau, replete with suckling pigs. In direct pit-fire cooking, hardwood embers are left in the pit, and steel rods are put across it, a few inches above the fire on rocks or logs set around its periphery; the rods, in turn, support a wire mesh grid on which the food is cooked.

A switch from direct pit-firing to fireless pit-cooking can achieve a completely different range of culinary effects. Fairly large-scale cookery of the latter type requires digging a pit not less than 2 feet deep, 3 feet across and 4 feet long. If pit-cooking is more than occasional and the locale does not vary, you may find it more convenient to build a surface pit by constructing a hollow rectangle of concrete blocks, about the same height as a true pit is deep.

The next step is to line the bottom and sides of the pit with medium-sized flat rocks, ▶ never with shale, which may explode when heated. Toss in another loose layer of rock. Now spread over the rocks a substantial bonfire of hardwood deadfall or driftwood. Hickory, beech, maple and ironwood are prime for this purpose. And grapevine cuttings lend grilled food special distinction. The French, incidentally, regard food broiled over grape wood, or *sarments de vigne,* as extraordinarily choice. When the fire has completely burned down—this should take not less than 2 hours—rake out the red embers and the top rocks. Now, sprinkle a quart or so of water over the hot rocks remaining and add a two-inch layer of fresh leaves—grape, beech, paw-paw—or of corn husks or seaweed for a shore dinner. If you have remembered to bring along some handfuls of aromatic herbs, add them too.

▶ Work quickly at this point, so that the rocks do not lose their stored heat. On the bed of packed foliage, arrange the elements of your meal: fish, cuts of meat, green peppers, onions, corn in its husks, unpeeled potatoes, acorn squash. Pile over them a second layer of green leafage, then a second grouping of food, and finally a third layer of green leafage. Cap off the stratification with the remaining hot rocks, a tarpaulin or canvas cover, and four inches of earth or sand to weight things down and to keep heat and steam at work inside—cooking your meal. How long this will take depends, of course, on what's cooking—maximum time will probably be required for a small pig; it should test 190° when done and takes about 20 minutes per pound.

The whole pit-cookery operation, whether it is carried out on the beach or in the woods, has a distinctly adventurous character. And periodic tests for doneness performed on the foods closest to the edge of the pit are an essential part of the process. In lifting the tarp and in removing it altogether when you are ready to serve, be extremely careful not to get food fouled up with sand or earth.

A modified form of pit-cookery is described in Smoking Food, (II, 634).

For shore dinners, with seaweed as filler, wire mesh is often placed over at least one layer to better support small crustaceans, clams and oysters. For details of a Clambake, see 447.

Far and away the most popular technique for outdoor cookery involves direct heat from reduced charcoal. We prefer portable rather than built-in cookers. ▶ **If using any charcoal-fired equipment indoors, be sure to put it within a fireplace where the carbon monoxide fumes can be carried off completely. Do not use charcoal burners ever in a tent, cabin, garage or any enclosed area: insufficient ventilation may prove fatal.**

The most common cookout stove is a portable brazier-type, of which the **hibachi,** shown below, is the Far-Eastern representative. But, to accommodate a main dish for groups of four or more, only the larger western-

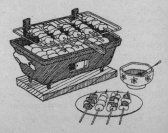

ized brazier offers an adequate cooking surface. A hibachi-type broiler or two will supplement this larger grill in the preparation of side dishes such as hors d'oeuvre and vegetables. The circular grills shown at right have fairly good-sized wheels for easy transport, as well as a lid or a collar to shield the grill surface from wind. The grills may be turned to expose food to the most active areas of heat, and both are equipped with a device which raises and lowers the grill for varied exposures. The lidded model can double as a device for smoke-flavored cooking. Before use, soak wood chips of hickory, apple, oak or cherry about two hours in water and add a few at a time to the charcoal during the cooking period.

Some braziers with horizontal grills have superimposed over them additionally a **spit,** in which case they are commonly protected from wind by a three-sided metal shield with a roof. Without an electrical connection or the use of a cumbersome counterweight system, the only practical way to turn a spit is by hand; and this—make no mistake—is a real chore. On the whole, should you go in extensively for spit-cooking, we advise either an electric oven equipped with a spit, or a separate rotisserie. If you do cook out of doors electrically, you may want to make use of a vertical broiler similar to that shown on 483, which exposes a maximum of food surface to the heat source. Whatever brazier equipment you use, pay close attention to the directions furnished by its manufacturer.

Remember that in all spit-cooking, the weight losses due to shrinkage are great, and flare-up from lost fats and juices may be frequent. Flare-ups can be avoided in part by careful trimming of surplus fat. Some short

flare-ups may be desired for browning; slight unwanted ones can be doused with a sprinkle of water from a sprinkling bottle or a water gun. To minimize the fall of fat onto the

embers, adjust the spit so that it revolves away from you and releases its fat into a small trough of heavy-duty foil.

Equipment for a full-scale brazier operation should include: a bellows or a fan to encourage the embers; a kettle for boiling water; a black iron pot for burgoos, stews or beans; a skillet or two; hinged wire basket grills with long handles—especially desirable for broiling fish and hamburgers; some sharp knives; a metal fork with an insulated handle; a spatula; tongs; a long pastry brush for glazing; a chopping block; skewers—these must be nonrusting, ♦ square or oval, not round and sharp-pointed; a roll of heavy-duty aluminum foil; a supply of pot holders or a couple of pairs of asbestos mitts; individual serving trays; a pail of water and, with it, a flare-up quencher. If you plan to roast a fowl or a joint, you will need also a baster, 554, and a meat thermometer.

♦ To prepare a brazier fire with

charcoal, be sure that you build a big enough bed of coals to last out the cooking operation. We find prepared hardwood briquets most uniform and convenient. They should be put into the brazier approximately two deep—preferably over a layer of gravel, enough to level the bed out to the edge of the bowl.

A circle of aluminum foil, cut to size and put down under the gravel, will protect the brazier from grease. To ready fuel for an extended firing period, arrange an extra circle of briquets around the edge. As the center of your fire burns to embers, these may be pushed inward. For short-term cookery you may group briquets at about two-inch intervals. To help ignite the charcoal, put a few briquettes in a dry waxed milk carton along with a few scraps of paper. ▶ When the charcoal is covered with a fine white ash, you are ready to begin cooking. Flick off the ash, which acts as insulation.

Judging the heat of a brazier fire is strictly a matter of manual training. Hold your hand above the grill at about the same distance from the coals that the food will be while cooking, and think of the name of a four-syllable state—"Massachusetts" or "Mississippi" will do nicely. If you can pronounce it once before snatching your hand away, your coals are delivering high heat; twice, medium heat; if three times, low heat.

What food should be cooked out of doors? Just as we recommend simple cooking equipment in the open, so we now urge simple outdoor menus. Do remember to have your meat at 70° before cooking, and protect it and the other foods against insects. For further menu suggestions, see (II, 31–33).

Also throughout this book you will find recipes which we regard as suitable for outdoor cookery marked with this grill-like symbol ▤. While, obviously, pan-broiled and pan-cooked food may be prepared over a brazier out of doors, you will not find such recipes singled out by the distinctive outdoor cookery symbol. We have, in large part, selected only those in which the flavor is actually improved by the outdoor cooking medium. ▤ For cooking vegetables, see 286. ▤ For cooking on skewers, see 94.

Steaks and chops are extraordinarily well suited to flat-broiling on a brazier. ▶ Choose well-marbled meat, 547. But by this we definitely do not mean meat that has a rim or collar of fat. On the contrary, it is important ▶ to trim off all excess fat before broiling to reduce the risk of flare-ups. Also, cut through encircling sinew—being careful not to slice into the meat itself—so that the meat does not curl up under the high heat which initiates its cooking. ▶ Avoid excessively thick cuts: an inch and a half should be the limit for individual servings. Grease the grill first with some of the meat fat or with a vegetable oil. ▶ To sear the meat and seal in its juices, lower the grill close to the coals before laying the meat on it or use a bellows to increase the heat momentarily.

Searing to seal is even more essential in flat-broil grilling than in pan or oven broiling, because the meat juice, once lost, is irrecoverable. After searing, raise the grill to about three inches from the fire and broil the meat until done. No specific time schedule for doneness can be set up, because so much depends not only on the degree of heat itself, but on the age of the animal, how long the meat has been hung, the nature of the cut and, of course, individual preference.

Here are a few things to keep in mind: Just as in any meat cookery, large cuts take, weight for weight, proportionately less cooking time. If the cut is large, testing for doneness with a thermometer is safer than testing with a knife or fork or with your thumb, 555. We would like to spare you the ordeal of an old friend of ours whose enthusiasm for outdoor grilling is repeatedly dampened by his wife's low-voiced but grim injunction: "Remember, Orville, medium-burned, not well-burned."

♦ If you flat-broil chicken or other fowl, restrict the weight of the bird to two pounds or under. Split it in half, coat both sides with cooking oil, and set the halves on the grill, cavity side down. The bony structure of the bird will transmit heat to the flesh above and at the same time provide insulation. Finish the cooking with the fleshy side down; but ♦ to keep the skin from sticking, make sure to cook farther from the heat source.

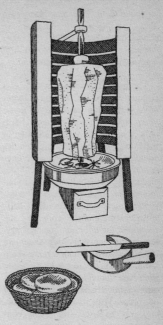

in the neighborhood of ten pounds for roast meat and up to fifteen for fowl. Smaller birds should be strung transversely on the spit, larger ones head to tail along the spit's axis, as illustrated left.

For spareribs, get your butcher to cut them in half crosswise, forming two long strips; prebake or parboil them in the kitchen and then string them like an accordion on your outdoor spit, as shown. Fowl and certain other types of meat must be trussed, 510, before spitting. Especially if they are heavy or of irregular shape, it is necessary, while adjusting them to the skewer, to determine their approximate center of gravity so that the birds balance well in turning. Fowl on a spit should be carefully coated in advance with melted butter

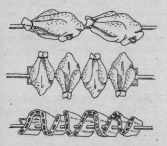

**Spit** and **rotisserie** cooking are best for very small or large fowl; for joints, like leg of lamb; and for other chunky cuts of meat. Here again, consult the directions that come with your equipment to determine maximum weight, which will probably be

or cooking oil. You may baste with butter or oil during the cooking period, but ▶ do not apply any barbecue sauce until the last 15 to 20 minutes of cooking. For Barbecue Sauces, see 404.

The **gyro,** illustrated on 113, is a strikingly functional method of large-scale barbecuing we observed some years ago at the American Farm School in Thessalonica. Common in the Middle East, it is an updated descendant of ember-roasting techniques as old as that part of the world. An electrically powered merry-go-round rotates an impaled mass of compressed meat before a vertical half-cylinder of "ember" coils. As the outside of the tall chunk reaches perfect succulence, very thin slices are cut off lengthwise with a razor-sharp knife. The slices are cut into a scoop and each individual portion is inserted with relishes into a pocket of flat bread. With its cut surfaces successively exposed, the meat continues to turn, to brown—and to diminish happily.

## ABOUT INDOOR COOKING EQUIPMENT

Certain cooking effects we have admired overseas and would like to bring back with us seem to defy stateside domestication. Part of the difficulty may have to do with the way food is grown elsewhere or with the fact that it is sometimes impossible to buy ingredients of comparable freshness. But, just as often, the loss in translation may be traced to special techniques which simply cannot be duplicated in the average American kitchen. This is true of the following: the quick, intense, short-lived fires and the huge pans that are essential to Chinese stir-frying; the very low, long-retained heat chamber called *étuve* in old French kitchens— so ideal for drying out meringues or for simmering foods in covered pots; and, for that matter, the open-air charcoal grilling in our own country, which imparts its distinctive aroma to a steak, or the seaweed-smother which gives that authentic touch to lobsters pit-cooked at the shore. Conditions like these may be approximated in cooking on modern ranges, but never completely reproduced.

If you grew up using gas for cooking heat, you appreciate its dynamic flexibility of control. If your experience has been with electric ranges, you value the evenness of their broiling heat and the stored warmth of their surface units. The relatively new electronic devices have attracted favorable attention because of their ability to reduce heating time to a fraction of its former length. If you are considering investing in this type of equipment, you would do well to see first the section on microwave cooking, 116; and if you do invest, be sure to read the manufacturer's booklet with care.

Indeed, whatever your source of cooking heat, learn thoroughly the characteristics of your range. Find out if the broiling elements need a preheating period; if broiling in the oven requires an open or a closed

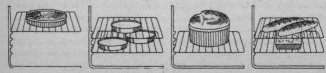

door. Some new electric ovens have a double unit for broiling in which the racked meat is placed midway between the heating elements—a horizontal version of the outdoor double broiler shown 483. A dripping pan is inserted below the lower coils. This broiling unit cuts timing by about half.

In purchasing, consider the safety value of controls. If located along the front of a range, they may be dangerous to small children. If at the rear, they may be obstructed by tall pans or cause accidents by bringing the hand and clothing too close to the burners. Pay particular attention, also, to the quality of oven insulation in the range you plan to buy, and to its venting characteristics.

For loading ovens, we make the following suggestions: ◗ Place oven racks where you want them before heating, not after. To brown a sauce or a gratinéed casserole, place the pan—briefly—close under the broiler, as shown first on the left on 114. Few cooks realize the importance of air circulation in ovens: overcrowding results in uneven baking. Make sure that the pans or sheets you are using fit the oven shelf comfortably, with at least two inches of space between the pans as well as between pans and oven walls. Never use two shelves if you can avoid it, but if you must, stagger the pans as shown second from the left. For a discussion of heat and pan-size relationships, see (II, 401).

For cake baking in general, the best position for the pan is just above center. But for angel food cakes, torten or soufflés, the placement is below center, as shown third in the sketch, for often, in modern ovens, the slight heat provided by a top element is enough to harden the surface of a soufflé, if it is set too close, preventing expansion.

Some commercial ovens feature devices for introducing moisture into an oven as needed. In the home range, a practical substitute, should the recipe require it, is a shallow pan partially filled with water, as shown on the right.

In baking, set the oven thermostat to the desired temperature. Preheat 10 to 15 minutes if there is no indicator light to inform you when the temperature is reached. Insert the pans as quickly as possible. Try not to peek until the time is up—or almost up.

If you use a thermostatically controlled gas or electric oven, don't think you are speeding things up by setting the thermostat higher than the recipe indicates. You will get better results at the specified temperature. And don't, incidentally, press a thermostatically controlled oven into service as a kitchen heater. This will throw the thermostat out of gear. Ovens vary, however, and even under normal use, thermostats need frequent adjustment—at least once every 12 or 14 months.

Keep in mind always that a clean oven will maintain temperature and reflect heat more accurately than an untidy one, and in buying a new range, you may want to consider one equipped with a self-cleaning system.

As to the range top, here again, as with its interior, familiarity breeds assurance. Questions about its use are almost without exception answered fully in the booklet that comes with the equipment. But if you are confronted with a range for which printed instructions are lacking, or if special problems arise, call your local utility company. They frequently maintain a staff of obliging and well-trained consultants, prepared to give you advice free of charge. A most important determination to make in electric ranges is whether your surface heating units—one or several—are thermostatically controlled to level off disconcertingly when you most need sustained heat for a sauté. Also, learn if they are so differentiated as to provide all the potentials of an electric skillet.

In using gas burners, watch the relation of flame to pan. ♦ The flame should never come closer than 1/2 inch to the outer edge of the pan bottom.

Before using such a specialized utensil as a wok or any utensil that would concentrate unusual heat onto the surface of a range, check with the manufacturer as to its practicality; enamel may craze or chrome discolor.

One-piece ceramic range-tops are now available. One has its own ceramic cookware engineered to exactly fit the heating areas; the pots are so flat-bottomed that no heat is lost. Other ceramic tops use any flat-bottomed cookware. Another even more revolutionary concept has been developed: a one-piece ceramic range-top with magnetic coils beneath that leave the cooking surface cool. Energy is generated only in the iron or magnetic stainless steel pans in which the cooking is done.

MICROWAVE COOKING

Our experience with microwave has followed a familiar contemporary pattern: inadequate response to great expectations. For who among us, on the long summer afternoons, has not harbored the recurring and roseate dream of prolonging to the very last minute the joys of gardening—or of tennis, or beachcombing with the children—before returning to the kitchen and putting dinner together in a trice? Even microwave's most obvious advantage—defrosting and

reheating frozen foods—has proved of limited value, and in any case it takes care of only an inconsequential fraction of our cooking schedule. Because no matter what particular microwave equipment you own, you may have to be on hand during much of the reheating period—to rotate the dish, to alternate cooking and withdrawal so that the outside of the food will not cook before the center thaws, or to stir the food intermittently and so vary the electronic impact.

Cooking fresh foods by microwave is also not without disappointments, especially when one compares the eating quality or appearance with that of more conventionally cooked foods. In order to arrive at fair conclusions, we divided into two equal parts each category of food—fresh vegetables, refrigerated or frozen casseroles and leftovers, fresh or frozen meats and fish, pie doughs and cakes—then cooked each by microwave and conventional method respectively. Formulas for cakes and cookies, which, baked by microwave, require less riser, were properly adjusted. We found that timing varied greatly from that prescribed in the manuals of microwave instruction, and almost all types of food tended to toughen. Meats have been shown to dry out and lose more nutrients than when properly roasted by conventional methods. Microwave-baked cakes turned out coarse in texture and over-moist, with pallid tops; those in which egg is the sole riser can only be regarded as failures. If milk or milk-mixtures are cooked in a microwave oven, they must be constantly watched, as they tend to boil over very quickly.

Browning—which in many traditional cooking processes is responsible for both the flavor and the aesthetic pleasure of the food—is not truly achievable with microwave equipment. Attempts have been made through the use of special browning dishes or pre- and post-browning techniques with a unit combining conventional electric heat, but they often complicate procedures or add to the cooking time so that the microwave cooking period may be longer than that of the older methods. Even expedients like dusting with paprika or brushing with soy sauce must often for best results be combined with the use of conventional equipment.

Other limitations of microwave cookery are freely acknowledged by its partisans. Only those tender meat, fowl, and fowl cuts which cook by dry heat respond adequately, and only those that have been boned—like rolled roasts—prove really trouble-free. For bony or uneven cuts, metal foil, which is not penetrated by the microwaves, must be used for part of the cooking time to cover the thinner portions; but the foil must be kept at least two inches away from the walls of the unit to prevent arcing, as described later. Many cooks make a practice of covering food in the microwave oven with plastic or paper wrapping to hold in steam and prevent spatter. Cooking whole hams, except for the reheating of fully cooked types, is not recommended. As we have implied, meat cuts and fowl requiring moist heat are apt to be more tender when cooked by conventional methods—and take no more time. The time factor is similar for foods like rice or pasta, which require large quantities of liquid in cooking.

To understand why the foregoing limitations exist, you must be aware of how microwaves function. Electromagnetic waves originate in a tube and are distributed to all metal parts of the oven interior; from these surfaces they bounce off into the food and are absorbed by it, provided the food is on or in certain materials discussed below. These penetrating waves cause the water molecules in the food to vibrate at an intense rate, and the resulting friction produces the heat, which in turn cooks the food. Since this friction continues after the food is removed from the oven—sometimes in a roast for as long as 30 minutes—microwave-cooked food is in effect undercooked, then allowed to stand outside the oven afterward to complete the process. Care must be exercised in choosing the material on which food is microwave-cooked. The molecular structure of glass, some plastics, ungreased white paper, and some ceramics is such that energy input is not impaired; the food cooked in or on such materials absorbs the waves without adverse effects on them or on the oven. A simple test for cookware suitability is to set it in the oven empty: if it is hot to the touch after 15 seconds of "cooking," it should be discarded. In any event metal or metal-trimmed dishes must be avoided, as they cause an arcing interaction with the oven walls which damages the magnetron tube. Very shallow freezer containers and TV trays made of foil, however, may be used, provided the cooking period is relatively short and they are kept at least two inches from oven sidewalls.

It is true that microwave ovens do not heat up the kitchen, and that the cookware indicated above remains cool during the cooking procedure itself, almost all heat being absorbed by the food. But at the end of the cooking period the hot food very quickly transfers its heat to the dish, and—especially if the dish is quite full—pot holders may be necessary to remove it, and lids or wrappings should be cautiously removed to avoid steam burns.

Because foods of varying types cook at different rates, it is usually necessary to microwave such dishes in succession, holding those finished until the rest have had their turn. In any case, in most portable ovens no more than four servings of any given food can be cooked at one time, nor more than one layer of cake. With the latter handicap, it will readily be seen, the microwave model loses the layer-cake race to the old-fashioned oven in which three or four layers can be simultaneously accommodated.

There are many safety factors one must keep aware of. To avoid danger, door mechanism and switches should be in flawless working order. Air filters must be clean and the oven interior unpitted. Any sign of irregularity should be occasion enough for a service call.

There are available in stationary and professional sizes combination microwave and conventional ovens which dispel some of the disadvantages described earlier. Also to shorten cooking time there are new **convector ovens** which by the use of fans force electrically heated air into oven areas for more rapid baking and roasting. But neither of these is apt to bring to the average household cook the freedom she dreams of via a kitchen robot, for heat is a subtle medium that for best results will always demand intelligent human attention.

So, all things considered—and at the risk of being put down as unadventurous or just plain not with it—we still prefer conventional techniques over those involved in microwave cookery. We find them less demanding, more flexible, and productive o more nutritious and appealing food.

## ABOUT THE TIME ELEMENT IN COOKING

How long to heat food? There are many answers. They lie in the inter action of the heat source, the equip ment and the medium—air, liqui or fat.

Consider the following rates o heat transferral. A dough that eithe bakes at 400° or steams at 212° fo 20 minutes will cook in deep fa heated to 400° in 3 minutes. A hard cooked egg will cool off in 5 minute if plunged into ice water, but wil need 20 minutes to cool in 32° air. A vegetable that will cook in 20 min utes in water at 212° will need onl 2 minutes steaming under 15 pound pressure at 250°.

In timing, a great deal depends o the freshness of food—this is espe cially true of vegetables; on the agin and fat content of meat; and on th size of the food unit. Large, thick ob jects like roasts need lower heat and longer cooking period than do cut lets, to allow the heat to penetrat deep into the center. The amount o surface exposed is also a factor, a you have learned from experienc with whole as compared with dice vegetables.

Still another determinant is th reflective and absorptive quality o the pan. Recent tests have shown tha a whole hour can be cut from th roasting time of a ten- or twelve pound turkey if it is cooked in one o those dark enamel pans that absor heat rather than in a shiny metal on that reflects it. And we have dis cussed elsewhere, 104, the insulativ qualities of foil when used in wrap cooking. Personal preference affect timing, of course, as well as the idiosyncrasies of equipment. Even placement in an oven, 115, makes a difference and, last but not least, the temperature of food at the onset of heating. For all these reasons it is with some trepidation that we have indicated cooking periods in our individual recipes. We know from our fan mail that timing is among the most worrisome of all problems for the beginning cook. Therefore, if our timing and yours do not jibe, we beg you to look for solutions in the facts we have set down above, before you take pen in hand.

## HOLDING FOOD AT SERVING TEMPERATURES AND REHEATING FOOD

Everyone knows that food which is held hot or reheated is not so tasty or nutritious as that served immediately after preparation. Unfortunately, laggards and leftovers are frequently a cook's fate. Here are a few hints on the best procedures:

There are two ways to reheat dishes that are apt to curdle when subjected to direct high temperatures. These include au gratin, egg or creamed dishes or any other dish rich in fat. One way is to put them in the oven in a container of hot water about two-thirds the depth of the cooking pan. Or place under the pan a cookie tin or a piece of foil—shiny side down—so that the heat is deflected. The latter suggestion is particularly handy to avoid overbrowning when reheating pies or cakes.

Reheat other cream- and egg-sauced foods in a double boiler ♦ over—not in—boiling water.

To retain color in vegetables reheated in a double boiler, use a vented lid.

If reheating whole roasts, bring them to room temperature and then heat through in a moderate oven.

If reheating roasted meat, slice it paper thin and put it on hot plates just before pouring over it boiling-hot gravy. ♦ Any other method of reheating will toughen it and make it taste second-hand.

To reheat deep-fat-fried foods, spread them on racks ♦ uncovered, in a 250° oven.

To hold pancakes, place them on and between cloth towels in a 200° oven.

To reheat casseroles, make certain the container is ovenproof before placing it in a 325° oven directly from the refrigerator.

To reheat creamed or clear soups or sauces, heat to boiling point and serve immediately.

Other devices that hold foods for short periods are electrically controlled trays, individual retractable infrared lamps, the age-old chafing dish, and the bain-marie or steam table. None of these should be used for a protracted period, however, if you hope to preserve real flavor and avoid bacterial growth. ♦ Holding temperatures should be at about 140°.

## ABOUT UTENSILS

The material of which pots and pans are made, as well as their sizes and shapes, frequently determines success or failure. So, often in this book we not only caution about too high heat, but especially warn against combining it with thin cooking pans. The latter may develop hot spots and cause sticking, or they may require an undue amount of stirring to avoid scorching. ♦ Choose a pan, then, of fairly heavy gauge—not so heavy as to make for difficult handling, but heavy enough to diffuse heat evenly. Note, too, that we distinguish in recipes between **flame- or heatproof ware** that can be used on direct heat—except for heatproof glass, which needs a trivet—and **ovenproof ware,** which is designed for oven use only.

### HEAVY ALUMINUM

The advantage here is good diffusion, but aluminum will pit—no matter how expensive. And it will not only tend to become discolored itself but will adversely affect the color of some foods. Don't clean aluminum with harsh soaps, alkalis or abrasives. To remove discoloration, boil in aluminum pans for 5 to 10 minutes a solution of 2 teaspoons cream of tartar to 1 quart of water.

### COPPER

Best in heavier gauges. It gives a quick, even heat distribution if kept clean. But unless well tinned, or lined with stainless steel on surfaces contacting the food, it is affected by acids and can prove poisonous. To clean, keep handy a squeeze bottle filled with a vinegar-and-salt mixture. Place some on a cloth and rub discolored copper until bright, then rinse in hot water.

### STAINLESS STEEL

Of course, this is the easiest material of all to keep clean. Its poor heat-conductivity is usually offset by thinning down the gauge, so that hot spots develop and food cooked in it is apt to burn easily. But stainless steel with an inner core of aluminum or copper which increases heat diffusion makes one of the choicest of utensils for surface cooking.

### IRON

Heavy but low in conductivity, iron rusts easily and discolors acid foods. To treat new commercially preseasoned skillets or Dutch ovens, wash with soapy water, rinse and dry. Coat frequently with unsalted vegetable oil, and just before using, wipe with paper toweling. To reseason an old iron skillet, scour and wash with soap—not detergent. Dry; then coat with an unsalted shortening, and place in a 350° oven about 2 hours.

### TEMPERED GLASS AND PORCELAIN ENAMEL

Both are poor heat conductors. The glass is apt to crack and the enamel scratches and chips. Unless of best quality and treated to resist acid foods, the glaze of enamel ware is quickly affected by them. It also is marked by metal utensils; only wooden or nylon hand tools should be used with it. High heat may make the enamel stick to the heating element, so a trivet is advisable.

### EARTHENWARE

While a poor conductor of heat, glazed or unglazed earthenware holds heat well and doesn't discolor foods. But it is heavy and breaks easily with sudden temperature changes. There are recent discoveries that indicate some danger of lead transference to food from soft glazes and even from certain unglazed earthenwares. To season and use an earthenware casserole, see 102.

### TINWARE

This has good conductivity but is apt to mar, and it rusts quickly. It turns dark after use and is affected by acid foods.

GREASELESS PANS

These are a delight to people suddenly put on fat-free diets. The soapstone griddle illustrated, (II, 141), is age-old. There is newer equipment with nonsticking silicone and fluorocarbon resin surfaces which can withstand temperatures up to 450°. These surfaces do not affect heat distribution but will help to keep food from sticking. As some scratch easily, use a nylon or wooden paddle for turning, and a nylon or wooden spoon for stirring. When cooking eggs, breaded fish and meat you may need added fat.

If you are on a fat-free diet and tired of broiling or of using greaseless utensils, poach food in skim milk, fruit juice, stock or wine for variety in flavor.

PLASTICS

There are plastics which can stand relatively high heat but not high enough for cooking or ◆ even for containing hot liquids that may dissolve the plastic and seriously burn the cook. Many storage containers, funnels and other kitchen utensils cannot even be washed in water over 140°. Others are ruined by oil and grease. The surfaces of all plastic utensils retain grease, ◆ so don't try to get egg whites to whip in a plastic bowl, (II, 207).

You will wonder after reading these pros and cons what pan materials to choose. Fortunately there are on the market today a number of brands of cooking ware with good flat bottoms made of alloys that take advantage of the superior diffusion of aluminum, the quick conductivity of copper, and the noncorrodible quality of stainless steel. But while we are speaking of combinations of metal, let us say that ◆ pots of copper, even when tin-lined, and of iron must not be covered with aluminum foil if the food to be cooked is very acid, as the foil can be dissolved into it. In fact, it is usually best to avoid dissimilar metal pots and lids when cooking any very acid foods. In the final analysis, you may still prefer a heavy iron Dutch oven for stews, an earthenware casserole for fondues, a heatproof glass vessel for sauce-making. ◆ Don't invest in large pan sets of a single material until you know what your preference really is. Be sure the pot handles are metal-reinforced at the jointure and are replaceable.

When you cook, choose a pan that fits the size of the heat unit. This correlation gives better cooking results and is more economical of fuel. Be certain, too, that the lid, if the process calls for one, is tight fitting. ◆ Be sure the cooking pan is appropriate in size to its contents. Especially in braising and baking, the relation of pan size to contents is vital, see 554 and II, 401.

In baking, round pans will give you more even browning; square pans tend to cause heavier browning at the corners. Note, too, that shiny metal baking pans deflect heat and that dark enamel or glass ones both catch and hold the heat more. ◆ Therefore, food cooked in glass or enameled pans needs at least a 25° reduction in the oven temperatures given in our recipes. While vitreous or dark metal materials may brown cookies too rapidly, they will ensure better browning for pies and puff pastries. If cooking fuel is scarce, a great saving can be effected by the use of these heat-retaining pans.

In pan-broiling or using a griddle, utensils should be brought up slowly to cooking temperature. ◆ Do not place an unfilled pan on high heat unless it has fat or liquid in it.

And should you scorch food by some unlucky chance, the scorched taste is greatly lessened by plunging the pan first into cold water before transferring the food to a clean container. To clean scorched pots, except those coated with silicone or a similar material, use a nylon pouf or a nylon brush with a built-in detergent container. If that is not sufficient, soak overnight with some detergent in the water. If that still isn't enough, in the scorched pot bring to a boil 1 teaspoon washing soda or cream of tartar for each quart of water.

There is a certain pace in food preparation that an experienced cook learns to accept. This doesn't mean she scorns short cuts, but she comes to know when she has to take the long way 'round to get proper results. She senses not only the demands of her equipment but the reactions of her ingredients.

A man once summed up his wife's life with the epitaph, "She died of things." It might have happened to any of us. We are constantly encouraged to buy the latest gadget that will absolutely, positively make kitchen life sublime. No kitchen can ever have enough space at convenient levels to take care of even a normal array of equipment. So think hard before you buy so much as an extra skewer.

Get pans that nest well. And if you can't resist a bulky mold, see that it hangs on an out-of-the-way pegboard panel, or make it a decorative feature for an odd, unused nook. Buy square rather than round canisters for economical use of storage space. Keep canisters with spices and staples in alphabetical arrangement for quick identification. And place these close to the areas where you will be using them most.

## BASIC KITCHEN EQUIPMENT

We all enjoy and expect shining, easily cleaned kitchen surfaces. Some traditional ones like crosscut or laminated wood chopping blocks, even when sanded daily, can harbor harmful bacteria. It is hard but wise to toss out slightly crazed or chipped pottery, but you can relegate it to the flower department. Choose shapes that are free from grooves and jointures that catch food, and select materials that are impervious to acids and rust.

Kitchens today are fairly scientifically laid out. Everyone is aware that the big kitchen is a time and energy waster; and that a U-shape or a triangular relationship of sink, stove and refrigerator—with their accompanying work spaces—is a step-saver. We may have to live with the kitchens we have, but it pays occasionally to think about your work habits. See if you can make them more efficient.

Well-designed nonrusting hand tools save your towels and your temper. The following is a reasonably comprehensive basic equipment list for which illustrations can be found as noted.

4 saucepans of assorted sizes with lids, 134
2 frying pans—large and small—with lids, 187
Large stewing or soup kettle, 126
Double boiler, 410
Pressure cooker, 281
Mold for steaming, 74
Deep-fat-frying equipment, 95
3 strainers, 175, 281, 376
Steamer, 281
Colander, (II, 197)

Coffee maker, 26
China teapot and teakettle, (II, 57)
Candy thermometer, (II, 581)
Deep-fat-frying thermometer, 95
Griddle, (II, 142)
Bean pot, 236
Oven roasting pan with rack, 510
3 round 9-inch cake pans, (II, 402)
2 square 9-inch cake pans, (II, 402)
2 loaf or bread pans, (II, 299)
2 cake racks for cooling, (II, 220) ·
Muffin tins, (II, 315)
2 pie pans—tin or glass, (II, 359)
2 cookie sheets, (II, 472)
Small ovenproof dish, 236
Large ceramic or glass casserole, 506
6 custard cups, (II, 509)
9-inch tube pan, (II, 405)
Shallow 9 x 12-inch pan, (II, 487)
8-inch soufflé baking dish, 211
Set of mixing bowls, (II, 207)
Set of metal measuring cups, (II, 210)
8-oz. dry-measure glass cup, (II, 210)
8-oz. liquid-measure glass cup, (II, 199)
Set of measuring spoons, 376
Large and small metal spoons, (II, 400)
Slotted wooden spoon, (II, 281)
Large fork, (II, 565)
Small fork, 343
2 paring knives, (II, 92)
Serrated bread knife, (II, 219)
Carving and slicing knives, 559
French chopping knife, (II, 237)
Grapefruit knife, 288
Knife sharpener, 559
Spatula, (II, 472)
Eggbeater, 376
Ladle, 126
A 4-sided and a rotary grater, 374, 376
Meat grinder, (II, 607)
Sugar or flour scoop, (II, 211)
Funnel, (II, 580)
Tongs, 95
Kitchen shears, 128
Flour sifter, (II, 211)
Potato ricer and food mill, 186

Potato masher, 343
Wooden chopping bowl and chopper, 430
Salad bowl, 42
Doughnut cutter, 95
Biscuit cutter, (II, 351)
Pastry blender, (II, 359)
Pastry board, (II, 299)
Pastry brush, (II, 359)
Vegetable brush, 282
Rolling pin, (II, 359)
Pastry cloth and cover for rolling pin, (II, 359)
Pancake turner, (II, 142)
Apple corer, 54
Vegetable slicer or parer, 310
Rubber scraper, (II, 297)
Weighing spoon or scales, (II, 205)
Ice cream freezer, (II, 548)
Citrus fruit juicer, (II, 54)
Electric mixer, (II, 398)
Blender, 374
Waffle iron, (II, 149)
Impervious cutting board, see (II, 237)
Asbestos pad or trivet, 410
Bottle openers, below
Corkscrew, below
Can openers, below
Nutcracker, (II, 238)
Salt shaker and pepper grinder, 105
Pot holders, 124
Plastic detergent dispenser with nylon brush, below, and nylon pouf, 124
Jar unscrewers, below

## OTHER USEFUL ACCESSORIES

4 or more canisters
Cake cover and carrier
Dish drainer
Dutch oven or enameled metal-lidded casserole
Garbage can
Wastebasket
Meat thermometer
Toaster
Vegetable bin
1 or more trays
Bucket
Wooden picks for testing cakes
Refrigerator containers
Waxed paper and paper toweling
Plastic storage bags
Aluminum foil
Dishpan
12 dishtowels
4 dishcloths
Plastic sponges

Small kitchen amenities for which we are enduringly grateful are those extensions of power like can openers, lid lifters, jar unscrewers and the nylon brush-topped detergent dispenser, 123, and the jar lifter and pot holders, below.

We end these lists with a reminder. ◖ Always clean off tops before opening cans, as they may be dusty or may have been sprayed with poisonous insecticides while in the store. Also in opening a can ◖ avoid metal slivers by starting beyond the side seam and stopping before you cut through it. Food may be stored safely in opened cans, covered and refrigerated, for a few days.

## ABOUT BURNS AND BURNING

In the foregoing pages we have supplied, among other information, enough facts to keep our readers from ever burning the food they heat. Now a few safeguards against burning the cook—and what to do should such an emergency occur.

Never throw water on a grease fire. Use salt or soda, or if the area is a small one, cover with a metal lid.

Choose a range, if you can find one, on which the burners are level with the surrounding platform so pots cannot tip.

Use flat-bottomed, well-balanced pans that are steady when empty. Be sure handles are not so heavy that the pot will tip, or so long that they can catch on a sleeve.

When deep-fat frying, please note the precautions given on 94–97.

Put boiling liquid to the back of the stove, out of reach of small children.

In pan-frying, keep a colander handy to place over the pan should the fat begin to sputter.

Keep heavy pot holders and metal tongs near the range for removing hot objects and hot foods.

Watch that your hands or the cloths you are to use are not damp when touching or wiping electrical equipment or hot handles or lids.

Have polarized attachments put on your electrical appliances to avoid shock.

Should you receive an extensive or painful burn, seek immediate help from your physician or the emergency room of your local hospital. Lie down, remain calm, and keep warm until skilled help is available.

The first aid treatment of the wound itself is much the same for large or small burns. Loosen clothing or other material over or near the wound and remove it. Take care not to cut or remove the burned skin or any material adhering to the burned surface. If blisters are present, they should not be broken or cut.

Submerge the burned area in cold water or apply cold water as soon as possible after injury for periods up to one or two hours. This will help to relieve the pain. Then apply a dry sterile gauze dressing as a protective bandage. If sterile gauze is not readily available, clean linen can be used. Larger burn wounds should be covered by a clean sheet for protection and comfort until medical help is provided.

Do not use antiseptic preparations, ointments, sprays, butter, or home remedies on the burn wound, since these substances may interfere with treatment by the physician later.

Individuals with face burns should be observed continuously to assure that they are breathing normally.

After first aid treatment has been initiated, further medical care should be under the direction of a physician.

## STAIN REMOVAL

We give here a partial list of removal instructions for those stains most encountered in the kitchen and dining room. These directions are for natural linens and cotton. If wool or synthetic fibers are involved, avoid hot water and bleaches. For other stains we recommend consulting the Home and Garden Bulletin No. 62 of the USDA, Washington, D.C.

**Alcoholic Beverages:** Sponge stain with cool water or soak 30 minutes or longer. Wash with soap or detergent.

**Butter, Margarine or Mayonnaise:** Regular washing removes some stains; others will need soap or detergent rubbed into the stain, then rinsing with warm water. For large stains use a commercial grease solvent and follow manufacturer's directions.

**Catsup and Chili Sauce:** See Alcoholic Beverages, above.

**Chocolate and Cream:** Sponge with cool water or soak 30 minutes or longer. Rub gently with soap and rinse. If stain remains, apply a commercial grease solvent.

**Coffee and Tea:** Boiling water poured from a height of 2 feet is good for fresh stains. Stretch stained material over a washbowl and ♦ be very careful not to scald yourself.

**Fruit, Fruit Juices and Wines:** Boiling water as for coffee stains; or try bleaching in sun after moistening with lemon juice and salt.

**Lipstick:** Apply undiluted detergent to stain, rub well and rinse. Repeat if necessary.

**Mustard:** See Lipstick, above.

**Soft Drinks:** See Alcoholic Beverages, above.

**Wax or Paraffin:** Scrape cloth to remove hardened wax. Place blotting paper or facial tissues both over and under the cloth and press with warm iron. Sponge with a commercial grease solvent.

# SOUPS

In the good old days, when a "soup bunch" cost a nickel and bones were lagniappe, pounds and pounds of meat trimmings and greenstuff were used in the household to concoct wonderful essences for everyday consumption. The best soups are still based on homemade stocks. ♦ Please read About Stocks, the foundation of soup, meat and sauce cookery, and therefore found under Ingredients, (II, 167). Note the suggestions offered for the long slow cooking of meat stocks or the rapid cooking of fish fumets and vegetable stocks, which also apply to soup making. Fish and vegetable stocks are especially important in *au maigre* or meatless cooking.

Because not everyone wants to bother with the painstaking methods often required to extract soup stock, and because soups are such an interesting addition to or base for meals, we suggest toward the end of this chapter a large number of time-saving prepared soup combinations. Have on hand a supply of canned, dried or frozen bases to bring quick and revivifying soups into the range of even the most casual cook. No one can afford to be without a varied store of these consistently good, and often excellent, products. Learn to use herbs and seasonings, (II, 265 and 246). Keep your own economical stockpot to dilute condensed soups and to enrich them with added minerals and vitamins. Astound your friends with effortlessly made and unusually flavored soup sensations!

To minimize cooking time, use your ⅃ blender for the processing of raw vegetables, and your ♎ pressure cooker for suitable meat scraps, fresh or leftovers. See Quick Household Stock, (II, 173).

No matter by what method it is made, soup should complement or contrast with what is to follow; and however enticing its name, it will fit into one of the categories below:

Some of the above are served hot, some cold, some either way, like bouillons, borsch, vichyssoise and fruit soups. ♦ To serve soups piping hot, use tureens, lidded bowls or well-heated cups. Especially if drinks and hors d'oeuvre have been offered first, a hot soup helps to recondition the palate.

♦ Cold soups should be very well chilled, and served in chilled dishes— especially jellied soups, which tend to break down more rapidly, being relatively light in gelatin. Cold soups, when not jellied, may be prepared quickly by using a ⅄ blender and chilling briefly in the freezer. On informal occasions, they may be chilled in a tall jug and served directly from it into chilled cups or bowls.

You should be able to count on about 6 servings from a quart of soup unless it is the mainstay for a lunch, as is frequently the case with a soup rich in solids. ♦ The quantities noted in the individual recipes are consistently given in standard 8-ounce cups; servings in about 6-ounce cups.

There are some classic dishes— Petit Marmite, 131, New England Boiled Dinner, 584, and Goulash, 582—that occupy middle ground between soups and stews.

▲ Above 2500 feet, soups need longer cooking periods than called for in the regular recipes, as the liquids boil at a lower temperature.

## SOUP SEASONINGS

Soup is as flavorful as the stock on which it is based. Please read About Stocks, (II, 167), and Seasonings for Stocks, (II, 169).

The addition of wine to soup frequently enhances its flavor, but ♦ do not oversalt soups to which wine is added, as the wine intensifies saltiness. A not-too-dry sherry or Madeira blends well with veal or chicken soup. A strongly flavored soup prepared with beef or oxtail is improved by the addition of dry red table wine—1/2 cup wine to 1 quart soup. A dry white table wine adds zest to a fish, crab or lobster bisque or chowder. Add 1/4 to 1/2 cup unfortified wine to 1 quart soup. Fortified wines should be added to the hot soup shortly before it is served. To add wine to soups containing cream or eggs, see individual recipes.

♦ Do not boil the soup after adding the wine.

Beer adds a tang to bean, cabbage and vegetable soups. Use 1 cup for every 3 cups soup. Add the beer just before serving. Reheat the soup well, but ♦ do not boil.

## COLORING SOUP

If soup has been cooked with browned onion skins or browned onions, and if the amount of meat used is substantial, it should have a good, rich color. Tomato skins also lend color interest. Caramelized Sugar III, (II, 232), may be added if necessary. We prefer it to commercial soup coloring, which is apt to overwhelm a delicately flavored soup with its own pervasive, telltale aroma. Also read About Vegetable Stock Making, (II, 174).

## REMOVING FAT FROM SOUP

**I.** Chill the soup. The fat rises at once and will solidify when cold. It is then a simple matter to remove it.

**II.** Float a paper towel on the surface of the soup, and when it has absorbed as much fat as it will hold, discard; or roll a paper towel and use one end to skim over the soup surface to remove the fat. When the end becomes coated with fat, cut off the used part with scissors and repeat the process as shown below.

**III.** Use your meat baster, 553, with the bulb as a suction device for grease removal.

## ABOUT CEREALS FOR THICKENING SOUPS

Noodles and dumplings and precooked cereal garnishes such as rice give an effect of body to a clear soup. But for intriguing texture and elegance of flavor, they do not compare to the thickeners added raw and cooked as an integral part of the soup.

To add any of the following, bring the soup to a boil and then reduce the heat to a simmer as soon as the addition has been made. Stir ♦ raw cereals into soup for the last hour of cooking. For a light thickening, allow to the original amount of liquid approximately:

- 1 **teaspoon barley to 1 cup liquid**
- 1 **teaspoon green kern to 1 cup liquid**
- 1 **teaspoon rice to 1 cup liquid**
- 1 **teaspoon oatmeal to 1 cup liquid**
- 2 **tablespoons wheat germ flour to 1 cup liquid**
- 2 **tablespoons peanut flour to 1 cup liquid**
- 2 **tablespoons soya flour to 1 cup liquid**
- 1/2 **teaspoon quick-cooking tapioca to 1 cup liquid**

If you wish to thicken cooked soup with flour, allow:

- 1 1/2 **teaspoons flour to 1 cup soup**

Make a paste of the flour with about:

**Twice as much cold stock, milk or water**

Pour the paste slowly into the boiling soup, while stirring. Simmer and stir 5 to 10 minutes.

Or make a roux, 378. To 1 cup soup allow:

- 1 1/2 **teaspoons butter**
- 1 1/2 **teaspoons flour**

Pour the soup over this mixture, stirring constantly until smooth and boiling.

Or add in the same proportions as above:

**Flour and butter**

to cooled soup in a 🥄 blender—then reheat the soup. Bring to a boil, lower heat and simmer 5 minutes.

Additional thickenings for soup are dry, crustless French bread or Panades, 146. Also, thick cream or a White Sauce, 383, may be used.

## ABOUT OTHER THICKENINGS FOR SOUPS

**I.** Egg yolks are one of the richest and best of soup thickeners—but they must be added just before serving. ▶ Take care that the soup is not too hot when this is done.

Allow for each cup of soup:

    1 **egg yolk, beaten with**
      1 **tablespoon cream or**
       **sherry**

To avoid curdling, it is wise to add to this beaten mixture a small quantity of the hot soup before incorporating it into the soup pot. ▶ When using egg or cream-based thickeners, it is always essential that the soup, after their addition, be kept below the boiling point.

**II.** Or, allow for each cup of soup:

    2 **riced hard-cooked egg**
      **yolks**

Add at the last minute and, of course, do not allow the soup to boil.

**III.** A good soup thickener, for those whose diet does not include flour, consists of:

    3 **tablespoons grated raw**
      **potato**

for each cup of soup. Grate the potato directly into the soup about 15 minutes before it has finished cooking. Then simmer until the potato is tender, when it will form a thickener.

**IV.** Soups cooked with starchy vegetables ▶ such as dried beans, peas or lentils, will separate and must be bound. To do this, blend:

    1 **tablespoon melted butter**
    1 **tablespoon flour**

with a small amount of:

    **Cold water, stock or milk**

This mixture will thicken about:

    3 **cups strained boiling soup**

Stir in and simmer at least 5 minutes before serving.

**V. Miso**

This favorite Japanese seasoning, heavy in salt, is used in many dishes as a protein extender. Made from fermented soybeans, which may be combined with rice or barley, it ranges in color and taste from beige and sweet to dark brown and savory. For each cup of clear soup, stir in as it heats:

    1 **tablespoon Miso**

It will hold well, sealed and refrigerated.

## ABOUT SOUP MEAT

Any meat that is ▶ immersed in cold water and simmered for a long period is bound to give its best flavor to the cooking liquor. But some food values remain in the meat, and it may be heightened in flavor by serving it, when removed from the soup, with one of these sauces:

    **Horseradish Sauce, 386**
    **Hot Mustard Sauce, 390**
    **Quick Tomato Sauce, 400**
    **Brown Onion Sauce, 392**

## ABOUT CLEAR SOUPS

Because so much valuable material and expert time go into the making of clear soups and because they taste so delicious, most of us assume that they have high nutritive value. It disappoints us to have to tell you that, while they are ◗ unsurpassed as appetite stimulators, the experts give them an indifferent nutritional rating. We suggest, therefore, combining them with egg garnishes, 134.

**I.** For chicken broth use:
   **Light Stock from Poultry, (II, 172)**

**II.** For game broth use:
   **Fowl, Rabbit or Game Stock, (II, 172)**

**III.** For fish broth use:
   **Fumet or Fish Stock, (II, 173)**

**IV.** For vegetable broth use:
   **Vegetable Stock, 524**

◗ Be sure to see Garnishes for Soups, 170.

## CONSOMMÉ

Prepare:
   **Brown Stock I, (II, 171)**
and clarify it by Method I, (II, 170). This will give you a clear, thin consommé. For double strength, clarify the stock by the second method. Before serving add:
   **(3 tablespoons Marsala, II, 48)**

## CONSOMMÉ BRUNOISE

**3 Cups**
Make a mixture of the following finely diced vegetables:

   1  **rib of celery**
   1  **small carrot**
   ¹/₂  **small turnip**
   ¹/₂  **small onion**
Sauté them gently in:
   1  **tablespoon heated butter**
Enough time should be allowed to let the vegetables absorb the butter, but ◗ do not let them brown. Add:
   1  **cup consommé**
and continue cooking, covered, until the vegetables are tender. Pour the above into:
   2  **cups hot consommé**
Remove fat and:
   **Season to taste**
Just before serving, add:
   1  **tablespoon finely chopped chervil**
   1  **tablespoon cooked peas**
   1  **tablespoon finely diced cooked green beans**

## CONSOMMÉ MADRILÈNE

**About 4 Cups**
Heat to the boiling point and strain:
   2  **cups tomato juice**
   ¹/₂  **teaspoon grated onion**
   2  **cups Light Stock from Poultry, (II, 172)**
      **A piece of lemon rind**
      **Salt and pepper**
Flavor with:
   **Lemon juice, dry sherry or Worcestershire sauce**
Or garnish with:
   **Cultured sour cream**
dotted with:
   **Red caviar**

## CHICKEN OR TURKEY BROTH

◗ See the many cream soups, 149, and egg-garnished soups, 134, based on this simple broth. Prepare:
   **Fowl, Rabbit or Game Stock, (II, 172)**

or use canned stock. When it is boiling, remove from heat. You may add for each 4 cups:

　　½ **cup cream**

Reheat but ♦ do not boil. Serve with Chiffonade of Herbs, 172, or with Dumplings, 182.

## CHICKEN BROTH OR BOUILLON WITH EGG

　　　　　　**Individual Serving**

A good dish for a convalescent, but not to be scorned by those in the best of health. Remove fat, clarify, and heat:

　　**Chicken Broth, 130**
　　**Season to taste**

For every cup add:

　　(1 **teaspoon lemon juice**)
　　(1 **tablespoon chopped**
　　　**parsley**)

When the soup is hot, add:

　　**An egg drop, 134**

allowing 1 egg per serving. Serve at once.

## POT-AU-FEU, POULE-AU-POT OR PETITE MARMITE

　　　　　　**About 10 Cups Broth**

A marmite is an earthenware lidded pot, higher than it is wide. Its material accounts in part for the flavor of the soup. This pot is conditioned by boiling clear water in it 12 hours. Traditionally, it is always washed out only with clear water. In pot-au-feu, another name for petite marmite, the major meat is beef, with an addition of chicken wings and gizzards. In making poule-au-pot, a juicy hen—the chicken which Henri IV wanted for every pot—is substituted for the giblets. Marrowbones are usually included, tied in cheesecloth. The vegetables may be seasonally varied.

Blanched cabbage is often served as a side dish.

Put into a marmite:

　　2½ **quarts cold water**
　　　2 **lb. shank or chuck beef, cut**
　　　　**into chunks, chicken wings**
　　　　**and giblets**

Tie in cheesecloth and add:

　　(1 **marrowbone**)

Bring this mixture ♦ slowly to a boil and ♦ skim off both foam and fat. Cut Parisienne style, 280, and add:

　　2 **carrots**
　　1 **small turnip**
　　3 **leeks: white parts only**
　　3 **small ribs celery**
　　1 **whole onion stuck with**
　　　**3 cloves**
　　1 **teaspoon salt**
　　1 **Bouquet Garni II, (II, 253)**

Bring these ingredients to a boil. ♦ Skim again. Cover and cook slowly about 3 hours in a 350° oven. The bouillon should be clear and amber in color.

To serve, start with the clear soup and offer the meat and vegetables on the side with the marrowbone and:

　　**Small pieces toasted French**
　　**Bread, (II, 306)**

## BOUILLON

Bouillon is an unsalted strong beef stock, not so sweet as consommé. Clarify and reduce by one-third:

　　**Brown Stock I or II, (II, 171)**
　　**Season to taste**

Serve with:

　　**A Garnish for Clear**
　　**Soups, 171**

## TOMATO BOUILLON

　　　　　　**About 3 Cups**

Bring to the boiling point and simmer 5 minutes:

3 cups strained tomato juice
½ small bay leaf
¼ cup cut-up celery, with
        leaves
2 tablespoons chopped fennel
2 whole cloves
1 tablespoon fresh basil
(1 small skinned, chopped and
        sautéed onion)

Strain.

**Season to taste**

Serve hot or cold in cups, topped with a teaspoon of:

**Whipped cream or cultured
sour cream**

## BEEF TEA

**About ¾ Cup**

Grind twice:

1 lb. lean round steak or neck
        bone meat

Place in a quart mason jar and add:

1 cup cold water
½ teaspoon salt

Cover the jar lightly. Place it on a cloth in a pan containing as much cold water as possible without upsetting the jar. Bring the water slowly to a gentle boil and continue boiling 1 hour. Remove the jar. Place on a cake rack to cool as quickly as possible. Strain the juice. Store it in a covered container in the refrigerator until ready to heat and serve.

## BROTH ON THE ROCKS

For the guest who shuns an alcoholic drink, offer a clear broth such as:

**Chicken broth or bouillon**

combined with:

**(Tomato and orange juice)**

poured over ice cubes. ◗ Be sure the broth is not too rich in gelatin, or it may suddenly congeal.

## VEGETABLE BROTH

**About 6 Cups**

Quickly made and very good. Serve strained or unstrained, hot or chilled. Chop:

3 cups or more Vegetables for
        Stock Making, (II, 174)

Sauté them gently and slowly 5 minutes in:

3 tablespoons butter

◗ Do not let them brown. Add:

4 cups boiling water or part
        water and tomatoes or
        tomato juice

Simmer the soup partially covered about 1 hour. You may add:

(1 bouillon cube)
**Season to taste**

## MUSHROOM BROTH

### I.

**About 6 Cups**

⚴ Blend or chop until fine:

¾ lb. mature mushrooms

Add them to:

6 cups Light Stock from
        Poultry, (II, 172), or beef
        consommé

Simmer partially covered about 15 minutes, or only 5 if you have used the blender. Strain, if you like, or thicken, see 128–129. Serve very hot. Add to each cup:

1 tablespoon dry sherry

### II.

**About 6 Cups**

Prepare:

¾ lb. diced mature
        mushrooms
2 ribs celery, diced
½ skinned and diced carrot
¼ skinned and diced onion

Cover these vegetables with:

3 cups water

◗ Simmer partially covered 45 minutes. Strain the broth. Add to make 6 cups of liquid:

> **Light Stock from Poultry, (II, 172), or beef consommé**

Add, if needed:

> **Salt and paprika**

Serve as for I, on 132.

## ONION SOUP

**6 Cups**

Onion soup, with vegetable stock, fish fumet or water substituted for meat stock, is used for meals *au maigre*.

Sauté until very well browned, but not scorched:

> **1½ cups thinly sliced onions**

in:

> **3 tablespoons butter**

Add:

> **6 cups beef or chicken broth**
> **¼ teaspoon freshly ground black pepper**

Cover and cook over low heat 30 minutes. The soup is now put into a casserole. Add:

> **(A dash of cognac or dry sherry)**

Cover with:

> **6 slices toasted French bread**

The toast should be crisp. Sprinkle over the toast:

> **1 cup mixed grated Parmesan and Gruyère cheese**

Heat in a 275° oven about 5 minutes or until the cheese is melted.

## CLEAR WATERCRESS SOUP

**About 5 Cups**

Simmer together:

> **5 cups hot chicken broth**
> **1½ cups chopped watercress**

about 4 to 6 minutes or until watercress is just dark green—not an olive green. Serve at once.

## COLD TOMATO SOUP OR GAZPACHO

**About 6 Cups**

Chilled clear soup full of fresh vegetables with fresh herbs—a summer delight from the caves of Spain, where it is held cooled. Just before serving, a few cubes of ice are added. Peel and seed:

> **2 large ripe tomatoes**

Seed and remove membrane from:

> **1 large sweet green pepper**

Peel:

> **1 clove garlic**

Wash:

> **½ cup or more fresh mixed herbs: chives, parsley, basil, chervil, tarragon**

Place all ingredients in a wooden chopping bowl. Chop them. Stir in gradually:

> **½ cup olive oil**
> **3 tablespoons lemon or lime juice**
> **3 cups chilled consommé or light beef stock**

Add:

> **1 peeled, thinly sliced sweet Spanish onion**
> **1 cup peeled, seeded, diced or grated cucumber**
> **1½ teaspoons salt, or more if needed**
> **½ teaspoon paprika**

Some cooks prefer to use their ⅃ blender for the vegetables. Others like to serve the soup unblended with a bowl of additional chilled, finely diced vegetables. Chill the soup about 2 hours or more before serving.

To serve, place in each bowl:

> **2 ice cubes**
> **1 tablespoon chopped parsley**

Add the soup and sprinkle the tops with:

> **½ cup crumbled dry bread**

## EGG DROPS FOR CLEAR SOUPS

If your travels have led you to the Mediterranean or China, you probably know the trick of turning a cup of broth into a midmorning pickup or a light nourishing lunch. Our friend Cecily Brownstone gave us these infallible directions for Egg Drops.

### I.

**2 Servings**

Heat in a quart pan, until boiling vigorously:

**2 cups chicken broth or beef stock**

Reduce the heat, so the broth ▶ simmers. This means that the bubbles form slowly and collapse below the surface of the liquid. Break into a cup:

**1 egg at room temperature**

▶ Beat it with a fork, just long enough to combine yolk and white. When the egg is lifted high, it should run off the tines of the fork in a watery stream. Now, with the broth ▶ simmering, hold the cup with one hand, 5 inches above the rim of the saucepan. Pour a little of the beaten egg slowly in a fine stream into the broth. With fork in the other hand, describe wide circles on the surface of the broth to catch the egg as it strikes and draw it out into long filmy threads. Rather than pour the egg in one fell swoop, break its fall 3 or 4 times, so as not to disturb the simmering. If you have a helper he can pour the egg through a strainer instead of from a cup. Simmer about 1 minute.

**Season to taste**

Add:

**(A generous squeeze of lemon)**

Serve at once in hot cups.

### II.  Greek Lemon Soup

**6 Servings**

The egg drops in this Avgolemono do not "flower" so profusely. Heat to a rolling boil:

**3 cups chicken broth**
**¾ cup cooked rice or cooked fine noodles**

Beat in a large bowl, just long enough to combine and be uniform in color:

**2 eggs**
**2 to 3 tablespoons lemon juice or wine**

Stir in 2 tablespoons of the hot broth; then from on high ▶ gradually, so as not to curdle the eggs but to allow them to shred, pour the eggs into the hot ▶ but not boiling soup, stirring constantly. Serve at once in hot cups.

### III.

**8 Servings**

A still stauncher mix is made in Germany and is called **Baumwollsuppe**. ▶ Simmer:

**4 cups strong brown stock**

Mix together:

**2 eggs**
**1 tablespoon flour**
**¼ cup cream**
**(1 tablespoon butter)**
**(Pinch of nutmeg)**

Mix and cook as described in I. Serve in hot cups.

**IV.**

**4 Servings**

In Italy a ragged, fluffy drop is made by beating until well combined:

> 1 egg
> 1½ teaspoons grated Parmesan cheese
> 1 tablespoon grated dry bread crumbs
> (½ pressed clove garlic)

Stir this mixture rapidly into:

> 3 cups ▶ simmering consommé

Continue to simmer and stir until egg is set. Serve at once.

## HARD-COOKED EGG DROPS

Crush with a fork:

> 2 hard-cooked egg yolks

Add to them and blend well:

> 1 tablespoon soft butter
> 1 raw egg yolk
> A few grains of cayenne
> A light grating of nutmeg
> ⅛ teaspoon salt

Form these ingredients into ½-inch balls. Roll them in:

> Flour

Cook the drops in ▶ simmering consommé about 1 minute.

## SOUP CUSTARD OR ROYALE

These tender drops are used in clear soups. Bake them as for Cup Custard, (II, 508), poured to ½-inch thickness into a well-buttered 9-inch pie pan. Because of their fragile consistency, they must always be ▶ well cooled before handling. Any slight crusting may be trimmed.

Preheat oven to 325°.

Beat well:

> ½ cup milk or stock
> ⅛ teaspoon each salt, paprika, and nutmeg

> 1 egg
> (1 egg yolk)

Bake about 25 minutes, then ▶ cool before cutting into dice or fancy shapes. Simmer the soup and drop the royales into it, just long enough to heat them through. Serve at once, allowing 3 or 4 small drops to each cup of broth.

## KREPLACH SOUP

**About 6 Cups**

Prepare:

> Noodle Dough, 199

This will make about 20 pastries. Do not allow the dough to dry, however, before cutting it into 3-inch squares. Put about 1½ tablespoons of one of the following fillings in the center of each square, as shown on the next page.

**I.** Sauté in:

> 1 tablespoon vegetable oil
> ½ cup minced onions
> ½ lb. ground beef

Add:

> ¾ teaspoon salt
> ¼ teaspoon pepper

**II.** Or combine:

> 1½ cups minced cooked chicken
> ¼ cup minced sautéed onion
> 1 egg yolk
> ¾ teaspoon salt
> 1 tablespoon chopped parsley

Fold the dough over the filling into a triangular shape. Press the open edges carefully with a fork to seal them completely. Before cooking ▶ allow the kreplach to dry on a flour-dusted towel 30 minutes on each side. Then drop them into:

> About 1 gallon rapidly boiling broth or salted water

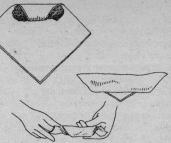

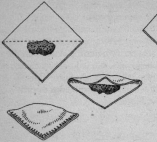

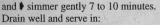

and ♦ simmer gently 7 to 10 minutes. Drain well and serve in:

**6 cups strong broth**

## WON TON SOUP

**About 4 Cups**

Prepare:

**Noodle Dough, 199**

Cut into 3½-inch squares. The fillings may be of cooked pork, veal, chicken, shrimp, crab meat or Chicken Farce, 437.

Combine:

**½ lb. cooked meat, see above**
**2 finely chopped green onions, white parts only**
**1 cup chopped spinach**
**1 beaten egg**

There are many fancy wrappings for won tons, which in most cases produce a high proportion of paste to meat. If truly Chinese, won tons emerge with a rather loose shape and fluttery outline. Try the one illustrated top right. Place cylindrically shaped filling well above the diagonal. Roll until contained. Insert index finger first in one end and then in the other to give a twist that seals the ends. Cook by putting all the won tons at once into:

**About 1 gallon rapidly boiling water**

Now ♦ lower the heat to medium.

When the water again comes to a boil, add:

**2 cups cold water**

to temper the dough. About 10 minutes should elapse from the time the won tons are first added to the boiling water until they are ready to serve. Put 5 won tons for each serving into a soup bowl. Sprinkle them with:

**(Soy sauce)**

Have ready and pour over them:

**3 cups seasoned, hot, clear chicken broth or bouillon**

A few prettily cut Chinese vegetables or partially cooked spinach leaves with center stems removed usually garnish the broth.

## ABOUT JELLIED CLEAR SOUPS

These delicious warm-weather soups may be more highly seasoned than hot soups, but ♦ watch their salt content. If you prepare them in advance, their saltiness is intensified.

Serve with:

**A lemon and parsley garnish**

You may add to the soup before jelling:

**A few drops of Worcestershire sauce**

Or allow per cup:

1 tablespoon sherry or
1 teaspoon lemon juice

If you add more lemon juice, be sure
you have allowed sufficient gelatin.
Stock made from veal knuckle and
beef bone may jell enough naturally
to be served without added gelatin.
We have learned that if canned consommé is from a new pack, it too has
enough gelatin in it to respond favorably to mere chilling. If the pack is as
old as two years, it must be treated as
though it had no gelatin. ◗ Do not
freeze it, but try it out by refrigerating for at least 4 hours, to see how
much additional thickening it will
need. Keep in mind that if too stiff,
soup jellies are not very attractive.
Allow, if necessary:

1½ teaspoons gelatin

to each:

2 cups consommé or broth

For rapid chilling, you may place
clear soups in a bowl over cracked
ice, or give them a start by leaving
them in the freezer ◗ for a few minutes but not longer, as intense cold, if
continued, destroys the texture.

## JELLIED TOMATO BOUILLON

**About 5 Cups**

Soak 5 minutes:

2 tablespoons gelatin

in:

½ cup cold water

Heat to the boiling point and strain:

2 cups tomato juice
½ teaspoon grated onion
2 cups Light Stock,
(II, 171–172)
A piece of lemon rind
Salt and pepper

Dissolve the gelatin in the hot stock.
Cool. Flavor with:

Lemon juice, dry sherry or
Worcestershire sauce

Pour stock into a wet mold. Chill.

The bouillon may be beaten slightly
before serving garnished with:

Lemon slices, chopped
chives, mint, small
nasturtium leaves, chopped
olives, hard-cooked riced
eggs, relish, horseradish,
parsley, watercress or dill

## JELLIED BEET CONSOMMÉ

**4 Servings**

Combine and heat:

1 cup beet juice
1 cup consommé

Add:

1 tablespoon gelatin
dissolved over hot
water, (II, 234)
Season to taste

When about to jell, add:

1 cup minced cooked beets
(1 tablespoon lemon juice)

Pour gelatin mixture into cups. In
serving, garnish each cup with:

(1 teaspoon caviar)
A slice of lemon decorated
with minced fresh tarragon
or basil, or a dab of
cultured sour cream

## ABOUT THICK SOUPS

Purée, cream, bisque, velouté, potage—to the connoisseur each of these
is a quite distinctive embodiment of
the indispensable thick soup.

If you like to attach a label to your
creations, know that a **purée** is a
soup which gets its major thickening
from the vegetable or other food put
through a sieve or blender and has
butter swirled into it at the very last
moment. By omitting the butter or
lessening the amount of it and adding
cream and sometimes egg yolk, you
get—guess what?—a **cream soup**! If
that soup is on a shellfish base—and

only if it is—you may call it a **bisque.**
If you add both eggs and cream and a
Velouté Sauce, 387, to a purée base,
you achieve a **velouté soup.**

**Potages,** the most variable of
soups, are likely to have the phrase
*du jour* added, meaning that they are
both the specialty of the day and, from
the cook's point of view, seasonal
and convenient to compose. Potages,
which tend to be hefty, taste best
when their vegetables are first braised
in butter and are then put through a
fine sieve before serving. For ways to
thicken soups, see 128–129.

Here are a few practical hints
that will help you make the most of
thickened soups. Be sure to scrape
the purée off the bottom of the
strainer. ◗ If you use a ⚙ blender,
first parblanch or cook any vegetables with strings, like celery, or
skins, like peas. After butter, cream
or eggs are ◗ added never allow the
soup to reach a boil. If you are not
serving at once, heat it in a double
boiler. Thick soups should not be
served as the first course of a heavy
meal. The wonderful thing about
them is that they are nearly a meal in
themselves. Balanced by a green salad or fruit, they make a complete
luncheon.


BARLEY SOUP
**I.**
                          **About 8 Cups**
A favorite of French farmers. For the
best flavor use stock from country-
cured hams, but not aged ones like
Smithfield, Kentucky, or Virginia.
Melt in a skillet:

   **2 tablespoons salt pork**
Add and cook until translucent:

   **3 tablespoons diced shallots
   or onions**

Add:
   **½ cup barley**
Agitate the pan to coat the barley
well in the hot fat. After about 5 minutes, add:

   **1 quart hot stock from
   country-cured ham**
Cook the mixture, covered, until the
barley is tender, about 1 hour. Bind or
not as you like, depending on how rich
and thick you want the soup, with:

   **(3 well-beaten egg yolks)**
   **(1 cup cream)**
◗ Heat, but do not boil, after adding
the eggs and cream. Before serving,
add as a garnish:

   **2 tablespoons finely chopped
   parsley**
   **1 cup sautéed, coarsely
   chopped mushrooms**


**II. Scotch Broth**
                          **About 15 Cups**
Soak 2 hours:
   **½ cup pearl barley**
in:

   **2 cups water**
If you use other barley, soak it 1 hour.
Add this to:

   **3 lb. mutton or lamb with
   bones**
   **10 cups water**
Simmer, covered, 2 hours or until the
meat is tender. Add for the last half
hour of cooking:

   **2 cups sautéed vegetables, see
   Consommé Brunoise, 130
   (A dash of curry)**
Remove the meat from the soup.
Dice it. You may use a flour or egg
thickener, 129, to bind the soup. Re-
turn the meat to the soup. Reheat it.
   **Season to taste**
Serve garnished with:
   **Chopped parsley**

## GREEN KERN SOUP

**About 15 Cups**

If you are English, corn means wheat;
if you are Scottish it means oats; if
you come from "down under" or are
American, you know corn grows on a
cob. Kern sounds as though it too
might be somebody's word for corn,
but it isn't. It's dried green wheat and
makes a favorite European soup.
Soak for ½ hour:

**½ to 1 cup green kern**

in:

**4 cups water**

Then cook as for Barley Soup II, 138,
replacing the lamb with beef.

## VEGETABLE SOUP OR SOUPE PAYSANNE

**5 Cups**

Place in a large kettle or pressure
cooker:

**2 tablespoons bacon fat or
butter**

Sauté briefly in the fat:

**¼ cup diced carrots**
**½ cup diced onions**
**½ cup diced celery**

Add:

**3 cups hot water or stock**
**1 cup canned tomatoes**
**(½ cup pared, diced potatoes)**
**(½ cup pared, diced turnips)**
**1 tablespoon chopped parsley**
**½ teaspoon salt**
**⅛ teaspoon pepper**

Cover and cook about 35 minutes;
then add:

**(½ cup chopped cabbage,
spinach or lettuce)**

Cook about 5 minutes more. If using a ♥ pressure cooker, cook at
15 pounds pressure 3 minutes. Remove from heat and let stand 5 minutes, then reduce pressure instantly.

**Season to taste**

and serve with:

**Melba Cheese Rounds,
(II, 354)**

## ⅃ BLENDER VEGETABLE SOUP

**About 4 Cups**

Blend in:

**¼ cup stock**
**2 cups coarsely cut mixed
vegetables**

If cucumbers, celery, asparagus or
onions are used, blanch them first to
soften seeds or fibers and to make the
onion flavor more agreeable. Heat the
blended vegetables until tender in:

**3 cups boiling stock**

Serve at once.

## VEGETABLE CHOWDER

**About 6 Cups**

Cut the stems from:

**1 quart okra**

Slice the okra. Prepare:

**2 cups diced celery**

Seed, remove membrane and dice:

**1 green pepper**

Skin and chop:

**1 small onion**

Sauté the vegetables 5 minutes in:

**¼ cup butter or bacon
drippings**

Skin, chop and add:

**2 large ripe tomatoes or
1 cup canned tomatoes**

and:

**1 teaspoon brown sugar**
**¼ teaspoon paprika**
**4 cups boiling water**

Simmer the vegetables gently until
they are tender, about 30 minutes.
Add, if required:

**Salt and paprika**

Cooked chicken, meat, fish or crisp
bacon may be diced and added to the
chowder. Serve with:

**Boiled Rice, 189**

## BEET SOUP OR BORSCH

### About 5 Cups

There are probably as many versions of borsch as there are Russians. For good quick versions, see 166.
Chop until very fine:

    1/2 cup pared carrots
    1 cup skinned onions
    2 cups pared beets

Barely cover these ingredients with boiling water. Simmer gently, covered, about 20 minutes. Add and simmer 15 minutes more:

    1 tablespoon butter
    2 cups beef or other stock
    1 cup very finely shredded
        cabbage
    1 tablespoon vinegar

Place the soup in bowls. Add to each serving:

    1 tablespoon cultured sour
        cream

mixed with:

    (Grated cucumber)
    Season to taste

and serve hot or cold with:

    Pumpernickel bread


## CABBAGE SOUP

### About 6 Cups

This superb cabbage soup, quick and inexpensive, is from Herman Smith's book, *Kitchens Near and Far.* You will find it, as well as his incomparable *Stina,* most rewarding.
Sauté gently in a saucepan until tender and yellow:

    1 large minced onion
    1 1/2 tablespoons butter

Grate or shred and add:

    1 small head green cabbage:
        about 3/4 lb.

Bring to a boil:

    4 cups Brown Stock I, (II, 171)

Add the stock to the vegetables. Season as needed with:

    Salt and pepper

Simmer the soup about 10 minutes. If you wish, use this delicious topping:

    1/2 cup cultured sour cream
    1 tablespoon minced parsley
    (1/2 teaspoon caraway seeds)

Place a spoonful of the sour cream mixture on the top of each serving of soup.


## CHICKEN CURRY OR SENEGALESE SOUP

### About 4 Cups

Melt:

    2 tablespoons butter

Add to it:

    1 1/2 to 2 teaspoons curry
        powder

Stir in, until blended:

    1 1/2 tablespoons flour

Stir in slowly:

    3 cups chicken broth

When the soup is boiling, season it with:

    Paprika

Reduce the heat. Beat:

    2 egg yolks
    1/2 cup cream

When the soup is no longer boiling, stir these ingredients into it. Stir over low heat until the egg yolks have thickened slightly ▶ but do not boil. Add also, still not allowing the soup to boil:

    1/2 cup slivers of cooked white
        chicken meat
    (3 to 4 tablespoons chutney)

Serve hot or chilled, garnished with:

    Chopped chives


## CHICKEN GUMBO

### About 12 Cups

Cut into pieces and dredge with flour:

    1 stewing chicken

Brown it in:

    1/4 cup bacon drippings

Pour over it:

**4 cups boiling water**

Simmer, uncovered, until the meat falls from the bones. Strain the stock and reserve, and chop the meat. Place in the soup kettle and simmer, uncovered, about 30 minutes or until the vegetables are tender:

**2 cups skinned seeded tomatoes**

**1/2 cup fresh corn cut from the cob**

**1 cup sliced okra**

**(1 large green pepper, seeds and membrane removed, or 2 small red peppers)**

**1/2 teaspoon salt**

**1/4 cup diced onion**

**1/4 cup rice**

**5 cups water**

Combine these ingredients with the chicken meat and stock.

**Season to taste**

Classic gumbo recipes then read— Add:

**(1 to 2 teaspoons filé powder, moistened with a little water)**

After adding the filé ♦ do not boil the soup, as it will become stringy. To-day, we are told filé powder, based on sassafras, is a carcinogen. So, for a similar texture, a tapioca thickening may be substituted. Two tablespoons of quick-cooking tapioca may be added when you start to cook the vegetables.

## ABOUT LEGUME SOUPS

**Lentils, Beans, Peas**

♦ Please read About Dried Legumes, 294.

Some packaged dried legumes do not require soaking. Follow directions on the label. Cook legumes in ham or other stock to which tomato juice or purée may be added, along with ham scraps, bacon or fresh pork fat. Try out the pork, (II, 204). Brown an onion in the fat. The cracklings may be added to the soup or used as garnish. For vegetables and seasonings, see the following recipes.

For easy removal of fat, chill the soup, see 128. Legume soups may be served unstrained, although they are usually more digestible if strained. They may be thinned with stock, tomato juice or milk. Navy bean soup always calls for milk.

Legume soups, whether made of fresh or dried materials, should be bound. See Thickenings for Soups IV, 129.

♀ We do not recommend the use of a pressure cooker for legume soups.

## DRIED BEAN SOUP

**4 Cups**

If you use marrow beans and add the optional mashed potato, you will have come close to reproducing the famous United States Senate Bean Soup. Soak, see above:

**1/2 cup dried navy, kidney, lima or marrow beans**

Add:

**A small piece of ham, a ham bone or 1/8 lb. salt pork**

**4 cups boiling water**

**1/2 bay leaf**

**3 or 4 peppercorns**

**3 whole cloves**

Cook the soup slowly until the beans are soft, 2 1/2 to 3 hours. For the last 30 minutes, add:

**1 diced carrot**

**3 ribs celery with leaves, chopped**

**1/2 sliced onion**

**(1 minced clove garlic)**

**(1/8 teaspoon saffron)**

(½ cup freshly cooked mashed
    potatoes)
(½ cup chopped sorrel)

Remove and mince the meat. Put the
soup through a food mill, ♣ blender
or sieve. Thin the soup, if required,
with boiling water or milk.

    **Season to taste**

Serve with the meat and garnish with:

    **Croutons, 174**
    **Chopped chives or parsley**


## BLACK BEAN SOUP

        **About 9 or 10 Cups**

Follow the recipe for Split Pea Soup,
143. Substitute for the peas:

    **2 cups black beans**

As this soup is drier, add:

    **3, instead of 2, tablespoons
      butter**

Just before serving, you may add:

    (1 tablespoon dry sherry for
      each cup)

Serve garnished with:

    **2 teaspoons deviled or
      Smithfield ham for each
      cup
      Thin slices of lemon
      Thin slices of hard-cooked
      eggs**


## BEAN SOUP WITH VEGETABLES
## OR GARBURE

        **About 10 Cups**

A highly variable soup. Perhaps the
most famous version comes from
Béarn. It includes preserved goose
and is cooked in a glazed casserole.
Exotic? It is made in season with
freshly hulled haricot beans. Soak
overnight:

    **1 cup dried haricot or navy
      or fava beans**

You may blanch, 106–107, or not, depending on its maturity:

    **2 lb. green or white cabbage**

Shred the cabbage finely the length
of the leaf. Peel and slice:

    **1½ cups potatoes
    1 cup carrots
    1 cup white turnips
    ¼ cup leeks, using white
      portion only
    ½ cup onion
    1 sprig thyme
    (A ham bone)**

Place all the above ingredients in a
heavy pan and cover with:

    **Liquid**

Use water if you plan to add salt pork;
game stock, (II, 172), with game.
Add:

    **1 lb. diced salt pork or
      sausage or boneless game
      or veal**

♦ Simmer, partially covered, 2½ hours
or until the meat is tender.

    **Season to taste**

Pour the soup over:

    **Garlic-buttered
      croutons, (II, 219)**


## MINESTRONE

        **About 3 Quarts**

An Italian soup made with many
kinds of vegetables, even zucchini
blossoms. Sometimes elbow macaroni or other pasta and sometimes
rice is added instead of dried beans.
Sweet sausages and smoked spareribs may also be put in at the end.
Soak and cook until tender, see 294:

    **½ cup dried kidney beans
    ½ cup lentils or chick-peas**

Drain the beans. Sauté in:

    **3 tablespoons olive oil
    ¼ lb. diced salt pork**

When the cracklings are crisp, remove and reserve them. Then sauté
in the remaining fat:

    **¼ cup diced white onion**

When the onion is golden, add and
continue to sauté briefly:

1 **cup chopped Savoy**
  **cabbage**
1 **diced leek**
1/2 **cup diced carrots**
1 **cup diced zucchini or**
  **vegetable marrow**
1 **pressed clove garlic**
Remove from heat and add:
  1/2 **cup fresh peas**
  1 **cup diced Italian tomatoes**
  1 **teaspoon salt**
Have ready:
  2 **quarts Brown Stock,**
  **(II, 171)**
Add the drained legumes. Bring
slowly to a boil. Reduce heat and
simmer about 30 minutes. Add the
mixed vegetables and continue to
cook about 15 minutes longer. Add:
  **A generous grating of black**
  **pepper**
  **Season to taste**
Serve garnished with the reserved
cracklings and pass:
  **Grated Parmesan or Asiago**
  **cheese**

## LENTIL SOUP

**About 8 Cups**

Wash well and drain:
  2 **cups lentils**
Add:
  10 **cups boiling water**
  1/4 **lb. salt pork or a piece of**
  **ham or a ham bone**
▶ Simmer about 4 hours. During the
last hour, add:
  1 **large minced onion**
which has been sautéed in:
  3 **tablespoons butter**
  **Season to taste**
and serve puréed or not, as you prefer. If you purée, bind the soup with
Thickenings for Soup IV, 129.

## SPLIT PEA OR LENTIL SOUP

**About 8 Cups**

Try this on a cold winter day.
Wash and soak, 294:
  2 **cups split peas or lentils**
Drain the peas, reserving the liquid.
Add enough water to the reserved liquid to make 10 cups. Adding peas
again, cook, covered, 2 1/2 to 3 hours
with:
  **A turkey carcass, a ham**
  **bone or a 2-inch cube salt**
  **pork**
Add and simmer, covered, 30 minutes longer until tender:
  1/2 **cup chopped onions**
  1 **cup chopped celery with**
  **leaves**
  1/2 **cup chopped carrots**
Add:
  (1 **clove garlic**)
  (1 **bay leaf**)
  (1 **teaspoon sugar**)
  (**A dash of cayenne or a pod**
  **of red pepper**)
  (1/4 **teaspoon thyme**)
Remove bones, carcass or salt pork.
Put the soup through a sieve. Chill.
Remove fat. To bind the soup, melt:
  2 **tablespoons butter or soup**
  **fat**
Stir in it until blended:
  2 **tablespoons flour**
Slowly add a little of the soup mixture.
Cook and stir until it boils, then stir
it into the rest of the reheated soup.
  **Season to taste**
Serve with:
  **Croutons, or sour black**
  **bread and Jellied Pigs'**
  **Feet, 657**

## ⅄ BLENDER SPLIT PEA SOUP

**About 1 Quart**

Simmer about 45 minutes or until
tender:

**1/2 cup split peas**

in:

**2 1/2 cups water**

When slightly cooled, pour into a blender and add:

**1 cup chopped luncheon pork sausage**

**1 small sliced onion**

**1 diced rib celery with leaves**

**1 clove garlic**

**1 teaspoon salt**

**2 teaspoons Worcestershire sauce**

**A pinch of rosemary**

**1/8 teaspoon pepper**

Blend until smooth. Return the soup to saucepan to heat. Rinse the blender with:

**1 cup water**

Add this to the soup and simmer about 10 minutes. Garnish with:

**Pieces of crisp bacon**

**Cultured sour cream**


## SPLIT PEA SOUP AU MAIGRE

Use the recipe for Split Pea Soup to make either a thick or a thin soup. During the last 20 minutes of cooking, substitute for the fowl or ham bone any clean fish scraps—such as heads, tails and fins.


## GREEN PEA SOUP OR POTAGE ST. GERMAIN

**About 6 Cups**

We never hear the French name of this soup without being reminded of the *New Yorker* vignette of lunchtime at prison—and the disconsolate cry of one of the zebra-striped inmates on the arrival of the inevitable steaming tub: "Aw, shucks, purée St. Germain aux croutons again!" It's a comment you're not likely to hear if the soup is made with fresh peas—which are in fact the first essential; do not try to make it with canned or frozen peas. If you do not have fresh peas, it is better to try the good Quick Pea Soup, 166.

Hull:

**3 lb. green peas**

There should be about 3 cups hulled peas.

Sauté gently until tender:

**1 head Boston lettuce, shredded**

**1 peeled diced onion**

**1/2 cup or more chopped celery with leaves**

**2 sprigs parsley, chopped**

in:

**2 tablespoons butter**

Add:

**2 1/2 cups chicken stock**

**2 cups of the hulled peas**

**10 or 12 pea pods**

**(1/3 bay leaf)**

Simmer these ingredients, covered, until the peas are very soft. Put the soup through a food mill or a potato ricer. Simmer until tender the remaining:

**1 cup hulled peas**

in:

**1 1/2 cups chicken stock**

Add them to the strained soup. To bind the soup, see Thickenings for Soups IV, 128–129.

**Season to taste**

You may color the soup with a drop or two of:

**Green vegetable coloring**

and serve it with:

**Butter Dumplings, 183, or Croutons, (II, 219)**

**(2 teaspoons chopped mint, or 1 tablespoon horseradish and slices of water chestnut)**

## BOULA-BOULA

**5 Cups**

◗ Simmer in boiling water until
tender:

   2 cups green peas

Purée them through a fine sieve or in
a 🔗 blender.
Reheat and add:

   2 tablespoons sweet butter

Add:

   2 cups canned green turtle
      soup
   1 cup dry sherry

Heat ◗ but do not boil the soup.
Spoon soup into heated cups. Top
each serving with:

   2 tablespoons whipped cream

Place briefly under broiler. Serve
at once.

## MULLIGATAWNY SOUP

**About 7 Cups**

Sauté lightly, but do not brown:

   1/2 cup diced onion
   1 diced carrot
   2 diced ribs celery

in:

   1/4 cup butter or tried-out
      lamb fat, (II, 204)

Stir in:

   11/2 tablespoons flour
   2 teaspoons curry powder

Stir and cook these ingredients about
3 minutes. Pour in and simmer 15
minutes:

   4 cups chicken or lamb broth
   1 bay leaf

Add and simmer 15 minutes longer:

   1/4 cup diced tart apples
   1/2 cup Boiled Rice, 189
   1/2 cup diced cooked chicken
      or lamb
   1 teaspoon salt
   1/4 teaspoon pepper
   1/8 teaspoon thyme
   1/2 teaspoon grated lemon rind

Immediately before serving, stir in:

   1/2 cup hot cream or coconut
      milk, (II, 244)

## OXTAIL SOUP

### I.

**About 7 Cups**

Brown:

   1 disjointed oxtail or 2 veal
      tails: about 2 lb.
   1/2 cup sliced onions

in:

   2 tablespoons butter or fat

Add to the above and ◗ simmer, uncovered, about 41/2 hours:

   8 cups water
   11/2 teaspoons salt
   4 peppercorns

Strain, chill, remove fat, and reheat
the stock. The meat may be boned
and diced and added to the soup later.
Add to the stock and simmer 1/2 hour
longer or until the vegetables are
tender:

   1/4 cup chopped parsley
   1/2 cup diced carrots
   1 cup diced celery
   1/2 bay leaf
   1/4 cup barley
   1/2 cup tomato pulp
   1 teaspoon dried thyme,
      marjoram or basil

Brown in a skillet:

   1 tablespoon flour

Add and stir until blended:

   2 tablespoons butter

Add the stock slowly, then the reserved meat and vegetables.

   Season to taste

When thoroughly heated, add:

   (1/4 cup dry sherry or Madeira
      or 1/2 cup red wine)

Serve the soup with:

   Fritter Garnish, 173, or
      slices of lemon

**II.** ♀

About 3 Cups

Brown in a pressure cooker:

1 oxtail, joints separated
1 small diced onion

in:

3 tablespoons fat

Add:

4 cups hot water or ½ water,
½ tomato juice
1 teaspoon salt
2 peppercorns

Adjust cover. Cook at 10 pounds pressure 1 to 1¼ hours. Reduce pressure quickly. Remove the cover. Remove ox joints. Add to liquid in cooker:

1 diced carrot
4 ribs celery, diced

Readjust cover. Pressure-cook the soup 5 minutes longer. Remove fat after chilling the soup. Reheat and:

Season to taste

You may add:

(2 tablespoons dry sherry or
tomato catsup)

Separate meat from the joints. Add to soup. Reheat and serve with:

Chopped parsley

PANADES

About 4 Cups

These filling vegetable soups are a very good way to utilize leftover bread. Panades combine well with leeks, celery and sorrel; but leafy vegetables like watercress, spinach, lettuce and cabbage may be substituted.

Cook slowly until soft, but not brown:

1 cup finely chopped celery,
leeks or onions

in:

1 tablespoon butter

Cover. If a leafy vegetable is used, add it to the butter, cover and cook slowly until wilted and reduced to about one-fourth. Add:

2 cups hot water or milk
½ teaspoon salt
3 cups diced fresh or dry
bread

Stir well and let the mixture boil. Then ♦ simmer ½ hour. Beat it well until smooth with a wire whisk or in a ⅄ blender. Combine:

1 cup light cream
1 egg

Stir this slowly into the hot soup. Heat until the egg thickens but ♦ do not let the soup boil. Serve with:

Chopped parsley
Freshly grated nutmeg

PEPPER POT

About 10 Cups

Cut into small pieces and sauté in a heavy saucepan until translucent:

4 slices bacon

Add and simmer about 5 minutes:

⅓ cup minced onion
½ cup minced celery
2 minced green peppers,
seeds and membranes
removed
(1 teaspoon marjoram or
summer savory)

Wash, cut into fine shreds and add:

¾ lb. cooked honeycomb
Tripe, 653

Add:

8 cups Brown Stock, (II, 171)
1 bay leaf
½ teaspoon freshly ground
pepper

Bring these ingredients to the boiling point. Add:

1 cup pared and diced raw
potatoes

Gently ♦ simmer the soup, uncovered, until the potatoes are tender. Melt:

2 tablespoons butter

Stir in until blended:

**2 tablespoons flour**

Add a little of the soup. Bring these ingredients to the boiling point, then pour them into the rest of the soup.

**Season to taste**

Shortly before serving, reheat and add:

**1/2 cup warm cream**

## COCK-A-LEEKIE

**5 to 6 Cups**

Old recipes for this leek, chicken and cream soup start with a fowl or cock simmered in strong stock, and wind up with the addition of prunes. The following version is delicious, if not traditional.

Remove and discard the dark green part of the tops and the roots from:

**6 leeks**

Wash carefully—they may be sandy. Cut them in half lengthwise, then crosswise in 1/8-inch slices. There should be about 4 cups. Place in a pan with:

**3 cups boiling water**
**1 1/2 teaspoons salt**

Simmer from 5 to 7 minutes or until tender but not mushy. Add and heat to a boil:

**2 tablespoons chicken fat or butter**
**1 1/2 cups well-seasoned strong chicken broth**

Reduce heat and stir in:

**1/2 cup cream**
**Season to taste**

Serve the soup at once.

## GHANIAN PEANUT OR GROUNDNUT SOUP

**About 3 Quarts**

Cut up and place in a soup kettle:

**A 5 1/2- to 6-lb. stewing chicken**

**2 skinned whole medium-sized onions**
**4 pared whole carrots**
**1 teaspoon salt**
**2 quarts water**

Bring slowly to a boil, then reduce heat and simmer, partially covered, about 50 minutes or until chicken is tender. Remove the chicken and reserve for other use or cut up into bits to serve in the soup. Strain the stock. Blend together with a small amount of stock:

**6 oz. tomato paste**
**1 cup smooth peanut butter**
**1 pinch cayenne**
**1/4 teaspoon pepper**

Add the remaining stock and simmer slowly until oil rises to the top, about 20 minutes. Skim off the oil, see 128, and add:

**1/4 cup diced cooked pimientos**
**Season to taste**

and serve hot or well chilled, with or without the bits of chicken.

## SAUERKRAUT SOUP

**About 7 Cups**

Sauté until golden brown:

**1/2 cup chopped onion**

in:

**3 tablespoons bacon fat**

Add:

**1/2 clove minced garlic**
**1/2 lb. diced lean pork**

Cover and cook over low heat about 20 minutes.

Add:

**1 lb. chopped sauerkraut**
**6 cups stock**

Cook until soft, about 45 minutes. Melt:

**1 1/2 tablespoons butter**

Stir in:

**1 1/2 tablespoons flour**

Stir in slowly a little of the hot soup,

blend and return the mixture to kettle.
Add:

(1  teaspoon sugar)
Season to taste

and garnish with:

Diced ham or salami

## SPINACH SOUP

About 6½ Cups

Pick over, wash, drain thoroughly,
then chop fine or blend:

2  lb. tender young spinach

You may use instead 4 cups cooked
or two 14-ounce packages of frozen
spinach, defrosted and drained. Melt
in a saucepan:

¼ cup butter

Sauté in it until golden brown:

¼ cup minced onion

Add the spinach. Stir to coat it well
with the butter. Cover and cook gently
till the spinach is just tender. ♪ Blend
or put the spinach through a food mill
or sieve. Return to pan and add:

4  cups chicken stock
A grating of nutmeg
Salt or paprika

Bring the soup slowly to a boil and
serve; or you may serve it cold, garnished with:

Diced, seeded cucumbers
or chives and cultured sour
cream

## NETTLE SOUP

About 5 Cups

Using rubber gloves to protect you
from the stinging nettles, remove the
central stem from:

1  quart young nettle tops

Have boiling:

5  cups stock

Blend in:

2  tablespoons cooked rice or
oatmeal

Add the nettles and simmer about

10 to 15 minutes, during which period any sting from the nettles is
eliminated.

Season to taste

and serve.

## GREEN TURTLE SOUP

About 8 Cups

It is a timesaver to buy canned or
frozen turtle meat. But if you can turn
turtles, feel energetic and want to
prepare your own, see 467.
Place in a saucepan and bring to the
boiling point:

1  lb. green turtle or terrapin
meat, cut into pieces
3  cups water
3  cups Brown Stock, (II, 171)
1  bay leaf
1  sprig fresh thyme
2  cloves
¼  teaspoon ground allspice
Juice and thinly sliced peel
of ½ lemon
A few grains cayenne
¼  teaspoon freshly ground
black pepper
½  teaspoon salt
4  whole corianders

These latter pods will rise to the top
by the end of the cooking period and
can be skimmed out before serving.
Simmer the soup, covered, until the
meat is tender, at least 2 hours.
Heat:

2  tablespoons vegetable oil

Sauté in this 2 minutes:

2  chopped medium-sized
onions

Stir in:

1  tablespoon flour

Add:

1½ cups skinned, seeded fresh
tomatoes

Let these ingredients cook 10 minutes. Combine them with the turtle
mixture and add:

1 **tablespoon chopped parsley**

2 **minced cloves garlic**

ou may add a few drops of caramel
loring. Add to each serving:

1 **tablespoon dry sherry**

arnish the soup with:

2 **chopped hard-cooked eggs**
  **Lemon slices**

**OCK TURTLE SOUP**

**About 16 Cups**

his full-bodied, nourishing soup,
rved with crusty rolls, can be the
ain dish for any meal.

over:

5 **lb. veal bones**

ith:

14 **cups water**

ring to the boiling point. Add and
simmer, covered, about 3 1/2 hours:

6 **chopped celery ribs with**
  **leaves**

5 **coarsely cut carrots**

1 **cup chopped onion**

2 **cups canned tomatoes**

1 **small can tomato paste:**
  **6 oz.**

6 **crushed peppercorns**

1 **tablespoon salt**

6 **whole cloves**

2 **bay leaves**

1/2 **teaspoon dried thyme**

emove bones and fat. Sauté about
minutes in a greased skillet:

2 **minced cloves garlic**

2 **lb. ground beef**

2 **teaspoons salt**

dd the meat to the stock with:

1/4 **teaspoon Worcestershire**
  **sauce**

4 **teaspoons sugar**

ring to a boil, reduce heat and ▶
immer about 30 minutes. Blend:

6 **tablespoons Browned**
  **Flour, 379**

1 **cup cooled stock**

tir this paste into the simmering

soup. Let it simmer 5 minutes more.
Add:

2 **thinly sliced lemons**

1 **set chopped, parboiled calf**
  **brains, 645**

Reheat but do not boil. Serve the
soup garnished with:

3 **sliced hard-cooked eggs**

## NEW YEAR'S SOUPS

Served just before parties break up,
these are also known as hangover
soups, or Lumpensuppe, and are sometimes helpful for the morning after.

**I. Onion Soup, 133,** with the addition of:

1 **cup red wine**

**II. Lentil Soup, 143, with sour
cream and sausage.**

## ABOUT CREAM SOUPS

These favored luncheon soups are
also sometimes served at dinner. In
this latter role, they satisfy, as often
as not, a functional rather than a nutritional need. Like hors d'oeuvre,
they act as a stabilizer for the cocktails that have just been drunk or as a
buffer against the wines that are
about to come.

For the richest of cream soups—
the veloutés—first, sauté the vegetables in butter, purée them and combine
the purée in equal parts with Velouté
Sauce, 387. Bind with egg yolk, allowing 2 to 4 yolks for each pint of
soup. Simpler cream soups may be
made on a White or Béchamel Sauce
base, 383, or on this quick Béchamel:
use 2 tablespoons butter to 1 1/2 tablespoons flour, plus 2 cups cream and
3/4 to 1 cup vegetable purée. Should
you wish to thin these ingredients,
use a little well-flavored stock.

For everyday cream soups, we find we can purée the tender vegetables raw, or cook the more mature, fibrous ones and process them in a 🗶 blender. The soup is served without straining. ❥ If seafood or fowl is blended it tends to be unpleasantly stringy; and the entire soup will need straining before serving.

❥ All cream soups, whether bound with egg or not, are ruined by boiling, so be sure to heat just to the boiling point, or cook them in the top of a double boiler ❥ over—not in—boiling water. Reheat them this same way.

## CREAM OF ASPARAGUS SOUP

**About 6 Cups**

Wash and remove the tips from:

**1 lb. fresh green asparagus**

Simmer the tips, covered, until they are tender, in a small amount of:

**Milk or water**

Cut the stalks into pieces and place them in a large saucepan. Add:

**6 cups Veal or Poultry Stock, (II, 171–172)**
**¼ cup chopped onion**
**½ cup chopped celery**

Simmer these ingredients, covered, about ½ hour. Strain them through a sieve. Melt in the top of a double boiler:

**3 tablespoons butter**

Stir in until blended:

**3 tablespoons flour**

Stir in slowly:

**½ cup cream**

Add the asparagus stock. Heat the soup, adding the asparagus tips. Season immediately before serving with:

**Salt, paprika and white pepper**

Garnish with:

**A chopped hard-cooked egg**

## CREAM OF CAULIFLOWER SOUP

**About 8 Cup**

Prepare:

**1 large Steamed Cauliflower, 311**

Drain it, reserving the water and about one-third of the florets. Put the remainder through a food mill, blender or sieve. Melt:

**¼ cup butter**

Sauté in it, until tender:

**2 tablespoons chopped onion**
**3 minced celery ribs**

Stir in:

**¼ cup flour**

Stir in slowly and bring to the boiling point:

**4 cups Veal or Poultry Stock (II, 171–172), and the reserved cauliflower water**

Add the strained cauliflower and:

**2 cups milk or cream**

Reheat but do not boil. Add the florets and:

**A grating of nutmeg**
**Salt and paprika**

Garnish with:

**(Grated cheese)**

## CREAM OF CELERY SOUP

**About 4 Cup**

Melt:

**1 tablespoon butter**

Add and sauté 2 minutes:

**1 cup or more chopped celery with leaves**
**(⅓ cup sliced onion)**

Pour in and simmer about 10 minutes:

**2 cups Veal or Poultry Stock, (II, 171–172)**

Strain the soup. Add and bring to the boiling point:

**1½ cups milk**

Dissolve:

**1½ tablespoons cornstarch**

in:
　½ cup cold milk
Stir these ingredients gradually into the hot soup. Bring to the boiling point. Stir and simmer about 1 minute. Serve with:
　(2 teaspoons chopped fresh
　　dill or 2 tablespoons
　　chopped parsley)

## CHESTNUT SOUP

About 4 Cups

Prepare:
　1 lb. Boiled Chestnuts, 313
Mash and beat them until smooth in:
　2 cups milk
Melt:
　¼ cup butter
Add and simmer until soft and golden:
　1 minced onion
Sprinkle with:
　1 tablespoon flour
　1 teaspoon salt
　⅛ teaspoon each nutmeg and
　　white pepper
　½ cup chopped celery leaves
Stir and slowly add the chestnut and milk mixture. ▶ Simmer about 10 minutes. Pour in:
　1 cup cream
Heat ▶ but do not boil. Serve immediately, garnished with:
　Chopped parsley
　Croutons, 174

## CREAM OF CHICKEN SOUP

About 4½ Cups

Simmer:
　3 cups Poultry Stock, (II, 172)
　½ cup finely chopped celery
When the celery is tender, add and cook 5 minutes:
　½ cup Boiled Rice, 189
Add:

　½ cup hot cream
　1 tablespoon chopped parsley
　　Salt and paprika
▶ Do not boil the soup after adding the cream. For a fresh approach, see Cream of Watercress Soup II, 156.

## CREAM OF CORN SOUP

About 5 Cups

Put through a food mill or coarse sieve:
　2½ cups cream-style canned
　　corn or 2½ cups corn, cut
　　from the ear and simmered
　　until tender in 1 cup milk
Melt:
　3 tablespoons butter
Simmer in it until translucent:
　½ sliced medium-sized onion
Stir in:
　3 tablespoons flour
　1½ teaspoons salt
　　A few grains freshly ground
　　white pepper
　　(A grating of nutmeg)
Stir in the corn and:
　3 cups milk, or 2½ cups milk
　　and ½ cup cream
Serve the soup sprinkled with:
　3 tablespoons chopped
　　parsley or chives
　　(Grated Parmesan cheese)

## CORN CHOWDER

About 7 Cups

Sauté slowly until lightly browned:
　½ cup chopped salt pork
Add and sauté until golden brown:
　3 tablespoons chopped onion
　½ cup chopped celery
　3 tablespoons chopped green
　　pepper, seeds and
　　membrane removed
Add and simmer:
　1 cup diced pared raw
　　potatoes

2 cups water
1/2 teaspoon salt
1/4 teaspoon paprika
1/2 bay leaf

When the potatoes are tender, in about 45 minutes, combine until blended, bring to the boiling point, and add to the above:

3 tablespoons flour

and:

1/2 cup milk

Heat about 5 minutes and add:

1 1/2 cups hot milk
2 cups whole-kernel corn

Reheat but do not boil the soup. Serve it sprinkled with:

**Chopped parsley**

## BULGARIAN COLD CUCUMBER SOUP

**About 3 Cups**

*"Nazdrave,"* as the Bulgarians say for *"Bon appétit."*

Two to 6 hours before serving, refrigerate, covered:

1 1/2 cups pared seeded cucumbers

marinated in a mixture of:

1 teaspoon salt
1/4 teaspoon white pepper
1/4 to 1 cup chopped walnuts
2 tablespoons olive oil
1 minced clove garlic
2 tablespoons chopped fresh dill

♦ The fresh dill is the essential touch. When ready to serve, add:

1 to 1 1/2 cups thick yogurt or cultured sour cream

Place 1 or 2 ice cubes in each soup bowl. Pour in the mixture. It should have the consistency of chilled borsch. If not thin enough, it can be thinned with a small amount of light stock. Serve at once.

## CHILLED CUCUMBER-HERB CREAM SOUP

**6 Cups**

Pare, seed and slice into a saucepan:

2 medium-sized cucumbers

Add:

1 cup water
2 slices onion
1/4 teaspoon salt
1/8 teaspoon white pepper

Cook the cucumbers, covered, until very soft. Put them through a fine strainer or an ⅃ electric blender. Stir until smooth:

1/4 cup flour
1/2 cup chicken stock

Stir into this flour paste:

1 1/2 cups Poultry Stock, (II, 172)

Add the cucumber purée and:

1/4 bay leaf or 2 cloves

Stir the soup over low heat. Simmer 2 minutes. Strain and chill in a covered jar. Before serving, stir in:

3/4 cup chilled cream, cultured sour cream, or yogurt
1 tablespoon finely chopped dill, chives or other herb, or grated lemon rind
Season to taste

Serve the soup very cold.

## CREAM OF MUSHROOM SOUP

**About 4 1/2 Cups**

The flavor of mushrooms is more pronounced if they have begun to color. Prepare for cooking:

1/2 lb. mushrooms with stems

Sauté lightly in:

2 tablespoons butter

Add them to:

2 cups Poultry Stock, (II, 172), or water
1/2 cup chopped tender celery
1/4 cup sliced onion
2 tablespoons shredded parsley

immer, covered, 20 minutes. Drain
he vegetables, reserving the stock.
⅄ Blend or put them through a food
hopper. Prepare:

**White Sauce I, 383**

Pour the liquid slowly into the cream
sauce, cook and stir until the soup
ust reaches a boil. Add the ground
vegetables. Heat ▶ but do not boil.
Season the soup with:

 ½ **teaspoon salt**
 ⅛ **teaspoon paprika**
 (⅛ **teaspoon nutmeg)**
 (3 **tablespoons dry white
 wine)**

Serve topped with:

 **(Whipped cream)**

Garnish with:

 **Paprika**
 **Sprigs of parsley or
 chopped chives**

## CREAM OF ONION SOUP OR ONION VELOUTÉ

**About 4 Cups**

Melt:

 3 **tablespoons butter**

Add and sauté till a golden brown:

 1½ **cups thinly sliced onions**

Stir in:

 1 **tablespoon flour**
 ½ **teaspoon salt**

Add:

 4 **cups milk or cream and
 Light Stock, (II, 171–172)**

Simmer, covered, until the onions are
very tender. Add a small amount of
hot soup to:

 4 **beaten egg yolks**

Add the egg mixture to the soup.
Heat but ▶ do not boil. Season with:

 **Salt and paprika**
 **Freshly grated nutmeg or
 Worcestershire sauce**

Place in each cup:

 1 **teaspoon chopped parsley**

Pour the hot soup over it.

## POTATO SOUP

**About 5 Cups**

Pare and slice:

 2 **medium-sized potatoes**

Chop:

 2 **medium-sized onions**
 4 **ribs celery**

Sauté these ingredients in:

 1½ **tablespoons butter**

Add:

 **Boiling water to cover**
 ½ **teaspoon salt**
 (½ **bay leaf)**

Boil the vegetables until the potatoes
are tender, or ♥ pressure-cook them
3 minutes at 15 pounds pressure. Put
them through a ricer or ⅄ blender.
Beat into them:

 2 **tablespoons butter**

Thin the soup to the desired consistency with:

 **Light cream and/or Poultry
 Stock, (II, 172)**

Add if required:

 **Salt and paprika**
 **A dash Worcestershire
 sauce**

Serve with:

 **Chopped parsley, chives or
 watercress**
 1 **cup sliced frankfurters or
 chopped cooked shrimp or
 diced cooked ham**

## POTATO SOUP WITH TOMATOES

**About 12 Cups**

A more sophisticated version of the
previous recipe.
Sauté very gently until translucent:

 2 **cups sliced onions**

in:

 ¼ **cup butter**

Add the onions to:

 2 **cups sliced potatoes**
 6 **cups boiling water**

Simmer about 30 minutes. Add and simmer, covered, about 20 minutes:

>5 **cups seeded sliced tomatoes or 3 cups canned tomatoes**
>2 **teaspoons sugar**
>1 **teaspoon salt**
>1/8 **teaspoon paprika**
>**A pinch of chervil**

Put the soup through a fine strainer or ⅄ blender.
Reheat and:

>**Season to taste**

Scald:

>1 **cup cream**

Stir the tomato mixture into the cream. Serve at once.

## VICHYSSOISE OR LEEK-POTATO SOUP

This leek soup may be served hot or very cold. Yes, the last "s" *is* pronounced like a "z," but most Americans shun it, in a "genteel" way, as though it were virtuous to ignore it. Be sure to serve the soup reduced to a velvety smoothness.

### I.

About 8 Cups

Mince:

>3 **medium-sized leeks: white part only**
>1 **medium-sized onion**

Stir and sauté them 3 minutes in:

>2 **tablespoons butter**

Pare, slice very fine and add:

>4 **medium-sized potatoes**

Add:

>4 **cups Poultry Stock, (II, 172)**

Simmer the vegetables, covered, 15 minutes or until tender. Put them through a very fine sieve, food mill or ⅄ blender. Add:

>1 **to 2 cups cream**
>(1/4 **teaspoon mace)**
>**Salt and white pepper**
>**Chopped watercress or chives**

### II.

About 4 Cups

Superlative! Less rich and made in about 20 minutes by using a ⅄ blender and a ♥ pressure cooker. Serve it hot or chill it quickly by placing it briefly in the freezer.
Prepare as above:

>**Vichyssoise**

using half the amount of ingredients given. After adding the potatoes and stock, pressure-cook the soup 3 minutes at 15 pounds. Cool. Add:

>1 **cup pared, seeded and diced cucumbers**

Blend covered until smooth, about 1 minute. Place the soup in a jar. Chill it thoroughly. You may add the cream called for above, but you may just like the result as well without it. Hot or cold, serve it sprinkled with:

>**Chopped chives**

## PUMPKIN SOUP

About 6 Cups

A flavor that keeps your guests guessing. Place:

>3 **cups canned or 2 lb. cooked fresh pumpkin**

in:

>3 **cups scalded milk or chicken broth**

Knead together and add:

>1 **tablespoon butter**
>1 **tablespoon flour**

Add:

>1 **tablespoon sugar or**
>2 **tablespoons brown sugar**
>**Salt and pepper**
>**(Ginger and cinnamon)**
>1/2 **cup finely julienned ham**
>(3/4 **cup light cream if you have used the chicken broth)**

Heat ▶ but do not boil. Serve at once

## WINTER MELON SOUP

### About 4 Servings

In China, the outside of a winter melon is laced with delicate carvings. Steamed with the broth in it, the melon serves as the soup tureen. Although not so appealing to the eye, the following recipe is as appealing to the taste.

Reconstitute in warm water 20 minutes:

**4 dried mushrooms, 326**

Combine and heat in a large saucepan:

**4 cups Poultry Stock, (II, 172)**
**1/3 cup diced cooked chicken breasts**
**1 cup shelled cleaned shrimp**
**1 lb. peeled, seeded winter melon cut into 1-inch squares**
**1 small diced leek**
**1 diced bamboo shoot**
**1/4 teaspoon grated fresh ginger**

and the drained chopped mushrooms. Bring the soup to a boil, cover and lower the heat. Simmer about 15 minutes. Before serving, add:

**1/3 cup diced cooked ham**

## CREAM OF SORREL SOUP

### 5 to 6 Cups

Also known as **Potage Germiny** and a favorite combination with veal and fish dishes. Because of the oxalic acid in sorrel ▶ use a stainless steel or enamel pan, and do not increase the proportion of sorrel to lettuce as given below.

Clean, shred from the midrib and chop:

**1/2 cup sorrel leaves**
**1 1/2 cups leaf lettuce**

Sauté them until wilted in:

**1 to 2 tablespoons butter**

When they are sufficiently wilted, there will be only about 3 tablespoons of leaves. Add:

**5 cups Poultry Stock, (II, 172)**
**(1 tablespoon fresh green pea purée)**

Simmer about 2 minutes. Remove from the heat and add a small amount of the soup to:

**1/2 cup cream**
**3 beaten egg yolks**

Combine all ingredients and heat until the soup thickens slightly ▶ but do not boil. Serve garnished with:

**Chopped chervil**

## CREAM OF SPINACH, ESCAROLE OR LETTUCE SOUP

### About 5 Cups

Pick over and wash:

**1 lb. spinach or escarole or**
**1 lb. leaf lettuce**

Or you may use:

**(1 cup frozen spinach)**

Place it, while moist or frozen, in a covered saucepan. Cook about 6 minutes. Drain. Put through a strainer or ⅄ blender. Melt in a saucepan:

**2 tablespoons butter**

Add and sauté 3 minutes:

**1 tablespoon grated onion**

Stir in and cook until blended:

**2 tablespoons flour**

Stir in gradually:

**4 cups milk and/or stock**

Season with:

**3/4 teaspoon or more salt**
**1/4 teaspoon paprika**
**(A grating of nutmeg)**

Add the spinach or lettuce. Heat the soup well. Serve sprinkled with:

**(Grated Parmesan cheese or sieved egg yolk)**

## CREAM OF TOMATO SOUP

**About 5¹/₂ Cups**

Simmer, covered, about 15 minutes:

> 2 **cups canned or seeded,
> skinned, cut-up fresh
> tomatoes**
> ¹/₂ **cup chopped celery**
> ¹/₄ **cup chopped onion**
> 2 **teaspoons white or brown
> sugar**

Prepare:

> 4 **cups White Sauce I, 383**

Strain into this the tomato and vegetable stock.

> **Season to taste**

and serve with:

> **Croutons, 174**
> **Chopped parsley, burnet or
> basil**

If served chilled, garnish with:

> **Chopped chives or whipped
> cream and paprika**

## CREAM OF WATERCRESS OR PURSLANE SOUP

### I.

**About 4 Cups**

Sauté until just wilted:

> 1 **cup chopped watercress or
> purslane**

in:

> 1 **tablespoon butter**

Add and cook gently about 3 minutes:

> **Salt, white pepper and
> paprika**
> ¹/₂ **cup white wine**

Remove from heat and add:

> 4 **cups light cream**

Heat but do not boil. Serve at once.

### II.

**About 5 Cups**

To:

> 5 **cups hot Cream of Chicken
> Soup, 151**

add:

> 1¹/₂ **cups chopped or ⅃
> blended watercress or
> purslane**

The latter was Gandhi's favorite vegetable.
Simmer the soup about 5 minutes.
Add and stir a small quantity of the soup into:

> 2 **well-beaten eggs**

Add this to the rest of the soup, stirring it in slowly. Heat the soup ▶ but do not boil. Serve at once.

An interesting taste variation results by adding:

> 2 **slices fresh ginger**

which have been lightly sautéed in:

> **Butter**
> **Salt**

Remove ginger after reheating and before serving the soup.

## MILK TOAST OR SOUP

**Individual Serving**

While not exactly a soup, this dish can bring something like the same cozy comfort to the young or the ailing.
Toast lightly on both sides:

> **A slice of bread ³/₄ inch
> thick**

Spread it lightly with:

> **Butter**

Sprinkle it with:

> **(Salt)**

Place it in a bowl and pour over it:

> 1 **cup hot milk**

## ABOUT FISH SOUPS

Making a broth or fumet of fish, (II, 173), is like making a stock of any kind of meat in that the process toughens the meat. It differs in that it takes a good deal less time. Extraction is limited to a ▶ 20- to 30-minute period ▶ over relatively high heat, instead of the slow simmering recommended for warm-blooded meat. ◗ As a consequence, most fish soups are quick soups. When fisherman's stews are served, the meat is often presented on the side; and in the preparation of delicate bisques based on shellfish, the shrimp or lobsters are often poached separately, then pounded in a mortar or minced before incorporation into a separate stock, cream and egg base.

The original stock may be used as a court bouillon for cooking other fish or reduced for use in *au maigre,* or meatless, sauces. Bisques, as well as oyster, clam and mussel soups and stews, need so little heat that the stock bases are warmed first and the shellfish then just heated through in them, preferably in a double boiler ◗ over—not in—boiling water. Serve fish soups at once. If you must hold or reheat, be sure to do so ◗ over— not in—boiling water.

## CLAM BROTH OR SOUP

**About 4 Cups**

Clams are of various types, see About Clams, 445. The broth is delicious when fresh. It may also be frozen until mushy and served in small glasses or on the shells with wedges of lemon. The meat of the clams themselves may be used in various seafood dishes, 447–449.
Prepare as described on 445 and 446, then place in a kettle:

    **2 quarts clams in shells**
Add:

    **1³/4 cups water, chicken broth
    or tomato juice**
    **3 cut-up ribs celery with
    leaves**
    **A pinch of cayenne**

◗ Cover the kettle closely. ◗ Steam the clams until the shells open. Strain the liquor through wet double cheese-

cloth to remove any sand. It may be heated and diluted with warm cream or rich milk.

    **Season to taste**
Each cup of broth may be topped with a spoonful of:

    **(Unsweetened whipped
    cream)**
sprinkled with:

    **(Chopped chives)**

## COQUINA BROTH

If you are lucky enough to be on a beach in Florida, collect in a sieve at ebb tide:

    **Coquinas**
the little native periwinkle clams, in their rainbow-hued shells. Rinse them clean of sand, then barely cover with:

    **Water**
Bring slowly to a boil and ◗ simmer about 10 minutes. Pour the broth through a fine sieve. When you imbibe it, remember the advice of an old German who urged, when serving a fine vintage, "Don't gullop it, just zipp it!"

## SPINACH SHELLFISH SOUP

**About 4 Cups**

Sauté until golden in:

    **3 tablespoons butter**
    **1 tablespoon finely chopped
    shallots**
Add and cook until reduced by one-half:

    **1 cup dry white wine**
Gradually stir in until smooth:

    **3 tablespoons flour**
    **1¹/2 cups clam or oyster broth**
    **(A pinch of dry mustard)**
After the mixture thickens, add and heat but ◗ do not boil:

    **1¹/2 cups light cream**
    **1/4 cup cooked puréed spinach**
    **Season to taste**

Serve in ovenproof soup bowls. Garnish each bowl with a topping of:

**1 tablespoon whipped cream**
**1 teaspoon Parmesan cheese**

and place the bowls under the broiler about 2 minutes until the cheese browns lightly.

## SHE-CRAB SOUP

**6 Servings**

Steam and remove the meat and roe from:

**2 blue she-crabs**

Reserve the roe. Prepare a roux by melting in a saucepan:

**2 tablespoons butter**

Blend in:

**1 tablespoon flour**

Gradually add, stirring constantly:

**4 cups milk or half cream and half milk**

When the sauce is heated through, add the crab meat with:

**1/2 teaspoon onion juice**
**1/2 teaspoon Worcestershire sauce**
**1/8 teaspoon mace**
**Season to taste**

When ready to serve, divide the roe and place it in the bottom of 6 heated bowls.

Pour the soup into the bowls. Garnish the soup with:

**Freshly chopped chervil**

## CRAWFISH BISQUE

**About 6 Cups**

Wash and scrub with a brush under running water:

**3 dozen live crawfish**

Soak 30 minutes in salted water, using 1 tablespoon salt to 4 cups of water. Repeat once or twice. Rinse thoroughly. Place the crawfish in a saucepan with:

**6 cups boiling water**

**A few grains of cayenne**
**1/2 teaspoon salt**

Bring to a boil, then ♦ simmer 15 minutes. Drain, reserving the stock. Separate the heads and tails. Remove the fat from the heads. Devein the tails and remove the meat. Clean the remaining foreign matter from 18 heads and refrigerate the meat, the fat and the cleaned heads. Return all remaining heads to the stock. Bring to a boil. Add:

**4 ribs celery, chopped**
**2 tablespoons chopped parsley**
**1/2 carrot, diced**
**1/8 teaspoon thyme or a sprig of fresh thyme**

♦ Simmer 30 minutes. Strain, discarding the cooked heads. Meanwhile, prepare the stuffing for the chilled heads. Mince the refrigerated crawfish meat. Sauté until golden:

**2 tablespoons minced onion**

in:

**2 tablespoons butter**

Add and cook 3 minutes:

**2 tablespoons finely minced celery**
**1 tablespoon finely minced parsley**

Remove from heat and add half the crawfish meat and:

**1/2 cup bread crumbs**

Beat and add:

**1 egg**
**Salt and paprika as required**

Stir lightly with a fork. Stuff the chilled heads with this mixture. Place them on a greased shallow pan. Dot each head with butter. For 10 minutes, before serving the soup, bake the heads in a preheated 325° oven. Melt:

**2 tablespoons butter**

Sauté in it until delicately browned:

**1/4 cup minced onion**

Add and stir until lightly browned:

2 tablespoons flour

Add the fish stock slowly, stirring until smooth. Add the remaining crawfish meat and the fat from the heads.

**Season to taste**

♦ Simmer the bisque about 5 minutes, stirring it often. To serve, place the heated heads in hot soup plates, then pour the bisque over them.

## LOBSTER BISQUE

**About 8 Cups**

Remove the meat from:

2 medium-sized boiled
lobsters, see 455

Dice the body meat and mince the tail and claw meat. Reserve it. Crush the shells. Add to them the tough end of the claws and:

2½ cups Poultry Stock,
(II, 172), or
Fish Fumet, (II, 173)
1 sliced onion
4 ribs celery with leaves
2 whole cloves
1 bay leaf
6 peppercorns

Simmer these ingredients for 30 minutes. Strain the stock. If there is coral roe, force it through a fine sieve. Combine it with:

¼ cup soft butter

Blend in:

¼ cup flour

Gradually pour into this mixture:

3 cups heated milk
¼ teaspoon nutmeg

When the sauce is smooth and boiling, add the lobster and the stock. ♦ Simmer the bisque, covered, 5 minutes. Turn off the heat. Stir in:

1 cup ♦ hot but not boiling
cream
**Season to taste**

Serve at once with:

Minced parsley
Paprika

## MUSHROOM AND CLAM BISQUE

**About 3 Cups**

Sauté:

½ lb. chopped mushrooms

in:

2 tablespoons butter

Stir in:

2 tablespoons flour

Stir in slowly:

2½ cups clam broth

Simmer 5 minutes. Remove from the heat. ♦ Heat but do not boil:

¾ cup cream

Add to the other ingredients.

**Season to taste**

and serve with:

Chopped parsley or chives

## SHRIMP BISQUE

**About 5 Cups**

Remove shells and intestines from:

1½ lb. Poached Shrimp, 462

Put the shrimp through a meat grinder or ⚒ blender. Cook, covered, in the top of a double boiler ♦ over—not in—boiling water 5 minutes:

6 tablespoons butter
2 tablespoons grated onion

Add the ground shrimp and:

3 cups warm milk

Cook 2 minutes. Stir in slowly and heat ♦ but do not boil:

1 cup cream

Add:

Salt, if needed, and paprika
or freshly ground white
pepper
A grating of nutmeg
2 tablespoons parsley or
chives

Serve at once.

## OYSTER STEWS AND BISQUES

Here are two good recipes which differ in nutritive value and effort of preparation. The first calls for milk and cream and is unthickened; the second, a bisque, calls for milk, cream and egg yolks. To clean oysters, see 439–440.

### I.

**About 4 Cups**

Our instructions are foolproof, as the use of a double boiler prevents overcooking the oysters.

Combine in the top of a double boiler and sauté lightly over direct heat:

> 2 to 4 tablespoons butter
> 1/2 teaspoon or more grated onion or leek, a sliver of garlic or 1/2 cup cooked celery

Add:

> 1 to 1 1/2 pints oysters with liquor
> 1 1/2 cups milk
> 1/2 cup cream
> 1/2 teaspoon salt
> 1/8 teaspoon white pepper or paprika

Place the pan ♦ over—not in—boiling water. When the milk is hot and the oysters float, add:

> 2 tablespoons chopped parsley

### II.

**About 4 Cups**

This is a true oyster bisque.

Prepare:

> **Oyster Stew I, above**

Before adding the parsley, remove the soup from the heat and pour a small quantity over:

> 2 beaten egg yolks

After mixing, add them slowly to the hot bisque. Heat slowly for 1 minute but ♦ do not allow to boil. Serve at once.

## MUSSEL STEW

Clean the mussels and remove the beard, 445. Steam them. Strain and reserve the liquor. Use either recipe for Oyster Stew, left, substituting mussels for oysters.

## LOBSTER STEW

**About 5 Cups**

Sauté 3 or 4 minutes:

> 1 cup diced fresh lobster meat

in:

> 3 tablespoons butter

Add slowly:

> 4 cups scalded milk or 3 cups milk and 1 cup cream
> 2 teaspoons onion juice

♦ Do not allow to boil. A Maine correspondent writes that this stew is much improved by the addition, at this time, of:

> (1/2 cup clam broth)
> Season to taste

and serve.

## SHRIMP, CRAB AND OYSTER GUMBO

**About 8 Cups**

Melt:

> 1 tablespoon butter

Stir in and cook until golden:

> 1/4 cup chopped onion

Stir in until blended:

> 2 tablespoons flour

Add and stir until smooth:

> 1 1/2 cups strained tomatoes
> 4 cups Light Stock, (II, 171–172), or Fish Fumet, (II, 173)
> 1 quart thinly sliced okra

Break into small pieces and add:

> 1/2 lb. shelled, cleaned shrimp
> 1/2 lb. crab meat

◆ Simmer these ingredients until the okra is tender. Add:

**16 shelled oysters**
**Season to taste**

and serve the gumbo as soon as the oysters are plump. Sprinkle with:

**Chopped parsley**

Pass:

**Hot Boiled Rice, 189**

which may be spooned into the gumbo.

## ABOUT BOUILLABAISSE AND OTHER FISHERMAN'S STEWS

Necessity is the mother of invention; and convenience gave birth to the can and the frozen package. Use frozen or canned fish, if you must, but remember that ◆ the fragrant, distinctive and elusive charm of fisherman's stew can only be captured if the fish which go into them are themselves freshly caught. Curnonsky reminds us of the legend that bouillabaisse, the most celebrated of these stews, was first brought by angels to the Three Marys of the Gospels when they were shipwrecked on the bleak shores of the Camargue.

Divinely inspired or not, it is true that bouillabaisse can only be approximated in this country, even if its ingredients are just off the hook. For its unique flavor depends on the use of fish native to the Mediterranean alone: a regional rockfish, high in gelatin content, for example, which gives a slightly cloudy but still thin texture to the soup, and numberless finny tidbits, too small for market. We offer a free translation of bouillabaisse into American, realizing fully that we have succeeded only in changing poetry to rich prose.

A similar accommodation has been made for matelote or freshwater fish stew, in which eel, carp, bream, tench

and perch are combined with wine. A certain amount of freewheeling must be the rule, too, in concocting chowders and stews of both sea and fresh fish, which are milk-based and often have potatoes added. Whatever fish you use, see that it is as ◆ fresh as possible and experiment with combinations of those that are most easily available.

## BOUILLABAISSE

**8 Cups**

◆ Please read About Bouillabaisse, left. Have ready:

**¼ cup finely chopped onion**
**4 finely julienned leeks, white**
**portions only**

Squeeze out the seeds, 366, and then dice:

**4 medium-sized skinned**
**tomatoes**

Combine:

**5 minced cloves garlic**
**1 tablespoon finely chopped**
**fresh fennel**
**½ to 1 teaspoon saffron**
**2 crushed bay leaves**
**1 teaspoon grated orange**
**rind**
**2 tablespoons tomato paste**
**⅛ teaspoon celery or fennel**
**seed**
**3 tablespoons chopped**
**parsley**
**1 teaspoon freshly ground**
**white pepper**
**1 to 2 teaspoons salt**

Heat in a large casserole:

**¼ to ½ cup olive oil**

When the oil is hot, add the ingredients above and cook until the vegetables are transparent. Meanwhile, cut into 1-inch dice and add:

**4 lb. very fresh fish in**
**combination:**
**red snapper, halibut,**

pompano, sea perch,
scallops. Also—all in the
shell and well-scrubbed—
clams and mussels, whole
shrimp and 1-inch pieces of
lobster

You may prefer to leave the fish in
2-inch-thick slices and use some of
the smaller fish whole. If so, add the
thinner pieces or small scrubbed
shellfish to the pot slightly later than
the thicker ones ♦ but do not disturb
the boiling. Cover the fish with:

**4 cups hot Fish Fumet,
(II, 173), or water**

♦ Keep the heat high and force the
boiling, which should continue to be
rapid for 15 to 20 minutes.

**Season to taste**

To serve, have already arranged in
the bottom of 8 hot bowls:

**3/4 -inch slices French bread**

which has been dried in the oven and
brushed with:

**Garlic butter**

When the bouillabaisse is ready,
arrange attractively some of each
kind of fish on and around the bread.
You may remove the lobsters from
the shell and remove the upper shells
from the clams and mussels. Then
pour the hot broth into the bowls and
serve at once. Or, you may strain the
broth onto the bread and pass the seafood on a separate platter. Plan the
meal with a beverage other than wine.

## MATELOTE

**8 Cups**

Depending upon the amount of stock
and wine used, this dish can be either
a soup or a stew.

Cook separately and have ready to
add as a garnish, just before serving
the matelote:

**12  small Steamed Onions, 334**

**1/2  lb. Sautéed Mushrooms, 328**
**1/2  lb. shelled Poached
Shrimp, 462**

Now, clean and cut into 1-inch slices:

**3  lb. freshwater fish: eel,
carp, tench, bream or perch**

Cover first the fish that need the longest cooking with a combination of
one-half:

**Good red wine**

and one-half:

**Fish Fumet, (II, 173), or
meat stock, (II, 171)**

If you are serving the matelote as a
soup, you will need about 3 quarts of
liquid, for this will be reduced by
one-third later on. Add:

**2  teaspoons chopped parsley**
**1/2  cup chopped celery**
**1  small bay leaf**
**2  cloves garlic**
**1/4  teaspoon thyme**
**1  teaspoon salt**

Bring the mixture to a boil, remove
from heat and float on the surface:

**2  tablespoons warm brandy**

Ignite the brandy, and when the flame
dies down, return the mixture to heat,
add the remaining fish, cover the pan
and simmer the soup about 15 minutes. Now, remove the fish to a serving dish and keep it warm. Strain the
liquid into another pan. Reduce the
liquid by one-third. Thicken the soup
with a Beurre Manié, 381, of:

**3  tablespoons butter**
**2 1/2  tablespoons flour**

adding it a little at a time to the hot
soup. Bring the soup just to a boil, stirring constantly. It should be creamy in
texture, but will go thin if boiled.

**Season to taste**

To serve, put the fish into soup bowls
and cover first with the onions and
mushrooms, then with the sauce; garnish the whole with the shrimp. Be
sure to serve over:

**Sautéed Soup Croutons, 174**

## MANHATTAN CLAM CHOWDER

**About 8 Cups**

Chowder should be allowed to ripen refrigerated; it is always better the following day.

Prepare as described, 445:

**1 quart quahog clams**

Then wash them in:

**3 cups water**

Drain through cheesecloth. Reserve liquid. Cut the hard part of the clams from the soft part. Chop finely:

**The hard part of the clams**

**A 2-inch cube of salt pork**

**1 large onion**

Sauté the salt pork very slowly. Remove and reserve the cracklings. Add the minced onions and hard part of the clams to the fat. Stir and cook slowly about 5 minutes. Sift over them and stir until blended:

**3 tablespoons flour**

Heat and stir in the reserved liquid. Prepare and add:

**2 cups pared raw potatoes, diced**

**3 cups cooked or canned peeled tomatoes**

**(½ cup diced green pepper)**

**(½ bay leaf)**

**(¼ cup catsup)**

Cover the pan and simmer the chowder until the potatoes are done, but still firm. Add the cracklings, the soft part of the clams and:

**3 tablespoons butter**

Simmer 3 minutes more. Place the chowder in a hot tureen.

**Season to taste**

Serve with:

**Oyster crackers**

You may substitute for the fresh clams:

**(2½ cups canned minced clams)**

to be added with the cracklings, above. Strain the juice. Add water to make 3 cups of liquid. Use this liquid in place of the water measurement given above.

## NEW ENGLAND CLAM CHOWDER

**About 8 Cups**

Most New Englanders consider the above recipe an illegitimate child. They omit the tomatoes, green peppers and catsup, but pour in:

**4 cups hot, ▶ not boiling, milk**

after the cracklings have been added. ▶ Do not let the mixture boil. Serve with large crackers.

## CONCH CHOWDER

Prepare:

**Manhattan Clam Chowder, left**

using conch meat to replace the clams. ▶ To prepare conch in the shell, cover:

**5 to 15 conchs or large whelks**

with cold water and ▶ simmer 20 to 30 minutes. Remove from shell and beat the white body meat in a canvas bag until it begins to disintegrate. Marinate 2 hours in:

**¼ cup lime juice**

After adding the conch meat to the chowder, simmer 3 to 5 minutes longer than directed for Manhattan Clam Chowder.

## ABOUT QUICK SOUPS COCKAIGNE

When we were very young, we were more appalled than edified by *Struwwelpeter,* a book of rhymed fables for children, which had been written in Germany by a Korpsbruder of our great-grandfather. We are still haunted by the story of Suppenkaspar, a little boy who resolutely refused to eat his soup, wasted away for his stubbornness and was buried with a tureen as his headstone. Looking back and taking note of our wonderful present-day battery of canned, frozen and dried soups, we can see that Kaspar was born a century too soon and, beyond a doubt, in this generation would have chosen to live.

We suggest here a process rather than a recipe for achieving very special effects. Mingle canned and frozen soups in your repertory with the vegetable stocks that are precious by-products of daily cooking. And, if you have on hand some leftover bones, lean fowl or meat trimmings, put your ♥ pressure cooker to work at building a soup base, see Quick Household Stock, (II, 173). Remember in this connection that most fish soups, 156, are quick soups, even when you start with raw materials. There is also the possibility that you are harboring some refrigerator scraps that could constructively respond to ⚒ blender treatment. Before processing, add to them a few mushrooms or a few leaves of spinach, lettuce or cress and a small amount of milk and cream. Lacking these, do not scorn a bouillon cube. And if you have a plot or some pots of fresh herbs, now is the time to commandeer a clipping. Or use parsley lavishly, or dried herbs discreetly.

Words of caution: ♦ Normally, we dilute ready-prepared soups considerably less than their manufacturers recommend, whether we use home-cooked stocks, milk or—less desirably—just plain water. But we find that the more concentrated the soup, the more likely it is to taste oversalted. Test your mix and correct this tendency, see (II, 247). ♦ Be sure, too, if you blend uncooked vegetables, that they are tender enough not to spoil the texture of your soup with stringy fibers or bits of hull. Add to a clear soup a canned consommé or chicken broth, diluted as suggested above, or one of several quickly confected egg drops, 134. If you fancy a more filling dish, serve Blender Borsch, 166, or Quick Cucumber Soup Cockaigne, 167. For other sturdy potages and casseroles, see suggestions in Brunch, Lunch and Supper Dishes, 236. Then perhaps a naïve house guest will say, as did a restaurant diner: "I like your soup du jour, but why is it different every day?"

## QUICK CANNED CONSOMMÉ VARIATIONS

**I.** A clear soup is supposed to be as bracing as a clear conscience.
Add to each serving of consommé, hot or cold:

> A slice of lemon, or
> 1 tablespoon sherry or
> Madeira, or some diced
> avocado
> A dollop of cultured sour
> cream

Or add to hot comsommé:

> Egg Drops, 134, Marrow
> Balls, 174, or Noodles, 200

**II.**

About 4½ Cups

For a cold-day pick-me-up, serve piping hot in mugs; and for a hot-day refresher, serve well chilled in old-fashioned glasses, see (II, 35), garnished with sprigs of fresh herbs.
Mix together:

> 2 cups tomato juice
> 1 can condensed consommé
> 1 can condensed chicken
> broth
> Juice of one lemon

## III.

### About 3 Cups

A cool drink with a tropical tang.
Combine and heat:

    **1 can condensed consommé**
    **1 can condensed Madrilène**

Stir in:

    **The juice of 1 large orange**

Serve chilled on the rocks.

## ⅃ QUICK CONSOMMÉ FONDUE COCKAIGNE

### About 2 Cups

Blend together:

    **1 can condensed consommé**
    **8 oz. cream cheese**
    **1 pressed clove garlic**

Chill and garnish with:

    **Chopped parsley**

Pass a bowl of:

    **Toasted French bread cubes**

and dip as for fondue.

## ⅃ BLENDER GAZPACHO

### About 1 Cup

Blend together 2 or 3 minutes:

    **¼ cup pared, seeded cucumbers**
    **¾ cup skinned, seeded tomatoes**
    **¼ cup condensed consommé or water**
    **½ teaspoon chopped red pimiento**

Add and blend for a shorter time:

    **1 teaspoon to 1 tablespoon olive oil**

Add, but do not blend, as the flavor would be too strong:

    **1 teaspoon chopped chives**
    **Season to taste**

and serve by pouring the broth over 2 ice cubes. A good garnish is:

    **Garlic croutons**

## QUICK VEGETABLE SOUP

### About 2½ Cups

Melt:

    **2 tablespoons butter**

Add and stir until blended:

    **1¼ tablespoons flour**

Add and stir until smooth:

    **1½ cups vegetable stock**

You may utilize the water in which vegetables, below, have been cooked. Bring to a boil and cook 2 minutes. Lower the heat and add:

    **½ cup cream or stock**

Add:

    **½ cup cooked, diced or strained vegetables**
    **2 tablespoons chopped parsley**
    **(A dash of celery salt)**
    **Season to taste**

Heat thoroughly ▶ but do not boil if you have chosen to add the cream.

## ⅃ BLENDER CREAM OF VEGETABLE SOUP

### 4 to 5 Cups

Blend:

    **1 can condensed cream of vegetable soup**
    **1 can condensed chicken rice soup**
    **1 cup canned or strong asparagus stock**
    **(¼ cup cream)**

Heat ▶ but do not boil and serve at once.

## QUICK CREAM OF ASPARAGUS SOUP

### 5 to 6 Cups

Combine:

    **1 can condensed cream of asparagus soup**
    **1 can condensed chicken broth**

(1  can condensed cream of
    mushroom soup)
1½ cups milk
Heat, stirring until smooth.

## ☘ QUICK CHILLED CREAM OF AVOCADO SOUP

**3 Cups**

Combine in a blender:

2  cups condensed cream of
    chicken soup
½  cup puréed avocado

When ready to serve, stir in:

¾  cup chilled milk
⅛  teaspoon white pepper

Serve in cups, sprinkled with:

1  teaspoon chopped chives or
    chervil

## ☘ BLENDER BORSCH

### I.

**4 to 5 cups**

Combine in a blender:

1  can condensed consommé
1  can condensed cream of
    chicken soup
1  can beets: No. 2½
(1  minced clove garlic)

Half of the liquid from the beets may
be drained if a thick soup is desired.
Blend until smooth and chill. Serve
with a garnish of:

Cultured sour cream and
chopped Fines Herbes,
(II, 253)

### II.

**About 4 Cups**

Combine in a blender:

2  cups tomato juice
2  cups canned beets
3  small dill pickles
3  tablespoons finely grated
    onion
1  drop hot pepper sauce

(1  minced clove garlic)

Chill the soup and serve garnished
with:

4  thinly sliced hard-cooked
    eggs
    Cultured sour cream
    Chopped fresh dill or
    fennel

## QUICK PEA SOUP

**About 6 Cups**

Combine and bring to the boiling
point:

1  can condensed consommé
1  can clear chicken broth
1  can condensed pea soup

Add:

1⅓ cups water or stock
¼  cup finely diced cooked
    ham
1  teaspoon grated onion
(4  oz. fine Boiled Noodles, 200)
(1  tablespoon Worcestershire
    sauce)
(1  tablespoon chili sauce)

Simmer, covered, until hot.

## QUICK CREAM OF CHICKEN SOUP

Easy to make and very good.
Heat in a double boiler ♦ over—not
in—boiling water:

Chicken bouillon
Cream—about ¼ the
amount of the bouillon

Add if you wish:

A dash of nutmeg
Chopped parsley

And if you want to be really luxurious add:

Ground blanched
almonds—use about
2 tablespoons to 1 cup soup

## QUICK CUCUMBER SOUP COCKAIGNE

**About 5 Cups**

Bring to a boil:

**2½ cups strong chicken broth**

Drop in about:

**1½ cups pared, seeded and diced cucumbers**

Simmer until translucent, about 15 minutes. Add:

**1 can condensed cream of chicken soup**

Again bring to a boil. Now add:

**½ cup canned crab meat, shrimp or minced clams**

**1 teaspoon fresh parsley or chervil**

Heat ◗ but do not boil, and serve at once.

## QUICK COLD CUCUMBER SOUP

**About 5 Cups**

Combine in a saucepan:

**1 can frozen condensed cream of potato soup**
**An equal amount of milk**
**1 chicken bouillon cube**
**1¾ cups finely chopped pared cucumber**

Heat slowly, stirring until very hot and until the cucumber is partially cooked, about 10 minutes. ⚘ Blend or put through a food mill and refrigerate, covered, until chilled. Shortly before serving, stir in:

**1 cup light cream**

## QUICK CREAM OF CAULIFLOWER SOUP

**About 3½ Cups**

Heat:

**2 tablespoons butter**

Cook in the butter about 4 minutes:

**¼ cup sliced onion**
**2 minced small ribs celery with leaves**

Add:

**1½ cups chicken broth**
**1 cup mashed or riced cooked cauliflower**

Heat to the boiling point. Add:

**1 cup light cream**

◗ Do not let the soup boil after adding the cream.

**Season to taste**

and serve with:

**1 tablespoon chopped parsley**
**A light grating of nutmeg or a pinch of coriander**

## QUICK CHEESE SOUP

**About 4 Cups**

Combine and stir over low heat until the cheese is melted:

**1 can condensed cream of celery soup**
**1 can condensed consommé**
**1¼ cups water or milk**
**½ cup shredded cheddar or pimiento cheese**

Add:

**(1 tablespoon chopped onion)**
**(¼ teaspoon Worcestershire sauce)**

◗ Do not let the soup boil. Serve with:

**Chopped parsley**

## QUICK TOMATO CORN CHOWDER

**3 Cups**

Combine and heat, but ◗ do not boil:

**1 can condensed tomato soup**
**An equal amount of milk**
**½ cup cream-style corn**
**½ teaspoon sugar**
**(¼ teaspoon curry powder)**
**Season to taste**

and serve.

## QUICK MUSHROOM SOUP

**I.**

**About 4 Cups**

Combine, stir and heat:

1 cup condensed cream of
  mushroom soup
1 cup condensed beef or
  chicken bouillon or
  consommé
1¼ cups water or milk

**II.**

**5 Cups**

Reconstitute:

1 oz. dried mushrooms, 328

in:

2 cans condensed consommé

Add:

1 can condensed mushroom
  soup
1 cup milk

Heat and serve.

## QUICK ONION SOUP

**About 2 Cups**

Heat:

1 can condensed onion soup

Add:

2 teaspoons lemon juice
A grating of lemon rind
½ pressed clove garlic
⅛ teaspoon nutmeg
(¼ cup sherry)
Season to taste

Top each serving with:

Melba Cheese Rounds,
(II, 354)

## QUICK OXTAIL SOUP WITH WINE

**About 2½ Cups**

Combine:

1 cup water
1 can condensed oxtail soup
1 teaspoon grated onion
3 strips lemon rind: 2 inches
  each

◗ Simmer these ingredients for 5 minutes. Remove the lemon rind and:

Season to taste

Reduce the heat. Stir in:

½ cup claret or
  ¼ cup very dry sherry
1 tablespoon minced parsley

Serve at once with:

Toasted crackers

## QUICK SPINACH SOUP

**About 2 Cups**

Combine:

½ cup puréed Boiled Spinach,
  358
1 can condensed cream of
  chicken soup

If the spinach has already been
creamed, use instead:

(1 can chicken broth)

You may thin the soup with:

Spinach water, stock or
  milk
Season to taste

Heat and serve.

## QUICK TOMATO SOUP

**About 4 Cups**

◗ Simmer, covered, 15 minutes:

2½ cups canned tomatoes
¼ cup sliced onion
½ cup chopped celery with
  leaves

Strain and reserve the tomato stock.
Melt:

2 tablespoons butter

Add and stir until blended:

2 tablespoons flour

Add, cook and stir until smooth and
boiling:

2 cups Brown Stock, (II, 171),
  or canned bouillon
½ teaspoon sugar
⅛ teaspoon paprika
The strained tomato stock
Season to taste

and add, just before serving:

> (1 tablespoon chopped fresh
> basil or 3/4 teaspoon
> anchovy paste or a dollop
> of whipped cream)

## QUICK CHILLED FRESH TOMATO CREAM SOUP

### I. ⚲

About 3 Cups

One way to use surplus garden tomatoes. Peel, seed and chop coarsely
into a blender:

> 2 1/2 cups very ripe fresh
> tomatoes

Blend briefly with:

> 1 cup cream
> 1 tablespoon parsley
> 1 tablespoon basil
> Season to taste

Chill and serve with:

> Lemon slices

### II.

About 3 Cups

Combine in a cocktail shaker:

> 2 cups chilled tomato juice
> 1 cup chilled cream
> 4 or more ribs raw celery,
> grated
> 1 teaspoon grated onion
> A few drops hot pepper
> sauce
> A few grains cayenne

Or, you may omit the onion and use:

> (1/4 teaspoon dry ginger)
> (1/8 teaspoon allspice)
> Season to taste

and add:

> 1/4 cup chopped ice

Shake well.

## QUICK CLAM AND CHICKEN BROTH

Combine equal parts of:

> Clam broth

> Chicken stock

If the clam broth is very salty, you
may have to use more chicken stock
or water. Season lightly with:

> White pepper

When the soup reaches a boil, remove from heat and place in hot
cups. Top each cup with:

> 1 tablespoon whipped cream

Have the cream at room temperature.
For color, sprinkle the top with:

> Paprika or chopped chives
> or parsley

Serve at once.

## QUICK CRAB OR LOBSTER MONGOLE

About 4 Cups

Sprinkle:

> 3 tablespoons dry white wine
> or 1 teaspoon
> Worcestershire sauce

over:

> 1 cup flaked canned crab or
> lobster

Combine and heat to the boiling
point:

> 1 can condensed cream of
> tomato soup
> 1 can condensed cream of
> green pea soup

Stir the above mixture slowly into:

> 1 1/4 cups hot light cream or
> part cream and part
> bouillon

Add the crab. Heat the soup ❯ but do
not let it boil.

## QUICK LOBSTER SUPREME

About 5 Cups

Combine and heat:

> 1 can condensed asparagus
> soup
> 1 can condensed cream of
> mushroom soup
> 3 tablespoons dry sherry

Add:

**2 cups light cream**

Pick over and add:

**6 to 8 oz. canned lobster meat**

Heat this soup ▶ but do not let it boil.

## QUICK LOBSTER CHOWDER

**About 8 Cups**

An easy-to-get soup meal.

Sauté in a saucepan about 5 minutes:

**¼ cup finely diced onion**
**½ cup finely diced celery**

in:

**2 tablespoons butter**

Add:

**1½ cups water**
**1 small bay leaf**
**1 package frozen mixed vegetables, defrosted**

▶ Cover and bring to a boil. Cook the vegetables until barely tender, about 5 minutes. Remove the bay leaf. Drain, but reserve the liquor from:

**1 can chopped broiled mushrooms: 3 oz.**

Stir into the liquor until smooth:

**1 tablespoon cornstarch**

Add this to the mixture in the saucepan, stirring constantly until it thickens. Add the drained mushrooms and:

**1 cup tomato sauce**
**2 cups milk**
**1 cup canned lobster**
**Season to taste**

and heat slowly ▶ but do not boil. Serve with an assortment of:

**Cheese**

or, as they do in France, with:

**Crusty bread and sweet butter**

## QUICK SEAFOOD TUREEN

**About 6 Cups**

Melt in a saucepan:

**¼ cup butter**

Add:

**2 cups flounder fillets, cut into pieces**
**1½ cups dry white wine**

▶ Cover and simmer about 10 minutes. Add:

**1 cup cooked shrimp**
**1 cup cooked lobster meat**
**1 small can sliced mushrooms**
**1½ cups condensed cream of mushroom soup**
**2 tablespoons chopped canned pimientos**
**1 crushed clove garlic**
**⅛ teaspoon saffron**

Simmer about 5 minutes longer. Add:

**(½ cup dry sherry)**
**Season to taste**

Serve in a tureen with:

**Buttered toast or French bread**

## ABOUT GARNISHES FOR SOUP

Adding marrow balls instead of a chiffonade of cress to the same clear soup can change the temper of a meal. Scan the parade of breads and garnishes on pages 171–172 to determine your pace-setter du jour. If serving an informal buffet, arrange a group of garnishes around a tureen to give your guests a choice among rich, lean or green. Whip up some more satisfying dumplings, 182, for hungry children or pass a rice ring. Tempt a finicky appetite with an egg drop, 134. ▶ Be sure none of the garnishes is chilled, unless the soup is an iced one.

To turn individual servings into added visual and taste treats, decorate soup bowls as illustrated or as described on the next page. The most popular soup garnish for clear or thick soups is lemon—shown first, with a notch-edged slice. For other

lemon cuts, see (II, 252). Flowers such as calendula and nasturtium lend color to pale cream soups; a small nasturtium and its piquant leaf floated on vichyssoise are shown next. Japanese clear broths are endlessly fascinating with their bits of vegetables and greens swirling across the top. Usually minimal in material like the turnip rosettes shown next, or the tofu barge with its herb cargo, they add inexpressible charm. Strengthen the color of a shrimp bisque with a whole shrimp garnished with an avocado slice and parsley. Float on a spinach soup tiny raw mushroom caps filled with sour cream amid a few sprigs of young burnet. Or as shown next, carved-carrot flowers with stems made of blanched chives.

## FOR CLEAR SOUPS
Drop into the soup:

> Thin slices of lemon or orange
> Thin slices of avocado drenched in lemon
> Minced parsley, chives, watercress, onion, mint, basil or chervil floated on the surface or concentrated on a dab of whipped cream
> Podded or snow peas
> Thin slices of cooked root: parsley, chervil or celeriac
> Consommé Brunoise, 130
> Cucumber balls
> Noodles, 200
> Gnocchi, 185–186
> Won Ton, 136
> Kreplach, 135
> Dumplings, see many varieties, 182–184
> Ravioli, 204
> Farina Balls, 184
> Spätzle, 186
> Nockerln, 183
> Quenelles, 187
> Meatballs, Marrow Balls, Sausage Balls, 173–174
> Cheese Balls, 174
> Pesto, (II, 251)
> Bean Curd or Tofu, (II, 192)
> Bean Sprouts, (II, 241)

## FOR CREAM SOUPS
Garnish with:

> Salted whipped cream or sour cream and a dusting of finely chopped mixed herbs
> Chiffonade of Herbs for Soup, 172
> Blanched, shredded, toasted almonds or cashews
> Flavored popcorn or puffed cereals

## FOR THICK SOUPS
Use:

> Thin slices of orange, lemon or lime

Sliced small sausages or
thin slices of
hard sausages
Sliced hard-cooked eggs
Croutons, 174 and (II, 219)
Sour cream
Meatballs, 173
Gnocchi, 185–186
Julienned strips of ham,
tongue, chicken or
bits of seafood
Grated cheeses
Pesto, (II, 251)

## BREADS TO SERVE AS A SIDE DISH WITH SOUPS

Fancy shapes in toasted
white, rye or
whole wheat
Melba Toast, (II, 355)
Toasted rye sticks
Plain or toasted garlic
bread, (II, 354), or
other herbed breads
Crackers, hot and plain or
spread with herb butters,
cheese spreads or
fish pastes
Cheese Wafers or
Straws, (II, 363)
Pastry Snails, (II, 69)
Hush Puppies, (II, 344)
Corn Dodgers, (II, 342), or
Corn Zephyrs, (II, 342)
Croutons, 174 and (II, 219)
Small Choux Paste
Puffs, (II, 370)
Rissoles, (II, 69)
Turnovers, (II, 69)
Seeded Crackers, (II, 354)

## CHIFFONADE OF HERBS FOR SOUPS

For a chiffonade, always use the
freshest and most tender of greens—
being sure ♦ to remove stems and
coarse midribs of lettuce, sorrel or
parsley—alone or in combination
with whatever fresh herbs you have
on hand that are compatible with the
flavor of your soup. Allow:

1 or 2 tablespoons fresh
herbs or greens

to:

1 pint soup

Add the herbs to a small quantity of
broth and chop in a ⅄ blender until
fine. Combine the blended herbs with
the remaining broth. If you have
no blender, mince a combination of
herbs very, very fine.

## CHOUX PASTE GARNISH

About 1½ Cups

For either of these garnishes, you
may add:

(4 to 6 tablespoons grated
Parmesan cheese)

to the dough.

**I.** Use a pastry bag with a ¼-inch-
diameter tube. Fill with:

Unsweetened or cheese-
flavored Choux Paste,
(II, 370)

Squeeze onto a greased baking tin
pea-sized bits of dough. Bake in a
preheated 400° oven about 10 minutes. Add these to the soup the instant
before serving.

**II.** Fill a pastry bag with:

Unsweetened Choux
Paste, (II, 370)

Make 1-inch rounds. Flatten carefully with a moistened finger any
points remaining after the bag is
lifted off. Glaze with:

French Egg Wash, (II, 503)

Bake in a preheated 400° oven about
10 minutes. Be sure the puffs are well
dried out before removing them from
the oven. ♦ Fill them, the last minute

before serving, with a farce that combines well with the soup. ♦ Place in soup the instant before serving to avoid sogginess.

## FRITTER GARNISH

**About ³/4 Cup**

♦ Please read About Deep-Fat Frying, 94.

Beat until light:

 1 egg

Add:

 ¹/4 teaspoon salt
 ¹/8 teaspoon paprika
 ¹/2 cup flour
 2 tablespoons milk

Drop the batter through a colander into deep fat heated to 365°. Fry until the garnish is brown. Drain on paper toweling. Place in the soup just before serving.

## LIVER DUMPLINGS OR LEBERKLÖSSE

Please read About Dumplings, 182. Being the descendants of South Germans, we cannot well compile a cookbook without including a recipe typical of that neck of the woods—not exactly a handsome dish, but it has qualities.

## I.

**About 3 Cups**

Skin and remove the fiber from:

 1 lb. calf liver or chicken livers

Grind or chop until very fine. Slightly frozen liver is easy to grind. Soak in water 3 minutes, then wring the water from:

 2 slices white bread

Mix bread and liver thoroughly, then add and beat:

 2 egg yolks
 ¹/4 cup soft butter

 2 teaspoons chopped onion
 2 tablespoons chopped parsley
 1¹/2 teaspoons salt
 ¹/2 teaspoon pepper
 2 tablespoons flour

Beat until stiff ♦ but not dry, then fold in:

 2 egg whites

Shape this mixture into 1¹/2-inch balls. Drop them into gently boiling soup or stock. ♦ Simmer 5 or 6 minutes. Serve them with the soup.

## II. Liver Sausage Dumplings

**About 1 Cup**

Combine and work with a fork:

 ¹/4 lb. liver sausage
 ¹/2 egg or 1 egg white or yolk
 ¹/2 cup cracker crumbs
 1 tablespoon chopped parsley or chives
 (1 tablespoon catsup)

Shape the mixture into 1-inch balls. ♦ Simmer gently about 2 minutes in soup stock.

## MEATBALLS FOR SOUP

A superb main dish may be had by adding these to vegetable soup. Make up half the recipe for:

 **German Meatballs, 621**

You may use more bread if desired. Mix the ingredients lightly with a fork. Shape them without pressure into 1-inch balls and drop into boiling soup or stock. ♦ Simmer them until done, about 10 minutes.

## SAUSAGE BALLS FOR SOUP

**About 1¹/2 Cups**

Good in pea, bean or lentil soup. Combine:

 ¹/2 lb. raw sausage meat
 1 egg white
 2 teaspoons chopped parsley

½ teaspoon fresh basil
¼ teaspoon fresh rosemary
3 tablespoons toasted bread
    crumbs

Roll this mixture into 1-inch balls. Drop them into boiling stock. Reduce the heat at once and ♦ simmer the soup until the balls are done, about 30 minutes. Skim the fat from the soup before serving.

## MARROW BALLS

**About ¾ Cup**

These delicate drops may be prepared several hours in advance and refrigerated.
Combine and beat until creamy:

¼ cup fresh marrow
2 tablespoons butter

Add:

3 egg yolks
¼ teaspoon salt
⅛ teaspoon paprika
2 tablespoons chopped
    parsley
Cracker crumbs

Use at least ½ cup cracker crumbs to make the mixture of a stiff consistency to shape into balls with:

3 stiffly beaten egg whites

Cook the balls in ♦ simmering soup about 15 minutes or until they rise to the surface.

## CHEESE BALLS FOR SOUP

**About 1½ Cups**

Combine:

2 beaten egg yolks
2 tablespoons grated cheese,
    preferably Parmesan
2 tablespoons dry bread
    crumbs
⅛ teaspoon paprika
½ teaspoon dried herbs or
    1 teaspoon chopped fresh
    chives or parsley

Beat until stiff ♦ but not dry, then fold in:

2 egg whites
⅛ teaspoon salt

Drop the batter from a spoon into ♦ simmering soup. Simmer only 1 or 2 minutes.

## SOUP CROUTONS

For other croutons, see (II, 219).
To retain the crispness of these ever-popular diced toasts, serve them in individual dishes and let the guests add them to their soup. Or, use them diced small, so they are much like buttered toasted crumbs, to garnish spinach, noodles or game. They may be flavored by sautéing in:

Butter and olive oil

or dusting them with:

Grated cheese

while still hot.

# CEREALS AND PASTAS

On a train trip from Palermo to Syracuse, a stranger leaned toward us to say in the most casual tones that this was the field from which Pluto abducted Proserpina. True or false, this brought to mind the lamentations of her mother, Ceres, and the surprises in store for her should she survey her domain today. She might rightly mourn that her noble way of grinding grain between stones is scorned, and, instead, grains divested of their rich germs are mercilessly swirled and crushed between high-speed hot rollers. But she might rejoice in some of the new higher protein hybrids, 6, and the fact that four-fifths of the world now relies on grains for nourishment. There are some recent discoveries in cereal research, both in plant breeding and in the combining of cereals when serving, that we cannot help but feel are hopeful for man's future. Cereals—including the high-durum wheats—when eaten alone lack certain essential aminos present in complete-protein foods, 4. But they do contain varying amounts of incomplete-protein elements, and when cereals are skillfully combined, 4, or are served with the addition of meat, fish, egg, cheese or soy products, the protein elements of the cereal itself are enhanced. Note that such combinations have for centuries been instinctively and skillfully used in lands where cereals form the overwhelming staple of the diet. Without benefit of science, the Asians have realized the importance of incorporating into rice bits of seafood or soybean substances; the North Africans add to their couscous morsels of meat or fish; and in Italy a thousand forms of pasta based on high-durum wheat have proliferated since the days of Ceres, and are customarily served with sauces or fillings containing meat, seafood or cheese. From Italy, too, come fanciful and melodic names: fettucine, lasagne, macaroni, mostaccioli, spaghetti, linguine, vermicelli. The glass jars shown, 175, contain a few of these, with a ravioli roller in the foreground. To cook pastas, see 199; for the rice ring, see 189.

In America, ready-to-eat cereals, our classic morning eye-openers, are found in mountainous piles of boxes in every supermarket and are shouted about daily from the mountaintops on TV. They are either exploded into puffs under high steam, pressed and dried in myriad forms from moist pastes, or malted, sugared and shattered into flakes. You pay as much for all this processing and for the expensive packaging to retain crispness as you pay for the cereals themselves. It takes more time to cook whole grains yourself or to make up cereal snacks, see below, but there is no question of the increased nutritive value and economy.

All cereals should be stored covered against insect or rodent infestation and moisture absorption. Raw whole cereals also require storage in a cool place, as even mild heat promotes development of rancidity. Some cereals like rice and oats are sold partially precooked to destroy the enzymes that hasten spoilage. If using precooked cereals, finish the cooking according to the directions on the label.

## ABOUT COLD WHOLE-GRAIN MIXTURES AND SNACKS

Grain combinations supplemented with seeds, nuts and dried fruits—raisins, dates, prunes and apricots—for their iron content, and fruit sugar for sweetening, have long been popular in health and vegetarian circles and prized by campers and climbers for their high energy potential. Snackers love them for their delicious flavors but must watch their intake because of the heavy caloric content. If the grains are toasted before being added to the other ingredients, the mix is often called **granola;** and if the grains are mixed raw the term is usually **müsli,** see 177. There is some vitamin loss in the toasting, but some people find the untoasted grains indigestible. Whatever mixture you decide suits your taste, balance it by drinking milk or eating cheese with it; or include enough soybean substances, milk solids and wheat germ to furnish adequate complete protein, 4.

## GRANOLA

### I.

About 6 Cups

Preheat oven to 300°.

Stirring frequently, toast in a 13 x 9-inch pan 10 minutes:

   **1 cup buckwheat groats**

Add and continue to stir frequently for 15 minutes:

   **1 cup rolled oats or cornmeal**
   **1 cup wheat flakes**

mixed with:

   **1/2 cup heated vegetable oil**

Add:

   **1/2 cup sesame seeds**
   **1/2 cup hulled sunflower seeds**
   **1 cup coarsely chopped almonds, pine nuts or walnuts**

Stir and toast 10 minutes longer. Remove from oven and add:

   **1/2 cup wheat germ**
   **1 cup chopped dates or apricots**

Store covered and refrigerated. Serve with:

   **Milk or yogurt**

## II.
### About 7 Cups
A sweetened version.
Preheat oven to 300°.

Scatter in a 13 x 9-inch pan and toast about 15 minutes, stirring frequently:

**3 cups rolled oats**

Mix in a large bowl:

**1½ cups wheat germ**
**½ cup dry milk solids**
**1 cup coarsely chopped almonds**
**1 cup shredded or flaked coconut**
**½ cup sesame seeds**
**1 cup hulled sunflower seeds**

Heat slowly and combine with the above:

**½ cup vegetable oil**
**½ cup honey or maple syrup**

Combine with the toasted oats and spread thinly in the pan, continuing to toast and to stir frequently another 15 minutes or until the ingredients are all toasted. Cool and store tightly covered and refrigerated.

## III.
### About 10 Cups
An easier formula but with somewhat more loss of nutrient value.
Preheat oven to 300°.

Heat slowly in a 9 x 13-inch pan:

**½ cup vegetable oil**
**½ cup honey or molasses**

Mix into the oil and honey:

**3 cups rolled oats**
**½ cup rye flakes**
**2 cups wheat germ**
**1 cup hulled sunflower seeds**
**½ cup sesame seeds**
**2 cups coarsely chopped mixed nuts: pecans, hazelnuts or peanuts**
**1 cup dry milk solids**
**½ cup soy flour**

Toast about 35 minutes, stirring frequently. Remove from oven and mix in:

**1 cup raisins**

Cool and store as above.

## MÜSLI OR SWISS OATMEAL
### 4 Servings
Soak overnight covered:

**1 cup rolled oats**
**(¼ teaspoon salt)**
**1 cup boiling water**

Before serving, combine the oat and water mixture with:

**2 to 3 tablespoons honey**
**½ cup raisins**
**¼ cup chopped pitted prunes**
**¼ cup chopped dried apricots**
**⅓ cup chopped nuts**
**½ cup grated apple**
**2 tablespoons lemon juice**

Serve with:

**Milk or cream**

## ABOUT COOKING CEREALS

Scientists tell us that cereals are edible as soon as the starch granules have swollen to their full capacity in hot liquid. This state they speak of glibly as gelatinization, although it remains something of a chemical mystery. To cooks, this phenomenon is evident in the thickening of cereals and sauces. While the technical-minded insist that the starch and protein in cereals are adequately cooked in a short period of time, many cooks claim that the results are not so nutty and sweet as when the older, slow-heat methods are used. Whether you back the cook or the scientist, on these points they agree: cereals must be added ♦ slowly to ♦ sufficient rapidly boiling water and ♦ stirred in, so that each individual grain is surrounded and quickly penetrated by the hot liquid. The boiling point of the water ♦ 212°, must be maintained throughout as the cereal is added. If you cook cereals or starches in an acid liquid like fruit juice, the thickening power is lowered.

With cereals that tend to gumminess, this slow addition to the boiling water allows the outer starch layers to stabilize and keeps the granules separated after swelling. The cereal is done when it looks translucent. The granules should still be separated, retaining their individual shape even though they are soft. Serve at once.

Cereals increase in bulk depending on the amount of water they absorb. You may count 4 to 6 servings for each cup of uncooked cereal. For particulars see equivalents, (II, 287). If you cook cereal in advance of serving ♦ cover it at once while it is still hot from the first cooking, so no crust forms on the top. If you plan to use it more than an hour after the first cooking, refrigerate it. ♦ To avoid lumps on reheating, place the cereal over—not in—boiling water and allow the cereal to heat thoroughly before stirring.

To make a **gruel** for the baby or an invalid, cook the cereal with 3 times the amount of water or milk called for and cook twice as long. Strain and serve.

To cook finely ground, coarsely ground, and whole-grain cereals, see below. For more details about some individual cereals, see Ingredients, (II, 287–288).

## FINELY MILLED CEREALS

### About 4 to 6 Servings

♦ Please read About Cooking Cereals, 177. To prepare fine-granule cereals, have water boiling in the bottom of a double boiler. In the top of the boiler, over direct heat, bring to a rolling boil:

4 to 6 cups water or milk or a mixture of both
1 teaspoon salt

Use the lesser amount of water for finest grains. Very slowly, ♦ without disturbing the boiling point, sprinkle into the liquid:

1 cup dry cornmeal, farina or hominy grits

Continue to cook over direct heat 2 to 3 minutes, then cook over—not in—boiling water 5 to 20 minutes. To avoid gumminess ♦ do not stir. During the last few minutes of cooking, you may fold in:

3 tablespoons dry skim-milk solids
2 teaspoons Nutritional Yeast, (II, 224)

for each cup dry cereal. These ingredients make no noticeable change in taste and are a great addition in food value. You may at this time also add:

Dates, figs, raisins or cooked dried fruits

Or serve with:

Cold or hot sliced canned or fresh fruits
A cinnamon-sugar mixture
Sugar and cream
Maple syrup
Jams and preserves

## COARSELY MILLED AND WHOLE CEREALS

### About 4 to 6 Servings

Coarsely ground or cracked grains have many different names, but all are cooked the same way. The wheats, whole-grain and cracked, also include **triticale**, (II, 213), and **bulgur**, a parboiled, dried and cracked whole-grain wheat. **Groats** may be **cracked wheat, buckwheat** or **oats.** Coarsely ground **buckwheat, barley** or **millet** is also called **kasha.** Millet can replace rice in most recipes.

**Cracked corn** is called **samp. Coarse oats** come in a number of forms, steel-cut or rolled. It is best to pre-soak all these cereals, covered, from 4 to 8 hours. To cook, use:

> **2 to 4 cups water, milk or fruit juice**
> **1 teaspoon salt**

for every:

> **1 cup dry cereal**

Use the lesser amount of water for finer grains. Using the same method as given on 178 for Finely Milled Cereals, cook, covered, 40 to 60 minutes or until translucent and tender.

## HOMINY

**Yield 1 Quart**

Hominy is corn with the hull and germ removed. In an attempt to give it calcium values, it is sometimes also soaked in wood ash lye. It has recently gained favor as an antistrontium absorbent. Hominy can be dried and ground into a coarse flour for baking, cooked as a cereal, or used in any recipe calling for corn. **Hominy grits,** also called **corn grits,** are the broken grains.

To prepare hominy from corn, shell and wash:

> **1 quart dried corn**

Put it into an enamel or stainless steel pan. Cover with:

> **2 quarts water**

Add:

> **2 tablespoons baking soda**

Cover the pan and let this mixture sit 12 hours. Then bring it to a boil in the liquid in which it has soaked. Simmer about 3 hours or until the hulls loosen. If necessary, add water. Drain and plunge into cold water. Rub corn until hulls are removed. Bring to a boil in:

> **2 quarts cold water**

Drain and rub again. Repeat this boiling process again in fresh water, adding:

> **1 teaspoon salt**

Drain once more and serve. Season with:

> **Melted butter**

## BAKED HOMINY

### I. With Ham

**4 Servings**

Preheat oven to 375°.
Combine:

> **¹/₂ cup water**
> **1 can condensed tomato soup**

Or you may use:

> **(2 cups White Sauce I, 383)**

Add:

> **1 cup diced cooked ham**
> **¹/₂ teaspoon salt**
> **¹/₂ teaspoon sugar**
> **¹/₈ teaspoon paprika or pepper**

Drain and add:

> **2¹/₂ cups canned or cooked hominy, above**

Heat these ingredients. Combine:

> **1 cup soft bread crumbs**
> **1 cup shredded cheese**
> **¹/₈ teaspoon paprika**
> **¹/₄ teaspoon salt**

Place half the hominy mixture in a greased baking dish; cover it with half the bread mixture. Dot the top with:

> **1 tablespoon butter**

Repeat the process. Bake until the top is brown, about 12 minutes.

### II. With Bacon

**6 Servings**

Preheat oven to 400°.
Combine and place in a greased baking dish:

> **2 cups drained, cooked hominy, above**
> **1 cup Cheese Sauce, 385**
> **¹/₂ cup minced green pepper, seeds and membrane removed**

Cover the top with:
    **Strips of bacon**
Bake about 20 minutes.


## HOMINY GRITS CHEESE CASSEROLE

Preheat oven to 325°.
Bring to a boil:
    **1 cup quick-cooking hominy
    grits**
    **3 cups milk**
    **1 teaspoon salt**
Add and cook until thickened:
    **2 beaten eggs**
    **3/4 cup milk**
Stir in and blend well:
    **1 cup shredded cheddar or
    garlic-flavored cheese**
    **1/2 cup butter**
    **(1/4 cup chopped chives)**
Bake in a buttered baking dish 45 to
50 minutes. Serve hot.


## CORNMEAL MUSH

                              **4 Servings**
Combine and stir:
    **1 cup white or yellow
    cornmeal**
    **1/2 cup cold water**
    **1 teaspoon salt**
Place in the top of a double boiler:
    **4 cups boiling water or water
    and milk**
Stir cornmeal mixture in gradually.
Cook and stir the mush over quick
heat from 2 to 3 minutes. Steam,
covered, over—not in—hot water 25 to
30 minutes. Stir frequently. Serve with:
    **Maple syrup, honey,
    molasses, milk or cream**
Or pour the mush into a loaf pan to
chill. When firm, slice and sauté in
cooking fat until slightly crisp and
browned. Serve with:
    **Honey, maple syrup or
    molasses**


## POLENTA

Just as our greatest architectural surprise in Italy was to find St. Francis's
first church a log cabin, so were we
amazed to discover that even more
delicious and interesting things are
done with cornmeal in Italy than in
our deep South.

Cheese is sometimes cooked with
it or served sprinkled over it. Or
serve cornmeal with a tomato sauce
or meat sauce.


**I.** Prepare:
    **Cornmeal Mush, above**
Add to it for the last 15 minutes of
cooking:
    **1/8 teaspoon paprika**
    **A few grains red pepper**
    **(1/2 cup shredded cheese)**

**II.** Prepare as above and sauté sliced
mush in:
    **Olive oil or butter**


## TAMALES

                              **24 Tamales**
A curious call used to rend the air on
hot summer nights, one that brought
a sense of adventure to our limited
childhood world. It was the cry of the
Mexican tamale man, whose for-
bidden, hence desirable, wares long
remained a mystery. These varied
leaf-wrapped confections, like individual puddings, may be filled with
spicy mole, with cheese and peppers,
or with almond, citron and coconut.

Tamales steam slowly to allow the
wrapping, either corn husks or banana leaves, to both protect and flavor the contents. Most tamales have
two components not easily obtained
north of the Rio Grande. First, a pas-
tate or tortilla base—that moistened
mixture of unslaked lime and dried

corn which is ground into flour in a matate; and second, a combination of tequesquite and transparent green tomato parings which makes the puddings puff up. The procedure that follows makes a concession to Gringo ingredients.

Remove outer husks from:

**10 ears fresh or dried corn**

Soak the leaves 5 minutes in hot water and drain. Combine:

**2 cups fine-ground cornmeal, preferably masa harina**

**2 teaspoons double-acting baking powder**

**1 teaspoon salt**

Cream in an electric mixer:

**1/3 cup lard**

When it is very fluffy, beat the corn mixture in gradually, about 2 tablespoons at a time, until well combined. Slowly add, beating constantly:

**1 1/2 cups meat or poultry stock**

until a small bit of dough is light enough to float in a glass of water. Lay out enough 4 x 9-inch softened leaves to make 24 tamales, or, if the leaves are narrow, overlap them, see 103. Using a spatula, spread on each leaf about 1 tablespoon of the dough in a rectangle about 3 inches wide and 4 inches long. Have ready as a filling:

**1 1/2 cups Turkey Casserole Mole, 524**

dicing the turkey finely after deep-frying. Or use uncooked:

**(1 1/2 cups filling for Sloppy Joes, 623)**

Drop a tablespoon of the filling in the center of each dough-lined leaf. Wrap by overlapping the edges of the leaves lengthwise and folding up the ends as shown, 103. Layer the folded husks seam side down in a flat-bottomed steamer colander, 281.

Fill the lower pan of the steamer with water to within about 1 inch of the colander base. Bring to a rolling boil and cover tightly. Reduce the heat so the tamales continue to steam 1 to 1 1/2 hours or until the dough is firm enough to pull away easily from the leaves. Serve the tamales in the leaves on a heated platter, allowing about 3 to a person; the leaves are discarded. If tamales are made in advance, resteam them for 1/2 hour. If frozen, bring to room temperature before resteaming.

## BUCKWHEAT GROATS OR KASHA

### I.

4 Servings

Brown in a hot skillet with:

**2 tablespoons hot chicken fat or butter**

**1 cup kasha, 178**

Using a fork, stir until each grain is coated. Add:

**2 1/2 cups boiling water**

Cover and simmer about 30 minutes.

### II.

Combine in a bowl:

**1 cup buckwheat groats or kasha**

**1 egg**

**2 teaspoons salt**

Brown this mixture in:

**2 tablespoons hot chicken fat or butter**

Add:

**2 1/2 cups boiling water**

Cover and simmer 15 minutes.

Preheat oven to 350°.

Sauté:

**1 medium-sized chopped onion**

in:

**1 tablespoon chicken fat or butter**

Add:

**1 cup stock or chicken broth**

and the cooked kasha. Pour into a 2-quart casserole and bake 15 to 20 minutes.

## BULGUR PILAF

**4 Servings**

Bulgur wheat, sometimes called parboiled wheat, has had some bran removed before being cracked into coarse angular fragments. It makes a fine substitute for rice or potatoes. Sauté until translucent:

**¹/₂ cup sliced onions**

in:

**2 tablespoons vegetable oil**

Stir in until the granules are coated:

**1 cup bulgur**

Slowly add and bring to a boil:

**2 cups Poultry Stock, (II, 172), or canned chicken broth**
**(¹/₂ cup chopped celery)**
**¹/₄ teaspoon sweet marjoram**

Cover and simmer about 40 minutes or until tender and fluffy. Add:

**Chopped parsley**
**Season to taste**

## ABOUT DUMPLINGS

This category of cereal dish, sometimes reinforced with protein, is one of winter's comforts when combined with soups or stews. We have also included here dumpling types based on potatoes.

The secret of making light dumplings is to keep them steaming on top of ◗ simmering liquid. And be sure the temperature of the stock, gravy or water in which you are cooking them never exceeds a simmer. Most dumplings are bound together by egg, and the protein in the egg must not be allowed to toughen. Use ample liquid in a wide-topped cooking vessel, giving each ball or drop a chance to expand. ◗ Never crowd the pan.

The minute the batter is floating in the liquid ◗ cover the pot, so the steam can begin functioning. ◗ Do not lift the lid until the dumpling is done. This is not so hard as it sounds if you cover the pan with a tight-fitting heat-resistant glass pie pan or lid, illustrated below, left, so you can watch the swelling of the batter. When the dumplings look fluffy, test them for doneness as you would a cake, by inserting a wooden pick. If it comes out clean, the dumplings are

done. Once you are expert at timing, try simmering dumplings in a ◗ pressure pan. Drop the batter from a spoon into at least 3 cups hot stock or water. Instead of the glass cover, use the pressure pan lid. ◗ Keep the vent open as shown above, right, and cook about 5 minutes. Some good additions to dumpling dough are parsley or other herbs, cheese or grated onion.

We give dumpling amounts in cups, for some people like large dumplings, others small. ◗ A cup of dough will usually yield about eighteen to twenty 1-inch balls, but marrow, liver and meatballs do not expand as do those high in cereal and egg.

## DUMPLINGS

**2 Cups**

◗ Please read About Dumplings, above. Measure, then sift:

**1 cup cake flour**
**2 teaspoons double-acting baking powder**

½ teaspoon salt

Break into a measuring cup:

> 1 egg

Add until the cup is half full:

> Milk

Beat well and stir the liquid slowly into the sifted ingredients. Add more milk if necessary but keep the batter as stiff as possible. You may add:

> (¼ cup finely chopped parsley,
> or 1 tablespoon fresh
> chopped herbs, or
> ½ teaspoon grated onion
> and 3 tablespoons minced
> green peppers)

Bring just to a boil in a 9-inch saucepan:

> 2 or 3 cups stock

To drop dumpling batter from a spoon easily, dip the spoon in stock first; then dip the spoon in the batter, fill it and drop the batter into the stock. Continue doing this until the dumplings are barely touching. Then cover them and simmer 10 minutes. They should be served at once.

## CHEESE DUMPLINGS

To the above recipe for:

> Dumplings

Add:

> 2 tablespoons shredded
> cheese

Cook the dumplings in:

> Tomato juice

## BUTTER DUMPLINGS OR BUTTERKLÖSSE

### About ¾ Cup

Beat until soft:

> 2 tablespoons butter

Beat and add:

> 2 eggs

Stir in:

> 6 tablespoons flour
> ¼ teaspoon salt

Drop the batter from a spoon into ▶ simmering soup and simmer the dumplings, covered, about 8 minutes. You may also simmer them in the soup about 4 minutes in a ✿ pressure cooker, keeping the vent open the entire time.

## NOCKERLN

### About 1 Cup

Beat until creamy:

> ¼ cup soft butter
> 1 egg

Stir in:

> 1 cup all-purpose flour
> ⅛ teaspoon salt

Add gradually, until a firm batter is formed, about:

> 6 tablespoons milk

Cut out the batter with a teaspoon to form small balls. Drop them into boiling water or directly into the clear soup in which they will be served. Reduce the liquid to a ▶ simmer and continue to simmer, covered, for about 10 minutes. For a stew, cook nockerln in water, drain, and drop them into the meat mixture just before serving.

## MATZO MEAL OR CRACKER MEAL DUMPLINGS

### About 2 Cups

These light Passover soup drops are made with the finely crushed crumbs of special unleavened crackers.

Beat until thick and well blended:

> 2 egg yolks
> 3 tablespoons soft chicken fat

Pour over them and beat well:

> ½ cup hot stock

Stir in gently a mixture of:

> ¾ cup matzo meal or cracker
> meal
> ½ teaspoon salt
> (⅛ teaspoon ginger)

(1/8 teaspoon nutmeg)
 (1 tablespoon finely chopped
    parsley)
 (1 tablespoon finely grated
    onion)

Beat until ▶ stiff, but not dry:

 2 egg whites

Fold the egg whites into the cracker mixture and chill, covered, 1/2 to 1 hour. About 1/2 hour before you are ready to serve, form this dough lightly into small balls. If you will wet your hands with cold water, the job will be easier. Drop them into:

 6 cups boiling stock

Reduce heat at once to a ▶ simmer and cook, covered, about 15 minutes.

## FARINA BALLS COCKAIGNE

                            6 Servings

Please read About Dumplings, 182. These remain after many tests the queen of dumplings. Though usually served in soup, they may be simmered in stock or boiling water, then served with meat gravy. Or they may be drained, placed in a greased baking dish and covered with a cup of White Sauce I, 383, to which you may add onion juice and parsley, or chopped chives. Sprinkle the top with 1/4 cup grated Parmesan cheese, dot it with butter and bake the dish in an oven about 15 minutes.

Heat to the boiling point:

 2 cups milk

Add, stir and simmer until thick:

 1/2 cup farina
  1 tablespoon butter
 1/2 teaspoon salt
 1/8 teaspoon paprika
 (1/8 teaspoon nutmeg)

Remove the batter from the heat and beat in vigorously ▶ one at a time:

 2 eggs about 70°

The heat of the mixture will thicken the eggs. Drop the batter, a generous teaspoon at a time, into ▶ simmering soup stock. Cook, covered, about 2 minutes and serve.

## CORNMEAL DUMPLINGS

Cooking in the United States is undoubtedly up-and-coming, but it seemed to us that a peak was reached in a small Kentucky town where we were served chicken with dumplings—the latter light as thistledown. "Oh, yes!" said the hotel proprietress wearily when we exclaimed over them. "They are always like that when our cook is drunk."

Far be it from us to limit your sources of inspiration, but we are convinced that the following recipe will give you superlative results without prior dissipation.

Set a steamer rack into:

 5 or 6 cups simmering corned
    beef stock, consommé or
    any clear soup or stock

Sift together:

 1/2 cup cornmeal
 3/4 cup all-purpose flour
  2 teaspoons double-acting
    baking powder
 1/2 teaspoon salt

Cut in with a fork or pastry blender:

 1 tablespoon butter

Beat together:

 1 egg
 1/3 cup milk

Combine all ingredients until just blended. Drop teaspoonfuls of batter onto the hot, steaming rack. Cover the pan closely. Simmer the dumplings about 20 minutes. Serve them while hot with the soup.

## POTATO DUMPLINGS OR KARTOFFELKLÖSSE

These are light and tender, especially good with beef à la mode or other

roast with gravy. It is traditional to serve them with Sauerbraten.
Boil uncovered in their jackets until tender:

**6 medium-sized mature baking potatoes**

Peel and rice them, see ricer, 186. Add:

**2 eggs**
**1½ teaspoons salt**
**½ cup flour**

Beat the batter with a fork until it is fluffy. Roll it lightly into balls 1 inch in diameter. Many cooks prefer to put a crouton in the center of each ball. Drop the balls into gently boiling salted water and cook about 10 minutes. Drain them well. Melt:

**½ cup butter or drippings**

Stir in:

**¼ cup dry bread crumbs**

Or, if you did not place croutons in the dumplings, prepare:

**(½ cup Croutons, (II, 219)**

Pour the crumbs or croutons over the dumplings.

## GNOCCHI

Serve in place of potatoes or as a soup garnish

### I. With Flour

**4 Servings**

Scald:

**1 cup milk**

Melt in a skillet:

**2 tablespoons butter**

Stir and blend in until smooth:

**2 tablespoons flour**
**2 tablespoons cornstarch**
**½ teaspoon salt**

Stir in the scalded milk. Reduce the heat and add:

**1 egg yolk**
**(½ cup shredded cheese)**

Beat the batter until the egg has thickened and the cheese has melted. Pour it onto a shallow greased platter or pan.
Preheat oven to 375°.
When the batter is cool, cut it into strips 2 inches long. Place the strips in a pan and pour over them:

**Melted butter**

Sprinkle with:

**(Grated cheese)**

Heat them in the oven.
We prefer poaching to baking the batter after it has been cut into strips. Poach in gently boiling water or stock 1 or 2 minutes. Drain the strips and serve with melted butter.

### II. With Farina

**4 Servings**

Scald:

**2 cups milk**

Stir in, all at once:

**¾ cup farina**

Stir the mush over low heat until thick. Remove from heat and beat in until smooth:

**1 tablespoon butter**
**1 egg yolk**
**¼ teaspoon salt**

You may spread the mixture evenly in an 8 x 8-inch pan lined with foil for easier handling. Chill about 3 hours.
Preheat oven to 425°.
Cut the farina mixture into 1½-inch squares. Place the squares in a well-greased ovenproof dish, letting them overlap slightly. Dot with:

**2 tablespoons butter**

Pour over them slowly:

**1 cup Hunter's Sauce, 392, or Aurore Sauce, 387**

Sprinkle the top with:

**6 tablespoons grated Parmesan cheese**

Bake about 10 minutes.

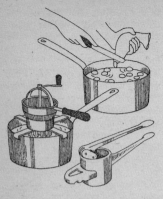

### III. With Potatoes

**6 Servings**

♦ The potatoes must be freshly cooked and used at once. Boil, then put through a ricer as shown above, in the foreground:

    **2 medium-sized peeled potatoes**

Heat to the boiling point:

    **1/2 cup milk**
    **5 tablespoons butter**

Stir in, until the dough forms a ball:

    **1 cup flour**

Remove from heat. Beat in:

    **2 eggs**
    **1 teaspoon salt**
    **1/4 teaspoon paprika**
    **(3 tablespoons grated cheese)**

and the potatoes. Sprinkle the dough with flour. Roll it into sticks 1/2 inch thick. Cut into 1-inch lengths. Drop the gnocchi into simmering salted water. Or force the dough through a pastry bag, cutting into desired lengths as shown above, as the gnocchi fall into the water. Simmer, uncovered, 3 to 5 minutes. Drain. You may place them on a greased pan in a hot oven about 3 minutes; the baking is optional. Serve the gnocchi dressed with melted butter and grated cheese.

## SPÄTZEN, SPÄTZLE OR GERMAN EGG DUMPLINGS

**4 Servings**

Spätzen are good at any time, but they are particularly good served with roast veal or in soup.

Beat:

    **2 eggs**

Combine them well with:

    **1 1/2 cups all-purpose flour**
    **1/2 cup water**
    **1/2 teaspoon salt**
    **1/4 teaspoon double-acting baking powder**
    **(A small grating of nutmeg)**

Drop small bits of the batter from a spoon into simmering salted water or stock. Or put the batter through a colander or a spätzle cutter, opposite left, or use a pastry bag as shown. Spätzen should be very light and delicate. Try a sample; if it is too heavy, add water to the batter. Simmer until they are done. When served with meat, drain, place them in a dish and cover with:

    **Croutons, or 1/4 cup bread crumbs sautéed in 1/2 cup butter**

## ABOUT QUENELLES

Once encountered, never forgotten is the texture of a well-made quenelle. Success lies not only in the mixing but in the very shaping. The ground mixture—of fish, chicken, veal or game—is placed in a large bowl ♦ set in ice, see top of page 187, and worked into a smooth paste with a wooden spoon.

To shape, you may roll quenelles in flour, but this is not the best method. We suggest the following classic spoon-molding, illustrated on 187; the size of the spoon determines the size of the quenelles. They will

expand to about double their original size. Have ready a well-buttered cooking pan and 2 spoons of equal size. Put one spoon in a bowl of hot water. With the other spoon, lightly scoop out enough of the quenelle mixture to just fill it. Invert the other hot, moist spoon over the filled spoon, shaping as shown. ♦ Do not press hard; only smooth the surface. After shaping the point, invert the little egg shapes into the buttered pan. Continue to shape and place the quenelles in neat rows, allowing for expansion space.

To poach the quenelles, pour almost boiling salted water or stock very gently into the pan from the sides so as not to dislodge them. The stock should half cover the quenelles. ♦ Simmer gently 8 to 10 minutes; the water should be barely quivering. As the undersides cook, the quenelles become light, rise and turn over; but the weight of the uncooked portion will keep them half submerged until they are thoroughly done, and floating.

Although not quite so delicate as when served at once, quenelles may be held several hours, poached as described above. Place them gently in a bowl of cold water to cool, then drain off onto a cloth and place on a plate. ♦ Butter the surfaces to keep them from crusting.

If you want very small quenelles for a garnish, cut a parchment paper the size of the pan in which you plan to poach them. Use a decorating bag with a small round tip, fill with the quenelle mixture and force out small units onto the parchment paper in uniformly spaced rows. Lift the whole paper into the pan and, as with larger quenelles, pour the water gently from the side of the pan until the quenelles are only half-covered. As they simmer for 5 to 8 minutes, they will float free and roll over. When floating, skim them off and place in a bowl of warm, mildly salted water until ready to use.

If fancy shapes are desired, pack the quenelle mixture into buttered decorative individual molds. To poach, place the molds in a pan of hot water so that they are completely covered. When the quenelles are cooked, they will release themselves and rise to the surface and then can be removed for serving.

Reheat quenelles by ♦ simmering them in the sauce or soup in which they are to be served.

## POACHED OR BAKED QUENELLES

**6 Servings**

♦ Please read About Quenelles, 186.
Run through the finest blade of a food chopper 3 times:

    **1½ lb. fresh pike, sole, shrimp or lobster**

Place the ground mixture in a large

bowl ◗ set in a bowl of ice. With a wooden spoon, work it to a smooth paste. Gradually work in ◗ by small additions:

**2 egg whites**

Season with:

**Grated fresh nutmeg**
**Salt**
**White pepper**
**Dash of cognac**
**Dash of cayenne or hot pepper sauce**

Mix well. At this point the quenelle mixture should be very firm. Still over ice, add ◗ very, very gradually and mix well with a wooden spoon:

**2 to 2¹/₂ cups well-chilled whipping cream**

The consistency now should be that of a firm whipped cream. To form and poach, follow directions above. Serve with:

**Newburg Sauce, 413**
**Poulette Sauce, 390**

## YORKSHIRE PUDDING COCKAIGNE

**Six 3-Inch Squares**

It was customary to cook this delicious dish in the pan with the roast, letting the drippings fall upon it. As many of us no longer want extravagant drippings, we recommend cooking Yorkshire pudding separately in the hot oven required to puff it up almost instantly. Serve it from the dish in which it was cooked, cut into squares. In Yorkshire it is served before the meat course as a hefty pudding. We substitute it for the usual starch served with a main course.
◗ Have all ingredients at 75°.
Stir into a bowl:

**⁷/₈ cup flour**
**¹/₂ teaspoon salt**

Make a well in the center, into which pour:

**¹/₂ cup milk**
**¹/₂ cup water**

Stir in the liquid. Beat until fluffy and add:

**2 eggs**

Continue to beat until large bubbles rise to the surface. Let stand covered and refrigerated at least 1 hour and beat again ◗ after bringing it back to 70°.
Preheat oven to 400°.
Have ready a hot ovenproof dish about 9 x 13 inches, containing about ¹/₄ cup ◗ hot beef drippings or melted butter. Pour in the batter. It should be about ¹/₂ inch high. Bake the pudding 20 minutes. ◗ Reduce the heat to 350° and bake about 10 to 15 minutes longer. Serve at once.

## ABOUT RICE

"May your rice never burn" is the New Year's greeting of the Chinese. "May it never be gummy" is ours. So many people complain to us about the variability of their results in rice cookery. Like flour, the rice itself may have more or less moisture in its makeup. In Japan the standard ratio is 8 cups of water to 8 cups of rice for the first six weeks after harvest. The amount of water then rises steadily. And when the rice is 11 months old, 8 cups of rice need 10 cups of water.

Not only is there moisture variability in rice, but the type must also be reckoned with. Brown rice, which retains its bran coat and germ, is much slower to tenderize, although more valuable nutritionally, than highly polished white rice.

There are also differences in the grain hybrids. Use short- or medium-grain types—which cook up tender and moist—in recipes calling for sauces, rings, croquettes and puddings. Long-grain types are best for salads, soups and main dishes, where each grain should be separate and fluffy. Also on the market are pre-processed rices; follow the directions on the label. Some of these that are parboiled before milling have greater nutritive value than polished white rice. Wild rice is not a true rice. The seed comes from a strictly American plant and needs its own recipes, see 198.

♦ To keep rice white when cooking in hard water, add 1 teaspoon lemon juice or 1 tablespoon vinegar to the cooking water.

♦ One cup raw rice equals 3 cups when cooked. One cup brown rice yields 3 to 4 cups cooked rice. If using preprocessed rice, the volume will be less, about 1 to 2 cups cooked for 1 cup uncooked. This is also true for recipes in which rice is browned in a skillet, with or without fat, prior to cooking it with moisture. But this browning helps to keep the grains separate and does contribute to good flavor.

## BOILED RICE

**6 to 7 Servings**

**I.** Bring to a ♦ rolling boil:

>   **2 to 2¹/₂ cups water, stock or consommé**

Use the larger amount for brown rice. Add:

>   **³/₄ teaspoon salt**

You may add:

>   **(1 tablespoon melted butter)**

to the rice, before cooking, to keep it from sticking to the pot. Stir slowly into the water, so as not to disturb the boiling:

>   **1 cup white or brown rice**

Cover and cook over slow heat. White rice will take from 25 to 30 minutes, brown from 40 to 50. If the rice becomes too dry, add ¹/₄ cup or more ♦ boiling water. When the grains have swelled to capacity, uncover the pot for about the last 5 minutes of cooking. Continue to cook the rice over ♦ very low heat, shaking the pot from time to time until the grains have separated. Or fluff the cooked rice with a fork. Enliven the above by cooking with the rice:

>   **(Chopped celery)**
>   **(Chopped scallions)**
>   **(Chopped spinach)**
>   **(Grated carrots)**

**II.** A moist Oriental-type rice.

**3 Servings**

Wash and drain:

>   **¹/₂ cup short- or medium-grain rice**

Place in a deep, heavy kettle with:

>   **1¹/₂ cups cold water**

Boil 5 minutes or until most of the surface water is gone and air bubbles can be seen on the surface of the rice. ♦ Reduce the heat and continue to cook ♦ covered about 20 minutes longer. Remove from heat and let the rice stand covered about 20 minutes more. It is then ready to serve.

## RICE RING OR MOLD

A molded rice ring, shown filled in the chapter heading, is a handsome way to enclose the food comprising your main course. For color, include chopped parsley with the cooked rice.

**I.**

**6 Servings**

Preheat oven to 350°.

Boil:

>   **1 cup short- or medium-grain rice, 206**

Season with:

>   **¹/₂ teaspoon grated nutmeg**

Place in a well-greased 7-inch ring mold. Melt and pour over it:

**¼ cup butter**

You may add:

**(¾ cup coarsely chopped
blanched almonds)**

Set the mold in a pan of hot water. Bake the rice for about 20 minutes. Loosen the edges and invert the contents of the mold onto a platter. Fill the center with:

> **Creamed Chicken, 257
> Creamed Mushrooms, 328,
> or a creamed or buttered
> vegetable**

## II.

We have had success packing hot cooked rice firmly into a well-buttered ring mold. Rest it 3 or 4 minutes and then turn it out onto the serving platter to be filled with the hot entreé. Do not use this method if egg is called for in the recipe—use instead I, above.

## MUSHROOM RICE RING

**6 Servings**

No need to bake this mold.
Boil:

**1 cup short- or medium-
grain rice, 189**

Grind, chop fine or ↀ blend:

**½ to 1 lb. mushrooms**

Sauté them 2 or 3 minutes in:

**2 tablespoons butter**

Add:

**¼ cup hot stock or water**

Combine the mushrooms and rice.
Add:

**(¾ cup coarsely chopped
blanched almonds)
Season to taste**

Press the rice firmly into a greased 7-inch ring mold and let stand 3 or 4 minutes. Invert the rice onto a plat-

ter. Fill the center with a buttered vegetable, creamed fish, etc.

## CHEESE RICE RING

**3 Servings**

Preheat oven to 350°.
Combine:

**1½ cups Boiled Rice, 189
1 beaten egg
2 tablespoons olive oil or
melted butter
¼ cup milk
⅓ cup shredded sharp cheese
¼ tablespoon grated onion
1 teaspoon Worcestershire
sauce
¼ teaspoon salt
3 tablespoons chopped
parsley**

Grease a 7-inch ring mold. Fill it with the rice mixture. Bake it, set in a pan of hot water, about 45 minutes.

## RICE AND HAM RING

**6 Servings**

Preheat oven to 375°.
Combine:

**2 cups Boiled Rice, 189
1 cup diced cooked ham**

Combine and beat:

**1 egg
⅔ cup condensed mushroom
soup
½ cup milk
¼ teaspoon salt
(½ teaspoon dried basil)**

Grease a 9-inch ring mold. Place in it layers of rice and ham. Pour the liquid ingredients over them. Sprinkle the top with:

**1 cup crushed potato chips or
bread crumbs**

Bake the mold in 1 inch of hot water about ½ hour. Invert it onto a platter. Fill the center with:

**A cooked vegetable: carrots
and peas, or green beans**

## RICE BAKED IN CHICKEN STOCK

**6 to 7 Servings**

Preheat oven to 375°.
Sauté:

**¹/₂ chopped onion**

in:

**¹/₄ cup butter**

until translucent. Add and stir until
well coated:

**1 cup long-grain rice or
brown rice**

Add:

**2 cups boiling chicken stock
or broth**

Cover and bake 20 to 25 minutes.
Gently mix with the rice:

**2 tablespoons melted butter**

Serve the rice at once.

## BAKED GREEN RICE

**3 Servings**

Outstanding alone or as a stuffing for
breast of veal. This amount will fill a
7-inch ring mold.
Preheat oven to 325°.
Beat:

**1 egg**

Add and mix well:

**1 cup milk
¹/₂ cup finely chopped parsley
1 finely chopped clove garlic
1 small minced onion
2 cups Boiled Rice, 189
¹/₂ cup shredded sharp cheese
or 2 tablespoons butter
¹/₈ teaspoon curry powder
Salt to taste**

Place these ingredients in a baking
dish, into which has been poured:

**2 tablespoons olive oil**

Bake about 30 minutes.

## BAKED PINEAPPLE RICE

**6 Servings**

This versatile dish may be served
with baked ham or fried chicken or as
a dessert with cream.
Preheat oven to 350°.
Boil:

**1 cup rice, 189**

Drain, then cut into pieces:

**3¹/₂ cups cubed pineapple**

Place one-third of the rice in a buttered baking dish. Cover with half the
pineapple. Repeat the layer of rice
and pineapple. Place the last third of
the rice on top. Dot each layer with:

**1¹/₂ tablespoons butter
¹/₄ cup brown sugar**

Use in all 5¹/₂ tablespoons butter and
³/₄ cup sugar.
Pour over all:

**³/₄ cup pineapple juice**

Bake the rice covered about 30 minutes.

## CURRIED RICE

**3 Servings**

An unusual and delicious rice dish.
Its popularity is undoubtedly due to
the restraint with which the spice
is used.
Pour:

**2 cups hot water**

over:

**¹/₂ cup rice**

Place the rice where it will remain hot,
but will not cook, about 45 minutes.
Preheat oven to 350°.
Add to the rice:

**¹/₂ cup drained, chopped
tomatoes
³/₄ teaspoon salt
¹/₄ cup finely sliced onion
¹/₄ cup sliced green peppers
2 tablespoons melted butter
³/₄ teaspoon curry powder**

Bake these ingredients in a baking

dish 1 1/2 hours or until down. Stir them from time to time. At first, there will be a great preponderance of liquid, but gradually the rice will absorb it. Remove the dish from the oven while the rice is still moist. Good served with beer.

## CHEESE RICE

**6 to 7 Servings**

A good dish to serve with a cold supper.
Boil:

> 1  cup rice, 189

When the water is nearly absorbed, add:

> 1/2 to 3/4 cup or more shredded cheese
> 1/4 teaspoon paprika
> A few grains cayenne

Add:

> 1 cup condensed tomato or mushroom soup

Stir the rice over low heat until the cheese is melted.

## RICE WITH SPINACH AND CHESTNUTS

**6 to 8 Servings**

Preheat oven to 350°.
Combine:

> 1 cup Boiled Rice, 189
> 1 cup cooked chopped spinach
> 1 cup Boiled Chestnuts, 313
> 1/2 to 1 cup shredded cheese

Cover with:

> Au Gratin II, (II, 221)

Bake about 35 minutes or until thoroughly heated. Before serving, garnish with:

> Sprigs of watercress and ribbons of pimiento

## BACON AND RICE CUSTARD

**4 Servings**

Preheat oven to 325°.
Sauté until partly done:

> 8  slices bacon

Line each of 4 muffin tins with 2 slices of bacon. Fill them with the following mixture. Combine:

> 2  cups Boiled Rice, 189
> 1  beaten egg
> 2  tablespoons cream
> 1  tablespoon melted butter
> 1  tablespoon grated onion
> 1  tablespoon chopped parsley
> 1/8 teaspoon salt
> 1/8 teaspoon paprika

Bake until the custard is firm, about 1/2 hour. Serve with:

> Tomato or other sauce

## CHINESE FRIED RICE

**6 Servings**

The rice for this recipe must be ▸ cooked, fluffy, and prepared at least one day before use. Heat in a heavy skillet:

> 1/4 cup vegetable oil

Toss in it:

> 3 cups Boiled Rice, 189

until hot and golden. Add:

> 4 minced scallions
> 3/4 teaspoon salt
> (1/2 cup julienned cooked roast pork or ham or 1 cup diced cooked shrimp)

When these ingredients are well mixed, hollow a center in the rice. Break:

> 3 eggs

into the hollow and scramble until semicooked, then stir into the rice mixture. Sprinkle with:

> 1 1/2 tablespoons soy sauce
> (1/4 cup minced coriander leaves)

and serve with:

> Podded Peas, 339

## ITALIAN RICE OR RISOTTO ALLA MILANESE

**8 to 10 Servings**

This dish needs fairly constant watching for about 20 minutes and ◗ must be served at once to prevent gumminess. Melt in a heavy pan:

**¼ cup Clarified Butter, 396**

Sauté in it, until golden:

**1 small minced onion**

Add and stir well with a wooden spoon until all the butter is absorbed:

**2 cups rice**

Have ready:

**8 to 10 cups hot beef or chicken stock**
**(½ cup Italian white wine)**

After the rice is well coated with the fat, add 1 cup of the stock. Continue to stir, adding about two-thirds of the hot stock over a 10-minute period. Dissolve in a little of the stock:

**(A pinch of saffron or**
**½ teaspoon fennel seed)**

Continue to stir and add stock about 5 to 8 minutes longer, when the rice should have absorbed all of the liquid. ◗ Do not let it dry out.

**Season to taste**

Place the rice in a hot serving dish. Pour over it and mix:

**¼ cup melted butter**
**(Sautéed chicken livers and giblets)**

Sprinkle over it:

**1 cup grated aged Parmesan cheese**

## SPANISH RICE

**3 to 4 Servings**

Sauté until crisp:

**3 slices bacon, minced**

Remove the bacon. Stir and cook in the drippings until browned:

**½ cup rice**

Add and cook until golden:

**½ cup thinly sliced onions**

Add the bacon and:

**1¼ cups canned tomatoes**
**½ teaspoon salt**
**1 teaspoon paprika**
**1 seeded and minced green pepper**
**(1 pressed clove garlic)**

Steam the rice in a double boiler about 1 hour. Stir it frequently. Add water or stock if the rice becomes too dry. It may be served with:

**Cheese Sauce, 385**

## ROMBAUER RICE DISH

**4 Servings**

Freely varied each time it is made, but in such demand that we shall try to write a general rule for it. Boil:

**½ cup rice, 189**

Prepare:

**Veal stew: 1½ lb. meat, 590**

Pare, slice and add the last 20 minutes of cooking:

**½ parsnip**
**2 carrots**
**2 onions**

and:

**6 ribs celery, sliced**
**3 sprigs parsley**

Drain the stew. To make the gravy, see 382. There should be about 3 cups of stock. If there is not enough, add chicken bouillon, a bouillon or vegetable cube and water, rice water, or sweet or sour cream to make up the difference. If there is not enough fat, add butter. The better the gravy, the better the dish. Combine rice, meat, vegetables and gravy and reheat. Garnish with:

**Parsley**

You may add a dash of curry powder and some herbs—thyme, basil, etc.,

(II, 265). You may use leftover meat, gravy and vegetables. You may serve the stew in a baking dish, au gratin or in individual baking dishes.

A deluxe dish is this recipe made with rice, chicken, sauce—with cream and chicken gravy—and blanched slivered almonds. An everyday dish is this recipe made with corned beef and some canned soup to substitute for gravy.

## PILAF

#### 4 Servings

A rice dish combined with shrimp or chicken livers, etc. It has many variations, some with grits, millet, or dried or split peas to replace the rice.
Boil:

> 2/3 cup long-grain rice, 189

Sauté until golden and add to the rice:

> 3 tablespoons chopped onion

in:

> 1 to 2 tablespoons butter

In a separate pan, simmer:

> 2 1/2 cups tomatoes
> 1/3 teaspoon salt
> 1/4 teaspoon paprika
> 1/2 teaspoon brown sugar

and a Bouquet Garni, (II, 253), of:

> 1/2 bay leaf
> 3 ribs celery with leaves

When the tomato mixture is thick, remove the bouquet garni. Add to the tomato mixture:

> 1 cup cooked shrimp, lobster meat, crab meat, or sautéed chicken livers
> (1/2 cup chopped pecans)

Combine these ingredients with the rice.

> Season to taste

Place the rice in a greased baking dish. Sprinkle with:

> 1/4 cup grated cheese and bread crumbs

Place under a heated broiler to brown.

## PAELLA

#### 8 Servings

If you do not own a paellero, the vessel to which this dish gives its name, you will need a generous lidded casserole in which to cook and serve it. Preheat oven to 350°.
Have ready:

> 2 cups cooked chicken, cut in 1- to 1 1/2-inch pieces
> 4 cups hot chicken stock

Heat until golden in the casserole:

> 1/4 cup olive oil
> 1/2 cup thinly sliced onions

Over moderate heat add, stirring until lightly browned:

> 2 cups rice

Add the hot stock, in which has been dissolved a small quantity of:

> Saffron

Add:

> 2 pressed cloves garlic
> 2 sliced sweet red peppers, seeds and membranes removed
> 1 teaspoon paprika
> 1/4 teaspoon oregano
> Thin slices chorizo or hard Spanish sausage
> Season to taste

Also put in the chicken, arranging it toward the top of the mixture. Cover and bake in a 350° oven about 15 minutes. Add, arranging them attractively on the top:

> Raw shrimp
> Well-scrubbed clams in their shells

Cover and steam about 10 minutes longer. Serve at once.

## FRUIT, NUT AND RICE CASSEROLE

**10 Servings**

Cover with water and soak ½ hour:

    **2 cups dried apricots**

    **1 cup golden raisins**

In the meantime, boil:

    **1 cup rice, 189**

Preheat oven to 375°.

In a skillet, melt:

    **½ cup butter**

Sauté:

    **1 cup minced onion**

    **½ cup chopped green pepper, seeds and membrane removed**

    **(½ teaspoon curry powder)**

Add:

    **(1 cup toasted almonds)**

and the drained, chopped apricots and raisins and cooked rice.

    **Season to taste**

Put into a greased baking dish to bake covered about 30 minutes.

## RICE AND NUT LOAF

**4 Servings**

Serve with broccoli or any green leafy vegetable.

Preheat oven to 375°.

Melt:

    **3 tablespoons butter**

Sauté in it until soft:

    **1 minced onion**

    **1 seeded chopped green pepper, seeds and membrane removed**

Add:

    **1 cup Boiled Rice, 189**

    **⅓ cup bread crumbs**

    **1 cup drained, chopped tomatoes**

    **1 cup chopped or ground walnuts or other nutmeats**

    **1 beaten egg**

    **2 tablespoons chopped parsley**

    **¾ teaspoon salt**

    **¼ teaspoon paprika**

    **(1 teaspoon grated lemon peel)**

Bake these ingredients in a greased baking dish about 30 minutes. Cover the top with:

    **Au Gratin II, (II, 221)**

Brown under a broiler. Serve the loaf with:

    **A tomato sauce**

## RICE LOAF OR CASSEROLE

**I.**

**5 Servings**

Boil:

    **⅔ cup rice, 189**

Line a buttered mold with it. Reserve ½ cup for the top. Cook:

    **1 cup White Sauce II, 383**

Stir in and thicken slightly over low heat:

    **1 egg yolk**

Add:

    **1 cup diced canned salmon, cooked fish or meat**

    **½ cup bread crumbs**

    **1 tablespoon chopped parsley**

    **1 tablespoon chopped onion**

    **½ cup chopped celery**

    **1 teaspoon lemon juice or 1 teaspoon Worcestershire sauce**

    **Salt, paprika, nutmeg**

Preheat oven to 375°.

Fill the rice mold and place the reserved rice over the top. Cover with a piece of buttered paper. Set the mold in a pan of hot water and bake or steam until set, about 30 minutes. Invert the loaf onto a platter. Garnish it with:

    **Sprigs of parsley**

Serve it with:

    **A tomato sauce, or Quick Mushroom Sauce, 395**

**II.**

**6 Servings**

Boil:

2/3 cup rice, 189

There should be about 2 cups cooked rice.

Drain:

1 cup canned tuna fish

Break the tuna into pieces with a fork.

Cook:

2 cups White Sauce II, 383

Add:

1/2 teaspoon salt—more if rice is unsalted

1/2 teaspoon paprika

A few grains red pepper

Reduce the heat to low. Stir in until melted:

2 cups shredded cheese

Preheat oven to 400°.

Place in a baking dish alternate layers of rice, fish and sauce. Dot the top with:

Au Gratin II, (II, 221)

Bake the dish until the crumbs are brown. If preferred, bake the ingredients in a ring, invert and serve with the center filled with Sautéed Mushrooms, 328.

## VEGETABLE RICE OR JAMBALAYA

**4 Servings**

Ideal for a picnic supper.

Boil:

2/3 cup rice, 189

Sauté lightly in butter:

3/4 to 1 lb. mushrooms

Chop and add:

2 medium-sized green peppers, seeds and membrane removed

1 medium-sized onion

1 rib celery

2 diced pimientos

1 1/4 cups fresh or drained canned tomatoes

Season these ingredients with:

3/4 teaspoon salt

A few grains cayenne

1/2 teaspoon paprika

Add:

1/4 cup melted butter

These proportions may be varied.

Preheat oven to 300°.

Combine the rice and other ingredients. Place in a greased baking dish. Bake ◗ covered 30 to 40 minutes. The sautéed mushroom caps and the pimientos may be used to garnish the top of the dish. They are highly decorative with a bunch of parsley in the center.

## JAMBALAYA WITH MEAT OR FISH

**6 to 8 Servings**

Have ready:

3 cups Boiled Rice, 189

Sauté lightly in a saucepan:

2 diced slices bacon

Add and sauté until golden:

1/4 cup chopped onion

Stir in:

1 tablespoon flour

Add:

1 cup tomato pulp

1/3 cup water

Bring these ingredients to the boiling point. Stir in the rice and:

2 cups coarsely diced cooked ham, chicken, sausage, tongue, shrimp or crab, alone or in combination

Add:

1/4 teaspoon thyme (Worcestershire sauce)

Season to taste

Stir over very low heat about 10 minutes or heat over boiling water about 1/2 hour. Serve sprinkled with:

Chopped parsley

## CHICKEN JAMBALAYA

**4 to 6 Servings**

Cut into pieces:

> **A young chicken**

Sauté about 5 minutes in:

> **¹/4 cup vegetable oil or butter**

Remove meat from pan. Sauté in the fat, about 3 minutes:

> **¹/3 cup minced onion**
> **¹/2 cup skinned, seeded and chopped tomato**

Stir in:

> **1 diced green pepper, seeds and membrane removed**
> **¹/2 cup diced celery**
> **1 cup rice**

When the rice is well coated with fat, stir in the sautéed chicken. Cover these ingredients well with:

> **About 3 cups boiling water**

Add:

> **1 bay leaf**
> **¹/4 teaspoon thyme**
> **¹/4 cup chopped parsley**
> **1 teaspoon salt**
> **¹/4 teaspoon pepper**

Simmer these ingredients until the chicken is tender and the rice almost done. Add:

> **¹/2 lb. finely diced cooked ham**
> **Season to taste**

Dry out the jambalaya by placing it about 5 or 10 minutes in a 350° oven.

## RICE TABLE OR RIJSTTAFEL

**8 Servings**

As this Javanese dish is very filling, it is ideal for suppers served with ice-cold beer, followed by salad. It may be made as elaborate or as simple as you wish. If you object to coconut or do not like the flavor of curry, do not discard this dish. Instead, carry out the idea of the rijsttafel by substituting creamed chicken, ragoût fin or a lamb stew you do like, followed by

vegetables and condiments served in some attractive way.

Grate:

> **A fresh coconut, or use about 2 cups unsweetened canned coconut**

Heat but do not scald:

> **4 cups milk or coconut milk, (II, 244)**

Add the coconut. Let these ingredients stand 2 hours in a cool place. Melt:

> **1 tablespoon butter**

Sauté in it, until light brown:

> **¹/2 cup finely chopped onion**

Add:

> **Chopped gingerroot: 2-inch length**
> **1 chopped clove garlic**
> **1¹/2 tablespoons curry powder**

Strain and add the coconut. Add to the cooled, strained milk:

> **1 cup milk or Poultry Stock, (II, 172)**

With 3 tablespoons of this liquid, mix:

> **1 tablespoon flour**
> **1 tablespoon cornstarch**

Heat the remaining liquid and stir the starch paste into it. Cook and stir the sauce until it is hot and thickened.

> **Season to taste**

Place half the sauce in the top of a double boiler. Add the coconut-curry mixture and:

> **3 cups cooked diced chicken, shrimp, fish, veal, sweetbreads or mushrooms, either alone or in combination**

Heat remaining sauce in another double boiler.

Have ready and rather dry and flaky:

> **2 cups Boiled Rice, 189**

The ceremony of serving this dish is part of its charm. In Java one refers to it by the separate dishes, as a "One-boy curry" or a "Twenty-two-boy curry," each boy representing one dish. Pass the rice first. Spread it generously over your plate, forming a base or "table." Pass the food in the sauce next. Follow this with:

> **Onion rings**
> **Sieved hard-cooked eggs**
> **Grated peanuts or toasted almonds**
> **Grated coconut, if there is none in the sauce**
> **Relish**
> **Chutney, raisins, preserved ginger or kumquats**
> **Halved fried bananas**
> **Mixed pickles**

Now pass the extra heated sauce.
To simplify matters, the last four or five may be served from one large condiment dish. Servings from these various dishes are placed on the rice table. Cut through the layers and proceed to feast.

## ABOUT WILD RICE

Wild rice is the seed from a grass growing wild in the northern United States, and nutritionally it is closer to wheat than to rice. It remains a luxury because of the difficulty of harvesting. For economy you may combine cooked wild rice with cooked white or brown ice.

One cup of wild rice equals 3 to $3^{1}/_{2}$ cups of cooked wild rice.

## WILD RICE

**4 Servings**

Wash well in several waters, pouring off the foreign particles from the top:
> **1 cup wild rice**

Drain it. Stir it slowly into:
> **4 cups boiling water**
> **1 teaspoon salt**

Cook without stirring about 40 minutes or until tender.

## WILD RICE RING

**4 Servings**

Cook as directed above:
> **1 cup wild rice**

You may add:
> **1 pressed clove garlic**

When the rice is tender, add:
> **$^{1}/_{4}$ cup butter**
> **$^{1}/_{2}$ teaspoon poultry seasoning or freshly grated nutmeg**
> **(1 cup sautéed onions and mushrooms)**
> **($^{1}/_{4}$ cup dry sherry)**

Preheat oven to 350°.
Place rice in a well-greased 7-inch ring mold set in a pan of hot water in the oven. Bake about 20 minutes. Loosen the edges with a knife, invert the contents onto a platter and fill the center with one or more of the following:

> **Creamed Mushrooms, 328**
> **Chicken Livers Lyonnaise, 639**
> **Sautéed Onions, 335**
> **Snow Peas, 339, and**
> **Water Chestnuts, 372**

## "LONG RICE" OR HARUSAME

This is not a rice at all, but an oriental pasta made of soybean powder, also known as bean thread noodles, Saifun, or dried cellophane noodles. We infinitely prefer its native name of "Spring Rain."
To prepare, pour:
> **Boiling water**

over:
> **Harusame**

Let stand 15 minutes or until it is limp. Cut into desired lengths and drain. Add as a garnish for soup, meat or vegetables. It should then ▶ simmer during the last 15 minutes of the cooking of these foods.

# COOKING PASTAS

Freshly made pastas are an incomparable treat. Noodles are those most frequently made in the home, as they do not require the difficult-to-purchase high-gluten flours that other pasta forms demand. To make noodles and casings for filled pastas like Ravioli, 204, Kreplach, 135, and Won Ton, 136, see Noodle Dough, opposite.

Because pasta shapes are so variable we give the weight rather than the volume for amounts to be cooked. And at meals where pasta is the predominant ingredient of the main dish, the individual serving is more generous than the usual meat or vegetable serving, so we allow ♦ ¼ pound of dry pasta per serving. For more detailed information, please see Equivalents and Substitutions, (II, 287).

All pastas should be added ♦ gradually to a large quantity of rapidly boiling water so that the boiling is not disturbed. As in the cooking of all cereals, it is essential that the outer surfaces be penetrated as quickly as possible. This requires a kettle large enough to accommodate about 7 quarts of rapidly boiling water for a pound of pasta. Add 1 tablespoon salt and 1 tablespoon olive oil. Long pastas are immersed as shown below; the dry material softens as it is gradually lowered into continuously boiling water, until all the pasta floats

free. No matter which pasta you are cooking ♦ do not overcook. The timing can be gauged only by tasting—not once, but several times. If the noodles are very thin or freshly made, a few minutes suffice. The perfect state any Italian recognizes as *al dente* is reached when ♦ no taste of raw flour remains and the pasta still offers slight resistance to the bite. Thick forms of commercial pastas with uncertain shelf histories may need cooking as long as 15 or 20 minutes. When the *al dente* state is reached, remove the pasta from the water with a pasta scoop similar to the one shown in the chapter heading and let the pasta drip-dry momentarily over the pot before releasing it into a large warm buttered bowl or spooning it with a pasta server, shown also in the chapter heading in the foreground. When all the pasta is drained and tossed in butter, portion it into hot bowls; served thus without a sauce, it is called *al burro*. Pass the grated cheese. For ways to garnish and serve pastas, see suggestions for Boiled Noodles, 200, Pasta Sauces, 209, and Pasta Fillings, 208.

# WHITE OR GREEN NOODLE DOUGH OR FETTUCINE

### About ½ Pound Dry or 4 Cups Cooked Noodles

If you are a beginner, do not try to make noodles in damp weather. This dough may be used for Won Ton, Ravioli or Kreplach cases, but cut it into squares without allowing it to dry, and fill at once. To fold and cook, see individual recipes.

On a large pastry board or marble tabletop make a well, (II, 366), of:

**⅔ cup all-purpose flour**

Drop into it:

**1 egg**

barely combined with:

>    1 **tablespoon water**
>    ½ **teaspoon salt**
>    1 **teaspoon oil**

Work the mixture with your hands, folding the flour over the egg until the dough can be rolled into a ball and comes clean from the hands. If you want to make green noodles, add at this point:

>    (2 **to 4 tablespoons very well**
>    **drained and dried, finely**
>    **chopped cooked spinach)**

Knead the dough as for bread, (II, 298), about 10 minutes. Then let it stand, covered, about 1 hour. Now roll the dough, stretching it a little more with each roll. Between each rolling and stretching, continue to sprinkle it with flour to keep the dough from sticking to the pin or board or developing holes. Repeat this procedure about 10 times or until the dough is paper-thin and translucent. Let it dry about 30 minutes. You can hang it as the Neapolitans do, like laundry, with a piece of foil or plastic underneath. Before it becomes brittle, roll it into a scroll and cut it on the bias as shown below into strips of any width you prefer: ⅛ inch for soup or 2 inches for lasagne. Allow about 3 tablespoons uncooked noodles for each quart of soup. Cook the noodles in ▶ rapidly boiling salted water about 10 minutes. Drain and add them to the soup before serving.

## BOILED NOODLES, SPAGHETTI, MACARONI AND OTHER PASTAS

**5 Servings**

Please read about Cooking Pastas, 199. Drop:

>    2 **cups pasta**

into:

>    3 **quarts boiling, salted**
>    **water—½ teaspoon salt to**
>    **the quart—or chicken**
>    **stock, consommé, etc.**

Boil 8 to 10 minutes, depending on size and your taste preference. Drain in a colander and immediately put back into the cooking pot, set over very low heat and toss generously in:

>    **Melted butter**

**I.** If served at once without sauce, they may be called **Fettucine al Burro.** With the pasta, pass:

>    (**Grated Asiago, Romano or**
>    **Parmesan cheese)**

**II.** You may prefer instead of the butter to mix with them:

>    ¾ **cup cultured sour cream**

Add:

>    (3 **tablespoons chopped**
>    **parsley)**
>    (2 **tablespoons poppy seed)**

or:

>    (½ **cup blanched slivered**
>    **almonds sautéed in**
>    **1 tablespoon butter)**

**III.** Or make **Good Friday Noodles.** Add:

>    **Buttered Croutons, (II, 219)**

and pass a bowl of:

>    **Stewed prunes**

**IV.** Or prepare:

>    **Welsh Rarebit I or II,**
>    **240–241**

and when hot, stir in:

> 1/2 **lb. freshly cooked, drained**
> **noodles**
> 1 **to 2 cups diced cooked ham**
> **or cooked smoked tongue**

## NOODLE RINGS

### I.

**4 Servings**

Boil in salted water:

> 1 1/2 **cups Noodles, 199**

Drain them. Beat:

> • 2 **egg yolks**
> 1/2 **cup milk**
> 3/4 **tablespoon melted butter**
> 1/4 **teaspoon salt**
> 1/8 **teaspoon paprika**
> (1/2 **cup shredded cheese)**
> (1/8 **teaspoon nutmeg)**

Combine this mixture with the noodles.
Preheat oven to 350°.
Beat until stiff ♦ but not dry:

> 2 **egg whites**

Fold lightly into the noodles. Butter a 7-inch ring mold or individual ring molds. Fill with the noodle mixture. Place in a pan of hot water and bake until done, about 45 minutes for a large mold or 30 minutes for the small ones. Invert the contents of the molds on hot plates and fill the centers with:

> **Creamed spinach, peas,**
> **mushrooms, hash, stewed**
> **tomatoes or Chicken à la**
> **King, 257**

### II.
Made with cheese, this is our favorite. Follow the recipe above. Use in all:

> 3/4 **cup milk**

Add to the noodle mixture before folding in the egg whites:

> 1 1/2 **teaspoons Worcestershire**
> **Sauce, (II, 688)**

> 1/2 **tablespoon catsup or**
> **sautéed onions**
> 3/4 **cup grated cheddar cheese**
> **or cottage cheese**

### III.

**10 Servings**

Use a 9-inch ring. For 5 servings prepare half the recipe and use a 7-inch ring. Boil in salted water:

> 2 **cups fine Noodles, 199**

Drain. Beat and pour over the noodles:

> 4 **egg yolks**
> 1/4 **teaspoon paprika**
> 1/2 **cup melted butter**

Preheat oven to 350°.
Whip until stiff:

> 4 **egg whites**
> 1/4 **teaspoon salt**

Beat until stiff:

> 1 **cup whipping cream or**
> 1 **cup cultured sour cream**

Fold the egg whites and the cream lightly into the noodle mixture. Fill a well-greased ring. Place it in a pan of hot water. Bake until firm, about 1 hour or more. Invert the ring and fill as above.

## FRIED NOODLES

To be served instead of a starchy vegetable or as a garnish on vegetables or other dishes, notably Chinese.
Boil in salted water about 5 minutes:

> **Thin noodles**

Place them in a colander and rinse with cold water to rid them of surface starch. Drain, separate and dry well. In deep fat heated to 390°, fry a small amount at a time, until they are a delicate brown. Drain on paper toweling. Sprinkle lightly with:

> **Salt**

Keep them hot or reheat in a 400° oven.

## NOODLE BASKETS

For these you need a tea strainer about 3 inches in diameter and a second strainer about 3/8 inch smaller that fits into it but leaves space for the swelling of the noodles. Prepare:

**Noodle Dough, 199**

Before the dough is dry, fold it over and cut it into 1/4-inch strips. Dip the strainers in hot fat to keep the noodles from sticking. Line the larger strainer with 2 layers of noodles in crisscross effect. Snip off the ragged edges. Place the smaller strainer over the noodle basket. Fry the noodle basket in deep fat heated to 390° until lightly browned. Remove it carefully from the strainers and fry the next one. You may fill the fried baskets at once with creamed food, etc., or you may cool and reheat them later by dipping briefly in hot fat without the strainers. Drain on paper toweling.

## HAM NOODLES

**6 Servings**

This recipe is capable of wide interpretation and its proportions may be varied.
Preheat oven to 350°.
Have ready:

**3 cups Boiled Noodles, 200**

Grease a baking dish. Place in it layers of noodles sprinkled with:

**3/4 cup diced or ground cooked ham**
**(1/2 cup shredded cheese)**
**(1/2 cup shredded green pepper and diced celery)**

Combine:

**1 1/2 cups milk**
**1 or 2 eggs**
**1/4 teaspoon paprika**
**1/4 to 1/2 teaspoon salt—omit if the ham is very salty**

Pour this over the noodles. Cover with:

**Bread or cracker crumbs**
Bake about 45 minutes.

## LEFTOVER NOODLE DISH

**I.** Follow the previous recipe. Substitute for the ham:

**Diced cooked roast beef, chicken, crab, shrimp, chipped beef, mushrooms and other vegetables**

## TUNA, NOODLE AND MUSHROOM SOUP CASSEROLE

**4 Large Servings**

An excellent emergency dish.
Preheat oven to 450°.
Have ready:

**2 cups Boiled Noodles, 200**

Drain:

**1 can tuna fish: 7 oz.**

Separate it with a fork into large flakes. Do not mince it. Grease an ovenproof dish. Arrange a layer of noodles, then sprinkle it with fish and so on, with noodles on top. Pour over this mixture:

**1 cup condensed mushroom soup**

Season the soup with:

**Worcestershire sauce, curry powder or dry sherry**
**1/4 cup chopped parsley**

Cover the top with:

**Buttered cornflakes or cracker crumbs**

Bake until the top is brown.

## ROMANIAN NOODLE AND PORK CASSEROLE

**8 Servings**

Preheat oven to 350°.
Have ready:

**1 lb. fine Boiled Noodles, 200**

Combine:

**1 lb. cooked ground pork**

**1 slice bread, soaked in milk
and wrung out
1 minced leek
1/2 to 1 teaspoon fennel seeds
1/4 cup chopped parsley
1 teaspoon salt
1/2 teaspoon pepper**

In a shallow large baking pan, arrange alternate layers of noodles and pork mixture, ending with noodles. Beat together:

**4 eggs
2/3 cup cream
1/4 cup grated hard cheese**

Pour this mixture over the noodles and dot with:

**1/4 cup butter**

Bake about 45 minutes.

## QUANTITY NOODLE AND CHEESE LOAF

**18 Servings**

Boil in salted water:

**5 cups Noodles, 199**

and drain them. Have ready:

**1 lb. shredded sharp cheese
1 1/2 cups dry bread crumbs**

Mix together half the cheese and 1 cup of the crumbs with:

**1/4 cup melted butter**

Mix the rest of the crumbs, the cheese and the noodles with:

**7 beaten eggs
1 3/4 cups milk
3 tablespoons grated onion
1/3 cup chopped pimiento
1/3 cup chopped green pepper,
seeds and membrane
removed
1 teaspoon salt
1/2 teaspoon white pepper
(1 cup finely chopped celery)
(1/2 cup sliced stuffed olives)**

Preheat oven to 325°.

Divide the mixture into two parts and place in two 9 x 9-inch baking pans.

Cover with the cheese, butter and crumb mixture. Bake about 25 minutes or until the custard sets and the top is golden brown. To test the custard for doneness, see (II, 507).

Serve with:

**Quick Mushroom Sauce,
395, Marinara Sauce, 403,
or Creole Sauce, 394**

## LASAGNE

**16 Servings**

These 2-inch wide, rather thick noodles often have a wavy ridge along one or both edges.

▶ Please read about Cooking Pastas, 199. Have ready a double portion of:

**Italian Meat Sauce for
Pasta I, 402**

Also have ready:

**3/4 lb. Ricotta cheese
1/3 lb. thinly sliced or
crumbled Mozzarella
cheese
1/2 lb. grated Parmesan cheese**

Cook barely to the *al dente* stage, 199, in salted water:

**3/4 lb. lasagne noodles**

using about 2 tablespoons olive oil in the boiling water. Stir occasionally. Drain and separate the lasagne strips. Preheat oven to 350°.

Spread a thin layer of the sauce, then a layer of pasta, in each of two 13 x 9 x 2-inch baking dishes. Cover with a sprinkling of each of the three cheeses. Spoon another layer of sauce over all, then another layer of pasta placed crisscross, and a layer of cheeses. Continue to build layers, reserving enough sauce to cover the final layer of pasta and enough Parmesan cheese to dust the top. Bake about 30 to 40 minutes. Let stand briefly before cutting and serving.

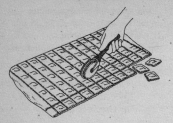

## RAVIOLI

If you make this filled pasta often, use a wooden roller such as the one shown in the foreground of the chapter heading, 175. Otherwise roll out a sheet of:

**Noodle Dough, 199**

Place the sheet on a floured board and divide into 2 equal oblongs. Depending on how large you prefer your ravioli, partly score half the strips to indicate 2-inch or 3-inch squares. Place in the center of each square:

**2 to 3 teaspoons Pasta Filling I, II or III, 208**

Place the unscored strips of pasta over the scored strips and with your fingers press down to seal the filling firmly on four sides in separate little mounds. With a pie jagger, first cut along the lengthwise edges of the strips to reinforce the closures. Then cut between the strips to separate the ravioli as shown above. Put the squares on a rack to dry about 1½ to 2 hours, turning once. Have ready a pot of:

**Boiling water or chicken stock**

**1 tablespoon salt**

Without disturbing the boiling, place about 6 ravioli in the pot. Reduce the heat at once and simmer until the pasta is *al dente,* 199. Remove with a skimmer and place them in a heated bowl. Continue cooking the remaining ravioli. Serve covered generously with:

**Melted butter**
**Freshly grated Parmesan cheese or a tomato sauce**

## CANNELLONI OR MANICOTTI

**4 to 5 Servings**

When they are wrapped around fillings and baked in a sauce, the charm of these "channels" or "little muffs" lies in the delicacy and freshness of the dough. The pasta, however, can be made a few hours in advance and refrigerated in foil or plastic to cover and separate the pieces.

Prepare a double portion of:

**Noodle Dough, 199**

After kneading the dough until very smooth, rest it ◗ covered with a cloth 10 minutes. Divide the dough in half. Roll each portion to a ⅛-inch thickness. For Cannelloni, cut into 4 x 4½-inch pieces. For Manicotti, cut into 4 x 6-inch oblongs. In either case, dry thoroughly on a cloth-covered surface; cover with a cloth about 1 hour.

To cook this pasta, have ready a kettle with at least:

**5 quarts boiling salted water**

Drop about 3 pieces at a time into the water so as not to disturb the boiling, and cook almost to the *al dente* stage, 199. Remove with a skimmer and dry quickly on a cloth-covered surface. Preheat oven to 350°.

Place in the center of each piece of cooked pasta:

**A heaping tablespoon Pasta Filling, 208–209**

For Cannelloni, roll into pipelike "channels." For Manicotti, fold up the ends before rolling to make the "little muffs." In either case place them seam side down in a buttered ovenproof dish. Cover generously with:

        **A tomato sauce**
or:

        **Melted butter**
        **A sprinkling of fresh basil**
        **Grated Parmesan cheese or**
        **Allemande Sauce, 390**
Bake about 10 minutes and serve at
once with additional:
        **(Grated Parmesan cheese)**

## PASTA WITH EGG AND CHEESE

                        **8 to 10 Servings**
Not the usual cheese sauce, but an
Italian version. ♦ Please read about
Cooking Pastas, 199.
Boil in salted water:
        **1 lb. spaghetti, macaroni or**
            **noodles, 200**
In the meantime, cook in a small
skillet:
        **2 tablespoons olive oil**
        **6 slices finely cut bacon**
until the bacon is crisp. Add:
        **1/3 cup dry white wine**
and reduce until the wine has evaporated. Beat together:
        **3 eggs**
        **2/3 cup grated mixed**
            **Parmesan and Romano**
            **cheese**
Drain the pasta and return it to the
hot saucepan. Add the egg and cheese
mixture and the hot bacon fat and
bits, stirring them in quickly. The
heat of the pasta will cook the egg
mixture.
        **Season to taste**
Serve immediately.

## BOILED MACARONI WITH CHEESE

                        **4 to 6 Servings**
♦ Please read about Cooking Pas-
tas, 199.
Boil in salted water until tender:
        **1/2 lb. macaroni: 2 cups, 200**

Drain. Return it to the saucepan.
Over low heat stir in:
        **1/2 cup light cream**
Place the macaroni in a dish and
sprinkle with:
        **1/2 cup or more grated cheese**
Serve with any of the Pasta Sauces
on 209–210.

## BAKED MACARONI

                        **4 Servings**
♦ Please read about Cooking Pas-
tas, 199.
Boil in salted water:
        **4 oz. macaroni: 1 cup, 200**
Drain it.
Preheat oven to 350°.
Place layers of macaroni in a buttered
baking dish.
Sprinkle the layers with:
        **1 cup shredded cheddar**
            **cheese**
Beat until blended:
        **1 or 2 eggs**
        **2/3 cup milk**
        **1/4 teaspoon salt**
        **1/8 teaspoon paprika**
            **A few grains cayenne**
        **(1 sliced pimiento)**
        **(1/4 cup chopped green peppers**
            **or 2 tablespoons chopped**
            **parsley)**
        **(1 tablespoon grated onion)**
Pour this mixture over the macaroni.
Sprinkle the top with:
        **Au Gratin III, (II, 221)**
Bake the macaroni about 40 minutes.

## MACARONI WITH TOMATOES, LIVERS, MUSHROOMS AND CHEESE

                        **About 1 1/2 Quarts**
♦ Please read about Cooking Pas-
tas, 199.
Boil in salted water:
        **1/2 lb. macaroni: 2 cups, 200**

Drain. Place in a deep casserole.
While the macaroni is cooking, sauté:

**1/2 lb. mushrooms, 328**

Sauté or boil until tender:

**1/2 cup chicken livers or calf
liver**

Chop the mushrooms and the liver.
Simmer until fairly thick:

**4 cups canned tomatoes**

Strain them. Season with:

**3/4 tablespoon salt**
**1 teaspoon brown sugar**
**A few grains cayenne**
**(1 teaspoon dried basil)**

Sauté:

**1 minced onion**
**(1/2 minced clove garlic)**

in:

**2 tablespoons butter**

Combine these with the other ingredients and pour them over the macaroni. Mix them well with 2 forks.
Sprinkle the top with:

**Grated cheddar cheese**

Preheat oven to 400°.
Bake the macaroni until the cheese is
golden.


## MACARONI WITH SHELLFISH

**4 Servings**

▶ Please read about Cooking Pastas, 199.
Boil in salted water:

**1 1/2 cups macaroni, 200**

Drain it. Sauté:

**1 tablespoon minced onion**

in:

**3 tablespoons butter**

Stir in until blended:

**1 1/2 tablespoons flour**

Stir in until smooth:

**1 1/2 cups milk**
**3/4 cup shredded cheese**
**1 teaspoon Worcestershire
sauce**
**1/2 teaspoon lemon juice**
**1 teaspoon salt**

**1/4 teaspoon paprika**
**A few grains cayenne**

Preheat oven to 350°.
Have ready:

**1 1/2 to 2 cups cleaned shrimp,
oysters or clams**

Place layers of macaroni and fish in a
baking dish. Pour the sauce over
them. Cover the top with:

**Au Gratin III, (II, 221)**

Bake about 30 minutes.


## QUICK SPAGHETTI MEAT PIE

**4 Servings**

Preheat oven to 375°.
Sauté lightly:

**2 cups cubed or ground
cooked meat**
**2 teaspoons grated onion**

in:

**2 tablespoons butter**

Add:

**1/4 cup cream**

Season it with:

**Salt and pepper**
**(1/2 teaspoon basil)**

Place in a greased baking dish:

**1 can spaghetti: 24 oz.**

Make a depression in the center.
Place the meat in it. Sprinkle the top
with:

**Au Gratin III, (II, 221)**

Bake about 25 minutes.


## QUICK SPAGHETTI WITH TUNA,
SALMON OR BEEF

**4 Servings**

Drain and reserve the oil from:

**1 can tuna fish or salmon:
7 oz.**

Sauté in the oil and add to the fish:

**1/3 cup chopped onion**

Or if you are preparing a meat dish,
sauté the onion and:

**(1/2 lb. ground beef)**

in:

(¼ cup shortening)

Combine:

**1 cup condensed tomato soup**
**2½ cups canned spaghetti**

Fold in the flaked fish or beef. Season with:

**½ teaspoon sugar**
**A few grains cayenne**
**Salt and pepper**

Cook until thoroughly heated. You may rub a bowl with:

**(A cut clove garlic)**

Add the spaghetti mixture. Garnish it with:

**2 tablespoons chopped**
**parsley**

## CHICKEN OR TURKEY TETRAZZINI

**8 to 10 Servings**

A fan writes that she prefers using ¼ pound macaroni and 1 pound mushrooms. A bit more extravagant but very good. ◗ Please read about Cooking Pastas, 199.

Cut the meat from the bones of:

**A boiled chicken**

There should be 2 to 3 cups shredded meat. Boil in salted water:

**½ lb. macaroni or spaghetti:**
**2 cups, 200**

Drain and add to this:

**(½ cup blanched, slivered**
**almonds)**
**½ to ¾ lb. Sautéed**
**Mushrooms, 328**

When sautéing the mushrooms, add to the pan:

**3 tablespoons dry white wine**

Make a sauce of:

**3 tablespoons butter or**
**chicken fat**
**2 tablespoons flour**
**2 cups chicken broth**
**Season to taste**

Remove from heat. Stir in:

**1 cup heated whipping cream**

Preheat oven to 375°.

Add half the sauce to the chicken and half to the macaroni and mushrooms. Place the macaroni in a greased baking dish. Make a hole in the center. Place the chicken in it. Sprinkle the top with:

**Grated Parmesan cheese**

Bake until lightly browned and heated through.

## SEAFOOD TETRAZZINI

**8 Servings**

◗ Please read about Cooking Pastas, 199.

Boil in salted water:

**½ lb. spaghetti: 2 cups, 200**

Sauté until golden:

**6 tablespoons chopped onion**

in:

**2 tablespoons olive oil**

Add:

**2 cups cream of mushroom**
**soup**
**1⅓ cups water**
**¼ cup grated Romano cheese**

Stir in and heat thoroughly:

**2 cups chopped drained tuna,**
**shrimp or clams**
**⅔ cup sliced pitted ripe olives**

Add:

**2 tablespoons chopped**
**parsley**
**2 teaspoons lemon juice**
**⅛ teaspoon each thyme and**
**marjoram**

Preheat broiler.

In a buttered casserole, mix the sauce and the drained spaghetti. Top with another:

**¼ cup grated Romano cheese**

Heat under the broiler until golden brown.

## MOSTACCIOLI

**5 Servings**

Manicotti are little muffs, cannelloni are pipes, linguine are tongues, fettucine are ribbons, vermicelli are wormlets; but we think these "little mustaches" have the most fetching name of all.

◗ Please read about Cooking Pastas, 199.

Reconstitute:

>　1/4　lb. dried mushrooms,
>　　　(II, 255)

Melt:

>　1　tablespoon butter

Stir and brown in it:

>　3/4　to 1 lb. ground round steak
>　1　large chopped onion
>　1　clove garlic cut into halves

Cover these ingredients with boiling water. Add:

>　3/4　teaspoon salt
>　1/8　teaspoon pepper

Simmer covered until almost dry. Fish out the garlic. Add:

>　2　cups canned tomatoes
>　(1/2　teaspoon each basil and
>　　　oregano)

Continue to simmer, stirring frequently. Cook until the sauce is thick, from 1 to 1 1/2 hours. As it thickens, add mushrooms, and when the sauce is almost done, add:

>　1/4　cup olive oil

Boil in salted water until tender:

>　1/2　lb. mostaccioli: about
>　　　2 cups

Serve the mostaccioli on a hot platter: first a layer of the pasta, then a layer of sauce, then a layer of the pasta and again a layer of sauce. Sprinkle each meat sauce layer generously with:

>　Grated Parmesan cheese
>　Freshly grated black
>　　pepper

## PASTA FILLINGS AND TOPPINGS

There can be much leeway in the makeup of pasta fillings, with combinations of meats and vegetables of your preference. Use for Cannelloni, Ravioli, Tortellini, Manicotti, large seashells, and other pastas.

### I.

**About 2 Cups**

Our favorite Ravioli filling.
Combine:

>　1/2　cup cooked puréed spinach
>　1　cup cooked meat: ground
>　　　veal and lean pork
>　2　eggs
>　1/4　cup lightly toasted bread
>　　　crumbs
>　1/2　cup grated Romano or
>　　　Parmesan cheese
>　1/2　teaspoon dried basil or
>　　　marjoram
>　(1/2　minced clove garlic)
>　2　teaspoons finely chopped
>　　　parsley
>　　　Salt and pepper

and enough:

>　　　Stock, cream or gravy to
>　　　form a stiff paste

### II.

**About 2 1/2 Cups**

Beat:

>　1　lb. Ricotta cheese

Add, one at a time, and continue to beat:

>　2　eggs

Add:

>　1　tablespoon chopped parsley
>　1/2　cup grated Parmesan
>　　　cheese
>　　　Salt and pepper to taste

### III.

**About 4 Cups**

Our favorite Cannelloni filling.
Lightly sauté together:

2 tablespoons butter
¼ cup finely chopped onion
¼ lb. finely chopped
   mushrooms

Add and simmer about 5 minutes:

1 cup drained, chopped
   cooked spinach
2 cups minced cooked white
   chicken meat
¼ teaspoon nutmeg
   Salt and pepper

After the mixture has cooled somewhat, add:

¾ cup Ricotta or dry cottage
   cheese
2 tablespoons cream

Mix thoroughly and:

Season to taste

## IV.

**About 2 Cups**

Combine thoroughly after putting through a fine grinder:

¼ lb. Italian bologna
2 oz. prosciutto
⅛ lb. lean beef
⅛ lb. pork

Sauté the mixture over medium heat in:

2 tablespoons olive oil

When thoroughly cooked, remove from heat and mix in enough:

Dry seasoned bread
   crumbs

to make a stiff mixture. Add:

¼ cup chopped parsley
¼ teaspoon nutmeg
   Salt and pepper

Chill for easier handling before filling pasta.

## EGG AND CHEESE TOPPING FOR PASTA

**About 1 Cup**

This is a good topping for spaghetti or noodle casserole dishes which have to wait for tardy guests, as it prevents the spaghetti from drying out.

Beat until light yellow and foamy:

3 eggs

Stir in, to form a thick paste:

⅔ cup grated Parmesan
   cheese

Spread over the top of the dish and bake in a 400° oven until the eggs and cheese are set and browned.

## CHICKEN LIVER TOPPING FOR PASTA

Sauté until just done:

1 cup chicken livers

in:

¼ cup vegetable or olive oil

Remove the livers from the pan and cut up coarsely. In the same pan, sauté 5 minutes:

1 cup sliced mushrooms

then add:

½ cup halved pitted ripe
   olives

and the chicken liver pieces. Stir and deglaze the pan with:

½ cup dry sherry

Spread the topping over the pasta in an even layer and sprinkle as evenly as possible with:

½ cup chopped hard New
   York cheese

Place under the broiler until the cheese is toasted, about 2 minutes.

## SUGGESTED PASTA SAUCES

The following are not the only sauces to enhance a pasta, so search our Sauce chapter for others that may appeal to your ingenuity.

Unthickened Tomato
   Sauce, 400
Thickened Tomato
   Sauce, 400
Quick Tomato Sauce, 400

# EGG DISHES

For a philosopher or a mathematician, the sphere is the most satisfactory of all forms. But for humankind in general, the ovoid—or egg-shape—exerts an even greater fascination. Ovoids crop up in architecture, from the earliest Greek moldings to the latest of Late Renaissance cartouches. The egg's significance as a symbol of the Resurrection and its importance to the Eastern Church led to the wildly extravagant, exquisitely wrought golden Easter eggs which the Imperial Russian Court commissioned during the decades preceding the Revolution. While the results of our American efforts to paint eggs may prove more homely, they are made easier if the eggs are held in a wire treelike form, shown above.

It is not surprising that so elegant a package should turn out to hold a small treasure of balanced nutrients—proteins, fats and minerals. Eggs and egg dishes may be acceptably served at any meal, fried, scrambled, boiled, poached, baked, or incorporated into omelets or into a soufflé, as shown above. And, almost unlimited variations of meat, vegetables or fish may accompany or be folded into them. For more about eggs, see About Eggs, (II, 204).

No egg dish really succeeds, however, unless the eggs are "strictly fresh" and are cooked with due respect for their delicacy and sensitive response to heat. ◗ In only one type of preparation should the heat be high and brief—for omelets. ◗ Otherwise, dishes in which eggs predominate invariably do best if gently cooked and carefully timed, see the egg timer illustrated on (II, 205). In combining eggs in custards, soufflés and sauces, let them partially cook on the stored heat in the pan. Do not put them back on direct heat, because they never will have so satisfactory a texture.

## SOFT-COOKED, HARD-COOKED AND CODDLED EGGS

The difference among these three is more a matter of timing than of method.

For soft- and hard-cooked eggs, place in a saucepan, preferably glass or enamel:

### Unshelled eggs
Cover them with:

### Cold water

Put the pan over medium heat and bring the water to the boiling point. ◗ Lower heat to a simmer. Now watch your time, which will depend on how large and how cold your eggs are. The following timings are for 70° eggs. Right out of the refrigerator, they will require at least 2 minutes more. After the heat is reduced, eggs will be **soft-cooked** in 2 to 3 minutes; **medium-cooked** in about 4; **hard-cooked** in 10 to 15. Hard-cooked eggs should be plunged into cold water at once to arrest further cooking and to prevent the yolks from discoloring.

To **coddle** eggs, lower them carefully into boiling water with a tablespoon. Cover the pan and remove from the heat. Allow 6 to 8 minutes for delicately coddled eggs. If you want the eggs to remain shapely when opened, turn them several times within the first few minutes of coddling so that the white of the egg solidifies evenly in the air space and the yolk is centered.

◗ To shell hard-cooked eggs, crack the shell and roll the egg between the palms of the hands to free the thin tough skin from the egg and make shelling easier. If eggs are very fresh, they are more difficult to shell. If you want to slice the eggs smoothly, dip a knife into water before slicing.

Soft-cooked eggs may be served shelled, in the various ways suggested for Poached Eggs, 213.

Recipes and suggestions for serving hard-cooked eggs follow. Others will be found in the chapters on Hors d'Oeuvre, (II, 81) and Salads, 42.

## SAUTÉED OR FRIED EGGS

**4 Servings**

Melt in a skillet over low heat:

### 1 or 2 tablespoons butter
Break carefully into the skillet:

### 4 eggs

Baste the eggs with the hot butter. Cook them over a very low heat until done. To get a firm white ◗ cover the pan with a lid at once. If you like a softer white, you may at once pour over the eggs:

### 1 tablespoon boiling water
then cover the skillet and cook about 1 minute. When the eggs are firm, serve them seasoned with:

### Salt and pepper
If you prefer "once-over-lightly" to "sunny-side-up," proceed as above; but when the whites are firm, insert a slotted spatula under the egg, supporting the yolk area, and cautiously reverse it in the skillet. Cooking the second side should take only a matter of moments.

## ADDITIONS TO SAUTÉED EGGS

It is often the extras that give punch to eggs, especially in brunch and luncheon dishes. Try eggs on a small mound of:

> **Boiled rice, noddles or potatoes, or on rounds of toast**

Pour over any of these:

> **A mushroom, tomato or onion sauce, see Index**
> **A canned soup sauce, 394**
> **White sauce seasoned with**

**mustard or curry powder,
herbs, onion, celery, green
peppers, capers, anchovies
or cheese
Black Butter, 397, or
Brown Butter, 397**

## POACHED EGGS

**Individual Serving**

**I.** Poached eggs, unless made in individual molds—in which case cook them over—not in—boiling water—are apt to produce "streamers" that you may trim off with scissors before serving.
Grease the bottom of a 6- to 8-inch pot. Put in enough slightly salted water to fill to twice the depth of an egg. While the water is coming to a boil, break into a small bowl:

**1 egg**

Swirl the water into a mad vortex with a wooden spoon. Drop the egg into the well formed in the center of the pot. ◗ The swirling water should round the egg. ◗ Reduce the heat. ◗ Simmer 4 to 5 minutes or let stand off the heat for 8 minutes. By this time the white should be firm and the yolk soft. Remove with a skimmer and drain well. If not using the egg immediately, plunge it at once into cold water to stop the cooking. Repeat the process for each egg. To store, see II, below. To reheat the eggs, drop them into hot—not boiling—water.

**II.**

**4 Servings**

Have ready:

**4 eggs**

Place in a skillet 1 1/2 inches of water. Bring it to a rolling boil, then reduce heat until water is quiet. Break an egg into a cup and bring the edge of the cup level with the surface of the water. Slide the egg in gently. Do this with each egg. Simmer eggs from 3 to 5 minutes or until the whites are firm and yolks appear pink. With practice, you will be able to judge the right degree of doneness. With a slotted spoon or pancake turner, lift out the eggs. Let drain well before serving. Eggs may be poached in a small amount of milk, cream or stock. For other additions, see below. To store for later use—but not later than 24 hours after the original cooking—put the poached eggs in a bowl of ice-cold water in the refrigerator. This is the professional way to prepare eggs in advance for use the following day in Eggs Benedict, 214, or any other recipe calling for poached eggs. The heat from the platter, toast and sauce warms up the egg.

## ADDITIONS TO POACHED EGGS

**I. Poached Eggs Mornay**
Arrange poached eggs in a shallow buttered baking dish.
Cover with:

**Mornay Sauce, 384**

Sprinkle with:

**Grated cheese
Bread crumbs**

and brown quickly under a hot broiler.

**II.** Cover the bottom of a shallow buttered baking dish with:

**Creamed Spinach, 359**

Arrange the poached eggs on the spinach and proceed as for Poached Eggs Mornay, above, to produce **Eggs Florentine.**

**III.** Hollow out a hard roll, insert egg, cover with:

**Quick Seafood Spaghetti
Sauce, 395**

and garnish with:

**Cooked shrimp, mussels and oysters**

IV. Serve on toast, covered with:
   **Hunter's Sauce, 392, or Aurore Sauce, 387**

V. Poach eggs in:
   **Creole Sauce, 394**

## EGGS POACHED IN SOUP

**4 Servings**

The following recipe makes an attractive light meal, prepared in a few minutes. Combine in an 8-inch skillet and heat to the boiling point over low heat:

   **1 can condensed tomato soup: 10½ oz.**

diluted with:
   **½ cup water**
Add:
   **(½ teaspoon dried basil)**
   **(¼ teaspoon sugar)**

♦ Reduce the heat and keep the liquid below boiling point. Slide into the soup from a saucer, one at a time:

   **4 eggs**

♦ Simmer 4 to 5 minutes or until the eggs firm up. Serve on:
   **Rounds of toast**
covered with the soup. Sprinkle with:
   **Chopped parsley or basil**

## EGGS POACHED IN WINE

**6 Servings**

Combine in a skillet:
   **1 cup dry red wine**
   **1 crushed clove garlic**
   **2 tablespoons minced onion or shallot**
   **¼ teaspoon salt**
   **⅛ teaspoon pepper**
   **A Bouquet Garni, (II, 253)**

Heat to boiling point, ♦ reduce heat and simmer about 3 minutes, then remove the bouquet. Slide into the wine from a saucer, one at a time:

   **6 eggs**

Poach them until the whites are firm. Remove and put them on:
   **Slices of fried bread (rubbed with garlic)**
Strain the wine, put it back into the skillet and thicken with:
   **Kneaded Butter, 381**
Pour the sauce over the eggs.

## EGGS BENEDICT

**6 Servings**

Try this substituting oysters for eggs. Have ready:
   **6 Poached Eggs, 213**
Toast:
   **6 rounds of bread or halves of English muffins**
Cover each with:
   **A thin slice of hot ham, minced cooked bacon or deviled ham**
Top each with one of the poached eggs.
Serve them hot, covered with:
   **Hollandaise Sauce, 410**

## POACHED EGGS BLACKSTONE

**6 Servings**

Have ready:
   **6 Poached Eggs, 213**
Sauté, then mince:
   **3 slices bacon**
Reserve the drippings. Cut:
   **6 slices tomato, ½ inch thick**
Season them with:
   **Salt and white pepper**
Dip the slices in flour and sauté them in the bacon fat. Sprinkle with the minced bacon. Cover each slice with a poached egg.
Pour over the eggs:
   **Hollandaise Sauce, 410**

# EGGS WITH SMOKED SALMON

A genial winter breakfast or luncheon dish.

Prepare:

**Buttered toast or slices of pumpernickel bread**

Dip into boiling water:

**Very thin slices of smoked salmon**

Dry them. Place them on the toast. Cover with:

**Poached or sautéed eggs**

Sprinkle with:

**(Dill seed)**

# HUEVOS RANCHEROS OR COWBOY EGGS

**4 Servings**

A traditional Spanish and Latin American dish. These eggs can be baked in the following sauce, or poached or sautéed with the sauce poured over afterward. Heat in a skillet:

**¼ cup olive oil**

and sauté in it for 5 minutes:

**1 crushed clove garlic**

Remove the garlic and add, sautéeing until soft:

**2 medium-sized finely chopped onions**

**1 large finely chopped green pepper**

Add:

**1 cup peeled, seeded and chopped fresh tomatoes**

**½ teaspoon salt**

**¼ teaspoon freshly ground black pepper**

**2 teaspoons chili powder**

**¼ teaspoon oregano**

**⅛ teaspoon powdered cumin**

Simmer covered until thick and well blended.

**Season to taste**

The sauce should be very hot and well flavored. Pour it over:

**8 poached or sautéed eggs**

allowing 2 eggs per serving.

Or, to bake, preheat oven to 450°.

Pour the sauce into a heatproof shallow dish or 4 individual casseroles and nest the uncooked eggs in the same. Garnish with:

**Strips of red pimiento**

Sprinkle with:

**A little grated cheese**

Bake until eggs are set.

# SCRAMBLED EGGS

For proper results, eggs should not be below room temperature. To achieve more fluffiness, beaten whites may be added to whole eggs in the proportion of 1 additional white to 3 whole eggs.

## I.

**2 Servings**

Melt in a skillet over low heat:

**1 to 2 tablespoons butter**

Have ready by the time the butter is hot and add the following mixture, beaten with a fork until the eggs are uniform in color:

**3 eggs**

**¼ teaspoon salt**

**⅛ teaspoon paprika**

**(2 tablespoons milk or cream)**

As the eggs heat through, increase the heat somewhat, and with a spoon shove the eggs about gently but with accelerating speed, turning them if necessary, until they have thickened but are still soft.

## II.

**2 Servings**

A slower but quite foolproof alternative. Melt in a double boiler ◗ over—not in—boiling water:

**1 tablespoon butter**

Have ready:

> **The seasoned egg mixture
> in I, 215**

When the butter is hot, pour in the egg mixture. Stir repeatedly with a wooden spoon until eggs have thickened into soft creamy curds.

You may serve the eggs on:

> **Hot toast lightly buttered
> or spread with fish paste,
> deviled ham or liver
> sausage; or in a hollowed-
> out hard roll**

Another attractive way to present scrambled eggs is to put them in warm, well-buttered individual ring molds while the eggs are still rather creamy in consistency. Let them finish cooking in their own heat, which will set them. Turn them out and fill the centers with any of the additions listed below.

## ADDITIONS TO SCRAMBLED EGGS

Small amounts of the following may be stirred into the egg mixture before scrambling. Ingredients should be about 70°.

> **Freshly ground mace
> Grated or crumbled cheese
> Chopped, peeled, seeded,
> sautéed tomatoes
> flavored with basil
> Cultured sour cream and
> chives
> Canned chopped sardines
> Crab meat, seasoned with
> curry powder
> Capers
> Chopped canned anchovies
> Chopped sautéed onions
> Crisp bacon bits
> Small pieces of broiled
> sausage
> Sautéed mushrooms**

> **Poached calf brains and
> parsley**

## EGGS SCRAMBLED WITH CREAM CHEESE

**4 Servings**

Melt in a double boiler over simmering water:

> **1 package cream cheese:
> 3 oz.**
> **1 tablespoon butter**

Scald and stir in:

> **1 cup cream**

Add:

> **1/2 teaspoon salt**
> **1/4 teaspoon paprika**

Break into the sauce:

> **6 eggs**

Before the egg whites are firm, stir the eggs gently with a fork until thick. Add:

> **1 1/2 tablespoons sherry**

## SCOTCH WOODCOCK

**2 Servings**

Toast:

> **2 slices bread**

Butter well and spread with a thin layer of:

> **Anchovy paste**

Cut the toast into fingers. Beat together:

> **3 or 4 egg yolks**
> **1/2 cup cream**
> **1/8 teaspoon pepper**
> **1/8 teaspoon salt**

Melt in a double boiler:

> **2 tablespoons butter**

Add the egg mixture and scramble until creamy. Arrange the anchovy toast on a hot dish and cover with the egg mixture. Garnish with:

> **Chopped parsley**

## SHIRRED OR BAKED EGGS OR EGGS EN COCOTTE

### Individual Serving

Baked eggs always have great "eye appeal" served in little ramekins, casseroles or cocotte dishes. Care must be taken not to overcook them, for the ramekin will retain the heat and continue to cook the egg after it is removed from the oven. If you put a poaching paper, 101, over the ramekin, it will return enough heat to the top side of the egg to set it. The yolks should be soft, the whites just set. Don't try to hurry baked eggs.

Preheat oven to 350°.

Grease small bakers or ramekins. Break carefully into each one:

> 1 egg

Add lightly:

> Salt

Sprinkle over the top:

> 1 teaspoon cream or melted butter

Place ramekins in a pan of hot water. Bake about 6 to 7 minutes, depending on the thickness of the ramekin. You may garnish with:

> Chopped sautéed chicken livers, well-seasoned

or serve covered with:

> A tomato sauce, 400–403

## BAKED EGGS ON TOAST

### Individual Serving

Carefully prepared, this makes a delectable dish.

Preheat oven to 325°.

Grease warmed individual molds with:

> Butter

Place in each one:

> 1 teaspoon chopped celery, chives or parsley

Break into each one:

> 1 or 2 eggs

Season with:

> Salt and paprika

Cover each mold with a small poaching paper, 101. Place the molds in a pan of hot water, to a depth of ½ inch from the top of the mold. Bake until the eggs are firm. Turn them out on:

> Rounds of hot buttered toast

Serve with well-seasoned:

> White Sauce I, 383, with a little mustard added, or
> Sauce Dijonnaise, 385

or with one of the Additions to Baked Eggs listed below.

## ADDITIONS TO BAKED EGGS

For interesting variations to baked eggs try adding: cooked mushrooms, asparagus tips, tomatoes or other vegetables, such as creamed spinach. Or add chicken hash, small bits of bacon, sausage or anchovy. Or place a round of toast covered with Gruyère cheese in the bottom of the baker before the eggs are added. You may cover the eggs with a cheese or tomato sauce before baking. Other tasty additions are: Creamed Mushrooms, 328, or Creamed Onions, 334.

## EGGS IN A NEST

### 1 to 2 Servings

A gala-looking dish.

Preheat oven to 350°.

Beat until very stiff:

> 2 egg whites

Heap them in a greased ovenproof dish. Make 2 cavities equally distant from but not too near the edge. Slip into them:

> 2 unbroken egg yolks

Bake 10 minutes or until the eggs are set. Season with:

> Salt and white pepper

Sprinkle with:
(Chopped chives)

## EGGS BAKED IN BACON RINGS

**Individual Servings**

Preheat oven to 325°.
Sauté or broil lightly:
Strips of bacon
Grease the bottoms of muffin pans.
Line the sides with the bacon. Place
in each pan:
(1 tablespoon chili sauce)
Drop into it:
1 egg
Pour over the egg:
1 teaspoon melted butter
Sprinkle with:
Salt and paprika
Bake about 10 minutes or until the
eggs are set. Turn them out onto:
Rounds of toast or warm
slices of drained pineapple
Garnish with:
Parsley

## EGGS IN HAM CAKES

**4 Servings**

Preheat oven to 325°.
Combine:
1 cup ground cooked ham
1 egg
1 tablespoon water
1/8 teaspoon paprika or pepper
Press these ingredients into 4 greased
muffin tins. Leave a large hollow in
each one. Drop into the hollows:
4 eggs
Bake the cakes until the eggs are
firm. Turn out the cakes on:
Rounds of toast
Garnish with:
Parsley or chopped chervil

## HARD-COOKED EGG AND VEGETABLE CASSEROLE

**5 Servings**

Preheat oven to 350°.
Combine:
1 cup cooked vegetables
1 cup White Sauce I, 383, or
Creole Sauce, 394
You may add:
(2 teaspoons chopped fresh
parsley, thyme or basil)
A sprinkling of dill or celery seed is
wonderful.
Prepare:
5 Hard-Cooked Eggs, 212
Slice them. Grease a baking dish.
Place alternate layers of vegetables
and eggs in the dish. Top with:
Au Gratin III, (II, 221)
Bake about 15 minutes.

## CURRIED EGGS

**4 Servings**

Cook:
6 Hard-Cooked Eggs, 212
Shell and slice or cut them in half
lengthwise.
Prepare:
2 cups Curry Sauce, 390
You may chop and add:
(1/4 cup blanched almonds)
Add the eggs. Heat well and serve on:
Hot buttered toast
garnished with:
Parsley

## CREAMED EGGS AND ASPARAGUS COCKAIGNE

We use both versions, depending
on the time available. The texture is
lovely if the asparagus is well drained
and the sauce not overheated.

## I.

**6 Servings**

Drain well, reserving the liquid, and cut in 1-inch pieces:

    **2 cups cooked or canned asparagus tips**

Have ready:

    **6 Hard-Cooked Eggs, 212**

Prepare:

    **2 cups Quick White Sauce, 384**

using milk and the reserved asparagus liquor. When the sauce is hot, gently fold in the asparagus and sliced eggs. Either heat this mixture further in the top of a double boiler ▶ over—not in—boiling water, or preheat oven to 350° and place in a greased baking dish. Cover with:

    **Au Gratin I, (II, 221)**

and bake until the eggs and asparagus are heated through, about 10 minutes. Serve with:

    **Slices of ham**
    **Hot French Bread, (II, 306)**

## II.

**4 Servings**

Preheat oven to 350°.
Reserve the asparagus liquor and have ready:

    **4 to 6 sliced Hard-Cooked Eggs, 212**
    **1½ cups well-drained canned asparagus, cut in 1-inch lengths**
    **1 can condensed cream of chicken soup: 10½ oz., diluted with ¼ cup asparagus liquor**

In 4 individual baking dishes place alternate layers of eggs and asparagus. Top each dish with equal amounts of soup mixture. Cover with:

    **Au Gratin III, (II, 221)**

and bake about 15 minutes or until thoroughly heated.

## CREAMED EGGS AU GRATIN

**4 Servings**

Preheat broiler.
Slice into a baking dish:

    **4 Hard-Cooked Eggs, 212**

Combine:

    **1½ cups White Sauce II, 383**
    **¼ cup Chili Sauce, (II, 686)**

Pour this mixture over the eggs. Top with:

    **Au Gratin III, (II, 221)**

Place the dish under the broiler until the crumbs are golden.

## MASKED EGGS

**Allow 1 Egg to a Person**

Chill:

    **Hard-Cooked Eggs, 212**

Cut them into halves lengthwise. Place them cut side down on:

    **Watercress or shredded lettuce**

Pour over them:

    **Mayonnaise, 419, thinned with a little lemon juice or cream; Mayonnaise Collée, 427; or Sauce Chaud-Froid, 428**

Sprinkle them with:

    **Capers, chopped anchovies, or bits of cooked ham or cooked bacon**

## STUFFED EGGS ON ROSETTES WITH SAVORY SAUCE

**8 Servings**

This dish is elaborate but capable of prefabrication. The rosettes and the sauce may be made and the eggs cooked the day before.
Prepare:

    **8 Hard-Cooked Eggs, 212**

Cut them crosswise into halves. Remove the yolks, and mash. Combine the yolks with an equal part of:

Finely chopped seasoned
cooked spinach or
Creamed Spinach, 359

Fill the egg whites with the mixture.
Prepare:

2 cups White Sauce I, 383

Season it with:

1 tablespoon Worcestershire
Sauce, (II, 688)
2 tablespoons dry sherry
3/4 cup Chili Sauce, (II, 686)
Salt and pepper

When the sauce is smooth and
hot, add:

2 cups cooked or canned
shrimp or diced cooked
sweetbreads

Prepare:

16 Rosettes, (II, 160)

Place a stuffed egg half on each
rosette and cover with sauce. Serve
at once while the rosettes are crisp.
If you have made the sauce and
the rosettes ahead of time, reheat the
sauce in a double boiler, and the
rosettes briefly in a 400° oven.

## DEVILED OR STUFFED EGGS

The blandness of hard-cooked eggs is
a challenge to adventurous cooks.
Here are a few suggestions to enliven
this basic ingredient with supplies
from your pantry shelves.
Prepare:

Hard-Cooked Eggs, 212

Cut the eggs in half lengthwise or
slice off both ends, which leaves
a barrel-shaped container. Remove
yolks carefully so as not to damage
the whites. Crush the yolks without
packing them and moisten them
pleasantly with:

French dressing or
mayonnaise; sweet or
cultured sour cream; soft
butter with vinegar and

sugar; lemon juice or sweet
pickle juice

Season to taste with:

Salt and paprika

or one or more of the following:

(A little dry mustard)
(Catsup)
(A dash of cayenne, curry,
or hot pepper sauce)
(Worcestershire
Sauce, (II, 688)

Exotic additions to the yolks are:

Anchovy or sardine paste
Liver sausage paste or Foie
Gras, 629
Chopped sautéed chicken
livers
Chopped ginger and cream
cheese
Chutney
Caviar
Smoked salmon
Deviled ham or tongue
Grated Roquefort cheese
Chopped chives, tarragon,
chervil, parsley, burnet or
basil

Put the filling back in the whites. You
may use a pastry tube for elaborate
effects. For improved flavor and texture, remove the eggs from the refrigerator 1/2 hour before serving.
Garnish with:

Olives, capers or truffles

## DEVILED EGGS IN SAUCE

4 Servings

Preheat oven to 425°.
Prepare:

4 Deviled Eggs, above

Place the halves in a greased dish.
Pour over them:

1 cup Quick Tomato Sauce,
400, or Mornay Sauce, 384,
Béchamel Sauce I, 383, or
Quick Mushroom Sauce,

**395, or Tomato Shrimp Sauce, 386**

Coat the sauce with:

**Au Gratin II or III, (II, 221)**

Bake until the top is brown.

## ABOUT OMELETS

The name "omelet" is loosely applied to many kinds of egg dishes. In America, you often get a great, puffy, soufflélike, rather dry dish in which the egg whites have been beaten separately and folded into the yolks. In France an entire mystique surrounds a simple process in which the yolks and whites are combined as unobtrusively as possible to avoid incorporating air, and this marbleized mixture is quickly turned into a two-fold miracle. In an Italian frittata, the food is often mingled at once with the stirred egg, and this thin pancake-like disk is cooked in a little oil, first on one side and then on the other, with a result not unlike a large edition of Eggs Fooyoung, 224.

Since omelet-making is so rapid, see that you have ready everything you are going to serve the omelet with or on, and be sure you have your diners captive. For more details about equipment, see About Omelet Pans, 222.

The success of all of these so-called omelets demands that ▶ the pan and the fat be hot enough to bind the base of the egg at once so as to hold the softer egg above, but not so hot as to toughen the base before the rest of the egg cooks.

▶ Eggs, therefore, and any food incorporated with them, must be at least 70° before being put into the pan. More omelet failures are due to eggs being used direct from the refrigerator than to any other cause. There is always, too, the problem of salting. As salt tends to toughen the egg structure, it should, in general, be added to the fillings or garnishes you choose to fold into the omelet.

Glazing omelets makes them look prettier but also tends to toughen them. ▶ To glaze an omelet, brush it with butter. Or, if it is a sweet omelet, sprinkle it with sugar and run it under the broiler briefly, or use a hot salamander, 91, or brander. It you want a really sophisticated job, put the omelet on a warm ovenproof server, coat it lightly with a thin Mornay Sauce, 384, and run it under a broiler 2 minutes.

To fill a 3-egg omelet, have ready about 1/2 to 3/4 cup cooked or creamed mushrooms, seafood, ham or tongue. Place one-fourth on the upper surface of the omelet while still in the pan and fold. Reserve the remainder for a final garnish on top. Or, a simple method is to fold the omelet as sketched below, then cut an incision along the top and insert the hot food. Herbs or finely grated cheese may be added to the beaten eggs before cooking. For other fillings, see Additions to Scrambled Eggs, 216.

## ABOUT OMELET PANS

Omelet pans generate more tempests than teapots do. Doctrinaire omelet-makers contend that one pan should be used solely for their specialty and that it should never be washed—simply rubbed with soft toweling and a handful of salt. The argument for the exclusive pan goes further. Any pan used for frying or braising is apt to develop hot spots. Yet those of us who resent giving kitchen space to a pan for a single function find an all-purpose skillet—cleaned with modern detergents—entirely feasible for omelet preparation ♦ provided the pan surface remains smooth so the eggs can slide freely over it. For this reason coated pans are preferred by some cooks, but if this type of pan is used in omelet-making, you may reduce the butter by not more than one-third. The pan should be moderately heavy, and slowly but thoroughly heated. Otherwise the egg cannot stand what one French authority calls "the too great brutality" of the quick heat that is so essential.

The next thing to consider is the omelet in relation to pan size. Since French omelets are made so quickly, we never try more than 2 to 3 eggs at a time—cooked in 1 tablespoon of sweet butter. If more than one omelet is needed, have some extra butter already melted to save preparation time. We use a skillet with a long handle and a 5-inch base flaring gently to a 7-inch top, as shown in the sketches on page 221. For larger omelets—and they can be made successfully with up to 8 or 10 eggs—see that the similarly shaped pan is big enough to keep the egg, when poured, no deeper than 1/4 inch; and add a proportionate amount of butter.

## FRENCH OMELET

Andrew Carnegie once counseled: "Put all your eggs in one basket. Then watch that basket!" When the container is a skillet and the objective an omelet, his advice is especially apt.

♦ Please read About Omelets, 221. Remember that an omelet of the French type takes only 30 to 50 seconds to make, depending on your preference for soft or firm results. Mix briefly in a bowl with a dinner fork:

> 3 eggs

Put in a 7-inch omelet pan:

> 1 tablespoon clarified sweet
> butter, 396

To avoid sticking, clarified butter is best. Roll it over the bottom and sides of the pan. When it is hot and ♦ has reached the point of fragrance, but is not brown, pour in the eggs. Meanwhile, agitate the pan forward and backward with the left hand. Keep the egg mass sliding as a whole over the pan bottom. With a dinner fork, quickly swirl the eggs with a circular motion, as shown on the preceding page. Hold the fork so the tines are parallel to, but not scraping, the base of the pan. At this point the heat in the pan may be sufficient to cook the eggs, and you may want to lift the pan from the heat as you gently swirl the eggs, as illustrated, in circular scrolls from the edges to the center. Pay no attention to the ridges formed by the fork. The rhythm of the pan and the stirring is like a child's trick of patting the head while rubbing the stomach. ♦ Have ready a hot serving plate, which helps to inflate the omelet; choose a heat-resistant one if you plan to glaze, see About Omelets, 221. Whether you fill your omelet or leave it plain, grasp the handle of the pan so the left palm is up, as shown. Tip the pan down away from the handle and, with the fork, flip about one-third of the omelet over, away from the handle, as shown in the center. If the omelet shows any tendency to stick, discard the fork and give the pan handle a sharp rap or two with the fist, as sketched. The omelet will flip over without the use of a fork and will start to slide. Slant the pan to 90° or more until the omelet makes a second fold in sliding out of the pan and lies with its ends folded under on the plate—ready to serve. Glaze and garnish, if you wish, and serve at once. For fillings, see About Omelets, 221.

## FLUFFY OR SOUFFLÉED OMELET

**4 Servings**

If you have 1 or 2 extra egg whites, add these and omit the baking powder. You may add some grated Parmesan cheese or chopped parsley, chives and chervil to the egg mixture before cooking it, or sprinkle these on top before putting the omelet in the oven.

Combine and beat with a fork:

    1/4 cup milk
    4 egg yolks
    1 teaspoon double-acting
      baking powder

Beat until stiff, but not dry:

    4 to 6 egg whites

Melt in a heavy skillet over slow heat:

    1 tablespoon clarified sweet
      butter, 396

Fold the yolk mixture lightly into the egg whites. Pour the batter into the skillet. Cover the skillet with a lid. As the omelet cooks, slash through it several times with a knife to permit the heat to penetrate the lower layer. When the omelet is half done—after about 5 minutes—it may be placed uncovered on the center rack of a 350° oven until the top is set. Jet-propel this to the table as it comes out of the oven, because it will collapse quite quickly.

Cut the omelet in pie-shaped wedges, serving single segments garnished with any of the fillings or sauces suggested under About Omelets, 221. Or double the omelet over the fillings, sandwich-style. Sprinkle with:

    **Chopped parsley**

## FIRM OMELET

**4 Servings**

For the beginner, the texture of this omelet is a little more manageable. Beat with a fork until blended:

    4 eggs

Beat in:

    1/4 cup milk, cream or stock
    1/2 teaspoon salt
    1/8 teaspoon paprika

Melt in a skillet:

    1 1/2 tablespoons clarified sweet
      butter, 396

When the butter is fairly hot, add the egg mixture. Cook over low heat. Lift the edges with a pancake turner and tilt the skillet to permit the un-cooked mixture to run to the bottom, or stick the egg mixture with a fork in the soft spots to permit the heat to penetrate the bottom layer. When it is all an even consistency, fold the omelet over and serve it. For a festive occasion, fold into the omelet before serving:

    (3 tablespoons cultured sour
      cream)
    (1 1/2 tablespoons red caviar)

## SWEET OMELET

See (II, 520–521) for other sweet omelets.

**I.** Follow the recipe for:
> **Fluffy Omelet, 223**

Add to the yolk mixture:
> **1  tablespoon sugar**

Just before serving, spread the omelet with:
> **Jam or jelly**

Sprinkle the top with:
> **Confectioners' sugar**

Fruit juice may be substituted for the milk and the omelet spread with cooked or raw sweetened fruit instead of jelly.

**II.** Prepare:
> **Fluffy Omelet, 223**

Add to the egg yolks:
> **1  tablespoon brandy**
> **1  tablespoon curaçao**

When finished, sprinkle with:
> **Confectioners' or castor sugar**

and flambé, 108.

## EGGS FOOYOUNG WITH SHRIMP

Fooyoung is really a rich omelet made with additions of cooked vegetables, fish and meat.

Clean or drain:
> **2  cups bean sprouts**

Heat:
> **A little vegetable oil**

in a skillet and stir-fry, 281, until translucent and crisp:
> **1  minced sliced gingerroot**
> **6  chopped green onions**
> **1  rib celery, thinly sliced**
> **1  cup chopped cooked fish, shrimp or finely diced cooked meat**

Have ready and combine the above ingredients and the sprouts with:
> **6  well-beaten eggs**
> **1  teaspoon salt**
> **1/2 teaspoon pepper**

Heat an additional:
> **1  tablespoon vegetable oil**

in another small skillet. Drop the above mixture into it to form small omelets, golden brown on both sides.

Serve with:
> **Soy sauce**

## SPANISH OMELET

> **2 Servings Without Potatoes**
> **4 Servings With Potatoes**

A true Spanish omelet always includes potatoes. We find that we get best results by cooking them separately, keeping them warm, and adding them to the rest of the vegetables at the last moment. Without potato, and with the addition of a dozen or so julienned strips of cooked ham, this omelet becomes a **piperade**, or **Basque omelet**.

If using potatoes, heat in a 10-inch skillet until it reaches the point of fragrance:
> **1/2 cup olive oil**

Add:
> **1  cup thinly sliced potatoes**

Turn them constantly until well coated with the oil. Reduce the heat and, turning occasionally, continue to cook the potatoes about 20 minutes. After starting the potatoes, heat in a heavy skillet to the point of fragrance:
> **2  tablespoons olive oil**

Add, stirring constantly, and cook about 5 minutes:
> **1/2 cup thinly sliced onions**
> **1/2 cup julienned green pepper strips**

Add:
> **1  pressed garlic clove**

Salt and pepper to taste
⅓ cup peeled, seeded,
    drained, chopped tomatoes

Continue to cook about 15 minutes. If you are adding potatoes, combine them now with the above and keep the mixture hot. When the filling is ready, prepare a French Omelet, 222. When the omelet is cooked, do not fold, but slide onto a heated plate so that it retains the flat shape it assumed in the pan. Cover with the hot vegetables and serve at once.

## FRITTATA

**3 Servings**

This Italian omelet usually has the filling mixed into the eggs before they are cooked. You may use any of the suggested fillings under About Omelets, 221, except the creamed or sauced ones, allowing about 1 cup of filling to 3 eggs.

Prepare and keep warm:

2 cups diced cooked
    vegetables, chicken,
    seafood or ham—in any
    desired combination

Beat with a fork until blended:

6 eggs

Stir in the filling and:

Season to taste

How much salt and pepper you add will depend on how highly seasoned your filling is. Have ready a 10-inch greased omelet pan. Into another 10-inch pan which has been heated, put:

1½ tablespoons olive oil

Pour in the egg mixture and proceed as in the basic French Omelet, 222, until the bottom of the frittata is set and the top is still like creamy scrambled eggs. Place the greased skillet with the greased side over the frittata like a lid. Reverse the position of the skillets so the frittata falls into the "lid," which is then heated to complete the cooking of the dish, a matter of 1 to 2 minutes more. Serve at once on a hot platter.

## ABOUT SOUFFLÉS

The soufflé is considered the prima donna of the culinary world. The timbale, 229, is her more even-tempered relative. With closer cultivation both become quite tractable and are great glamorizers for leftover foods. ◗ Cooked foods are best to use in both soufflés and timbales, as they release less moisture into the mixture than do raw ones.

Soufflés have a duration as evanescent as the "breath" for which they are named; some last a bit longer than others, but all have a built-in limit for holding their puff. If the soufflé is well made, you can count on about 10 short minutes in a holding oven ◗ but beware of drafts. Since they depend on egg white and steam for their ascent ◗ not a second should be wasted from the beating of the whites until the soufflé is popped quickly into the ◗ preheated oven. With very few exceptions, every action, including ◗ immediate serving after baking, should contribute to holding their "breath" as long as possible. These tours de force, often based on a white sauce with egg yolks and whipped whites, are easy to make if the pointers are carefully heeded. The white sauce should be a rather firm one ◗ heated just to a boil. Remove it from the heat for ½ minute before the 70° eggs and any other ingredients—also at 70°—are added. The egg whites should be ◗ stiff, but not dry, (II, 206). ◗ Soufflés can always be made lighter if an extra egg white is added for every 2 whole eggs.

♦ To prepare a souffle dish for baking, use a straight-sided ovenproof baking dish, shown in the chapter heading, 211. Grease the bottom and sides well with butter and then coat the buttered surface with a thorough dusting of flour, sugar or dry grated cheese, depending on the flavor of your souffle. It will also climb up the sides of an ungreased baker, but it will not rise so high, and the lovely brown crust will stick and have to be scraped off the sides rather than forming the glossy coating that adds so much to the look of the individual serving.

Next, be sure the oven is heated to the indicated temperature. ♦ A souffle needs quick bottom heat. ♦ If your electric oven is an old model, you may need to remove the top element, as the heat in it is often enough to stiffen the top surface of the souffle too quickly and not allow for its fullest expansion during the baking period. ♦ For oven placement of souffle baking dishes, see sketch on 114. Some recipes suggest making souffles in the top of a double boiler ♦ over—not in—boiling water. This is advisable only if an oven is not available, as the resulting texture is closer to that of a timbale than a souffle. To make a souffle with a crown—a "high-hat souffle"—just before putting the souffle into the oven, take a large spoon or a rubber scraper and run a groove about 1 1/2 inches deep all around the top, about 1 1/4 inches from the edge of the dish. A crown may also be made by extending the height of the baking dish with a piece of parchment paper tied firmly around the dish. We find this satisfactory only with so-called cold souffles based on cream gelatins.

## CHEESE SOUFFLÉ COCKAIGNE

**4 Servings**
♦ Please read About Souffles, 225.
Preheat oven to 350°.
Prepare:
**1 cup White Sauce II, 383**
Bring to a boil. Remove from heat 1/2 minute. Add, stirring well:
**5 tablespoons grated Parmesan cheese**
**2 tablespoons shredded Gruyère cheese**
**3 beaten egg yolks**
Beat until stiff, but not dry:
**4 egg whites**
Fold into the cheese mixture. Pour into one 7-inch or four individual prepared souffle baking dishes. You may decorate the souffles before baking with:
**Paper-thin slices of aged Swiss cheese cut into fancy shapes**
Bake 25 to 30 minutes or until set.

## ⚘ BLENDER CHEESE SOUFFLÉ

**4 or 5 Servings**
A somewhat firm but very acceptable souffle.
♦ To prepare baking dish, please read About Souffles, 225.
Preheat oven to 325°.
Dice into cubes:
**6 oz. sharp cheddar cheese**
Heat to just below boiling:
**1 1/2 cups milk**
Pour milk into blender container and quickly add:
**2 tablespoons butter**
**6 to 8 pieces crustless bread, torn into large pieces**
**1/2 teaspoon salt**
**1/8 teaspoon pepper or a few grains of cayenne**
**(1/8 teaspoon dry mustard)**
Blend until thickened. Add the cubed

heese. Beat in a large bowl until
emon-colored:

**4 egg yolks**

Add the cheese mixture ▶ very
slowly, beating constantly. Beat until
stiff, but not dry, and fold in gently.

**4 egg whites**

Place the mixture in a prepared 8-inch
soufflé baking dish and bake about 50
minutes or until set.

## ADDITIONS TO CHEESE
## SOUFFLÉS

For a more complete dish, consider
adding one of the following to cheese
soufflé:

1/2 **cup ground or finely
chopped cooked ham**

1/2 **to 1 cup well-drained
chopped or ground cooked
vegetables, such as celery
or carrots**

3 **tablespoons Italian tomato
paste**

## VEGETABLE SOUFFLÉ

**4 Servings**

Please read About Soufflés, 225.
Cooked oyster plant, eggplant, cauliflower, peas, onions, carrots, canned
or fresh scraped corn, or asparagus
may be used alone or in chosen combinations. The addition of small quantities of finely minced raw carrots,
celery, onions, olives and pimiento
freshens the flavor.
Preheat oven to 350°.
Prepare and bring to a boil:

1 **cup White Sauce II, 383,
using** 1/3 **cup cream and**
2/3 **cup vegetable stock**

Stir in:

1 **cup minced drained
vegetables**

When the vegetables are hot, reduce
the heat and add:

3 **beaten egg yolks**

Cook and stir 1 minute longer to
let the yolks thicken. Season as required with:

**Salt and pepper
(Nutmeg)**

Cool this mixture slightly. Whip until
stiff, but not dry:

3 **egg whites**

Fold them lightly into the vegetable
mixture. Bake the soufflé in a prepared
7-inch baking dish about 40 minutes or
until firm. If you would like a dish that
is a course in itself, serve the soufflé
with one of the following:

**Mushroom Wine
Sauce, 392
Soubise Sauce, 387
Paprika Sauce, 388
Sauce Indienne, 388**

## ONION SOUFFLÉ

**4 Servings**

One of our pet accompaniments to a
light meal.
Please read About Soufflés, 225.
Preheat oven to 325°.
Prepare:

1 **cup Steamed Onions, 334**

Drain and mince them. Melt:

2 **tablespoons butter**

Stir in until blended:

2 **tablespoons flour**

Combine and stir in slowly:

1/2 **cup milk**

1/2 **cup evaporated milk or
cream**

When the sauce is smooth, add the
minced onions and heat thoroughly.
▶ Remove onions from heat and
stir in:

3 **beaten egg yolks**

Cook ▶ but do not boil, and stir about
1 minute longer to let the yolks
thicken. Season with:

**Salt, paprika and nutmeg**

2 **tablespoons chopped**

**parsley or ¹/₂ teaspoon
dried basil**

Cool these ingredients slightly. Whip until stiff, but not dry:

**3 egg whites**

Fold them lightly into the onion mixture. Bake the soufflé in a prepared 7-inch baking dish until it is firm, about 40 minutes.

## SWEET POTATO AND PINEAPPLE OR APPLESAUCE SOUFFLÉ

**6 Servings**

Superlative with cold or hot ham. Please read About Soufflés, 225. Preheat oven to 350°.

Prepare:

**3 cups Boiled Sweet Potatoes, 355**

While still warm, add and beat with a fork until the potatoes are fluffy:

**3 tablespoons butter**
**¹/₂ teaspoon salt**
**¹/₂ teaspoon grated lemon rind**
**2 beaten egg yolks**

Fold in:

**¹/₂ to ³/₄ cup drained crushed pineapple or tart applesauce**

Cool these ingredients slightly. Whip until stiff and fold in:

**2 egg whites**

Bake the soufflé in a prepared 7-inch baking dish about 35 minutes.

## CHICKEN SOUFFLÉ

### I.

**5 Servings**

Please read About Soufflés, 225. Preheat oven to 325°.

Prepare:

**1 cup White Sauce II, 383**

using chicken stock and cream for the liquid. When the sauce is hot, add:

**1 cup solids: minced cooked chicken, nutmeats, minced and drained cooked vegetables**

Remove from heat and add:

**3 beaten egg yolks**

Season with:

**Salt and pepper**
**Freshly grated nutmeg**

Let cool slightly. Whip ▶ until stiff, but not dry:

**3 or 4 egg whites**

Fold them lightly into the chicken mixture. Bake in a prepared 8-inch soufflé baking dish until firm, about 35 minutes.

### II.

**16 Individual Soufflés**

A favorite luncheon soufflé, having more "body" than most others. Serve in individual baking dishes.

▶ Please read About Soufflés, 225. Preheat oven to 325°.

Mince:

**2¹/₄ cups cooked chicken**

Prepare:

**3 cups White Sauce II, 383**

using chicken fat to replace the butter, and stock or cream as the liquid. Stir in the minced chicken and:

**1 cup chopped nutmeats**
**1 cup chopped cooked vegetables or raw celery, carrots and onions**

When these ingredients are hot, remove from the heat and add:

**9 beaten eggs yolks**

Season with:

**Salt and pepper**
**Nutmeg**

Let cool slightly. Whip ▶ until stiff, but not dry:

**9 egg whites**

Fold them lightly into the chicken

mixture. Fix prepared soufflé baking dishes, 211, two-thirds full. Bake until firm, 20 to 25 minutes. Serve the soufflés with:

> **Mushroom Wine Sauce,
> 392, or
> Poulette Sauce, 390**

## MEAT OR FISH SOUFFLÉ

> **4 Servings**

◗ Please read About Soufflés, 225.
Preheat oven to 325°.
Prepare:

> **1 cup White Sauce II, 383**

When it is smooth, stir in:

> **3/4 to 1 cup flaked cooked fish:
> tuna, crab, clams, lobster
> or shrimp, or finely
> chopped cooked meat**
> **1/4 cup each finely chopped
> raw carrots and celery**
> **(2 tablespoons chopped
> parsley)**

When these ingredients are hot, remove from the heat and stir in:

> **3 beaten egg yolks**

Season with:

> **Salt and paprika
> Nutmeg
> Lemon juice,
> Worcestershire Sauce,
> (II, 688), or Tomato
> Catsup, (II, 686)**
> **(1/3 cup sliced stuffed olives)**

Let cool slightly. Whip ◗ until stiff, but not dry:

> **3 to 4 egg whites**

Fold them lightly into the mixture. Bake in a prepared 7-inch soufflé baking dish until firm, about 35 minutes. Serve the soufflé with:

> **A tomato sauce, 400–401,
> or Nantua Sauce, 385, or
> Anchovy Sauce, 386**

## OYSTER SOUFFLÉ

> **4 Servings**

Please read About Soufflés, 225.
Preheat oven to 325°.
Drain, but save the liquor from:

> **1/2 to 1 pint oysters**

Dry them on a towel. Prepare:

> **1 cup White Sauce II, 383,
> using part cream and part
> oyster liquor**

When it is hot, remove from heat and add the oysters. Add:

> **3 beaten egg yolks**

Season with:

> **Salt and pepper
> Nutmeg
> (Lemon juice)**

Let cool slightly. Whip ◗ until stiff, but not dry:

> **3 to 4 egg whites**

Fold them lightly into the oyster mixture. Bake in a prepared 7-inch soufflé baking dish until firm, about 35 minutes.

## ABOUT TIMBALES AND TIMBALE RING MOLDS

A virtually indispensable mainstay of that sterling American institution, the ladies' luncheon, the timbale is a soufflé with a more equable disposition and greater stamina because of the steaming of the molded custard-like dish—often referred to as a **savory mousse**. The recipes that immediately follow include those in which a timbale mixture is incorporated into a custard, as well as those in which the custard is baked separately in a ring mold to surround a vegetable or meat combination. Or, the mold can be reversed onto a hot dish or onto a previously baked pastry shell. It is often coated or served with a sauce.

Butter individual or larger molds

lightly, and fill them about two-thirds full with the timbale mixture. ◗ Place on a rack in a pan of hot, but not boiling, water. The water should be as high as the filling in the molds. If a rack is not available, fold several thicknesses of paper and place the molds on them. ◗ Check the heat occasionally to make sure the water around the mold never boils—just simmers. It is wise to protect the top of the timbale with a poaching paper, 101.

Bake the timbales in a ◗ moderate oven, about 325°, 20 to 50 minutes, depending on the size of the mold. They are done when a knife blade inserted in the center of the mold comes out uncoated. They are then ready to invert onto a serving platter.

## BASIC TIMBALE CUSTARD

**4 Servings**

Preheat oven to 325°.
Combine and beat with a wire whisk:

**1½ cups warm cream or ½ cup cream and 1 cup chicken stock**
**4 eggs**
**¾ teaspoon salt**
**½ teaspoon paprika**
**(⅛ teaspoon grated nutmeg or celery salt)**
**(1 tablespoon chopped parsley)**
**(A few drops onion or lemon juice)**

To bake and unmold, see About Timbales, 229.
Serve with:

**Creamed vegetables or Mushroom Wine Sauce, 392**

For a brunch, garnish with:

**Crisp bacon**
**Parsley**

## VEGETABLE TIMBALES

### I. Spinach, Broccoli or Cauliflower Timbale

**5 or 6 Servings**

Preheat oven to 325°.
Prepare:

**Basic Timbale Custard, left**

Add to the custard:

**1 to 1½ cups well-drained cooked spinach, broccoli or cauliflower, chopped or put through a food mill**
**(½ cup grated cheese)**

Add seasoning if required. To bake, see About Timbales, 229. Garnish with:

**Hollandaise Sauce, 410**

### II. Mushroom Timbale

**5 or 6 Servings**

Preheat oven to 325°.
Prepare:

**Basic Timbale Custard, left**

Add:

**2 cups drained, chopped, sautéed mushrooms**

To bake, see About Timbales, 229.

### III. Asparagus Timbale

**4 Servings**

Preheat oven to 325°.
Grease 4 deep custard cups or a 7-inch ring mold. Place around the sides of each container:

**3 to 5 well-drained canned or cooked asparagus tips, heads down**

Fill the cups with:

**Basic Timbale Custard, left**

To bake, see About Timbales, 229.
Place between the inverted timbales:

**Hollandaise Sauce, 410**

Garnish them with:

**Parsley**

and surround with:

**Broiled or boiled link sausages**

## EGGPLANT TIMBALE

Preheat oven to 325°.
Prepare for stuffing:

**An eggplant, 322**

Cut it lengthwise and hollow out the pulp, leaving shells about 1/2 inch thick.
Combine the cooked mashed pulp with:

**3/4 cup soft bread crumbs
2 beaten egg yolks
1 tablespoon melted butter
1/2 cup chopped nutmeats or
   shredded cheese
Salt and pepper
Grated nutmeg**

If the filling seems stiff, add:

**1 tablespoon or more milk**

Whip until ◗ stiff, but not dry:

**2 egg whites**

Fold them lightly into the other ingredients. Fill the eggplant shells. Cover the tops with:

**Buttered crumbs or
   cornflakes**

Place them in a pan with a little water and bake about 30 minutes.

## CELERIAC RING MOLD

**6 Servings**

◗ Please read About Timbales, 229.
Preheat oven to 325°.
Cook:

**4 medium-sized celery
   roots, 313**

Drain well. Put them through a grinder, using a coarse blade, or through a ricer. Soak:

**2 slices white bread**

in:

**3 tablespoons milk**

Stir this into the celery and add:

**2 tablespoons melted butter
1 teaspoon grated onion
2 tablespoons cream
4 beaten egg yolks**

**3/4 teaspoon salt
1/2 teaspoon paprika
A fresh grating of nutmeg
   or 1 teaspoon horseradish**

Whip until ◗ stiff, but not dry:

**4 egg whites**

Fold them into the celery mixture. Bake the mixture in a greased ring mold set in a pan of hot water about 45 minutes. Invert the mold onto a hot plate. Fill the center with:

**Buttered peas or sautéed
   mushrooms**

## MEAT-AND-VEGETABLE TIMBALE

**5 or 6 Servings**

Use any interesting combination of cooked vegetables and cooked meat.
Preheat oven to 325°.
Follow the rule for:

**Basic Timbale Custard, 230**

using milk instead of cream. Omit the seasoning. Cut into small pieces and add:

**1 to 1 1/2 cups leftover food
   (Chopped parsley)
   (Grated onion)
   (1/4 cup ground ham)
   (A few chopped stuffed
   olives)**

After the above have been added to the timbale mixture, season it to taste. If the food is dry, no additional thickening is needed. If it is slightly moist, add to the leftovers, before combining them with the custard, until they form a moderately thick paste:

**Cracker crumbs or bread
   crumbs**

To bake, see About Timbales, 229.
Serve with:

**A tomato sauce, 400–401,
Sauce Albert, 386, or
Ravigote Sauce, 389**

## CHEESE TIMBALE OR CRUSTLESS QUICHE

For a classic Quiche, see 244.
Preheat oven to 325°.
Prepare the filling for:

**Cheese Custard Pie, 244**

To bake, see About Timbales, 229.
Good served with:

**Green peas, spinach or broccoli**

## CHICKEN OR HAM TIMBALES

**6 Servings**

Preheat oven to 325°.
Grind twice or blend:

**2 cups cooked white chicken meat or 1 cup each chicken and cooked ham**

Stir in very slowly to form a paste:

**¾ cup cold cream**
**¼ teaspoon salt**
**⅛ teaspoon paprika**

Whip until stiff:

**4 egg whites**

Fold them lightly into the meat mixture. Line 6 greased timbale molds with:

**(Pieces of truffles, ripe olives or pimiento)**

Add the timbale mixture. To bake, see About Timbales, 229. Serve with:

**Mushroom Wine Sauce, 392, or**
**chicken gravy with chopped parsley**

## CHICKEN LIVER TIMBALE

**4 Servings**

Very light and delicate.
Preheat oven to 325°.
Put through a ricer, grinder or 人 blender:

**¾ cup cooked chicken livers**
**½ cup Boiled Rice, 189**

Add:

**A scant ¼ teaspoon salt**
**A few grains cayenne and nutmeg**
**½ teaspoon prepared mustard**

Whip until stiff:

**2 egg whites**

In a separate bowl, whip until stiff:

**¼ cup whipping cream**

Fold these ingredients lightly into the chicken-liver mixture. To bake, see About Timbales, 229. Serve with:

**Caper Sauce, 390, Poulette Sauce, 390, or**
**Smitane Sauce, 389**

## VEAL TIMBALE

**4 Servings**

Preheat oven to 325°.
Grind twice or blend:

**1¼ cups cold cooked veal**

Beat slightly and add:

**3 egg yolks**

Stir the ingredients well. Continue to stir while adding:

**⅓ cup whipping cream**
**¼ cup dry white wine or 2 tablespoons lemon juice**
**⅛ teaspoon paprika**
**Salt, as needed**

Beat until stiff:

**3 egg whites**
**(¼ teaspoon mace)**

Fold these into the other ingredients. To bake, see About Timbales, 229. Serve with:

**Mushroom Wine Sauce, 392, or**
**A tomato sauce, 400–403**

FISH TIMBALE

## I.

**6 Servings**

Cooked fish may be substituted as in III, but uncooked fish gives a better result. Pike is preferred, but a combination of pike and sole is more than acceptable.

◗ Please read About Timbales, 229.

Preheat oven to 350°.

Grind, put through a ricer or 𝖩 blend:

**1 lb. uncooked fish: 2 cups**

Over low heat, melt:

**1¹/₂ tablespoons butter**

Stir in until blended:

**1 tablespoon flour**

then add:

**¹/₄ cup milk**

◗ Remove from heat. Beat and stir in:

**2 egg yolks**

Season the egg mixture with:

**¹/₂ teaspoon salt**
**¹/₈ teaspoon white pepper**
**¹/₈ teaspoon nutmeg**

Stir the yolks 1 or 2 minutes. Add the ground fish. Cool. Whip ◗ until stiff, but not dry:

**2 egg whites**

Whip until stiff:

**1 cup whipping cream**

Fold these ingredients lightly into the fish mixture. Garnish a greased 9-inch ring mold with:

**Strips of pimiento**
**(Strips of green pepper)**

Pour the mixture into the mold. Set the mold in a pan of hot water. Bake about 45 minutes, or until set. Let stand 5 minutes. Unmold. Serve with:

**Hollandaise Sauce, 410,**
**Horseradish Sauce, 386, or**
**Oyster Sauce, 386**

## II.

**4 Servings**

A less rich version. This recipe is highly recommended for conversion into a ring mold.

Preheat oven to 350°.

Combine and cook to a paste:

**1 cup bread crumbs**
**¹/₂ cup cream**

When the mixture is hot, add:

**¹/₂ lb. finely chopped raw**
**halibut or salmon**

Season with:

**¹/₄ teaspoon salt**
**¹/₈ teaspoon paprika**

Cool these ingredients slightly. Whip until ◗ stiff, but not dry:

**2 egg whites**

Fold them lightly into the fish mixture. Place the mixture in a 7-inch buttered baking dish and set it in a pan of hot water. Bake about 40 minutes. Serve with:

**Oyster Sauce, 386, Nantua**
**Sauce, 385, or Anchovy**
**Sauce, 386**

Garnish with:

**Tomatoes**
**Watercress**

## III.

**5 or 6 Servings**

Preheat oven to 325°.

Flake and chop until very fine:

**2 cups cooked fish**

Season it with:

**¹/₄ teaspoon salt**
**¹/₈ teaspoon paprika**
**¹/₂ teaspoon grated lemon rind**
**1¹/₂ teaspoons lemon juice**

Whip until stiff:

**¹/₂ cup whipping cream**

In a separate bowl, whip until stiff:

**3 egg whites**

Fold the cream into the fish mixture, then fold in the egg whites. To bake, see About Timbales, 229. Serve with:

**Béchamel Sauce, 383, or
Tartare Sauce, 421**

## SHAD ROE TIMBALE

**4 Servings**

◗ Please read About Timbales, 229.
Preheat oven to 375°.
Poach 3 to 5 minutes:

**1 fresh shad roe**

Remove outer integument and veins.
Crumble the roe and combine it
with:

**2 beaten eggs
1 cup whipped cream
A grating of nutmeg
Season to taste**

Fill individual molds three-fourths
full of this mixture. Set molds in a
pan of hot water. Bake about 25 minutes. Serve with:

**Allemande Sauce, 390, or
Béarnaise Sauce, 412**

## CHESTNUT RING MOLD

**4 Servings**

A delightful way to use chestnuts.
The egg white lightens the consis-
tency of the mixture.
◗ Please read About Timbales, 229.
Preheat oven to 325°.
Combine:

**2 tablespoons flour
1 teaspoon salt
1/4 teaspoon paprika
1 cup riced Boiled
Chestnuts, 313
1/2 teaspoon grated
onion**

Add gradually:

**1/2 cup milk**

Stir and cook these ingredients over
low heat about 5 minutes. Cool
slightly. Whip until ◗ stiff, but not
dry, then fold in:

**3 egg whites**

Bake the mixture about 1/2 hour in a
7-inch ring mold set in a pan of hot
water. Invert it onto a hot plate. Fill
it with:

**Buttered green peas
Chopped parsley**

It may be served with:

**Mushroom Wine
Sauce, 392**

## MUSHROOM RING MOLD WITH
SWEETBREADS OR CHICKEN

**8 Servings**

◗ Please read About Timbales, 229.
Preheat oven to 325°.
Blanch, 106:

**1 pair sweetbreads, or use
1 cup cooked minced
chicken**

Remove the skin and membrane and
mince the sweetbreads. Prepare:

**1 cup White Sauce II, 383**

Melt in a pan:

**2 tablespoons butter**

Add and sauté about 3 minutes:

**2 slices onion**

Remove the onion. Add to the pan:

**1 1/2 cups finely minced
mushrooms**

and the sweetbreads or chicken.
Heat the white sauce to the boiling
point and combine it with the mushroom mixture. Remove from heat and
stir in:

**1/4 cup dry bread crumbs
1 chopped pimiento
1/4 teaspoon salt
2 beaten egg yolks**

Cook and stir about 1 minute longer
to let the yolks thicken. Cool these
ingredients slightly. Whip until ◗
stiff, but not dry:

**2 egg whites**

Fold them lightly into the mushroom
mixture. Place the mixture in a
greased ring mold set in a pan of hot
water and bake covered with a piece

of buttered paper 35 minutes or until
firm. Invert the mold onto a platter
and serve filled with:

**Asparagus spears or peas**
and pass with:
**Suprême Sauce, 388**

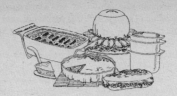

# BRUNCH, LUNCH AND SUPPER DISHES

How we love this grab-bag chapter—
for the ease and speed with which
most of its dishes, elegant or plebeian, may be prepared; for its tricks
with already cooked foods, and for
the stimulus it gives to the attractive
serving of leftovers. Shown on the
left in the sketch above is a sausage
and millet casserole, 251; next to it,
in the rear, a bean pot containing a
quick bean-and-fruit mixture, 296,
surrounded by buttered brown bread.
In the foreground are a tempting
Quiche Alsacienne, 244, and a hefty
Reuben Sandwich on a well-seeded
rye roll, 272. The nesting flame-proof,
lidded casseroles, right, are great
storage-space and serving-time savers.
In this chapter, too, are last-minute
ways to combine staples from your
larder—dried, preserved, canned or
frozen—many of them perked up with
onions, cheese, herbs and fruit—great
emergency fare for unexpected guests!

Do not neglect other combinations
in the egg, cereal and griddle-cake
chapters. From many of these recipes
attractive meals may be prepared in
less than half an hour's time. Keep in
mind that many fresh fish and shellfish recipes are almost as rapidly

cooked as those involving a preprocessed food. For other quick
dishes, refer also to the section on
Ground Meats, 616, and Variety Meats,
638. For the quickest of sauces, see
soup-based sauces, 394.

Care in cooking and skill in seasoning and presentation can make
even a tin of tuna memorable. The
large gratinéed casserole, the individual lidded baking dish or one of
the following cases for food—as
well as garnishes made from simple
materials—all lend distinction in
making a quick dish a gracious one.

## CASES FOR FOOD

We have left behind the era of
trenchers, those coarse, gravy-
soaked loaves that served as both
dishes and food—and whence came
the word "trencherman." But none of
us has lost a taste for sauce-flavored
pastry, pancake, tortilla or toast. All
manner of creamed foods—meat,
vegetable or fish mixtures, cheese
concoctions, as well as farces and
stews—can be placed in one of the
following cases and served with a
sauce:

**Patty Shells, (II, 369)**
**Popovers, (II, 347)**
**Brioches, (II, 320)**
**Rounds of buttered and**
**toasted bread or**
**French Toast, (II, 355)**
**A loaf of bread that has**
**been hollowed,**
**buttered lightly and toasted**
**in a 300° oven**
**A Rice Loaf, 195**
**Large or individual Rice**
**Rings, 189**
**Pies or Tart Shells, (II, 360)**
**Large or individual Noodle**
**Rings, 201**
**Noodle Baskets, 202, or**
**Potato Baskets, 352**
**Biscuits or Shortcakes,**
**(II, 350)**
**A Mashed Potato Ring, 344**
**A Bread Dressing Ring, 256**
**Stuffed Pancakes, (II, 144)**
**Waffles, (II, 150)**
**Stuffed Vegetables, 284**
**Sandwich Loaf, (II, 66)**
**Barquettes, (II, 68)**
**Turnovers, (II, 69) and 238**
**Leaf-Wrappings, 103**
**Coconut shells, (II, 245)**
**Sea shells, 438**

See also the recipes that follow.

## ROLL CASES

Preheat oven to 300°.
Hollow out:

**Small rolls**

Spread the hollows with:

**Melted butter**

Toast in the oven until crisp.

## BREAD CASES OR CROUSTADES

Preheat oven to 300°.
With a biscuit cutter make rounds
from:

**1¼-inch-thick slices of bread**

With a smaller cutter, press out an
inner round, but do not cut deeper
than 1 inch. Hollow out these smaller
rounds and brush the hollows with:

**Melted butter**

Toast the cases in the oven until
crisp and golden, or make them into
croustades by deep-frying them, 94,
at 350°.

## MELBA TOAST BASKETS

Preheat oven to 275°.
Lightly butter on both sides:

**Thin crustless bread slices**

Press them into muffin tins, letting
the corners of the bread protrude
slightly. Toast in the oven until crisp
and golden.

## CHINESE EGG ROLLS

**12 Egg Rolls**

Egg rolls are frequently used for
hors d'oeuvre, or you may serve them
as the main dish at luncheon. The
pancakelike skins are available at
Chinese grocery stores, or you may
make the following dough.
Sift into a bowl:

**1 cup all-purpose flour**

Add gradually to make a thin, smooth
batter:

**2 cups water**

Beat in:

**2 eggs**
**½ teaspoon salt**

Grease a 6-inch-diameter skillet and
put over ♦ low heat. Beat the batter
again and pour 1 tablespoon into the
pan. Let it spread over the surface of
the pan to form a very thin, flexible
pancake. When it shrinks away from
the sides, turn it and let it set on the
other side. Do not let it become
brown or crisp. Remove pancakes to
a dish when done and cover with a
damp cloth until ready to use.

Heat in a skillet or wok:

> 3 tablespoons vegetable oil

Stir-fry in it briefly:

> 1/2 cup finely chopped celery
> 3/4 cup shredded cabbage
> 4 finely chopped scallions

Add and stir-fry for 3 minutes:

> 1/3 cup diced shrimp
> 1/2 cup diced cooked pork

Add and stir-fry 5 more minutes:

> 1/2 cup drained, finely chopped
>    water chestnuts
> 1/2 cup bean sprouts
> 1 minced clove garlic
> 1/4 cup soy sauce
>    A grating of gingerroot
> 1/2 teaspoon sugar

Cool the filling. Place 4 tablespoons of filling in rectangular shape on the center of each pancake and fold up envelope-style, sealing the last flap with a paste made of:

> 1 tablespoon flour
> 2 tablespoons cold water

Fry until golden brown in deep fat heated to 375°. Or use oil about 1 inch deep in a skillet and fry the egg rolls until golden brown. Serve with:

> Chinese mustard
> Soy Sauce
> Oriental Sweet-Sour
>    Sauce, 405

## TURNOVERS, PIROSHKI, OR MEAT-FILLED PASTRIES

6 Servings

▶ Please read About Meat Pie Toppings, 557.

This recipe and the following one make excellent hot canapés. For canapés, cut the dough into small, attractive shapes. For hot luncheon sandwiches, make them a more generous size. If prepared in advance, keep chilled until ready to bake.

Preheat oven to 450°.

Prepare, using about 2 cups flour:

> Biscuit Dough, (II, 348), or
> Pie Dough, (II, 360), or
> Vienna Pastry Dough,
>    (II, 362)

Pat or roll it until thin. This is a matter of taste—about 1/4 inch for biscuit dough, 1/8 inch for Vienna pastry dough. Cut 3 x 3-inch squares, or cut into rounds. Place on each piece of dough as much filling, below, as will fit. Moisten the edges, fold over and pinch together with a fork. Place the triangles or crescents in a pan. Brush lightly with:

> (Soft butter)

Bake until the dough is done, about 20 minutes. This may be served with:

> Brown Sauce, 391

### Fillings

I. Lightly moisten:

> Ground or minced cooked
>    meat

with:

> Gravy or cream, Brown
> Sauce, 391, or a canned
> soup sauce, 394

Season well with:

> Salt and pepper
> Worcestershire sauce or
> chili sauce

II. Moisten braunschweiger sausage with chili sauce or tomato soup.

III. Use:

> 1 1/2 cups cooked ground ham
> 1/2 cup White Sauce II, 383,
>    thick cream or evaporated
>    milk
> 2 tablespoons chopped
>    pickles or olives
> 1 tablespoon chopped onion
> 1 1/2 tablespoons catsup
>    Salt and pepper, if needed

IV. Sauté gently until yellow:

> 2 cups chopped onion

in:

>3 tablespoons olive or
anchovy oil

Add:

>1/4 cup or more chopped ripe
olives
>6 or 8 chopped anchovies

**V.** Use any good cooked seafood filling; taste before seasoning.

## MEAT PIE ROLL OR PINWHEELS

**4 Servings**

This is a palatable, quickly made
everyday dish—an attractive way to
serve a small quantity of leftover
meat.

◗ Please read About Meat Pie Toppings, 557.

Preheat oven to 450°.

Prepare, using 2 cups flour:

>Biscuit Dough, (II, 348), or
Pie Dough, (II, 360)

If you use biscuit dough, make it a little drier than for ordinary biscuits or
it will be difficult to handle. Roll the
dough until very thin. Cut it into an
oblong. To prevent sogginess, use a
pastry brush and brush it lightly with:

>1 egg white or soft butter

Spread the dough with:

>A cooked meat filling, 238

Leave about 1 inch at the sides uncovered. Roll it loosely. Moisten the
end with water to bind it together.
Moisten the sides and pinch them
together. This roll may be prepared
in advance and placed in the refrigerator until ready for use. Bake the
roll on a greased cookie sheet until
done, about 20 minutes. Or cut the
roll into 3/4-inch pinwheel slices. Dot
the tops with:

>Butter

Bake the pinwheels until the dough is
done, about 20 minutes. Serve the
roll or pinwheels with:

>Brown Sauce, 391, or a
tomato sauce

## QUICK CHICKEN OR BEEF POT PIE

◗ Please read About Meat Pie Toppings, 557.

Preheat oven to 400°.

Have ready:

>A lightly baked pie shell
and baked pie crust
top, (II, 360)

formed to fit your casserole or individual baking dishes. We find the
prebaked shell more convenient and
tastier than the prefilled unbaked
crust which has to be exposed to
longer, slower cooking. Heat:

>Creamed chicken, Chicken
or Turkey Hash, 257, or
Beef Hash, 255

Fill the shell with the meat filling and
cover with the baked pie topping.
Bake until the filling is thoroughly
heated and the top is light brown.

## CORN BREAD TAMALE PIE

**6 Servings**

Sauté in a lightly greased skillet:

>1 pound ground beef
>1 chopped onion

When the meat is highly browned
and the onion translucent, add:

>1 cup cream of tomato soup
>1 cup water or stock
>1/4 teaspoon pepper
>1 teaspoon salt
>1 tablespoon chili powder
>1 cup drained whole-kernel
corn
>1/2 cup chopped green pepper,
seeds and membrane
removed

Simmer 15 minutes.

Preheat oven to 425°. Meanwhile,
sift and mix together:

³/₄ cup cornmeal
1 tablespoon flour
1 tablespoon sugar
¹/₂ teaspoon salt
1¹/₂ teaspoons double-acting
    baking powder

Moisten with:

1 beaten egg
¹/₃ cup milk

Mix lightly and stir in:

1 tablespoon vegetable oil

Place meat mixture in a greased 2-quart casserole and cover with the corn bread topping. The topping will disappear into the meat mixture, but will rise during baking and form a layer of corn bread. Bake about 20 to 25 minutes or until corn bread is brown.


## ENCHILADAS

**About 2 Dozen**

Preheat oven to 350°.
Have ready:

Hot Tortillas, (II, 343)

In a heavy saucepan, heat:

2 tablespoons olive oil

Sauté until golden:

¹/₂ cup chopped onion
1 minced clove garlic

Add:

2 teaspoons to 1 tablespoon
    chili powder
1 cup tomato purée
¹/₂ cup chicken or beef stock

Season with:

Salt and pepper
1 teaspoon cumin

Spread some sauce over the tortillas and fill the centers with equal quantities of:

Finely minced raw onion
Shredded Mozzarella or
    longhorn cheese

Roll the tortillas and place them ▶ seam side down in an ovenproof dish. Pour more sauce over the tops and sprinkle with:

Shredded Mozzarella or
    longhorn cheese

Heat thoroughly in the oven about 15 minutes.


## QUICK TOMATO TART

**6 Servings**

Preheat oven to 350°.
Have ready:

6 baked unsweetened
    2¹/₂-inch tart shells, (II, 363)

Slice ¹/₂ inch thick:

6 skinned seeded fresh
    tomatoes

Mix and heat well:

¹/₄ cup sautéed sliced
    mushrooms
¹/₄ cup canned cream of
    chicken soup
¹/₄ cup Italian tomato purée
¹/₄ teaspoon sugar
¹/₄ cup softened liver sausage
4 large chopped stuffed olives
2 teaspoons fresh chopped
    basil
¹/₄ teaspoon salt

First place a layer of heated sauce in each tart shell, then a tomato slice. Cover with the remaining hot mixture. Dust each tart with:

Grated Parmesan cheese

Heat the filled tarts on a baking sheet in the oven about 15 minutes.


## WELSH RAREBITS

Our correspondence is closed on the subject of rarebit vs. rabbit. We stick to rarebit because rabbit already means something else. But we can only answer the controversy with a story. A stranger mollifying a small crying boy: "I wouldn't cry like that if I were you!" Small boy: "You cry your way and I'll cry mine."

## I. With Beer

**6 to 8 Servings**

Grate or shred:

    **1 lb. aged yellow cheese**

Melt in a double boiler over—not in—boiling water:

    **1 tablespoon butter**

Stir in:

    **1 cup beer**

When the beer is warm, stir in the cheese. Stir constantly with a fork until the cheese is melted. Beat slightly and add:

    **1 egg**

Season the rarebit with:

    **1 teaspoon Worcestershire sauce**

    **1 teaspoon salt**

    **(1/2 teaspoon paprika)**

    **A few grains red pepper**

    **(1/4 teaspoon curry powder or a pinch of saffron)**

    **1/4 teaspoon dry mustard**

Serve the rarebit at once on:

    **Crackers, hot toast or Grilled Tomatoes, 367**

## II. With Milk

**4 Servings**

Melt in a double boiler over—not in—boiling water:

    **1 tablespoon butter**

Stir in and melt:

    **1 1/2 cups diced aged yellow cheese**

Add:

    **1/4 teaspoon salt**

    **1/4 teaspoon dry mustard**

    **A few grains cayenne**

    **1 teaspoon Worcestershire sauce**

Stir in slowly:

    **1/2 to 3/4 cup cream**

When the mixture is hot, remove the pan from the heat. Beat in:

    **1 egg yolk**

Serve the rarebit at once over:

    **Hot toasted crackers or bread**

## TOMATO RAREBIT OR WOODCHUCK

### I.

**4 Servings**

Combine and bring to the boiling point:

    **1 cup condensed tomato soup**

    **1/2 cup water**

You may add:

    **(3/4 cup thinly sliced Sautéed Onions, 335)**

Add and stir until melted:

    **3/4 lb. or more shredded aged yellow cheese**

Remove pan from heat. Combine, beat and add:

    **2 egg yolks**

    **1 teaspoon Worcestershire sauce**

    **1 teaspoon dry mustard**

    **1 teaspoon salt**

    **1/4 teaspoon paprika**

    **1/8 teaspoon white pepper**

Stir these ingredients over low heat 1 or 2 minutes to let the yolks thicken slightly. Whip until ▶ stiff, but not dry:

    **2 egg whites**

Fold them into the hot cheese mixture. Serve the rarebit on:

    **Hot toast or crackers**

### II.

**4 Servings**

Stir and melt over low heat:

    **1/2 lb. shredded aged cheddar cheese: 2 cups**

Add, stir and heat:

    **1 cup condensed tomato soup**

    **3 tablespoons water**

    **1/2 teaspoon salt**

    **A few grains cayenne**

Serve the rarebit on:

    **Toast or toasted crackers**

## CHEESE CASSEROLE

A most appetizing luncheon or supper dish when balanced by a green vegetable, a salad, or orange and grapefruit cups.

### I.

**4 Servings**

Preheat oven to 350°.
Cut ½ inch thick:

**7 slices bread**

Spread the slices lightly with:

**Butter**

Cut 2 of the slices twice across on the bias, making 8 triangular pieces. Cut the remaining bread into cubes. There should be about 4 cups of diced buttered bread. Place layers of diced bread in a buttered baking dish. Sprinkle the layers with:

**1 cup shredded cheese**

Combine and beat:

**2 eggs**
**1 cup milk**
**1 teaspoon salt**
**¼ teaspoon paprika**
**A few grains cayenne**
**½ teaspoon dry mustard**

Pour these ingredients over the cheese. Place the triangles of bread upright around the edge to form a crown. Bake about 25 minutes. Serve at once.

### II.

**4 Servings**

Trim the crusts from:

**8 slices bread**

Cut them in half on the bias. Place half of them in the bottom of a greased 8-inch ovenproof dish, spiral fashion, not letting them overlap. They should resemble a pinwheel. Cut into slices ¼ inch thick:

**6 oz. aged cheddar cheese**

Cover the bread layer with the cheese slices, not letting them overlap. Cover the cheese with the rest of the bread, again in spiral fashion.
Beat lightly:

**3 eggs**

Add and beat well:

**¼ teaspoon salt**
**⅛ teaspoon paprika**
**A few grains cayenne**
**2 cups cream**
**(1 teaspoon grated onion,**
**1 tablespoon parsley or**
**chives, or ¼ teaspoon dry**
**mustard)**

Pour this mixture over the bread. ◗ Let the dish stand 1 hour. Bake in a 350° oven about 1 hour or until well browned. Serve hot.

## CHEESE, NUT AND BREAD LOAF

**6 Servings**

Preheat oven to 350°.
Combine well:

**2 cups fresh bread crumbs**
**1 cup minced walnut or**
**pecan meats**
**1 cup shredded American**
**cheese**
**1 cup milk**
**¾ teaspoon salt**
**½ teaspoon paprika**
**1 tablespoon finely chopped**
**onion**
**1 tablespoon minced parsley**
**1 beaten egg**

Shape these ingredients into a loaf in a greased bread pan. Bake about 25 minutes. Serve it with:

**Quick Tomato Sauce, 400,**
**Quick Mushroom Sauce,**
**395, or White Onion**
**Sauce, 387**

## ABOUT CHEESE FONDUE

For so simple an affair, the controversy involved in the making of this dish is vast indeed. Its confecting is a ritual that varies with each Swiss household. Experiment has led to the following conclusions, no matter how simple or how complex a version you choose to make. Use a heavy pot and both high and low heat. The cheese or combination of cheeses used must be ◖ natural cheeses, not pasteurized types. The wine must be ◖ a dry white wine. Although kirsch is traditionally de rigueur, you may substitute a non-sweet liqueur like slivovitz, cognac or applejack. ◖ Measure all ingredients and have them ready to add with

one hand, for your other hand will be busy stirring the mixture with a wooden spoon—from the time the wine is hot enough for the cheese until the fondue is ready to eat. Altogether, this is a matter of about 10 minutes of cooking. ◖ Never make this dish in advance.

Have ready a breadbasket or bowl filled with crusty French or Italian bread cut into 1 x 1 x ³/₄-inch pieces, making sure that each piece has one side of crust. The guests, each equipped with a heatproof-handled fork—preferably two- or three-tined—spear the bread from the soft side and dip the impaled bit into the well-warmed cheese. The fondue will at first be on the thin side, but will

thicken as the process progresses. There is seldom much left by the time another 10 minutes has elapsed. Serve with fresh fruit and tea.

FONDUE

**4 Servings**

Shred:

**1 lb. Emmenthaler, or**
**¹/₂ lb. Emmenthaler and**
**¹/₂ lb. Gruyère cheese**

Rub a heavy saucepan with:

**A clove of garlic**

Put into the pan:

**2 cups dry white wine**

While this is heating ◖ uncovered, over moderately high heat, pour into a cup:

**3 tablespoons kirsch**

This is the classic flavoring, although one of the other dry liqueurs mentioned above may be used. Stir into the kirsch until well dissolved:

**1 teaspoon cornstarch**

By this time the wine will begin to show small foamy bubbles over its surface. When it is almost covered with this fine foam ◖ but is not yet boiling, add the coarsely shredded cheese gradually ◖ stirring constantly. Keep the heat high, but do not let the fondue boil. Continue to add the cheese until you can feel a very slight resistance to the spoon as you stir. Then, still stirring vigorously, add the kirsch and cornstarch mixture. Continue to cook until the fondue begins to thicken. Add to taste:

**Nutmeg, white pepper or**
**paprika**

Quickly transfer it to a heatproof heavy pan and place the container over an alcohol lamp or in a fondue pot or a chafing dish. Or use an electric skillet adjusted to ◖ low heat. After this transferral the cooking continues on low heat and the guests take over as described above.

## ABOUT QUICHES

Early recipes for Quiche called for bacon and cream, but later cheese was added. When sautéed onions were included, the dish was dubbed **Alsacienne**. Cool the onions before adding them.

Other ingredients have found their way into this delicious custard base: tomatoes, nuts, and cooled, well-drained braised endive.

Quiche makes a hefty brunch or an hors d'oeuvre baked in tiny tarts no larger than the lining of muffin tins. As it is always served lukewarm, time it accordingly. Following are several variations on a Quiche theme:

## QUICHE LORRAINE

**6 servings**

Preheat oven to 375°.
Prepare a 9-inch pie shell of:

> **Pâte Brisée, (II, 362), or
> any rich pie dough**

Brush it with:

> **The white of an egg**

and prick it well. Chop into 1-inch lengths:

> **¼ lb. sliced bacon**

Cook the bacon in a heavy skillet, stirring constantly, until the fat is almost rendered out, but the bacon is not yet crisp. Drain on paper toweling. Scald to hasten the cooking time:

> **2 cups milk or cream**

Cool slightly, then beat together with:

> **3 eggs
> ¼ teaspoon salt
> ⅛ teaspoon white pepper
> A fresh grating of nutmeg
> 1 teaspoon chopped chives**

Sprinkle in the bottom of the pie shell the bacon and:

> **½ cup diced Swiss cheese**

Pour the custard mixture over it. Bake 35 to 40 minutes or until the top is a golden brown. For doneness, you may test as for Custard, (II, 507).

## CHEESE CUSTARD PIE OR FLAN

**4 Servings**

Preheat oven to 325°.
Prepare:

> **An 8-inch baked pie crust
> shell, (II, 360)**

at least 2 inches deep. When cool, brush with:

> **Egg white**

Scald:

> **1¾ cups milk or cream**

Reduce the heat and add:

> **1 cup shredded cheese**

Stir until the cheese is melted. Add:

> **½ teaspoon salt
> ¼ teaspoon paprika
> ½ teaspoon grated onion
> A few grains cayenne**

Remove the mixture from the heat and beat in, one at a time:

> **3 eggs**

You may add:

> **(¾ cup diced cooked seafood)**

Fill the pie crust and bake it until the custard is firm, about 45 minutes.

## ONION SHORTCAKE

**6 Servings**

Preheat oven to 425°.
Peel and slice:

> **10 medium-sized white onions**

Sprinkle them with:

> **½ teaspoon salt**

Melt in a saucepan:

> **3 tablespoons butter**

Add the onions, cover and simmer until tender.
Add:

> **¼ teaspoon paprika
> 2 teaspoons chopped parsley**

(½ cup diced cooked ham)
    A grating of nutmeg or
        white pepper
Place the mixture in a casserole and
cover with:

    1 cup White Sauce I, 383

into which you have beaten:

    1 egg
    (¼ cup grated cheese)

Prepare half the amount of:

    Fluffy Biscuit Dough,
        (II, 350)

omitting the sugar. Spread the dough
over the onion mixture. Bake about
20 minutes or until the dough is done.

## ONION OR LEEK PIE

Preheat oven to 450°.
Line a 9-inch pie pan with:

    Pie Dough, (II, 360)

Prick and chill it. Skin and slice
thinly:

    2½ lb. Bermuda onions or
        leeks

Melt in a heavy saucepan:

    3 tablespoons butter

Add the onions. Stir and cook over
low heat until they are translucent.
Cool them well. Combine and heat
slowly until blended:

    3 eggs
    1 cup cultured sour cream
    1 teaspoon salt
    ¼ teaspoon freshly ground
        pepper
    (1 tablespoon minced fresh
        herb or 1 teaspoon dried
        dill or celery seed)

Stir this mixture into the onions.
Brush the bottom of the cooled pie
shell with:

    1 slightly beaten egg white

Fill it with the slightly cooled onion
mixture.
Place over the top:

    (4 strips bacon, diced, or
        crumbled cooked sausage)

Bake the pie in a 450° oven 10 minutes. ◗ Reduce the heat to 300° and
bake until the crust is light brown,
about ½ hour. Serve it piping hot
with a:

    Tossed green salad

## SOY OR LIMA BEAN CASSEROLE

4 Servings

Preheat oven to 325°.
Have ready:

    2½ cups cooked lima beans or
        1½ cups lima beans and
        1 cup cooked soybeans

Stir into them:

    ½ cup chicken stock

Or melt:

    (2 tablespoons butter)

You may add and sauté 3 minutes:

    (¼ cup minced onion)

Stir into the stock or butter, over low
heat, until melted:

    ½ lb. shredded cheese

Add the beans and:

    ½ teaspoon salt
    ¼ teaspoon pepper
    1 teaspoon dried basil or
        thyme
    A few grains cayenne
    (1 cup chopped nutmeats)

Bake the beans about ½ hour.
Serve with:

    Quick Tomato Sauce, 400

## SOY CAKES

4 Servings

Sauté in:

    3 tablespoons butter or
        vegetable oil
    ¼ cup chopped onion
    ¼ cup finely chopped green
        pepper, seeds and
        membrane removed
    ¼ cup finely diced celery

Mix with:

>    1 cup cooked dried
>      soybeans, 294
>    1 cup Boiled Rice, 189
>    1 or 2 eggs
>    Season to taste

Form into 4 patties and roll in:

>    Sesame seeds

Sauté gently in:

>    2 tablespoons sesame or
>      vegetable oil

until the seeds are golden.

## MIXED VEGETABLE GRILL

Preheat broiler.
Cut into slices:

>    Tomatoes

Brush them with:

>    Melted butter

Season them with:

>    Salt and pepper
>    Brown sugar

Prepare for cooking:

>    Sliced mushrooms
>    Sliced green peppers, seeds
>      and membrane removed

Brush them with:

>    Melted butter

Season lightly with:

>    Salt
>    (Lemon juice)

Grease the broiler. Place on it the
tomato slices, and on the slices the
mushrooms, peppers and:

>    (Sliced bacon)
>    (Sausages)

Broil these ingredients until done.
Meanwhile sauté or poach:

>    Eggs

Serve the eggs on a hot platter on:

>    Toast rounds

surrounded by the grilled food. Garnish the platter with:

>    Parsley and olives

## CREAMED LEFTOVER VEAL

**6 Servings**

Melt in a chafing dish or electric
skillet:

>    1/4 cup butter

Add and sauté about 5 minutes:

>    1/2 lb. sliced mushrooms
>    1/4 cup diced green pepper,
>      seeds and membrane
>      removed

Add and stir well:

>    1/4 cup flour

Pour over the mixture and stir until
thickened:

>    1/2 cup cream
>    1 cup veal or chicken stock

Add:

>    2 cups diced cooked veal
>    2 tablespoons minced
>      pimiento
>    1/4 teaspoon marjoram
>    1/2 cup dry white wine
>    Season to taste

Simmer about 5 minutes longer and
serve over:

>    Rice, noodles or macaroni

Garnish with:

>    Chopped parsley

## VEAL OR LAMB AND SPINACH CASSEROLE

Preheat oven to 425°.
Place in a casserole a 1-inch layer or
more of:

>    Creamed Spinach, 359

which has been delicately flavored
with a little:

>    Grated onion

Place over it:

>    Slices of roast veal or lamb

If you have gravy, pour a little of it
over the meat, or use some thick
cream. Cover the top with:

>    Au Gratin III, (II, 221)

Bake until the top is brown. Garnish with:

>    Parsley

## COOKED CURRIED VEAL OR LAMB AND RICE

**4 Servings**

Peel and slice:

    **1 cup onions**

    **(½ cup diced celery)**

Core, pare and slice:

    **2 medium-sized apples**

Melt in a saucepan:

    **3 tablespoons butter**

Add:

    **½ to 1 teaspoon curry powder**

Caution: use only ½ teaspoon curry to begin with if you are unfamiliar with it. Add the onions and apples and sauté until the onions are tender. Remove them from the pan. Brown lightly in the pan about:

    **2 cups sliced or diced cooked veal or lamb**

Remove from the pan. Stir into the pan juices:

    **2 teaspoons flour**

Stir in slowly:

    **1 cup stock**

    **(½ cup raisins)**

When the sauce is smooth and boiling, add the onions, apples and meat. Stir in:

    **1 tablespoon lemon juice**

    **Season to taste**

and serve with:

    **Boiled Rice, 189**

## LAMB TERRAPIN

**4 Servings**

Chop or rice:

    **2 hard-cooked eggs**

Combine the eggs with:

    **2 cups diced cold cooked lamb**

    **2 tablespoons olive oil**

    **1 tablespoon lemon juice**

Melt:

    **2 tablespoons butter**

Stir in until blended:

    **3 tablespoons flour**

    **1 teaspoon dry mustard**

Stir in slowly:

    **2 cups lamb stock or milk**

Add:

    **1 teaspoon Worcestershire sauce**

    **Season to taste**

Cook and stir the sauce until it is boiling. Add the lamb and egg mixture. Reduce heat and simmer until reheated. Serve on:

    **Hot toast**

Garnish with:

    **Mint**

## CHOP SUEY OR CHOW MEIN

**4 Servings**

These vaguely Chinese dishes which can be made with cooked pork, chicken or seafood differ in that Chop Suey is served over steamed rice, and Chow Mein over fried noodles. Both are— like some of the old Chinese porcelain patterns—strictly for export. To get the feeling of true Chinese food, read Mrs. Buwei Yang Chao's delightful *How to Cook and Eat in Chinese*. To prepare the dish below please read about Stir-Frying, 98. Cut into 2-inch julienne strips about ¼ inch wide:

    **2 cups cooked pork roast**

Slice diagonally, see 279:

    **½ cup celery with tender leaves**

    **½ cup green onions**

Chop coarsely:

    **1 green pepper, seeds and membrane removed**

    **1 cup mushrooms**

Drain:

    **1 cup bean sprouts**

Heat well in a deep heavy skillet:

    **2 tablespoons cooking oil**

Stir-fry the onion and celery about 3 minutes. Then add the mushrooms, pork, peppers and bean sprouts. Continue to stir-fry 2 to 3 minutes longer. Add:

> (½ cup peeled, seeded and slivered fresh tomatoes)
> Jellied juices from the roast or a bit of Meat Glaze, 427
> 1 cup strong consommé

Season with:

> Salt and pepper
> 1 tablespoon soy sauce
> 3 tablespoons dry sherry

You may thicken the juices with cornstarch, 379.
Serve at once.

## POLYNESIAN PORK OR CHICKEN

**4 Servings**

Prepare and keep warm:

> Oriental Sweet-Sour Sauce II, 405

Stir-fry, 98, in a wok or skillet:

> 1 tablespoon vegetable oil
> 1 cup finely diced cooked chicken or pork

When thoroughly heated, put meat into a heated dish. In the wok, stir-fry briefly:

> 1 cut-up orange
> 1 small cubed banana
> (¼ cup grated coconut)

in:

> 1 tablespoon vegetable oil

Add the meat and the warm sauce. Mix lightly until all ingredients are coated and hot. Serve at once over:

> Chow Mein noodles

## LETOVERS IN BACON

Preheat oven to 450°.
Moisten lightly three parts of:

> Cooked ground meat or meat loaf

and one part of:

> Boiled Rice, 189

with:

> Gravy or cream

Season well with:

> Salt and pepper
> Minced onion or onion juice

Roll the mixture into small balls, flatten slightly and wrap around them:

> Slices of bacon

Secure the bacon with wooden picks. Place the patties in a greased baking dish and bake until the bacon is crisp, about 15 minutes. Serve with:

> A tomato sauce

## COOKED GROUND HAM LOAF

**6 Servings**

Preheat oven to 350°.
Combine:

> 2 cups cooked ground ham
> 1 cup bread or cracker crumbs or crushed cornflakes
> 2 eggs
> 2 tablespoons grated onion
> ⅛ teaspoon pepper
> 1 cup milk
> 2 tablespoons chili sauce
> 2 to 4 tablespoons chopped parsley or celery

Bake these ingredients in a greased loaf pan about 30 minutes. Serve the loaf with:

> Horseradish Sauce, 386,
> Hot Mustard Sauce, 390,
> Mushroom Wine Sauce, 392, or a tomato sauce, 400–401

## STUFFED HAM ROLLS

### I.

**4 Servings**

Make these when you have leftover rice.
Preheat oven to 400°.
Trim:

8  **thin slices baked or boiled
    ham**
Spread them lightly with:
    **Mustard**
Place on each slice part of the following filling.
Combine:
  1½  **cups cooked rice**
   ⅓  **cup chopped raisins**
    1  **beaten egg**
   ¼  **teaspoon paprika**
   ½  **teaspoon Worcestershire
       sauce**
  (¼  **cup chopped celery)**
  (½  **teaspoon basil)**
Roll the slices and secure them with
wooden picks. Brush with:
    **Milk**
Bake the rolls until they are thoroughly heated.
Serve with:
    **Hot Cumberland Sauce, 407**

**II.**  Prepare, as for above:
    **Slices of ham or prosciutto**
Place on each slice:
    4  **asparagus tips**
Roll, brush and heat the ham as di-
rected above.
Serve the rolls with:
  1½  **cups Cheese Sauce, 385**

**III.**
                   **4 Servings**
Preheat oven to 350°.
Prepare, as for above:
    8  **large slices ham**
Combine and mix well:
   ¾  **cup cultured sour cream**
    1  **cup sieved creamy cottage
       cheese**
    1  **slightly beaten egg**
   ¼  **cup minced onions**
   ½  **cup drained chopped
       cooked spinach**
   ½  **teaspoon dry mustard**
   ¼  **teaspoon salt**
Place about 2 tablespoons filling on

each slice of ham. Roll and tuck in
the edges. Put in a shallow baking
dish and cover with a mixture of:
    1  **cup cream of mushroom
       soup**
   ¼  **cup cultured sour cream**
Bake 20 to 25 minutes.

## GROUND HAM ON PINEAPPLE SLICES

                   **4 Servings**
Preheat oven to 400°.
Combine:
    1  **cup ground cooked ham**
    1  **teaspoon prepared mustard**
    2  **tablespoons mayonnaise**
Spread this mixture on:
    4  **slices drained pineapple**
Bake the slices in a greased pan
about 10 minutes.

## HAM AND POTATO CAKES

                   **4 Servings**
Combine:
    1  **cup mashed potatoes**
    1  **cup ground cooked ham**
    1  **tablespoon chopped parsley**
   ½  **teaspoon grated onion**
   ⅛  **teaspoon pepper**
     **Salt, if needed**
Shape this mixture into flat cakes.
Dip lightly in:
    **Flour**
Sauté in:
    **Bacon drippings or other
       fat**

## HAM CAKES WITH PINEAPPLE AND SWEET POTATOES

                   **6 Servings**
Prepare:
    3  **large Boiled Sweet
       Potatoes, 355**
Preheat oven to 375°.
Combine:

2 cups chopped or ground
    cooked ham
1/2 cup dry bread crumbs
2 eggs
1/8 teaspoon salt
(1 teaspoon prepared
    mustard)

Shape these ingredients into 6 flat cakes. Melt in a skillet:

5 tablespoons bacon
    drippings

Brown lightly in the skillet:

6 slices drained pineapple

Remove them and brown the ham cakes in the skillet. Place the pineapple slices in a baking dish and cover each slice with a ham cake. Skin the sweet potatoes. Cut them lengthwise into halves. Combine and sprinkle over them:

1/4 teaspoon cloves
1/4 cup brown sugar

Cook the potatoes slowly in the skillet until well caramelized. Place them over the ham cakes in the baking dish. Baste with:

Pineapple juice

Bake about 10 minutes.

HAM À LA KING

6 Servings

Prepare:

2 cups White Sauce I, 383

When the sauce is boiling, add:

2 cups diced cooked ham
2 diced hard-cooked eggs
1 cup Sautéed Mushrooms,
    328, or canned mushrooms
    with sliced stuffed olives
1 tablespoon chopped green
    pepper
1 tablespoon chopped
    pimiento

Serve the ham very hot on:

Rounds of toast, on rusks,
    in bread cases or on corn
    bread squares

Garnish with:

Chopped parsley

## ☰ BARBECUED FRANKFURTERS, WIENERS OR HOT DOGS

I. Preheat broiler or grill.
Grill:

Frankfurters, wieners or
    hot dogs

or put under the broiler on a rack in a roasting pan. During the cooking baste them ▶ constantly with:

A Barbecue Sauce, 404

II. Cut lengthwise:

Frankfurters, wieners or
    hot dogs

Fill with:

A strip of sharp cheese

Wrap spirally with:

A strip of bacon

Grill, turning often, until bacon is crisp. Serve with:

A Barbecue Sauce, 404

## ☰ FRANKFURTER KEBABS

8 Servings

Cut into about 4 pieces each:

8 frankfurters

Marinate about 30 minutes in:

French Dressing, 413

Preheat grill or broiler.
Skewer the pieces alternately with bits of:

Bacon
Small canned pickled
    onions
Green pepper

Grill or broil, turning often.

## FRANKFURTERS OR SAUSAGES IN SAUCE

### I.
**3 Servings**

Preheat oven to 400°.
Place in a shallow pan:

**6 frankfurters**

Prepare:

**1 cup Quick Tomato Sauce, 400 or Barbecue Sauce, 404**

You may add:

**(Chopped green peppers, seeds and membranes removed)**
**(Grated onions or chives)**

Pour these ingredients over the frankfurters. Bake them until they swell and the sauce thickens.

### II. Prepare, using no salt:
**Quick Tomato Sauce, 400**

Season it well with:

**Paprika**

Sauté, 97:

**Vienna Sausages**

Drain them. Heat them in the sauce. Serve with:

**Boiled Rice, 189,**
**Boiled Noodles, 200, or**
**Mashed Potatoes, 344**

## SAUSAGE BAKED WITH APPLES
**4 Servings**

Preheat oven to 400°.
Arrange in a baking dish:

**8 partly sautéed pork sausages**

Core:

**6 tart apples**

Cut them into 1/4-inch slices and place around the sausages. Sprinkle with:

**3/4 cup brown sugar**

Bake at 400° for 10 minutes. ◗ Reduce the heat to 350° and continue baking about 15 minutes longer. Baste with the drippings.

## SAUSAGES AND MUSHROOMS

Prepare:

**Mashed Potatoes, 344,**
**or Mashed Boiled Chestnuts, 313**

Heap them in a mound on a hot platter. Keep them hot. Sauté:

**Sausages, 633**

Place them around the potatoes. Sauté in the drippings:

**Sliced Mushrooms, 328**

Garnish the platter with them and:

**Sprigs of parsley**

Pour drippings over the potatoes or chestnuts.

## SAUSAGE AND ONIONS
**4 Servings**

Heat in a skillet:

**2 tablespoons vegetable oil or shortening**

Add:

**1 1/2 cups sliced onions**

Cook and stir over low heat about 15 minutes or until golden. Cut a lengthwise slit in:

**8 hot dog sausages or frankfurters**

Fill them with the onions. Fasten with wooden picks. Broil slowly on both sides. Remove picks and place stuffed sausages on:

**Toast or toasted buns**

## SAUSAGE AND MILLET CASSEROLE

Using millet, prepare:

**Rice or Millet Spoon Bread, (II, 343)**

While the spoon bread is baking, sauté:

**Small link sausages**

Fry long enough to remove most of the fat. About 10 minutes before the spoon bread is done, place the sausages on top. Coat with:

Chili Sauce, (II, 686), or
Quick Tomato Sauce, 400

Continue to bake about 10 minutes longer.

## CANNED BAKED BEANS WITH BACON OR FRANKFURTERS

**6 Servings**

Preheat oven to 350°.

To put zing into this dish, and to make it moist and palatable, add to:

2½ cups canned beans:
21-oz. can

approximately:

¼ cup catsup
2 tablespoons molasses
2 tablespoons brown sugar
2 tablespoons bacon
drippings
Minced onion, celery and
green pepper
Salt, if needed
(3 drops hot pepper sauce, a
few grains of red pepper, or
1 tablespoon prepared
mustard)

Place the beans in a greased shallow ovenproof dish. Cover the top with:

Bacon or skinned sliced
frankfurters

Bake covered about 30 minutes. Uncover and bake 30 minutes more.

## LENTIL OR LIMA BEAN SAUSAGE CASSEROLE

**4 Servings**

This dish, puréed, makes a fine stuffing for peppers or onions.
Preheat oven to 375°.
To:

1 cup cooked or canned lima
beans or lentils

add:

6 sliced frankfurters or
cooked sausages
1 chopped green pepper,
seeds and membrane
removed
2 chopped tomatoes

You may wish to purée the beans or lentils. Place these ingredients in a baking dish and cover with:

Au Gratin II, (II, 221)

Bake about 15 minutes.

## PIGS IN POTATOES

**3 Servings**

▶ Please read about Deep-Fat Frying, 94.

Combine and beat well:

1 teaspoon minced onion
1 teaspoon minced parsley
2 cups Mashed Potatoes, 344
1 egg yolk

Sauté:

6 small Vienna sausages

or use:

Precooked pork sausages

Coat them with the potato mixture.
Roll in:

Finely crushed bread
crumbs

then in:

1 egg diluted with
1 tablespoon water or milk

then again in the crumbs. Fry the piggies in deep fat heated to 375° until they are a golden brown.

## CREAMED CHIPPED BEEF

**4 Large Servings**

▶ Do not salt this dish.
Pull apart:

8 oz. chipped beef

Melt:

3 tablespoons butter

Sauté until the onions are golden:

3 tablespoons minced onion

3 **tablespoons minced green
  pepper**
Sprinkle with:
   3 **tablespoons flour**
Add slowly, stirring constantly:
   2 **cups milk**
Add the beef. Simmer these ingredients until they thicken. Remove from
the heat and season with:
   1 **tablespoon chopped parsley
     or chives**
   1/4 **teaspoon paprika**
   2 **tablespoons dry sherry**
   (2 **tablespoons capers or
     chopped pickles)**
Serve the beef on:
   **Hot buttered toast**


CHIPPED BEEF IN CREOLE
SAUCE

                        **3 Servings**
♦ Do not salt this dish.
Prepare and keep hot:
   **Quick Creole Sauce, 401**
Melt:
   1 **tablespoon butter**
Sauté 1 minute:
   4 **oz. shredded chipped beef**
Add the sauce. Serve on:
   **Buttered toast**


CHIPPED BEEF IN CHEESE
SAUCE

                        **2 Servings**
♦ Do not salt this dish.
Prepare:
   1 **cup Cheese Sauce, 385**
Add to it:
   4 **oz. or more shredded
     chipped beef**
Heat it. Serve over:
   **Hot corn bread squares or
   pancakes**


CHIPPED BEEF AND SWEET
POTATO CASSEROLE

                        **5 Servings**
Preheat oven to 375°.
♦ Do not salt this dish.
Cut into cubes:
   5 **cooked or canned sweet
     potatoes**
Shred:
   4 **oz. dried beef**
Prepare:
   1/4 **cup grated onion**
   1 1/2 **cups White Sauce I, 383, or
     a canned cream soup**
Place these ingredients in layers in a
greased casserole. Cover the top with:
   **Crushed cornflakes**
Dot with:
   **Butter or cheese**
Bake about 20 minutes.


CHIPPED BEEF OR CORNED
BEEF IN CANNED SOUP

                        **4 to 5 Servings**
♦ Do not salt this dish.
Combine and heat:
   1 **cup cream soup—
     mushroom, celery or
     asparagus**
   6 **tablespoons milk or stock**
   1/8 **teaspoon freshly ground
     nutmeg
     A grating of black pepper**
Add:
   8 **oz. shredded chipped beef
     or 1 cup diced canned
     corned beef**
   (1 **cup leftover vegetables:
     onions, artichoke hearts or
     asparagus)**
Heat these ingredients. Serve on:
   **Toast or hot biscuits**
sprinkled with:
   **Chopped parsley, chives or
   grated cheese**

## CORNED BEEF HASH AND POTATOES

### 6 Servings

Grind, using coarse blade, or dice:

1½ lb. cooked or canned
       corned beef: about 3 cups

Dice:

2 cups boiled potatoes

Melt in a large saucepan:

2 tablespoons butter

Stir in and simmer until tender:

½ cup chopped onion
1 diced green pepper, seeds
   and membrane removed
2 ribs celery, chopped
(1 clove garlic)
(1 cup mushrooms)

Add the beef and potatoes and:

1 teaspoon Worcestershire
   sauce
2 tablespoons minced parsley
   or chives

Stir lightly over medium heat while adding gradually:

⅓ to ⅔ cup White
   Sauce III, 383
   Season to taste

Stir and cook till well blended and thoroughly heated. Place on a hot platter and serve topped with:

6 Poached Eggs, 213

## CANNED CORNED BEEF HASH PATTIES

### 4 Servings

Sauté:

3 tablespoons chopped onion

in:

2 tablespoons butter

Add:

2 tablespoons horseradish
½ teaspoon thyme
2 cups canned corned beef
   hash

Form patties of this mixture. Sauté them on both sides in:

Hot butter or drippings

Sauté in the same pan:

(Sliced firm tomatoes)

Season with:

Brown sugar
Salt and pepper

Arrange the tomatoes and patties on a platter, garnished with:

Parsley

Or, if you omit the tomatoes, serve the patties with:

1½ cups White Sauce I, 383

to which you may add:

(2 chopped hard-cooked eggs)
(2 tablespoons chopped
   pickles)

## ABOUT HASH

The Irish cook, praised for her hash, declared: "Beef ain't nothing. Onions ain't nothing. Seasoning's nothing. But when I throw myself into my hash, that's hash!" The usual way to make hash is to cut the meat from a chicken or turkey carcass or from a beef roast, combine it with leftover gravy, reheat it briefly and season it acceptably. ◗ Never allow it to boil or overcook once the meat is added. There should be about half as much gravy as other ingredients. Have sauce or gravy at the boiling point. Put in the solids, then ◗ reduce the heat at once and let them warm through thoroughly. If heating hash in the oven, be sure to use a topping to prevent the drying out of the top layer of meat or vegetables. Covering with a lid may develop steam, which will thin the gravy. See Au Gratins, (II, 221).

You may add to the meat cooked mushrooms, celery or potatoes, chopped olives, green peppers, parsley or some other herb. The proportions may be varied; this is a matter of taste and expediency. In the absence of gravy, sweet or sour cream or a sauce—white, tomato or creole—may be substituted. Or you may add a sauce or cream to the gravy to obtain the desired amount. When using cream, reheat the hash in a double boiler, because boiling thins it. Sherry or Madeira may be added, or, for each 2 cups of gravy, a tablespoon each of vinegar and sugar to give a sweet-sour effect. Serve hash in a pastry shell or a rice or noodle ring or in individual Bread Cases, 237.

## BEEF HASH WITH POTATOES AND MUSHROOMS

Cut into cubes equal parts of:
> **Cooked roast beef**
> **(Diced cooked ham)**
> **Pared raw potatoes**

Reserve the beef. Place in a saucepan the potatoes, plus the ham if used. Cover with:
> **Brown Sauce, 391**

Cover the pan and simmer 15 minutes. Add:
> **½ lb. or more sliced mushrooms**

Simmer covered 15 minutes longer. Add the beef. Reheat the hash, but do not let it boil. Season with:
> **A pinch of basil, thyme or savory**
> **Dry sherry**
> **Salt or garlic salt**

Serve the hash on:
> **Hot toast**

garnished with:
> **Chopped parsley**

## SAUTÉED OR BROWNED HASH

**4 Servings**

Combine and grind:
> **1½ cups cooked meat**
> **½ cup cubed raw potatoes with or without skins**

> **1 medium-sized onion**

Season with:
> **Salt, pepper, celery seed**

Turn these ingredients into a skillet in which you have melted:
> **2 tablespoons butter**
> **1 tablespoon vegetable oil**

Cook the hash over medium heat until a crust forms on the bottom; turn it and brown the other side. Stir from time to time to let the hash brown throughout. Shortly before it is done, pat it down firmly to form an unbroken cake. This mixture requires about ½ hour's cooking in all. Serve the hash with:
> **Catsup or a tomato sauce**

## QUICK HASH

**4 Servings**

Heat and stir over very low heat:
> **1 cup cream of mushroom soup**
> **¼ cup milk**

Add:
> **1 cup cubed cooked meat: ham, frankfurters, hamburgers, etc.**
> **2 sliced hard-cooked eggs**

Season the hash with:
> **A pinch dried basil or thyme**
> **Salt and pepper**
> **(Chopped parsley)**

Serve it over:
> **Hot corn bread or toast**

## HASH WITH VEGETABLES

**6 Servings**

This is an excellent combination. Preheat oven to 350°.
Combine:
> **½ cup diced cooked potatoes**
> **⅓ cup diced cooked onions**
> **⅓ cup parboiled sliced green peppers**

¹/₃ **cup parboiled chopped
celery**
3 **tablespoons diced pimiento**
2 **cups cold cooked meat, cut
into ¹/₃-inch cubes**

Combine and heat just to the boiling
point:

1 **cup leftover gravy or
canned cream soup**
¹/₃ **cup tomato purée**
1 **tablespoon butter**
1 **teaspoon Worcestershire
sauce**

Add the meat and vegetables.

**Season to taste**

Pour the hash into 1 large baking dish
or into 6 individual baking dishes.
Sprinkle the top with:

**Au Gratin III, (II, 221)**

Brown in the oven.

## HASH IN CREAMED CABBAGE

Preheat oven to 400°.
Prepare:

**Creamed Cabbage II, 304**

Place half the cabbage in a greased
ovenproof dish. Place on top of it a
layer of:

**Hash moistened lightly
with gravy or cream**

Cover with the remaining cabbage.
Sprinkle the top with:

**Au Gratin II or III, (II, 221)**

Bake the cabbage until the topping is
light brown.

## SHEPHERD'S PIE

Preheat oven to 400°.
Prepare:

**Hash**

Spread it in one large baking dish or
in smaller individual ones. Cover
with fresh hot:

**Mashed Potatoes, 344**

Coat with:

**Melted butter**

Bake until the potatoes are browned.

## BREAD DRESSING IN A RING
FILLED WITH HASH

Preheat oven to 400°.
Grease a ring mold. Fill it with:

**Bread Dressing, 431, or
Apple and Onion
Dressing, 434**

Bake until brown. Invert it onto a hot
plate. Fill the center with:

**Hash or stewed creamed
fresh or leftover vegetables**

Serve with:

**Leftover gravy or some
other sauce**

## ROAST BEEF IN SAUCE

**I.**

4 Servings

Cut into ¹/₂-inch cubes:

2 **cups cooked roast beef**

Prepare:

**Hot Cumberland
Sauce, 407**

Add the beef and heat in the sauce,
but do not boil. Serve at once on:

**Hot toast**

**II.** Prepare:

**Quick Creole Sauce, 401, or
Curry Sauce, 390**

Arrange very thin slices of:

**Cooked roast beef**

on a hot platter. Pour the hot sauce
over them. Sprinkle the top with:

**Chopped parsley or
chopped chives**

## BOEUF MIROTON

Melt:

2 **tablespoons butter**

Sauté in it until golden:

1 **coarsely sliced onion**

Sprinkle over all and mix rapidly
with a wooden spoon:

1 **tablespoon flour**

Add and stir until boiling:

**1 cup bouillon**
**Season to taste**

Reduce the heat and add:

**1 to 2 tablespoons vinegar**

Simmer about 15 minutes. Arrange on a hot platter:

**Thin slices of boiled or**
**roasted beef**

Cover the slices with the above hot sauce and serve.

## CHICKEN OR TURKEY HASH

**4 Servings**

▶ Please read About Hash, 254.
Combine and heat:

**1½ cups diced cooked chicken**
**or turkey**
**½ cup drained cooked celery**
**or boiled potato cubes**
**1 cup leftover chicken or**
**turkey gravy or other sauce**
**1 tablespoon chopped parsley**
**or chives**
**Season to taste**

## CREAMED CHICKEN OR VEAL

**4 Servings**

Prepare:

**1 cup White Sauce I, 383**

using cream and chicken stock or vegetable water for the liquid, or use part gravy and part milk.
Add:

**2 tablespoons chopped**
**parsley**
**2 cups minced cooked**
**chicken or veal**
**(½ cup Sautéed Mushrooms,**
**328, or cooked peas)**

Season these ingredients with:

**1 teaspoon lemon juice or**
**½ teaspoon Worcestershire**
**sauce or 2 teaspoons dry**
**sherry**

**(3 tablespoons chopped pickle**
**or olives)**
**¼ teaspoon celery salt or salt**
**and pepper as needed**

Grease a baking dish and put the creamed mixture in it. Sprinkle the top with:

**Au Gratin II or III, (II, 221)**
**(½ cup shredded blanched**
**almonds)**

Place the dish under the broiler until the crumbs are brown. Or serve the creamed ingredients unbreaded on:

**Hot Waffles (II, 150) or**
**in a Noodle or Rice Ring,**
**201 or 189**

## CHICKEN À LA KING

**4 Servings**

Dice:

**1 cup cooked chicken**
**½ cup Sautéed**
**Mushrooms, 328**
**¼ cup chopped pimiento**

Melt:

**3 tablespoons chicken fat or**
**butter**

Stir in and blend:

**3 tablespoons flour**

Add slowly:

**1½ cups Chicken Stock,**
**(II, 172), or cream**

When the sauce is smooth and boiling, add the chicken, mushrooms and pimiento. Reduce the heat. Pour some sauce over:

**1 beaten egg yolk**

and return mixture to pan. Stir until it thickens slightly. Add:

**Seasoning, if required**
**(¼ cup blanched slivered**
**almonds)**
**(1 tablespoon dry sherry)**

Fill:

**Patty Shells, (II, 369)**

with the chicken and serve at once.

## TURKEY OR CHICKEN CASSEROLE WITH VEGETABLES

**4 Servings**

Prepare by cutting into cubes:

>    **2  cups cooked turkey or chicken**

Melt:

>    **3  tablespoons butter**

Stir in and sauté gently until onions are golden:

>    **½  cup diced celery**
>    **⅓  cup thinly sliced onions**
>    **⅓  cup thinly sliced green pepper, seeds and membrane removed**

Sprinkle over the top, stir in and cook slowly 5 minutes:

>    **3  tablespoons flour**

Stir in gradually:

>    **1½  cups turkey or chicken stock**

Remove the pan from the heat. Stir in:

>    **2  lightly beaten egg yolks**

and the turkey meat. Stir over low heat just long enough to let the sauce thicken slightly. You may add:

>    **(3  tablespoons dry white wine)**
>    **Season to taste**

Place the mixture in one large or in individual casseroles. Sprinkle the top with:

>    **Minced chives, parsley, or nutmeats**

Serve at once. Good with rice or spoon bread or on toast.


## QUICK CHICKEN CREOLE

**8 Servings**

Melt:

>    **3  tablespoons chicken fat**

Sauté in it:

>    **2  tablespoons chopped onion**
>    **(1  minced clove garlic)**

Stir in:

>    **3  tablespoons flour**
>    **¼  teaspoon salt**
>    **¼  teaspoon paprika**

Add:

>    **½  cup tomato purée or strained tomatoes**
>    **1  cup chicken broth**

Stir and cook these ingredients until they boil. Add:

>    **1  teaspoon lemon juice**
>    **½  teaspoon horseradish**
>    **2  cups diced cooked chicken meat**
>    **½  cup sliced Sautéed Mushrooms, 328**
>    **½  cup chopped pimiento**
>    **Season to taste**

Serve the chicken in a:

>    **Rice Ring, 189, or Noodle Ring, 201**


## COOKED TURKEY, CHICKEN OR VEAL LOAF

**4 to 6 Servings**

Preheat oven to 350°.

Cook and stir 1 minute:

>    **1½  tablespoons grated onion**

in:

>    **1  tablespoon butter**

Add it to:

>    **2  cups diced cooked turkey, chicken or veal**
>    **½  teaspoon salt**
>    **1  cup cracker crumbs**
>    **¾  cup gravy or thickened Chicken Stock, (II, 172)**
>    **¾  cup milk**
>    **2  beaten eggs**
>    **(½  cup finely chopped celery)**
>    **(¾  teaspoon chili powder)**

Place these ingredients in a well-greased loaf pan set in a pan of hot water. Bake about 40 minutes. Serve with:

>    **Leftover gravy with chopped olives,**

Quick Mushroom Sauce, 395, or White Sauce IV, 384, with lots of chopped parsley or chives

## CHICKEN OR TURKEY DIVAN

**4 Servings**

Preheat oven to 400°.

Butter a 9 x 12-inch shallow heat-proof dish. Place on the dish:

(**4 slices hot buttered toast**)

Next place a layer of:

**Sliced cooked chicken or turkey**

The white meat is best. Allow 2 or 3 slices per serving. Cook until almost done and lay on top the contents of:

**1 package frozen broccoli or asparagus spears, well drained**

Or use leftover cooked broccoli or asparagus.

Cover the whole with:

**2 cups Mornay Sauce, 384**

Sprinkle with:

**Grated Parmesan cheese**

and heat in the oven until the sauce is browned and bubbling. Serve at once.

## HOT CHICKEN SALAD

**4 Servings**

This recipe enlarges well for quantity service.

Preheat oven to 350°.

Combine:

**2 cups cubed cooked chicken**
**1 cup finely diced celery**
**1/2 teaspoon salt**
**1/4 teaspoon tarragon**
**1/2 cup toasted almonds**
**1 tablespoon chopped chives**
**2 tablespoons lemon juice**
**1/2 cup mayonnaise**
**1/2 cup White Sauce I, 383**

Bake in very shallow individual bak-ing dishes 10 to 15 minutes or until heated through. Garnish with:

**Parsley or small sprigs of lemon thyme**

## QUANTITY CHICKEN LOAF

**16 to 24 Servings**

This is a wonderfully stretchable recipe to serve at group meetings. It is rather firm, slices well and is attractive covered with a sauce.

Preheat oven to 350°.

Remove meat carefully from:

**A 4- to 5-lb. stewed chicken**

Dice it. Combine lightly with a fork:

**2 to 4 cups dry bread crumbs**
**1 to 3 cups cooked rice**
**1 1/2 to 2 cups chicken broth, depending on how much rice and crumbs are added**
**3 to 4 lightly beaten eggs**
**Season to taste**
(**1/2 cup chopped ripe olives**)
(**1/2 cup slivered pistachio nuts**)

Bake ▶ uncovered in a 9 x 13-inch ovenproof pan 25 to 30 minutes. Serve with:

**Poultry Pan Gravy, 383, seasoned with a little lemon rind, parsley and 1/16 teaspoon saffron**

or with:

**Quick à la King Sauce, 395, or Quick Mushroom Sauce, 395, or Poulette Sauce, 390**

## SEAFOOD À LA KING

**4 Servings**

Combine:

**1 cup canned lobster, crab meat or tuna**
**3 diced hard-cooked eggs**
**1 chopped pimiento**

Sauté and add:

**1/2 cup chopped mushrooms, 326**

Cook in boiling water until tender; drain and add:

> **¼ cup chopped sweet red peppers, seeds and membrane removed**

Prepare:

> **White Sauce I, 383**

When the sauce is smooth and boiling, add the above ingredients:

> **Season to taste**

and add:

> **1 teaspoon Worcestershire sauce, 1 tablespoon lemon juice or 2 tablespoons dry white wine**

Serve the seafood over:

> **French Toast, (II, 355), or rusks, or in patty shells, or au gratin in ramekins**

Or garnish with toast triangles spread with:

> **Mashed avocado and lemon juice**

## CREAMED SEAFOOD

**4 Servings**

Prepare:

> **1½ cups White Sauce I, 383, or Poulette Sauce, 390**

Add:

> **1 cup canned tuna, shrimp or clams**

Just before serving, heat the seafood through and add:

> **½ to 1 cup coarsely chopped watercress**
> **1 diced avocado**

Serve over:

> **Toast or rusks**

## CREAMED SEAFOOD AU GRATIN

**6 Servings**

Preheat oven to 350°.

Combine 3 or 4 kinds of raw fish or shellfish, for example:

> **½ lb. chopped lobster meat**
> **1 cup drained oysters**
> **1 cup minced fillet of haddock**

Prepare:

> **1½ cups Sautéed Mushrooms, 328**
> **4 cups White Sauce I, 383**

using cream as the liquid. When the sauce is smooth and hot, fold in the fish. Add the mushrooms.

> **Season to taste**

Fill ramekins or shells with the mixture. Cover the tops with:

> **Au Gratin II, (II, 221)**

Bake the fish about 25 minutes.

## CREAMED SEAFOOD WITH VEGETABLES

**4 Servings**

Preheat broiler.

Cook one or more of the following:

> **1 cup chopped celery, eggplant or cucumber**

Drain well. Prepare:

> **¾ cup White Sauce I, 383**

When the sauce is boiling, add the vegetable and:

> **¾ lb. cooked shrimp, crab meat or tuna**

Season with:

> **Salt, if needed**
> **⅛ teaspoon paprika**
> **(½ teaspoon Worcestershire sauce)**

Place these ingredients in greased ramekins. Cover with:

> **Au Gratin I, (II, 221), or unsweetened grated coconut**

Heat under the broiler until golden.

## KEDGEREE OR LOBSTER OR OTHER FISH

**6 Servings**

Combine:

**2 cups cooked rice
1 lb. cooked flaked lobster, cod fillets or skate
4 minced hard-cooked eggs
1/4 cup butter
1/4 cup cream
2 tablespoons minced parsley
Salt and cayenne**

Heat these ingredients in a double boiler.

## SEAFOOD CASSEROLE IN CREOLE SAUCE

**4 Servings**

Prepare:

**3/4 lb. cooked shrimp or other seafood**

Melt in a skillet:

**2 tablespoons butter**

Toss the seafood in the hot butter about 2 minutes. Add:

**2 cups Creole Sauce, 394
1/4 cup dry white wine**

Simmer the shrimp covered about 5 minutes. You may add:

**(Salt and pepper)
(A few grains cayenne)
(3 diced hard-cooked eggs)**

Serve the shrimp with:

**Boiled Rice, 189**

## WEST AFRICAN TUNA CASSEROLE

**6 Servings**

Have ready:

**2 cups cooked dried black-eyed peas, 294**

Preheat oven to 350°.

Place peas in an ovenproof baking dish. Sauté:

**1/2 cup finely chopped onions**

in:

**3 tablespoons vegetable oil**

Add to the peas with:

**1 large chopped tomato
2 teaspoons crushed hot red peppers**

Bake covered 15 minutes. Add:

**2 cans flaked tuna: 7 oz. each
2 tablespoons tomato paste
1/2 teaspoon salt**

Cover dish, return to oven and bake 10 minutes without stirring. Remove cover, stir, sprinkle with:

**Au Gratin II, (II, 221)**

and bake 5 minutes longer uncovered. Serve with:

**Baked Bananas, (II, 120)**

omitting the sugar.

## QUICK SEAFOOD DIVAN

**4 Servings**

Preheat oven to 325°.

Prepare and heat:

**1 1/2 cups White Sauce I, 383, or Quick Canned Soup Sauce II or III, 394, or Quick Creole Sauce, 401**

Have ready:

**1 cup cooked shrimp, crab meat or tuna
Season to taste**

Put into a hot baking dish:

**2 cups cooked asparagus, broccoli or cauliflower
1/2 cup Sautéed Mushrooms, 328
2 teaspoons diced pimientos**

Cover the vegetables with the seafood. Pour the hot sauce over the seafood. Garnish with:

**Grated cheese**

Bake about 25 minutes.

## QUICK CRAB MEAT OR LOBSTER MONGOLE

**4 Servings**

For a perfect luncheon or supper, serve with rice and a salad.
Combine and heat in a double boiler ♦ over—not in—boiling water:

> 3/4 cup canned tomato soup
> 3/4 cup canned pea soup
> 3/4 cup cream
> 1 cup canned crab or lobster meat

When hot, serve as a thick soup over:

> **Croutons**

or pour the Mongole over:

> **Boiled Rice, 189**

Garnish with:

> **Parsley**

## CRAB MEAT CUSTARD

**8 Servings**

Preheat oven to 325°.
In the bottom of a large buttered casserole place:

> 4 slices crustless bread

Place on top of the bread:

> 2 cups canned flaked crab meat
> 1/2 cup shredded cheddar cheese
> Season to taste

Beat together:

> 4 eggs
> 3 cups milk
> 1/2 teaspoon salt
> Dash of cayenne

Pour this mixture over the fish and top with:

> 1/2 cup shredded cheddar cheese

Bake as for a Custard, (II, 507), until done. Serve with:

> **A mixed green salad**

## DEVILED CRAB

**4 Servings**

Flake and pick over:

> 1 1/2 cups canned or cooked crab meat

Sauté:

> 1/4 cup finely chopped onions
> 1/4 cup finely chopped green peppers, seeds and membrane removed
> 1/4 cup finely chopped celery

until onions are golden in:

> 2 tablespoons butter

Add:

> 1/4 cup cracker crumbs
> 3/4 cup milk, cream or clam broth

Cook these ingredients until thick. Remove from the heat. Beat and add:

> 2 eggs
> 1/4 teaspoon salt
> 1 1/2 teaspoons prepared mustard
> A few grains cayenne or 1/8 teaspoon hot pepper sauce

Add the crab meat. Pack these ingredients into crab shells or ramekins. Brush the tops with:

> **Melted butter**

Brown in a 400° oven or under a broiler.

## INDIVIDUAL FISH-PIES

**6 Servings**

Bake 6 individual Pie Shells, (II, 360). Combine and heat:

> 1 cup flaked cooked tuna or salmon
> 1 to 1 1/2 cups thick White Sauce II, 383, or canned cream soup slightly diluted with milk

Season with:

> 2 tablespoons fresh chopped parsley or chervil

¼    teaspoon curry powder
½    teaspoon Worcestershire
       sauce

Just before serving, place the hot mixture in the hot pie shells. Serve garnished with:

**Chopped chives**


## QUICK FISH LOAF

**4 Servings**

Preheat oven to 400°.
Drain, then flake:

1    lb. cooked or canned fish:
       2 cups

Combine and beat:

1    egg
¼    cup undiluted evaporated
       milk or whipping cream
¾    cup soft bread crumbs
½    teaspoon salt
¼    teaspoon paprika
2    teaspoons lemon juice or
       1 teaspoon Worcestershire
       sauce
1    tablespoon melted butter
3    tablespoons minced parsley
2    tablespoons chopped celery,
       onion, green pepper or
       olives

Add the fish. Place these ingredients in a greased baking dish. Bake about 30 minutes. This loaf may be served hot with:

**Quick Tomato Sauce, 400,
Cheese Sauce, 385, or
Caper Sauce, 390**

or cold with:

**Mayonnaise**


## EMERGENCY FISH CAKES

Excellent cakes may be made quickly by combining cooked seafood with canned cream soup. Keep your mixture rather stiff. Treat it as you would any other fish ball or cake. See recipes below.


## FISH BALLS OR CAKES

**About 4 Servings**

Also use as a hot hors d'oeuvre.
Combine and mix well:

1    cup grated or flaked
       canned tuna or salmon
1    cup mashed potatoes
6    chopped olives
8    capers
½    minced clove garlic or
       1 teaspoon grated onion
1    tablespoon minced parsley
       Salt and paprika
1    teaspoon brandy or dry
       sherry
(1   teaspoon dried or
       1 tablespoon freshly
       chopped basil)

Shape the mixture into 1-inch balls or into flat cakes. Sauté them 2 or 3 minutes in:

½    cup hot olive oil or butter

Drain, then roll in:

¾    cup ground nutmeats


## SEAFOOD POTATO CAKES

**6 Servings**

Prepare:

**Leftover Potato Cakes, 354**

Use the egg and 2 cups mashed potatoes.
Add in small flakes:

1    cup or more canned salmon
       or tuna

Season with:

**Chopped parsley, onion
juice or celery seed**

Shape the mixture into cakes. Roll in:

**Crushed cornflakes or
bread crumbs**

Sauté them slowly in:

**Butter or vegetable oil**

## CRAB, CLAM OR OYSTER CAKES

**Six 3-Inch Cakes**

Melt:

    **2 tablespoons butter**

Add, stir and simmer 3 minutes:

    **2 tablespoons minced onion**

Combine and add:

    **2 beaten eggs**

    **1/2 cup cream**

    **1/2 cup soft bread crumbs**

    **2 cups minced oysters, canned clams or flaked crab meat—separately or combined**

    **1/2 cup finely minced celery**

    **1/2 teaspoon dry mustard or 1 tablespoon lemon juice**

    **2 tablespoons chopped parsley**

    **1/2 teaspoon salt**

    **1/2 teaspoon paprika**

Chill this mixture 2 hours. Shape into cakes. Lightly dust with:

    **Flour or bread crumbs**

Melt in a skillet:

    **1 tablespoon butter**

Quickly brown the cakes on both sides. ◗ Lower the heat and cook the cakes slowly about 6 minutes longer. Or you may deep-fat-fry the cakes, first coating with:

    **Bound Breading à l'Anglaise, (II, 220)**

Let dry, then fry until golden in fat heated to 375°, about 15 minutes.

## SALMON CAKES

**6 Servings**

Drain and flake:

    **2 cups canned salmon**

Stir in:

    **1/2 cup cracker crumbs**

    **2 beaten eggs**

    **1/2 teaspoon salt**

    **1/8 teaspoon paprika**

Form these ingredients into cakes. Sauté until brown in:

    **Butter**

Serve the cakes with:

    **quick mushroom sauce, 395, or a celery soup sauce, 394**

to which you have added:

    **Chopped fresh fennel**

## SALMON PUFFS

**6 Servings**

Preheat oven to 350°.

Remove skin and bones, drain, then flake:

    **2 cups canned salmon**

Add and stir lightly to blend:

    **1/2 cup fresh bread crumbs**

    **2 tablespoons grated onion**

    **1 tablespoon lemon juice**

    **1 tablespoon melted butter**

    **Season to taste**

Beat together:

    **1 egg**

    **1/2 cup milk**

Combine with the salmon mixture. Place in 6 well-greased baking cups set in hot water. Bake about 45 minutes. Unmold onto a hot platter. Serve with:

    **Velouté Sauce, 387, or Quick Tomato Sauce, 400**

## SEAFOOD AND CHEESE LOAF

**6 Servings**

Preheat oven to 350°.

Prepare:

    **1 cup Cheese Sauce, 385**

Grease a baking dish and spread in it:

    **1 1/2 cups Mashed Potatoes, 344**

Cover them with half the sauce. Drain, skin, then flake:

    **2 cups canned salmon or tuna**

Place it over the sauce. Cover with the remaining sauce. Bake about 30 minutes. Serve with:

**Quick Tomato Sauce, 400**

## SEAFOOD POT PIE

**8 Servings**

Prepare:

**Biscuit Dough, (II, 348)**

Prepare:

1 cup chopped cooked celery
1 cup cooked peas

Drain the vegetables, reserving the liquid.

Preheat oven to 425°.

Drain and flake if necessary:

2 cups canned salmon,
shrimp or tuna

Melt:

¼ cup butter

Sauté in it about 2 minutes:

1½ tablespoons minced onion

Stir in until smooth:

6 tablespoons flour

Stir in until boiling:

¾ cup vegetable water
1½ cups milk

Add:

1 teaspoon salt
⅛ teaspoon paprika
1 tablespoon lemon juice or
1 teaspoon Worcestershire
sauce
1 teaspoon or more chopped
parsley or chives

Fold the vegetables and the seafood into the cream sauce.

**Season to taste**

Place the mixture in a large casserole. Roll the biscuit dough ¼ inch thick. Cut it into rounds. Top the salmon mixture with biscuits. Bake until done, about 12 minutes.

## SEAFOOD AND TOMATO SCALLOP

**4 Large Servings**

Preheat oven to 375°.

Drain:

2 cups canned salmon, tuna
or shrimp

Combine them with:

3 cups soft bread crumbs
2 tablespoons butter
¼ cup chopped onion
½ teaspoon salt
1 teaspoon sugar
¼ teaspoon paprika or pepper
2½ cups chopped, drained
tomatoes
(1 chopped seeded green
pepper, membrane
removed)
(1 beaten egg)
(1 teaspoon Worcestershire
sauce or lemon juice)
(¼ cup white wine)

Place these ingredients in a greased baking dish. The top may be sprinkled with:

**Grated cheese**

Bake until the top is golden and the interior heated.

## SEAFOOD IN PARSLEY SAUCE WITH RICE OR NOODLE RING

**6 Servings**

Drain:

2 cups canned salmon, tuna
or other seafood

Remove skin and bones. Break into large flakes.

Combine:

1½ teaspoons dry mustard
½ teaspoon salt
⅛ teaspoon pepper
½ teaspoon paprika
3 tablespoons flour

Combine and beat into the dry ingredients:

...ler ♦ over—not
...nd beat with a

**2 tab...ns lemon juice**

Add the milk mixture and stir and cook until the sauce has thickened. Add the salmon and:

**2 tablespoons butter**
**¹/₂ cup finely minced parsley**
**1 teaspoon Worcestershire sauce**

Heat well and serve in:

**Rice Ring, 189, or Noodle Ring, 201**

## PROSCIUTTO STUFFED WITH LOBSTER OR CRAB MEAT

**6 Servings**

Have ready:

**6 large thin slices prosciutto**

Melt in a skillet to the point of fragrance:

**¹/₄ cup butter**

Add and cook 2 minutes:

**2 tablespoons finely chopped shallots**
**2 tablespoons finely chopped celery**

Add:

**2 cups canned crab meat or lobster in small chunks**

Heat the mixture until blended. Remove skillet from heat and add:

**2 teaspoons finely chopped tarragon**
**3 tablespoons chopped parsley**
**Salt and pepper to taste**

Spoon the mixture on half of each ham slice and fold the other half over it. Garnish the tops with:

**A sprig or two of watercress**

Serve with:

**Crisp hot Rye Rolls, (II, 320)**

## CREAMED SHAD ROE

**2 Servings**

Sauté:

**1 cup canned shad roe**

in:

**Butter**

with:

**¹/₂ teaspoon curry powder**

Add:

**Salt and paprika**
**³/₄ cup cream**

Reheat but do not boil the roe. Serve on:

**Toast**

See other roe recipes on 497–498.

## BROILED SHAD ROE

**2 Servings**

Preheat broiler.
Separate into pieces:

**1 cup canned shad roe or other canned fish roe**

Dry with paper toweling. Brush with:

**Melted butter**

Sprinkle with:

**Lemon juice**
**Paprika**

Place roe in a shallow greased pan or on a greased broiler. Broil gently about 10 minutes, turning once. Baste frequently with:

**Melted butter**

Serve on toast, garnished with:

**Slices of lemon**
**Chopped parsley**

## FISH ROE IN RAMEKINS

**3 Servings**

Preheat oven to 325°.
Combine:

**1 cup drained canned fish roe**
**1¹/₂ teaspoons bread crumbs**

1½  teaspoons butter
 1  beaten egg
    Salt, if needed
 ¼  teaspoon paprika
 2  teaspoons chopped parsley
 ½  cup milk

Fill three greased ramekins. Bake them in a pan of hot water until firm—about 20 minutes. Serve the roe with:

Slices of lemon

## ABOUT SANDWICHES

Innumerable hostesses—not to mention quick-lunch stands—keep green the memory of Lord Sandwich, whose mania for gambling, from which he didn't want to be disturbed long enough to eat, gave the world the convenient concoction that bears his name.

Sandwiches range widely in size and complexity. ◗ Don't neglect the Canapé chapter, where many delectable smaller versions are found. To keep sandwiches fresh, wrap in wax paper, foil or a well-wrung-out dampened cloth.

## GRILLED OR SAUTÉED SANDWICHES

Especially good when a thin slice of cheese spread with mustard, salt and paprika is put between the bread slices; or use deviled ham, meat mixtures, jam or jelly.
Melt in a small skillet large enough to accommodate one sandwich:

1½  teaspoons butter

Sauté a sandwich ◗ slowly on one side until browned. Add to the skillet:

1½  teaspoons butter

Brown the second side slowly and serve at once.

## TOASTED OR WAFFLE SANDWICHES

Cut into thin slices:

White or dark bread

Spread it lightly with:

Soft butter

Cut off the crusts and spread between the slices:

Cheese Spread or other
sandwich fillings, (II, 73–75)

Cut the sandwiches to fit the sections of a waffle iron. Wrap them in a moist cloth ready to toast. Heat a waffle iron, arrange the sandwiches upon the iron, lower the top and bake until crisp.

## TOASTED SANDWICHES

These are offered as luncheon suggestions. Many of the sandwich fillings given in the chapter on Canapés may be spread between slices of toast. The sandwiches may be served with a hot sauce or a cold dressing.
Put between:

2  slices of toast

any of the following combinations:

Sliced chicken
Sautéed bacon
Shredded cheese
Quick Mushroom
Sauce, 395

Creamed chicken
Parmesan cheese
Grilled tomatoes and
bacon

Sliced baked ham
Creamed chicken and
mushrooms

Sliced ham
Sliced chicken
Mayonnaise
Lettuce

Braunschweiger
Sliced tomatoes
Lettuce
Tart mayonnaise

Sliced tongue
Sliced tomatoes or
cucumbers
Sautéed bacon
Mayonnaise

Lettuce, French dressing
Sliced tomato and avocado
Crisp sautéed bacon

Asparagus tips
Crisp bacon
Welsh Rarebit, 240–241

Sliced chicken
Lettuce, sliced tomato
Crumbled Roquefort
cheese
Crisp bacon

5. Bamboo shoots with grapefruit sections and sliced pimiento
6. A parsley fringe surrounding a tomato slice, topped by a cucumber slice, topped by a dab of Andalouse Sauce, 421
7. Belgian endive hearts spread generously with Guacamole, (II, 91)
8. Small caviar-filled beets, (II, 91), accented with watercress
9. Artichoke heart garnished with parsley or lemon and filled with Tartare Sauce, 421, or with Crab Salad, 65.

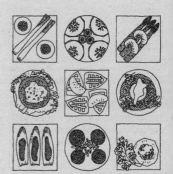

## OPEN-FACED SANDWICHES

These have great appeal, especially when glazed, (II, 70), and attractively garnished like those shown on the right. Vary the bread shapes as well as the bread varieties. For other toppings see Canapés, (II, 63). Reading from left to right in the drawing are:
1. Scallions or tiny hearts of celery or Florence fennel stalks with slices of caviar-covered hard-cooked egg
2. Halves of radish or cucumber slices unpeeled or partially peeled as shown, with slices of stuffed olives in the center
3. Asparagus tips mounted by cooked shrimp
4. A thick slice of tomato topped with seafood salad on lettuce leaves taken from the heart of the head

## BREAD ROLL FILLINGS

Recommended for picnic sandwiches, as they are easy to handle.
Cut into lengthwise halves:

Soft rolls

Hollow them slightly. Fill the hollows with any palatable sandwich spread, such as:

Chicken Salad, 68
Tuna Fish Salad, 67
Braunschweiger sausage
Canapé Fillings, (II, 70)
Chopped celery, nuts and
mayonnaise
Chopped olives and cream
cheese

## HOT BISCUITS BAKED WITH FILLINGS

**About Eighteen 2½-Inch Biscuits**

Combine:

> 1 **cup shredded cooked meat: chicken, fish, ham, veal, or beef**
>
> ½ **cup thick gravy, White Sauce I, 383, or condensed cream soup**
>
> 1 **tablespoon grated onion**
>
> 1 **chopped hard-cooked egg**
>
> 2 **tablespoons chopped pickles or olives**
>
> **Season to taste**

Preheat oven to 450°.

Prepare:

> **Rolled Biscuit Dough, (II, 349)**

Roll it to the thickness of ¼ inch. Cut it into rounds. Place on one round 1 tablespoon of the meat mixture. Moisten the edges and cover with another round. Seal the edges by pressing with a fork. Prick the tops. Place the biscuits on a baking sheet and bake until brown. You may serve these with:

> **(Quick Mushroom Sauce, 395)**

## MEAL-IN-ONE SANDWICH

**4 Servings**

On your toes when you make this. It's easy if you have all your ingredients ready before you poach the eggs.

Prepare:

> 4 **large slices of toast**
>
> 8 **sautéed bacon slices**
>
> 4 **skinned and sliced large tomatoes**
>
> ½ **cup French Dressing, 413**
>
> 1 **cup White Sauce I, 383**
>
> 1 **cup shredded cheese**

Place the toast on a baking sheet; cover it with the bacon, tomatoes and dressing. Poach:

> 4 **eggs**

Place an egg on each piece of garnished toast and cover with the white sauce and grated cheese. Place the toast under the broiler until the cheese melts and the sauce begins to color. Serve piping hot.

## HOT ROAST BEEF SANDWICH

**4 Servings**

Slice:

> **Cold roast beef**

Prepare:

> 1 **cup Brown Sauce, 391**

Add to it:

> 1 **tablespoon finely minced sour pickle or ½ cup chopped olives**

Cut:

> 6 **thin slices of light or dark bread**

Beat until soft:

> 2 **tablespoons butter**
>
> ¼ **teaspoon prepared mustard or 1 teaspoon horseradish**

Spread the bread with this mixture. Dip the beef slices in the hot sauce. Place them between the slices of bread. Serve on a hot platter and garnish with remaining sauce.

## CORNED BEEF OR CHIPPED BEEF AND CHEESE SANDWICHES

**6 Servings**

Cream well together:

> ¼ **cup shredded sharp cheddar cheese**
>
> 2 **tablespoons mayonnaise**

Shred finely and add:

> 4 **oz. canned corned beef or chipped beef**

Add:

¼ cup finely chopped sweet-
   sour pickles
1 tablespoon grated onion
(2 tablespoons minced celery
   or parsley)
Season the spread, as needed, with:
   Salt and pepper
   Prepared mustard or
   Worcestershire sauce
Spread it between:
   Slices of bread
The sandwiches may be toasted or
served with sliced tomatoes and let-
tuce between the layers.

## SAVOYARDE SANDWICH

**1 Serving**

Preheat broiler.
Place on a shallow baking dish or
cookie sheet:
   ½ English muffin
topped with:
   A large thin slice of ham
Make a:
   French Omelet, 222, using
   2 eggs
large enough to cover the ham. Do
not fold the omelet, but slip it flat
onto the ham. Sprinkle with:
   Shredded Gruyère or Swiss
   cheese
Place under broiler until cheese
melts. Serve at once.

## WESTERN SANDWICH

**1 Serving**

For each sandwich, mix the following ingredients:
   1 beaten egg
   2 tablespoons milk
   2 tablespoons chopped
      cooked ham
   1 tablespoon finely minced
      onion
   1 tablespoon finely chopped
      green pepper

Season to taste
In a 9-inch skillet melt:
   2 teaspoons butter
Pour the egg mixture into the hot pan
and cook until almost set, then turn
and cook 1 minute longer. Serve on:
   A large warm hard roll

## CROQUE MONSIEUR
## SANDWICH

**1 Serving**

Make a sandwich of:
   2 slices white bread
Place between them, trimmed to the
same size as the bread:
   A ½-inch slice Gruyère
   cheese
   A ¼-inch slice baked ham
You may spread the ham lightly with:
   (Dijon mustard)
Top with another:
   Slice Gruyère cheese
Melt in a skillet just large enough to
hold the sandwich:
   2 tablespoons butter
Generously brush the upper side of
the sandwich with melted butter; then
place the sandwich with the unbut-
tered side in the skillet and brown it
slowly. Turn and brown the other
side. Place the skillet in a 350° oven
and let the sandwich heat until the
cheese is thoroughly melted. Serve
at once.
   To make a **Croque Madame Sandwich,** substitute thinly sliced chicken
for the ham, and Emmenthaler for the
Gruyère.

## HAM OR TONGUE SALAD
## SANDWICHES

I. Combine:
   Ground cooked ham or
   tongue
   Chopped onion or chives

**Chopped celery or bean sprouts**

Moisten with:

**Cream or salad dressing**

If cream is used, season with:

**Paprika and salt, if needed**

Spread the filling between:

**Thin slices of bread**

II. Combine and mix:

2 tablespoons chopped onion
2 tablespoons catsup
2 tablespoons chopped green pepper
2 tablespoons chopped pickles
1/2 lb. chopped sharp cheese
3 oz. deviled ham or 1/2 cup finely minced cooked ham
1/4 cup cream or a little melted butter

Serve in hollowed hard rolls.

## HAWAIIAN TOAST WITH BACON SANDWICH

**4 Servings**

Cut:

4 to 6 slices dry bread, 1/2 inch thick

Beat until light:

2 eggs

Beat in:

1 cup pineapple juice
1/2 teaspoon salt

Dip the bread in the egg mixture. Soak it well. Sauté in a skillet:

8 slices bacon

Remove them to a hot platter. Keep them hot. Fry the bread in the bacon drippings, browning one side, then the other. Remove the bread to the hot platter. Sauté in the bacon drippings:

4 slices drained pineapple, cut into halves

Garnish the platter with the bacon and the pineapple. Serve toast at once.

## HAM AND PINEAPPLE FRENCH TOAST SANDWICH

Combine equal parts:

**Ground ham**
**Drained crushed pineapple**

Season these ingredients with:

**Dijon mustard**

Spread this filling between slices of:

**Buttered bread**

Prepare an egg mixture as for French Toast, (II, 355); spread on the outside of the sandwiches and sauté as directed.

## HAM, TOMATO AND EGG SANDWICH

Slice and butter:

**Rye bread**

Place on it:

**Boiled ham slices**
**Lettuce leaves**
**Sliced tomatoes**

Garnish the sandwiches with:

**Hard-cooked egg slices**
**Parsley sprigs**

Serve with:

**Cream Horseradish Dressing, 408, or Russian Dressing, 420**

## TOAST ROLLS WITH HAM AND ASPARAGUS

**4 Servings**

A fine luncheon or supper dish with a molded grapefruit salad and coffee.

Preheat oven to 400°.

Drain and reserve liquid:

12 to 16 asparagus tips

Remove the crusts from:

8 thin slices of bread

Brush lightly on both sides with:

**Melted butter**

Place on each piece of bread:

**A slice of boiled ham**

and three or four of the asparagus

tips. Roll the bread around the tips or bring 2 corners together. Fasten the bread with wooden picks. Bake these rolls on a baking sheet until lightly browned. Use the asparagus liquor and cream to make:

**White Sauce I, 383**

Serve the rolls piping hot with the sauce.

## TOASTED DEVILED HAM AND CHEESE SANDWICHES

Cover:

**Thin slices of toast**

with a paste made of:

**Deviled ham**
**Dijon mustard or horseradish**

Cover the ham with thin slices of:

**Cheddar cheese**

Dot with:

**Capers**

Press the sandwiches and sauté until heated through, in:

**Butter**

Serve hot.

## POOR BOY OR SUBMARINE OR HERO SANDWICH

**4 Servings**

Native to New Orleans, where you can find in the filling fried oysters, chili sauce and chicken, as well as the ingredients below. Similar also is the Italian Hero Sandwich served with a tomato-meat sauce.

Cut in half lengthwise a long loaf of:

**French Bread, (II, 306 )**

Spread both cuts with:

**Butter**

On the bottom half, arrange layers of:

**Sliced salami sausage**
**Sliced sharp cheese**
**Thinly sliced boiled ham**
**(Thinly sliced tomato)**

Put on the top half of the loaf to make a sandwich, and cut into 4 pieces. Mix together:

**¼ cup dry mustard**
**1 tablespoon dry white wine**

Serve this with the sandwich.

## REUBEN SANDWICH

**1 Serving**

Preheat oven to 400°.

Lightly butter on one side only:

**2 slices sour rye bread or a cut rye roll**

Layer between the slices of bread or roll:

**Thinly sliced corned beef**
**Sauerkraut**
**1 slice Swiss or Gruyère cheese**

Spread generously with:

**Russian Dressing, 420**

Wrap in foil and heat in oven until cheese is melted and sandwich is heated through. You may also grill this sandwich under the broiler or brown in a skillet.

## TOASTED BRAUNSCHWEIGER SANDWICH

Braunschweiger is a refined version of the rather heavy smoked liver sausage.

Combine and stir to a smooth paste:

**Braunschweiger sausage**
**Canned cream of tomato soup or tomato paste**
**(A few drops of cream or Worcestershire sauce)**

Cut the crusts from:

**Thin slices of bread**

Spread them with the sausage mixture. Roll the bread or make double-deck sandwiches. Toast and serve very hot.

## BACON AND CHEESE SANDWICH

**4 Servings**

Preheat broiler.
Toast either on one or on both sides, or use untoasted:

**4 slices of bread**

Place on each slice:

**(A thick slice tomato)**
**(Chopped onion and green peppers)**
**(Sliced olives or pickles)**
**A slice of cheddar cheese**

Spread with:

**Mustard or Chili Sauce, (II, 686)**

Cover each sandwich with:

**2 slices crisp broiled bacon**

## EGG AND CHEESE SANDWICH WITH TOMATO SAUCE

**4 Servings**

Rub:

**4 slices French Bread, (II, 306)**

with:

**(Garlic)**

Dip them quickly in:

**Milk seasoned with a pinch of salt**

Brown in a skillet in:

**Olive oil**

Place them on a hot ovenproof plate. Cover with:

**4 chopped hard-cooked eggs**
**6 or more chopped olives**
**1 cup or more grated cheese**

Place the open-faced slices under a broiler until the cheese is melted. Serve with:

**Quick Tomato Sauce, 400**

## FRENCH TOAST AND CHEESE

**4 Servings**

Preheat oven to 350°.

Prepare, omitting the sugar:

**French Toast, (II, 355)**

Then toast the bread in the oven on a buttered ovenproof plate about 5 minutes. Stir over very low heat until smooth:

**1/2 lb. shredded or minced cheese**
**1/2 teaspoon salt**
**A few grains cayenne**
**1/4 cup milk**
**3 tablespoons butter**

Spread the toast with the cheese mixture. Return it to the oven to brown lightly.

## TOMATO FRENCH TOAST

**6 Servings**

Beat until light:

**2 eggs**
**1/2 teaspoon salt**
**1/4 teaspoon paprika**
**1/2 cup canned cream of tomato soup**

Dip in this:

**6 bread slices**

Sauté the bread in hot:

**Butter or drippings**

When brown, serve with:

**Cheese Sauce, 385**
**Minced parsley or chives**

## CHEESE SANDWICH WITH MUSHROOM SAUCE

Trim the crusts from:

**Light or dark bread slices**

Spread with:

**Butter**

Place on each piece:

**Slices of cheese**
**Lettuce leaves**
**Tomato or cucumber slices**
**Hard-cooked egg slices**
**Olive or pickle slices**

Serve the sandwiches open-faced with:

Quick Mushroom
Sauce, 395

## PUFFED CHEESE WITH MUSHROOMS ON TOAST

**6 Servings**

Preheat oven to 375°.
Melt in a saucepan:

**1 tablespoon butter**

Add and sauté until tender:

**1/2 cup finely sliced
mushrooms
1 teaspoon grated onion**

Combine and heat:

**2 egg yolks
1/2 lb. shredded Swiss or
Gruyère cheese: 2 cups
3/4 teaspoon salt
1/4 teaspoon pepper
A few grains cayenne**

Stir in the mushroom and onion mixture. Beat until stiff ♦ but not dry:

**2 egg whites**

Fold them into the mixture. Toast on one side:

**6 slices bread**

Place them untoasted side down on a cookie sheet. Spread the toasted sides lightly with:

**(Butter)**

Heap the cheese mixture on the bread. Bake the slices until firm to the touch and well puffed.

## PEANUT BUTTER AND TOMATO SANDWICH

Preheat broiler.
Toast on one side:

**A slice of bread**

Spread the untoasted side with:

**Peanut butter**

mixed with:

**Chopped cooked bacon
Bacon drippings**

Top this with:

**A thick slice of tomato**

Season the tomato with:

**1/4 teaspoon brown sugar
Salt and paprika**

Put the sandwich under a broiler for a minute or two.

## PEANUT BUTTER AND BACON SANDWICH

**4 Servings**

Virtue, however admirable, is frequently dull. Peanut butter needs enlivening. Try this mixture on the unconverted.
Preheat broiler.
Combine:

**3/4 cup peanut butter
1/4 cup mayonnaise
1/4 teaspoon salt
2 tablespoons pickle relish or
chili sauce
1/4 cup cooked minced bacon**

Toast on one side:

**4 slices bread**

Spread the untoasted side with the mixture. Broil the sandwiches until the tops are golden. Slice them diagonally.

## FRUIT STICKS

**I.** Cut into strips 3 x 1 x 1 inch thick:

**White bread**

Toast them on 3 sides. Place them on a baking sheet with the untoasted side up. Drain:

**Pineapple or apricot slices**

Place on the untoasted sides. Sprinkle them well with a mixture of:

**Brown sugar and cinnamon**

Dot with:

**Butter**

Brown lightly under a broiler:

**II.** Preheat oven to 450°.
Prepare:

**Pie Dough, (II, 360)**

Roll it until very thin. Cut it into oblongs. Sprinkle:

> **Drained pineapple or apricot slices**

with:

> **Cinnamon and brown sugar**

Wrap the slices in the oblongs. Moisten the edges with water. Bake the slices about 20 minutes.

## CLUB SANDWICH

**Individual Serving**

Spread:

> **3 large square slices of toast**

on one side only with:

> **Butter, mayonnaise or Russian Dressing, 420**

Cover the spread side of slice 1 with:

> **A lettuce leaf**
> **3 crisp slices hot bacon**
> **Tomato slices**
> **(Drained pineapple slices)**

Over this place slice 2, its spread side covered with:

> **Slices of cold cooked chicken**

Place the spread side of slice 3 over the chicken.

Cut the sandwich on the bias.

## LAMB OR CHICKEN SANDWICH

Trim the crusts from:

> **Large slices rye bread**

Spread them with:

> **Butter**

Place on each piece:

> **Cold lamb or chicken slices**
> **Lettuce leaves**
> **Tomato slices**
> **Hard-cooked egg slices**

Serve the sandwich with:

> **Russian Dressing, 420, or Mayonnaise, 419**

## CHICKEN AND CREAM CHEESE SANDWICHES

Spread:

> **Slices of whole wheat bread**

with:

> **Cream cheese softened with cream**

Add:

> **Slices of cooked chicken**
> **Chopped green olives**
> **Salt, if needed**

## HOT CHICKEN SANDWICHES

**I.** Cut into slices:

> **Cold cooked chicken**

Dip the slices in:

> **Mayonnaise**

Prepare:

> **Biscuits, (II, 348)**

While hot, open and spread with:

> **Butter**

Place the chicken slices in the biscuits. Serve hot with:

> **Poultry Pan Gravy, 383, Cheese Sauce, 385, or Quick Mushroom Sauce, 395**

**II.** Using biscuits as in the previous recipe, fill with:

> **Chicken Salad, 68**

or combine:

> **1/2 cup cooked minced chicken**
> **1 chopped hard-cooked egg**
> **6 chopped stuffed olives**
> **1/4 cup mayonnaise**
> **(2 tablespoons chopped parsley)**

Serve hot with one of the sauces mentioned previously.

**III.**

Preheat oven to 375°.

Prepare:

> **Buttered toast**

Cover the toast with:

> **Sliced chicken**

Sprinkle with:
> **Crumbled Roquefort**
> **cheese**

Cover with:
> **Strips of bacon**

Bake about 10 minutes, until the bacon is crisp.

## TOASTED ROLLS WITH CRAB MEAT AND CHEESE

**4 Servings**

Preheat broiler.
Cut into halves:
> **4 rolls**

Cover the 4 lower halves with:
> **Lettuce leaves**

Combine:
> **³/₄ cup canned crab meat**
> **¹/₄ cup mayonnaise**

Spread this on the lettuce. Spread the remaining halves with:
> **Butter**
> **Slices of cheese**
> **(Mustard)**

Toast the cheese halves under a broiler until the cheese is soft. Combine the halves.

## LOBSTER SANDWICHES

Flake:
> **6 oz. canned lobster or other**
> **seafood**

Sprinkle over it:
> **1 teaspoon lemon juice**

Add:
> **¹/₂ cup minced celery**
> **1 tablespoon minced onion or**
> **chives**
> **¹/₂ cup mayonnaise**

Mayonnaise, if too thick, may be thinned with sour cream. Season with:
> **(Worcestershire sauce or**
> **curry powder)**

Add:
> **(Capers, chopped olives,**
> **pickles or parsley)**

Spread these ingredients on:
> **Buttered rye bread**

You may add:
> **(Crisp lettuce leaves)**

## SHRIMP SANDWICHES WITH CHEESE SAUCE

**6 Servings**

Clean and chop:
> **1¹/₂ cups cooked shrimp**

Melt:
> **2 tablespoons butter**

Add:
> **1 tablespoon grated onion**
> **(1 sliced pimiento)**

and the shrimp. Stir over low heat for 1 minute.
Prepare:
> **6 slices toast**

Heap the shrimp on the toast. Serve with:
> **Cheese Sauce, 385**

# VEGETABLES

Rumor has it that the Baron Eduard de Rothschild never sent word to his gardener what vegetables he had chosen for dinner until an hour before mealtime to ensure their appearing at table absolutely fresh. If you "grow your own" you don't have to be one of the richest men in the world to know how spectacularly delicious corn on the cob can be if gathered while the water for it is coming to a boil. To preserve true, delicate flavor as well as natural sugars and nutrients, and to enjoy green vegetables at their wholesome best, wash them just before cooking. Cook only to the point of doneness, not a moment more, and transfer them at once from cook to consumer.

If you grow your own vegetables, you can choose seeds specifically listed for the home gardener, seeds that usually produce a harvest of superior texture and flavor. Grow them in organically enriched soil, and control their moisture requirements through mulching and watering during dry periods when they need a boost. The longer it takes vegetables to mature, the coarser their cellulose. These slowpokes and overdeveloped vegetables will demand a longer cooking period and incur consequent loss of nutritive value, color and eating quality.

Some unusual vegetables are shown above. Reading left to right, in the foreground are a lotus pod, okra and kohlrabi; in the front of the basket is a bamboo shoot to the left, salsify to the right. Behind these, from left to right, are Florence fennel or finocchio, Jerusalem artichokes and celeriac or knob celery. But vegetables don't have to be unusual to be of the utmost importance in your diet. They are essential for many vitamin, enzyme and mineral factors and often furnish a surprising amount of protein, see 4.

While few things could make us happier than to branch out at this point with how our readers might successfully produce for themselves at least the basic repertory of garden vegetables, the subject is too broad for inclusion here. If you live in the Northeast you might consult Catherine Osgood Foster's *The Organic Gardener,* and for more generalized information *The Basic Book of Organic Gardening* by E. R. Rodale or *Growing Food the Natural Way* by Ken and Pat Kraft.

Because, on the other hand, the growing of a dozen-odd culinary herbs can be achieved in small outdoor areas or even in window pots on an all-year 'round basis; because fresh herbs are so rarely obtainable at market, and since they so greatly enhance the savor of vegetables as well as that of other foods, we have given explicit instructions for their culture on pages (II, 262–265).

Newly in vogue but almost as old as the hills is the collecting of "greens," 323, and of wild fruits, roots and blossoms. This enterprise is not without peril for the uninitiated. Indeed, in looking into the "bag" of the bolder explorers we are sometimes reminded, unfairly we know, of Oscar Wilde's description of a foxhunt: "The unspeakable in pursuit of the inedible." For the fact that the birds and the beasts seem to be thriving on certain kinds of native verdure does not necessarily prove them fit for human consumption.

We have included in the pages which follow those "far-out" vegetables we have found, on close inspection, to be most palatable and troublefree. Even some of these have toxic elements when raw which must be carefully dispersed by heating or leaching: see, for example, About Mushrooms, 326, and About Wild Greens, 323. Where the use of regional names might produce dangerous confusion, we have identified edible varieties by supplying scientific names and specific descriptions. In the field be sure that plants taken from roadside habitats have not been coated with poisonous sprays.

On your more conventional quests—trips to market—use the tests for ripeness we describe under individual vegetable listings. If store stocks are uneven, give preference to a fresh garden-type lettuce over a pale green watercress, or a crisp bunch of carrots over darkened leathery artichokes. Care in cooking, piquancy in seasoning and ingenuity in combining familiar varieties can compensate for the more commonplace choice. But the choices are constantly increasing. It is amazing how many airborne "out-of-season" and exotic vegetables are becoming available almost all year 'round from the controlled-temperature bins of our "fancier" grocers. While most of these novelties are identified in the pages which follow, the inquisitive reader is referred to D. Hawkes's *A World of Vegetable Cookery* for an even more comprehensive count-down.

Should fresh vegetables of any description be in drastically short supply or altogether unavailable the next best bets are—in order of preference those frozen, canned or dried. To compare nutritive values in these categories, see "The Foods We Keep" (II, 607).

In all vegetable cookery involving moisture, be sure to utilize the resulting liquids in sauces or as stocks. Otherwise, nutritional losses are great. For vegetable combinations, often protein-enriched, consult Brunch, Lunch and Supper Dishes, 236, where you will discover a host of recipes in which cooked vegetables make up the principal ingredient.

## STORING VEGETABLES

Certain vegetables and fruits should not be stored together. Apples give off an ethylene gas that makes carrots bitter, and onions hasten the spoilage of potatoes. Watch for other such relationships. Do not wash vegetables until you are ready to use them. Cut the leaves from all root vegetables at once, for the flow of sap continues to the leaf at the expense of the root. We have found that even in the vegetable-keeper of the most modern refrigerators lettuces, celery and endive, for example, hold over much better if encased in plastic bags. For storing watercress and mushrooms, see 45 and 327–328. Vegetables like salad greens, including celery and endive, are best held in moderate humidity at about 35°—as are salsify, turnips and parsnips. Between 35° and 40° is best for most other vegetables, including the cabbage family. Potatoes and tomatoes are best around 40°. Potatoes should always be stored in a dark place to keep them from turning green and so activating poisonous qualities. Held under dry conditions between 35° and 40° are dried peas and beans. Onions and garlic, also stored in dry air, need about 35°. To ripen sweet potatoes and tomatoes, store in warm dry air at about 60° to 70°.

## PREPARING VEGETABLES FOR COOKING

Prepare vegetables as close to cooking time as possible. Most thin-skinned vegetables may be rinsed, scrubbed if necessary, and cooked unpared. If vegetables are to be pared before cooking, trim them as thinly as possible unless the individual recipe indicates otherwise. Also, unless the individual processing requires it, never soak vegetables after paring or slicing if conserving nutrients is of prime importance. Should vegetables tend to brown after paring, sprinkle them with lemon juice or acidulated water, (II, 167). Whether you cook vegetables whole or pared and sliced, see that the pieces are uniform in size so they will all cook through in the same length of time.

You will avoid trouble if, when slicing round vegetables like onions, you first cut them in half and place the flat side down on the cutting surface. Whatever the object to be sliced, hold it as sketched below. Many chopping and slicing devices are advertised, but nothing can replace a skilled relaxed wrist and a sharp knife. Acquire this indispensable trick and you will be forever grateful. Practice with a mushroom, which is yielding and not slippery when placed cap down, and work up to an onion, which can be both resistant and evasive.

♦ The point of the knife is never lifted from the cutting board but forms a pivot. The cutting edge, in turn, is never lifted above the first joint of the left forefinger, as shown on page 279. The handle end of the knife is raised high enough to be eased gently up and down, its wide blade guided by the perpendicular left forefinger and mid-finger. As the slicing progresses, inch a slow retreat with the left hand without releasing a firm grasp on the object.

Should a vegetable like celery or Chinese cabbage be sliced on the diagonal, the two guide fingers are set at an angle, as shown next. But the knife in the right hand continues its relaxed accurate slicing, while the left makes way without losing control of the stalks. To pare very hard, round vegetables, see 372.

In making a really determined effort to lure your family into eating vegetables, you will find that they will respond more readily if the vegetables are appealing in shape. Think of the irresistible charm of vegetables floating like flowers in a Japanese lacquered bowl. The French are also very adept at presentation, if more lavish, and they disguise the same old carrots, beans and potatoes under a mass of impressive modifiers. As **printanière** they are spring-grown, young, tender and thinly sliced. As **brunoise, salpicon, mirepoix** and **macédoine** they are ageless, and sliced respectively from 1/8 to 1/4 to 3/8 inch, which latter size we call just plain **diced**. As **jardinière, julienne** or **allumette**, they are taller and thinner, about 2 to 3 inches long and 1/8 inch through. When they are round in shape and small, you may call them **pearls;** if they are elliptical, **olivette** at 3/8 inch, **noisette** at 1/2 inch, and **Parisienne** if about 1 inch at their narrowest diameter. Utilize whatever scraps are left over in ♣ blender

soups or, unless they are starchy ones, in the stockpot.

## RETAINING NUTRIENTS, FLAVOR AND COLOR DURING VEGETABLE COOKING

Some enthusiasts go so far as to insist that vegetables are best if not cooked at all. But carrots and spinach, for example, among a good many other varieties, will have more nutrients available for body absorption when cooked, despite the inevitable losses due to heating. No one method of vegetable cookery can claim complete superiority. Some vegetables may be scrubbed, then steamed or baked unpeeled, minimizing vitamin loss—provided the cooking is not overly prolonged. Pressure steaming, 281, like stir-frying and pan-steaming, is both quick and efficient; as is steaming with only the water which adheres to the vegetables after rinsing, plus a small quantity of butter or oil. Other methods are discussed at length in the following pages.

Probably the greatest loss of vitamins, especially of vitamin C—from one-fourth to one-half—occurs in mashing and puréeing. The water-soluble vitamins, C and the B-complex group, are the hardest to retain during the application of any type of heat; and this points up again the importance of utilizing all the vegetable juices which result, unless they are bitter or off-flavored. Be sure to drain these stocks as shown on the next page, and store refrigerated for later use.

Both steaming and stir-frying help to retain good color, provided the vegetables are not kept covered after the point of palatable tenderness. Color should never be maintained

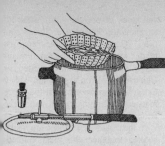

by the addition of baking soda, for this procedure not only destroys nutrient values but makes the vegetable mushy. Color may also be lost through cooking in hard water, (II, 166). Retention of color as well as flavor can be helped along by salting just after the onset of cooking. Allow about 1/4 teaspoon salt to each cup of water.

Since older vegetables tend to lose their natural sugars, they often profit by a pinch of sugar during cooking, as well as by dressing with seasoned butters, herbs, spices and sauces. Dried legumes and canned vegetables in particular profit greatly by bold seasoning. But vegetables in their prime may simply be tossed in butter, allowing not more than one to two teaspoons per cup, so that the full flavor of the vegetable still prevails.

## PRESSURE-COOKING AND PRESSURE-STEAMING VEGETABLES

The use of a pressure cooker saves both time and nutrients, especially if you pressure-steam, a process involving a rack as illustrated above. Allow a minute or two longer than the times given for pressure-cooked vegetables in the individual recipes. Also please read more about Pressure Cooking, 99.

## STEAMING VEGETABLES

Some cooks find the supervision of a pressure cooker worrisome. If you are of this number, use the special steaming pan shown at right above. Be sure the water in the lower element is boiling briskly before setting in place the perforated top with its vegetables. Cover at once and cook the vegetables until tender.

## SKILLET-PANNING AND STIR-FRYING VEGETABLES

Asian cooks are justifiably partial to these methods of cooking vegetables, which preserve freshness of flavor and crisp texture. Please read more about Stir-Frying, 98, and see drawing on the next page.

The slow part of both of these similar methods is the preparation.

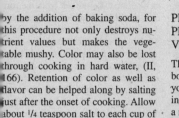

For best results the vegetables must be finely sliced to uniform thickness. Those that tend to stringiness are cut on the diagonal. Stem ends and midribs should be removed from coarse-leaf vegetables and sliced separately. The vegetables are then grouped so the tougher ones go into the pan first. For 4 servings allow about 1 pound of kale, cabbage, okra, celery or celery cabbage; about 1½ pounds of spinach or chard, and about ¾ pound of beans. Cucumber, tomato, zucchini, spinach, Chinese cabbage and salad greens need no water during the cooking period. Have ready for green beans and young root vegetables about ¾ cup boiling water per pound and allow 5 to 8 minutes for cooking. Maturer root vegetables are better steamed, as discussed above.

Use about 1 to 2 tablespoons of cooking oil—sesame is a great favorite—or oil and butter combined, per pound of vegetables. Heat the pan well, put in the cooking oil and heat to the point of fragrance. You may add a slice or two of garlic or fresh gingerroot briefly and discard before the vegetables are put into the pan. Stir the vegetables rapidly with a large flat spatula, coating them with oil until they show signs of wilting slightly. Some cooks like to season at this point with a dash of soy sauce

and stock before clapping on the lid to maintain succulence. Lower the heat. When the vegetables are just tender, you may stir in a small quantity of additional stock if needed, or Chinese Sauce for Vegetables, 396. ▶ Cover the pan briefly until the sauce reaches the boiling point, and serve at once.

If meat and vegetables are to be cooked together, the meat, 546, is cooked first. Remove it from the pan and add it again with the vegetables for reheating. If cooking vegetables in the pod either in a skillet or wok, no oil is needed. Allow for 4 servings 1½ to 2 pounds per person, depending on how full the pods are. Depending also on the thickness of the pods, have ready ½ to ¾ cup boiling water for each pound of vegetable and cook, covered, 5 to 15 minutes or until tender. Shell after cooking and butter before serving. For snow peas, see 339. To ensure crispness, serve immediately. Make certain also that lidded dishes from which the food is served are preheated.

## DEEP-FAT-FRYING VEGETABLES

The French have made the fried potato famous as **French fries**, 351; the English as **chips**, 352. The Ital-

ians, by using either a beaten-egg coating or a batter, produce their famous fried vegetable and other mixtures as **Fritto Misto**, (II, 154); and the Japanese, who learned this trick from Portuguese sailors way back in the sixteenth century, prepare them today under the term **Tempura**, (II, 155).

Since success depends so largely on the ◗ quality of the fat and avoiding its excess absorption, please read About Deep-Fat-Frying, 94. After preparing the vegetables, be sure to sprinkle with lemon juice any that may discolor. Check to see that the vegetables are ◗ dry before applying a coating. It is also best to let the coating dry for about 10 minutes before immersing the food in fat heated to between 350° and 375°. Cook until the vegetables are golden.

Vegetables suitable for this type of cooking are long green beans; 1/3-inch-thick eggplant slices barely nicked with tiny knife marks at 1/2-inch intervals all around the bands of skin; mushrooms and tiny green peppers, whole or cut in half vertically; cucumber, squash, zucchini or sweet potato rounds; sliced lotus roots or bamboo shoots; small bundles of julienned onions or very young green onions; asparagus tips; cauliflower or broccoli florets; artichoke hearts or stems.

## GLAZED ROOT VEGETABLES

Vegetables produced by this method are suitable for garnishing and require no further saucing.
Choose:

> **2 cups young vegetables:**
> **onions, carrots, turnips or**
> **potatoes**

Simmer, covered, in a very heavy pan with:

> **1 cup veal or chicken stock**
> **1/2 teaspoon salt**
> **2 teaspoons sugar**
> **2 tablespoons butter**

When the vegetables are nearly done and the liquid has been almost absorbed, ◗ uncover and continue to cook, shaking the pan continually over brisk heat until they are coated with a golden glaze.

## ABOUT VEGETABLES FOR A ROAST

To cook vegetables for a roast, it is better on several scores to process them separately. For one thing, if they are placed in the roasting pan, the steam they release tends to give a moister oven heat than is desirable for meat roasting. For another, typical root vegetables such as potatoes, carrots, onions and turnips profit by separate cooking. Steam them, 281, until partially tender, then drain and dry. Finish cooking them in butter in a ◗ heavy, covered pan until tender, and complete the browning uncovered.

## ABOUT CREAMED, BUTTERED AND SAUCED VEGETABLES

Practically any vegetables may be served in or with a sauce. They may be steamed or even deep-fried before saucing. ◗ Drain them well before combining with sauces or butter. The amount to allow for garnishing will depend largely on the richness of the sauce, from 1 teaspoon to 1 tablespoon of butter per cup of cooked vegetables, on up to 4 tablespoons of a cream sauce. If the vegetable is heated in the sauce, allow about 2 to 3 tablespoons for each cup of vegetables, using less if it is a rich sour cream dressing—more, perhaps, if based on cream soup. Consider, too, if the vegetable is to be presented in individual deep dishes or from a big serving bowl onto a flat plate.

If you are casseroling the vegetable in a sauce, allow enough sauce to just cover the vegetables. Such casseroles are often finished off Au Gratin, (II, 221).

You may add to vegetable butters and sauces, if not already indicated in the recipe, citrus juices and pinches of zests, (II, 252), fresh or dried herbs, curry powder, mustard, chili powder, horseradish or grated cheese; and don't forget the onions, (II, 272).

## ABOUT STUFFED VEGETABLES

Tomatoes, peppers, squashes, cucumbers, onions, mushrooms, all make decorative and delicious vegetable cases. For a "new dimension," fill them with other vegetables, contrasting in color or flavor; or point up the bland ones with a farce of cooked food, with buttered, crumbed, cooked vegetables or with creamed mixtures. Raw foods that need long cooking should not be used in vegetable stuffings.

Since vegetable cases need different timing when blanched, see recipes under individual vegetables for this information. Other factors remain the same. After draining, place the filled cases on a rack in a pan containing about 1/4 inch of water.

Heat the cases through in a 400° oven, unless otherwise indicated, before serving. Or, if you want to serve them Au Gratin I or II, (II, 221), you may find they have better color if you run them first under a broiler and then bake as above. With Au Gratin III, the cheese will probably brown the tops

sufficiently in the baking alone without the use of a broiler at all.

## ABOUT VEGETABLE FONDUES

Although the term fondue is usually associated with cheese, 243, it applies if you are French to Boeuf Fondu Bourguignonne, 570, or if Spanish to Bagna Cauda, (II, 102). The term is also used for vegetables reduced to a pulp by very, very slow cooking in butter, as for Tomato Pudding (II, 369). Some other vegetables that lend themselves well to such dishes are carrots, celery, eggplant, sweet peppers, onions, leeks and lettuce.

To prepare vegetables for fondueing, first rid them of excess moisture in one of the following ways. Except for tomatoes, they may be parblanched, 106, from 3 to 5 minutes. Eggplant and cucumber may be sliced, salted generously and allowed to drain on a rack. Salting clears them of the rather unpleasant astringent quality they sometimes acquire. They may also be thinly sliced, salted, placed in a bowl and weighted to force out excess moisture. Mushrooms and green onions may be wrapped in a dish towel and wrung out. Tomatoes for fondues may be cut at the stem end and squeezed toward the cut end to eject both moisture and seeds. Cook fondue vegetables in the butter, covered, over very low heat until they reach a naturally puréed state.

## ⅄ ABOUT BLENDED PURÉED VEGETABLES

The blender is a real find for mothers of young children who want to cook fresh vegetables all at once for the whole family and then purée the very young children's portion. In either case, more nutrients are retained if the vegetables are cooled before blending. As an alternative, well-washed and scrubbed, tender raw vegetables may be blended and then cooked to the boiling point. Tough ones should be parboiled, cooled and then blended. You may reheat briefly in butter or cream before serving.

## VEGETABLES À LA GRECQUE

These mixed vegetables, left whole if small or cut into attractive shapes, 280, become aromatic as the result of simmering in a court bouillon of highly seasoned oil and water. ▶ They are served at between 70° and 90°, so that the oil will not be evident. They make convenient hors d'oeuvre, meat tray or salad garnishes, as they keep well if covered and refrigerated. They are excellent, too, for an antipasto tray. Prepare one of the following court bouillons or hot marinades in which to cook:

  1 lb. mixed vegetables

Suitable varieties include artichoke hearts, julienned carrots, cauliflower florets, celery, fennel, green beans, leeks, mushrooms, pearl onions, peppers and whole olives. Cucumber and eggplant slices or strips are delicious, but these should have excess moisture removed, 319.

Squeeze over the cut vegetables, to prevent browning:

  Juice of 2 lemons

I. Place in a 3-quart stainless or enamel pan:

  4 cups water
  1/3 to 1/2 cup olive oil
  1 teaspoon salt
  2 peeled cloves garlic
  (3 peeled shallots)

and the following herbs and spices, tied in a cheesecloth bag:

  6 sprigs parsley
  2 teaspoons fresh thyme
  12 peppercorns
  (3 coriander seeds or
    1/4 teaspoon oregano)
  (1/8 teaspoon fennel or celery
    seeds)

Add for flavor 2 of the squeezed lemon halves. Bring the mixture to a boil, then remove from the heat to season for about 15 minutes. Remove the spice bag and garlic. Bring the court bouillon again slowly to a simmer. Add in turn the most delicately flavored of the prepared vegetables. Once more bring the liquid just to a boil, reduce the heat and let the vegetables heat through and then cook in the marinade. Drain and place them in a jar, using a slotted wooden spoon. Now, cook the next most delicately flavored vegetable. Continue till each one has been cooked and cooled in the marinade. When they are all in the jar, mixed or separate, cover them with the marinade to store. After the vegetables have been eaten, use the marinade for sauces.

II. Combine in a stainless or enamel pan:

  1 cup wine
  2 cups olive oil
  1/2 cup vinegar
  1/2 to 3/4 cup water
  2 cloves garlic
  3 sprigs parsley
  6 peppercorns
  2 sliced lemons
  1/4 teaspoon salt

Cook the vegetables in the heated mixture, as in I.

III. This rather offbeat version is a pleasant change.

Combine in a stainless or enamel pan:

³/₄ **cup olive oil**
¹/₂ **cup wine vinegar**
³/₄ **cup catsup**
¹/₂ **cup chili sauce**
1 **clove garlic**
1 **teaspoon Worcestershire sauce**

Cook the vegetables in the heated mixture, as in I.

## ❀ COOKING FROZEN VEGETABLES

Please read About Thawing and Cooking of Frozen Foods, (II, 646). To cook these convenience foods so they lie flat and are all heated through at the same time, we prefer using a rectangular frozen-food steamer.

✪ To pressure cook frozen vegetables, allow about ¹/₂ as long as for the regular pressure cooking times given in individual recipes, but use the same amounts of water.

If using an electric skillet, place the hard-frozen vegetables—except for spinach and corn on the cob, which must be partially thawed—in the skillet and then cover. Set at 350° until steam escapes. Reset to 300° until the vegetable is tender.

## ABOUT REHEATED AND CANNED VEGETABLES

Delicious, often, are the uses of leftovers, but reheated vegetables have lost much of their nutritive value. If you do reheat them, put them in the top of a covered double boiler with a few teaspoons of water or stock, or reheat or bake them in a hot sauce. Allow about ¹/₄ to ¹/₂ as much sauce as vegetables. ◗ Be sure to retain the canning or cooking water for use in soup or sauce or as the medium in which to reheat. Making leftover vegetables into soufflés, 227, tim-

bales, 229, omelets and frittatas, 225, both glamorizes and stretches them. The sautéing and browning of cooked vegetables diminish vitamin content. Try serving leftover vegetables vinaigretted in a salad, remembering—contrary to at least one precept we learned at mother's knee— that cold food is as nutritious as hot. Canned or frozen vegetables have, of course, already suffered some loss of flavor and vitamins. Reheating before serving increases this loss.

◗ Always clean off tops before opening cans, as they may be dusty or may have been sprayed with poisonous insecticides while in the store.
◗ Once opened, cans should not be used to store food. Lead may leach from the cans into the contents, especially if the food is acid.

## COOKING VEGETABLES BY MICROWAVE

Please read about Microwave Cooking, 116. In electronic cooking, most vegetables are casseroled with a small quantity of water and are cooked covered. Because they need moisture, the cooking periods are generally comparable to pressure steaming, 281. If the vegetable can be baked like a potato, cooking time is saved. Scientific tests seem to show that nutrients are well retained, although the majority of taste panels rate vegetables cooked by other methods superior in flavor and texture. For timing follow manufacturer's directions.

## ▤ ABOUT CAMPFIRE AND BARBECUE VEGETABLES

Here are two simple, potless ways to cook vegetables for an outdoor barbecue. For the first, use frozen or sliced and washed vegetables. Place

them on heavy-weight aluminum foil
and season them. Use the drugstore
wrap, (II, 644). Place the foil-wrapped
vegetables on a grill or under or on hot
coals for 10 to 15 minutes. For the
second method, place—directly on a
greased grill above the coals—thick
slices of tomato, mushroom, pepper,
parboiled onion. Cover with an inverted colander. Cook until tender.

## ▲ COOKING VEGETABLES
AT HIGH ALTITUDES

In baking vegetables at high altitudes, use approximately the same
temperatures and timing given for
sea-level cooking. In cooking vegetables at high altitude by any process
involving moisture, both more liquid and a longer cooking time are
needed, as the vegetables boil at
lower temperatures. Frequently, the
longer time can be reduced if the
vegetables are thinly sliced or cut
into small units. To avoid tough
stems and overcooked leaves on
leafy vegetables, remove the midrib
and use it in the stock pot.

Make these adjustments as an approximate time guide: for each 1000
feet of elevation, add to the cooking
time given in the recipes about 10%
for whole beets, carrots and onions
and about 7% for green beans,
squash, green cabbage, turnips and
parsnips. ✿ In cooking frozen vegetables at high altitudes, whole carrots
and beans may require as much as
5 to 12 minutes of additional cooking, while other frozen vegetables
may need only 1 to 2 more minutes.

The extension division of most
land grant colleges will test the gauge
of your pressure cooker and probably
provide a pressure chart for your area
free of charge.

♥ In pressuring vegetables at high
altitude, you will have to increase
the liquid in your cooker $1/4$ to $1/2$ cup
for every 2 cups of vegetables, depending on their respective length
of cooking time. As with other
vegetable-cooking at high altitudes,
sliced or shredded vegetables, as well
as peas, corn and spinach may cook
almost as rapidly as at sea level, at
15 lbs. pressure. But you may find
that, with some of the leafy greens,
10 lbs. of pressure and a slightly
longer cooking period give a better
result. This has been found true for
asparagus, celery, turnips and cauliflower. Don't be surprised if whole
potatoes, beets, yams and beans need
considerably more time than at sea
level.

## ABOUT ARTICHOKES

Artichokes of the globe type, sketched
on 288, differ in shape, taste and
method of cooking from Jerusalem
artichokes, 289. If the leaves are
spreading or discolored, artichokes
are not tender. Sometimes, when immature, they are cooked, pickled (II,
676) and eaten whole. The mature
vegetable, after cooking, is most
frequently served one to each diner
and eaten with the fingers. The leaves
are removed singly and dipped into
a sauce, the lower end of the leaf
being simply drawn through the teeth
to extract the tender edible portion,
and the leaf then discarded. Continue
this procedure until a light-colored
cone of young leaves appears. Pull
this up with one movement. Then,
with a knife, cut out cleanly the fuzzy
center below and discard it. Eat the
remaining heart with a fork, dipping
each piece first into a sauce. Artichoke hearts, with bottoms neatly
trimmed, make delicious salad mate-

rial, as well as bases for stuffing, see below.

## UNCORED ARTICHOKES

To wash, hold by the stem end and dash up and down quickly in a deep bowl of water. To prepare:

**Artichokes**

cut off the stems. Trim the top leaves by one-fourth with scissors. Snap off the tough bottom row of leaves by bending them back from the core. To avoid discoloration, dip the trimmed base in:

**Lemon juice**

Place the artichokes top down on a trivet over 1 to 2 inches of boiling water. Add to the water:

- 1 **sliced onion or 1 mashed clove garlic**
- 2 **celery ribs with leaves**
- 1¹/₂ **tablespoons lemon juice, wine or vinegar**
- (2 **tablespoons vegetable oil)**
  **(A bay leaf)**

Steam, 281, covered 45 minutes or until tender. Drain and serve hot with:

**Melted butter, Mayonnaise, 419, Hollandaise Sauce, 410, Béchamel Sauce, 383, or Sauce Vinaigrette, 413**

Cooked artichokes may be served chilled.

❂ Pressure cook large artichokes at 15 lbs. about 15 minutes, small ones 8 minutes.

## CORED ARTICHOKES

Clean and trim as described above:

**Artichokes**

Turn them upside down. Press hard to force the leaves apart. Reverse and insert a curved knife, as shown left, to cut out and remove the choke. Tie artichokes into shape with string. Cook as in previous recipe but upright on the trivet. Drain well, untie and serve warm, the centers filled with:

**Hollandaise Sauce, 410**

If the artichokes are too hot when filled, the Hollandaise may separate. Or fill the centers with:

1 **cup cooked cocktail shrimp or small chunks of lobster**

heated in:

**Newburg Sauce, 413**

You may also serve these cored artichokes cold and stuffed as salad. Incidentally, the very tender leaves usually discarded in the coring, if trimmed and cooked, make delectable flavorings for an omelet or a casserole.

## ARTICHOKE HEARTS

For a good way to stuff cold artichoke hearts, see Artichoke Salads, 55.

**I.** Remove all leaves and chokes, as shown above, from:

**Artichokes**

Steam the hearts, 281, or drop them into 1 inch of:

**Boiling water**

to which you may add:

**Lemon juice**

Simmer covered for 20 minutes or until tender. Serve with:

**Brown Butter, 397, or
Hollandaise Sauce, 410**

**II.** Cooked or canned artichoke hearts, well drained, may be sautéed until hot in:

**Butter or drippings**

to which you may add:

**Garlic, shallots or onions**

Season with:

**Salt and paprika
Lemon juice**

Serve hot or cold.

## STUFFED BAKED ARTICHOKES

Preheat oven to 350°.

**I. Roman Style**

Clean, trim and blanch, 106:

**Artichokes**

Drain well. Make a dressing of:

**Bread crumbs
Minced garlic or onion
Chopped celery
Chopped anchovies or
anchovy paste
Grated Parmesan cheese
Chopped parsley
Salt and paprika**

Push the dressing down between the leaves. The choke may be removed, as described previously, if desired, and the center filled with the dressing. Pour over the artichokes a little:

**Olive oil**

Place them on a rack in a baking dish and cover the bottom of the dish with 1 inch of:

**Boiling water or stock**

Bake covered about 1 hour.

**II.** Or fill the artichokes with either:

**Ham Stuffing, 435 or
sausage stuffing, 433**

## JERUSALEM ARTICHOKES

Vegetable nomenclature abounds in double or doubtful terms—endive, chicory, pepper, yam and "wild rice" being examples; but "Jerusalem artichoke," seen in the chapter heading, center rear, should get some sort of prize in the misnomer sweepstakes. It is not even a thistle, like the true artichoke, but the tuber of a sunflower; and "Jerusalem" is a corruption of the Italian "girasole," or "turn-to-the-sun," as the sunflowers, like heliotropes, are obliged to do. They may be eaten raw, peeled, or may be prepared as for Saratoga Chips, 352, or as below.

Wash:

**1½ lb. Jerusalem artichokes**

Steam, 281, or drop them into:

**Boiling water**

To prevent discoloration, add:

**1 teaspoon mild vinegar or
white wine**

Cook covered until ◗ tender only. If permitted to cook beyond this point, they will again become tough. Test with a fork after 15 minutes. Drain. Rub off the peel. Melt:

**2 to 3 tablespoons butter**

Add:

**2 drops hot pepper sauce
2 tablespoons chopped
parsley**

Pour these ingredients over the artichokes or cream them, 283. Or cut into halves and ♀ pressure cook 10 minutes at 15 lbs.

## ASPARAGUS

The Romans used to say if they wanted something in a hurry, "Do it in less time that it takes to cook asparagus." Hilled, blanched asparagus, grown by heavy fertilization and deep mulching, is now available in American markets. This is a thick white variant which, though less nutritious than the green, has a distinctive succulence all its own. "Whites"—familiar to us all in their canned state—must be peeled, cutting from below the head and increasing the depth of cut as you go downward. This is also sometimes necessary with the larger older "greens" to eliminate bitterness in the skins.

## I.

**4 to 6 servings**

Wash:

    **2 lb. asparagus**

Snap off the lower part of the stalks where they break easily. Keep the trimmings for soup. Tie the asparagus in serving bunches with white string. Place them upright in an asparagus steamer or in the bottom part of a double boiler, the lower ends in:

    **½ cup boiling water**

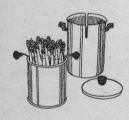

Cook the asparagus ❧ closely covered 12 minutes or until tender. An in-

verted double boiler top may be used. The steam will cook the tips. Drain well, reserving the liquid. Add:

    **½ teaspoon salt**

Melt:

    **⅓ cup butter or Brown Butter, 397**

Sauté in it, for 1 minute:

    **1 cup bread crumbs**

Pour this mixture over the tips of the asparagus, or serve them with:

    **1 cup White Sauce I, 383, made with half cream and half asparagus liquid, or Hollandaise Sauce, 410**

**II.** For real speed, slice diagonally ¼ inch thick:

    **Asparagus**

Stir-fry, 281, and garnish with:

    **Buttered bread crumbs**

**III.** Sometimes, if asparagus must be held, both the color and the texture are improved if this recipe is used—although we do not guarantee nutritive value.

Arrange in a flat pan:

    **2 lb. cleaned asparagus**

Place them not more than 3 or 4 deep. Add:

    **½ teaspoon salt**

Cover with cold water, then with a poaching paper, 101. Bring to a boil, reduce heat at once and ❧ simmer about 15 minutes. Keep lukewarm until ready to serve, then drain before serving.

## BAMBOO SHOOTS

In Asian dishes, these slightly acid shoots complement mushrooms and meat. They must be young and tender and from an edible bamboo plant. See illustration in chapter heading on 277. If fresh, boil:

**Bamboo shoots**

in:

**Water**

about 10 to 15 minutes. Texture should remain somewhat crisp. Discard the water. If using canned shoots, scrape off the calcium deposits. If using only part of a can, store the remainder by pouring off the original liquid, replacing it with cold water and refrigerating, covered, for not more than a few days.

## ABOUT FRESH BEANS

Fresh beans are of many varieties. **Snap beans**, seen below at left, can be eaten whole. Formerly called **string,** because their strings had to be removed, they have in many instances been hybridized so that they snap clean and need only have the ends snipped off. True **haricots verts**, with their okralike overtones, shown next, are a tenderer and slimmer version of snap beans. **Kentucky Wonders** and **wax beans**, not shown, still require both snipping and stringing. **English runner beans**, third from the left, respond to the same cooking procedures as snap beans. Any stringy portions should be cut off, and, before cooking, the bean should always be sliced into pieces no bigger than 1/2 inch. If they do not snap easily, they should be hulled and their red-streaked seeds cooked as for **lima beans**, 298, seen third from the right. Hulled also if they are larger than a pea are **fava beans** or **European broad beans,** second from the right, which are then cooked as for li-

mas. If under pea size, the filled pods may be sliced two or three times and prepared as for snap beans. Cook **edible soy beans**, shown at far right, as described, 293. To avoid toughening any fresh beans, add salt when cooking is half finished.

GREEN OR SNAP BEANS

**5 Servings**

This vegetable is available fresh the year 'round and lends itself to endless variations.

**1 lb. green beans**

Snip off the ends. You may then sliver them, French them on the diagonal or leave them whole. If the last, tie them in individual bunches before cooking. When cooked and drained, arrange them on a platter and cover with one of the garnishes or sauces suggested on 292. To cook green beans, steam, 281, or drop them into:

**Boiling water or part water**
**and part stock**

Reduce the heat at once. Cook partially covered if you wish to preserve the color; or covered if you wish to preserve more nutrients. Simmer until barely tender, no longer—about 20 minutes. Drain and:

**Season to taste**

Cover with:

**1 tablespoon melted butter**

✪ Pressure cook 3 minutes at 15 lbs. We note here that one of our very favorite ways of second-guessing a quantity of cooked green beans is to make them into a salad, 53.

## ADDITIONS TO GREEN BEANS

To further flavor beans during the cooking, add:

**1 small cut-up onion**
**1- to 2-inch cube of salt pork**

To garnish or sauce, use for 1 lb. of beans:

**1 tablespoon butter or Brown Butter, 397,**
**or ¼ cup buttered crumbs,**
**or 2 tablespoons brown onion butter,**
**or 2 tablespoons crumbled bacon and drippings**

Add to the above fats:

**½ teaspoon celery or dill seed, or**
**1 teaspoon fresh summer savory or basil,**
**or 2 teaspoons chopped chives**

Or garnish with:

**Anchovy Butter or Oil, 397, or Almond Garnish, (II, 221)**

Or add:

**½ cup Sautéed Mushrooms, 328**
**⅓ to ½ cup cultured sour cream**
**2 tablespoons chopped parsley**

Or add:

**2 tablespoons wine vinegar**
**¼ teaspoon mustard**
**1 tablespoon Worcestershire sauce**
**A drop of hot pepper sauce**

Or add:

**2 tablespoons butter**
**¼ cup toasted slivered almonds**
**¼ cup sliced water chestnuts**

If the beans are not served at once, reheat in:

**A White Sauce variation, 383, or**
**canned cream of chicken or mushroom soup seasoned with herbs,**
**or Quick Tomato Sauce, 400**

## GREEN BEAN CASSEROLE

### I.

**6 Servings**

What becomes of the onions and peppers? They frequently disappear, leaving marvelously seasoned beans. An easy dish for the hostess who cooks her own dinner.

Preheat oven to 350°.
Trim:

**1 lb. green beans**

Skin and chop:

**4 medium-sized white onions**

Remove the seeds and membrane from:

**2 medium-sized green peppers**

Chop the peppers. Butter a baking dish. Place in it alternate layers of the vegetables, beginning and ending with a layer of beans. Sprinkle each layer with:

**Salt and paprika**

Dot each layer with:

**Butter**

Bake the vegetables covered for about 1 hour, or until the beans are tender. Before serving, garnish with:

**Au Gratin II, (II, 221)**

### II.

**6 Servings**

Preheat oven to 350°.
Prepare for cooking:

**1 lb. green beans**

Place them in a buttered casserole. Cover with:

**1 can cream of tomato soup: 10½ oz.**
**3 tablespoons prepared horseradish**

1 teaspoon Worcestershire
   sauce
¼ teaspoon salt
¼ teaspoon paprika

Bake covered about 1 hour or until tender. Remove the lid and garnish with:

   **Au Gratin III, (II, 221)**

Serve when the cheese is melted.


## GREEN BEANS, POTATOES AND SMOKED MEAT

**8 Servings**

Cook until nearly tender in water to cover:

   **A small piece of smoked
   meat: ham, Canadian
   bacon or link sausage**

Or if using already cooked or leftover ham or bone, bring just to a boil before adding:

   **1 lb. green beans
   4 halved, pared, medium
     potatoes
   (1 onion)**

Simmer, covered, about 20 to 25 minutes. Drain.

   **Season to taste**

Serve from a large platter, garnished with:

   **Lemon wedges**


## SWEET-SOUR BEANS

**5 Servings**

Trim and shred lengthwise:

   **1 lb. green beans**

Steam them, 281, or drop them into:

   **Boiling water**

to barely cover. Cook covered about 20 minutes. Now render the fat slowly from:

   **3 pieces lean bacon**

Cook with it:

   **2 tablespoons chopped onion**

When the bacon is lightly browned, remove it and swirl in the pan:

1 tablespoon white wine
   vinegar
1 tablespoon sugar
½ teaspoon salt

Drain the liquid from the beans and add it to the skillet mixture. Then combine with the beans and cut-up bacon and serve. A happy variation is the addition of:

   **(Bean Sprouts, 294)**


## PURÉED GREEN BEANS, PEAS OR LIMAS

**4 Servings**

Puréed, these lend a fresh note if used as a base for soup, as a ring in serving sautéed mushrooms, or as a vegetable garnished with parsley.
Purée:

   **2 cups cooked fresh beans or
     peas**

Use a ⚬ blender or a food mill. Add:

   **2 tablespoons butter
   Season to taste**

and serve as soon as possible after puréeing. If the purée must be held over, cover it while hot with whipping cream and, in reheating in a double boiler ⚬ over hot water, beat in the cream before serving.


## GREEN SOYBEANS

Use the edible vegetable type, not field varieties of beans. The fuzzy pods, shown on 291, should still be green. They can be eaten hot or as an informal cold snack. Let the diner pop them from the pod. To serve hot, immerse them in boiling water. Cover the pot. Cook in boiling water until tender, approximately 10 to 15 minutes. Use the shelled beans as in any recipe for lima beans, 298.

The cooked beans may also be spread in a greased pan, dotted with butter and roasted in a 350° oven until brown; or they may be browned in deep fat, 94.

Soy milk, (II, 192), and bean curd, (II, 192), can also be made from the raw beans.

## COOKED BEAN SPROUTS

8 Servings

Sprouted beans eaten raw, just after sprouting, see (II, 241), have more vitamin C than when cooked. Bring to a boil:

3/4 cup water

Add:

4 cups sprouted beans, Mung or edible soybeans or lentils

Simmer, covered, until almost soft, just long enough to remove the raw bean flavor. Season with:

Salt

(Soy sauce)

Bean sprouts, fresh or cooked, immediately recall the Chinese-American cuisine, and suggest such added ingredients as chicken, shrimp, scallions, mushrooms or water chestnuts.

## ABOUT DRIED LEGUMES

Dried peas and beans, being rather on the dull side, respond readily—like a good many dull people—to the right contacts. Do not upstage them, for they have valuable, if incomplete, proteins, 4. Mix them with tomatoes, onions, chili, meat and cheese. They are also much more temperamental than one would think. Their cooking time depends on the locality in which they were grown and on their age—usually two unknowns for the cook; plus the type of water used in cooking them, see About Water, (II, 165). Wash, unless the package states otherwise. Do not use soda, see 280–281. Soak in 3 to 4 times as much water as beans. Remove any that float or that ▶

may be moldy. If not preprocessed, the beans are usually soaked overnight. Bring them to a slow boil in the water in which they were soaked, unless it is bitter, as happens sometimes with soybeans. Reduce the heat and ▶ simmer. All beans should be cooked until tender. One test, provided you discard the beans you have tested, is to blow on a few of them in a spoon. If the skins burst, they are sufficiently cooked.

If you have forgotten to soak, a quick method to tenderize for cooking is to cover beans with cold water, bring to a boil and simmer for 2 minutes. After removing them from heat let them stand, tightly covered, 1 hour. Alternatively, blanching for 2 minutes is almost equivalent to 8 hours of soaking.

You may use preprocessed beans which require no soaking. But remember that some nutrients have been lost in the preparation. Lentils and split peas are the better for soaking but do not require it. Remember, too, that 1 cup of dried beans, peas or lentils will expand to 2 to 2½ cups after cooking.

There are over 25 types of beans and peas available in our stores. They include broad, black or turtle, cranberry, scarlet runner, red, kidney, black-eyed peas or beans, edible soys, pinto, cowpeas or Mexican frijoles, chick-peas or garbanzos, flageolets—which are the French haricots, dried—and adzuki beans from which Asian bean paste is made. Each variety has, for the connoisseur, its own slightly different but satisfyingly hefty charm.

White beans, which the white man learned of from the Indians and then took sailing, became our navy beans. They are usually the toughest of the lot and take up to 3 hours simmering. Dried limas, after soaking for

8 hours, may cook almost as rapidly as fresh ones—in about ¹/₂ hour. Lentils take about 1¹/₂ hours to cook.

## PURÉE OF DRIED LEGUMES

Please read About Dried Legumes, 294. Cook until tender:

**Dried lentils, beans or peas, see above**

You may add:

**(A clove of garlic)**

After draining the lentils, put them through a fine sieve, a purée strainer or ⚒ blender. Allow to every cup of purée:

**1 tablespoon butter**
**¹/₄ to ¹/₂ teaspoon salt**
**¹/₄ teaspoon pepper or paprika**
**or**
**¹/₈ teaspoon cloves**

You may brown in the butter:

**1 tablespoon flour**

Whip the purée over a high heat. Serve in a mound, garnished with:

**Sautéed Onions, 335, or chutney**
**Chopped parsley**

## HOPPING JOHN

Eaten on New Year's Day, this dish is supposed to bring good luck.
Bring to a boil in a large covered saucepan:

**1¹/₄ cups dry black-eyed peas**
**4 cups water**

After boiling 2 minutes, remove pan from heat and let stand 1 hour. Add:

**1¹/₂ cups chopped onions**
**¹/₂ teaspoon pepper**
**¹/₄ teaspoon crushed dried red pepper**
**1 minced clove garlic**
**1 bay leaf**

After bringing to a boil, cover and simmer 1 hour, stirring occasionally. Stir in:

**8 oz. coarsely chopped salt pork**

Simmer another hour, uncovered, stirring frequently. Remove the salt pork and the bay leaf. Slightly mash the pea mixture.

**Season to taste**

Serve with:

**Boiled Rice, 189**

## REFRIED BEANS OR FRIJOLES REFRITOS

**4 Servings**

Melt in a heavy skillet:

**4 tablespoons lard or vegetable oil**

Add:

**2 cups cooked pinto beans**

If they are very dry you may add several tablespoons of:

**(Hot stock)**

While the beans are frying, stir to heat them through and then shape them, with the back of a wooden spoon, into a large cake. Cook until they are glazed enough to shake loose as one mass. Move the mass to one side of the pan and flip over in pancake style. Continue to turn and heat until a glazed loaf is formed. Top with cubes of:

**Mild cheddar**

Let the beans stay in the pan until the cheese is melted. Serve garnished with:

**Shredded lettuce**

on triangles of:

**Tortillas**

## DRIED BEAN PATTIES

**4 Servings**

Grind and mash:

**2 cups cooked dried beans: soy, lima, or navy**

Add to them:

**1 small chopped onion**

¼ cup chopped parsley

Beat and add:

   2 egg yolks
   2 tablespoons cream or
      evaporated milk
   ¼ teaspoon pepper
   1 teaspoon salt

Shape these ingredients into balls. Flatten them. Dip them in:

   Flour

Chill the patties for 1 hour or more. Sauté slowly, until brown in:

   Butter, drippings or
      other fat

Serve with any:

   Barbecue Sauce, 404

## DRIED BEAN CASSEROLE

**4 Servings**

Preheat oven to 350°.

Combine:

   1 cup cooked corn
   1 cup cooked navy beans
   1 cup lightly drained canned
      tomatoes
   ¾ teaspoon salt
   ¼ teaspoon paprika
   ½ teaspoon brown sugar
   1 teaspoon grated onion

Place in a greased casserole. Sprinkle the top with:

   Browned bread crumbs or
      grated peanuts

Bake covered about 45 minutes.

## BAKED BEANS

Did you know that baked beans are as traditional in Sweden as they are in Boston? Please read About Dried Legumes, 294.

**6 Servings**

If quick-cooking or precooked beans are used, follow directions on the package. Otherwise, soak:

   1½ cups dried beans

Cover them with water. Bring to a boil, then simmer slowly for ½ hour or more, until tender.

Preheat oven to 250°

Drain the beans, reserving the cooking water, and add:

   ¼ cup chopped onion
   2 tablespoons or more dark
      molasses
   2 or 3 tablespoons catsup
   1 tablespoon dry mustard
   1 teaspoon salt
   ½ cup boiling bean water or
      beer
   (½ teaspoon vinegar)
   (1 teaspoon curry powder)
   (1 tablespoon Worcestershire
      sauce)

Place beans in a greased baker, decorate them with:

   ¼ lb. sliced salt pork

and bake covered 6 to 9 hours. If they become dry, add a little:

   Well-seasoned stock or
      reserved bean water

Uncover the beans for the last hour of cooking.

## CANNED BAKED BEANS WITH FRUIT

**6 Servings**

Preheat oven to 300°.

Arrange:

   2½ cups canned beans

in layers in a casserole with:

   2 sliced apples
   2 sliced oranges or 6 canned
      apricot halves or pineapple
      slices
   (2 large onions, sliced)

Top with:

   ¼ lb. salt pork

Cover with:

   ¼ to ½ cup molasses or
      brown sugar

Bake 1 to 1½ hours, depending on how dry you like baked beans.

## BOILED BEANS

**5 Servings**

Soak, 294, then drain:

    **1 lb. dried beans: kidney, navy, or marrowfat**

Place them in a heavy saucepan. Cover with water. Add:

    **6 tablespoons butter**
    **1/3 cup chopped onion**
    **3 whole cloves**
    **2 teaspoons salt**
    **1/4 teaspoon freshly ground pepper**
    **1/4 teaspoon dried thyme**

Simmer the beans, covered, from 1 to 1 1/2 hours. Stir from time to time. Add and cook for about 20 minutes longer:

    **1 cup dry red wine or stock**

When the beans are tender, serve hot, garnished with:

    **Chopped chives or parsley**

◗ We do not recommend the pressure cooking of dried beans because of the danger of frothing and blocking the vent.

## ▤ CAMPFIRE BEANS

Have ready at least 2 to 3 quarts of hot coals. Dig a hole deep enough and wide enough to hold a covered iron kettle, allowing about 4 extra inches to the depth of the hole. Get ready for cooking:

    **Baked Beans, 296**

Put half the coals in the bottom of the hole. Sink the covered kettle. Cover the lid with a large piece of foil to keep out dirt. Put the rest of the coals on the kettle lid. Now, fill in the rest of the hole with dirt and put at least 3 inches of dirt on top of the kettle. Don't dig in to peek for at least 4 hours.

## CANNED KIDNEY BEANS AND TOMATOES

**4 Large Servings**

The mixture below may be used to stuff green peppers, 341.

Preheat oven to 350°.

Grease a baking dish. Have ready:

    **2 1/2 cups canned red kidney beans**
    **1 cup canned tomatoes or diluted tomato soup**
    **1/4 cup chopped onion**
    **1/4 lb. chopped bacon**

Cover the bottom of the dish with a layer of beans. Sprinkle it with some of the bacon and onions. Repeat the process. Pour the tomatoes over the whole. Cover the top with:

    **Bread crumbs or crushed cornflakes**

Dot with:

    **Butter**

or sprinkle with:

    **Grated cheese**

Bake the dish until the top is browned, about 30 minutes

## PINTO BEANS AND RICE

**4 Servings**

A combination relished in South American countries.

Soak, see 294:

    **1/2 cup pinto beans**

in:

    **3 cups ham stock**

Gently boil the beans in the stock until almost done. Add:

    **1/2 cup chopped cooked ham**
    **1/2 cup rice**

Cover and cook 20 to 30 minutes until the rice is tender.

LENTILS

## I.

**8 Servings**

Please read About Dried Legumes, 294.

Combine:

2 cups lentils

3 sprigs parsley or a celery
rib with leaves

¼ cup sliced onions

½ bay leaf
(A piece of fat corned beef,
ham skin or bacon rind,
tried-out pork fat or
smoked sausage)
(2 cloves without heads)
(A slice of garlic)

Cover with:

4 cups water

Simmer covered about 1½ hours.
Stir occasionally and add boiling water if necessary. Drain the lentils and
serve with:

Quick Tomato Sauce, 400

Or serve as a Purée, 284. If you omit
the bacon or pork flavorings above,
serve the lentils with:

Roast Pork, 601
Applesauce, (II, 118)

## II.

**4 Servings**

Wash but do not soak:

1 cup lentils

Sauté until golden brown:

1 minced onion

in:

¼ cup olive oil

Add the lentils and let them absorb
the oil. Pour over them:

3½ cups boiling water

Cover the pan and simmer about 1½
hours.

**Season to taste**

and serve hot or cold. If used for a
salad, garnish with French dressing
and hard-cooked egg slices.

LENTILS AND PRUNES

**4 Servings**

Please read About Dried Legumes,
294. Wash and prepare:

1 cup cooked lentils

Pit and mash:

1 cup cooked dried
prunes, (II, 108)

Add them to the lentils with:

¼ cup dry sherry

1 teaspoon salt
(Lemon juice and spices)

Stir over low heat until thoroughly
heated.

## ABOUT LIMA, BUTTER OR BROAD BEANS

The following cooked beans, whether
canned, frozen, fresh or dry, may be
substituted for one another in most
recipes: Fordhooks or baby limas;
Sieva types or fava, the European
broad beans, shown on 291—which
really taste more like peas. Both limas and favas have poisonous properties when eaten raw.

If you are hulling fresh limas, cut
a thin strip along the inner edge of
the pod to which the beans are attached. The beans will pop out easily.
One pound in the pods will yield
2 servings.

For that famous combination called
Succotash, see 317.

LIMA BEANS

## I.

**6 Servings**

Steam, 281, or cover:

1 quart shelled fresh lima
beans

with:

1 inch boiling water

Add:

1 tablespoon butter

Simmer the beans for 15 minutes. Add:

> 1 teaspoon salt

Simmer covered until tender, about 20 minutes more, depending on the age of the beans. Add:

> 1 tablespoon butter or olive oil
> 1½ tablespoons lemon juice
> 1 tablespoon chopped parsley, chives or dill

Or dress them with:

> Warm cultured sour cream and freshly ground white pepper

Or serve them with:

> Sautéed onions, creamed mushrooms, or a sprinkling of crisp bacon

♀ Pressure cook fresh lima beans about 2 minutes at 15 lbs.

## II.

**6 Servings**

Place in a heavy saucepan:

> 1 quart fresh shelled lima beans
> 1 small clove garlic
> 2 tablespoons skinned, seeded, finely diced tomatoes

Barely cover with:

> 1 inch water, or half water and half olive oil

Cover and simmer about 15 minutes. Remove garlic. Add:

> 2 tablespoons butter
> ½ teaspoon salt
> 1 tablespoon chopped parsley

Continue cooking covered until beans are tender.

## CHILI LIMA BEANS

**6 Servings**

Preheat oven to 300°.
Drain:

> 2 cups cooked lima beans

Add:

> ¼ lb. salt pork cut into strips
> 1 large minced onion
> 1 tablespoon molasses
> 2 cups drained cooked tomatoes
> 1 tablespoon brown sugar
> ¼ teaspoon chili powder or pepper
> 1 teaspoon salt

Bake these ingredients in a greased casserole about 1 hour.

## LIMA BEANS AND MUSHROOMS

**6 Servings**

Serve this with crisp bacon and grapefruit salad.
Have ready:

> 2 cups freshly cooked or canned lima beans

Drain and reserve the bean liquor.

> ½ lb. Sautéed Mushrooms, 328

Place in a skillet:

> 1 tablespoon butter

Stir in:

> 2 tablespoons flour

Cook and stir these ingredients until they are well blended. Stir in slowly:

> ½ cup chicken stock, or stock and bean liquor
> ½ cup cream
> Season to taste

Add the beans and mushrooms. Heat them. Add before serving:

> (1 tablespoon sherry)
> (½ teaspoon chopped fresh basil)

The dish may be served with:

> Au Gratin II, (II, 221)

Place it under a broiler until the crumbs are brown.

BEETS

**4 Servings**

Cut the tops from:

**1 lb. beets**

leaving 2 inches of stem. If the tops are young, reserve and cook; see Beet Greens, 301. Wash the beets. Steam them, 281, or half cover with:

**Boiling water**

Lid the pot and cook gently until tender. Allow 30 to 40 minutes for young beets, as much as 2 hours for old beets. Add boiling water if needed. When the beets are done, cool them slightly and slip off the skins. If small, serve whole. If larger, slice.

**Season to taste**

Then either pour over them:

**Melted butter**
**Chopped parsley**

or serve the beets in:

**White Sauce II, 383**

seasoned with:

**Mustard, curry powder, horseradish or ¼ cup sautéed onions**

Or prepare:

**White Sauce II, 383**

using in place of the milk half orange juice and half water. Add:

**3 tablespoons brown sugar**
**2 teaspoons grated orange rind**

♀ Pressure cook small beets 12 minutes, large beets 18 minutes at 15 lbs.

CASSEROLED BEETS

**8 Servings**

Preheat oven to 400°.

Pare, then slice or chop fine:

**2 lb. medium-sized beets**

Grease a 7-inch baking dish. Place the beets in it in layers. Season them with:

**(2 tablespoons sugar)**
**¾ teaspoon salt**

**¼ teaspoon paprika**

Dot them with:

**3 tablespoons butter**

Add:

**1 tablespoon lemon juice or a sliver of fresh ginger**
**⅓ cup water**
**(1 tablespoon grated onion)**

Cover the dish closely and bake the beets for 30 minutes or until tender. Stir twice.

SWEET-SOUR OR HARVARD BEETS

**6 Servings**

For a cold version of sweet-sour, see Pickled Beet Salad, 56.

Slice or dice:

**3 cups freshly cooked or canned beets**

Stir in a double boiler until smooth:

**½ cup sugar**
**1 tablespoon cornstarch**
**½ teaspoon salt**
**2 whole cloves**
**½ cup mild cider vinegar or dry white wine**

Cook and stir these ingredients until they are clear. Add the beets and place them ▶ over hot water for about 30 minutes. Just before serving, heat but do not boil the beets and add:

**2 tablespoons butter**
**(1 tablespoon orange marmalade)**

BOILED BEETS IN SOUR CREAM

**6 Servings**

Combine in a double boiler:

**3 cups cooked or canned sliced beets**
**½ cup cultured sour cream**
**1 tablespoon prepared horseradish**
**1 tablespoon chopped chives**
**Salt as needed**

(1 teaspoon grated onion)

Heat these ingredients ◗ over hot water.

## SWEET-SOUR APPLE BEETS

**4 Servings**

Preheat oven to 325°.

Grease a casserole. Mix together and put into it:

    **2 cups chopped cooked beets**

    **2 cups chopped tart apples**

    **1/4 to 1/2 cup thinly sliced onions**

    **1 1/2 teaspoons salt**

    **A generous grating of nutmeg**

If the apples are very tart, add:

    (1 tablespoon sugar)

If they are bland, add:

    (2 tablespoons lemon juice)

Dot with:

    **2 to 3 tablespoons butter**

Cover and bake about 1 hour.

## BAKED BEETS

**I.** Beets may be baked like potatoes—in their jackets.

Preheat oven to 325°.

Wash, taking care not to break the skin:

    **Beets**

Trim the tops, leaving 2 inches of stem. Place them on a pan and bake until tender. Allow at least 1/2 hour for young beets and 1 hour for old. Slip off the skins. Season the beets with:

    **Salt and paprika**

Serve them with:

    **Melted butter**

**II.** Have ready a preheated 325° oven or ▤ hot coals in the grill. Pare and slice:

    **Beets**

    **Season to taste**

and add:

    **Butter**

to individual servings before wrapping each one in aluminum foil. Bake until tender.

## BEET GREENS

**I.**

Beet greens may be prepared like Spinach, 358. If you are serving the greens with the beets, put the beets in a ring and serve the greens in the center, dressed with melted butter, and garnish with Horseradish Sauce, 386.

**II.**

**4 Servings**

Heat in a frying pan:

    **2 tablespoons butter or cooking oil**

Add and simmer until tender:

    **2 cups cooked chopped beet greens**

    **1 teaspoon grated onion**

    **1/4 teaspoon salt**

    **1/2 tablespoon prepared mustard**

    **1 tablespoon grated horseradish**

Remove from the heat and add:

    **1/2 cup cultured sour cream**

◗ Pressure cook beet greens 3 minutes at 15 lbs.

## BREADFRUIT

If ever your fate is that of Robinson Crusoe, remember that you can eat raw any breadfruit that has seeds. All seedless varieties must be cooked.

Breadfruit is 6 to 8 inches in diameter and greenish brown or yellow when ripe. The slightly fibrous meat is light yellow and sweet. You may remove the center core with its seed, if it has one, before or after cooking. Season and serve as you would sweet potato.

**I.**

**6 Servings**

To boil, choose mature firm fruit, with rind still green in color. Core and dice:

**4 cups peeled breadfruit**

Drop into:

**3 cups boiling water**

and simmer covered about 1 hour, until tender. Drain, season and serve.

**II.** Preheat oven to 375°.

To bake, place in a baking pan:

**1 unpeeled breadfruit**

Have enough water in the pan to prevent burning. Bake until tender, about 1 hour, when the stem and core will pull out easily. Discard them. Cut fruit in half. Season with:

**Salt and pepper or sugar and butter**

**III.** To steam, skin and core:

**1 breadfruit**

Cut into halves or quarters and place the pieces in a pan to steam, covered, 281, 2 hours. Drain. Season with:

**Butter**

**Salt and pepper**

You may steam 3/4-inch-thick breadfruit slices, roll them in flour and fry in deep fat until golden brown.

## BREADFRUIT SEEDS

These are so close to chestnuts in flavor and texture that they may be substituted in any chestnut recipe.

Wash well:

**1 lb. breadfruit seeds**

Drop them into:

**1 quart boiling water**

**3 tablespoons salt**

Cook covered about 45 minutes. Drain and serve hot.

## BROCCOLI

**4 Servings**

Choose heads that are all green. If yellow appears, the bloom is coming up and the broccoli is apt to be tough. Remove the large leaves and the tough parts of the stalks. Cut deep gashes in the bottoms of the stalks. It is worth remembering, in general, that broccoli leaves have a much higher vitamin A content than either the buds or the stalks and may be set aside and prepared like Greens, 323–324. If the broccoli is mature, cook it like Cabbage, 304. If it is young, steam it, 281, or place it upright so that only the stems are in water and the heads steam, see Asparagus, 289–290. Or, to retain excellent color, use a poaching paper, 101.

Soak in a cooking pot 10 minutes in cold water:

**2 lb. broccoli**

Drain well. Add:

**1 inch boiling water or chicken stock**

Cook the broccoli closely covered until barely tender, 10 to 12 minutes. Drain and sprinkle with:

**1/2 teaspoon salt**

Serve with:

**Buttered crumbs, melted butter or lemon juice**

to which add:

**(1/4 cup chopped salted almonds or walnuts)**

or try serving it:

**Au Gratin II, (II, 221)**

or with one of the following sauces:

**Hot Vinaigrette Sauce, 413**

**Hollandaise Sauce, 410**

**Cheese Sauce, 385**

**White Onion Sauce, 387**

**Sour Cream Dressing, 425**

**Allemande Sauce, 390**

♥ Pressure cook broccoli about 2 minutes at 15 lbs.

## QUICK CREAMED BROCCOLI

**4 Servings**

Preheat broiler.
Prepare:

**2 cups cooked broccoli**

Drain. Either cover it with:

**Quick Canned Soup
Sauce, 394**

or dice the broccoli and fold it gently
into the sauce. Place in a buttered
casserole and sprinkle with:

**Crushed cornflakes
(Grated Romano cheese)**

Run it under the broiler until golden

## DEEP-FRIED BROCCOLI

Prepare:

**Cooked broccoli**

Drain before it is tender; dry and cool
it. Cut it into quarters. Dip into:

**Fritter Batter for
Vegetables, (II, 155)**

Fry the broccoli in deep fat, 94,
heated to 375°, until golden brown.

## BRUSSELS SPROUTS

**6 Servings**

These are among the most prevalent
of winter cabbage types and all too
often suffer from simplistic treatment.
If wilted, pull the outer leaves from:

**1 lb. Brussels sprouts**

Cut off the stems. Soak the sprouts
for 10 minutes in cold water to which
a little salt has been added. Drain.
Cut crosswise gashes into the stem
ends. Steam, 281, or drop them into a
quantity of rapidly boiling:

**Water**

Reduce heat and simmer uncovered
until they are barely tender, about 10
minutes. ◗ Do not overcook. Drain
and serve with:

**1 tablespoon melted butter
(Grated Parmesan cheese**

and chopped parsley, or
1 tablespoon lemon juice,
or a grating of nutmeg)

or sauté in the butter:

**1 tablespoon grated onion, or
2 tablespoons bread
crumbs and ¼ teaspoon
dried mustard**

or serve with:

**Quick Canned Soup
Sauce III, 394**

into which you may put at the last
moment:

**(½ cup finely chopped fresh
celery)**

or, serve with:

**Sicilian Garnish, 424**

or, best of all, with lots of:

**Hollandaise Sauce, 410**

◗ Pressure cook Brussels sprouts
about 3 minutes at 15 lbs.

## BAKED BRUSSELS SPROUTS AND CHESTNUTS

**6 Servings**

Preheat oven to 350°.
Have ready:

**2 cups cooked Brussels
sprouts
½ lb. whole Boiled
Chestnuts, 313**

Butter a baking dish. Fill it with alternate layers of sprouts and chestnuts.
Dot the layers with:

**Butter
Season to taste**

Moisten lightly with:

**Stock**

Cover with:

**Au Gratin II, (II, 221)**

Bake uncovered 20 to 30 minutes.

## ABOUT CABBAGE

Cabbage types are as different as the
uses of the word. In France, "mon
petit chou" is a term of endearment;

but it is highly politic never to call a German a "Kraut." The recipes below—which, you will note, are many, as befits a vegetable so available, versatile and inexpensive—are guaranteed to give a boost to international good will.

Shown below from left to right is a range of cabbages: that firm old standby **head cabbage,** green or red; the soft-leaved crinkly **Savoy;** the clustered **cauliflower** and **broccoli;** columnar-fruiting **Brussels sprouts;** leafy **collards** and the similarly shaped **kale,** not illustrated; the stemmed **Swiss chard;** the elongated **bok-choi** and its better-known cousin **Chinese cabbage,** or **pe tsai.**

All cabbage types, if fresh, are a plentiful source of vitamin C, if you use the cooked cabbage water in sauces and soups. Choose firm cabbage heads and allow 1 lb. raw cabbage for 2 cups cooked. Old cabbage recipes called for long boiling, see 12. We recommend quartering a cabbage head and cooking it gently, uncovered, about 15 minutes; Savoy types about 20 minutes. Better still, shred the cabbage first, 49–50, and cook only 7 to 10 minutes respectively. You may prefer to stir-fry shredded cabbage, 281. And don't forget that cabbage lends itself to stuffing, as do the leaves, see Dolmas, 626. ❂ Pressure cook 2- to 3-inch wedges of cabbage 3 to 5 minutes at 15 lbs.

## CREAMED CABBAGE

### I.

**6 Servings**

Remove the outer leaves from:

**A 2-lb. head cabbage**

Drop it into a quantity of rapidly boiling:

**Water**

Reduce heat to a simmer. Cook ❂ uncovered until tender but still crisp. Drain. Add:

   **1 teaspoon salt**

Place in a serving dish and pour over it:

   ¼ **cup melted butter**
      **(Bread crumbs or caraway,**
      **chilis, or poppy seeds, or a**
      **few drops lemon juice and**
      **1 tablespoon chopped**
      **parsley)**

or place the cooked cabbage in a baking dish and cover with:

   **Creole Sauce, 394, or**
   **Au Gratin III, (II, 221)**

Heat through in a 350° oven.

### II.

**4 Servings**

All rules have exceptions, so try out this cabbage dish, which calls for little water. Cut into wedges:

**A 2-lb. head cabbage**

Trim off part of the core. Drop the wedges into:

   ½ **inch boiling water**

Cover and cook about 10 minutes. Drain well.

Dress with:

**1 cup White Sauce, 383**

to which has been added:

**1/2 teaspoon freshly grated
nutmeg or 2 teaspoons
prepared mustard or
1/2 cup shredded cheese**

or use:

**1 cup Horseradish Sauce, 386
or 1 cup creamed canned
condensed soup or
Allemande Sauce, 390**

### III.

**6 Servings**

This method makes young cabbage very delicate and is a great help in disguising the age of a mature one, but you may be losing some nutrients.
Cut into very fine shreds:

**3 cups cabbage**

Drop gradually into:

**3/4 cup boiling milk**

Boil for 2 minutes. Drain, and discard the milk. Drop the cabbage into hot:

**White Sauce I, 383**

Simmer 3 minutes longer and serve at once with:

**(Broiled sausages)**

### CABBAGE, POTATOES AND HAM

**4 Servings**

Cook until nearly tender in water to cover:

**A piece of smoked ham:
picnic, butt, shank or
cottage ham or roll**

If using already cooked or leftover ham, bring the water just to a boil before adding:

**1 large quartered cabbage
4 halved and pared medium-
sized potatoes**

Simmer covered about 20 to 25 minutes. Drain.

**Season to taste**

Serve from a large platter, garnished with:

**Lemon wedges**

### BAKED CABBAGE

**4 Servings**

Preheat oven to 325°.
Put in a buttered baking dish:

**3 cups shredded cabbage**

Pour over it a mixture of:

**3/4 cup cream
2 well-beaten eggs
1 tablespoon sugar
1/2 teaspoon salt
1/2 teaspoon paprika
(1/2 cup chopped nuts or
1 cup seedless green
grapes)**

Sprinkle the top with:

**Au Gratin III, (II, 221)**

Bake about 45 minutes.

### SAUTÉED CABBAGE

**4 Servings**

Preheat oven to 375°.
Shred:

**A 2-lb. head cabbage**

Sauté it lightly in:

**Butter or bacon drippings**

Season with:

**1/2 teaspoon salt
1/4 teaspoon paprika
Minced garlic or onion**

Place the cabbage in a greased baking dish. Pour over it:

**1 cup cultured sour cream**

Bake about 20 minutes.

### FRENCH-FRIED CABBAGE

▶ Please read about Deep-Fat Frying, 94.
Crisp in cold water:

**Finely shredded cabbage**

Drain and dry it. Dip in:

**Milk**

then in:
### Flour
Rest it for 10 minutes.
Fry a small amount at a time in deep fat heated to 365°. Drain on paper toweling.
### Season to taste

## CABBAGE OR LETTUCE AND RICE DISH

### 6 Servings

This is a "gleaner's" dish to make on the trail of a salad luncheon, using outer leaves. Melt:

- 2 tablespoons bacon drippings
- 2 tablespoons butter or 3 tablespoons other fat

Stir in, cover and cook gently about 10 minutes:

- 3 cups finely shredded cabbage or lettuce
- 1/2 cup finely chopped onion
- 1 chopped green pepper, seeds and membrane removed

Stir these ingredients frequently. Stir in and cook until well heated:

- 1 cup cooked rice
- 2 cups tomato pulp or thick stewed tomatoes
  Salt and pepper

This is enhanced by serving with it:
Crisp bacon or cold ham

## CABBAGE OR SAVORY STRUDEL

### 12 to 14 Servings

Prepare:
Strudel dough, (II, 373)
Steam blanch, 106, for 5 minutes:
4 lb. shredded cabbage
Press out any excess moisture and place on the dough with:

- 1 1/2 cups cultured sour cream
- (1 teaspoon caraway seed)

(4 chopped hard-cooked eggs)
To roll and bake the strudel, see (II, 373).

## SCALLOPED CABBAGE

### 8 Servings

Shred and prepare by any method for cooked cabbage:
A 4-lb. head cabbage
Drain it well. Prepare:
1 1/2 cups White Sauce I, 383
Prepare:

- 2 tablespoons chopped seeded green pepper
- 2 tablespoons chopped pimientos

Sauté and mince:
(6 slices bacon)
Preheat oven to 375°.
Melt:

- 2 tablespoons bacon fat or butter

Toss lightly in this:
1/2 cup bread crumbs
Place layers of drained cabbage in a greased baking dish. Sprinkle with the minced bacon and peppers and:
1 cup or less shredded cheese
Cover with the cream sauce. Top with the bread crumbs. Bake about 10 minutes.

## CABBAGE OR BRUSSELS SPROUTS WITH TOMATO

### 6 Servings

Preheat oven to 325°.
Cook for 5 minutes:

- 3 cups finely shredded cabbage or whole Brussels sprouts

Drain well. Have ready:

- 1 can condensed tomato soup: 10 1/2 oz.

mixed with:

- 1/4 teaspoon paprika
- 2 teaspoons brown sugar

Butter a baking dish. Place in it alternate layers of cabbage and the soup mixture. Sprinkle the top with:

**Au Gratin III, (II, 221)**

Bake the dish about ¹/₂ hour.

## CABBAGE STUFFED WITH CORNED BEEF HASH

**4 Servings**

Trim the outer leaves and the stem from:

**A 2-lb. head cabbage**

Cook it uncovered in:

**2 quarts boiling water**

until barely tender and slightly crisp. Drain well. Scoop out the inside, leaving a 1¹/₂-inch shell. Place the shell in a greased ovenproof dish. Keep it hot. Chop the removed part. Add it to the contents of:

**1 can minced corned beef hash: 16 oz.**

**¹/₄ cup or more Sautéed Onions, 335**

**A pinch of thyme**

Moisten it with a little:

**Cream, evaporated milk or bacon drippings**

Heat these ingredients. Fill the shell. Cover the top with:

**Buttered cornflakes**

The cabbage may be heated in a 425° oven about 10 minutes and served with:

**A Quick Canned Soup Sauce, 394**

## CABBAGE STUFFED WITH HAM

**6 Servings**

Preheat oven to 325°.

Cook and scoop out as for the above recipe:

**A firm 2-lb. head cabbage**

Combine:

**2 cups cooked ground or chopped ham**

**1 cup bread crumbs**

**³/₄ cup grated American cheese**

**¹/₂ teaspoon dried mustard**

**Salt, depending on saltiness of ham**

**¹/₂ teaspoon paprika**

**A few grains cayenne**

Place the cabbage on a rack in a greased ovenproof dish with ¹/₄ inch chicken stock in the bottom. Fill the hollowed cabbage with the ham mixture, cover closely, and bake about 30 minutes until heated through. Serve with:

**Cheese Sauce, 385**

## RED CABBAGE

**4 Servings**

An old favorite to serve with game—cooked either as in this recipe or for a shorter time as in the next.

Pull off and discard the outer leaves from:

**A head of red cabbage: about 2 lb.**

Cut the head into sections. Remove the hard core, shred the cabbage and soak briefly in cold water. Cook over low heat until some fat is rendered out:

**4 slices bacon, chopped, or use 3 tablespoons melted butter**

Sauté in the fat until golden:

**3 or 4 tablespoons finely chopped onion**

Lift cabbage from the water, leaving it moist. Place it in an enameled iron casserole, cover, and let it simmer 10 minutes. Then add:

**2 thinly sliced apples**

**(¹/₈ teaspoon caraway seeds)**

**¹/₄ teaspoon salt if bacon is used, or 1 teaspoon salt if unsalted butter is used**

**¹/₄ cup vinegar or ¹/₂ cup red wine or a mixture of**

2 tablespoons honey and
2 tablespoons vinegar

Add the sautéed onion and stir these ingredients. Cover pan and simmer the cabbage very slowly about 1 hour. Add boiling water during cooking if necessary. If liquid is left when the cabbage is done, uncover the pot and cook gently until it is absorbed.

## RED CABBAGE AND CHESTNUTS

**6 Servings**

A colorful dish when served in green peppers, see Stuffed Peppers, 341. Have ready:

1 cup chopped Boiled
Chestnuts I, 313

Shred until very fine:

1 small head red cabbage:
1 lb.

Place it in a bowl. Cover with:

Boiling water

Add:

1/4 cup dry white wine or
vinegar

Let it soak for 15 minutes. Drain well. Heat in a saucepan:

2 1/2 tablespoons bacon
drippings or butter

Add the cabbage. Sprinkle it lightly with:

Salt and pepper

Sauté the cabbage until it is limp. Cover and simmer for ten minutes. Sprinkle it with:

1 tablespoon flour

Add the chestnuts and:

1 cup water
1 1/2 tablespoons sugar
1/4 cup dry white wine or
vinegar
1/3 cup seedless raisins
1 peeled, cored, thinly sliced
apple

Simmer until well blended.

Season to taste

and serve hot.

## CHINESE OR CELERY CABBAGE

**6 to 8 Servings**

Use this vegetable raw as a salad or prepare it by any of the recipes for cabbage; or stir-fry it as the Chinese do, 281. If young, it may require only a few minutes' cooking.

Steam, 281, or place a stalk of:

Whole or shredded celery
cabbage

in:

1/2 cup boiling water

Cook until barely tender. Drain thoroughly. Add:

1/2 teaspoon salt

Serve with:

Melted butter or
Hollandaise Sauce, 410

or season with:

1/2 teaspoon turmeric

and garnish with:

1/4 cup freshly grated coconut

## SAUERKRAUT

**6 Servings**

The healthful quality of sauerkraut was recognized in 200 B.C. when, history records, it was doled out to the laborers working on that largest and longest of public works—the Great Wall of China. To retain its full flavor, sauerkraut should be served raw or barely heated through. Cooking makes kraut milder.

Melt in a skillet:

2 tablespoons butter or
bacon drippings

Add and sauté until clear:

1/2 cup sliced onion or shallots

Add and sauté for about 5 minutes:

1 quart fresh or canned
sauerkraut

Peel, grate and add:

1 medium-sized potato or
tart apple

Cover the kraut with:

**Boiling stock or water**
**(¼ cup dry wine)**

Cook uncovered 30 minutes; cover and bake in a 325° oven about 30 minutes longer. You may season with:

**1 or 2 tablespoons brown sugar**
**1 teaspoon caraway or celery seed**

Serve with:

**Frankfurters, roast pork or spareribs**

## SAUERKRAUT AND TOMATO CASSEROLE

**8 Servings**

Preheat oven to 350°.
Drain well:

**4 cups canned or fresh sauerkraut**

Put through a strainer:

**3½ cups canned tomatoes**

Melt:

**2 tablespoons bacon or other fat**

Add, cook and stir until golden:

**1 small chopped onion**

Add the strained tomatoes and:

**¼ cup brown sugar**
**Freshly ground pepper**

Add the drained sauerkraut. Place the mixture in a covered casserole and bake about 1 hour. ◗ Uncover the last 20 minutes of cooking. Garnish the top with:

**Crumbled crisp bacon**

## CARDOONS

A vegetable of the thistle family, like artichoke—but the tender stalks and root are eaten, rather than the fruiting head. Often used for soups. Allow 1 lb. to 2 persons. Wash well. Discard outside stalks; trim the strings as for celery. Leave the heart whole. Cut into 3-inch pieces:

**Tender stalks of cardoon**

Parblanch, 106, in:

**Court Bouillon Blanc, (II, 176)**

for 5 to 7 minutes to prevent discoloration. Drain and rinse at once in cold water to remove bitterness. Simmer covered for about 1¼ hours or until tender in:

**Boiling Acidulated Water (II, 167) to cover**

Drain and serve with:

**Cream, butter or White Sauce I, 383**
**Season to taste**

Slice the heart and arrange it as a garnish.

## CARROTS

Carrots continue to suffer from the jibes of people who like to dispense what H. W. Fowler called "worn-out humor." Their unsavory reputation is ill deserved. Look for the delicious "baby" carrots, now more and more beginning to appear at market. For jaded palates, combine carrots with onions, celery, green peppers, olives or mushrooms. Peel or scrape them, using the tool shown on 310—by far the most effective we have found for taking the hide off a coarse or bumpy vegetable. Or use them unpeeled, cut into slices or diced. If small, they may be served whole. If large, they may be more attractive if cut Parisienne, 280, or julienned as shown on 310.

Wash and scrape:

**Carrots**

Steam, 281, or place them in a small quantity of:

**Boiling water or stock**

Cook covered until tender, 20 to 30 minutes. Allow a shorter cooking period for cut-up carrots. Let them absorb the water in which they are cooked. If necessary add a small quantity of boiling water. Serve with:

**(Seasoned chopped parsley)
Bercy Butter, 398, or
White Sauce I, 383**

or add to 2 cups cooked carrots:

**1 or 2 tablespoons butter
1 to 2 tablespoons sugar,
honey or orange
marmalade
(¼ teaspoon cinnamon or
nutmeg)**

Simmer the carrots in this mixture until well glazed. Or use the glaze for:

**Candied Sweet
Potatoes, 356**

♥ Pressure cook carrots whole 4 minutes—sliced, 2½ minutes—at 15 lbs.

## CARROTS IN BUNCHES

Steam or cook as in preceding recipe:

**Small, shapely carrots in
their jackets**

Cool and skin them. Reheat by placing them over steam or by sautéing briefly in a little butter. Serve in 2 bunches—one at each end of a meat platter. Place at the blunt ends, to represent carrot greens:

**Sprigs of parsley**

Pour over them:

**Melted butter seasoned
with a dash of cloves**

## MASHED CARROTS OR CARROT RING

**4 Servings**

Cook as above:

**2 bunches young carrots in
their jackets**

Skin the carrots and mash or rice them or use a 🔧 blender. Beat in:

**1 tablespoon butter
Salt and pepper
1 tablespoon chopped
parsley, dillweed
or chives**

Add:

**½ cup sliced green grapes**

and heap the carrots in a mound with:

**Sprigs of parsley**

Or, to make a ring, beat in:

**1 to 2 egg yolks**

Place in a greased mold and heat ♦ over hot water in a 350° oven until set, 20 to 30 minutes. Invert mold. Fill center of the ring with:

**Green Peas, 338**

## CARROTS VICHY

**4 Servings**

Place in a saucepan:

**2 cups thinly sliced scraped
carrots
½ cup boiling water
2 tablespoons butter
1 tablespoon sugar
¼ teaspoon salt
(1 teaspoon lemon juice)**

Cover the pan closely. To form a glaze with the butter and sugar, simmer the carrots until the water is absorbed. Serve sprinkled with:

**Chopped parsley**

## BAKED CARROTS

**4 Servings**

Preheat oven to 350°.
Melt:

**3 tablespoons butter**

Sauté in it for about 3 minutes:

**¼ cup chopped onion**

Add and stir in:

**2 cups shredded peeled carrots**

Place these ingredients in a baking dish. Combine and pour over the carrots:

**¾ teaspoon salt**
**1 tablespoon brown sugar**
**1 teaspoon dry mustard or**
**¼ teaspoon cloves**
**(A few drops hot pepper sauce)**
**½ cup stock**

Cover the dish. Bake until tender.

## STEAMED CAULIFLOWER

**4 Servings**

Mostly white, these delicately flavored clustered "curds"; but occasionally encountered in green, or even purple, with no very noticeable difference in taste. Select firm heads lacking in brownish discoloration, although such blemishes may be pared off with only cosmetic damage.

Cut off the tough end of the stem, removing the leaves, and soak in cold salted water, head down, for 10 minutes:

**A 2-lb. cauliflower**

Drain it. You may break it into florets. Cut deep gashes into the stalks. Steam, 281, or place uncovered, head up, in about 1 inch of:

**Boiling water or milk**

The milk will help keep it white, as will:

**(Juice of ½ lemon)**

Reduce the heat to a simmer and cook ◖ partially covered, until the stalk is barely tender—about 12 minutes. Drain well and place in a serving dish. For **Cauliflower Polonaise,** cover it with:

**Brown Buttered Bread Crumbs, (II, 219)**
**(Chopped nuts sautéed in butter)**

Or cover with:

**Hollandaise Sauce, 410**
**Quick White Sauce, 384**
**(with crumbled bacon or chopped ham)**
**Creole Sauce, 394**
**Lemon Butter, 397**

✿ Pressure cook whole cauliflower about 7 minutes at 15 lbs.

## SAUTÉED CAULIFLOWER

**4 Servings**

Cook as above:

**Boiled or steamed cauliflower**

Break it into florets. Heat:

**2 tablespoons butter**
**2 tablespoons vegetable oil**

Add and cook for 2 minutes:

**½ clove garlic or 2 teaspoons grated onion**

Remove the garlic. Sauté the florets in the fat until they are well coated. Cover and cook for several minutes. Season with:

**Salt and paprika**
**A fresh grating of nutmeg**

or serve the cauliflower with:

**Chopped parsley or chives**

## DEEP-FRIED CAULIFLOWER

◖ Please read About Deep-Fat Frying, 94.
Drain:

**Cooked cauliflower**

Separate the florets
Dip each section of cauliflower into:

**Fritter Batter for
Vegetables, (II, 155)**

Drain, rest 10 minutes and deep fry
in fat heated to 365° until golden.
Serve with:

**Hollandaise Sauce, 410, or
Sour Cream Dressing, 425**

## CAULIFLOWER AND MUSHROOMS IN CHEESE SAUCE

**6 Servings**

Cook, see Steamed Cauliflower, 311:

**A 3-lb. cauliflower**

Drain well and put it in a greased
baking dish. Keep it hot. Melt in a
skillet:

**2 tablespoons butter**

Sauté in it for 2 minutes:

**1/2 lb. mushrooms**

Cook:

**1 1/2 cups White Sauce I, 383**

Stir into the hot sauce ♦ off the heat:

**3/4 cup shredded cheese**

When the cheese is melted, add the
sautéed mushrooms and pour the
sauce over the cauliflower. Serve at
once.

## CELERY

**4 Servings**

The unbleached green variety—
Pascal, so-called—is growing in popularity and, like all unbleached vegetables, has a higher vitamin content
than its paler counterpart. The golden
leafage, usually discarded, is well
worth reserving: chopped fine, it
makes a delicate component of an
Omelet aux Fines Herbes, (II, 253);
dried carefully in a slow oven and
rubbed through a sieve, it makes a
powder for flavoring sauces. For Celery Root, or Celeriac, see below.
Wash:

**2 cups chopped celery**

Steam, 281, or drop it gradually into:

**1/2 inch boiling water**

Cook covered until tender, about 8
minutes, allowing it to absorb the water. Should there be any liquid, drain
the celery and reserve the liquid for
the sauce. Brown the celery in:

**Seasoned butter**

Or drop the celery into:

**1 cup White Sauce I, 383,
made with cream and
celery liquor**

Season the sauce with:

**Curry powder, or celery,
dill or sunflower seeds, or
freshly grated nutmeg, or
herbs, (II, 265)**

♥ Pressure cook celery 1 1/2 minutes
at 15 lbs.

## BRAISED OR GLAZED CELERY OR ENDIVE

**4 Servings**

Not only celery and Belgian endive
but Boston lettuce is choice prepared
in this way. Do blanch the endive and
lettuce briefly first.
Wash and trim:

**1 1/2 lb. celery**

Cut into 3- to 4-inch lengths. Arrange
them attractively in the bottom of a
♦ flameproof glass or enamel casserole. Pour over them:

**3 tablespoons lemon juice**
**1/2 cup chicken or veal stock**
**1/2 teaspoon salt**
**1 tablespoon sugar**
**2 tablespoons butter**

Bring the liquid to a boil, then cover
with a poaching paper, 101. Now,
cover the casserole with a lid and
simmer for about 25 minutes or until
tender. Place the celery on a heated
serving dish and keep warm. Reduce
the pan liquid to about 1/2 cup. Add:

**1 tablespoon butter or
Beurre Manié, 381**

Pour this glaze over the celery.

## CELERY ROOT OR CELERIAC

**4 Servings**

This knobby tough root, also called **celeri-rave,** is often woody if too old, but can be one of the most subtly flavored of vegetables, see illustration in the chapter heading on 277. It is difficult to peel, so cut it into slices first, as shown on page 279. To make the flavor more delicate for use in salads and hors d'oeuvre, and to keep it white, blanch 1 to 2 minutes after peeling by using lemon juice in the water.

Scrub well and peel:

    **1½ lb. celery root**

Steam, 281, or cover with:

    **Boiling water**

Simmer uncovered until tender—about 25 minutes. Drain. Cover with:

    **1½ cups White Sauce II, 383**

or serve with:

    **Au Gratin III, (II, 221)**

✪ Pressure cook about 5 minutes at 15 lbs.

## SWISS CHARD

Prepare:

    **Chard**

by washing carefully and removing the midribs. Cook the leaves by any recipe for Spinach, 358. Cook the ribs as for Asparagus, 290.

## CHAYOTES

**4 Servings**

This pear-shaped vegetable belongs to the gourd family. Treat chayotes much as you would any squash, 360, after removing the long flattish central seed. They may be served with meats and seafoods and may even be used, like pumpkin, in desserts.

Pare and cut crosswise into ¾-inch slices:

    **1 lb. chayotes**

Drop into:

    **Boiling water to cover**

Reduce the heat at once and simmer 45 minutes, if young, or as long as 1 hour if mature. Drain. Dress with:

    **Butter, salt and pepper, or**
    **Black Butter, 397,**
    **Amandine Garnish**
    **(II, 221), or a cream sauce**
    **and grated cheese**

Chayotes are delicious if halved and steamed and stuffed with:

    **Mushrooms and cheese**

✪ Pressure cook whole chayotes at 15 pounds 6 to 8 minutes; if diced, 2 minutes.

## BOILED CHESTNUTS

**I.**

**4 Servings**

To prepare as a vegetable, shell and skin, (II, 239):

    **1 lb. chestnuts**

or ½ lb. shelled dried chestnuts that have been soaked overnight. Use this water. Drop the chestnuts into:

    **Boiling water or milk**

To which add:

    **3 chopped ribs celery**
    **1 small peeled chopped onion**
    **(1 tablespoon vinegar)**
    **(⅛ teaspoon anise)**

Cook until tender. Drain well. Mash with:

    **1 tablespoon butter**
    **Season to taste**

Add:

    **2 or more tablespoons warm cream**

Beat the chestnuts until fluffy. Keep them hot over hot water.

**II.** To prepare as a compote, shell, skin, cook as above:

    **1 lb. chestnuts**

in:

    **Boiling water or milk**

Drain. Save the liquid and add enough to make about 2 cups. Prepare a syrup by adding:

2 cups sugar
Juice and grated rind of 2 lemons
Juice and grated rind of 1 orange
4 whole cloves
1 stick cinnamon
1/4 teaspoon ground ginger
(1/2 cup raisins)
(1/2 cup chopped nuts)

Simmer the syrup gently until slightly reduced, add chestnuts and serve hot or chilled.

## BAKED CHESTNUTS

6 Servings

Prepare and cook:

3 cups chestnuts, 313

Preheat oven to 325°.
Grease a baking dish. Place the drained whole chestnuts in it. Pour over them:

1 3/4 cups chicken stock
(2 tablespoons or more brown sugar)

Cover and bake about 3 hours. Pour off the stock and reserve. Melt:

2 tablespoons butter

Stir in until blended:

1 tablespoon flour

Stir the stock in slowly. When the sauce is smooth and boiling, pour it over the chestnuts and serve.

## STEAMED CHESTNUTS

Our French friend Max Lachaux describes with contagious nostalgia a time-consuming method of preparing chestnuts that was used in his childhood home and which is traditional in his native Périgord.

Authenticity demands three pieces of equipment. First, the écuradour, a kind of wooden shears as illustrated below. This would make a good project for a whittling boy. Each arm is about 16 inches in length and 1 1/2 inches square; the arms are attached at the center with a nut, like scissors. The so-called blades have hand-carved sawtoothing on all edges for removing the inner skins of the chestnuts. Second, the oule, seen in the drawing below, a 10- to 20-quart round-bottomed three-legged cast-iron pot with a narrower neck, made especially for the chestnut-steaming process. Third, a sieve made of wire mesh on a wooden frame with sides a few inches high, the mesh slightly finer than the chestnut size.

Prepare by removing the outer shells with a knife. Place chestnuts in the oule after soaking them in water a few moments, and immediately place the oule over hot coals and leave it for about 10 minutes. The inner skin softens, swells and separates from the nuts. Take the oule from the fire and, without removing the chestnuts, "scissor" them in all directions with the écuradour. The nuts are not cooked and remain whole as the teeth of the shears pull off the skin. When almost all of it has come off, the chestnuts are placed in the sieve and the bits of skin pass through. Wash

the chestnuts, removing any remaining pieces of skin.

Line the oule with fig leaves and raves—a long French variety of turnip. Small potatoes may be substituted but are not as good. Place the wet chestnuts in the oule, adding no more water. Cover with muslin cloth in layers forming a thickness of at least an inch at the neck of the oule. Place the oule on hot fire until steam begins to escape from underneath the lid. Then move to low heat and cook slowly and continuously until no more steam appears.

The chestnuts must be eaten very hot and may be served with sweet cider or new white wine. Those at the bottom of the pot have been roasted—a children's favorite, to be eaten as an afterschool snack. The turnips or potatoes are perfumed with absorbed fragrances.

If you do not have an oule and if you have not found in your grandmother's attic a three-legged iron pot similar to that shown in the illustration on 314, try a Dutch oven elevated on bricks. Have fun—we did—and bon appétit!

## CHICORY

**Witloof** chicory, the **French** or **Belgian endive,** may be prepared by any recipe for cooked lettuce or celery. Differentiate it from the sunburst-centered, highly ruffled or frisée endive, or chicory, 44, common in our stores and usually used raw, and the wild chicory, 324.

## ABOUT CORN

One of the comic inventions of the late Ed Wynn was a corn-on-the-cob-eating machine, put together along the lines of a typewriter, with the ear of corn itself constituting the carriage. In truth, any device which speeds sweet corn to the "chomping" stage is to be encouraged, because its "bouquet," like that of a newly plucked ripe tomato, is fleeting.

The corn we usually find in our markets comes from two progenitors: "Country Gentleman" and "Golden Bantam"—white and yellow, respectively—the latter hybrids having a more robust flavor. But many years ago, when we were very young, we were captivated by the great diversity of color we encountered in the delicious "Indian corn" of northern Minnesota: kernels in red, brown, blue and purple.

When cooked corn is called for in the following recipes, it can be canned, fresh cooked or frozen. Try cutting fresh corn for puddings and fritters by scraping with the tool shown enlarged on the right below— and notice the superior results this kind of preparation gives. If you must use a knife to cut off the kernels, do not cut deeply. Then press down along the rows with the dull side of the knife to retrieve the richly flavored juice and heart of the kernel.

♦ To avoid toughness in cooking corn, add salt when the cooking period is half over.

If ⦿ pressure cooking ✽ frozen corn on the cob ♦ be sure to thaw partially before cooking about 4 minutes at 15 lbs.

## CORN ON THE COB

**I.** Remove the husks and silk from:

**Ears of fresh corn**

Steam, 281, or drop them, ear by ear, so as not to disturb the boiling, into:

**Boiling water to cover**

Boil the corn rapidly until tender, from 3 to 5 minutes, depending on maturity. Drain and serve with:

**Butter**
**Salt**
**Freshly ground pepper**

**II.** Remove the husks and silk from:

**Very young freshly picked corn**

In a large kettle which you can cover tightly, bring to a rolling boil:

**Enough water to cover corn generously**

Slip the ears into the water one by one. Cover the kettle and remove from the heat at once. Allow the corn to remain in the hot water for about 5 minutes or until tender. Drain and serve at once.

## FRESH CORN CUT FROM THE COB

Cut or grate from the cob:

**Fresh corn**

Simmer it covered for several minutes, until tender, in its own juice and a little:

**Butter**

Season with:

**Salt and white pepper**

Moisten with:

**Milk or cream**

You may devil it by adding:

**Worcestershire sauce**
**Minced garlic**

## ☰ GRILLED OR ROASTED CORN

Preheat oven to 475° or have ready a generous bed of coals.

**I.** Pull down husk to remove silk and any damaged portions of the ear on:

**Young roasting corn**

Replace the husk. Run into the husk as much:

**Water**

as it will hold. Drain and close the husk by twisting it. Put the ears on a rack over the hot coals or in the preheated oven and bake 20 to 25 minutes. Husk before serving.

**II.** Strip the husk and silk from:

**Roasting ears**

Remove any damaged portions. Rub with:

**Butter**
**Salt and white pepper**

Wrap in foil and roast 20 to 30 minutes, depending on the size of the ears.

## FRESH CORN PUDDING COCKAIGNE

**4 Servings**

This is a luscious dish, but it is a little difficult to give an exact recipe for it because the corn differs with the season. Early on, should the corn be watery, it is sometimes necessary to add a beaten egg. Later more cream may be required—up to 1 cup. When the corn mixture is right, it looks, after scraping, like thick curdled cream. Preheat oven to 325°.

Scrape as shown on 315, but ▶ do not cut:

**2 cups fresh corn**

Add:

**(1 teaspoon sugar)**
**¹/₂ to ³/₄ cup cream**
**Salt and white pepper**

Place these ingredients in a generously buttered flat baking dish. Dot the top with:

**Butter**

Bake the pudding for about 1 hour.
❉ This dish may be frozen, (II, 655).

## SOUFFLÉED CORN PUDDING

**5 Servings**

Sturdy and satisfying.
Drain:

1 No. 2 can kernel corn:
2½ cups

Reserve the liquid. Melt:

2 tablespoons butter

Stir in until blended:

2 tablespoons flour

Combine and stir in slowly:

**The corn liquid and enough cream to make 1 cup**

When the sauce is smooth and hot, stir in the drained corn and:

¼ cup chopped seeded green pepper with membrane removed
1 chopped pimiento

When this mixture reaches a boil ▶ reduce heat. Beat well:

2 egg yolks

Pour part of the corn mixture over them off the heat. Beat it and return to corn mixture. Stir and cook for several minutes ▶ over very low heat to let the yolks thicken slightly.
Add:

¾ teaspoon salt
¼ teaspoon paprika
(¼ cup minced ham or crumbled cooked bacon)

Preheat oven to 350°.
Place on a platter and whip ▶ until stiff but not dry:

2 egg whites

Fold them lightly into the corn mixture.
Bake the pudding in a baking dish pre-

pared as for a soufflé baker, 226–227, for about 30 minutes.

## SCALLOPED CORN

**4 Servings**

Preheat oven to 325°.
Combine:

2 cups uncooked corn, scraped or cut from the ear
2 beaten eggs
½ teaspoon salt
(¼ cup minced seeded green peppers with membrane removed, or chopped stuffed green olives)
¾ cup cream

Place in a baking dish prepared as for a soufflé baker, 226–227. Sprinkle with:

Au Gratin II, (II, 221)

Bake the corn for about ½ hour.

## SUCCOTASH

**4 Servings**

This is entirely acceptable made with canned or frozen vegetables.
Combine, then heat in a double boiler ▶ over—not in—boiling water:

1 cup cooked fresh corn
1 cup cooked fresh lima or finely shredded green beans
2 tablespoons butter
½ teaspoon salt
⅛ teaspoon paprika
Chopped parsley

## CORN CREOLE

**4 Servings**

Seed, remove membranes and chop:

¼ cup green pepper

Skin and chop:

1 small onion

Melt:

2 tablespoons butter

Sauté the vegetables in the butter until translucent. Heat in the top of a double boiler:

**1 cup drained canned or fresh cooked tomatoes**

Add the sautéed vegetables and:

**1/2 teaspoon salt**
**1/8 teaspoon pepper**
**A few grains cayenne**

Cook and stir these ingredients ▶ over—not in—boiling water about 5 minutes. Add:

**2/3 cup cooked corn**

Heat 2 minutes longer. Stir in until melted:

**1 1/3 cups shredded cheese**

## CORN FRITTERS WITH FRESH CORN

**4 Servings**

The author of the following account graciously permitted us to use it when we told him how much it pleased us.

"When I was a child, one of eight, my father frequently promised us a marvelous treat. He, being an amateur arboriculturist, would tell us of a fritter tree he was going to plant on the banks of a small lake filled with molasses, maple syrup or honey, to be located in our backyard. When one of us children felt the urge for this most delectable repast, all we had to do was to shake the tree, the fritters would drop into the lake, and we could fish them out and eat fritters to our hearts' content.

"Mother was a good cook and she duly developed this fabulous fritter." The following is, we hope, a faithful transcription of her recipe.

Scrape:

**2 1/2 cups fresh corn**

Add:

**1 well-beaten egg yolk**
**(2 teaspoons flour)**
**1/4 teaspoon salt**

Whip until ▶ stiff but not dry:

**1 egg white**

Fold the corn mixture into it. Sauté as for pancakes, (II, 142) until light brown and fluffy. Do not overcook.

## CORN OYSTERS

**About Sixteen 1 1/2-Inch Fritters**

For best results, make the batter immediately before using it. Have ready:

**1 cup freshly scraped corn or drained canned cream-style corn**

Add:

**2 well-beaten eggs**
**6 tablespoons flour**
**1/2 teaspoon double-acting baking powder**
**1/4 teaspoon salt**
**1/8 teaspoon nutmeg**

Melt in a small skillet:

**3 tablespoons butter**

When it has reached the point of fragrance, add a tablespoon of batter at a time. Let the bottom of the cakes brown, reverse them and brown the other side. Serve at once with:

**Quick Creole Sauce, 401, or maple syrup**

## ABOUT CUCUMBERS

How often the Japanese draw these highly decorative plants! And from the opposite corner of Asia the prophet Isaiah lamented their absence in bitter weather: "desolate as . . . a cottage cucumber garden abandoned in winter."

Among the varieties of this almost endlessly fascinating fruit are a very long virtually seedless Japanese type, and the round, yellowish "apple cucumbers," which are somewhat mellower to the taste than the greenskins.

A cucumber fit for use is rigid. It should have a lustrous skin—but do not be misled by the heavy, waxy, man-applied finish on some of those now in the markets. If the skin is not waxed, it is edible. Some people who are allergic to cucumbers find they can enjoy them if they are seeded and cooked. Use any recipe for summer squash or one of the following.

## MULLED CUCUMBERS

### I.

**4 Servings**

Pare, seed and cut into strips:

    **2 cups cucumbers**

Drop them into:

    **1½ cups boiling water**

▶ Simmer until nearly tender—but no longer, so as to retain their color. Drain well. While still in the pan, season the cucumbers with:

    **Salt and white pepper**
    **Freshly grated nutmeg or**
    **1 teaspoon chopped fresh**
    **herbs or dill or celery seeds**

and stir in:

    **2 tablespoons heavy cream**

Reheat briefly and serve at once.

### II. Prepare:

    **Mulled Cucumbers I,**
    **above**

Drain and serve with:

    **Lemon Butter, 397, with**
    **capers; or a tomato sauce**
    **with basil; or Soubise or**
    **White Onion Sauce, 387**

## CUCUMBER ANCHOVY CASSEROLE

**4 Servings**

Preheat oven to 400°.

Prepare:

    **2 cups Mulled Cucumbers,**
    **above**

Drain well. Prepare:

    **1 cup White Sauce, 383**

seasoned with:

    **1 tablespoon anchovy paste**

Place the vegetable in a baking dish. Pour the hot sauce over it. Cover with:

    **Au Gratin III, (II, 221)**

Bake the dish until the top is brown.

## CUCUMBER CREOLE CASSEROLE

**6 Servings**

Pare and seed:

    **3 cups cucumbers**

Cut them into ¼-inch slices. Combine with half the recipe for:

    **Creole Sauce, 394**

Preheat oven to 375°.

Place in the bottom of a greased ovenproof dish:

    **½ cup dry bread crumbs**

Add the cucumbers. Pour the sauce over them. Cover with:

    **Au Gratin I, (II, 221)**

Bake about 35 minutes.

## ABOUT EGGPLANT OR AUBERGINE

These vegetables, lovely when stuffed, also make beautiful individual servings with their green caps against the polished purple of the cases. We have tried alternating them with green and red stuffed peppers for an effective buffet platter.

There are several important things to keep in mind in cooking eggplant. It may become very watery. Get rid of excess moisture by salting and draining on a rack before using it in unthickened recipes; or stack the slices, cover with a plate, place a heavy weight on top and let stand until moisture is squeezed out. ▶ Eggplant discolors quickly when cut and should be sprinkled or rubbed with lemon juice. Also, because of discoloration ▶ cook in pottery, enamel, glass or stainless steel. One pound of eggplant equals 3 cups diced.

Eggplant has a blotterlike capacity for oil or butter, well pointed up by this Middle East tale. The imam or priest was so fetched by the eggplant dish his fiancée prepared that he asked that her dowry be the oil in which to cook it. Great Ali Baba jars of oil were stored in their new home. The first night the eggplant was delicious, also the second; but on the third night his favorite dish was not waiting for him. "Alas," said the wife, "the first two nights have exhausted the supply of oil." And then the priest fainted! If the newly wedded housewife had taken the precaution to keep the oil well heated, it would have lasted a great deal longer.

**Imam Baaldi,** the classic dish which caused the priest's downfall and carries his name, calls for halved eggplant, stuffed, soaked in oil and casseroled covered for 1½ hours.

## EGGPLANT SLICES

After frying, 281, sautéing, 97, or baking, eggplant slices can be used in the following ways.

**I.** Top with:
 **Creamed Spinach, 359**
Sprinkle with:
 **Grated Gruyère cheese**
and run under broiler.

**II.** Put in a casserole and cover with:
 **Creole Sauce, 394, or**
 **Au Gratin I, (II, 221)**
Run under broiler.

**III.** Place on each slice:
 **A slice of Tomato**
 **Provençale, 367**

**IV.** Place on eggplant slice:
 **A grilled tomato slice**
Cover with:
 **A poached egg and Cheese**
 **Sauce, 385**

**V.** Place on an eggplant slice:
 **Creamed ham or hash**

## BAKED EGGPLANT SLICES

     **4 Servings**
Preheat oven to 400°.
Pare:
 **A 1½- to 2-lb. eggplant**
Cut it crosswise into slices ½ inch thick. Spread the slices on both sides with a mixture of:
 **Soft butter or vegetable oil**
seasoned with:
 **Salt and pepper**
 **Grated onion or lemon**
 **juice**
Place on a baking sheet and bake until tender, about 12 minutes, turning once. Garnish with:
 **Chopped parsley or chervil**

## BAKED EGGPLANT HALVES

     **4 Servings**
Preheat oven to 325°.
Wash, dry, then cut into halves lengthwise:
 **A 2-lb. eggplant**
Crisscross the flat cut sides with gashes about 1 inch deep. Sauté the halves cut side down about 10 minutes in:
 **3 tablespoons hot olive oil**
Set them skin side down in a shallow ovenproof dish. Make a paste by mashing together until well blended:
 **8 minced anchovy fillets**
 **2 chopped cloves garlic**
 **¼ cup bread crumbs**
 **2 tablespoons beef stock**

$^1/_8$ **teaspoon freshly ground**
        **pepper**
Spread this over the tops of the egg-
plant. Sprinkle them with:
        **Au Gratin II or III, (II, 221)**
Bake about 20 minutes.


## SCALLOPED EGGPLANT

**4 Servings**

Pare and cut into dice:
        **A 1$^1/_2$- to 2-lb. eggplant**
Simmer it until tender in:
        $^1/_2$ **cup boiling water**
Drain well. Sprinkle with:
        **(2 tablespoons chopped**
        **parsley)**
Chop until very fine:
        **1 small onion**
Melt:
        **1 tablespoon butter**
Sauté the onion in this until it is
golden. Add it to the eggplant with:
        $^1/_2$ **cup milk**
        **(2 well-beaten eggs)**
Melt:
        **3 tablespoons butter**
Stir into it, until the butter is absorbed:
        $^3/_4$ **cup cracker crumbs or $^1/_2$**
        **cup bread crumbs**
Preheat oven to 375°.
Place layers of eggplant and layers of
crumbs in a baking dish. Season them,
if the crackers are unsalted, with:
        $^1/_4$ **teaspoon salt**
        $^1/_4$ **teaspoon paprika**
Wind up with a top layer of crumbs.
Place on it:
        **(Thin slices of cheese or**
        **grated cheese)**
Bake the eggplant for $^1/_2$ hour. Gar-
nish with:
        **Crisp crumbled bacon or**
        **thin strips of pepperoni**

## DEEP-FRIE[...]

♦ Please read A[...]
Vegetables, 282.
Pare and cut into
sticks:
        **An eggplant**
Dip them in:
        **Fritter Batter for**
        **Vegetables, (II, 155)**
Fry them in deep fat heated to 365°
until golden. Drain on paper toweling
and serve after adding:
        **Salt**


## SAUTÉED EGGPLANT SLICES

**4 Servings**

Peel and cut into $^1/_2$-inch slices,
cubes or sticks:
        **A 1$^1/_2$- to 2-lb. eggplant**
Dip the pieces in:
        **Milk**
Dredge them in:
        **Seasoned flour, crumbs or**
        **cornmeal**
For easier handling, place slices on a
rack to dry for 15 minutes before
cooking. Melt in a skillet:
        **Butter or oil**
Sauté the pieces until tender. Serve
while very hot with:
        **Chopped parsley or**
        **tarragon**
        **A sliced lemon or a tomato**
        **sauce, or a garnish of green**
        **pepper strips and pitted**
        **black olives**


## EGGPLANT CASSEROLE OR
## RATATOUILLE PROVENÇALE

**8 Servings**

This ends up looking in color like a
very successful Braque still-life.
Peel, slice and salt to get rid of excess
moisture, 319:

...s diced eggplant

...a deep skillet:

**¹/₃ cup olive oil**

Sauté until golden:

**³/₄ cup thinly sliced onions**

**2 cloves garlic**

Add:

**¹/₂ cup whole pitted black olives**

**4 julienned green peppers, seeds and membrane removed**

**3 cups zucchini in ¹/₂-inch slices**

**2 cups skinned, seeded, quartered tomatoes**

Add the drained eggplant. Sprinkle the mixture with:

**Olive oil**

Add:

**(¹/₂ teaspoon oregano or 2 teaspoons chopped fresh basil)**

Simmer covered over very low heat about 45 minutes. ◗ Uncover and continue to heat 15 minutes longer to reduce the amount of liquid. Add:

**Salt and a grating of fresh pepper**

Serve hot or cold with:

**Cultured sour cream**

## STUFFED EGGPLANT OR EGGPLANT FARCIE

### 4 Servings

Eggplant makes a wonderful "background" food due to its color and shape. Cut eggplant just under and following the lines of the leafy green cap, which then forms an attractive lid. Large cases may be filled with any desired combination of food, to which the cooked eggplant pulp is added. Smaller ones may be served individually.

Cut as described:

**A 2-lb. eggplant**

Scoop out the pulp, leaving a ¹/₂-inch shell. Drop the pulp into a small quantity of boiling water or stock and cook until tender. Drain well and mash it. Combine with:

**Farce, 437, of chopped or ground cooked meat: lamb or ham or rice and shrimp**

Preheat oven to 400°.

Fill the shell. Cover with the cap. Bake in a small amount of water until filling is heated.

## STUFFED EGGPLANT CREOLE

### 4 Servings

Cut into halves:

**A small eggplant**

Scoop out the pulp and chop it. Leave a shell ¹/₂ inch thick. Mince and heat in a skillet:

**2 strips bacon**

Add to it and sauté until the bacon is cooked:

**¹/₄ cup minced onion**

**¹/₄ cup minced seeded green pepper with membrane removed**

Add the eggplant pulp and:

**2 cups drained canned tomatoes**

**¹/₄ cup diced celery**

Simmer these ingredients until the eggplant is tender. Beat them with a fork until well blended. Thicken with:

**¹/₃ cup bread crumbs**

Season with:

**Salt and freshly ground pepper**

Add:

¹/₂ **cup Sautéed**
   **Mushrooms, 328**
Preheat oven to 350°.
Fill the eggplant shells with the mixture. Cover the tops with:
   **Au Gratin III, (II, 221)**
Place the eggplant on a rack in a pan with very little water and bake until thoroughly heated, about 15 minutes.

## ABOUT FENNEL OR FINOCCHIO

The anise-flavored root and stalks of the Florence fennel, illustrated in the chapter heading on 277, which can be found in season at Italian markets, may be eaten raw as a choice hors d'oeuvre, used as a substitute for celery in stuffings, or braised as for celery, 312. The leaves can also be used discreetly for seasoning, but the usual plant for this purpose is *Foeniculum vulgare*, (II, 269).

## FERN SHOOTS

Since we are now all dedicated environmentalists, we remind you that if fern clumps occur in any but very plentiful communities they should not be harvested at all. We might add that many people are allergic to ferns, and that ostrich fern fiddleheads are least likely to irritate.

In the spring, cut ferns while the shoots are still curled in crosiers. Wash and tie in bundles of 6 to 8 fronds. Stand upright and steam as for Asparagus, 290, about 20 minutes or until just tender. Serve with:
   **Hollandaise Sauce, 410**
Fiddleheads may also be deep-fat-fried in a batter, (II, 152).

## ABOUT CULTIVATED GREENS

Greens such as turnips, mustard, kale, collards, corn salad, comfrey and borage are seldom creamed. However, there is no reason why they should not be. The old-fashioned custom is to cook them to death, for an hour or more, with bacon, salt pork or ham hocks and to serve them with vinegar. We prefer to retain color and nutrients by the following methods. To reduce cooking time—when the green is unusually large and mature—strip the leafage from the midrib, which can then be cooked separately, much like Asparagus, 290. Collard greens, incidentally, are sweetest after the frost has hit them.

**I.** Prepare greens by washing carefully to remove grit and cut out any blemished areas or tough stems. Simmer for 2 hours in water to cover:
   **A 1-lb. piece side meat: salt**
      **pork or cottage ham**
Add:
   **2 to 3 lb. greens**
and simmer 25 to 40 minutes, until just tender.

**II.** If the greens are very young, prepare as for:
   **Panned Spinach, 359**
allowing about 10 minutes cooking time.

## ABOUT WILD GREENS, SHOOTS, ROOTS, SEEDS AND BERRIES

If you are in earnest about collecting edible wild foods, try to find a local expert. If such a person is not available, the best advice comes from the *U.S. Armed Services Survival Manuals* and *Poisonous Plants of the*

*United States and Canada* by John M. Kingsbury.

Many wild greens harbor large concentrations of oxalates, nitrates and other as yet unidentified but definitely toxic elements. Such irritants can be lessened by parboiling before final cooking. Generally, avoid all plants with milky or colored juices; all unknown plants with white or red berries; all unknown seeds, especially those which are three-angled or three-lobed; and any bulbs that do not smell like onion. Sample all wild greens sparingly, especially if your diet has been deficient. Remember, too, that all plants have seasons when they are succulent and periods when they are inedible; and that they all need careful washing to remove grit.

## COOKING WILD GREENS

Although many of them have been found to contain toxins, the greens listed below are those most popularly collected. Prepare as for Spinach, 358: young chickweeds, lamb's quarters, purslane, yellow rocket cress, mustards, miner's lettuce, tiny plantains, bladder campion, cleavers, cheese mallows, shepherd's purse, sheep sorrel, spiderwort and nettles. All these will cook down by at least half. Nettles, which have to be handled before cooking with tongs or impervious gloves, may be used as blanched shoots all winter if the roots are dug and grown on in boxes of soil in a cool cellar. Prepare these also as for spinach.

Parboil the plants listed below for about 5 minutes; then, after discarding the water, cook again for 10 minutes or so in fresh boiling water: dandelion leaves picked before the plant flowers, young sour and curly dock, young chicory leaves, evening primrose and escaped comfrey. Most of these, even after parboiling and cooking, will remain slightly bitter. Unless you are working up a real or imaginary survival program, their continued use is of questionable benefit.

## COOKING WILD SHOOTS

There are certain wild shoots that bring rave reviews—wild asparagus, of course, and stalks of bellwort. The latter are usually too scarce to consider cropping. In fact their own survival is due in large part to the difficulty of finding them, for it is often necessary to spot the clumps first in full leaf and mark them for the following season's devouring. This does not hold for such prevalent shoots as cattails, fireweed, burdock and the escaped Japanese butterbur, which grow in such thriving colonies that they are easy to locate. The roots of burdock and butterbur, or fuki, see 325, may be used, as well as the stems, which should be very carefully peeled prior to cooking. All the above may be prepared as for Asparagus, 290.

Then there are poke shoots, which must be cut very young, for both leaf and root are poisonous. The shoot should be parblanched, 106, in two waters, and the waters discarded, before cooking a third time until tender.

## COOKING WILD ROOTS

For survival, again, or if you still like to feel the squish of mud between your toes, are the gathering and preparation of certain watergrown roots. Bulrushes and cattails can be dug the year around. Use the root stalks. Scrape and remove the hairs. Parboil at least ten minutes, then boil for over an hour. Roasting in coals takes from

2 to 3 hours. Arrowhead tubers, dug in the fall, are treated as for bulrushes. All need lemon juice to prevènt discoloration after peeling. Boil the long spongy roots of the yellow spatterdock water lily about 30 minutes. You may also eat the unopened flowers of the fragrant white water lily, boiled very briefly, or the boiled green seeds of our beautiful native yellow lotus, which are really too precious to plunder. Among water plants, the root shoots of pickerelweed are the quickest to prepare, needing only about 8 minutes of boiling.

Among the land-based roots, Jerusalem artichokes, also found in cultivated forms, 289, are favorites. Cooked like them are groundnut roots, butterbur and burdock roots, and—after their runners are removed—the roots of the day lily. To prepare the buds and flowers, see II, 683. The first-year roots of evening primrose may also be prepared as for Jerusalem artichokes if they are parboiled ten minutes first. Spring beauty roots, which are sometimes found as sods in old lawns, may be treated as for potatoes; but patience and Lilliputian appetites are necessary prerequisites.

## JICAMA

A Mexican tuber with the crispness and whiteness of a turnip. Use it raw, sliced on hors d'oeuvre or salads, or slice thinly and cook as for or with Pan-Fried Potatoes, 347.

## KOHLRABI

**4 Servings**

These "knobs"—actually thickened stems—are superb in flavor, but, unless young, are frequently too fibrous in texture to be worth preparing; see illustration in chapter heading on 277. Wash:

**16 small kohlrabi**

Cut off the tops and pare the knobs. Slice the knobs and drop into a quantity of rapidly:

**Boiling water**

Cook uncovered until barely tender, about 20 minutes, and drain. Boil the tops separately in the same manner. After draining well, chop the tops until very fine or purée and combine them with the knobs. Prepare:

**White Sauce I, 383**

Add:

**(A grating of nutmeg)**

When the sauce is smooth and hot, add the kohlrabi.

## ABOUT LEEKS OR POIREAUX

How we wish that leeks were as common here as in France, where they are known, all too modestly, as the "asparagus of the poor." Leeks, like other onion types, (II, 272), make a wonderful seasoning. When cooked as a vegetable, they must be carefully washed to free the interlacing leaves from grit; and only the white portion is used. Cook as for Asparagus, 289–290, or braise as for Celery, 312.

## PURÉE OF LEEKS

**4 Servings**

Very special as a side dish with meat, or as a stuffing for tomatoes.

Prepare and cook as suggested above:

**8 leeks**

Drain them well. Chop them coarsely. For each cup add:

**2 tablespoons butter**

**1/2 cup fresh bread crumbs**

**Salt and pepper**

Stir and simmer them gently until blended. If they become too thick, add:

**A little cream**

Serve the purée very hot with:

**Finely chopped parsley**

## COOKED LETTUCE

Home gardeners in their enthusiasm often find themselves with sudden surpluses of lettuce and wish they had rabbits instead of children—failing to realize that a crisp nibble is not the only approach to this vegetable. Try these delectable alternatives after making sure that the leaves at hand are not bitter: cook lettuce as a Cream Soup, 149; cream it like Spinach, 359; cook with peas; stuff it like Cabbage, 307; cook and smother it with stewed tomatoes, or braise as for Celery, 312; allowing the lettuce to simmer only a few minutes before reducing the sauce; or cook, drain and casserole it in a Curry Sauce, 390, garnished with chopped filberts.

## LOTUS

The handsome seed pod of lotus shown first on the left in the chapter heading, 277, is symbolic of the fragrant delicacy of all parts of this majestic, versatile plant. The leaves, either fresh or dried, make vegetable, meat or rice wrappings. The peeled 2- x 8-inch jointed underwater stems can be sliced and stir-fried or stuffed and steamed. Soak them first in acidulated water, (II, 167), to avoid discoloration. The blanched 1/2-inch oval seeds may be eaten, but push out the bitter center portion first with a wooden pick. Also use these vitamin-rich seeds in soups or stews; or sautéed like Amandine Garnish, (II, 221); or in sweet dishes.

## ABOUT MUSHROOMS

Who would expect a lot of sunshine vitamin D in plants like these, which flourish in cellars, woods and caves? Another amiable trait of mushrooms is their ability to lend an air of elegance to every dish of which they become a part. They gratify many of us, too, with their almost total lack of calories. But they trick us, while cooking, with their sly habit of absorbing considerable amounts of butter, oil and cream.

Some of their trickery is, of course, of a very serious order. A number of poisonous mushroom types, during various stages of development, resemble edible forms. The quite innocent-looking and rather widely distributed **amanitas** are white-gilled and include varieties so deadly that they are frequently assumed to have furnished the murderous potions so useful to the princely houses of the early Renaissance. In sober truth, there is no simple way to identify harmless mushrooms and other related fungi. Even the experts often prefer to examine up to ten specimens of a single variety before announcing a verdict.

The novice should remember that there are bold mushroom hunters and old mushroom hunters, but no

bold old mushroom hunters, and begin his collecting with a safe and obvious—if not very thrilling—family like the **puffballs,** which have neither stems nor gills. They are edible if they grow above ground and the flesh inside is white throughout. **Lycoperdon giganteum,** shown first on the left on 326, varies from marble to watermelon size, and **Lycoperdon craniforme,** not shown, resembles a skull slightly shriveled even when in prime eating condition.

**Agaricus campestris,** shown in the center, is the type most often found fresh at market. The young pale buttons are succulent; the older drier ones are best for sauces, as the flavor intensifies as the gills darken. The dried **Gyromitra esculenta,** not shown, usually imported from Europe, is very strong in flavor when reconstituted, see opposite. Strangely enough, it can never be eaten raw, as it has a poisonous alkaloid which disappears entirely in drying or parboiling—a quality which also characterizes most varieties of **morel,** shown second from left, on 326. ◗ But cooking will not destroy the toxins within most poisonous types.

Morels grow in the spring. Second from the right is **chanterelle,** which appears in summer. On the far right is **Boletus edulis,** a great European favorite known to gourmets as **cèpe** or **Steinpilz.** For **truffles,** those black diamonds of the kitchen, see 331–332. ◗ Never use any mushroom that shows signs of decay. It harbors ptomaines and toxins just like any other decaying vegetation. ◗ Never cook light-colored mushrooms in aluminum, as it darkens them. Don't worry about mushrooms packaged by reputable firms, who guard their beds intensively against harmful invad-

ing spores. And don't bother to buy spawn blocks to grow your own mushrooms if your cellar is warmer than about 55°. To preserve seasonal mushrooms, see (II, 625).

In preparing fresh mushrooms, brush or wipe them with a cloth. If they must be washed, dry thoroughly. As the skins harbor much of the flavor, do not remove them. Some people use only the caps, since the stems tend to be tougher. Should you be so extravagant, turn the mushroom on its side and cut the stem so enough is left within the cap to prevent subsequent shrinkage at the center during cooking. Be sure to use the stems in Stock Making, (II, 167), in Farces, 430, or in Duxelles, (II, 255). Another way to keep the mushrooms plump and to

use most of the stem is to turn them, as sketched above, and slice lengthwise.

One of the best-looking food garnishes is the channeled mushroom. Shown also in the above sketch are decorative mushrooms under glass. To carve curving lines on the rather firm but spongy-textured mushroom evenly with a sharp knife requires considerable skill, but we find the point of a curved grapefruit knife quick and easy for the amateur. We have even been tempted to use a V-shaped linoleum-carving tool.

To store mushrooms temporarily,

keep them refrigerated in a ventilated container. To keep mushrooms light in color, sprinkle with lemon juice or white wine, or cook à blanc, 555. To reconstitute dried mushrooms, soak from 1/2 to 4 hours in tepid water to cover. Drain and use as for fresh mushrooms. Use the water, if not gritty, for sauces or soups.

Store dried mushrooms uncovered in a glass container in a light but not sunny place. ◆ Three ounces dried mushrooms reconstituted equals 1 pound fresh. To keep fresh mushrooms or truffles impaled on food as a garnish, use tiny branches of fresh lemon thyme as picks.

## STEAMED MUSHROOMS

**4 Servings**

This is a fine way to prepare very large mushrooms for stuffing.
◆ Please read About Mushrooms, 326.
Prepare:

    **1 lb. mushrooms**

Place them in the top of a double boiler ◆ over—not in—boiling water. Dot with:

    **2 tablespoons butter**

Add:

    **1/4 teaspoon salt**
    **1/8 teaspoon paprika**
    **1/2 cup milk**

Cover closely. Steam about 20 minutes or until tender. The broth that results is superlative. Serve it with salt or use in sauces.

## SAUTÉED MUSHROOMS

**4 Servings**

Prepare for cooking, using caps or pieces sliced to uniform thickness:

    **1 lb. mushrooms**

Melt in a skillet over moderately high heat until they reach the point of fragrance:

    **2 tablespoons butter**
    **1 tablespoon vegetable oil**

or use:

    **(3 tablespoons clarified butter, 396)**

Add the mushrooms and ◆ shake the pan, so the mushrooms are coated without scorching. Drop in:

    **(1 clove garlic)**

Continue to cook over moderately high heat ◆ uncovered, shaking the pan frequently. At first the mushrooms will seem dry and will almost invisibly absorb the fat. Continue to shake the pan for 3 to 4 minutes, depending on the size of the pieces. Remove garlic. If you are holding the mushrooms to add to other food, do not cover, as this will draw out their juices. If using as a garnish or vegetable, serve at once on:

    **Toast rounds**
    **Grilled tomatoes or eggplant**

or on a bed of:

    **Puréed Peas, 339**

## CREAMED MUSHROOMS

**4 Servings**

Sauté as for Sautéed Mushrooms, above:

    **1 lb. sliced mushrooms**
    **1 tablespoon finely chopped onion**

Add:

    **2 tablespoons dry white wine**

Cook briefly, remove from heat and combine the above with:

    **1 cup hot White Sauce II, 383 or Velouté Sauce, 387**

Season with:

    **Salt and paprika**
    **A pinch of herbs**

Marjoram is the traditional touch. Chives and parsley are also recommended. Serve over a baked potato or in a casserole, covered with:

**Au Gratin III, (II, 221)**

## MUSHROOMS À LA SCHOENER

**4 Servings**

A Viennese specialty.

▶ Please read About Deep-Fat-Frying Vegetables, 282.

Wipe off with a clean cloth:

**1 lb. button mushrooms**

Choose mushrooms with about a 1- to 1½-inch cap and cut off the stems ¼ to ½ inch below the caps. Sprinkle with:

**Lemon juice**
**Salt**

Dip in:

**Fritter Batter for**
**Vegetables, (II, 155)**

and deep-fat-fry them in oil heated to 365° until golden brown. You may hold them, covered with a paper towel, for a very short time in a 200° oven. Just before serving, dust with:

**Chopped parsley or chervil**

Serve with:

**Tartare Sauce, 421**

## BROILED MUSHROOMS

Preheat broiler.

Wipe with a dry cloth and remove the stems from:

**Mushrooms**

Brush generously with:

**Butter or oil**

Broil stem side down on a hot greased broiler about 2½ minutes. Turn and put in each cap a small lump of:

**Butter or a dab of ground**
**ham**

Season the mushrooms with:

**Salt and paprika**
**Chopped parsley and**
**lemon juice**

Continue to broil, stem side up, until tender. Serve at once on:

**Hot toast**

## BROILED STUFFED MUSHROOMS COCKAIGNE

**4 Small Servings**

Farces in which the main ingredient is finely chopped sweetbreads, ham, or sausage make wonderful mushroom stuffing; or just seasoned puréed peas, garnished with a sprig of lemon thyme. The mushroom stems may be incorporated into the stuffing. Our favorite formula is given below.

Remove stems. Wipe with a damp cloth:

**12 large mushroom caps**

Chop the stems and simmer them for 2 minutes in:

**1 tablespoon butter**

Add:

**1½ cups dry bread crumbs**
**¼ cup chopped pecans or**
**other nutmeats**
**(1 pressed clove garlic)**
**1½ tablespoons chopped**
**chives, basil or tarragon**

Bind these ingredients with:

**2 tablespoons cream, stock or**
**part stock and part sherry**

Season with:

**Salt and paprika**

Preheat broiler.

Brush the mushroom caps with:

**Butter or olive oil**

Fill them with the above dressing and sprinkle with:

**Grated Parmesan cheese**

to which you have added a pinch of:

**Paprika**

Place them stem side up on a well-greased pan. Broil about 5 minutes and serve sizzling hot on:

**Toast**

## MUSHROOMS STUFFED WITH CLAMS OR OYSTERS

Preheat broiler.
Prepare as for Broiled Mushrooms, above:

**Large mushrooms**

After cooking, stem side down, place in each one:

**A clam or oyster**

Cover each clam with:

**1 teaspoon or more mayonnaise**

seasoned with:

**Horseradish and Worcestershire sauce**

Continue to broil about 6 inches from the source of heat until the sauce begins to color. Serve hot.

## MUSHROOMS FLORENTINE

**4 Servings**

Preheat broiler.
Prepare as for Broiled Stuffed Mushrooms Cockaigne, 329:

**12 large mushrooms**

Add to the stems and the juice in the pan:

**2 teaspoons grated onion**
**2 tablespoons chopped parsley**
**(1 teaspoon anchovy paste)**

Cook these ingredients gently about 3 minutes. Add:

**1/2 to 3/4 cup Creamed Spinach, 359**

Brush the caps with:

**Butter or olive oil**

Fill them with the above mixture and broil stem side up on a greased pan about 5 minutes. Serve as a garnish for individual steaks or scrambled eggs.

## MUSHROOMS STUFFED WITH SEAFOOD OR SNAILS

**8 Servings**

Preheat broiler.
Remove the stems from:

**24 large mushrooms**

Wipe caps and stems with a dry cloth. Chop the stems. Shell, then chop:

**1/2 lb. cooked shrimp, snails or crab meat**

Melt:

**2 tablespoons olive oil or butter**

Stir in:

**2 tablespoons flour**

Add:

**1 cup shrimp, chicken or clam stock**

Add the mushroom stems. ◗ Lower the heat. Stir and simmer the sauce for 2 minutes. Add the seafood or snails and:

**2 teaspoons chopped chives or other herbs**

Stir gently until well blended and add:

**1/8 teaspoon curry powder or 1 tablespoon sherry
Season to taste**

Brush the mushroom caps with:

**Butter or olive oil**

Fill them with the above dressing, place stem side up on a well-greased pan and broil about 5 minutes. Prepare:

**8 rounds buttered toast, each large enough to hold 3 mushrooms**

Place the cooked caps on the toast. Serve garnished with:

**Parsley and broiled bacon**

## MUSHROOMS AND ONIONS IN WINE

**4 Servings**

Fine for a chafing dish.
Prepare for cooking, 326:

**1 lb. mushrooms**

Melt:

**½ cup butter**

Skin, add, stir and sauté 5 minutes:

**16 tiny white onions**

Add the mushrooms. When they are coated with butter, add:

**2 tablespoons flour**
**¼ cup chopped parsley**
**½ bay leaf**
**¼ teaspoon freshly grated nutmeg**
**½ cup bouillon or stock**

Cook and stir these ingredients until the onions are tender. Add:

**¼ cup Madeira or dry sherry**

Serve garnished with:

**Croutons, (II, 219)**

## MUSHROOM RING OR MOUSSE

**6 Servings**

Chop finely:

**1 lb. mushrooms**

Melt:

**2 tablespoons butter**

Stir in:

**2 tablespoons flour**

Brown the flour slightly. Sauté the mushrooms in this mixture for 2 minutes. Cool them. Beat in:

**4 beaten egg yolks**
**½ teaspoon salt**
**¼ teaspoon paprika**

Preheat oven to 325°.

Whip until stiff:

**½ cup whipping cream**

In another bowl ♦ whip until stiff, but not dry:

**2 egg whites**

Fold the cream lightly into the mushroom mixture. Fold in the egg whites. Butter a 9-inch ring mold. Pour in the mousse. Cover it with a piece of buttered paper. Place the ring mold in a pan of hot water. Bake about 1 hour.

Remove paper. Invert the mousse onto a platter. Fill center with:

**Buttered peas and parsley**

## MUSHROOMS UNDER GLASS

**4 Servings**

This supposedly "posh" specialty, shown as served on 327, is quite within the reach of anyone with an ovenproof glass bowl that fits closely over a baking dish.

Preheat oven to 350°.

Trim the stems from and channel, see 327:

**1 lb. mushrooms**

Beat until creamy:

**¼ cup butter**

Stir in very slowly:

**2 teaspoons lemon juice**

Add:

**1 tablespoon chopped parsley**
**⅓ teaspoon salt**
**¼ teaspoon paprika**

Cut with a biscuit cutter and toast:

**4 rounds bread, ½ inch thick**

When cold, spread both sides with half the butter mixture. Spread the rest on the tops of the mushroom caps. Place the toast in the bottom of a small baking dish and heap the mushrooms upon it. Pour over them:

**½ cup cream**

Cover closely with a glass bowl. Bake about 20 minutes. Add more cream if the mushrooms become dry. Just before serving, add:

**2 tablespoons dry sherry**

Serve the mushrooms—still under the glass—garnished with:

**Parsley**

## ABOUT TRUFFLES

So precious are these nubbly unattractive-looking fungi that in Southern Europe, where they are exclusively found—or rather strip-mined—they are locked up in hotel safes. On the other hand, they have become so widely distributed in the canned state that we are reminded of a friend of ours who asked the proprietor of a small fruit store in her neighborhood if he had any truffles; at which the fruiterer, who was a little hard of hearing, shrugged his shoulders eloquently and replied: "And who hasn't?"

Truffles defy cultivation. The French type—the blacks—like the rest of the genus, grow underground. As in Italy, where a "white" variety occurs, they are rooted out by trained pigs or dogs. Too bad for us humans that we haven't invented a truffle Geiger counter; but at least we know in general where to start digging: truffles are symbiotic with oaks. And— another hint—the "season" is October to March!

The terms **Périgourdine, Piémontaise** and **Lucullus** are often applied to truffled dishes. Dishes frequently seasoned with truffles are: pâté de foie in pastry; scrambled eggs; garnishes for hors d'oeuvre; farce for artichokes.

To prepare fresh truffles, wash in several waters. As the skin is rough, you may have to scrub them clean. Pare them with care, or rub off the skin, which should be saved for seasoning sauces or for the garnish below. Truffles should be sliced very thin, for their aroma is overpowering. To take advantage of it, place thin slices on food and store overnight in a closed container in the refrigerator. Add truffles to dishes at the end of the cooking period to avoid overcooking. If you are working with canned truffles, merely heat them with the food or use them as a garnish. If you open a can and use only a portion, place the remainder, covered with oil or sherry, in a tightly lidded

glass container. It will keep refrigerated about a month.

❀ Truffles may be frozen in their own juice; or add some Madeira wine if juice is lacking.

### ⼈ TRUFFLE GARNISHES

**I.** To produce black truffles in economical quantity for decorating, put in a blender:

> 7 tablespoons truffle bits,
>   peelings, rubbings and
>   juice
> 1 tablespoon gelatin

dissolved in:

> ³/4 cup water

If this blended mixture is not dark enough to suit you, heat it over hot water until it colors to your satisfaction. Spread the mixture thin on a cookie tin and cool it in the refrigerator. Cut into any desired form and use on cold food, see Chaud-Froid, 428. This same process may be used for pimientos.

**II.** Bits of white truffle may be used raw over risotto or fondue, puréed for canapés, processed in foie gras or cooked 2 to 3 minutes in butter.

## OKRA

This vegetable, see illustration in chapter heading on 277, is often combined in stews, where its gluey sap helps thicken the sauce and gives to such dishes the name of **Gumbo.** See Chicken Gumbo, 140.

### STEWED OKRA

**3 Servings**

Wash:

> 2 cups young okra

If the pods are small, leave them whole, in which case less sap is released. If large, cut off the stems and slice into 1-inch pieces. Drop into a small amount of:

**Boiling water**

enough to cover the bottom of the pan by 1/8 inch. Simmer covered until tender, if whole about 8 minutes, if cut about 5. Drain if necessary.

**Season to taste**

Serve hot with:

**2 tablespoons melted butter**

or with:

**Hollandaise Sauce, 410**

or if cooled with:

**Sauce Vinaigrette, 413**

◗ Pressure cook okra cut into 1-inch slices 4 minutes at 15 lbs.

## SAUTÉED OKRA

**6 Servings**

Wash:

**1 quart okra: 1 lb.**

Dry it well, cut off the stem ends and slice crosswise thinly. Melt:

**2 tablespoons butter**

Add the okra, cover and simmer gently about 5 minutes. Stir frequently. Add:

**1/4 cup finely chopped green peppers**
**1/2 cup finely chopped onion**
**1 cup skinned, seeded, chopped tomatoes**
**1/2 teaspoon sugar**
**1/2 teaspoon fresh basil**

Simmer covered about 20 minutes longer. Remove the cover and continue cooking until tender.

## ABOUT ONIONS

An elderly cousin of ours maintained that onions are the secret of health; to which our grandfather liked to rejoin, "But how on earth can you keep the secret?" For various suggestions to disguise their outspokenness and exploit their potential, please read about onions as seasoning, (II, 272), where you will also find a full discussion of this marvelous family with the qualities each member contributes.

Carl Sandburg contended that life itself is like an onion: it has a bewildering number of layers; you peel them off, one by one, and sometimes you cry. To prepare onions without tears, you may drop them into rapidly boiling water for about 8 seconds, then drain and chill them; after which the skins should slip off easily. Or you may work under running water as shown below, to keep the irritants diluted. For the unskilled there is the closed chopping device, but this, of course, must be cleaned. Also shown is a special grater. But, again, a skilled wrist and a sharp knife as shown at the top of 334 are the quickest approach. Peel the onion, leaving the tuft at the root end intact.

Cut the onion in half from stem to stern. Place one half cut side down. Start slicing it perpendicular to the root end in 1/8-inch parallels but leave about 1/2 inch of the root end in one piece. Then turn your knife so the

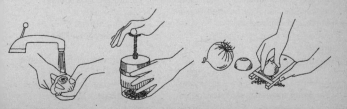

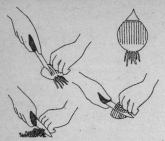

blade is parallel to the table surface and again make 1/8-inch parallel incisions to the 1/2-inch demarcation at the root end. Finally make 1/8-inch slices from the top perpendicular to the longitudinal slices starting at the stem end of the onion. When you reach the demarcation line your onion will fall into dice. To remove onion odors you may rub your hands—and the cutting board—with a slice of lemon or a little powdered mustard; then rinse them in water.

Onions all rebel under high heat or too long a cooking period by discoloring and giving off an unpleasant odor caused by the breakdown of their sulfur component. In sautéing them, be sure they are evenly sliced so they all cook golden at the same time and none remains raw and harsh in taste.

Several kinds of onions are generally available: the small whites, ideal for creaming and stews; the big full-flavored "globes," yellows, and red and white Creoles; as well as the Bermudas, the sweet Spanish and the Italian reds, which are so much milder that they can be used raw in salads and sandwiches.

STEAMED ONIONS

**5 Servings**

We prefer this method to stewing because it avoids the dangers of overheating.

Place on a rack ◗ over—not in—boiling water:

> **10 medium-sized dry unpeeled onions: about 1 1/2 lb.**

Cover the pan and cook until tender, 30 minutes or more. Peel and serve them with:

> **(1 cup browned buttered bread crumbs)**

or dress them with:

> **1/4 cup melted butter**
> **1/2 teaspoon salt**
> **1/2 teaspoon cinnamon or cloves**
> **(1 teaspoon sugar)**

CREAMED ONIONS

**5 Servings**

Prepare:

> **Steamed Onions, above**

Cover with one of the following:

> **1 cup White Sauce I, 383, and Au Gratin III, (II, 221)**
> **1 cup Allemande Sauce, 390; or 1 cup Quick Tomato Sauce, 400**

You may use 1/4 onion water and 3/4 cream in the white sauce. Cook the onions and the sauce together for 1 minute. Add:

> **1/4 cup chopped parsley**
> **A dash of cloves**
> **1/4 teaspoon paprika**
> **(2 tablespoons sherry)**

You may also add:

> **(1/2 cup Sautéed Mushrooms, 328)**

or:

> **(Minced celery, cooked or raw)**

Serve the onions on:

> **(Toast)**

## YOUNG GREEN ONIONS OR SCALLIONS

**4 Servings**

Rinse and trim, allowing 3 inches of green:

**3 bunches scallions**

Place them in a heavy skillet with:

**½ cup boiling water**
**2 tablespoons butter**

Cook covered until nearly tender, about 5 minutes. Drain well. Place them in rows on:

**4 very thin slices toast**

Season with:

**Salt and freshly grated white pepper or nutmeg**

Pour over them:

**Melted butter, Cheese Sauce, 385, or Hollandaise Sauce, 410**

Or cut the onions into small pieces, cook them and combine them with other cooked vegetables—peas, beans, or new potatoes.


## WHOLE BAKED ONIONS

**I.** Preheat oven to 375°.
Wash:

**Medium-sized onions: 8 oz. each**

Bake on a rack in a pan above ¼ inch water about 1½ hours. Cut a slice from the root end. Discard the outer shells. Pour over the onions:

**Melted butter**

Season with:

**Salt and paprika**

Cover with:

**(Grated Parmesan cheese or chopped parsley)**

**II.** ⊟ Cook, as you would potatoes, in a bed of coals about 45 minutes:

**Whole onions**

The outer skin forms a protection. When the onions are tender, puncture the skin to let the steam escape. Scoop out the centers and serve with:

**Salt and pepper**


## SAUTÉED ONIONS

**2 Servings**

These can be useful also as a garnish for a greater number than two.
Skin:

**4 medium-sized onions**

Cut them into very thin slices or chop them. Melt in a skillet:

**2 tablespoons butter or bacon drippings**

Add the onions and sauté until golden brown. Stir frequently to prevent burning. Before serving, season with:

**Salt**
**(Worcestershire sauce)**


## SMALL BRAISED ONIONS

Skin:

**Small onions**

Pour over them to the depth of ½ inch:

**Boiling stock**

Simmer covered over low heat. Let them absorb the liquid until they are tender, about 25 minutes. Add additional stock if necessary. When the onions are almost tender:

**Season to taste**

and add:

**(Seeded golden raisins)**


## GLAZED ONIONS

**4 Servings**

Boon companions for a pork roast.
Skin:

**12 small onions**

Prick them through the center and place them on a rack above:

**1 inch boiling water**

Cook covered until nearly tender,

about 25 minutes. Dry on paper toweling. Melt:

**¼ cup butter**

Add:

**½ teaspoon salt**
**2 tablespoons brown sugar**

Cook this syrup 1 minute. Add the onions and move them about until they are well coated. Cook over low heat 15 minutes, using an asbestos mat under the pot, if needed, to prevent scorching.

## SCALLOPED ONIONS WITH CHEESE

**6 Servings**

Peel, slice crosswise and poach in:

**Milk**

until tender:

**6 large white onions: about 4 lb.**

Drain them well.
Preheat oven to 350°.
Place in a buttered baking dish:

**4 slices buttered toast**

Arrange the onions on the toast. Sprinkle with:

**½ cup grated American cheese**

Beat well:

**1 egg**
**1 cup milk**
**½ teaspoon salt**
**⅛ teaspoon paprika**

Pour this mixture over the onions. Dot the top with:

**1 tablespoon butter**

Bake about 15 minutes. Serve with:

**Crisp bacon**
**Parsley**

## FRENCH-FRIED ONION RINGS

**4 Servings**

◗ Please read About Deep-Fat Frying, 94.

Skin and cut crosswise into ¼-inch slices:

**4 large white onions: about 3 lb.**

Combine:

**1 cup milk**
**1 cup water**

Soak the onions in the liquid for 1 hour. Drain them, spread on paper toweling and dredge in:

**Fritter Batter for Vegetables, (II, 155)**

Pick up a group of the rings on a fork and let excess batter drip off before frying them in deep fat heated to 365° until light brown. Drain on paper toweling before serving.

## STUFFED ONIONS

Onions make attractive garnishes or individual servings when filled. Asians often give very special dishes fanciful names, like "Phoenix Bursting Through Clouds" or "Lady's Grace." We call this one "Cultured Pearls."
◗ Please read About Stuffed Vegetables, 284.
Skin and parboil, 106, about 10 minutes:

**Large onions**

Drain well. Cut a slice from the top and remove all but ¾ inch of shell. Chop the removed pulp with:

**Seasoned bread crumbs or cooked rice, chopped cooked fish, meat or sausage, baked beans, mushrooms and bacon, or Deviled Ham Spread, (II, 77), and nutmeats**

Moisten these ingredients with:

**White Sauce I, 383, a tomato sauce, melted butter, stock, cream or gravy**
**Season to taste**

and add:

**Chopped fresh herbs**

Fill the onion cases. Cover the tops with:

**Au Gratin III, (II, 221)**

Place the filled onions in a pan on a rack with enough water below to keep them from scorching, and bake in a preheated 375° oven until tender, about 30 to 40 minutes, depending on size.

## ONIONS STUFFED WITH SAUERKRAUT

**4 Servings**

Not for a ladies' luncheon.
Prepare:

**6 onion cases, above**

Preheat oven to 400°.
Combine the chopped onion pulp and:

**1 cup drained sauerkraut**
**1/2 cup soft bread crumbs**
**1/4 teaspoon salt**
**(1/4 teaspoon caraway or celery seed or a few juniper berries)**

Heap the mixture into the onion cases. Sprinkle the tops generously with:

**Buttered crumbs**

Bake the onions in a pan with a very little water until well heated and tender, about 35 minutes.

## ONION AND APPLE CASSEROLE

**4 Servings**

Preheat oven to 375°.
Peel and cut crosswise into 1/8-inch slices:

**4 large onions: about 3 lb.**

Peel, core and cut in the same way:

**4 medium-sized apples**

Sauté, remove from the pan and mince:

**8 slices bacon**

Take out all but 2 tablespoons of the bacon fat.

Toss in the fat left in the pan and reserve:

**1/2 cup soft bread crumbs**

Grease a baking dish. Arrange the onions, apples and bacon in alternate layers. Combine and pour over them:

**3/4 cup hot stock or water**
**1/2 teaspoon salt**

Bake the dish covered 30 minutes. Uncover and dot the top with the reserved bread crumbs. Bake about 15 minutes longer.

## ABOUT HEARTS OF PALM

Not all palm "hearts" are edible. Most of those eaten in this country are taken from the palmetto, and the same variety furnishes almost all the canned product, which comes from Florida or Brazil. Since the plant is of slow growth and cannot survive removal of the heart, conservation-minded cooks are presented with a problem.

Hearts generally weigh between 2 and 3 pounds when trimmed. They must be prepared quickly to preserve color and flavor.

▶ To boil, remove the outer covering of the heart, leaving a cylindrical portion, the base of which should be tested for bitterness. Remove fibrous upper portion. Slice thin and soak for 1 hour. Use the same water to blanch the palm à blanc, 555, 5 minutes—if there is any trace of bitterness. Now drain and plunge into boiling water again. Cook covered about 45 minutes. Drain and serve with:

**Hollandaise Sauce, 410**

or in:

**White Sauce I, 383**

▶ To roast, leave the heart in its sheath. Roast in a 400° oven until tender. Lay back the sheath. Slice the heart crosswise and serve with:

**Lemon juice and salt**

## PARSLEY

During the earlier years of this century parsley, in most American households, was regarded as a purely decorative plant—like asparagus fern or smilax—except for an occasional light sprinkling over boiled potatoes. Now, nutritionally, it has come into its own, (II, 276). The so-called turnip-rooted or Hamburg parsley can be occasionally found at market. It makes an interesting change from other types of root vegetable and is cooked similarly.

## DEEP-FRIED PARSLEY

◗ Please read About Deep-Fat Frying, 94. When parsley takes the following form it is really quite irresistible. Care is the watchword, though: it becomes limp if the fat is not hot enough and olive green if the fat is too hot. The finished product should be at once crisp and a bright dark green. To achieve both objectives, have at least 2 to 3 inches of fat per cup of parsley. The parsley must first be carefully stemmed, washed and placed between towels until absolutely dry. Put in a frying basket:

**1 cup fresh curly parsley**

Immerse the basket in deep fat which has been heated to between 400° and 425° and leave it 1 to 2 minutes or until no hissing noise is heard. Remove and drain on paper toweling. Serve immediately!

## PARSNIPS

**4 Servings**

To bring out the best flavor of parsnips, store them for several weeks at temperatures just above 32°. Parsnips discolor easily. To avoid this see Salsify, 357.

Preheat oven to 375°.
Pare, then cut into halves, discarding cores if woody:

**4 medium-sized parsnips: 1 lb.**

Place them in a buttered oven-proof dish.
Brush with:

**2 1/2 tablespoons butter**

Sprinkle with:

**1/2 teaspoon salt**

Add:

**3/4 cup stock or water**

Cover the dish and bake until the parsnips are tender, about 30 to 45 minutes. Serve with:

**Chopped parsley and butter, or Lemon Butter, 397**

◐ Pressure-cook parsnips 7 minutes at 15 pounds.

## FRENCH PARSNIPS

Prepare as for:

**Carrots Vichy, 310**

## GREEN PEAS

**2 Servings**

Young peas, with good reason, have always brought forth paeans of praise; but how to cope with the older ones, with their often dismayingly tough skins? Try salting when cooking is about half over, or try Purée of Peas, 339. One pound of well-filled pea pods will yield about 1 1/4 to 1 1/2 cups hulled peas. Wash, then hull:

**1 lb. green peas**

Steam them, 281, or cook covered in:

**1/8 inch boiling water or light stock**

to keep them from scorching. Add:

**1/2 teaspoon lemon juice**

to help preserve color. There is a tradition that one must add to peas:

**(A pinch of sugar)**

Two or three pods may be cooked with the peas for flavor. Simmer 7 to 10 minutes. When the peas are tender, drain them if there is any water left. Remove the pods. Season with:

**Melted butter or hot cream**

to which you may add:

**Chopped parsley or mint**

♥ Pressure cook peas 2 minutes at 15 lbs.

## GREEN PEAS COOKED IN LETTUCE

**4 Servings**

Steaming in a lettuce casing tenderizes peas and imparts to them a subtly delicious flavor.
Wash and remove the heart from:

**A head of lettuce**

leaving a deep shell reinforced by 3 or 4 thicknesses of leaves. Reserve the heart for salad. Wash, then hull:

**2 cups green peas**

Season with:

**Salt**

**Pinch of sugar**

Fill the head of lettuce with the peas and place it in a heavy pan narrow enough to support the lettuce case. Add a small quantity of:

**Boiling water or light stock**

Simmer covered until the peas are tender, about 30 minutes. Drain off any liquid. The lettuce leaves may be chopped and served with the peas. Dress with:

**Melted butter or cream**

## PURÉE OF PEAS

This makes a lovely base on which to place stuffed mushrooms.
Prepare:

**2 cups cooked frozen peas**

🡾 Blend when tender with:

**3 tablespoons cream**

**Season to taste**

and serve at once.

## PEAS AND CARROTS

Disdainfully dubbed "Keys and Parrots" by a cousin of ours, a devout anti-vegetarian; but a classic just the same.
Combine in any proportion:

**Hot drained cooked Carrots, 309**

**Hot canned or cooked green peas**

Drain the vegetables well.

**Season to taste**

Pour over them:

**Melted butter**

**Chopped parsley**

Serve at once.

## PEAS AND MUSHROOMS

Prepare as for:

**Peas and Carrots, above**

substituting for the carrots:

**Sautéed Mushrooms, 328**

but omit additional butter.

## PODDED PEAS

**4 Servings**

These sought-after varieties, known also as **sugar peas, snow peas** and **mange-tout,** are often available in Chinese shops. If they are mature, slice the pods diagonally.
Wash, cut off the ends and any strings adhering to:

**1 lb. podded peas**

Cook as for:

**Green Beans, 291**

or you may stir-fry about 1½ minutes. Serve while still crisp.

## ABOUT PEPPERS OR PIMIENTOS

"Pepper" is one of those confusing designations so frequent in the world of vegetable cookery. The term "pimiento" is commonly used to describe the cooked, fully ripened sweet pepper, which turns red in color and which is used as a garnish or seasoning, (II, 276). The recipes that follow all basically refer to the less mature fruits known as **sweet, green, globe** or **bell** peppers—sometimes, to add to the confusion, called **mangoes** in the Midwest—and have nothing to do with the fruit, the condiment, or the red-hot chili pepper. For more details, see (II, 276). Peppers of all types are chock-full of vitamin C. To peel peppers, put under the broiler and turn often until they blister.

These are one of the few vegetables that can be ✿ frozen without blanching. So buy when they are plentiful. Small packets of frozen chopped peppers can be counted on to add zest to any number of dishes. ◗ Never overcook peppers, as they become bitter.

Illustrated above are the mild bell peppers, which vary in shape from the long reds to the squat porcelain greens, and similar yellow types so well shaped for stuffing, shown on the left of the sketch, and also shown cut to reveal the fibrous membrane and seeds common to all *capsicum* peppers. These portions must be removed before eating. They also cause severe discomfort if they come in contact with eyes or lips. From rather sharp to mild are the next two peppers used for **paprika** and **ancho**, a favorite for chili powder. The really hot ones next, like **Tabasco**, the small **Japanese santaka** and **cayenne**, are treasured as condiments.

## GREEN PEPPERS IN SAUCE

Stewed green peppers combine well with other vegetables—for example, tomatoes, celery or onions. Remove stem, seeds and fibrous membranes from:

**Green peppers**

Cut them into oblongs or strips. Drop into:

**¹/₂ inch boiling water**

Boil until tender, about 10 minutes. Drain well. Serve in:

**Cheese Sauce, 385, or a**
**Canned Soup Sauce, 394**

Allow about half as much sauce as peppers.

## ONIONS AND GREEN PEPPERS

**4 Servings**

A sterling accompaniment to cold meat.

Skin, then cut into thin slices:

**6 medium-sized onions**

Cut coarsely, after removing seeds and membranes:

**3 green peppers**

Melt in a large skillet:

**3 tablespoons butter, ham fat or olive oil**

Sauté the onions about 10 minutes.

Add the peppers and sauté 5 minutes longer. Add:

**2 tablespoons stock or water**
**Season to taste**

Cover the skillet. Simmer the vegetables until the onions are tender, about 10 minutes. Serve with:

**Quick Tomato Sauce, 400**

## ABOUT STUFFED GREEN PEPPERS

Should you wish to fill peppers with heated precooked food, remove seeds and membranes. Parboil them, 106, until nearly tender, about 10 minutes. Fill and serve. Or cover the filling with Au Gratin I, II, or III, (II, 221), and run briefly under a broiler until the crumbs are golden. You may fill pepper cases with any of the fillings suggested for Stuffed Tomatoes, 369, or one of the following: parslied, buttered lima beans; creamed spinach, peas or celery; creamed asparagus with shredded almonds; or any stuffings of precooked food such as macaroni and cheese, Corn Creole, 317, Tomatoes Creole, 368, or those in the recipes which follow.

## GREEN PEPPERS STUFFED WITH ANCHOVY DRESSING

**4 Servings**

◗ Please read About Stuffed Green Peppers, above.

Preheat oven to 350°.

Prepare for stuffing:

**4 pepper cases**

Fill cases with a mixture of:

**1²/₃ cups dried bread crumbs**
**2 tablespoons melted butter**
**6 crushed anchovy fillets**
**2 tablespoons capers**
**¹/₂ cup sliced green olives**
**¹/₂ teaspoon salt**

**1¹/₄ cups drained canned**
**tomatoes**

Bake 10 to 15 minutes.

## GREEN PEPPERS STUFFED WITH RICE

**4 Servings**

◗ Please read About Stuffed Green Peppers, above.

Preheat broiler.

Prepare for stuffing:

**4 pepper cases**

Have ready:

**1 cup hot Boiled Rice, 189**

Add:

**¹/₂ cup stock, cream or tomato**
**pulp**
**Salt and pepper**
**A few grains cayenne**
**¹/₂ teaspoon curry powder or a**
**small pinch of oregano**
**¹/₂ cup or more grated cheese**

Fill the pepper cases. Cover the tops with:

**Au Gratin I or II, (II, 221)**

Brown briefly under a broiler.

## GREEN PEPPERS STUFFED WITH MEAT AND RICE

**4 Servings**

◗ Please read About Stuffed Green Peppers, left.

Preheat oven to 350°.

Prepare for stuffing:

**4 pepper cases**

Melt:

**2 tablespoons drippings or**
**butter**

Add, stir and sauté until light-colored:

**¹/₂ lb. ground beef**
**3 tablespoons minced onions**

Add:

**1 cup hot Boiled Rice, 189**
**2 well-beaten eggs**
**¹/₂ teaspoon salt**
**¹/₈ teaspoon paprika**

¹/₄ teaspoon celery seed, curry powder, dried herbs or Worcestershire sauce

Fill the pepper cases. Bake 10 to 15 minutes.

## GREEN PEPPERS STUFFED WITH CORN À LA KING

**6 Servings**

◗ Please read About Stuffed Green Peppers, 341.
Prepare for stuffing:

**6 pepper cases**

Place in a double boiler ◗ over—not in—boiling water:

**2¹/₂ cups drained corn niblets:
1 No. 2 can
1 chopped canned pimiento**

You may add:

**(4 slices sautéed minced bacon)
(2 tablespoons minced onion that has been sautéed in the bacon fat and drained)**

Combine, beat and add to the above:

**1 egg
¹/₂ cup milk
1 tablespoon soft butter
³/₄ teaspoon salt
¹/₈ teaspoon paprika**

Cook until the mixture is slightly thickened, about 15 minutes. Fill the peppers and serve.

## GREEN PEPPERS STUFFED WITH CREAMED OYSTERS

**4 Servings**

◗ Please read About Stuffed Green Peppers, 341.
Preheat broiler.
Prepare for stuffing:

**4 pepper cases**

Have ready:

**¹/₂ pint Creamed Oysters, 442 using half the recipe**

Add:

**2 tablespoons chopped parsley**

Fill the pepper cases with the hot oysters.
Cover the tops with:

**Au Gratin II or III, (II, 221)**

Brown briefly under a broiler.

## PLANTAIN

These 9- to 12-inch bananas, unlike their ubiquitous smaller cousins, must be cooked before eating, but never overcooked, since high heat releases an objectionable tannin component. They can be prepared in their green state, as well as when semi-ripe or quite mature, when the skins often become black and mottled. Cooked chopped ripe plantains also make a more than acceptable component of soups, stews and omelets.

Remove the fibrous strings from plantains before cooking, as they darken. Peel green plantains under running water to keep from staining the hands. Cut across into 2-inch-thick pieces; place at once in rapidly boiling water. Simmer 30 minutes. Season and serve with butter. If plantains are ripe, slice fine and cook in deep fat heated to 365°; or cook as for Candied Sweet Potatoes, 356. The purple bud end of plantain can be roasted in its husk. Only the heart is eaten. Serve with crumbled bacon or cracklings.

## ABOUT POTATOES

Anyone who has visited Hirschhorn, in the sweetly romantic Neckar Valley, and who has climbed the hill to the partly ruined castle that dominates the little village will remember being confronted by a monument dedicated piously, if unhistorically, "To God and Francis Drake, who brought to Europe for the everlasting benefit of the poor—the Potato."

Potatoes come in all shapes and sizes, but the two types generally found in markets across the country are the thin-skinned round "white" Katahdins, and the oblong russet Burbanks, or Idahos, higher in starch, and for this reason a better bet for baking and French frying and for pommes soufflés. Rising in popularity is a rather newly developed variety known as California long white, almost "eyeless," smooth-skinned, and moderate in starch content. Whatever the type, the older the potato the starchier.

In recent years, potatoes have been maligned as over-caloric—although they are only equal in this respect to the same-sized apple or a baking powder biscuit. They are full of B, C and G vitamins, plus many minerals and even some high-class protein. Don't use sprouted potatoes that are green from exposure to light, as the green portions as well as sprouts are poisonous; or frost-bitten ones, which are watery and have a black ring under the skin when cut in cross sections.

If you wonder why there are no recommendations for ❋ freezing potatoes in this chapter, let us say that this operation is not feasible with home equipment. Potatoes purchased frozen have all been treated to quick-vacuum partial dehydration and instant freezing, to which home equipment does not lend itself.

In the following recipes we have tried to give these delicious vegetables a renewed status. ◗ Be sure, if a potato type is specified, to use that type only—and remember that ◗ once a potato is cold, mealiness can never be returned to it.

Potatoes are often combined and mashed with other cooked vege-

tables, as: ²/₃ celeriac to ¹/₃ potato, or in equal parts with turnips, or ¹/₄ fresh avocado to ³/₄ potato.

Illustrated above are three implements we have found useful in preparing potatoes of various types. At left is a potato masher. Centered is a pickle spearer with tines of almost needlelike slenderness—an invaluable help in peeling new potatoes. The rack on the right has heavier tines on which potatoes may be impaled for baking. The inserted metal causes rapid penetration of heat, and at the same time releases steam, which assures a desirable flakiness.

## BOILED MATURE POTATOES OR POMMES ANGLAISE

**6 Servings**

Wash well, remove sprouts and blemishes, then pare:

**6 medium-sized potatoes: 2 lbs.**

When in haste, cut them into quarters. Cook covered 20 to 40 minutes in:

**4 cups boiling water**
**¹/₂ teaspoon salt**

When they are tender, drain well. Reserve the **potato water** for a thick soup base or for use in bread making.

To make the potatoes mealy, place a folded towel over the pot for 5 minutes. Shake the pot well. Remove the towel, which will have absorbed excess steam. Roll the potatoes in:

**2 to 3 tablespoons melted butter**
**3 to 4 tablespoons chopped parsley or chives**

🅿 Pressure cook large potatoes about 15 minutes at 15 lbs.

## BOILED NEW POTATOES

### 4 Servings

Few vegetables are as ingratiating as small new—which is to say, young—potatoes, especially when they are served in their tender skins, so that all their delicate goodness is held until the very moment they are eaten. We are put in mind of the character in *Patience* who developed "a passion à la Plato for a bashful young potato."

In the illustration, 343 center, is a pickle fork useful when peeling hot new potatoes.
Wash well:

**12  small new potatoes**
Drop them into:
**Boiling water to cover**
Cook covered until tender, 20 to 30 minutes. Remove the skins and serve with:
**Chopped parsley, mint or chives**
Or melt in a skillet:
**3 to 6 tablespoons butter**
Add the potatoes and shake them gently over low heat until well coated. Serve sprinkled with:
**Salt**
**Chopped parsley or chopped fresh dill or fennel**
Or add to the butter in the pan:
**3 to 4 tablespoons freshly grated horseradish**
and shake the potatoes until coated. This last is particularly choice with cold cuts.

🅿 Pressure cook small new potatoes about 2½ minutes at 15 lbs.

## TINY NEW POTATOES, SAUTÉED

### 4 Servings

Scrub and scrape well:
**24  very small whole new potatoes**
Heat in a heavy saucepan:
**2 to 3 tablespoons olive oil or clarified butter**
Turn the potatoes in the oil, cover closely and cook slowly until tender. Shake the pan from time to time. Sprinkle the potatoes with:
**Salt and paprika**
**(Chopped chives or parsley)**

## RICED POTATOES

### 6 Servings

A fine foil for meat with a rich gravy.
Prepare:
**Boiled Mature Potatoes, 343**
When they are tender and dried, put them through a food mill or a ricer, shown on 186. Heap them on a dish and pour over them:
**(2  tablespoons melted butter)**

## MASHED POTATOES

### 6 Servings

Mashed potatoes should be served at once but in a pinch can be kept warm by placing the pan in a larger pan of hot water. Or put them in a greased casserole, run a slight film of cream over the top and keep in a warm oven. The cream should brown to an attractive color.
Prepare:
**Boiled Mature Potatoes, 343**
You may add to the water a small onion or a cut clove of garlic, a piece of bay leaf and a rib of celery with leaves. Remove these ingredients before mashing potatoes with a fork or

a potato masher, seen shown on 343, or putting them through a food mill, ⚒ blender or electric mixer. Add to them:

> **3 tablespoons butter**
> **1 teaspoon salt**
> **¹/₃ cup hot milk or cream**

Beat with a fork or heavy whisk until the potatoes are creamy. Grated or sautéed onions with the drippings, minced crisp bacon, chopped parsley, caraway seeds, chives or watercress may be added to mashed potatoes. To help fluff the potatoes, cover the pan after they are mashed and place over very low heat about 5 minutes.

## MASHED POTATO CHEESE PUFFS

**6 Puffs**

This is a tempting potato dish and a good-looking one.
Preheat oven to 350°.
Beat:

> **2 egg yolks**

Add and beat until fluffy:

> **1¹/₃ cups hot or cold Mashed Potatoes, above**
> **3 tablespoons hot milk**
> **¹/₃ cup grated cheese**

Season these ingredients with:

> **¹/₄ teaspoon paprika**
> **¹/₄ teaspoon celery salt**
> **(¹/₂ teaspoon finely grated onion)**
> **(1 teaspoon chopped green pepper or parsley)**

Beat until stiff, then fold in:

> **2 egg whites**

Place the mixture in mounds in a greased pan. Brush the tops with:

> **1¹/₂ tablespoons soft butter**

Bake the puffs about 20 minutes. Should you want them evenly browned, turn once during the baking period.

## CHANTILLY POTATOES

**6 Servings**

The use of whipping cream is what makes a dish **Chantilly.**
Prepare:

> **3 cups Mashed Potatoes, 344**

Preheat oven to 375°.
Whip until stiff:

> **¹/₂ cup whipping cream**

Season it with:

> **Salt and white pepper**
> **A few grains cayenne**

Combine it with:

> **¹/₂ cup grated hard cheese**

Shape the potatoes into a mound on an ovenproof plate. Cover the mound with the whipped cream mixture. Bake until the cheese is melted and the potatoes are lightly browned.

## CREAMED POTATOES

Prepare:

> **Boiled New Potatoes, 343**

Drain and dry off potatoes over very low heat. Peel and cut into ¹/₂-inch dice. Serve at once in:

> **White Sauce II, 383**

flavored with:

> **(Dill seed)**

Should you wish to delay serving this dish, place the potatoes in a buttered casserole. Cover with Au Gratin III (II, 221), and bake in a 400° pre-heated oven until heated through.

## SCALLOPED POTATOES

**I.**

**6 Servings**

Preheat oven to 350°.
Drop into boiling water:

> **3 cups pared, very thinly sliced potatoes**
> **1 teaspoon salt**

Parboil about 8 minutes. Drain well. Grease a 10-inch baking dish. Place the potatoes in it in 3 layers, sprinkling each layer with flour and dotting with butter. Use in all:

**2 tablespoons flour**

**3 to 6 tablespoons butter**

There are many tidbits you can put between the layers. Try:

(**¼ cup finely chopped chives or onions**)

(**12 anchovies or 3 slices minced crisp bacon—but then reduce the salt in the recipe**)

(**¼ cup finely sliced sweet peppers**)

Heat:

**1¼ cups milk or cream**

Season with:

**1¼ teaspoons salt**

**¼ teaspoon paprika**

(**¼ teaspoon dry mustard**)

Pour the mixture over the potatoes. Bake about 35 minutes, testing for tenderness with a fork.

## II.

**6 Servings**

Preheat oven to 350°.

Pare and slice thin:

**3 cups potatoes**

Heat:

**1¼ cups hot condensed mushroom or celery soup**

Stir in:

**¼ cup grated cheese**

(**½ cup Steamed Mushrooms, 328**)

Pour the mixture over the potatoes. Bake about 1 hour, testing for doneness with a fork.

## BAKED POTATOES

We have always liked the snug phrase "baked in their jackets" to describe this process. But we are told that at least one young cook, after encountering it, called a home economist at the local utility company and complained that her grocer was unable to supply her with potato-jackets!

The best baked potatoes are flaky when served—so start with mature baking types like Idahos. Although new potatoes can be used and will need only about half as much baking time, they will never have the desired quality. The present rage for wrapping potatoes in foil inhibits flakiness, because too much moisture is retained. In fact, to draw moisture out of bakers, they are often placed on a bed of rock salt. See the potato baking rack shown on 343.

Preheat oven to 400°.

Wash and scrub even-sized, shapely:

**Baking potatoes**

Dry them and grease lightly with:

**Butter**

Bake for 40 to 60 minutes, depending on size. When potatoes are half done, pull out rack; quickly puncture skin once with a fork, permitting steam to escape. Return to oven and finish baking. When done, serve at once with:

**Butter or thick sweet or cultured sour cream, or chopped chives or parsley, or 1 tablespoon Deviled Ham Spread, (II, 77), or Cheese Sauce, 385**

## ▤ POTATOES COOKED IN ROSIN

**6 Servings**

Coming upon this sensational setup after an hour or two of skating or skiing will send the spirits soaring—and no other method turns out a potato so distinctively flaky. Allow a minimum of three hours for this recipe; because of the fumes, never try it indoors. Rosin can be purchased at athletic and dance supply stores. Place in a

3-gallon iron kettle or galvanized bucket:

**15 to 25 lb. rock rosin**

The rosin may be used repeatedly. Heat it to 275°F. over a grill or hot-plate. Carefully lower into it on a large slotted wooden-handled spoon, one at a time:

**6 large baking potatoes**

After about 45 minutes in the simmering rosin they will float to the surface. Simmer them 30 minutes longer. Remove one potato and wrap in heavy brown paper, twisting the ends tightly. Let cool 10 minutes and serve. If the texture is not exceptional, cook the remaining potatoes 10 minutes more before testing. Serve with:

**Butter, salt, and freshly ground pepper**

Avoid eating the rosin-covered skins.

STUFFED POTATOES

**6 Servings**

Prepare:

**6 Baked Potatoes, above**

Cut them in halves crosswise, lengthwise like boats, or leave them whole, cutting a small ellipse on the flat top. Scoop out the pulp. Add to it:

**3 to 4 tablespoons butter**

**3 tablespoons hot milk or cream**

**1 teaspoon salt**

**(2 tablespoon sautéed grated onion)**

Or, if you plan to serve these with fish, add for piquancy:

**(1 tablespoon horseradish)**

along with the butter and cream. Beat these ingredients until they are smooth. Whip until stiff:

**(2 egg whites)**

Fold them into the potato mixture.

Fill the potato shells. Sprinkle the exposed potato with:

**$1/2$ cup grated hard cheese**

**Paprika**

Broil under low heat until the cheese is melted.

BAKED POTATOES STUFFED WITH VEGETABLES

**8 Servings**

Preheat oven to 400°.

Prepare:

**4 Baked Potatoes, 346**

Have ready:

**1 cup White Sauce I, 383**

Mix into the sauce:

**$1/4$ teaspoon salt**

**$1/2$ cup grated hard cheese**

**$1/2$ cup cooked peas**

**$1/2$ cup cooked chopped carrots**

**$1/4$ cup diced green peppers, seeds and membrane removed**

**2 tablespoons diced pimientos**

Cut the potatoes lengthwise into halves. Remove the pulp without breaking the skin. Mash the pulp and fold in the sauce and vegetables. Heap the potato shells with the mixture. Cover with:

**Au Gratin II, (II, 221)**

Place the potatoes on a pan in the oven until the tops are brown. Serve with:

**(Hot or cold meat)**

LYONNAISE OR PAN-FRIED POTATOES

**4 Servings**

Prepare:

**6 medium-sized Boiled New Potatoes, 344**

While hot, peel and slice thinly and evenly. Sauté to an even brown in a heavy skillet in:

**2 tablespoons butter**
**2 tablespoons vegetable oil**
Meanwhile, sauté until golden in another pan:
**½ cup finely sliced onions**
in:
**2 tablespoons butter or beef
    drippings**
Mix onions and potatoes together gently.
**Season to taste**
Sprinkle with:
**Parsley**
and serve at once.

## FRANCONIA OR BROWNED POTATOES

**4 Servings**

We love browned potatoes but have an aversion to the hard-crusted, grease-soaked variety so often served. To ensure a tender crust, we suggest preparing:

**6 boiled mature potatoes:
    about 2 inches in diameter**
Cook them until they are ♦ not quite done, so that there is still resistance to the testing fork.
Preheat oven to 350°.
Melt in a small heavy skillet a mixture of:

**Butter and vegetable oil**
to a depth of about ¼ inch. When the fat is hot but not quite to the point of fragrance, put in the potatoes. Let them cook ♦ covered in the oven about 20 minutes, turning them for even coloring. On the last turn put in:

**2 tablespoons finely chopped
    parsley**
Bake ♦ uncovered about 10 minutes longer.

## POTATOES ANNA

A beautiful ware for a beautiful dish is the lidded copper Potatoes Anna

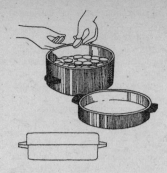

pan, shown above, about 8 inches in diameter and 3½ inches high. The lid, which has side handles, fits down over it to a 1½-inch depth during the oven period, but is reversed to hold the potatoes for serving. You may substitute a heavy lidded skillet.
Peel and cut large mature baking potatoes into even ³/₁₆-inch slices; then with a small biscuit-cutter cut them into enough equal-sized rounds to make:

**4 cups potatoes**
Soak them in ice water for 10 minutes. Drain. Dry carefully in a towel. Preheat oven to 375°. Heat in the Anna pan:

**2 to 3 tablespoons butter**
**2 tablespoons vegetable oil**
Do not brown the fats, but let them just reach the point of fragrance. Put the potatoes in the butter in slightly overlapping spirals until the base of the pan is filled. Shake occasionally while filling to make sure the potatoes are not sticking. Add a sprinkling of:

**Salt**
**Grated onion**
**Parmesan cheese**
The butter will bubble up. But make sure, before adding another layer of slightly overlapping potato slices,

that the first layer is coated with additional:
**Melted butter**
Continue this process for the first 2 layers, letting the potatoes color slightly. Be sure the layers are welded together. Add a sprinkling of salt, onion and butter each time. It is not necessary to continue adding butter if you have used about ¹/₂ cup. The moisture from the cooking potatoes will make it continue to bubble up so that in building the next layer or two you may omit the butter. Continue to shake the pan now and then to prevent sticking. Cover the pan and bake 45 minutes to 1 hour. Just before the potatoes are done, turn the entire mass over into the lid—to brown the upper side. Serve in the lid or turned out onto a platter.

## HASH BROWN POTATOES

**4 Servings**
Combine with a fork:
  **3 cups finely diced raw potatoes**
  **1 teaspoon grated onion**
  **1 tablespoon chopped parsley**
  **¹/₂ teaspoon salt**
  **¹/₄ teaspoon black pepper**
Heat in a 9-inch skillet:
  **3 tablespoons bacon drippings, oil or other fat**
Spread the potato mixture over the fat. Press it with a broad knife into a cake. Sauté the potatoes slowly, shaking them from time to time to keep them from sticking. When the bottom is brown, cut the potato layer in half and turn each half with 2 spatulas. Pour slowly over the potatoes:
  **¹/₄ cup cream**
Brown the second side and serve the potatoes piping hot.

## POTATO PANCAKES

**About Twelve 3-Inch Cakes**
◗ This recipe demands mature potatoes.
Pare and grate coarsely until you have:
  **2 cups grated potatoes**
Fold the gratings into a muslin towel and wring the towel to extract as much moisture from the potatoes as possible. Place them in a bowl. Beat well:
  **3 eggs**
Stir them into the potatoes.
Combine and sift:
  **1¹/₂ tablespoons all-purpose flour**
  **1¹/₄ teaspoons salt**
Add the flour to the potato mixture with:
  **1 to 3 teaspoons grated onion**
Heat in a heavy skillet:
  **¹/₄ inch or more beef drippings or oil**
Place spoonfuls of the potato mixture in the skillet, forming them into patties ¹/₄ inch thick and 3 inches in diameter. Brown, then turn and brown the second side until crisp. These are usually served hot with:
  **Applesauce, (II, 118)**
If you must hold until all the batter is cooked, place them on a rack above a baking sheet in a 200° oven. Then serve all of them at once after draining on paper toweling to remove any excess fat.

## PAN-BROILED GRATED POTATOES

**4 Servings**
Very good, quick—next best to a potato pancake. Wash, then grate on a medium grater, skin and all:
  **3 medium-sized mature baking potatoes**
  **2 tablespoons grated onion**

Melt in a skillet to the point of fragrance:

**2 tablespoons butter**
**2 tablespoons vegetable oil**

Spread the potatoes in the skillet to a depth of about ¼ inch. Cook covered over medium low heat until the bottom is brown. Reverse and brown the other side.

**Season to taste**

## SOUFFLÉ OR PUFFED POTATOES

**6 Servings**

According to legend—which we like to believe—Louis XIV, on campaign against the Dutch and, as major monarchs of the 17th century were wont to do, traveling in an exquisite little palace on wheels, had sent a courier ahead to his chef, detailing just what he desired for dinner. The roads were nearly impassable; the hour grew late; and the chef, who had managed to keep most of the elaborate menu in reasonably prime condition, found to his consternation as the King's party clattered into the courtyard that his *pommes frites* had gone utterly limp. In a frenzy, he immersed the potatoes in the hot fat a second time, madly agitated the pan, and behold!—the dish which was to make him rich and famous.

There were several more coincidences that the cook may not have been aware of. His potatoes must have been old, so that the starch content was just right to make them puff. He must have had a very systematic apprentice who cut the potatoes all with the grain and to a very uniform thickness, as sketched on 351. In his relief at having something to serve, he evidently didn't mind a 10% failure, for even experts who make this dish daily count on that great a percentage of spud-duds. All this is just to encourage you if, like us, you expect a 100% return on your efforts. The duds, by the way, are acceptable as French fries, even if they are not so glamorous as the puffs.

◗ Please read About Deep-Fat Frying, 94.

Choose:

**8 large mature potatoes**

Restaurants famous for this dish age their own to the point where you can no longer pierce or scrape the skin off with your fingernail, but must use a knife to pierce it. There should be about 80% starch in the potato. Pierre Adrian, who was very expert, maintained that there is nothing like a Holland potato, grown on Spanish soil; but we have been obliged to content ourselves with Idahos or Burbanks. Cut from the unpared potato the largest possible oblong ◗ with the grain—that is, the long way, as sketched on the next page—into ◗ ⅛-inch slices that are of uniform thickness from one end to the other. In restaurants this accuracy is produced by a slicing machine. Once you have these long even slices, you can cut them into the classic polygonal shape, as sketched, or even into triangles, circles or fancy ovals with crimped edges. Soak the slices for at least 25 minutes in:

**Ice water**

Dry them thoroughly. Have ready a deep-fat-frying kettle one-third filled with:

**Rendered beef kidney fat**
**or vegetable oil**

heated to 275°. Drop the slices in separately. ◗ Do not crowd the pan. The slices will sink. This next admonition is not without danger for the unskilled. ◗ When, after a few seconds, they rise, use a continuous shaking motion with the pan, which will set up a wavelike action to keep

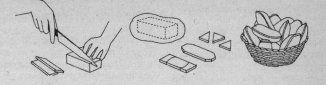

the floating strips bathed in the fat. Continue to cook them at 275°, turning them at least once, until they begin to clarify toward the centers and show a marked difference in texture at the cut edges, to a depth of about ¹/₁₆ inch. Drain on paper toweling. If you do not want to use them at once, they may be refrigerated before the second cooking, but ▶ bring them to room temperature before immersing in the hot fat the second time. If you want to proceed at once, let them cool off and drain for about 5 minutes before the second cooking.

Just before you are ready to serve, drop them again one by one into a fryer filled ¹/₃ full with the fat at 385°. Again agitate the pan as described. The once-fried slices should puff at once, although they always retain a seam wherever you have made an original perimeter cut. Cook to a golden brown. Drain. Dry on paper toweling. Salt and serve the puffed ones at once, preferably in a basket as shown above, to keep them crisp. If they are not crisp enough, return them to the fat for a few seconds. Drain again. Sometimes it is worth trying the duds once more, after they have cooled.

## NEVER-FAIL FRENCH FRIES

The following recipe, like Soufflé Potatoes, calls for a two-stage frying operation. After the first stage, you may drain and cool the potatoes on paper toweling. Cook the second stage just before serving.

▶ Please read About Deep-Fat Frying, 94.

As with all successful potato frying, much depends on the maturity of the potato, so choose:

### Mature baking potatoes

Pare and slice them into strips about 2¹/₄ inches long and about ³/₈ inch through. If you are using cold-storage potatoes and want a light-colored result, soak the slices for 15 minutes in 90° water. Wipe well with a towel to remove surface moisture and excess starch. Slowly heat to between 300° and 330°:

### Vegetable oil or rendered beef kidney fat

Drop the potatoes in—about 1 cup at a time—and cook about 2 minutes, until all sputtering ceases. Skim out the rather limp potatoes, drain on paper toweling and cool at least 5 minutes before starting the second stage. ▶ Heat the oil to 365°. Place the potatoes in a frying basket. This will assure quick and easy removal. Fry them for about 3 minutes. They should be golden brown and will be crisp when drained on paper toweling. ▶ Never cover them, as they will get flabby. Serve at once in a napkin-lined basket.

## SHOESTRING POTATOES

Cut into very thin strips, not more than ³/₁₆ inch thick:

### Mature baking potatoes

Cook as for:

> **Never-Fail French Fries, 351**

## OVEN "FRENCH-FRIED" POTATOES

**4 Servings**

Preheat oven to 450°.

Pare:

**4 medium-sized potatoes**

Cut them lengthwise into strips about 1/2 inch thick. You may soak them in cold water for 10 minutes. Dry well between towels. Spread in a single layer in a flat ovenproof dish. Pour over them:

**1/4 cup melted butter, bacon drippings or vegetable oil**

Stir them until coated. Bake about 30 to 40 minutes, turning several times during this period. Drain on paper toweling. Sprinkle with:

**1/2 teaspoon salt**
**1/4 teaspoon paprika**

## POTATO PUFFS

**3 to 4 Servings**

◗ Please read About Deep-Fat Frying, 94.

Combine:

**1/2 cup sifted flour**
**1 teaspoon double-acting baking powder**
**1/4 teaspoon salt**

Add and mix:

**1 cup Mashed Potatoes, 344**

The potatoes should be soft and at room temperature. If they are not, add a little hot milk or water and beat. Add:

**1 slightly beaten egg**
**1 teaspoon minced parsley**

Drop by spoonfuls into deep fat heated to 365°. Fry to a golden brown. Drain on paper toweling.

## POTATO OR SARATOGA CHIPS

◗ Please read About Deep-Fat Frying, 94.

As with Soufflé Potatoes, 350, and French Fries, 351, it is very important to have properly aged potatoes. Use these chips as a vegetable, a garnish or a cocktail snack.

With a vegetable slicer, slice as thinly as possible:

**Peeled Idaho potatoes**

Soak the slices 2 hours in cold water, changing the water twice. Drain and dry well. ◗ Very slowly heat to 380° in a deep fryer:

**Vegetable oil**

If you want a good luster on your cooled chips, allow the cooking oil to reach 75° before heating. Place a frying basket in the oil and drop the slices in one by one. Shake the basket or stir the potatoes several times to prevent the chips from sticking together. Cook until golden. Drain and place on paper toweling to get rid of excess fat.

## POTATO BASKETS

◗ Please read About Deep-Fat Frying, 94.

Use a shredder to cut into long 1/4-inch strips:

**Peeled potatoes**

Soak them for 30 minutes in ice water. Drain well and dry between towels. To form the baskets, please read about Noodle Baskets, 202. Heat to 380°:

**Vegetable oil**

Deep-fry the potato baskets 3 to 4 minutes. Remove from the fat and drain. Bring the fryer up to 380° again and immerse basket for 1 minute more. Drain on paper toweling and serve at once.

## DUCHESS POTATOES

**8 Servings**

Prepare:

**4 cups Riced Potatoes, 344**

Add while still hot:

**1/4 cup butter**
**2 beaten egg yolks**
**(A dash of dry mustard)**
**Season to taste**

and allow this mixture to cool briefly.
Preheat oven to 400°.
Shape the potato mixture into flat
cakes on a floured board. Place
the cakes on a buttered baking sheet.
Brush with:

**A slightly beaten egg**

Bake until golden and serve at once.

If you are using the above mixture
decoratively, do not allow it to cool
before inserting it into a pastry tube
and fluting it at once in wavy scallops
around the edge of a plank or a heat-
resistant platter, then browning it in
the oven.

## DAUPHINE POTATOES

If you add about 2 tablespoons of
grated Gruyère cheese to each cup of
potatoes called for in this recipe, you
will have **Potatoes Lorette.**
♦ Please read About Deep-Fat Frying, 94.
For every cup:

**Freshly Mashed
Potatoes, 344**

add:

**1/3 to 1/2 cup Pâte à Choux,
(II, 370)**

made without sugar and seasoned with:

**A grating of nutmeg**

Form the potato mixture by hand into
1- to 1 1/2-inch balls or insert in a pastry bag with a large plain tube, shaping as for Spätzle, 186.
Roll in:

**(Dry white bread crumbs)**

Heat to 350°:

**Vegetable oil**

Deep fry the balls 3 to 4 minutes and
allow the heat of the fat to increase to
370° until they are golden. Drain on
paper toweling. Add:

**Salt**

and serve at once.

## FRIED POTATO BALLS

**6 Servings**

A simpler version, not unlike Dau-
phine Potatoes, left.
♦ Please read About Deep-Fat Frying, 94.
Prepare:

**2 cups hot Riced Potatoes,
344: 4 medium-sized
potatoes**

Add to them:

**2 tablespoons butter**
**1/2 cup grated cheese**
**1/2 teaspoon salt**
**A few grains cayenne**
**2 tablespoons cream**
**2 beaten egg yolks**
**1/2 teaspoon any baking
powder**

Whip these ingredients until light.
Shape into balls. Roll the balls in:

**Flour**

then in:

**1 egg beaten with
2 tablespoons water**

and in:

**Fine bread crumbs**

Heat to 380°:

**Vegetable oil**

Deep fry the balls until golden. Drain
on paper toweling. Serve at once.

## ABOUT LEFTOVER
POTATOES

Not inappropriately is an unrespon-
sive person called a "cold potato."
Held over after cooking, potatoes

lose their mealiness and that subtle down-to-earth flavor. They are probably most effective when ⚒ blended into a soup base, in which the combining liquid should be hot. We give the following additional suggestions as better-than-nothing bargains.

## LEFTOVER GERMAN-FRIED POTATOES

**4 Servings**

Melt in a skillet:

> 2 **or more tablespoons vegetable oil**

Add:

> 2 **cups sliced leftover boiled potatoes**
> **Salt and paprika**
> 1 **or more teaspoons minced onion**

Sauté the potatoes slowly until light brown. Turn frequently.

## LEFTOVER POTATOES O'BRIEN

**6 Servings**

Preheat oven to 350°.
Dice:

> 6 **medium-sized leftover boiled potatoes**

Add:

> 1 **chopped seeded green pepper with membrane removed**
> 1 **minced onion**
> 1 **tablespoon flour**
> **Salt and pepper**
> **A few grains cayenne**
> (3/4 **cup grated cheese)**

Place these ingredients in a greased baking dish. Pour over them:

> 1 **cup hot milk**

Cover with:

> **Au Gratin II, (II, 221)**

Bake about 30 minutes.

## LEFTOVER POTATO CAKES

Shape into little cakes:

> **Leftover mashed potatoes**

Add for each cupful:

> **(A beaten egg)**
> **(Chopped parsley)**
> **(Chopped celery or celery seed)**
> **(Grated onion or 1/4 cup chopped sautéed onions)**
> **(A grating of nutmeg)**

Dip the cakes in:

> **Flour, bread crumbs or crushed cornflakes**

Melt in a skillet:

> **Butter or other fat**

Brown the cakes on one side, reverse and brown the other.

## LEFTOVER AU GRATIN POTATOES

Preheat oven to 400°.
Cut into dice:

> **Leftover boiled potatoes**

Prepare:

> **White Sauce I, 383, or Cheese Sauce, 385**

Make half as much sauce as there are potatoes. Combine potatoes and sauce. Add:

> **(Chopped parsley, minced onion or chives)**

Put the mixture in a greased baking dish. Cover with:

> **Au Gratin II, (II, 221)**

Bake until browned.

## ABOUT SWEET POTATOES OR YAMS

There are two quite distinct types of "sweet potato": a rather dry type with pinky-yellow flesh, and a sweeter, softer, much more moist and vividly orange-colored kind affectionately if mistakenly called **yam** in many parts of the country. Sweet potatoes are extremely high in vitamin A, while yams contain only a trace. Buy only enough of either type for immediate use, as they do not store well.

Sweet potatoes lend themselves to most of the cooking methods used for white potatoes and are delightfully enhanced by fruits and fruit flavoring. They reheat better than leftover white potatoes.

## BOILED SWEET POTATOES

To prepare sweet potatoes in their jackets, drop them into boiling water to cover and cook ◗ covered until tender, about 25 minutes. Peel and salt before serving.

## MASHED SWEET POTATOES

**4 Servings**

Prepare:

    **5 medium-sized Boiled Sweet Potatoes, above: 2 cups**

Skin and put them through a ricer, or mash with a potato masher. Add:

    **2 tablespoons butter**
    **1/2 teaspoon salt**
    **A little hot milk, cream, lemon juice or dry sherry**
    **(2 teaspoons brown sugar)**

Beat the potatoes with a fork or whisk until very light. Sprinkle with:

    **Grated orange or lemon rind, cloves or cinnamon**

Chopped dates and nutmeats may be added. To make attractive individual servings, heap the mixture into hollowed-out orange halves. Place these cups in a covered buttered baking dish and heat through in a 375° oven.

## BAKED SWEET POTATOES

Follow the recipe for:
    **Baked Potatoes, 346**
◗ Be sure to cut a small slice off one end or to puncture a sweet potato when half cooked as a safety valve to prevent its bursting.

## STUFFED SWEET POTATOES

**6 Servings**

Preheat oven to 375°.

**I.** Prepare and bake as for Baked Potatoes, 346:

    **3 large shapely sweet potatoes**

Cut lengthwise into halves and scrape out most of the pulp. Add to the pulp:

    **2 tablespoons butter**
    **1/4 cup hot cream or 3/4 cup crushed pineapple**
    **1/2 teaspoon salt**
    **(1 tablespoon dry sherry)**

Southern people say "use lots of butter, some brown sugar, nutmeg and black walnut meats; and replace the sherry with 2 tablespoons bourbon whisky."

Beat these ingredients with a fork until fluffy. Fill the shells and cover the tops with:

    **Au Gratin, (II, 221)**

Marshmallows may be substituted for the bread crumbs and butter. These are a matter of taste, or—in our strongly biased view—lack of it. Bake the potatoes until browned.

**II.** These make a heartening cold weather touch. Bake as for Baked Potatoes, 346:

    **Sweet potatoes**

Just before serving, insert in each potato:

    **1 tablespoon warm Deviled Ham Spread, (II, 77)**

## CANDIED SWEET POTATOES

**4 Servings**

Cook covered in boiling water to cover until nearly tender:

    **5 medium-sized sweet
    potatoes**

Preheat oven to 375°.

Pare and cut the potatoes lengthwise in ¹/₂-inch slices. Place in a shallow greased baking dish. Season with:

    **Salt and paprika**

Sprinkle with:

    **³/₄ cup brown sugar or ¹/₃ cup
    maple syrup**
    **(¹/₂ teaspoon grated lemon
    rind)**
    **1¹/₂ tablespoons lemon juice or
    ¹/₈ teaspoon ginger**

Dot with:

    **2 tablespoons butter**

Bake uncovered about 20 minutes, until glazed.

## CARAMELIZED SWEET POTATOES

**4 Servings**

Slice:

    **5 medium-sized Boiled Sweet
    Potatoes, 355**

Melt:

    **3 tablespoons orange
    marmalade or Sauce
    Cockaigne, (II, 564)**

Cook the potatoes gently in the sauce until glazed and brown.

## DEEP-FRIED SWEET POTATOES

◗ Please read About Deep-Fat Frying, 94.

Wash, then parboil for 10 minutes:

    **Large sweet potatoes**

Pare and cut them into strips. Heat to 365°:

    **Vegetable oil**

Deep-fry the strips until golden brown. Drain on paper toweling. Sprinkle with:

    **Brown sugar**
    **Salt**
    **Freshly grated nutmeg**

## SWEET POTATO PUFFS

**4 Servings**

Preheat oven to 500°.

Have ready:

    **2 cups riced cooked sweet
    potatoes**

Peel, mash and add:

    **1 large ripe banana**

Combine and add, stirring well:

    **1¹/₂ tablespoons melted butter**
    **1 beaten egg yolk**
    **1¹/₂ teaspoons salt**
    **3 to 4 tablespoons hot milk or
    cream**
    **(¹/₈ teaspoon nutmeg or ginger)**

Beat until stiff:

    **1 egg white**

Fold it lightly into the potato mixture. Drop the batter from a tablespoon in mounds—well apart—on a greased tin, or place the mixture in buttered ramekins. Bake about 12 minutes.

## SWEET POTATOES AND FRUIT

**6 Servings**

This tart dish is exceptionally good with roast pork, baked ham or game. Cook covered until nearly done in boiling water to cover:

    **6 medium-sized sweet
    potatoes**

Peel and cut them into ¹/₂-inch slices. Cook covered until nearly done in a very little boiling water:

    **1¹/₂ to 2 cups thinly sliced
    apples**

If the apples are not tart, sprinkle them with:

    **Lemon juice**

Preheat oven to 350°.

Grease a baking dish and place in it alternate layers of apples and sweet potatoes. Sprinkle the layers with:

> 1/2 **cup or more brown sugar**
> **A dash cinnamon or grated lemon rind**
> **(2 tablespoons seedless raisins)**
> **(2 tablespoons chopped pecans)**

Dot with:

> 1/4 **cup butter**

Pour over the top:

> 1/2 **cup of the apple water or water**

Bake about 30 minutes.
Or you may omit the sugar and substitute for the apples:

> 1/2 **cup puréed, sweetened apricots, (II, 111), Sauce Cockaigne, (II, 564), or crushed pineapple**

## RADISHES

Transforming red or white radishes into clever garnishes fascinates the young; and the allure endures. If you've read Pepys, you know that he ate buttered radishes at William Penn's—worth trying, too, especially with black ones. The jumbo-sized **daikon** sometimes exceeds 3 feet in length. It is so plastically promising that the Japanese, to whose country it is native, sometimes carve it into a fantastically intricate net, with which they cover a sizable baked fish. Daikon can be cooked by any recipe for Turnips, 372. So can any other radish, for that matter; or prepared as for Celeriac, 313. To store radishes before using, cut off the leaves.

## BOILED RUTABAGAS OR SWEDES

> **4 Servings**

Look for a new Laurentian hybrid of rutabaga developed in Canada and superior in texture and flavor. Rutabagas, also called **yellow turnips,** may be French-fried as for Shoestring Potatoes, 351, or baked like Potatoes, 346.
To boil, pare and dice:

> 2 **medium-sized rutabagas: 2 cups**

◗ Do not use the leaves. Drop the pieces into:

> **Boiling water**

Cook uncovered until tender, 20 to 30 minutes. Drain well. Add:

> 1/2 **teaspoon salt**

Serve with:

> **Melted butter**

to which you have added generously:

> **Lemon juice**
> **Chopped parsley**

Or mash the turnips and add them in any proportion to mashed potatoes with lots of:

> **Chopped parsley or cultured sour cream and nutmeg**

## ABOUT SALSIFY OR OYSTER PLANT

The salsify commonly found in the market is the white-skinned variety, see sketch on chapter heading, 277. But, if available, choose **scorzonera,** the black-skinned type, which is better flavored. Best results are obtained if the vegetable is stored for several weeks at temperatures just above 32°.

To avoid discoloration, cook this root unpeeled, or, if peeled, à blanc, as follows.

## SALSIFY À BLANC

Have ready:
> 3 cups boiling water

in which you have dissolved:
> 1 tablespoon flour
> 2 teaspoons lemon juice
> 1/2 teaspoon salt

Drop in:
> 2 cups peeled salsify

and cook 7 to 10 minutes. Serve in:
> White Sauce I, 383

or with:
> 2 tablespoons melted butter
> (Chopped chives or
> parsley)
> (A grating of nutmeg)

## SAUTÉED SALSIFY

Wash and peel:
> Salsify

Dip at once in:
> Milk

Drain and season with:
> Salt and pepper

Roll in:
> Flour, bread crumbs or
> crushed cornflakes

Sauté slowly until golden in:
> Butter

## SKIRRET

Cook as for any recipe using carrots, but always peel after boiling to retain flavor. Be sure also to remove the inner hard core before serving.

## SORREL

Because it is heavy in oxalic acid, this vegetable is usually parblanched, 106, for 3 minutes and drained before being cooked as for spinach or chard and combined with them rather than being served by itself. Alone, as a garnish, it lends itself to flavoring with meat glaze, eggs and cream; or puréed and seasoned with mustard and tarragon, it may form a bed for fish.

## ABOUT SPINACH

One of the more controversial greens, this is believed—with some scientific justification—to inhibit the body's absorption of calcium. It is also the most delectable of greens. We recommend throwing caution to the winds and enjoying it in moderation. Spinach is a special treat as a garnish with other foods, where its presence is usually heralded by the title **Florentine.**

Yield per pound varies from 2 servings if young, to 3 if old. Spinach requires little salt. Its astringent taste may be counteracted by a pinch of sugar.

♥ Pressure cook spinach 1 minute at 15 lbs.

## BOILED SPINACH

> 3 to 4 Servings

Pick over and cut the roots and tough stems from:
> 1/4 peck spinach: 1 lb.

Wash it quickly in several waters until it is free from sand and soil. If young and tender, cook as for Panned Spinach, opposite. If old, place the spinach in:
> 2 cups rapidly boiling water

◗ Reduce heat and simmer covered until tender, about 10 minutes. Discard the water if it is strong in flavor. If not, keep it for use in soups and sauces. Drain the spinach well. ⨺ Blend briefly or cut up the spinach with 2 sharp knives or a triple chopper until it is as fine as you like it. Sauté:
> 2 tablespoons diced sweet red
> pepper, 2 tablespoons

minced onion or a clove of
garlic

in:

**Butter or drippings**

Add:

**Lemon juice**
**Season to taste**

♦ being careful not to oversalt. Serve
the seasonings over the spinach.
Other garnishes for spinach include:

**Hard-cooked egg**
**Crumbled bacon**
**Fine buttered croutons**
**Hollandaise Sauce, 410**
**Au Gratin III, (II, 221)**

## CREAMED SPINACH

### I.

3 Servings

Prepare:

**2 cups Boiled Spinach, above**

⚗ Blend, rice or chop to a fine
purée. Melt in a skillet which may
be rubbed lightly with a clove of
garlic:

**1½ to 2 tablespoons butter**

Add and cook until golden:

**(1 tablespoon or more very
finely chopped onion)**

Stir in until blended:

**1 tablespoon flour or
2 tablespoons Browned
Flour, 379**

Stir in slowly:

**½ cup hot cream or stock**
**½ teaspoon sugar**

When the sauce is smooth and hot,
add the spinach. Stir and cook 3 minutes. Season with:

**Salt and pepper**
**(Freshly grated nutmeg or
grated rind of ½ lemon)**

Serve garnished with slices of:

**1 hard-cooked egg**

### II.

3 Servings

Cook and drain:

**Boiled Spinach, opposite**

⚗ Put it very briefly through a
blender with:

**¼ cup cultured sour cream or
condensed cream of
chicken soup**
**A grinding of nutmeg or
⅛ teaspoon prepared
mustard**
**(1 teaspoon horseradish)**
**Season to taste**

Heat briefly and serve.

### III.

4 Servings

⚗ Place in blender:

**¾ cup milk**
**(1 thin slice onion)**
**3 tablespoons soft butter**
**2 tablespoons flour**
**½ teaspoon salt**
**⅛ teaspoon paprika**
**A fresh grating of nutmeg
or lemon rind**
**(½ peeled clove garlic)**

Blend in small amounts, lidding blender after each addition:

**12 oz. spinach, coarse stems
removed**

When smooth, put this mixture into a
heavy skillet and stir over low heat
about 3 minutes until it bubbles and
the flour is cooked. Serve with:

**Buttered crumbs**
**4 slices cooked crumbled
bacon**
**2 sliced hard-cooked eggs**

## PANNED OR SICILIAN SPINACH

3 Servings

The seasonings in this dish help to
enliven even canned spinach.
Wash well and remove the coarse
stems from:

**1 lb. spinach**

Shake off as much water as possible. Heat in a large heavy skillet:

**1 tablespoon butter**

**2 tablespoons olive oil**

Add:

**(1 clove minced garlic)**

Add the spinach. Cover skillet and cook over high heat until steam appears. Reduce the heat and simmer until tender, 5 to 6 minutes in all.

**Season to taste**

To turn this into **Sicilian Spinach,** add:

**(2 or more chopped anchovies)**

## SPINACH WITH TOMATOES

**3 Servings**

Prepare:

**Boiled Spinach, 358**

Drain. ⚘ Blend or chop fine with:

**1/2 cup Italian tomato paste or tomato purée**

Sauté:

**1 pressed clove garlic**

in:

**(2 tablespoons olive oil)**

Add the spinach mixture and heat.

**Season to taste**

## SPINACH, TOMATO AND CHEESE LOAF

**8 Servings**

Preheat oven to 350°.

Place in a bowl:

**2 cups cooked drained spinach**

**2 1/4 cups drained canned tomatoes**

**1/4 cup chili sauce**

**1/2 lb. grated hard cheese or crumbled feta**

**1 cup cracker crumbs**

**Juice of 1/2 onion**

**1/4 teaspoon salt**

**1/4 teaspoon freshly ground pepper**

Toss these ingredients until blended. Place in a greased loaf pan. Bake the dish about 35 minutes. Serve garnished with:

**Crisp Bacon, 615**

## SPINACH IN PANCAKES

Prepare:

**Creamed Spinach, 359**

Prepare:

**French Pancakes, (II, 143)**

**Chopped Sautéed Mushrooms, 328**

Place the spinach and mushrooms on the pancakes. Roll them like a jelly roll. The tops may be sprinkled with:

**Grated cheese**

Place the rolls under a broiler until the cheese is melted. Serve at once.

## ABOUT SQUASHES

Easy cross-pollenization accounts for the myriad diversity of this family. It probably also accounts for occasional bitterness in the cultivated types, which may have interbred with their very bitter wild forebears. Unless squashes are to be stuffed, always choose the smaller specimens.

These plants divide into summer and winter types. We often call for special varieties of each type in the recipes which follow, but others may be substituted, as long as they belong to the respective type.

### SUMMER SQUASHES

Whether green, yellow, white; long, round or scalloped, these are all thin-skinned and easily punctured with a fingernail—the shopper's furtive assurance and the proprietor's despair. They should be firm and heavy. Avoid them if the rind is tough or the stem dry or black. If they are young, there is no need to pare them or to discard the seeds. Should only hard-rinded ones be available, do both. Summer squash do not store well, but a limited number of varieties can be found all year 'round at the "fancier" markets.

Our own favorite is zucchini. Try also the closely related cocozelle and vegetable marrow. Prepare these squash as for any cucumber and eggplant. Shown below in top row from left to right are **straight neck, crooked neck, cymling** or **pattypan, cocozelle** and **zucchini.** To stuff summer squash or squash blossoms, see below.

### WINTER SQUASHES

These, again, are of many colors and shapes and remain on the market from fall to early spring. Except for butternut, they have hard-shelled skins. Choose the others for their hard rinds. Watery spots indicate decay. The winter types, sketched below in the lower row, are **Golden Delicious acorn, buttercup** or **turban, butternut** and **Hubbard.** For ways to cook **pumpkin,** the most famous of all winter varieties, see 365.

Unless you bake squash whole, remove the seeds and stringy portions. Peel and cut into small pieces. Winter squashes need from 10 to 45 minutes of cooking.

Because squash is so bland in flavor, it will benefit from imaginative treatment. It may be cut lengthwise into "boats," scooped out, or cooked and the centers loaded with a succulent cargo. For fillings, see Stuffings, 430. If the squash is a tender summer type, you may combine the removed portion with the filling, which may include vegetables, bread crumbs, nuts, mushrooms or cooked meat.

### STEAMED SUMMER SQUASH

**4 Servings**

♦ Please read About Squashes, 360.

I. Wash and cut into small pieces:
   **2 cups any summer squash: zucchini; yellow crooked neck, etc.**
If very tender, the squash may even be left whole. Steam it covered, 281, until tender. Drain very well. Sprinkle generously with:

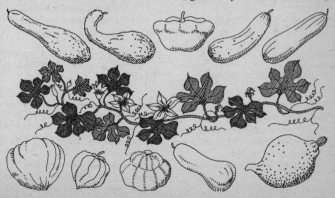

Grated Parmesan cheese
and melted butter

**II.** Prepare the squash as above, then
mash it with a fork. Beat until fluffy.
Beat in:

2 tablespoons cream
2 tablespoons butter or
olive oil
1/8 teaspoon white pepper
(2 teaspoons grated onion or
chopped fresh herb or a
touch of saffron)
1/2 teaspoon salt

Reheat the squash briefly and serve.

## STUFFED SQUASH BLOSSOMS

If you grow squashes, you may wonder why so many blossoms fall off
without maturing. These are male
flowers not retained for seed development. After they close and drop
they make decorative as well as edible cases for Forcemeat, 436. Open
each flower and put in only enough
of the forcemeat to allow the petals to
close again. Place stuffed blossoms
side by side on a greased baking dish
in a moderate oven until thoroughly
heated. Serve alone or as a platter
garnish.

Partially opened squash flower
buds may be sautéed in butter or
olive oil. Do not brown.

## BAKED SUMMER SQUASH

**4 Servings**

♦ Please read About Squashes, 360.
Preheat oven to 350°.
If summer squash is young, it need
not be pared. Cut into strips and place
in a greased baking dish:

3 cups any summer squash

Cover it with:

1/4 cup milk

Dot with:

2 tablespoons butter

Sprinkle with:

1 teaspoon salt
1/4 teaspoon paprika
(A grating of nutmeg or
1 teaspoon fresh lemon
thyme)

Cover the dish. Bake for about
1/2 hour or until tender. Garnish with:

Crisp crumbled bacon

## SAUTÉED SUMMER SQUASH

**4 Servings**

♦ Please read About Squashes, 360.
Wash and dice:

3 cups any summer squash

Melt in a skillet:

3 tablespoons butter or
olive oil

Add and sauté in it until golden:

1 cup minced onion

Add the squash and:

1/2 teaspoon salt
1/4 teaspoon freshly ground
white pepper

Cover the pan and cook until tender, about 6 minutes, shaking the pan
occasionally to prevent sticking. Remove lid and cook 3 minutes longer.
Serve sprinkled with:

Chopped parsley or basil
Grated Parmesan cheese or
Quick Tomato Sauce, 400

## STEAMED STUFFED SUMMER SQUASH

**I.**

**4 Servings**

♦ Please read About Squashes,
360.
Wash thoroughly, then cut the stem
ends from:

4 small summer squashes

Steam as for Steamed Summer
Squash, 361, but leave whole. When

almost tender, drain and cool. Scoop out the centers, leaving a shell about $1/2$ inch thick. . Chop the removed pulp. Add to it:

> $1/4$ **teaspoon paprika**
> $1/2$ **teaspoon Worcestershire sauce**
> **Minced garlic or onion**
> $1/4$ **teaspoon salt**
> 1 **tablespoon butter**
> 3 **tablespoons dry bread crumbs**
> $1/4$ **cup grated cheese**
> **A few grains cayenne**
> $1/8$ **teaspoon curry powder or dry mustard**

Preheat oven to 400°.
Refill the shells. Place them in a pan on a rack above $1/4$ inch of water. Bake until hot, about 10 minutes.

**II.** Or fill these cooked squash cases while hot with:

> **Heated creamed chicken, ham, fish or spinach**

Garnish with:

> **Parsley or tiny sprigs of lemon thyme**

## STUFFED BAKED SUMMER SQUASH

**4 Servings**

♦ Please read About Squashes, 360.
Preheat oven to 350°.
Wash:

> 4 **small summer squashes**

Cut them down the middle, either crosswise or horizontally. Scoop out the pulp, leaving a $1/2$-inch shell.
Sauté in:

> 2 **tablespoons butter**
> 2 **tablespoons chopped onions**

Add the squash pulp and:

> $1/2$ **teaspoon salt**
> $1/4$ **teaspoon paprika**
> **A dash of nutmeg or cloves**

Stir and cook these ingredients until hot. Remove from the heat. Add:

> 1 **beaten egg**
> $1/2$ **cup dry bread crumbs**
> $1/2$ **cup grated cheese**

You may rub the squash shells with:

> **Butter or drippings**

Fill them with the stuffing. Place in an ovenproof dish on a rack over $1/8$ inch of water or stock. Sprinkle the tops with:

> **Au Gratin II, (II, 221)**

Bake the squashes until tender, about 20 to 25 minutes, depending on their size.

## SUMMER SQUASH CREOLE

♦ Please read About Squashes, 360.
Have ready:

> $21/2$ **cups well-drained cooked zucchini, yellow crooked neck or pattypan squash**

Place it in a greased baking dish and proceed as for:

> **Stuffed Eggplant Creole, 322**

substituting squash for eggplant.

## DEEP-FRIED ZUCCHINI

♦ Please read About Deep-Fat Frying, 94, and About Squashes, 360.
Wash, dry and cut into $1/4$- to $1/2$-inch slices:

> **Zucchini**

Dry well. Dip in:

> **Fritter Batter for Vegetables, (II, 155)**

Heat in a deep fryer to 365°:

> **Vegetable oil**

Fry the squash until golden. Serve at once.

## SUMMER SQUASH CASSEROLE COCKAIGNE

**4 Servings**

We are particularly fond of zucchini in this dish. ▶ Please read About Squashes, 360.

Preheat oven to 375°.

Drain:

**2 cups cooked zucchini, 361, or other squash, cut into 3/4-inch slices**

Place zucchini in 4 buttered flat ramekins. Cover with a mixture of:

**1 can condensed cream of chicken soup: 10 oz.**

**1/2 cup cultured sour cream or yogurt**

Top with:

**Au Gratin III, (II, 221)**

**(Chopped nuts)**

Bake about 7 minutes or until thoroughly heated.

## SPAGHETTI SQUASH

For those on wheat-free diets, try this as a base for pasta sauces. Bake like potatoes, 346. Crack open the peeling and scoop out strings and seeds. Add butter, salt and pepper. Or boil without peeling in water to cover 20 to 30 minutes. Cut in half and remove seeds. Sauce and toss as for spaghetti.

## MASHED WINTER SQUASH

▶ Please read About Squashes, 360.

**I.**

Preheat oven to 375°.

Scrub:

**A Hubbard or other winter squash**

Place it on a rack and bake until it can be pierced easily with a wooden pick. Cut it in halves; remove the seeds. Peel the squash and mash the pulp. To:

**1 cup squash**

add:

**1 tablespoon butter**

**1 teaspoon brown sugar**

**1/4 teaspoon salt**

**1/8 teaspoon ginger**

Beat this well with enough:

**Warm cream or orange juice**

to make it a good consistency. Place in a serving dish. Sprinkle with:

**Raisins or nutmeats**

**1/4 cup crushed pineapple**

**II.** ❋ If using frozen or canned squash, you may season with:

**Sautéed onions**

**Cultured sour cream**

**A pinch allspice**

**Chopped parsley**

Heat in a double boiler over—not in—boiling water.

## BAKED WINTER SQUASH

▶ Please read About Squashes, 360.

Preheat oven to 375°.

If the squash is small, like:

**Acorn or butternut squash**

it may be washed, dried, greased and treated just like Baked Potatoes, 346. Bake at least 1 to 1 1/2 hours. Season as in the above recipe and garnish with:

**(Pimiento strips or Au Gratin II, (II, 221)**

The smaller baked winter squashes make attractive cases for the stuffings in the recipe below.

## STUFFED WINTER SQUASH

Small acorn or butternut squash are ideal for individual service. You may fill the raw shell, or bake it first as in Baked Winter Squash, above, and then fill it with the hot creamed foods suggested below.

◗ Please read About Stuffed Vegetables, 284, and About Squashes, 360. Prepare cooked:

> **Acorn squash cases, see 364**

Fill them with:

> **Creamed oysters, chicken, chipped beef, crab, fish, or mushrooms; spinach, hash, hash and vegetables, hot applesauce or crushed pineapple; cooked sausage meat or Ham à la King, 250**

Garnish the tops with:

> **Parsley**

Reheat in an ovenproof dish 10 to 15 minutes in a 350° oven.

## PUMPKIN

We Americans think of this squash first as pie, (II, 383), and next as soup, 154, but it is also surprisingly satisfactory as a vegetable. Cook by any recipe calling for a winter squash, or see (II, 383). About 1/2 pound will serve 1 person.

## TAMPALA OR CHINESE SPINACH

When the leaves of this tropical amaranth are about 6 inches tall, it is cooked as for Spinach, 358.

## ABOUT TARO OR DASHEEN

This versatile plant has leaves similar in form to the inedible elephant ears we grow decoratively, and a potato-like root that becomes grayish or violet when cooked. It is used as a vegetable or as a base for puddings and confections. The spinach-flavored leaves, if young, are cooked as for spinach; when mature, they may need about 45 minutes.

To bake, remove loose fibers and parboil the unpared root 15 minutes, then time as for potato baking, but make sure the oven is not over 375°. Uncooked taro may prove irritating to the skin, so handle it in water to which you add 1 tablespoon baking soda for every quart of water. To boil taro, treat as for Boiled Mature Potatoes, 343. Taro may also be fried as for Saratoga Chips, 352. Do not soak the slices—merely dry for 30 minutes on paper toweling.

## POI

**About 5 Cups**

Dice into 1-inch cubes:

> **2 1/2 lb. boiled, peeled taro roots, above**

Mash in a wooden bowl with a wooden potato masher until a starchy paste forms. Work in gradually with the hands:

> **2 1/2 cups water**

To remove lumps and fiber, force the poi through several thicknesses of cheesecloth. Serve promptly or let it stand 2 to 3 days in a cool place until it ferments and has a sour taste.

## ABOUT TOMATOES

Those of us accustomed to having the highest court in the land pronounce upon paramount issues of our national life will not be surprised to learn that as long ago as 1893 the Justices resoundingly declared the tomato a vegetable, not a fruit. Either way, it ranks with lemon as a perennial inspiration for culinary uplift— fresh or canned or as juice, purée, paste, catsup or chili sauce. To process for canning, see (II, 614).

In many sections of the country

fresh large-sized field-grown tomatoes are not available during the colder months, being supplanted by hydroponic or hothouse-grown kinds. We find most of these disappointingly mushy in texture. Try occasionally the meaty pear-shaped **Italian tomatoes**, which are sweeter than the American types.

When you use fresh tomatoes in cooking, their juiciness is seldom an asset. To avoid watery results, slit the stem end and remove it; then, holding your hand palm down above a bowl, squeeze the tomato to eject excess juice and seeds. When recipes call for strained canned tomatoes, be sure to force the pulp through the sieve well, to make the most of its thickening and seasoning power; and watch your brands—the cheaper ones are apt to be diluted. To skin fresh tomatoes, see 63.

Tomatoes have run the usual checkered gamut of vegetable introductions: they were regarded at one time or another as purely decorative, poisonous, and aphrodisiac. Now that they have become staples, it is nice to emphasize their solid virtues, one of which is high vitamin A and C content. These values as well as good color and condition may be preserved in ripe—not overripe—fruit for as long as 5 to 6 days after picking if stored in light—not sunlight—unwrapped, at between 65° and 75°, and upside down. Best practice, though, is to make use of only vine-ripened fruit and to store it at once in

the refrigerator. Similarly, to assure maximum food value, prepare tomatoes just before serving. Fruit of mature size but still green in color may be ripened on a windowsill but will lack the flavor and some of the nutritive value of its vine-ripened counterpart. Immature small-sized tomatoes will not ripen satisfactorily after harvesting. Use them, if at all, for pickling, (II, 681). Do not attempt to freeze tomatoes: no effective process has yet been developed.

Prepare tomatoes stuffed, not only for Salads, 63, but as cases for vegetables; see recipes on 369-371.

## STEWED TOMATOES

**4 Servings**

Wash, skin and quarter:

 **6 large tomatoes or 2½ cups canned tomatoes**

Place them in a heavy pan over slow heat—about 20 minutes for the fresh tomatoes, 10 for the canned. You may add:

 **(1 teaspoon minced onion)**
 **(½ cup chopped celery)**
 **(2 or 3 cloves)**

Stir occasionally to keep them from scorching. Season with:

 **¾ teaspoon salt**
 **¼ teaspoon paprika**
 **2 teaspoons white or brown sugar**
 **⅛ teaspoon curry powder or 1 teaspoon chopped parsley or basil**
 **1 tablespoon butter**

The tomatoes may be thickened with:

 **(½ cup bread crumbs)**

## STEWED GREEN TOMATOES

**4 Servings**

Sauté until light brown:

 **2 tablespoons minced onion**

in:

    **2 tablespoons butter**

Add:

    **2 cups sliced large green
    tomatoes**

Stir and cook the tomatoes slowly
until tender. Season with:

    **3/4 teaspoon salt**
    **1/4 teaspoon paprika**
    **1/2 teaspoon curry powder**

Garnish with:

    **1 tablespoon chopped parsley**

## CREAMED CANNED TOMATOES

              **4 Servings**

Simmer gently about 3 minutes:

    **2 cups drained canned
    tomatoes**
    **1 pressed clove garlic or
    2 teaspoons onion juice**
    **3/4 teaspoon salt**
    **1/4 teaspoon paprika**
    **2 teaspoons brown sugar**
    **(1/2 cup chopped celery)**

Combine until smooth and bring just
to a boil:

    **1 tablespoon flour**
    **1/2 cup cream or milk**

▶ To avoid curdling, add the tomato
mixture slowly to the cream or milk,
never vice versa. Stir constantly over
very low heat until the raw-flour taste
is gone, about 3 to 5 minutes.

## TOMATO PROVENÇALE

This dish looks very professional as a
platter-garnish. Choose:

    **Firm ripe tomatoes**

Slice off a deep enough section horizontally on the stem end to get an
even surface. Do the same on the
base. Divide the rest of the tomato
horizontally. Place these thick slices
on a rack to drain. Sprinkle on top
of each:

    **Salt and black pepper**

    **Chopped basil**
    **A slight pinch of oregano**

Melt enough:

    **Butter**

to coat the tomato slices. Place in the
butter:

    **A split clove of garlic**

Or, as an alternative to the butter,
squeeze a little garlic juice on a thin
square of:

    **(Parmesan cheese)**

that will almost cover the tomato
slice. Allow the seasoned tomatoes to
remain at 70° for 1 hour.
Preheat both broiler and oven to
350°. Put the slices on a greased baking sheet. Run them under a broiler
first to brown slightly and then bake
15 minutes. Serve at once.

## GRILLED TOMATOES

              **4 Servings**

Preheat broiler.
Wash:

    **4 large firm tomatoes**

Cut them crosswise into even 1/2- to
1-inch slices. Season well with:

    **1 teaspoon salt**
    **1/4 teaspoon pepper**
    **A pinch of white or brown
    sugar**
    **(Celery salt)**

Place in a greased pan and cover
closely with:

    **About 1 cup
    Au Gratin III, (II, 221)**
    **(2 tablespoons or more grated
    onion)**

Broil about 10 minutes ▶ approximately 5 inches from the heat source.
Or dip them in:

    **Bound Breading III,
    (II, 220)**

Bake on a greased sheet until nearly
soft, then broil as above, until brown,
turning once.

## TOMATOES CREOLE

**4 Servings**

Sauté until golden in:

**2 tablespoons butter**
**1 large minced onion**

Add:

**6 skinned, sliced, seeded**
**tomatoes or 2 cups drained**
**canned tomatoes**
**2 tablespoons minced celery**
**1 shredded green pepper**

Cook the vegetables until tender, about 12 minutes. Add:

**3/4 teaspoon salt**
**1/4 teaspoon paprika**
**2 1/2 teaspoons brown sugar**
**(3/4 teaspoon curry powder)**

Strain the juice from the vegetables and add to it enough:

**Cream**

to make 1 1/2 cups of liquid. Stir in:

**Beurre Manié, 381**

Simmer and stir the sauce until thick and smooth. Combine with the vegetables and serve hot on:

**Toast**

with:

**Sautéed bacon**

Or use the mixture to fill pepper or squash cases.

## TOMATO OLIVE CASSEROLE

**4 Servings**

If you have any prejudice against tapioca, please dismiss it long enough to try out this fine dish. Serve with ham, scrambled eggs or omelet.

Discard as many seeds as possible and place in the top of a double boiler:

**1 1/2 cups canned tomatoes**

Sauté until golden:

**1/4 cup minced onion**

in:

**1 tablespoon butter**

Add it to the strained tomatoes with:

**3 tablespoons quick-cooking**
**tapioca**
**1/2 teaspoon salt**
**1/2 teaspoon sugar**
**1/8 teaspoon paprika**

Cook and stir these ingredients in the double boiler ♦ over—not in—hot water about 7 minutes. Chop coarsely and add:

**18 stuffed or ripe olives**

Preheat oven to 350°.

Grease a baking dish. Fill it with the mixture.

Cover the top with:

**Au Gratin III, (II, 221)**

Bake about 30 minutes.

## TOMATO CUSTARD

**6 Servings**

Preheat oven to 325°.

Skin and squeeze well, 366, to expel excess liquid and seeds and put through a coarse sieve:

**Enough tomatoes to make**
**2 cups**

Beat together with:

**3 eggs**
**1 cup milk**
**1/4 cup sugar**
**1/2 teaspoon salt**
**1/8 teaspoon nutmeg**

Bake in custard cups about 30 minutes or until set. Serve hot or cold.

## TOMATO PUDDING
## COCKAIGNE

Either of these recipes should serve six, but we find the demand for this favorite makes four servings a safer count.

**I.** Preheat oven to 375°.

In winter, place in a saucepan:

**1 1/4 cups Tomato Purée,**
**(II, 619–620)**
**1/4 cup boiling water**

Heat to the boiling point and add:

¹/₄ **teaspoon salt**
6 **tablespoons brown sugar**
¹/₂ **teaspoon dried basil**
Place in a 9-inch baking dish:
1 **cup fresh white bread
crumbs, (II, 218)**
Pour over them:
¹/₄ **cup melted butter**
Add the tomato mixture and:
(2 **tablespoons chopped
stuffed olives)**
◗ Cover the dish closely. Bake the
pudding about 30 minutes. Do not lift
the lid until ready to serve.

**II.** Preheat oven to 325°.
In summer, substitute for the dried
basil:
1¹/₂ **to 2 teaspoons fresh
chopped basil**
1 **teaspoon chopped chives**
1 **teaspoon chopped parsley**
and for the tomato purée and water
substitute:
14 **skinned, seeded, sliced
tomatoes**
Bake the dish 2¹/₂ to 3 hours until
it has cooked down to a pastelike
consistency.

## SCALLOPED TOMATOES

**6 Servings**
Preheat oven to 350°.
Drain:
3 **cups canned Italian-type
tomatoes or peeled, diced
fresh tomatoes**
Sauté until golden in:
3 **tablespoons butter**
¹/₄ **cup finely chopped onions**
Add:
1 **tablespoon brown sugar**
1 **teaspoon salt**
¹/₄ **teaspoon pepper
(A grating of nutmeg)**
1³/₄ **cups toasted bread crumbs**
Place the tomatoes in a buttered bak-

ing dish alternately with layers of
the bread crumb mixture, ending
with a layer of crumbs. Bake about
30 minutes.

## TOMATO TART

**6 Servings**
Have ready:
6 **baked 2-inch Tart
Shells, (II, 360)**
Prepare a filling of:
³/₄ **cup Tomato Purée,
(II, 619–620)**
³/₄ **cup White Sauce III, 383**
3 **tablespoons sautéed
chopped onions**
¹/₂ **cup sautéed chopped
chicken livers**
2 **tablespoons chopped
stuffed olives**
Just before serving, preheat the
oven to 400°. Fill the tarts and bake
until thoroughly heated. Serve at once.

## ABOUT HOT STUFFED TOMATOES

To prepare cases for hot food, cut
large hollows in the stem ends of
very firm unpeeled tomatoes. Salt
and invert them on a rack to drain
about 15 minutes. Fill the tomato
cases with any of the following
cooked foods and cover with:
**Au Gratin I, II, or III
(II, 221)**
Place the cases on a rack in a pan
with enough water to keep them from
scorching and bake in a preheated
350° oven 10 or 15 minutes. If they
are very ripe, you may bake them in
well-greased muffin tins to keep them
shapely. For fillings, try:
**Creamed ham or cooked
sausage and mushrooms
Bread crumbs and
deviled ham**

Chestnuts and rice or wild
rice, seasoned with salt and
brown sugar
Creamed green peas or
mushrooms with parsley
Mashed potatoes and nuts
Creamed Spinach, 359

Or use one of the following recipes.

## TOMATOES STUFFED WITH PINEAPPLE

**4 Servings**

▶ Please read About Stuffed Tomatoes, 369.
Preheat oven to 350°.
Prepare:

4 medium-sized tomato cases

Sprinkle each hollow with:

1 teaspoon brown sugar

Place in each hollow some of the following mixture:

1 cup drained crushed
pineapple
2 tablespoons dry bread
crumbs
A grating of fresh ginger

Sprinkle the tops with:

Au Gratin II, (II, 221)

Bake as for Hot Stuffed Tomatoes, 369, and serve on:

Toast rounds

## TOMATOES STUFFED WITH CORN

**4 Servings**

▶ Please read About Stuffed Tomatoes, 369.
Preheat oven to 350°.
Prepare:

4 tomato cases

Sauté, then crumble:

4 slices bacon

Combine:

1 cup cooked drained corn

1 chopped pimiento
1/2 chopped green pepper,
seeds and membrane
removed
2 tablespoons chopped celery
1/2 cup bread crumbs
2 tablespoons corn liquor
or cream
1/2 teaspoon salt
1/4 teaspoon paprika
1/2 teaspoon sugar, if the corn
is green

Add the bacon. Fill the tomato cases.
Sprinkle the tops with:

Au Gratin I or III, (II, 221)

Bake as for Stuffed Tomatoes, 369.

## TOMATOES FILLED WITH ONIONS AND ANCHOVIES

**6 Servings**

▶ Please read About Stuffed Tomatoes, 369.
Preheat oven to 350°.
Prepare:

6 tomato cases

Melt:

2 tablespoons bacon
drippings or butter

Add and sauté until golden:

1/2 cup finely chopped onion

Chop the pulp taken from the tomatoes and combine it with the onions.
Add:

1 1/2 teaspoons brown sugar
1/2 teaspoon salt
1 tablespoon celery seed

Simmer these ingredients for about 10 minutes. Add:

2 tablespoons sautéed
chopped peppers
4 chopped anchovies

If the filling is too moist, it may be thickened with:

(Bread crumbs)

If too dry, it may be moistened with:

(Stock)

Fill the tomato cases. Cover the tops with:

Au Gratin I or III,

(II, 221)

Bake as for Stuffed Tomatoes, 369.

## TOMATOES STUFFED WITH CREAMED SWEETBREADS

**8 Servings**

▶ Please read About Stuffed Tomatoes, 369.

Prepare:

8 large tomato cases

Have ready:

1/2 cup chopped Sautéed Mushrooms, 328

Have ready:

1 cup Poached Calf Sweetbreads, 642

Bring to the boiling point:

1 cup White Sauce I, 383

Add the other ingredients to the sauce. Thicken with:

(1/4 cup bread crumbs)

Preheat oven to 350°.

Fill the tomato cases. Cover the tops with:

Au Gratin II or III, (II, 221)

Bake as for Hot Stuffed Tomatoes, 369.

## TOMATOES STUFFED WITH SEAFOOD

**6 Servings**

▶ Please read About Stuffed Tomatoes, 369.

Preheat oven to 350°.

Prepare:

6 tomato cases

Melt over low heat:

1 1/2 tablespoons butter

Add and cook for 3 minutes:

3 tablespoons minced green pepper

3 tablespoons minced onion

Stir in until blended:

1 1/2 tablespoons flour

Stir in slowly:

1 1/2 cups milk

When sauce is thick and hot, add:

1 1/2 cups crab meat, chopped shrimp or lobster

1/3 teaspoon salt

A few grains red pepper

2 teaspoons Worcestershire sauce

(1 cup grated cheese)

Simmer and stir these ingredients until the cheese is melted. Fill the tomato cases with this mixture. Bake as for Stuffed Tomatoes, 369.

## ABOUT TURNIPS

Children often enjoy these spunky, time-honored vegetables well-washed and raw, like apples; and the knowing choose them as an accompaniment to game. They make a good change, if browned, to serve instead of potatoes around a roast, 565. A favorite peasanty dish, **Himmel und Erde,** is made of mashed turnips, potatoes and seasoned apples, combined in any proportion.

Discard woody turnips and parblanch old ones 3 to 5 minutes before cooking. One pound of turnips will yield about 2 cups cooked.

Cut off the tops at once and store turnips in a dark cool place. The tops, if tender, may be used as greens, 323.

♦ Pressure cook whole turnips 8 to 12 minutes at 15 lbs.

## COOKED TURNIPS

### I.

**4 Servings**

Wash, slice as shown above, and to avoid bitterness pare past the dark line separating rind from the white center:

**1 lb. young turnips**

Steam, 281, 15 to 20 minutes. Drain.

**Season to taste**

and dress with:

**Butter**
**Lemon juice and vinegar or**
**Quick Tomato Sauce, 400**

or mash or cream as for potatoes.

**II.** If turnips are mature, you may parblanch, 106, 3 to 5 minutes:

**Pared sliced or whole**
**turnips**

Drop them into rapidly boiling water to cover. Add:

**½ teaspoon salt**
**½ teaspoon sugar**

Cook uncovered 15 to 20 minutes if sliced, 20 to 25 minutes if whole, or until tender. Serve as in I.

## GLAZED TURNIPS

Cook as directed above:

**Young turnips**

Drain and dry them well. Brown in:

**Hot melted butter**

Season with:

**Paprika and sugar or a**
**little Meat Glaze, 427**

which helps with the browning.

**Season to taste**

Serve at once, rolled in:

**Chopped parsley**

## SCALLOPED TURNIPS

Prepare as for:

**Scalloped Potatoes, 345**

substituting for the potatoes turnips alone or turnips and sliced onions or turnips and apples.

## STUFFED TURNIP CUPS

### I.

**8 Servings**

♦ Please read About Stuffed Vegetables, 284.

Preheat oven to 350°.

Pare, then blanch, 3 to 5 minutes:

**8 medium-sized turnips**

Hollow into cups, reserving and chopping the pulp. Melt:

**1 tablespoon butter**

Sauté in it about 3 minutes:

**1 tablespoon grated onion**
**2 tablespoons seasoned**
**cooked peas**

Combine the pulp with the onion and peas. Season with:

**Salt and white pepper**

Thicken slightly with:

**Cracker crumbs or bread**
**crumbs**

Fill the turnip cups with this mixture. Place them in a greased baking dish. Pour around them:

**½ cup milk**

Bake until tender, about 15 minutes.

**II.** Proceed as above, using a filling of leftover sauced foods, or a cooked stuffing, 430.

## WATER CHESTNUTS

Please read about water chestnuts, (II, 238).

These crisp vegetables are added usually as a garnish to other vegetables. ▶ Add for the last 2 or 3 minutes of cooking only.

## WATERCRESS

Usually thought of only as salad and sandwich material, watercress not only adds a distinctive flavor to soups and vegetables but lends piquancy to other cooked greens. Never overcook it, as it becomes stringy. Serve it puréed as a garnish with grills, chops or scallops.

# SAVORY SAUCES AND
# SALAD DRESSINGS

When Voltaire chose to contrast his native country with England by observing that France was a land of forty-two sauces and one religion, whereas Britain was a land of one sauce and forty-two religions, he was wrong on both counts. But the witticism throws an interesting light on which two cultural consolations even a free-thinking Frenchman instinctively brackets as enjoying top international priority.

Some sauces complement the food with which they are served: that is, they supply either the blandness or the piquancy which that food lacks. Others complement it, so to speak: they enhance or heighten its intrinsic flavor. All sauces, of whatever character, should be so perfectly smooth, so skillfully blended that, like successful soups, they can be eaten all by themselves. Basic prerequisites in sauce-making are ♦ never to use high heat; ♦ to remove sauces-in-progress from the heat before stirring in fresh ingredients; and ♦ always, if such ingredients are cold, to **temper** them by mixing them first in a separate container with a small quantity of the original hot liquid before returning both to the cook-pot. This last injunction is especially important for egg-based sauces. Other pointers to infallible sauce-making will be found in each sauce category, with suggestions for adding herbs, especially fresh herbs such as basil, above, rear right; and chervil, near the blender—which do not dry well—or a grating of lemon rind or gingerroot and a few minced shallots, all shown in the chapter heading.

By designating the sauces in this chapter as **savory,** we mean to differentiate them from the **sweet** types which are dealt with in Volume II, 563–573. The savory sauces that follow are themselves grouped into two general classes, hot and cold, although a few can be served both ways. It must be noted here, too, that Europeans—sensibly, we think—

do not carry temperatures to extremes, their "cold" savory sauces being served, for the most part, cool, never chilled; the "hot" ones generally luke-warm. As to content, the sequence runs as follows: white sauces; brown sauces, or gravies; soup-based sauces, which are simpler to make and less caloric than the classic *sauces brunes*, as well as surprisingly satisfactory; butter sauces, including seasoned butters; sauces in which tomato dominates; barbecue sauces; sweet-sours; cream sauces; hot egg-based sauces; those based on French dressing, or vinaigrettes—with a trail of other non-egg, non-cream sauces; cold egg-based sauces; some cold cream-based salad dressings; and decorative thick sauces, like glazes and glaçage.

After a number of these groups, we have set down formulas for low-calorie substitutes—or, to use a more appropriate term—makeshifts. Such sauces are based on gelatin, evaporated milk, bread crumbs, cream of rice, strong stocks, tomato juice, walnut and mustard catsup, etc. Slimmers might keep in mind that almost any zesty salad dressing may be pretty much defused if its butter, egg or flour content is sharply cut back or eliminated altogether; also that dressings made with lemon juice or yogurt, or *au maigre* constituents, such as fish fumet—indeed, all the boiled or sweet-sour sauces—make helpful allies for anybody who happens to be "thick and tired of it."

For Marinades, see (II, 180); Au Gratin, (II, 221); Tomato and other Catsups, (II, 686); Chili Sauce, (II, 686); Worcestershire Sauce, (II, 688); Pickled Horseradish, (II, 688). For sweet sauces of all types, see Sweet Sauces, (II, 563).

## ABOUT SAUCE TOOLS

Handy-sized simple tools hanging near the stove encourage the addition of interesting ingredients to sauces. ♦ The three hand beaters sketched on the left, on 376, make lumps vanish. The third is particularly useful for beating an egg in a cup. ♦ If the recipe calls for beating over ice, see illustration, 187. For adding flavorings, keep measuring spoons handy. For a quick grating of cheese, onion or bread crumbs, try the rotary grater shown next. Kitchen shears with a self-releasing hinge are easy to keep clean and unrusted. Snip herbs quickly, right into the sauce.

A garlic press, center, will squeeze enough juice to give an ineffable flavor to your sauces, and the hand grater is convenient for a touch of shaved lemon rind or a grating of nutmeg. Also have ready a bar-type strainer for the quick clearing of very small quantities of sauce. For larger ones, use a Chinese hat or conical strainer, illustrated last, and for very careful straining, line this with muslin.

By all means use very hard wooden spoons for the fragile sauces that may be broken down by the more vigorous metal tools. A sauce spoon with one pointed end, shown next to last, will easily scrape the pan edges clean and will help avoid lumping. If you should use a metal spoon, make sure it is stainless steel, so as not to discolor a delicate mixture.

Electric beaters and ⅃ blenders are great labor-savers in the kitchen and will beat out lumps very quickly. They do, however, change the texture and flavor of the sauce somewhat, as they whip in a good deal of air, which will tend to make a thickened sauce foamy and less tasty and a brown sauce rather lighter in color. At high

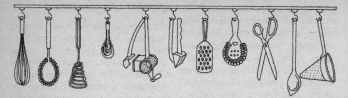

speed they also are likely to over-macerate herbs and so sharpen their flavor.

## ABOUT HOT SAVORY SAUCES

There are certain old dowagers who try to dominate "sauciety." Call them the mother sauces, as the French do, if you like. Each has her strong peculiarities of individual makeup; each traditionally queens it over a whole coterie of dishes. The leanest member of the clan, but one capable of much highly successful cross-breeding, is pan gravy.

Her roux-based cousins have more solid and dependable backgrounds and take greater abuse in heating, re-heating and storing, for their flour and butter base combines into as stable an alliance as any in the kitchen. There are the delicate pale members of the roux family, descended from Béchamel, who accept the company of eggs, cream and even shallots. There are the robust characters, originating in browned flours, who have picked up acquaintanceships with strange foreign spices, who love tomatoes, and who, on occasion, set their caps for garlic. Both rely for authenticity on two principles: ◗ Their roux base must be cooked to rid it and them of any trace of plebeian floury origin, and it must always be hot when added to cold liquids or cold when added to hot.

There are the plush sauce aristocracy who scorn flour altogether and derive their stamina from eggs. Like a lot of other sauces for cold food, the mayonnaise branch performs this elegant trick without requiring heat. While its cousins, the Hollandaise-Béarnaise group, must have heat, they need it only in small doses and only for short periods.

Most showy and demonstrative of all are the wine sauces, the vinaigrettes, the playful tenderizing sweet-sours or agrodolces, the barbecues, and of course the truly sweet dessert sauces, (II, 563), which are the simpering sentimentalists of the whole colony.

Do not limit your acquaintanceship with this far-flung family until you have met them all; and until you are clever enough even to spot a rare nonidentical twin—with arrowroot as thickener—or an occasional reveler in fancy dress, tricked out with Beurre Manié, 381, or Butter Swirls, 380. These wayward collaterals are among the most treasured, if fleeting, personalities of all.

When you once feel at home in sauce circles, you will learn rapidly how to make their charmed members your partners in a day-to-day campaign of culinary enhancement. You will learn how to skillfully blend the hot ingredients, so that they receive food without thinning. You will discover that ◗ adding the wine before—not after—the eggs and cream will avoid curdling, and that ♦ a mixture can be stabilized with that extra bit of cream when separation threatens.

Of course, there is always the ⚶ blender to fall back on in a crisis of this kind, but the texture of the sauce can never be so smooth or so thick as if it had been properly made in the first place. In sauces based on cornstarch ♦ overbeating itself can disturb consistency—and this factor alone may cause thinning, see Cornstarch (II, 214). The use of a light whisk or a wooden spoon is a help in avoiding this condition. Another reason for thinning in sauces may be the addition of acid in the form of fruit juice or wine. ♦ Sauces will also lose body if covered and held heated, for the excess steam created thins them and tends to cause separation. ♦ To lessen separation in frozen sauces, see Waxy Rice Flour, (II, 215). ♦ In preparing sauced foods, allow half as much sauce as solid ingredients.

## COLOR IN SAUCES

The vast majority of sauces, if well prepared, need no artificial coloring; the various ways ♦ to maintain and develop their natural color are described above. Rich beef stock combined with some tomato, browned meat—in the case of a stew—browned onions and carrots and a brown roux will result in a rich brown sauce needing no addition of caramel to bring up the color. If you feel obliged to add caramel, soy sauce or vegetable-based dyes to gravies, add them sparingly. Some cooks use yellow coloring for chicken gravies and sauces to try to hide the omission of chicken fat and egg yolks. Should you use saffron, do beware of its overpowering flavor. A tomato sauce will keep good color if you do not cook it too quickly or too long.

## SAUCES IN QUANTITY

♦ If you are making gravies or sauces in large amounts, it will take considerably longer to get rid of the raw flour taste after the liquid has been added to the roux than when you are making only 1 or 2 cups for immediate family use. We advise heating these large amounts ♦ uncovered in a slow oven 1/2 to 3/4 hour and straining the sauce before serving, to remove any crusting or lumps. But if you will stir the sauce from time to time, it may not be necessary to strain it.

♦ When doubling the ingredients in sauce recipes, taste before adding the full amount of seasoning. It is easy to overdo it.

## KEEPING SAUCES

You may keep Béchamel, Velouté, tomato and brown sauces in the refrigerator about a week. To store, strain the sauce, pour it into a container and cover with a thin layer of fat or sherry.

You can also ❀ freeze the sauces mentioned above in ice-cube trays and keep the cubes in your freezer in a plastic bag, taking out as many as you need for immediate use. They may be melted in a double boiler— 4 large cubes melt down to about 1/2 cup of sauce. You may also freeze Hollandaise Sauce, 410, and Béarnaise Sauce, 412, but be very careful when reheating. Do not try to freeze mayonnaise; it will break. And, in general, do not try to keep sauces made with eggs, cream or milk for more than 2 or 3 days in the refrigerator.

## ABOUT SAVORY SAUCE INGREDIENTS

Many savory sauces depend on some sort of pan gravy, because pan residues, unless derived from less-than-fresh fish or from strong variety meats like kidneys, are most desirable sauce ingredients. They may result from sautéing, roasting, braising or browning. Making pan gravies is described in detail in About Sauces Made by Degreasing and Deglazing, 381.

Good, strong, fat-free Stocks, (II, 167), are invaluable sauce ingredients, too, especially when reduced to a Glaze, 426. Where possible, the stock should reflect the food it is to flavor: chicken stock for chicken, lamb stock for lamb, etc. Although meat stocks, including those of poultry and game, are often combined in sauce-making—favorites being those of chicken and veal—fish and shellfish Fumets, (II, 173), should be reserved only for fish and shellfish dishes. Meat broths always make better sauce ingredients if refrigerated 24 hours and then defatted.

When pan residues or stocks are scanty, turn—with discretion—to wine. ♦ Please read About Wine for Cooking, (II, 176). Use, as a rule of thumb, dry white wines in sauces for fish or white meats; dry red wines for red meats. Strong game sauces sometimes support stronger liquors such as rum, brandy or Madeira, but whisky is not recommended. ♦ In any wine sauce, add egg, milk, cream or Butter Swirls, 380, after the wine has been incorporated.

## ABOUT THICKENERS FOR SAUCES

Sauces not made by deglazing with liquids, as described above, are generally thickened just enough to coat food lightly. Suggestions for thickening—other than those below—are found in Thickeners for Soups, 128–129.

### ROUX

The most common thickeners for savory sauces are the roux—white or brown. All of them are made of the same ingredients to begin with but change in character as heat is applied. These mixtures of flour and fats are blended gently ♦ over very low heat from 5 minutes to a considerably longer period, depending on your available time and your patience. White roux should not color; those to which stock is added, barely; while brown ones should reach the color of hazelnut and smell deliciously baked. ♦ Unless a roux is cooked long enough to dispel the raw taste of flour, this unpleasant flavor will dominate the strongest stocks and seasonings. And unless the flour and butter are stirred to distribute the heat and to allow the starch granules to swell evenly, they will later fail to absorb the liquid, and the sauce will be thin. ♦ This heated blending period is most important. Using excessive heat to try hurrying it will burn the flour, giving it a bitter taste; and it will shrink the starch, making it incapable of continuing to swell.

For white roux-based sauces, see Béchamel, 383; for those made of white sauce to which stock is added, see Velouté, 387; for brown sauces, see Sauce Espagñole, 391. Since most cooks use some form of roux every day, you may find it a time-saver to make one in advance and store it in tablespoon-sized units under refrigeration. It will keep in the ❄ freezer, too, for several months if you proceed as follows. When the roux has been cooked to the desired color and is still soft, measure it by tablespoons onto a baking sheet and freeze. Transfer the frozen wafers to a plastic bag or wide-topped container and store in the freezer. To thicken sauce, drop the wafers into the sauce until desired thickness is achieved. Or you may soften the wafers in a double boiler over hot water and proceed as usual to complete the sauce.

BROWNED FLOUR

A variant used in gravies to enhance color and flavor. The slow but inexpensive procedure by which it is made is worth trying. The flour, when ready, should smell nutty and baked. Place:

**1 cup flour**

in a dry heavy skillet. ❿ Stir constantly over very low direct heat, scraping the flour from the sides and bottom of the pan. Or, heat the flour in a very slow oven, 200° to 250°, in a very heavy pan. Shake the pan periodically so the flour browns evenly. Do not let it get too dark or, as with brown roux, it will become bitter and lose its thickening power altogether. ❿ Even properly browned flour has only about half the thickening power of all-purpose flour. It may be stored in a tightly covered jar in a cool place.

FLOUR PASTE

Sometimes pressed into service to thicken emergency gravies and sauces, but the results are never so palatable as when even a quick roux is used. Make a paste of flour and cold water or stock. Use about two parts water

and one part flour. Stir as much of the paste as needed into the boiling stock or drippings. Let the sauce heat until it thickens and ❿ simmer at least 3 minutes more to reduce the raw taste of the flour. Stir frequently with a wire whisk.

CORNSTARCH

Cornstarch, see (II, 214), is often used where translucency is desirable, as in some Chinese sauces. It should be mixed with a little cold water before being added to the hot liquid. One tablespoon cornstarch will thicken 1½ to 2 cups of liquid. Most Chinese sauces are finished over direct heat. ❿ Overbeating cornstarch-based sauces thins them.

ARROWROOT

Of all the thickeners, this makes the most delicately textured sauces. ❿ But use it only when the sauce is to be served within 10 minutes of preparation. It will not hold, nor will it reheat. Since the flavor of arrowroot is neutral and it does not have to be cooked to remove rawness, as do flour and cornstarch, and since it thickens at a lower temperature than either of them, it is ideal for use in egg and other sauces which should not boil. Allow 2½ teaspoons to 1 cup liquid.

POTATO STARCH OR FECULA

Preferred by some cooks to flour as a thickener in certain delicate sauces. When it is used, less simmering is required and the sauce gains some transparency. ❿ If heated beyond 176°, the sauce will thin out. Serve soon after it has thickened, as it has no holding power. One tablespoon of

potato starch will moderately thicken
1 cup of liquid.

### EGG YOLKS

Egg yolks not only thicken but also
enrich a sauce. ▶ Never add them directly to hot liquid. Stir them into a
little cream, then incorporate with
them some of the hot sauce in preparation. Stir this mixture into the
remainder of the hot liquid and continue to stir over low heat until the
sauce thickens. ▶ Do not allow the
sauce to boil, or it will curdle. If this
happens, plunge pot into cold water
and stir; or beat in a small amount of
chilled cream. It is generally safer to
add egg yolks to a mixture in a double boiler ▶ over—not in—boiling
water, unless you can control the heat
source very exactly. Two or three egg
yolks with a little cream will thicken
1 cup of liquid. Egg yolks added very
slowly to melted butter or oil with
constant stirring will produce an
emulsion that is quite thick. Suitably
seasoned, this becomes the base for
Hollandaise or mayonnaise. Hard-
cooked egg yolks and oil will also
emulsify, see Sauce Gribiche, 422.

### BLOOD

Blood from the animal or bird the
sauce will accompany is a desirable
thickener. To save the blood from a
freshly killed hare, rabbit or chicken,
see (II, 627). You may store it refrigerated a day or two, mixed with 1 or
2 tablespoons vinegar to prevent clot-
ting. Strain it and add it to the sauce
at the last minute just before serving,
swirling it in as you would butter,
right. Simmer gently, but ▶ never allow the sauce to boil after the blood
is added.

### REDUCTION

Another classic way to thicken
sauces. Béchamel and Espagñole
may be thickened during very slow
simmering by the evaporation of liquid to achieve more richness and
subtlety. If you intend to thicken a
sauce by reducing it, season ▶ after
you have brought it down to the right
viscosity; otherwise you may find it
highly overseasoned or unpleasantly
salty. There are a good many recipes
for tomato sauces which demand
long cooking and reducing. Unless
you can keep these sauces—or, in
fact, any thickened sauces—on very
low heat, they will cook too fast, and
flavor and color will be impaired. In
the case of roux-thickened sauces
which call for reducing, do use an
oven. It is a great labor-saver, and the
heat can be controlled much more exactly. ▶ Almost all reduced sauces, to
be perfect in texture, should be
strained before serving.

### BUTTER SWIRLS

These finish off many fine, rich
sauces, both white and brown, after
straining and final heating. But after
swirling, the sauce must be served at
once ▶ nor can it be reheated. In addition to improving the flavor, the butter swirl also very slightly thickens
the sauce. To make a sauce *finie au
beurre* after straining and heating,
add ▶ unsalted, unmelted butter bit by
bit, moving the pan in a circular motion, so that the butter makes a visible
spiral in the hot sauce as it melts. Remove the pan from the heat before
the butter is fully melted and continue to swirl. ▶ Do not use a spoon to
stir it and do not try to reheat it.
About 1 tablespoon butter is generally used to "finish" 1 cup of sauce.

### KNEADED BUTTER OR BEURRE MANIÉ

A magic panacea for rectifying sauces or thickening thin ones at the end of the cooking process. Avoid using it, though, for those which require long simmering. After adding kneaded butter ♦ do not boil the sauce. Simmer only long enough to dispel the floury taste. Manipulate with your fingers, as though you were rubbing for fine pastry, 2 tablespoons butter and 2 tablespoons flour. Form into small balls and drop into the hot liquid, stirring constantly until the ingredients are well blended and the sauce thickens. This amount will be sufficient for 1 cup of thin liquid.

### FILÉ

Filé powder, the classic thickener of Creole gumbos, has been banned by the FDA as carcinogenic. To reproduce its mucilaginous texture, use Tapioca Flour, (II, 216).

## WAYS TO SERVE SAUCES

See the sketch below of various containers for hot or cold sauces, but there are other attractive ways to serve them. Cold sauces and dips with a mayonnaise or sour cream base may be presented in a crisp hollowed-out cabbage, (II, 83), or individually in tomato or pepper cases, 63. Suggest the sea habitat of cold shrimp or poached salmon with a delicate pink Mayonnaise, 419, or Rémoulade Sauce, 420, by serving them in a large seashell.

Hot sauces may be served in ramekins, tiny tin-lined copper saucepans, and other small heatproof containers. The doll house instinct rises in all of us at the sight of these miniature individual pitchers and pots that are so appropriate when hot lobster, artichokes or asparagus is on the menu. Sauces on the buffet table may be kept hot in small three-legged French saucepans, placed over a candle, in chafing dishes, or in an enameled iron pot over heat, shown in the chapter heading on 374. Like the food it accompanies, sauce, if it is meant to be hot, must be kept hot. However, ♦ any sauce that is worth its salt won't keep indefinitely on a steam table or in a casserole. There is a point of maximum goodness at which it should be served.

Cold sauces and Seasoned Butters, 396, may be kept chilled on a mound of crushed ice; molds and pats of seasoned butter placed directly on the ice. Don't use ice cubes—the butter slips down between them.

## ABOUT SAUCES MADE BY DEGREASING AND DEGLAZING

These are a welcome change after the heavier and more familiar roux-based types. Residues and scrapings from sautéing, broiling, roasting and browning constitute the precious base for many delectable pan gravies that are to be served with sautéed or roasted fowl, meat dishes and fish. It is always best, if you sauté with butter—and the butter should be sweet, not salted—to clarify it, 396, or to combine it with a little cooking oil to raise its smoking point, and so prevent scorching. If margarine has been substituted for butter, you may wish to improve the flavor of the final product by finishing off the sauce with a Butter Swirl, 380. In roasting meat, be sure to grease the pans lightly at the start to keep from burning any juices which may drip into the bottom of the roasting pan before it receives a protective covering of rendered fat. Browning lends attractive color, and the incorporation of some fat from the pan will intensify the characteristic meat flavor. Even more effective in this respect is to add to the pan, after browning the meat, a cup of Mirepoix, (II, 254). When the meat is done, remove it from the pan and pour off the fat. There are several ways to do this quickly. One is to pour all the juices into a heatproof glass container and submerge it in cold water. The fat will rise at once and can be spooned off. Another, if there is more fat than stock, is to use a baster, 553: tip the pan and siphon off the good juices from underneath the top layer of grease. Pour off the grease. Return juices to roasting pan. Add ¼ cup or more hot water, wine or stock and cook on top of the stove, stirring and scraping the solidified juices from the bottom and sides. The addition of wine or dry sherry will hasten the deglazing process and heighten aroma. Use the stock appropriate to

your meat or fowl and the kind of wine you would normally drink with it. This, with a Butter Swirl, 380, Beurre Manié, 381, or a little cream, can make the finest of all sauces.

## MEAT PAN GRAVY

**1 Cup**

If you use drippings for sauces, you may want to strain them first and remove excess fat. Reheat some of the fat because it will absorb the flour better. Remove the meat from the pan. Place it where it will remain hot. Pour off all but:

> **2 tablespoons drippings**

Blend into them:

> **1 or 2 tablespoons flour**

Stir with a wire whisk until the flour has thickened and until the mixture is well combined and smooth. Continue to cook slowly and stir constantly, while adding:

> **The degreased pan juices and milk, water, stock, cream, wine or beer to make 1 cup**

The beer may be "flat." Season the gravy with:

> **Salt**
> **Pepper**
> **Fresh or dried minced herbs**
> **Grated lemon rind**

Color, if necessary, with:

> **A few drops Caramelized Sugar II, (II, 232)**

You may strain the gravy; reheat before serving. If you are using a thickener other than flour, please read About Thickeners for Sauces, 378, for the correct amount of cornstarch or arrowroot to be added for the above amount of liquid.

## POULTRY PAN GRAVY

**About 2 Cups**

Strain the juices from the roasted fowl. Pour off and reserve the fat. Heat in a saucepan:

**¼ cup of the fat**

Add and stir until blended:

**¼ cup flour**

Stir in slowly:

**Pan juices and enough Chicken or Poultry Stock, (II, 172), to make 2 cups**

Cook and stir the gravy until smooth and ◗ simmer 5 minutes. Add:

**Chopped cooked giblets (¼ cup or more cream)**

◗ If the gravy is very rich, it may separate. Add the cream slowly. Stir it constantly. This will usually forestall any difficulty. Should you wish to add the brown material in the original pan, pour a small quantity of the gravy into the pan to dislodge it, heating slightly if necessary. Stir well and return this liquid to the rest of the gravy.

**Season to taste**

and serve.

## WHITE SAUCE I OR BÉCHAMEL

**1 Cup**

Very basic: used not only for creaming foods like vegetables and fish but as a base for many other sauces. Melt over low heat:

**2 tablespoons butter**

For a delicate flavor, even commercial establishments have found no substitute for butter. Add and blend over low heat for 3 to 5 minutes:

**1½ to 2 tablespoons flour**

Stir in slowly:

**1 cup milk**

For better consistency, you may scald the milk beforehand; but be sure—to avoid lumping—that the roux is cool when you add it. Add:

**1 small onion studded with 2 or 3 whole cloves**
**½ small bay leaf**

Cook and stir the sauce with a wire whisk or wooden spoon until thickened and smooth. Place in a 350° oven for 20 minutes to cook slowly. The oven interval also saves your time and hands for other kitchen jobs. Strain the sauce.

**Season to taste**

Add:

**A grating of nutmeg**

and serve. For creamed dishes, use about one-half as much sauce as solids.

## WHITE SAUCE II OR HEAVY BÉCHAMEL

**1 Cup**

Used in soufflés.
Prepare:

**White Sauce I, left**

Use in all:

**3 tablespoons butter**
**3 tablespoons flour**
**1 cup liquid**

## WHITE SAUCE III OR BINDING BÉCHAMEL

**1 Cup**

For croquettes.
Prepare:

**White Cream Sauce I, left**

Use in all:

**3 tablespoons butter**
**⅓ cup flour**
**1 cup liquid**

## WHITE SAUCE IV OR ENRICHED BÉCHAMEL

For poached lean fish.
Reduce:

> **1 cup White Sauce I, 383**

to three-fourths of its volume. Stir in:

> **¼ cup heavy cream**

and bring to boiling point. If the sauce is for fish, add:

> **(½ to 1 teaspoon lemon juice)**

## QUICK WHITE SAUCE

This base can be flavored and modified in many ways. Melt over low heat:

> **2 tablespoons butter**

Add ◗ still over low heat, stirring about 3 to 4 minutes or until well blended and the taste of raw flour has vanished:

> **1½ to 2 tablespoons flour**

Stir in slowly:

> **1 cup milk, milk and light stock, light stock, or light stock and cream
> Season to taste**

and vary the flavor with one or more of the following:

> **Celery salt
> A grating of nutmeg
> 1 teaspoon lemon juice
> ½ teaspoon Worcestershire sauce
> 1 teaspoon sherry
> 1 teaspoon onion juice
> 2 tablespoons chopped parsley
> 2 tablespoons chopped chives**

◗ Simmer and stir the sauce with a wire whisk until it has thickened and is smooth and hot. Combine it with other ingredients just as it boils, so that it will not become watery. For creamed dishes, use about half as much sauce as there are solids.

## WHITE SAUCE WITH HARD-COOKED EGG

> **1¼ cups**

Delicious when made with half chicken stock and half cream.
Prepare:

> **White Sauce I, 383**

Add to it:

> **2 chopped hard-cooked eggs
> 1 tablespoon capers or chopped pickle**

## FLORENTINE SAUCE

> **About 2 Cups**

Combine:

> **1 cup White Sauce I, 383
> A dash of hot pepper sauce
> 2 drops Worcestershire sauce
> 1 cup finely chopped spinach
> A fresh grating of nutmeg
> 1 tablespoon finely chopped parsley**

If using the sauce cold for fish, do not thin. If using it hot, you may thin with:

> **(Cream or dry white wine)**

## MORNAY SAUCE

> **About 1¼ Cups**

Excellent for masking fish, egg and vegetable dishes. If you are using it in a dish to be browned in the oven or under the broiler, sprinkle a little grated cheese over the top first.
Prepare:

> **1 cup White Sauce I, flavored with onion or shallots, 383**

Beat until blended:

> **1 egg yolk
> 2 tablespoons cream**

◗ Add a little of the sauce to the egg yolk and cream, stirring constantly, then return the mixture to the rest of the sauce and cook until well heated. Then add:

2 tablespoons grated
    Parmesan cheese
2 tablespoons grated Gruyère
    cheese

Keep stirring with a small whisk to
help melt the cheese and to keep the
sauce smooth while it thickens.

Season to taste

with:

Salt and a few grains of
    cayenne

## SAUCE DIJONNAISE

About 2 Cups

For baked or boiled ham or a rather
coarse-grained fish.
Prepare:

1 cup White Sauce III, 383

omitting the whole onion. Reserve.
Sauté in:

2 tablespoons butter
¹⁄₃ cup finely chopped onions

until onions are translucent. Add to
skillet:

¹⁄₄ teaspoon thyme
¹⁄₄ teaspoon crushed garlic
¹⁄₂ bay leaf
1 teaspoon basil

stirring constantly. Put into a separate
pan:

1 can condensed chicken
    broth
1 cup drained canned
    tomatoes

and simmer until these ingredients
are reduced by half. Remove bay leaf
and combine all ingredients. Put
them through a sieve, if you like.
Bring mixture to a boil, remove from
heat and stir in:

1 tablespoon prepared Dijon-
    type mustard, (II, 271)
2 tablespoons Madeira
    Season to taste

When ready to serve, add:

A Butter Swirl, 380

## CHEESE SAUCE

About 2 Cups

Prepare:

White Sauce I, 383

When it is smooth and hot, reduce the
heat and stir in:

1 cup or less mild grated
    cheese

Season with:

¹⁄₂ teaspoon salt
¹⁄₈ teaspoon paprika
    A few grains cayenne
(¹⁄₂ teaspoon dry mustard)

Stir the sauce until the cheese is
melted.

## WHITE WINE SAUCE FOR FISH

About 1¹⁄₄ Cups

Reduce by half over medium heat a
mixture of:

¹⁄₄ cup white wine
1 bay leaf
2 cloves
2 black peppercorns
(1¹⁄₂-inch piece gingerroot)
¹⁄₄ cup Fish Stock, (II, 173)
1 teaspoon chopped shallots
    or mild onions

Strain and add to:

1 cup strained White
    Sauce I, 383

To make a sauce that coats well and
browns beautifully, add:

(2 tablespoons whipped
    cream)

## NANTUA OR SHRIMP SAUCE

About 1¹⁄₂ Cups

For fish.
Prepare:

1 cup White Sauce I, 383

Add:

¹⁄₂ cup whipping cream

Rub through a fine sieve:

2 tablespoons Shrimp
    Butter, 399

Instead of the shrimp butter, you may add 1 tablespoon finely ground shrimp made into a smooth paste with 1 tablespoon butter. Heat to boiling point.

**Season to taste**

Garnish with:

**Finely chopped shrimp**

## TOMATO SHRIMP SAUCE

**3¹/₂ Cups**

This sauce may be poured over a platter of baked or steamed fish, or may accompany either. It may also be served with a soufflé or a simple omelet.

Prepare:

**2 cups Thickened Tomato Sauce, 400**

Season the sauce well. Add and heat to the boiling point:

**1 teaspoon Worcestershire Sauce, (II, 688), or 2 teaspoons Chili Sauce, (II, 686)**

**2 tablespoons chopped parsley**

**¹/₄ cup chopped olives**

**¹/₂ cup boiled or canned shrimp**

**¹/₂ cup sautéed or canned mushrooms**

**¹/₄ cup finely chopped celery**

## OYSTER SAUCE

**About 2 Cups**

For fish.

Prepare:

**1 cup White Sauce II, 383**

Season it well with:

**Salt**

**(1 teaspoon Worcestershire sauce)**

Shortly before serving, bring the sauce to the boiling point and add:

**3 tablespoons chopped parsley**

**1 cup finely chopped poached oysters and juice**

## ANCHOVY SAUCE

**1 Cup**

For fish and bland vegetables.

Prepare:

**White Sauce I, 383**

Add to it:

**3 fillets of anchovy, washed and pounded to a paste**

Blend it well with the sauce.

## HORSERADISH SAUCE OR SAUCE ALBERT

**1 Cup**

A happy complement to boiled or corned beef.

Prepare:

**White Sauce I, 383**

Remove it from the heat. Add:

**3 tablespoons prepared horseradish**

**2 tablespoons whipping cream**

**1 teaspoon sugar**

**1 teaspoon dry mustard**

**1 tablespoon vinegar**

Reheat but do not boil. Serve immediately.

## LOW-FAT WHITE SAUCE

**About 2 Cups**

Combine and scald:

**2 cups skim milk**

**¹/₂ teaspoon salt**

**A dash of white pepper**

Sprinkle over the surface and stir in for 1 minute:

**3 tablespoons cream of rice**

Remove from heat, cover and let stand 4 minutes. Beat well until smooth. Reheat and serve, or store refrigerated and reheat for future use.

## BREAD SAUCE

**About 3 Cups**

The bread crumbs here substitute for flour. This sauce is usually served with small roasted wild birds or roast meat.

Skin:

**A small onion**

Stud it with:

**3 whole cloves**

Place the onion in a saucepan with:

**2 cups milk**
**2 tablespoons butter**

Bring the milk to a boil. Add:

**1 cup fresh white bread crumbs**

Simmer for 15 minutes. Remove the onion. Beat the sauce smooth and stir in until blended:

**3 tablespoons cream**

## WHITE SAUCE WITH STOCK OR SAUCE VELOUTÉ

**1½ Cups**

Another basic: a white sauce made from a roux in which a light stock usually takes the place of milk or cream. The stock may be chicken, veal or fish, depending on the dish the sauce is to accompany. A quick Velouté may be made like White Sauce I, 383, using stock in place of milk, but for a classic sauce of fine texture, proceed as directed below. ♦ The sauce should never be cooked in aluminum pans because they discolor it badly. Melt in the top of a double boiler:

**2 tablespoons butter**

Stir in:

**2 tablespoons flour**

When blended, add gradually:

**2 cups chicken, veal or fish stock**

and stir over low heat until well combined and thickened. Add:

**¼ cup mushroom peelings**

Place in the double boiler and simmer ♦ over—not in—boiling water about 1 hour, stirring occasionally. Strain through a fine sieve, then add:

**A pinch of nutmeg**
**Season to taste**

and stir occasionally during the cooling process to prevent a crust from forming. You may enliven a Velouté by adding combinations of very finely chopped fresh herbs.

## AURORE SAUCE

**About 2 Cups**

A sole-mate—Dover sole.

Prepare:

**Velouté Sauce, left**

Add:

**2 tablespoons tomato purée**

to the sauce and mix. Let boil a little before pouring through a sieve and adding:

**A Butter Swirl, 380**

## SOUBISE OR WHITE ONION SAUCE

**About 1½ Cups**

A delicate onion-flavored sauce for fish, poultry or vegetables.

Prepare:

**1½ cups Velouté Sauce, opposite**

Sauté until transparent:

**2 chopped medium-sized onions**

in:

**2 tablespoons butter**

Add the onions to the Velouté Sauce and simmer over low heat 30 minutes, stirring occasionally. Rub the whole sauce through a fine sieve, and finish it off with:

**2 tablespoons whipping cream**
**Season to taste**

## SUPRÊME SAUCE

**About 2 Cups**

For fish, poultry and eggs. Its special characteristics are its perfect whiteness and delicacy.
Prepare:

**1¹/₂ cups Velouté Sauce, 387, made with chicken stock**

Add:

**1 cup strong light chicken stock**

**¹/₄ cup mushroom peelings**

Bring to a boil, reduce the heat and simmer, stirring occasionally, until the sauce is reduced to 1¹/₂ cups. Strain through a fine sieve and add, stirring constantly:

**¹/₂ cup whipping cream**

Stir in:

**1 tablespoon butter**
**Season to taste**

## CHAMPAGNE SAUCE

**About 1¹/₄ Cups**

Not every householder has to worry about what to do with leftover champagne, but should this appalling dilemma be yours, there is no better way than this to solve it and make a light but rich sauce for fish or chicken.
Prepare:

**³/₄ cup Velouté Sauce, 387**

using fumet to replace the stock if the dish is fish. Have ready:

**¹/₂ cup butter divided into six portions**

Cook together until the mixture reduces almost to a glaze:

**1 cup champagne**
**¹/₂ cup minced shallots or mild onions**

Remove the mixture from the heat and add the butter, piece by piece, so that it softens but does not liquefy

and retains the texture of a Béarnaise sauce. Add:

**1¹/₂ teaspoons freshly chopped tarragon**

and combine the above with the heated but not boiling Velouté. Have the warm cooked fillets of fish or breast of chicken ready on a hot dish. Cover them with the sauce and serve at once.

## PAPRIKA OR HUNGARIAN SAUCE

**About 1¹/₂ Cups**

For fish, poultry or veal.
Sauté until golden in:

**1 tablespoon butter**
**1 finely chopped medium-sized onion**

Add:

**2 tablespoons mild Hungarian paprika**

and stir for 1 minute. Add gradually, stirring constantly:

**1 cup cream**
**¹/₃ cup Velouté Sauce, 387**
**Season to taste**

## SAUCE INDIENNE

**About 2 Cups**

Sauté slowly until tender in:

**¹/₄ cup butter**
**¹/₄ cup finely chopped onion**

Stir in and cook, without browning, for 4 or 5 minutes:

**2¹/₂ tablespoons flour**
**¹/₂ to 2 teaspoons curry powder**
**A pinch to ¹/₄ teaspoon saffron**

Add slowly, stirring constantly, and simmer until well blended:

**1 cup chicken broth**
**1 cup cream**
**¹/₂ teaspoon grated lemon peel**

If you wish to have a perfectly

smooth sauce, add the chicken broth and grated lemon peel only, cook 10 minutes, strain through a sieve, add the cream and bring back to a boil. You may liven up this sauce, if you like a hot curry, with dashes of:

> (Hot pepper sauce)
> (Cayenne)
> (Ginger)
> (Dry sherry)

or by adding:

> (Chopped chutney)
> (Very small gherkins)

## RAVIGOTE SAUCE

Served lukewarm over variety meats, fish, light meats and poultry. Chop until very fine:

> **2 shallots**

Add:

> **1 tablespoon tarragon vinegar**

Cook these ingredients rapidly about 3 minutes, stirring constantly. Add:

> **1 cup Velouté Sauce, 387**

to the shallots and simmer about 10 minutes. Stir frequently. Add:

> **Salt and freshly ground pepper**

Cool the sauce to lukewarm. Add:

> **1 tablespoon chopped parsley**
> **1 tablespoon chopped chervil**
> **1 tablespoon chopped capers**
> **1/2 teaspoon chopped chives**
> **1/2 teaspoon chopped tarragon**

Quaintly enough, the classic cuisine also includes a cold "Ravigote" sauce which is not based on Velouté at all, but is in essence an Herbed French Dressing, 414.

## SMITANE SAUCE

**About 2 Cups**

For roast poultry or wildfowl—especially pheasant—and for game if the brown base is used.

Melt in a saucepan:

> **1 tablespoon butter**

Add:

> **1/4 cup finely chopped onions**

and cook until transparent, then add:

> **1/2 cup dry white wine**

and cook until the mixture is reduced to one-half. Add:

> **1 cup Velouté, 387, or Brown Sauce, 391**

Blend and simmer 5 minutes, then add:

> **1 cup cultured sour cream**
> **Season to taste**

For a tarter effect, add:

> **(A little lemon juice)**

After adding the sour cream, do not allow the sauce to boil or it will curdle.

## WHITE WINE SAUCE

**About 1 Cup**

Serve over Sautéed Brains, 645, Sweetbreads, 642, or other light meats. If using with a fish dish, substitute a fumet, (II, 173), for the stock, below. Heat:

> **2 tablespoons butter**

Add and sauté until light yellow:

> **1 tablespoon chopped onion or shallots**

Stir in until smooth:

> **1 1/2 tablespoons flour**

Stir in gradually, until the sauce is smooth and very hot:

> **1/2 cup chicken or veal stock**
> **1/2 cup dry white wine**

You may add:

> **(1 tablespoon chopped parsley or chives)**
> **Salt, as needed**

## ALLEMANDE SAUCE OR EGG-THICKENED VELOUTÉ

1½ Cups

An enriched Velouté Sauce, to be used with poached chicken or vegetables. It becomes **Poulette** if, as a final step, you add finely chopped parsley. If, at the last minute, you add a generous tablespoon of drained chopped capers, you have **Caper Sauce**, which goes well with fish or mutton. ▶ Do not let an Allemande boil after the egg is added, or it will curdle.
Prepare:

1½ cups Velouté Sauce, 387

Stir in:

¾ cup strong chicken stock

Blend well and reduce to two-thirds its original volume, stirring occasionally. Remove from the heat and add:

1 egg yolk mixed with
2 tablespoons cream

Stir the sauce until slightly thickened. Just before serving, stir in:

1 tablespoon lemon juice
1 tablespoon butter

## CURRY SAUCE

1½ Cups

Pour over whole poached fish or fish fillets.
Prepare:

1½ cups Allemande Sauce, above

adding:

1 teaspoon curry powder

and replacing the ¾ cup chicken stock with:

¾ cup coconut milk, (II, 244)

## HOT MUSTARD SAUCE

1½ Cups

For poached or broiled fish.
Prepare:

1½ cups Allemande Sauce, left

Add, just before serving:

½ teaspoon dry mustard or 1 teaspoon prepared mustard
¼ teaspoon salt
½ teaspoon freshly ground black pepper

## SAUCE FOR WILDFOWL

After roasting the game bird which has been barded with salt pork or bacon and basted with equal quantities of butter and white wine, flambé it in:

⅛ cup brandy: 1 oz.

Remove the game and keep warm. Degrease the pan juices and reduce them over low heat for 1 minute. Then add, for each small bird:

1 egg yolk

Beat in:

½ cup whipping cream

Stir until thickened ▶ but do not allow the sauce to boil. Season well.

## PEANUT PEPPER SAUCE

About 1¼ Cups

Use over chicken or beans to enrich their protein content.
Combine in a heavy saucepan over low heat and stir constantly until the ingredients thicken:

½ cup milk
½ cup chicken broth or vegetable stock
4 tablespoons peanut butter
1 teaspoon soy sauce
½ clove garlic, pressed
2 tablespoons finely shredded green pepper or pimiento
(1 teaspoon sugar)
Season to taste

Serve at once.

# BROWN SAUCE OR SAUCE ESPAGÑOLE

**About 6 Cups**

Legion are the children of this mother-sauce, and only the cook's clumsiness or lack of ingenuity need convert them into the changelings we lump together as "gravy." Espagñole is the fundamental brown sauce, but its classic preparation is time-consuming, often involving slow reduction over an 8- to 12-hour period. Today many illustrious restaurants are basing their brown sauces on canned condensed soups, a heresy we have for years happily practiced. The decline in quality, we often think, is balanced by infinitely greater speed of preparation and a welcome drop in caloric content. The recipe below is a kind of compromise short-cut requiring 2 to 2½ hours.

Melt in a heavy saucepan:

> ½ **cup beef or veal drippings**

Add:

> 1 **cup Mirepoix, (II, 254)**

When this begins to color, add:

> ½ **cup flour**

and stir until the flour is thoroughly browned.

Add:

> 10 **black peppercorns**
> 2 **cups drained, peeled tomatoes or 2 cups tomato purée**
> ½ **cup coarsely chopped parsley**

Stir and mix well, then add:

> 8 **cups rich beef stock**

Simmer 2 to 2½ hours or until reduced by one-half. Stir occasionally and skim off the fat as it rises to the top. Strain and stir occasionally as the sauce cools to prevent the formation of a skin. The sauce should be the consistency of whipping cream, no thicker. If you are using this sauce "as is":

> **Season to taste**

Herbs, spices and mushrooms are frequent additions to any brown sauce.

# DEMI-GLAZE SAUCE

**About 4½ Cups**

The Espagñole, left, reduced to the $n$th degree. Serve with filet mignon or any meat with which Madeira Sauce, below, is generally used.

Combine in a heavy saucepan:

> 4 **cups Brown Sauce, left**
> 4 **cups rich beef stock, flavored with mushroom trimmings**

Simmer slowly until reduced by half. Strain into a double boiler and keep warm over hot water while adding:

> ½ **cup dry sherry**

# MADEIRA SAUCE

**About 1 Cup**

A dry sherry may be substituted. Highly sympathetic to game or fillet of beef.

Reduce:

> 1 **cup Brown Sauce, left**

to three-fourths its volume, then add:

> ¼ **cup Madeira**
> **(1 teaspoon Meat Glaze, 427)**

Finish with a:

> **Butter Swirl, 380**

and another:

> 2 **tablespoons Madeira**

Keep hot, but do not let boil after adding the butter. You may also make this in the pan in which you have cooked the meat. Remove meat and pour off fat. Deglaze the pan with the above quantity of Madeira until the wine is reduced by half, then add the Brown Sauce and cook 10 minutes before finishing, as described above.

## LYONNAISE SAUCE OR BROWN ONION SAUCE

**1¼ Cups**

An inspired choice for leftover meat. Melt in a saucepan:

**2 tablespoons butter**

Add:

**2 finely chopped onions**

and cook until golden brown. Add:

**⅓ cup dry white wine or**
**2 tablespoons vinegar**

If you use the wine, simmer until reduced by half. Then add:

**1 cup Brown Sauce, 391**

and simmer for 15 minutes. Just before serving, add:

**1 tablespoon finely chopped parsley**

## HUNTER'S SAUCE OR SAUCE CHASSEUR

**About 2 Cups**

Sauté gently until very tender:

**2 tablespoons minced onion or shallots**

in:

**2 tablespoons butter**

Stir in and sauté gently for about 2 minutes:

**1 cup sliced mushrooms**

Add:

**½ cup dry white wine**
**(2 tablespoons brandy)**

Simmer until reduced by half. Add:

**½ cup tomato sauce or purée**
**1 cup Brown Sauce, 391**

Cook 5 minutes, then:

**Season to taste**

and add:

**1 teaspoon chopped parsley**
**(¼ cup pine nuts)**

## BORDELAISE SAUCE

For sweetbreads, chops, steaks, grilled meats.

Cook together in a saucepan:

**½ cup dry red wine**
**4 or 5 crushed black peppercorns**

until reduced to three-fourths, then add:

**1 cup Brown Sauce, 391**

Simmer 15 minutes. Add, just before serving:

**¼ cup diced beef marrow, poached for a few minutes and drained**
**(½ teaspoon lemon juice)**
**½ teaspoon chopped parsley**

## MARCHAND DE VIN OR MUSHROOM WINE SAUCE

**About 2 Cups**

Serve with broiled steak. Sauté:

**1 cup finely sliced mushrooms**

in:

**2 tablespoons butter**

Add:

**½ cup hot beef stock**

▶ Simmer 10 minutes. Add:

**1 cup Brown Sauce, 391**
**½ cup dry red wine or Madeira**

▶ Simmer 20 minutes, then:

**Season to taste**

You may add:

**(Juice of ½ lemon)**

## ROSEMARY WINE SAUCE

**1 Cup**

Serve with Calf's Head, 655, or turtle meat, 467. Aptly enough, the strongly flavored combination of herbs which gives this sauce its special tang is known in France as herbs *à tortue*.

Heat to boiling point:

**½ cup Madeira or dry sherry**

Add:

1 teaspoon mixed dried
   marjoram, rosemary, sage,
   bay leaf, thyme and basil

Remove from heat and let stand
5 to 10 minutes. Strain off the herb-
flavored wine and add it to:

**1 cup hot Brown Sauce, 391**

## SAUCE PÉRIGUEUX

**1 Cup**

For croquettes, shirred eggs and
chicken.
Prepare:

**Madeira Sauce, 391**

Just before adding the butter swirl,
stir in:

**1 tablespoon chopped truffles**

Very similar is **Sauce Périgourdine,**
but the truffles are finely diced instead of chopped and a dice of foie
gras is added.

## PIQUANT SAUCE

**About 1¼ Cups**

Excellent for giving extra zip to
bland meats and for reheating leftover meat. A good sauce, too, for
pork and pigs' feet.
Lightly brown:

**2 tablespoons minced onions**

in:

**1 tablespoon butter**

Add:

**2 tablespoons dry white wine**
   **or 2 tablespoons vinegar or**
   **lemon juice**

and cook until the liquid is almost
evaporated. Add:

**1 cup Brown Sauce, 391**

and simmer 10 minutes. Just before
serving, add:

**1 tablespoon chopped parsley**
   **or chopped mixed parsley,**
   **tarragon and chervil**
**1 tablespoon chopped sour**
   **pickles**

**1 tablespoon chopped capers**
   **Season to taste**

## SAUCE ROBERT

**1¼ Cups**

Prepare:

**Piquant Sauce, left**

doubling the amount of onion and
omitting the parsley, chervil and tarragon. Just before serving, stir in:

**1 teaspoon prepared Dijon-**
   **type mustard**
   **A pinch of powdered sugar**

## POIVRADE OR PEPPER SAUCE

**3 Cups**

The traditional sauce to serve with
venison. It constitutes the basis of
several other game sauces.
Heat:

**¼ cup vegetable oil**

Sauté in it, until brown:

**1 chopped carrot**
**1 chopped onion**
   **(Game bones, trimmings**
   **and giblets, if available)**

Add:

**3 sprigs parsley**
**1 bay leaf**
   **A pinch of thyme**
**¼ cup vinegar or ¼ cup**
   **marinade liquid, if the**
   **game has been marinated**
   **before cooking**

Simmer until reduced to one-third
original quantity. Add:

**3 cups Brown Sauce, 391**

Bring to a boil ▶ reduce heat and simmer 1 hour. Add:

**10 peppercorns**

and simmer 5 more minutes. Strain
the sauce into another saucepan and
add again:

**¼ cup marinade liquid**

Cook slowly 30 minutes more,
then add:

½ cup dry red wine
Season to taste
adding enough:
Freshly ground black
pepper
to make a hot sauce.

## CREOLE SAUCE

About 2 Cups
Melt over low heat:
2 tablespoons butter
Add and cook covered about 2 minutes:
¼ cup chopped onion
1 minced clove garlic
6 minced green olives
Add and cook until the sauce is thick, about 50 minutes:
1½ cups canned tomatoes or
½ cup tomatoes and 1 cup
Brown Sauce, 391
½ chopped green pepper, with
seeds and membranes
removed
½ bay leaf
A pinch of thyme
1 teaspoon chopped parsley
1 teaspoon white or brown
sugar
⅓ teaspoon salt
A few grains cayenne
(1 tablespoon dry sherry)
(¼ cup chili sauce)
(2 tablespoons diced ham)
(½ cup sliced mushrooms)

## ABOUT QUICK CANNED SOUP SAUCES

Not only do unconcentrated canned consommés and broths perform a valuable impromptu role as strengtheners and flavoring for sauces: condensed canned soups may be used to furnish the very foundations for sauce as well. The results, of course, are not so subtle and delicate as roux-based sauces carefully constructed from fresh meat or poultry stock. But an impressive saving in time and a substantially lower caloric content go far toward offsetting loss of quality. Taste these mixtures before salting and final seasoning.

### I.

1¼ Cups
For chicken, veal and fish.
Heat:
1 cup condensed cream of
chicken soup
2 tablespoons butter
2 to 4 tablespoons rich
chicken or vegetable stock
A grating of lemon rind

### II.

1¼ Cups
For beef hash.
Heat:
1 cup condensed cream of
mushroom soup
2 to 4 tablespoons strong beef
stock
½ teaspoon Meat Glaze, 427
Few drops garlic juice
1 tablespoon butter

### III.

1¼ Cups
For creaming vegetables.
Heat:
1 cup condensed cream of
celery soup
2 tablespoons butter
2 to 4 tablespoons chicken
stock
1 tablespoon chopped chives

## QUICK BROWN SAUCE

About 1 Cup
You may rub your pan with:
½ clove garlic
Melt:

2 tablespoons butter
Stir in until blended:

2 tablespoons flour
Stir in:

1 cup canned bouillon, or
1 or 2 bouillon cubes
dissolved in 1 cup boiling
water

Permit the gravy to reach the boiling point. Stir constantly. Season as required with:

Salt and pepper or paprika
Dry sherry or
Worcestershire sauce
Lemon juice, catsup or chili
sauce
Dried herbs

## QUICK MUSHROOM SAUCE

**About 2 Cups**

For roast meat, chicken and casseroles.
Sauté:

1/4 lb. sliced mushrooms
in:

2 tablespoons butter

Remove the mushrooms from the skillet. Add to the drippings:

Quick Brown Sauce, 394

When the sauce is heated, add the sautéed mushrooms.

## QUICK À LA KING SAUCE

**About 1 1/2 Cups**

The stout stanchion under many a quickly trumped-up luncheon-bridge.
Sauté until tender:

1 minced green pepper
in:

1 tablespoon butter
Add:

1 cup condensed cream of
mushroom soup
1/4 cup milk

Heat the sauce and add:

1 pimiento, cut into strips
(2 tablespoons dry sherry)

## QUICK TOMATO CHEESE SAUCE

**About 1 1/2 Cups**

Good over eggs.
Heat in a double boiler:

1 cup condensed tomato soup
Add:

1/4 teaspoon salt
1/4 teaspoon pepper or paprika

Stir and cook these ingredients until they are hot. With a wire whisk beat in:

1 cup or more grated cheese
until the cheese is melted.

## QUICK SEAFOOD SPAGHETTI SAUCE

**About 1 Quart**

Heat:

1 1/2 cups condensed tomato
soup

Melt in a saucepan over low heat:

1/4 cup olive oil or butter

Stir in and cook until transparent:

1/4 cup or more chopped onion
3/4 cup chopped green pepper

Stir in slowly the hot soup and:

1/2 cup Fish Stock, (II, 173)

When the sauce is hot, add very slowly, stirring constantly:

1/2 lb. cooked or canned diced
lobster, crab, shrimp or
tuna

Remove from heat and add:

1/2 lb. diced cheese:
Mozzarella, Parmesan or
Scamorza
Season to taste

and stir in cheese until melted. Pour over cooked spaghetti.

## DRIED SOUP SAUCES

**4 Servings**

Not so speedy as canned ones, but they can provide a well-flavored base when reconstituted with half the

amount of liquid called for normally:
the dried vegetable components swell
during cooking.

Combine and heat:

> 1 package dried cream of
> leek, cream of mushroom
> or smoky pea soup
> 1½ cups light cream or top
> milk

Use with leftover chicken or veal,
with rice or noodles in a casserole. Or
combine and heat:

> 1 package dried onion soup
> 1½ to 2 cups water

and add to meat and vegetables in a
casserole. Again, do not salt—and go
easy on other seasonings—until these
sauces have cooked about 20 minutes
and you have tasted them.

## CHINESE SAUCE FOR VEGETABLES

**For About 1 Pound Vegetables**

Blend until smooth:

> 1 tablespoon cornstarch
> 3 tablespoons cold water

Add:

> ½ teaspoon salt
> 1 tablespoon soy sauce
> (½ teaspoon finely grated
> gingerroot)

Pour over vegetables that are cooking. Stir well until the whole mixture
comes to a boil.

## ABOUT SEASONED BUTTERS AND BUTTER SAUCES

These garnishes are quick, tasty and
simple to make. The main thing is to
use fresh, high-quality butter, preferably unsalted. For other seasoned
butters used as Spreads, see (II, 70).
For Seafood Butter, see (II, 71).

Allow about 1 tablespoon butter
per serving. A few butter sauces are
melted, but most of them are creamed
and reach the table in solid form, being allowed to melt on the hot fish,
meat or vegetables for which they are
designed. You may form the butter
into fancy shapes and molds, see (II,
201). Most solid seasoned butters
may be prepared more quickly and
taste almost as good as melted butter sauces. If you use melted butter,
dress the food in the kitchen. Make
sure you spoon out the seasonings
with the butter. They will sink to the
bottom if you serve the melted butter
at the table in a sauce boat. There are
some butters, such as shrimp and lobster, which are used to flavor and finish sauces but are rarely served by
themselves as sauces.

Seasoned butters may be ✳ frozen for several weeks. But they ◗
should not be refrigerated longer than
24 hours, as the herbs deteriorate
quickly.

## DRAWN OR CLARIFIED BUTTER OR GHEE

There need be neither mystery nor
mystique about this substance: it is
merely melted butter with the sediment removed. But, as it is used in so
many different ways—among others
as a sauce for cooked lobster, to
make brown and black butter and as a
baking ingredient—here is the recipe.

Melt completely over low heat:

> **Butter**

Remove from heat and let stand a
few minutes, allowing the milk solids
to settle to the bottom. Skim the butter fat from the top and strain the
clear yellow liquid into a container.

## BROWN BUTTER OR BEURRE NOISETTE

### 4 Servings

Brown or so-called black butters can only be made successfully with clarified butter, since otherwise the sediment always present in "raw" butter will tend to burn and make the resultant sauce speckled and bitter. Use for asparagus, broccoli and brains.
Melt in a saucepan and cook slowly until light brown:

**¼ cup Clarified Butter, 396**

## BLACK BUTTER OR BEURRE NOIR

### 4 Servings

For fish, eggs, vegetables, sweetbreads and brains.
Melt and cook very slowly, until dark brown:

**¼ cup Clarified Butter, 396**
Stir in at once:

**1 teaspoon vinegar or lemon juice**
If served with brains or fish, you may add:

**1 tablespoon chopped capers**
Serve immediately.

## MEUNIÈRE OR LEMON BUTTER

### 4 Servings

Prepare:
**Brown Butter, 391**
Add:

**1 tablespoon finely chopped parsley**
**1 teaspoon lemon juice**
**Season to taste**

## BURGUNDY SAUCE OR SAUCE BOURGUIGNONNE

### 1 Cup

For snails and egg dishes.
Reduce by half a mixture of:

**2 cups dry red wine, preferably red Burgundy**
**2 minced shallots or mild onions**
**A few sprigs parsley**
**A pinch of thyme**
**¼ bay leaf**
**(Mushroom peelings)**
Strain the mixture. When ready to serve, heat and add:

**1 to 1½ tablespoons Kneaded Butter, 381**
**(A dash of cayenne)**

## ALMOND BUTTER

### ⅓ Cup

Often used in cream sauces, for sautéed chicken and other "amandine" dishes. Another version is Amandine Garnish, (II, 221).
Cream:

**¼ cup butter**
Blanch:

**¼ cup almonds, (II, 238)**
Remove the skins and pound the almonds to a paste with:

**1 teaspoon water**
Add gradually to the butter, blending well. Rub through a fine sieve.

**Season to taste**

## ANCHOVY BUTTER

### 4 Servings

Fine spread over hot broiled fish, a steak or canapés.
Cream until soft:

**¼ cup butter**
Beat in:

**1 teaspoon anchovy paste**
**⅛ teaspoon onion juice**

¹/₄ teaspoon lemon juice
A few grains cayenne

## BERCY BUTTER

**About ¹/₄ Cup**

For broiled meats.
Cook together until reduced to about one-fourth the original quantity:

**2 teaspoons finely chopped shallots**
**²/₃ cup dry white wine**

Cool. Cream:

**4 tablespoons butter**

and add:

**2 teaspoons finely chopped parsley**

Combine the two mixtures and:

**Season to taste**

## CAVIAR BUTTER

**6 to 8 Servings**

A lovely fish garnish.
Cream:

**¹/₂ cup butter**

Add:

**1 tablespoon lemon juice**
**¹/₄ cup black caviar or salmon roe**
**Salt, if necessary**

Chill slightly, mold or cut into shapes and serve.

## MAÎTRE D'HÔTEL BUTTER

**4 Servings**

Good over broiled steak.
Cream until soft:

**¹/₄ cup butter**

Add:

**¹/₂ teaspoon salt**
**¹/₈ teaspoon white pepper**
**1 teaspoon finely chopped parsley**

Add very slowly, stirring the sauce constantly:

³/₄ to 1¹/₂ tablespoons lemon juice

## COLBERT BUTTER

**4 Servings**

Use on fish and roasted meats.
Cream together:

**¹/₄ cup Maître d'Hôtel Butter, above**
**¹/₂ teaspoon melted beef extract or Meat Glaze, 427**
**¹/₄ teaspoon finely chopped fresh tarragon**

## SNAIL BUTTER

**About 1 Cup**

Should any of this remain after stuffing the snails ✻ freeze for a short period for use on steaks, fish or vegetables.
Cream until soft:

**³/₄ cup butter**

Work into it:

**1 to 2 tablespoons minced shallots or mild onions**
**1 to 2 well-pressed cloves garlic**
**(1 tablespoon minced celery)**
**1 tablespoon minced parsley**
**¹/₂ teaspoon salt**
**Freshly ground pepper**
**(1 tablespoon lemon juice)**

## DEVILED BUTTER FOR SEAFOOD

**4 Servings**

Work until soft:

**¹/₄ cup butter**

Combine it with:

**¹/₂ teaspoon dry mustard**
**2 teaspoons wine vinegar**
**2 teaspoons Worcestershire sauce**
**¹/₄ teaspoon salt**

<sup></sup>1/16 teaspoon cayenne
2 egg yolks
Beat well.

## GARLIC BUTTER

**4 Servings**

For steak, if you are a garlic fancier, or for garlic bread. Boil in a little water 5 or 6 minutes:

1 to 3 cloves garlic

Drain, crush and pound well in a mortar with:

1/4 cup butter

## GREEN BUTTER

**About 1/4 Cup**

Use for broiled fish and to give white or cream sauces a green color.
Blanch the following ingredients 5 minutes, then plunge into cold water, drain and dry in a towel:

2 shallots or 1 tablespoon
mild onion
1 teaspoon fresh tarragon
1 teaspoon fresh chervil
1 teaspoon fresh parsley
6 to 8 spinach leaves

Chop until fine and pound them in a mortar. Work in gradually:

1/4 cup butter
Salt, if needed

## SHRIMP OR LOBSTER BUTTER

**1/2 Cup**

Delicately pink and deliciously flavored. Use for finishing cream sauces served with fish or by itself with the shellfish you have used in making the butter.
Dry the shells from:

1 lb. shrimp or 1 large
lobster

in a low oven for a short time. Pound in a mortar or put them through the

food grinder, breaking them up as finely as possible. Melt:

1/2 cup butter

in a double boiler ▶ over—not in—boiling water. Add the shells and:

2 tablespoons water

Simmer 10 minutes. ▶ Do not let the butter boil. Line a sieve with cheese-cloth or fine muslin and strain the hot butter into a bowl of ice water. Refrigerate and skim off the butter when it hardens.

## WHITE BUTTER

**4 Servings**

For poached fish. The fumet required is from the same type of fish. If you lack a fumet, a surprisingly effective alternative is an equal amount of clam juice, canned or fresh. Simmer until reduced to one-fourth its original volume:

1 teaspoon finely chopped
shallots
1/4 cup wine vinegar
1/4 cup Fumet, (II, 173)

Cool this mixture and add, a little at a time:

1/4 cup softened butter

beating constantly with a sauce whisk until the sauce is creamy and whitened, rather like whipped cream.

**Season to taste**

Add:

2 tablespoons mixture of very
finely chopped fresh fennel,
parsley, chives, basil,
chervil or tarragon, or
1 tablespoon of the dried
herbs

## POLONAISE OR BROWNED
## BUTTER CRUMB SAUCE

**4 Servings**

A topping for vegetables.
Brown:

**¹/₃ cup fine dry bread crumbs**
in:
**Meunière Butter, 397**
If you wish, you may sauté:
**(1 tablespoon minced onion)**
in the butter, until transparent, before adding the bread crumbs. Garnish the vegetable with:
**Finely chopped hard-
cooked egg**
and pour the sauce over it.

## BUTTER SAUCE FOR CANNED OR COOKED VEGETABLES

Drain the vegetables. Let the stock or juice boil until reduced by half. Add:
**Melted butter**
**Seasonings and lemon juice**

## UNTHICKENED TOMATO SAUCE

**About 4 Cups**
Place over low heat:
**3 tablespoons olive oil**
Add and stir about 3 minutes:
**1 large Bermuda onion,
chopped**
**2 chopped celery ribs with
leaves**
**1 carrot cut in small pieces**
**(¹/₂ chopped green pepper,
seeds and fibrous portions
removed)**
**(1 pressed clove garlic)**
Add:
**4 cups drained canned
tomatoes or 6 large fresh
tomatoes**
If the latter are very juicy, peel and squeeze slightly to get rid of excess liquid and seeds. Add:
**1 sprig thyme, basil or
tarragon**
**1 teaspoon salt**
**¹/₈ teaspoon pepper**
**1 teaspoon sugar**

Cook gently, uncovered, until the mixture is thick, about 45 minutes. ♦ Watch it, so that it does not burn. Put it through a fine strainer. Add seasoning, if needed. This sauce will keep several days.

## THICKENED TOMATO SAUCE

**About 1¹/₂ Cups**
Bring to a boil and then ♦ simmer 30 minutes before sieving:
**2 cups canned tomatoes**
**1 onion, stuck with 3 cloves**
**2 chopped celery ribs with
leaves**
**1 diced carrot**
**1 Bouquet Garni, (II, 253)**
**1 bay leaf**
**(¹/₂ chopped green pepper)**
♦ Be sure to pass through all the pulpy residue when sieving, so that only cloves, leaves and seeds remain behind. This well-flavored pulp helps thicken the sauce. Melt in a saucepan:
**3 tablespoons butter**
Stir in, until blended:
**2 tablespoons flour**
Add the strained thickish stock slowly with:
**¹/₄ teaspoon sugar**
♦ Simmer and stir the stock 5 to 10 minutes.
**Season to taste**
including, if desired:
**(1 tablespoon fresh basil)**

## QUICK TOMATO SAUCE

**About 2¹/₂ Cups**
Strain:
**1 large can Italian tomatoes:
16 oz.**
Add:
**3 oz. canned tomato paste**

½ teaspoon salt
1 tablespoon onion juice or
  2 tablespoons finely grated
  onion
½ teaspoon sugar

Bring to a boil and simmer gently 15 to 20 minutes.

## QUICK CREOLE SAUCE

**2½ Cups**

To:

2 cups Quick Tomato Sauce, 400

Add:

½ cup very finely chopped
  green pepper, onion, celery,
  olives and pimiento

## COCKTAIL SAUCE

**About 1 Cup**

For dunking or garnishing shellfish, small sausages or other hors d'oeuvre. Combine:

¾ cup Catsup, (II, 686)
⅛ to ¼ cup prepared
  horseradish
Juice of 1 lemon
1 dash hot pepper sauce

## MEXICAN TOMATO SAUCE

**About 1 Cup**

Just what you might expect. You will feel hot inside, down to your toes. Use with Cowboy Eggs, 215.
Place in a small saucepan and simmer until fairly thick:

¾ cup drained canned
  tomatoes or about 3 large,
  skinned and quartered,
  peeled and seeded fresh
  tomatoes
6 tablespoons Chili
  Sauce, (II, 686)

2 teaspoons prepared
  mustard
3 tablespoons grated or
  prepared horseradish
½ teaspoon sugar
¾ teaspoon salt
¼ teaspoon pepper
  A few grains cayenne
¾ teaspoon curry powder
6 tablespoons vinegar
1 teaspoon onion juice
1 sliced clove garlic

Strain the mixture. Add:

1 teaspoon dried or
  1 tablespoon fresh herbs

This sauce may be served—in discreet quantities—by itself, but it combines excellently with hot cream sauce or hot or cold mayonnaise. Add as much of it to these as you find palatable.

## ⚘ BLENDER TOMATO SAUCE

**About 1 Cup**

Serve over bland foods, sweetbreads, cold veal, hot or cold fish, or salads. Combine and blend:

¾ cup tomato purée or 2 large
  skinned tomatoes—the
  juice and seeds pressed
  from them
1 medium-sized onion
1 green pepper, seeds and
  membrane removed
¼ cup celery, or 1 teaspoon
  celery and/or dill seeds
2 tablespoons chopped
  parsley or chives
½ teaspoon salt
¼ teaspoon freshly ground
  pepper
(2 tablespoons French
  Dressing, 413)

Chill the sauce about ½ hour.

## ITALIAN MEAT SAUCE FOR PASTA

### I.

#### About 1 Quart

Heat:

    1/2 cup olive oil

Add:

    1 pressed clove garlic
    1 lb. ground round steak
    1/4 lb. ground lean pork
    2 cups Italian tomatoes
    1/2 cup Italian tomato paste
    1/2 cup beef or veal stock
    1 1/2 teaspoons salt
    1/4 teaspoon pepper
    1 bay leaf

Simmer the sauce uncovered about 1 hour. Add for the last 15 minutes:

    (1/2 cup sliced mushrooms)

Season with:

    1 to 2 tablespoons fresh basil
    or oregano

Serve over:

    Cooked spaghetti or
    noodles

with:

    Grated Parmesan or
    Romano cheese

### II.

#### About 1 1/2 Quarts

Mince and cook over very slow heat:

    3 slices bacon

Stir in and sauté:

    1/4 cup chopped onion
    1/2 lb. ground round steak

When the meat is nearly done, add:

    2 1/2 cups skinned tomatoes,
    pressed to expel seeds and
    juice
    1/2 cup chopped green pepper
    1 cup chopped canned
    mushrooms or 1/2 to 1 lb.
    sliced fresh Sautéed
    Mushrooms, 328

Season with:

    1 teaspoon chopped basil

    2 cups shredded cheese: 1/2 lb.
    Salt, cayenne or paprika

Simmer ▶ uncovered 20 or 30 minutes. If more liquid is needed, add:

    1/2 cup hot stock or canned
    bouillon

## BOLOGNESE PASTA SAUCE

#### About 2 Cups

An interesting variation, involving cream.

Reconstitute, (II, 255):

    6 dried mushrooms

reserving them and the liquor.

Melt in a large saucepan:

    1/3 cup butter

Add:

    1/4 cup minced lean ham or
    Canadian bacon
    1/4 cup finely chopped carrot
    1/4 cup finely chopped onion

Stir and cook for 1 or 2 minutes. Add:

    1 cup chopped lean beef

and brown over medium heat, stirring occasionally, then add the mushrooms, their liquor and:

    2 tablespoons tomato paste
    1 strip lemon peel
    A pinch of nutmeg
    1 cup beef stock
    (1/2 cup dry white wine)

Partially cover and simmer slowly 1 hour. Remove from heat, take out lemon peel and stir in:

    1/4 cup whipping cream

just before serving with:

    Green Noodles, 199

## SPAGHETTI SAUCE WITH LIVER

#### 4 Servings

Melt:

    2 tablespoons butter or
    drippings

Sauté in it until light brown:

    1/2 cup chopped onions

Add and sauté very lightly:

1 cup cubed calf liver or
chicken livers

Add and simmer about 15 minutes:

1/2 cup any tomato sauce for
pasta

Season with:

1 teaspoon salt
1/8 teaspoon pepper
(1/4 teaspoon basil)

Serve over noodles, spaghetti, etc.,
garnished with:

Parsley

## MARINARA SAUCE

**About 1 1/2 Cups**

Use a little on green beans or a lot
over spaghetti.

Sauté lightly:

1 minced clove garlic

in:

2 tablespoons olive oil and
the oil from the anchovies

Add slowly:

2 1/2 cups canned pressed and
drained whole or Italian
tomatoes

Stir in:

6 finely chopped anchovies
1/2 teaspoon oregano
1 tablespoon chopped parsley

Bring to a boil, then ◖ reduce heat
and simmer uncovered 15 to 20 minutes, stirring occasionally. If served
with spaghetti, pass with:

Grated Parmesan or
Romano cheese

Try omitting the oregano and adding:

(5 chopped canned artichoke
hearts)

Simmer 3 or 4 minutes more.

## OCTOPUS PASTA SAUCE

**For 1 Pound Linguini Pasta**

See About Octopus, 492.

Heat in a large saucepan:

1 to 1 1/4 cups olive oil

Add:

1 1/4 cups seeded, peeled fresh
tomatoes
2/3 to 1 cup finely chopped
parsley
1 teaspoon salt
2 cloves garlic

Simmer the mixture 15 to 20 minutes. Remove the garlic. Add:

1 1/2 cups cooked octopus, cut
into bite-sized pieces

Simmer another 15 to 20 minutes.
Toss with the cooked, drained pasta
and serve at once.

## QUICK SHRIMP AND CLAM
SAUCE FOR PASTA

**Enough for 1 Pound Pasta**

This sauce goes down well with
seafood addicts who don't care for
the usual tomato sauces.

Heat in a skillet:

6 tablespoons olive oil

Add:

3 minced cloves garlic

and cook gently 5 minutes. Add:

3/4 cup finely chopped parsley
1 cup minced clams or
mussels with liquid
1/2 lb. shelled raw shrimp, cut
into bite-sized pieces
(1/8 teaspoon oregano)

Heat until bubbling and the shrimp is
pink. Serve at once over hot cooked
seashell pasta—conchiglie—to complete the marine effect. Pass with:

Grated Parmesan or
Romano cheese

## LOW-CALORIE TOMATO SAUCE

**About 1 Cup**

Try this over raw or cooked vegetables or seafood.

Combine:

3/4 cup Italian tomato paste
1 teaspoon dry mustard

1 tablespoon sugar
1/2 teaspoon salt
1 tablespoon vinegar
1 tablespoon drained
  horseradish
(1 tablespoon chopped onion,
  chives or fresh herbs)

## BARBECUE SAUCES

Please read about skewer cooking,
94. It is important to ♦ baste with barbecue sauces only during the last 15
minutes of cooking. Longer cooking
will make the spices bitter.

### I.
                        About 2 Cups
Sauté until brown:
  1/4 cup chopped onion
in:
  1 tablespoon drippings or
    other fat
Add and simmer for 20 minutes:
  1/2 cup water
  2 tablespoons vinegar
  1 tablespoon Worcestershire
    sauce
  1/4 cup lemon juice
  2 tablespoons brown sugar
  1 cup Chili Sauce, (II, 686)
  1/2 teaspoon salt
  1/4 teaspoon paprika
  1/4 teaspoon pepper
  1 teaspoon mustard, or chili
    or curry powder

### II.
                        About 1 1/2 Cups
Simmer 15 minutes, stirring frequently:
  12 to 14 oz. Tomato
    Catsup, (II, 686)
  1/2 cup distilled white vinegar
  1 teaspoon sugar
    A few grains cayenne
    pepper
  1/4 teaspoon black pepper
  1/8 teaspoon salt

## FEROCIOUS BARBECUE SAUCE

Combine and heat:
  1 1/2 cups Barbecue Sauce II,
    left
  1/4 of a seeded lemon, diced
    fine
  1/2 teaspoon ground cumin
  1 teaspoon ground coriander
  1/8 teaspoon paprika
  1/8 teaspoon saffron
  1/4 teaspoon ground ginger

## BARBECUE SAUCE FOR FOWL
### I.
                        For 1 Fowl
Combine and heat:
  4 teaspoons lemon juice
  1 teaspoon Worcestershire
    Sauce, (II, 688)
  1 teaspoon Tomato
    Catsup, (II, 686)
  1 tablespoon butter

### II.
                        About 2 1/2 Cups
Cook slowly until golden:
  1 medium-sized onion,
    chopped
  1 minced clove garlic
in:
  3 tablespoons drippings or
    other fat
Add and simmer for 30 minutes:
  3 tablespoons soy or
    Worcestershire sauce
  1 cup water
  1 chopped red pepper
  2 tablespoons vinegar
  2 to 4 tablespoons brown
    sugar
  1 cup Tomato Catsup,
    (II, 686)
  1 teaspoon prepared mustard
  1/2 cup diced celery
  1/2 teaspoon salt
Then add:
  1/4 cup lemon juice

## SWEET-SOUR BACON SAUCE

**About 1 Cup**

Fine for green beans.
Slowly render until crisp:

    4 thin slices bacon, cut up

At the same time, you may cook until
transparent:

    (1 teaspoon minced onion)

Remove the bacon and onion and
pour off all but:

    2 tablespoons bacon fat

Add to the fat:

    ¼ cup of the bean or other
        stock
    2 tablespoons vinegar
    1 to 2 tablespoons sugar

Heat and pour over the vegetables.
Garnish with the bacon and onion bits.

## AGRODOLCE SAUCE

**About 1¼ Cups**

For sweetbreads, calf's head or diced
meat.
Slightly caramelize in:

    1 tablespoon vinegar
    1 tablespoon sugar

Add and cook until shallots are soft:

    ½ cup white wine
    1 tablespoon minced shallots
        or mild onion

Mix in:

    ½ cup Demi-Glaze Sauce, 391

and heat briefly with:

    ½ cup chopped seeded
        Malaga grapes or
    2 tablespoons chopped
        parsley

## ORIENTAL SWEET-SOUR SAUCE

For Chinese-type vegetables and
shellfish.

### I.

**1 Cup**

Heat:

    ½ cup pineapple juice

    3 tablespoons vegetable oil
    2 tablespoons brown sugar
    1 teaspoon soy sauce or salt
    ½ teaspoon pepper
    ¼ cup mild vinegar

### II.

**2½ to 3 Cups**

A Polynesian version, for luau food,
Chinese Meatballs, 622, or Sweet
and Sour Pork, 607.
Have ready a paste of:

    2 tablespoons cornstarch
    ½ cup chicken broth
    2 tablespoons soy sauce

Melt in a heavy pan:

    2 tablespoons butter

Add:

    1 cup chicken broth
    ¾ to 1 cup diced green
        peppers
    6 slices diced canned
        pineapple

Cover and simmer 5 minutes. Add
the cornstarch paste and the following ingredients to the peppers and
pineapple:

    ½ cup vinegar
    ¾ cup pineapple juice
    ½ cup sugar
    ½ teaspoon salt
    ¼ teaspoon ginger

Simmer, stirring constantly, until the
mixture thickens.

## SWEET-SOUR MUSTARD SAUCE

**About 2½ Cups**

For ham or tongue.
Combine in a double boiler ♦ over—
not in—boiling water:

    ½ cup sugar
    1 tablespoon flour
    4 teaspoons dry mustard

Add gradually:

    2 cups cream

mixed with:

    2 egg yolks

Cook until thick. Stir in gradually:

> 1/2 **cup vinegar**

## SWEET-SOUR ORANGE SAUCE

> **About 2 Cups**

For duck or goose turn this into a true **Bigarade Sauce** by using the rind and juice from the Seville or bitter orange, and omitting the lemon juice. Pour off the fat from the pan in which you have roasted the bird. Deglaze the pan with:

> 1 **cup Game Stock, (II, 172)**

Thicken with:

> 1 **teaspoon arrowroot or cornstarch**

mixed first with a little of the stock. In another pan, cook together until light brown:

> 2 **tablespoons vinegar**
> 2 **tablespoons sugar**

Add the sauce from the roasting pan and cook 4 or 5 minutes, then add:

> 2 **tablespoons julienned and blanched navel orange rind**
> 1/2 **cup hot orange juice**
> 1 **tablespoon lemon juice**
> 2 **tablespoons curaçao**
> **Season to taste**

Serve immediately over goose or wild or domestic duck and garnish with:

> **Orange sections**

## SWEET-SOUR CREAM DRESSING

> **About 1 Cup**

For green beans or cabbage.
Combine and stir over very low heat until the sauce thickens slightly:

> 1 **beaten egg**
> 1/2 **cup cultured sour cream**
> 2 **tablespoons sugar**
> 1/4 **cup vinegar**
> 1/2 **teaspoon salt**
> 1/4 **teaspoon paprika**

Serve hot over hot vegetables or cold over chilled ones.

## CARAWAY SAUCE

Really a garnish to enhance plain vegetables.
Cook until the water is absorbed:

> 1 **tablespoon caraway seeds**

in:

> 2 **tablespoons water**

Melt in a skillet:

> 4 **tablespoons butter**

Sauté seeds and:

> 1 **tablespoon grated onion**

in the butter just a few moments, until seeds brown slightly. Remove from heat.

> **Season to taste**

Add:

> 1 **teaspoon lemon juice**

Pour sauce over hot vegetables.

## MINT SAUCE

> **About 1 Cup**

The usual accompaniment to roast lamb.
Heat:

> 3 **tablespoons water**

Dissolve in it:

> 1 1/2 **tablespoons confectioners' sugar**

Cool the syrup and add:

> 1/3 **cup finely chopped mint leaves**
> 1/2 **cup strong vinegar**

This is best made 1/2 hour before serving.

## PLUM, PEACH OR APRICOT SAUCE

> **About 3/4 Cup**

For spareribs and Chinese dishes.
⚶ Blend:

> 1/2 **cup plum, peach or apricot preserves**

**¼ cup Chutney, (II, 685)**

To use as a marinade, dilute with a small quantity of vinegar.

## CHERRY SAUCE

**About 1 Cup**

For ham and roast pork.

⅄ Blend:

**1 cup drained, pitted canned sour red cherries**
**½ cup plum preserves**
**2 teaspoons soy sauce**
**¼ teaspoon dry mustard**

Stir in:

**(¼ cup finely chopped walnuts)**

Serve hot or cold.

## RAISIN SAUCE

**About 1½ Cups**

For ham or tongue.

Combine in a saucepan:

**2 tablespoons butter**
**2 tablespoons flour**

Add:

**1½ cups cider or fruit juice**
**½ cup seedless raisins**

Cook until mixture boils, stirring constantly. Simmer about 10 minutes, until thickened. Add:

**1 teaspoon grated lemon rind**
**(¾ teaspoon prepared mustard)**
**(1 tablespoon sherry)**

## CIDER OR BEER RAISIN SAUCE

**About 1½ Cups**

For hot or cold ham or smoked tongue.

Combine in a saucepan:

**¼ cup firmly packed brown sugar**
**1½ tablespoons cornstarch**
**⅛ teaspoon salt**

Stir in:

**1 cup fresh cider or beer**
**¼ cup raisins, cut in halves**

Put in a cheesecloth bag and suspend the bag in the sauce as it heats:

**8 whole cloves**
**2-inch stick cinnamon**
**¼ diced lemon**

Cook and stir about 10 minutes. Remove the spices. Add:

**1 tablespoon butter**

Serve the sauce very hot.

## CUMBERLAND SAUCE

I.

**About 2 cups**

A classic formula for cold ham and game. The sauce may be served cold. For quicker currant jelly sauces, see 408.

Combine:

**1 teaspoon dry mustard**
**1 tablespoon brown sugar**
**¼ teaspoon powdered ginger**
**A few grains cayenne**
**¼ teaspoon salt**
**¼ teaspoon ground cloves**
**1½ cups red wine, preferably port**
**(½ cup seedless raisins)**
**(½ cup slivered blanched almonds)**

Simmer the sauce, covered, 8 minutes. Dissolve:

**2 teaspoons cornstarch**

in:

**2 tablespoons cold water**

Stir this into the sauce. Let it simmer about 2 minutes. Stir in:

**¼ cup red currant jelly**
**1 tablespoon grated orange and lemon rind**
**¼ cup orange juice**
**2 tablespoons lemon juice**

For a rather exquisite final touch you may add:

**(2 tablespoons Grand Marnier)**

## II.

About ¾ Cup

Combine and blend well:

>   Grated rind of 1 lemon
>   Juice of 1 lemon
>   Grated rind of 1 orange
> 1 tablespoon confectioners'
>     sugar
> 1 teaspoon prepared mustard
> ½ cup melted red currant
>     jelly
> 1 tablespoon port wine

If the jelly is very stiff, it may have to
be diluted over heat with:

>   (1 or 2 tablespoons hot water)

## III.

About 1¼ Cups

For cold meats.
Heat in a double boiler just before
serving:

> ¾ cup currant jelly

Stir in:

> ½ cup Indian chutney
> 1 teaspoon lemon juice
> 1 tablespoon brandy
>   Salt

## IV.

About ½ Cup

Make a quickie version by mixing:

> ½ cup currant jelly
> 2 tablespoons horseradish
> ½ teaspoon dry mustard

## SOUR CREAM HORSERADISH DRESSING OR DRESDEN SAUCE

1 Cup

A fine change from the well-liked but
often monotonous butter or cream
sauce. Usually served with smoked
or braised fish.
Combine and stir:

> 1 cup cultured sour cream
> ½ teaspoon prepared mustard

> ½ teaspoon grated
>     horseradish
> ¼ teaspoon salt

## CREAM HORSERADISH DRESSING

About 1¼ Cups

Another cold-meat dressing.
Beat until stiff:

> ½ cup heavy cream

Add slowly, beating constantly:

> 3 tablespoons lemon juice or
>     vinegar
> ¼ teaspoon salt
> ⅛ teaspoon paprika
>   A few grains cayenne
> 2 tablespoons grated
>     horseradish
> (3 tablespoons mayonnaise)

## FROZEN HORSERADISH SAUCE

About 1½ Cups

This comes out rather like a sherbet
and is delicious with boiled beef.
Combine:

> ¼ cup grated horseradish
> ¼ cup fresh orange juice
> 1 teaspoon sugar

and fold into:

> 1 cup stiffly whipped cream

Freeze about 3 to 4 hours in a tray
and spoon out into a bowl to serve.
Do not hold frozen for long periods.

## CUCUMBER ALMOND SAUCE

About 1½ Cups

Mostly for aspics and mousses; but
also for cold meat or fish, especially
salmon.
Beat until stiff:

> ¾ cup heavy sweet or
>     cultured sour cream

If the cream is sweet, add slowly:

> 2 tablespoons vinegar or
>     lemon juice

Season the sauce with:

 1/4 teaspoon salt

 1/8 teaspoon paprika

Pare, seed, cut finely and drain well:

 1 large cucumber

Add it to the sauce with:

 Slivered almonds

 (2 teaspoons finely chopped chives or dill)

## SOUR CREAM SAUCE FOR BAKED POTATOES

**1 Cup**

Do not chill before serving—keep at room temperature.

Combine:

 1 cup cultured sour cream

 1 teaspoon Worcestershire sauce

 A dash of hot pepper sauce

 1/2 teaspoon salt

 Freshly ground black pepper

Garnish with:

 Chopped chives

## CAVIAR SAUCE

**About 1 1/3 Cups**

Try as a dip for cold vegetables, in hors d'oeuvre, or on salads or baked potatoes.

Combine:

 1 cup cultured sour cream

 1 teaspoon onion or shallot juice

 2 teaspoons capers

 1/4 cup red caviar

## COLD MUSTARD SAUCE

### I.

**About 1/4 Cup**

For boiled or cold meats or fish. This sauce is in the nature of a relish.

Combine:

 2 teaspoons grated onion

 1 tablespoon Dijon- or Düsseldorf-type mustard

 1 1/2 teaspoons sugar

 1 to 2 tablespoons vegetable oil

 2 tablespoons vinegar or lemon juice

 (2 hard-cooked egg yolks)

 (1 tablespoon cream)

### II.

**About 1/2 Cup**

A highly seasoned sauce lower in calories than I. For cold meats or broiled sausages.

Blend gradually:

 2 tablespoons or more dry mustard

with a little:

 Water

until it is the consistency of thick cream. Fold this paste into:

 1/2 cup evaporated milk, whipped, (II, 187)

Season, if desired, with:

 Salt and paprika

## ABOUT HOLLANDAISE AND OTHER HOT EGG-THICKENED SAUCES

Delicious and loaded with calories, these transform into a superb dish the plainest and simplest cooked vegetables or broiled or roasted meat. But they have their maddening caprices, too. To circumvent them, we offer some stratagems. Don't try to make Hollandaise or Béarnaise on a very humid day, unless you use Clarified Butter, 396. Cook these sauces ♦ over—not in—hot, but not boiling, water. If you use a heatproof glass double boiler you can see when the water begins to boil, at which time add 1 or 2 tablespoons of cold water to lower temperature slightly. Keep stirring the sauce constantly and ♦ add the melted butter very, very slowly at first. Scrape the mixture away from the sides and bottom of the pan as you stir, to keep the sauce smooth. As with Mayonnaise, 419, a wooden spoon or a whisk is the best tool for making Hollandaise. A professional chef will make it over a low direct heat, but don't try this unless you are prepared to act out a new definition of "stir-crazy." Some of our friends freeze Hollandaise just as they do roux-based sauces. If frozen, it must be reheated in a double boiler ♦ over—not in—hot water, stirring briskly to preserve consistency. Should any of these egg sauces break, beat into them at once 1 to 2 tablespoons chilled cream. A slightly curdled sauce can be rescued in a blender, although its texture will not be so smooth as that of an originally well made sauce. Or it can be reconstituted, using a fresh egg yolk, as for Mayonnaise, 419.

## HOLLANDAISE SAUCE

**1 Cup**

♦ Please read About Hollandaise Sauce, 409. Our cook calls this "holiday sauce"—isn't that a grand name

for it? If directions are carefully followed, it never fails.

Melt slowly and keep warm:

**¹/₂ cup butter**

Barely heat:

**1¹/₂ tablespoons lemon juice, dry sherry or tarragon vinegar**

Have ready a small saucepan of boiling water and a tablespoon with which to measure it when ready. Place in the top of a double boiler ♦ over—not in—hot water:

**3 egg yolks**

Beat the yolks with a wire whisk until they begin to thicken. Add:

**1 tablespoon boiling water**

Beat again until the eggs begin to thicken. Repeat this process until you have added:

**3 more tablespoons water**

Then beat in the warm lemon juice. Remove double boiler from heat. Beat the sauce well with a wire whisk. Continue to beat while slowly adding the melted butter and:

**¹/₄ teaspoon salt**
**A few grains cayenne**

Beat until the sauce is thick. Serve at once.

## ⚘ BLENDER HOLLANDAISE

**About 1 Cup**

Easy, but less flavorful and paler in color than handmade Hollandaise. ♦ Do not make it in a smaller quantity than given here: there will not be enough heat to cook the eggs properly. Have ready in your blender:

**3 egg yolks**
**2 tablespoons lemon juice**
**A pinch of cayenne**
**¹/₄ teaspoon salt**

Heat to bubbling stage, do not brown:

**¹/₂ cup butter**

Cover container and turn motor on "High." After 3 seconds, remove the lid and pour the butter over the eggs in a steady stream. By the time the butter is poured in—about 30 seconds—the sauce should be finished. If not, blend on "High" about 5 seconds longer. Serve at once or keep warm by immersing blender container in warm water. This sauce may also be frozen and reconstituted over hot water.

## QUICK WHOLE-EGG HOLLANDAISE

About 1 Cup

Even paler in color than the sauce in the preceding recipe; but it does, once and for all, solve the problem of what to do with those extra whites.
Place in a mixing bowl and whip with a fork until thoroughly blended and pale yellow:

> 3  whole eggs
> 4  or 5 teaspoons lemon juice
> 3  tablespoons water

In a heavy ♦ nonstick coated skillet melt ♦ over low heat:

> 6  or 7 tablespoons butter

Add egg mixture slowly, stirring continuously until sauce has thickened. ♦ Do not overcook. Before serving add:

> 1/2  teaspoon salt
>   Season to taste

## HOLLANDAISE VARIATIONS

For less rich versions, try one of the following; or if you are in a hurry, prepare Hot Mayonnaise, right.

### I.

About 1 1/4 Cups

Mix in the top of a double boiler:

> 1  cup cultured sour cream
>   Juice of 1 lemon
> 2  egg yolks
> 1/2  teaspoon salt

> 1/4  teaspoon paprika

Stir ♦ over—not in—hot water until thick.

### II.

4 Servings

Good over vegetables such as Brussels sprouts and cauliflower.
Place in a double boiler ♦ over—not in—hot water:

> 2  beaten eggs
> 1/4  cup cream
> 1/8  teaspoon salt
> 1/8  teaspoon freshly ground nutmeg
> 1  tablespoon lemon juice

Cook and stir these ingredients until they are thick, then add a little at a time:

> 2  tablespoons butter

Serve at once.

## HOT MAYONNAISE SAUCE

About 1 Cup

See Mayonnaise, 419. If you have mayonnaise on hand but no Béarnaise, try it sometime on steak or fish.
Heat in a double boiler and stir:

> 1  cup Mayonnaise, 419

Add:

> Lemon juice and capers

## SOUFFLÉD MAYONNAISE

Enough for a 3-Pound Fish

See Mayonnaise, 419. For fish or as a masking for broiled tomatoes.
Combine and beat well:

> 1/2  cup Mayonnaise, 419
> 1/4  cup pickle relish
> 2  tablespoons chopped parsley
> 1  tablespoon lemon juice
> 1/4  teaspoon salt
>   A few grains cayenne

Beat until stiff, but not dry:

> 2  egg whites

Fold them into the mayonnaise mixture. Spread the sauce evenly on hot cooked fish or tomatoes. Broil until the sauce is puffed and golden.

## MOUSSELINE SAUCE

**1¼ Cups**

Use with vegetables or fish as a change from Hollandaise.
Just before serving, add:

**½ cup whipped cream**

to:

**1 cup Hollandaise Sauce, 410**

Serve hot or cold.

## CHORON SAUCE

**1¼ Cups**

We have known adults who, understandably enough, used this sauce with as much abandon as a child with a bottle of restaurant catsup.
Prepare:

**1 cup Hollandaise Sauce, 410**

Beat in very slowly:

**¼ cup warm tomato purée, reduced until very thick**

Add:

**(1 to 2 tablespoons chopped parsley)**
**Season to taste**

and serve.

## MALTAISE SAUCE

**About 1 Cup**

Interesting on asparagus.
Add:

**2 to 3 tablespoons orange juice**
**1 teaspoon grated orange rind**

to:

**1 cup Hollandaise Sauce, 410**

## BÉARNAISE SAUCE

**About 1½ Cups**

Heavenly on most broiled red meat, especially beef tenderloin. It is also quite at home with fish and eggs.
Combine in the top of a double boiler:

**¼ cup white wine**
**2 tablespoons tarragon vinegar**
**1 tablespoon finely chopped shallots or onion**
**2 crushed white peppercorns**
**2 sprigs tarragon, chopped**
**1 sprig chervil, finely chopped**
**(1 sprig parsley, minced)**

Cook over direct heat until reduced by half. ♦ If you have used dried tarragon or coarsely chopped onion, strain the mixture. Allow it to cool. Then, beating briskly ♦ over—not in—hot water, add alternately a little at a time and beat steadily so that they are well combined:

**3 egg yolks**
**¾ cup melted butter**
**Season to taste**

When you have added all the butter, the sauce should have the consistency of Hollandaise.

## ⚘ BLENDER BÉARNAISE SAUCE

**About 1 Cup**

♦ Do not make in a lesser quantity than given here, as there is then not enough heat to cook the eggs properly.
Prepare as in the above recipe:

**The seasoned wine vinegar mixture**

Have ready in your blender the above mixture and:

**3 egg yolks**
**½ teaspoon salt**

Heat to the bubbling stage but do not brown:

**³/₄ cup butter**

Cover container and turn motor on "High." After 3 seconds, remove lid and pour the butter over the eggs in a steady stream. By the time the butter is poured in—about 30 seconds—the sauce should be finished. If not, blend on "High" about 5 seconds longer. Serve at once or keep warm by placing blender container in warm water. This sauce may be frozen and reconstituted over hot water.

## FOYOT SAUCE

Prepare:

**1 cup Bearnaise Sauce, 412**

Add:

**1 teaspoon melted Glace de Viande, 427, or**

**¹/₄ teaspoon concentrated meat extract**

Serve with grilled meats, chicken and eggs.

## NEWBURG SAUCE

**I.**

**About 1 Cup**

Melt in the top of a double boiler:

**¹/₂ cup Lobster Butter, 399**

Add and cook gently until translucent:

**1 teaspoon finely chopped shallots or mild onions**

Add and continue to cook about 3 minutes:

**¹/₄ cup sherry or Madeira**

Into:

**1 cup cream**

beat:

**3 egg yolks**

Add the two mixtures, stirring constantly until the sauce thickens. Use at once.

**II.** To turn this sauce a seductive pink, add:

**1 tablespoon tomato paste**

**(1 tablespoon brandy)**

## ABOUT COLD SAVORY SAUCES

These are salad and fruit dressings of two very different types, and there is a widely cherished notion that those in the first category—the French-dressing type, or vinaigrettes, as opposed to those based on the mayonnaise principle—are virtually noncaloric. The fact is that although a salad is in itself an unimpeachable slenderizer, a salad dressing most definitely is not. Commercial mayonnaise must by law consist of 65% fat, but the fat content even of commercial French dressings runs about 35 to 40%; and these amounts are almost always exceeded by their homemade counterparts. Whether simple or rich and complex, salad dressings, with the rarest exceptions, should never repeat in their composition the materials they grace. Please read About Tossed Salads, 46, About Oils, (II, 202), and About Vinegar, (II, 177). For heavier dressings, see About Dips, (II, 101).

## FRENCH DRESSING OR SAUCE VINAIGRETTE

**About 1 Cup**

This dressing is best made just before use and can become part of the salad-making if you like. See About Tossed Salads, 46. The classic proportions are 3 to 4 parts of oil to 1 part lemon juice, lime juice or vinegar, and salt and pepper to taste. However, you may find it satisfactory—and less caloric—to use a dry red wine instead of vinegar, wholly or in part: since the wine is less tart, the amount of oil may be substantially reduced. Many other condiments are often added to the time-honored ingredients in the recipe, including Worcestershire sauce, chili sauce, chutney, Roquefort cheese, spices, sweet and sour cream and, of course, herbs and garlic. Garlic cloves and herbs should be removed after 24 hours.

Place in the bottom of a jar:

<sub>1</sub>/2 teaspoon salt
<sup>1</sup>/8 teaspoon freshly ground pepper
<sup>1</sup>/4 cup vinegar or lemon juice
+<sup>1</sup>/4 to <sup>1</sup>/2 teaspoon prepared mustard

Lid and shake jar until these ingredients are blended. Add gradually, shaking between additions:

<sup>3</sup>/4 cup olive or walnut oil

If made in advance, cover jar and refrigerate. Shake well before using.

## HERBED FRENCH DRESSING

### About <sup>1</sup>/2 Cup

◗ Fresh herbs should be added only when the sauce is to be used at once, because they become strong and unpleasant if left in the oil for any length of time. This is also true for grated onions and capers.

Prepare and place in a jar with a screw top:

<sup>1</sup>/2 cup French Dressing, 413

using tarragon vinegar. Add:

<sup>1</sup>/2 teaspoon dry mustard
<sup>3</sup>/4 teaspoon each of the following fresh herbs: basil, thyme, sweet marjoram and chervil
<sup>1</sup>/4 teaspoon salt
<sup>1</sup>/8 teaspoon pepper

Lid and shake well and serve promptly.

## CHIFFONADE DRESSING

### About 1<sup>1</sup>/2 Cups

Prepare:

<sup>1</sup>/2 cup French Dressing, 413

Add to it:

2 chopped hard-cooked eggs
2 tablespoons julienned cooked beetroot
2 tablespoons chopped parsley
2 teaspoons chopped chives
1 teaspoon chopped onion

## SPINACH OR WATERCRESS DRESSING

### About 2 Cups

Excellent over salad greens or Cucumber Gelatin Salad, 76, and Shrimp or Lobster Mold, 67.

Combine:

2 tablespoons lemon juice
1 tablespoon tarragon vinegar
<sup>1</sup>/2 cup olive oil
1 teaspoon salt
<sup>1</sup>/8 teaspoon pepper

Chop finely and stir in:

2 cups watercress or very young spinach leaves

Use at once.

## ⅄ BLENDER CRESS DRESSING

Blend to a paste in an electric blender:

2 hard-cooked eggs
2 tablespoons olive oil
<sup>3</sup>/4 cup cut watercress, packed lightly

Dilute this paste with:

French Dressing, left

to the consistency you prefer. Use at once.

## LORENZO DRESSING

**About ³/₄ Cup**

For cold meat or fish.
Combine:

    **¹/₂ cup French Dressing, 413**
    **3 tablespoons Chili
    Sauce, (II, 686)**
    **3 tablespoons chopped
    watercress**

## FRENCH DRESSING FOR FRUIT SALAD

**About ¹/₂ Cup**

Prepare:

    **¹/₂ cup French Dressing, 413**

substituting for the vinegar:

    **3 tablespoons grapefruit or
    lemon juice**

## ANCHOVY DRESSING

**About ¹/₂ Cup**

For a leaf lettuce salad.
Prepare:

    **¹/₂ cup French Dressing, 413**

Beat into it:

    **1 tablespoon or more
    anchovy or other fish paste**

## ANCHOVY AND BEET DRESSING

**About 1 Cup**

For endive or crisp leaf lettuce salads.
Place in a jar with a screw top:

    **¹/₂ cup French Dressing, 413**
    **3 or 4 chopped anchovies**
    **2 small chopped cooked beets**
    **1 chopped hard-cooked egg**

Season the dressing highly.

## SALSA VERDE OR ANCHOVY CAPER SAUCE

**About 1¹/₄ Cups**

To be used with salads and fish.
Prepare:

    **French Dressing, 413**

Soak in it:

    **1 crustless slice white bread
    or 1 small riced boiled
    potato**

Add:

    **¹/₂ cup chopped parsley**
    **1¹/₂ tablespoons capers**
    **2 garlic cloves**
    **3 anchovy fillets or
    ¹/₂ teaspoon anchovy paste**
    **2 tablespoons sugar
    Season to taste**

Any of the following may be added:

    **(Horseradish or chopped
    pickles, green olives or
    green peppers)**

Beat well and serve at once.

## ROQUEFORT OR BLUE CHEESE FRENCH DRESSING

**About ²/₃ Cup**

Prepare:

    **¹/₂ cup French Dressing, 413**

Beat into it:

    **2 tablespoons or more
    crumbled Roquefort or
    blue cheese**

## ⅃ BLENDER ANCHOVY AND ROQUEFORT DRESSING

**About 1¹/₂ Cups**

Place in electric blender and blend
until smooth:

    **²/₃ cup olive or walnut oil**
    **1 can anchovies with oil:
    2 oz.**
    **3 tablespoons vinegar**
    **3 tablespoons lemon juice**
    **¹/₄ teaspoon paprika**

(1 clove garlic)
½ teaspoon prepared mustard
½ teaspoon sugar
½ teaspoon celery salt
A dash of Worcestershire sauce and hot pepper sauce
A 3-inch wedge Roquefort cheese

## FRENCH DRESSING WITH CREAM CHEESE

**About ⅞ Cup**

Serve this dressing over a green salad or one made with vegetables.
Mash with a fork and beat until smooth:

1 package cream cheese: 3 oz.

Beat in:

1 teaspoon finely minced onion
½ teaspoon prepared mustard
1 teaspoon salt
Freshly ground black pepper
2 tablespoons chopped parsley

Beat in gradually:

¼ cup vegetable oil
1½ tablespoons vinegar

## CHUTNEY DRESSING

**About 1 Cup**

Combine in a jar and chill:

1 tablespoon chopped hard-cooked egg
1 tablespoon chopped chutney
¼ teaspoon curry powder
1 tablespoon lemon juice
½ cup olive oil
3 tablespoons vinegar
¼ teaspoon salt
1 teaspoon sugar
A few grains black pepper

Shortly before serving this dressing, beat it well with a fork.

## HONEY DRESSING

**1 Cup**

For fruit salads.
Combine:

½ cup honey
½ cup lime juice
(A pinch of ground ginger)

## ITALIAN DRESSING

**About 1 Cup**

Its pedigree is shaky, this sauce being basically a French dressing with a strongly Neapolitan accent; but in recent years it has become highly popular. Steep 1 hour—no more—in:

⅓ cup white wine vinegar
2 sliced cloves garlic
½ teaspoon oregano
¼ teaspoon basil
¼ teaspoon dill
(¼ teaspoon fennel)

Strain the above mixture into:

⅔ cup olive or walnut oil
1½ teaspoons lemon juice

Chill. Shake well before using.

## AVOCADO DRESSING

### I.

**About ¾ Cup**

Great for sliced tomatoes.
Peel and mash:

½ avocado

Add gradually:

½ cup French Dressing, 413

and beat until smooth. Use immediately.

**II.** Use this variant as a heavy dressing or as a filling for tomatoes, cucumbers, celery or endive. See Salads, 42, and Hors d'Oeuvre, (II, 81).
Mash:

A ripe avocado

with:

Lemon juice or vinegar

and:

Season to taste

## HORSERADISH DRESSING

About 1/2 Cup

Prepare:

1/2 cup French Dressing, 413

Beat into it:

1 tablespoon or more fresh or
prepared horseradish

## CELERY SEED DRESSING

About 2 Cups

Add to fruit salad just before serving. This dressing may be made with an electric ⚙ blender or mixer. Constant beating, in any case, is a prerequisite. Combine:

1/2 cup sugar
1 teaspoon dry mustard
1 teaspoon salt
1 to 2 teaspoons celery seed

Add:

1 tablespoon grated onion

Gradually add, beating constantly:

1 cup vegetable oil
1/3 cup vinegar

Garnish with:

(A few finely cut sprigs
lemon thyme)

## LOW-CALORIE FRENCH DRESSING

About 1/2 Cup

No, it isn't a special treat, but it may be eaten by the bulging with a clear conscience.

Soak:

1 teaspoon gelatin

in:

1 tablespoon cold water or
tomato juice

Dissolve it in:

1/4 cup boiling water

Add:

1 tablespoon sugar
1/2 teaspoon salt

Cool this mixture. Add:

1 teaspoon grated lemon rind
1/4 cup lemon juice
1/8 teaspoon prepared mustard
1/4 teaspoon paprika
A few grains cayenne
1/8 teaspoon pepper
1/4 teaspoon onion juice
(1/8 teaspoon curry powder)

Shake the dressing. Chill it. Before serving, beat well with a wire beater. Add, if you wish:

(2 tablespoons minced
parsley)
(1 tablespoon minced chives)

## SWEET-SOUR LOW-CALORIE DRESSING

1 Cup

For a green salad.

Combine:

1/3 cup lemon juice
2/3 cup water
1 teaspoon sugar
1/4 teaspoon salt

## CHINESE LOW-CALORIE DRESSING COCKAIGNE

About 1/2 Cup

Good on sliced cucumber and tomato.

Combine:

4 tablespoons lemon or lime
juice
1/4 cup condensed bouillon or
reduced stock
2 tablespoons soy sauce
1/2 to 1 teaspoon sugar
(1 teaspoon grated fresh
gingerroot)

## LOW-CALORIE SALAD DRESSING WITH TOMATO

### I.

**About 1¼ Cups**

Combine in a glass jar:

1 cup tomato juice
2 tablespoons tarragon vinegar
1 teaspoon Worcestershire sauce
1 teaspoon onion juice
½ teaspoon salt
½ teaspoon fresh dill
½ teaspoon fresh basil

Beat into the above ingredients:

**Yolks of 2 hard-cooked eggs**

Shake well after making and before using. Chill.

### II.

**1¼ Cups**

Blend in a saucepan, using a wire whisk:

¼ cup water
2 teaspoons cornstarch

When the paste is smooth, add, beating constantly:

½ cup water

Simmer and stir over low heat until thickened—about 3 minutes. Cool. Add:

2 tablespoons lemon juice
1½ teaspoons sugar
2 tablespoons vegetable oil
1 teaspoon grated horseradish
1¼ teaspoons prepared mustard
1 teaspoon salt
¼ cup Catsup, (II, 686)
½ teaspoon paprika
½ teaspoon garlic powder or chili sauce

Beat well. Chill.

## MAYONNAISE

Mayonnaise is at its best when made by hand. But, with care, we can now abridge the process fairly satisfactorily in an electric mixer or a 🝆 blender. Blender mayonnaise is made more quickly and has greater volume and fluffier texture, but it cannot duplicate the smooth, rich-looking glisten of the hand-beaten product. We believe it is also slightly less adaptable to some mayonnaise variations, such as Mayonnaise Collée, 427. See also Hot Mayonnaise, 411. In making mayonnaise by any method ▶ eggs, oil and bowl or mixer must all be at room temperature, 70°. Warm the oil slightly if it has been refrigerated, rinse your bowl in hot water first and dry it. ▶ Don't try to make mayonnaise if a thunderstorm threatens or is in progress, as it simply will not bind.

Care must be used in ▶ storing all mayonnaise combinations under refrigeration, as they are subject to bacterial activity which may be very toxic without any evidence of spoilage. Cooked foods to be mixed with mayonnaise keep much better and help deter bacteria if they have been marinated in vinegar or lemon juice or are mixed with pickle. But, even if they have this added acid content, they must be kept thoroughly refrigerated. Freezing mayonnaise combinations is chancy, as the spoilage is only arrested, not destroyed, and accelerates when the food is defrosted.

If you have to resort to bottled mayonnaise, beating in 1 to 2 tablespoons good olive oil until all trace of it has disappeared will make it stiffer and heavier and will improve flavor. Sour cream, according to taste, can also do wonders for commercial mayonnaise—if well incorporated. Please note that commercial "Salad Dressing" is not mayonnaise, and the above suggestions will not work if it is used.

## I.

### About 1¼ Cups

Place in a medium-sized bowl and beat with a wire whisk or wooden spoon until lemon-colored:

    2 egg yolks

Beat in:

    ¼ to ½ teaspoon dry mustard
    ½ teaspoon salt
    A few grains cayenne
    ½ teaspoon vinegar or lemon
        juice
    ½ teaspoon confectioners'
        sugar

Beat in, very slowly, ½ teaspoon at a time:

    ½ cup olive oil

The mixture will begin to thicken and emulsify. Now you can relax! Combine in a cup or small pitcher:

    1½ tablespoons vinegar
    2 tablespoons lemon juice

Have ready:

    ½ cup olive, safflower, walnut
        or sesame oil

Alternate the oil ♦ drop by drop, with a few drops of the lemon and vinegar mixture. If the oil is added slowly during constant beating, this will make a good thick sauce. The sauce will break if you have either added your oil too fast toward the end or added too much of it—figure no more than ½ to ¾ cup oil to each large yolk. It may also break if your oil has been cold and your egg yolks warm. Do not despair. Try first stirring in a teaspoon of warm water. If this doesn't work, the mayonnaise can be salvaged by placing another egg yolk in a fresh bowl and adding the curdled sauce to it very, very slowly, beating the mixture all the

while, until it again thickens. If the dressing becomes too heavy, it may be thinned with cream.

## II.

### About 1½ Cups

You may make the above recipe following exactly the same procedure, in the same order, using an electric mixer on medium speed or the speed indicated for whipping cream.

## III. ⅄

### About 1¾ Cups

Blender mayonnaise differs from the first recipe in that it uses a whole egg. If your beating arm is rather weak, we suggest you try this method, as the emulsifying is produced by the action of the blender.

Put in blender container:

    1 egg
    1 teaspoon dry mustard
    1 teaspoon salt
    A dash of cayenne
    1 teaspoon sugar
    ¼ cup olive or vegetable oil

Cover and blend on "High" until thoroughly combined. With blender still running, take off the cover and slowly add:

    ½ cup vegetable oil

and then:

    3 tablespoons lemon juice

until thoroughly blended. Add slowly:

    ½ cup vegetable oil

and blend until thick. You may have to stop and start the blender to stir down the mayonnaise.

## MAYONNAISE GRENACHE

### About 2 Cups

Serve with smoked turkey or smoked tongue.

Combine:

    1 cup Mayonnaise, above
    ½ cup red currant jelly

3 tablespoons grated
    horseradish
1/4 teaspoon salt
1/8 teaspoon freshly ground
    pepper
2 tablespoons dessert sherry
    or Madeira

Fold in:

1/2 cup whipped cream

## HERB MAYONNAISE

**About 1 1/4 Cups**

Combine:

1 cup Mayonnaise, 419

with:

1 pressed clove garlic
1 teaspoon Worcestershire
    sauce

and 1/2 teaspoon of any 3 of the
following:

Chopped basil, chervil, dill,
burnet, tarragon or parsley

## GREEN GODDESS DRESSING

**About 2 Cups**

For fish or shellfish or vegetable
salads.
Combine:

1 cup Mayonnaise, 419
1 minced clove garlic
3 minced anchovy fillets
1/4 cup finely minced chives or
    green onions
1/4 cup minced parsley
1 tablespoon lemon juice
1 tablespoon tarragon
    vinegar
1/2 teaspoon salt
    Ground black pepper
1/2 cup cultured sour cream

## GREEN MAYONNAISE OR
## SAUCE VERTE

**1 Cup**

For cold shellfish or vegetables.
Chop, blanch, 106, 2 minutes and
drain in a sieve:

2 tablespoons parsley
2 tablespoons tarragon,
    fennel or dill
2 tablespoons chives
2 tablespoons spinach or
    finely chopped cucumber
2 tablespoons watercress

Rub through a sieve and combine to
make a paste with:

2 hard-cooked egg yolks

Add to:

1 cup stiff Mayonnaise, 419

## RÉMOULADE SAUCE

**About 1 1/3 Cups**

For cold meat and poultry—also
shellfish, with which it is especially
appropriate.
Combine:

1 cup Mayonnaise, 419
1 tablespoon drained, finely
    chopped cucumber pickle
1 tablespoon drained,
    chopped capers
2 teaspoons French mustard
1 teaspoon finely chopped
    parsley
1/2 teaspoon chopped fresh
    tarragon
1/2 teaspoon chervil
(1/2 teaspoon anchovy paste)

## RUSSIAN DRESSING OR
## RUSSIAN MAYONNAISE

**About 1 3/4 Cups**

Use on arranged salads, eggs and shellfish; or in chicken sandwiches, instead
of butter or a plainer mayonnaise.
Combine:

1 cup Mayonnaise, 419
1 tablespoon grated
    horseradish
(3 tablespoons caviar or
    salmon roe)
(1 teaspoon Worcestershire
    sauce)
¼ cup Chili Sauce, (II, 686),
    or Catsup, (II, 686)
1 teaspoon grated onion

## TARTARE SAUCE

### About 1⅓ Cups

A good old standby for fried fish.
Combine:

1 cup firm Mayonnaise, 419
1 teaspoon French mustard
1 tablespoon finely chopped
    parsley
1 teaspoon minced shallots
1 tablespoon chopped,
    drained sweet pickle
(1 tablespoon chopped,
    drained green olives)
1 finely chopped
    hard-cooked egg
1 tablespoon chopped,
    drained capers
    Season to taste

You may thin the sauce with:

A little wine vinegar or
lemon juice

## THOUSAND ISLAND DRESSING

### About 1½ Cups

Serve over iceberg lettuce wedges,
eggs, etc.
Combine:

1 cup Mayonnaise, 419
¼ cup Chili Sauce, (II, 686),
    or Catsup, (II, 686)
2 tablespoons minced stuffed
    olives
1 tablespoon chopped green
    pepper

1 tablespoon minced onion or
    chives
1 chopped hard-cooked egg
2 teaspoons chopped parsley

## LOW-CALORIE MOCK
## THOUSAND ISLAND DRESSING

### About 2 Cups

Combine in a large screw-top jar:

¾ cup tarragon vinegar
1 cup condensed tomato soup
1 minced garlic clove
    A few grains cayenne
2 tablespoons chopped dill
    pickle
2 tablespoons finely chopped
    celery
2 tablespoons finely chopped
    parsley
1 tablespoon Worcestershire
    sauce
1 teaspoon paprika
1 teaspoon prepared mustard

## ANDALOUSE SAUCE

### 2 Cups

For vegetable salads, cold fish or egg
dishes.
Combine:

2 cups Mayonnaise, 419
1 chopped tomato with seeds
    and juice removed, or
    ½ cup tomato purée
¼ julienned red pimiento

## FRUIT-SALAD MAYONNAISE

### 1½ Cups

Combine:

1 cup Mayonnaise, 419
½ cup pineapple juice
1 teaspoon grated
    orange rind
1 tablespoon orange curaçao

## CREAM OR CHANTILLY MAYONNAISE

**2 Cups**

Serve with fruit salad.
Prepare:

    1 cup Mayonnaise, 419

Shortly before serving, blend in:

    1 cup whipped cream

## CURRY MAYONNAISE

**About 1 Cup**

This dressing makes an interesting binder for a fruit, molded chicken or shellfish salad.
Combine:

    1 cup Mayonnaise, 419
    1/4 teaspoon ginger
    1/2 to 1 teaspoon curry powder
    1 mashed clove garlic
    1 teaspoon honey
    1 tablespoon lime juice

You may add:

    (1 tablespoon chopped
        chutney)
    (1 tablespoon chopped
        kumquats)
    (1 tablespoon blanched
        slivered almonds)

## WATERCRESS SAUCE OR SAUCE AU CRESSON

**About 1 Cup**

Excellent with cold fish dishes.
Combine:

    1/4 cup finely chopped
        watercress
    3/4 cup Mayonnaise, 419
    1 tablespoon lemon juice
        Season to taste

## SAUCE LOUIS

**About 2 Cups**

Especially relished with stuffed artichokes, shrimp or crab. It is the sauce used for Crab Louis, 65.

Combine:

    1 cup Mayonnaise, 419
    1/4 cup heavy cream
    1/4 cup chili sauce
    1 teaspoon Worcestershire
        sauce
    1/4 cup chopped green pepper
    1/4 cup chopped green onion
    2 tablespoons lemon juice
        Season to taste

## HALF-AND-HALF DRESSING

**About 2 1/2 Cups**

Serve on tossed salad, combination salads or hearts of lettuce.
Combine:

    1 cup Mayonnaise, 419
    1 cup French Dressing, 413
    1 minced garlic clove
    1 teaspoon mashed anchovies
    1/2 cup grated Parmesan
        cheese

## SAUCE GRIBICHE OR MAYONNAISE WITH HARD-COOKED EGG

**About 3 Cups**

For fish and cold meat.
Mash in a bowl until smooth:

    3 hard-cooked egg yolks

Add:

    1/2 teaspoon salt
        A dash of pepper
    1 teaspoon Dijon-type
        mustard

Add very gradually and beat constantly:

    1 1/2 cups olive oil
    1/2 cup vinegar

The mixture will thicken. Then stir in:

    3 finely julienned hard-
        cooked egg whites
    1/2 cup mixed finely chopped
        sour pickles and capers,
        with the moisture squeezed
        out

2  **tablespoons finely chopped
mixed parsley, chervil,
tarragon and chives**

## AIOLI OR GARLIC SAUCE

### 1 Cup

Very popular in France, where it is
sometimes known as **Beurre de Pro-
vence**. Serve over fish, cold boiled
potatoes, beet rounds and boiled beef.
Skin, then chop very finely the:

4  **garlic clove sections**

that give the sauce its original name.
Beat in:

2  **egg yolks**
1/8  **teaspoon salt**
(1  **slice dry French bread
without crust, soaked in
milk and wrung out)**

Add, as for mayonnaise, very slowly
and beating constantly:

1  **cup olive oil**

As the sauce thickens, beat in:

1/2  **teaspoon cold water**
1  **teaspoon lemon juice**

In case the sauce fails to thicken,
treat as a defeated Mayonnaise, 419.

## SKORDALIA

### 1 Cup

For soups.
Prepare:

**Aioli Sauce, above**

omitting the optional bread and adding, after the sauce has thickened:

1/4  **cup ground almonds**
1/4  **cup fresh bread crumbs or
1 small riced boiled potato**
3  **teaspoons lemon juice**
2  **tablespoons chopped
parsley**

## LOW-CALORIE MOCK MAYONNAISE

### About 2 1/2 Cups

On the gelatin principle.
Mix:

2  **tablespoons unflavored
gelatin**

in:

1  **tablespoon cold water**

Combine in a saucepan and bring to
a boil:

1/2  **cup herb vinegar**
1  **teaspoon prepared mustard**
1/2  **teaspoon salt**
1/4  **teaspoon white pepper**
3  **teaspoons liquid artificial
sweetener**

Add gelatin to above mixture, stirring
until completely dissolved. Add, continuing to stir:

2  **cups buttermilk**
1  **tablespoon onion flakes**

Cover and refrigerate until set. You
may flavor this dressing with:

(1/4  **cup or more tomato purée)**

## EGGLESS MOCK MAYONNAISE

### About 3/4 Cup

Combine in a mixing bowl:

3  **tablespoons evaporated
milk**
1/4  **teaspoon salt**
1/4  **teaspoon paprika**
1/4  **teaspoon prepared mustard**
**A few grains white pepper**

Beat in gradually:

1/2  **cup vegetable oil**

then:

3 to 4  **teaspoons lemon juice**

Keep covered in refrigerator.

## ROUILLE SAUCE

### About 1 Cup

Strongly flavored, served with fish
soups or bouillabaisse. Pound together

in a bowl or mortar to make a smooth paste:

> 1 blanched, seeded, skinned red pimiento or 1 canned pimiento
> 1 small red chili, boiled until tender, or a dash of hot pepper sauce
> 1/4 cup white bread crumbs soaked in water and squeezed dry
> 2 mashed cloves garlic

Beat in, very slowly, as in Mayonnaise, 419:

> 1/4 cup olive or vegetable oil

Thin the sauce just before serving with:

> 2 to 3 tablespoons of the soup you are serving

Pass with the soup.

## MOCK ROUILLE SAUCE

### About 1 Cup

For fish soups, bland meats and vegetables. Lower in calories than the genuine article. Prepare as on 423:

> Rouille Sauce

omitting the oil and substituting for the soup an equal amount of:

> Canned condensed consommé

## SICILIAN GARNISH

### 6 Servings

For vegetables.
Sauté until golden:

> 1 finely sliced large onion

in:

> 1/4 cup olive oil

Add and cook briefly:

> 1/2 crushed clove garlic

Add:

> 1/4 cup chopped black olives
> 4 mashed anchovy fillets
> A grating of black pepper

Pour over vegetables just before serving and finish off with a grating of:

> Parmesan or Romano cheese

## BOILED SALAD DRESSINGS

Note that the term "boiled," while traditionally used, is inaccurate: "double-boiled" comes closer. Of the three versions, I is the most economical, and more than acceptable for vegetable and potato salads; II is recommended for slaw, tomato salad and aspics; III for fruit salad. Keep all of them refrigerated.

### I.

#### About 1 1/4 Cups

Mix together:

> 1/2 to 1 teaspoon dry mustard
> 1 to 2 tablespoons sugar
> 1/2 teaspoon salt
> 2 tablespoons flour
> 1/4 teaspoon paprika

in:

> 1/2 cup cold water

Beat in the top of a double boiler:

> 1 whole egg or 2 yolks
> 1/4 cup vinegar

Add the above ingredients. Cook and stir the dressing ▶ over—not in—boiling water until thick and smooth. Add:

> 2 tablespoons butter

Chill the dressing. It may be thinned with:

> Sweet or cultured sour cream

### II.

#### About 1 1/2 Cups

Beat in the top of a double boiler:

> 2 egg yolks
> 2 teaspoons sugar
> 1 tablespoon melted butter
> 2/3 cup milk
> 1/4 cup vinegar

2  teaspoons salt
   A few grains cayenne
1  teaspoon dry mustard

Dissolve:

2  teaspoons cornstarch

in:

1/3  cup milk

Add it to the ingredients in the double boiler. Cook and stir the dressing ♦ over—not in—boiling water until thick. Cool it. You may add chopped parsley, chives or other herbs, celery or dill seeds, etc. Fold the sauce into:

2  stiffly beaten egg whites

## III.

### About 1 1/4 Cups

Beat in the top of a double boiler:

1  teaspoon salt
1/3  teaspoon paprika
1/4  to 1/2 cup sugar
2  tablespoons melted butter
6  tablespoons cream
3  eggs
(1/2  teaspoon prepared
   mustard)

Stir and cook the dressing ♦ over—not in—boiling water until thick. Add slowly:

6  tablespoons lemon juice

The dressing may be thinned with:

Fruit juice or cream

## ROQUEFORT SOUR CREAM DRESSING

### About 1 1/2 Cups

Combine in a bowl or ⅄ blender:

1/4  lb. Roquefort or blue
   cheese
1  tablespoon vinegar
1  tablespoon onions or chives
1  cup cultured sour cream

## SOUR CREAM DRESSING FOR VEGETABLE SALAD

### About 1 Cup

Beat until smooth:

1  cup thick cultured sour
   cream

Add to it:

1  teaspoon grated onion or
   fresh onion juice
1  teaspoon celery or dill seed
1/2  teaspoon salt
   A fresh grating of white
   pepper
(2  tablespoons chopped green
   or sweet red pepper)

## CREAM CHEESE DRESSING FOR FRUIT SALAD

### About 1 1/4 Cups

Mash with a fork and beat until smooth:

1  package cream cheese:
   3 oz.

Beat in slowly:

1  tablespoon lemon juice
2  tablespoons currant jelly
3/4  cup cream

Chill the dressing 1 hour or more before serving.

## CURRY DRESSING FOR FRUIT SALAD

### About 1 Cup

Combine:

2  tablespoons mild vinegar
1  tablespoon lemon juice
1/4  to 1/2 teaspoon curry
   powder
1  teaspoon sugar

Stir in:

1  cup cultured sour cream

See also Curry Mayonnaise, 419.

## YOGURT DRESSING

Yogurt, (II, 189), simple and unadorned, is excellent on honeydew and cantaloupe melon balls in a lettuce cup. Try it, too, with other fresh fruits or over crisp salad greens on hot summer days. Good for dieters, too.

## LOW-CALORIE YOGURT AND CUCUMBER DRESSING

**About 1½ Cups**

For salads.

⅄ Blend:

**1 large peeled seeded cucumber**

Fold in:

**1 cup Yogurt, (II, 189)**
**Salt and pepper to taste**
**Chopped fresh herbs**

## ABOUT GLAZES AND GLAÇAGE

These terms are among the trickiest in the cooking vocabulary. However, take heart: we have postponed the explanation of sweet glazes—by all odds the more confusing—to Desserts, Icings, Pastries, Ice Creams, Fruits and Candies. We shall deal here only with the somewhat simpler topic of savory glazes: those nonsweet maskings and coatings which impart so much color and glamor to meats, fish, salads and vegetables.

Savory glazing—particularly with meats and vegetables—can have, as we have warned it might, several connotations. Before sorting them out, we may as well remind you of "deglazing," which has already been described in this chapter, 381–382. The fat-free juices extracted in this effortless way from sautéed or braised foods, or those prepared à l'étouffée, 102, may be used just as they are, reduced, or as the liquid in roux-based sauces. But meats may be glazed also by the use of Glace de Viande, or Meat Glaze, described on 427—a substance yielded by a lengthy process of reduction. It is potent and delectable, but, like all other powerful essences, it must be used with moderation.

You may "glaze" vegetables by letting the butter in which they have been cooked combine with their reduced juices. This is best done over carefully controlled heat; often a little sugar or honey is added, see 283.

To glaze a sauce may mean to run it under a broiler until it turns golden brown. To glaze a tongue, an hors d'oeuvre or an open-faced sandwich may mean to apply an aspic coating to it. You may coat eggs or fish with a rich White Sauce, 383—a procedure which is then referred to as napping or glazing them.

## TO GLAZE A SAUCE ON A CASSEROLE

Try this only if you have preheated the broiler well. Then run your dish quickly under the heat, until it browns delicately. Should the sauce boil before it colors, it will separate into an oily, watery mass. ➧ Be sure the sauce does not touch the edge of the casserole. Allow an empty area all around for expansion. It is also a wise precaution to protect the casserole by putting it in a pan of hot water. Do not leave it longer than 3 minutes. A perfect all-over brown glaze on a sauce used to coat fish or chicken dishes can be achieved by the following method: Reserve some of a Béchamel or other white sauce and fold in whipped cream, at least 4 tablespoons to 1 cup of sauce. The more whipped cream, the smoother the browning. Put under a hot broiler and watch closely.

## MEAT GLAZE OR GLACE DE VIANDE

What a convenience and delight this substance is if you have the patience to make it.
Prepare:

> **Brown Stock, (II, 171)**

Reduce slowly until the stock forms an even coating on a spoon inserted into it. Remove from heat and cool, at which point the mass solidifies and becomes very glutinous. Covered and refrigerated, a meat glaze will last for several weeks.

Or you may cut it in squares equivalent to 1 tablespoon or more and freeze them in individual packets for use in preparing sauces.

## SPIRIT GLAZE FOR HAM

Combine:

> 1/2 to 1 cup dry red wine
> 1/2 to 1 cup bourbon whisky
> 1 cup brown sugar
> 6 bruised cloves
> 2 tablespoons grated orange peel

Spread on the ham after it is skinned and continue to baste during the last 1/2 hour of cooking.

## CRANBERRY GLAZE FOR FOWL

Combine:

> 1 cup canned cranberry sauce
> 1/2 cup brown sugar
> 2 tablespoons lemon juice

## HONEY GLAZE FOR MEAT OR ONIONS

Combine:

> 1/4 cup honey
> 1/4 cup soy sauce
> 1 teaspoon prepared mustard

## ASPIC GLAZE

Spoon this over the flat surfaces of cold sliced meat or open-faced sandwiches.
Soak:

> 1 tablespoon gelatin

in:

> 1/2 cup meat or vegetable stock

Dissolve it over hot water. Add it to:

> 1 1/2 cups clarified stock

Season mildly. Chill until the glaze thickens somewhat. ◗ Be sure you have the food to be glazed and the tools you are working with well chilled. Apply a thin even coat of aspic which has begun to jell. Chill the food. Repeat, if needed, with a second layer and chill again.

## MAYONNAISE COLLÉE OR GELATIN MAYONNAISE

This coating, also known as **Mayonnaise Chaud-Froid,** is ordinarily used to coat or mask aspics, cold fish, meat or fowl dishes. But if you make it fairly stiff, it can be piped through a pastry tube, and you can achieve the same rococo flights of fancy as when icing a wedding cake. You may also use delicately tinted Mayonnaise Collée, made from Green Mayonnaise, 420, but please avoid highly colored low-relief effects, which look unappetizingly artificial. Note that this stiffened mayonnaise serves much the same purpose as the Béchamel-based Chaud-Froid Sauce, 428, but it does not hold well or long, for the

heavy oil content may cause oozing.
♦ The dish you wish to coat should be
well chilled and dry.

**I.** Soak:

**1¹/₂ to 2 teaspoons gelatin**

in:

**1¹/₂ to 2 tablespoons water**

Beat this mixture into:

**1 cup heavy Mayonnaise, 419**

To color the mayonnaise pink, you
may add:

**(Tomato purée or Lobster
Butter, 399)**

To color it green:

**(Spinach purée)**

**II.** Or beat:

**¹/₄ cup Aspic Glaze, 427**

into:

**1 cup Mayonnaise, 419**

The Aspic Glaze should be at about
70°—tepid and still liquid. Once it
has begun to jell, it will not incorporate with the mayonnaise properly.
Spread the mayonnaise as you would
frosting, with firm strokes of a spatula,
working quickly, for it tends to congeal even at room temperature. Chill
the dish, then decorate as described
below. After the decorations have
also set, place the whole dish on a
rack with a platter under it and glaze
it with aspic glaze, which should be
about the consistency of thick syrup.
Your food must be very cold, so that
the aspic sets almost at the moment
of contact. Use a ladle which holds
about 1 cup glaze and pour it on with
the motion illustrated for Petits
Fours, (II, 447), giving the whole
dish two or three coats, which should
be perfectly smooth, with no streaks
or lumps. The aspic which has fallen
through the rack onto the platter may
be reused, after straining, for the second and third coats.

## SAUCE CHAUD-FROID

Chaud-Froid is so called because it
begins as a heated sauce and is served
as a cold one. It differs from Mayonnaise Collée in emphasizing the flavor
of the dish to which it is applied, since
it is made with the selfsame stock.
Chaud-Froid is often used to coat
whole cooked chickens, ham or veal
roasts, fish or other cold buffet items.
Prepare:

**2 cups Béchamel Sauce,
383–384, slightly
overseasoned**

substituting for the milk Light Stock
or Fumet, (II, 171–172)—according
to the dish you intend to mask.
Chaud-Froid may also be made with
a Brown Sauce, 391, for meats or
chicken. Many people find the dark
color more appetizing. Add:

**2 tablespoons gelatin**

softened in:

**3 or 4 tablespoons stock**

again using the appropriate flavor for
the dish. Stir constantly over medium
heat until thoroughly combined. Remove from heat and cool, stirring
from time to time to keep a skin from
forming. ♦ When cool enough to coat
a spoon, but not set, ladle it over the
cold chicken or fish in the manner described above. Chill to set. The dish
may need more than one coat of the
sauce. Decorate and glaze.

## QUICK PINK CHAUD-FROID

**1¹/₂ Cups**

Especially good as a sauce or glaze
for fish.

Combine, stir, then chill:

**1 cup mayonnaise**

**¹/₂ cup catsup**

**1¹/₂ tablespoons lemon juice
A few drops hot pepper
sauce
Salt to taste**

## ABOUT DECORATIONS FOR CHAUD-FROID

Decorations on dishes masked with Sauce Chaud-Froid or Mayonnaise Collée can be as fanciful as you wish. And professional chefs achieve masterful effects. With a little practice, you can produce the same elegantly curving sprays of flowers, leaves and stems, using as basic material leeks, chives, eggplant skin or green peppers. To make them pliable, they must be blanched about 3 minutes in salted water, then cooled immediately on crushed ice to retain color. Chives form the stems, and leeks, etc., can be cut into leaf shapes—freehand or with the fancy cutters shown on 54.

Lemon rind, carrot and red pepper, blanched as above, can be used for flower petals—or paper-thin slices of ham. Other materials suitable for decoration are: truffles or black olives—you can use the skins of ripe olives as a truffle substitute; pickles; hard-cooked eggs and grapes; parsley and other herbs, blanched 1 minute; peas, capers and wilted cucumber slices.

These decorations are first dipped in clear Aspic Glaze, 427, then applied to the dish to be ornamented as described on 428. If they slip after the first application of clear glaze, replace them carefully with tweezers. If the decorating proves slow, be sure to chill periodically so that the Chaud-Froid does not darken.

Chaud-Froids are often garnished with aspic jelly, chopped or cut in fancy shapes. For Chaud-Froid poultry dishes, decorate the platter with foie-gras balls rolled in chopped nuts or Truffles, 331. Lemon wedges sprinkled with finely chopped parsley and other fancy lemon shapes are shown on (II, 252). To garnish with hard-cooked eggs, see 212.

## LOW-FAT TOFU DRESSING

**About 1 Cup**

This base makes a fine medium for several seasonings—add pickles, nuts, raisins or various herbs and spices. Perishable! Use within one or two days.

⅄ Purée in a blender:
  ⅔ **cup drained Tofu, (II, 192)**
  3 **tablespoons lemon juice or wine vinegar**
  3 **to 4 tablespoons oil or olive oil**
  ½ **teaspoon salt or 2 teaspoons soy sauce**
  **Pepper**

# STUFFINGS AND FORCEMEAT

"No more turkey," announced the little boy at the Thanksgiving dinner table, "but I'd like another helping of that bread he ate." Not all stuffings are made of bread; but all, if delicately and interestingly put together, are quite delicious enough to lure a budding gourmet away from even the most tradition-hallowed main dish. Some of the "makings," which may include those shown above, are celery, spices, herbs, oysters, giblets, sausage, mushrooms, olives, nuts and fruits, as well as the essential members of the onion family. They enrich the bread crumbs, rice, chestnuts and other cereals that bind stuffings, dressings and **farces** together.

Many foreign and old-fashioned stuffing recipes call for bread soaked in a liquid and then pressed before using. We find that most commercial American breads are already so soft in texture that soaking produces too pasty a dressing. For best results we recommend day-old bread in any case, and, unless otherwise indicated,

the use of homemade white, whole wheat or corn bread.

The quality of the crumbs used is very important, so check page (II, 218) to differentiate between fresh and dry. ◗ Never grind bread, as the stuffing will be too compact. It is important, too, ◗ to stuff food just before cooking; ◗ to handle stuffings lightly so as not to compact them; and ◗ to allow space when stuffing, so the mixture can swell and stay light. Should there be extra dressing that does not fit the cavity of fish, fowl or roast, cook it separately in a greased baking dish.

A useful rule of thumb in judging the amount of stuffing needed is ◗ to allow ½ cup of stuffing for each pound of bird or fish.

◗ Never use raw pork in dressings. Dressings are done when they reach an internal temperature of 165° to 170°.

For stuffings for vegetables, see individual stuffed vegetable recipes and page 284.

Make dressings just before cooking stuffed foods to achieve superior texture, but particularly to ◗ avoid danger from spoilage. If made in advance, stuffings should be refrigerated separately from the meat, fowl or fish. To take off the chill, remove the dressing from the refrigerator about 20 minutes before stuffing and cooking. Remember too ◗ to allow extra cooking time for stuffed food, see for fish, 476, for meat, 430, for poultry and game, 512. Should there be any stuffing left after serving, remove it promptly from the cavity of the meat, fish or fowl and refrigerate it separately.

## BREAD DRESSING WITH MUSHROOMS, OYSTERS, NUTS, GIBLETS, ETC.

### About 5 Cups

There are no set proportions for ingredients in bread dressing. It should be palatable, light and slightly moist, well flavored but bland. Chopped green peppers, nutmeats, sautéed mushrooms and drained or slightly sautéed oysters may be added to it. Stock or oyster liquor may be substituted for milk.

Chop:

**Giblets**

Melt:

1/4 **cup butter**

Add and sauté about 2 minutes:

(2 **tablespoons or more chopped onion**)

and the chopped giblets. Combine these ingredients with:

4 **cups crustless day-old or slightly toasted, diced white, whole wheat or corn bread crumbs**

1/4 **cup chopped parsley**

1/4 **to 1 cup chopped celery**

1 **teaspoon crushed dried tarragon or basil**

3/4 **teaspoon salt**

1/2 **teaspoon paprika**

1/8 **teaspoon nutmeg**

**Milk, stock or melted butter to moisten the dressing very lightly**

(2 **or 3 eggs**)

You may add:

1 1/2 **cups nutmeats: Brazil, pine, pecan or walnut**

and one of the following:

1 **cup browned sausage meat**

1 **cup or more sliced mushrooms, sautéed with onion**

1 **cup chopped or whole drained oysters**

1 **cup chopped or whole soft-shell clams**

1 **cup cooked chopped shrimp**

## DRY DRESSING

### About 5 Cups

This name was given by our cook, Sarah Brown, to a dressing she frequently made, which is by no means dry when served. Chopped pecans, oysters and olives may be added to it. Make of day-old white or whole wheat bread:

**About 3 1/2 to 4 cups soft bread crumbs, (II, 218)**

Combine with:

**About 1 cup chopped celery**

**About 1/2 cup chopped sautéed onion**

Season with:

**Salt and paprika**

Partly fill chicken or turkey with the dressing.

Melt:

3/4 **to 1 cup butter**

Pour half of it onto the dressing in the cavity. Fill it lightly with the remaining dressing and pour the remaining butter on it. Sew up the opening.

## SHERRY BREAD DRESSING

**1½ Cups**

Soak 10 minutes:

    1 cup bread crumbs, (II, 218)

in:

    ½ cup dry sherry

Wring the wine from the bread. Stir and sauté 3 minutes:

    ¼ cup finely chopped green
        pepper
    ½ cup finely chopped onion

in:

    3 tablespoons butter

Add the bread crumbs and:

    2 teaspoons Chili Sauce,
        (II, 686)


## OYSTER BREAD DRESSING

**2½ Cups**

Enough for a 4-pound fish or the crop of a turkey.

Melt:

    6 tablespoons butter

Sauté in the butter until brown:

    ¼ cup chopped onion

Add:

    1 tablespoon chopped parsley
    2 cups dry bread crumbs,
        (II, 218)
    1 cup drained whole or
        chopped oysters: ½ pint
    ¾ teaspoon salt
    ¼ teaspoon paprika
    2 tablespoons capers
    (½ cup drained chopped
        spinach)


## BREAD DRESSING FOR FISH

**2 Cups**

A fine but plain, unsophisticated dressing.

Combine:

    1½ cups soft bread crumbs,
        (II, 218)
    2 tablespoons chopped onion
    ½ cup chopped celery
    2 tablespoons chopped
        parsley
    1 or 2 beaten eggs

Season these ingredients well with:

    ½ teaspoon salt
    ⅛ teaspoon paprika
    ½ teaspoon dried tarragon or
        dill seed
    2 tablespoons capers
    (¼ teaspoon nutmeg)

Use enough:

    Milk, melted butter or soup
        stock

to barely bind the ingredients.


## GREEN DRESSING FOR FISH OR FOWL

**About 1½ Cups**

This has a tempting pistachio-green color.

Sauté until transparent:

    2 tablespoons chopped
        shallots

in:

    2 tablespoons butter

Cool slightly. Place this in a blender and 🡒 blend to a paste with:

    1 egg
    ½ cup tender celery with
        leaves
    ½ cup parsley tops
    ¼ cup watercress tops
    ½ cup crumbled crustless
        bread
    ½ teaspoon salt
    ⅛ teaspoon dried basil

Blend in with a fork:

    ½ cup pulled crustless bread
        crumbs, (II, 218)
    ¼ cup pistachio nuts, sliced
        water chestnuts or seeded
        peeled grapes

## SEAFOOD DRESSING

For filling fish or for use in Vegetable
Cases, 284.
Combine:

> 1  cup flaked crab meat,
>    drained oysters or mussels
> 2  slightly beaten eggs

Melt:

> 2  tablespoons butter

Sauté in it:

> ½  cup chopped onion
> ¾  cup chopped celery
> 2  slices bacon, minced
> 1  cup fresh bread crumbs

Combine with the seafood.

> **Season to taste**

Add:

> (1 teaspoon Worcestershire
>  sauce, 1 tablespoon dry
>  sherry, ⅛ teaspoon ginger
>  or ½ teaspoon grated
>  lemon rind)

## SAUSAGE DRESSING

**About 2½ Cups**

Heat and stir in a skillet until done:

> ½  cup sausage meat

Drain off the surplus fat. Add:

> ½  cup chopped celery
> 2  cups cracker crumbs or
>    1 cup soft bread crumbs
>    and 1 cup corn bread
>    crumbs
> ¼  teaspoon minced onion
> ¼  teaspoon salt
> ⅛  teaspoon paprika
> (½ cup chopped tart apple)

Moisten the dressing with:

> ½  cup stock or water

## STUFFING FOR CROWN ROAST OF PORK

This stuffing is added for the last
hour of the baking of the roast, 602.

Combine:

> 2½ lb. cooked pork sausage
> ½  cup dry bread crumbs,
>    (II, 218)
> ¼  cup chopped onions
> ½  cup chopped celery

Moisten these ingredients with a very
little:

> **Milk**

Season with:

> **Savory**
> **Paprika**

Fill the crown with this dressing.

## CHESTNUT DRESSING FOR GAME

**About 4 Cups**

Rice:

> 2½ cups Boiled Chestnuts, 313

Combine them with:

> ½  cup melted butter
> 1  teaspoon salt
> ⅛  teaspoon pepper
> ¼  cup cream
> 1  cup dry bread or cracker
>    crumbs
> 2  tablespoons chopped
>    parsley
> ½  cup chopped celery
> (1 tablespoon grated onion or
>  ¼ cup seedless raisins)

You may add, but remember this will
increase the amount:

> (½ cup liver sausage, ¼ cup
>  chopped Chipolata sausage
>  or 2 cups raw or creamed
>  oysters)

## ONION DRESSING

**About 4 Cups**

Prepare:

> 2  cups chopped onions

Drop them into:

> 4  cups boiling salted water

Simmer for 10 minutes. Drain. Mix
the onions and:

3 cups dry bread crumbs,
   (II, 218)
1 beaten egg
¹/₂ cup melted butter
³/₄ teaspoon salt
¹/₈ teaspoon paprika
¹/₂ teaspoon poultry seasoning
(1 cup chopped tart apple or
   ¹/₂ cup sliced olives)

Moisten the mixture slightly with:
   Stock, (II, 171–172)


## ONION AND SAGE DRESSING

### About 4¹/₄ Cups

Prepare:
   Onion Dressing, 433
Add:
   ¹/₄ cup cooked pork sausage
   2 teaspoons chopped fresh
      sage leaves or ³/₄ teaspoon
      dried sage


## FENNEL DRESSING

### About 1 Cup

Brown:
   1 cup bread crumbs, (II, 218)
in:
   1 tablespoon butter
   1 teaspoon Meat Glaze, 427
Cut into julienned strips:
   1 carrot
   1 white base of leek
   2 ribs celery
Add the above to the butter mixture.
Add:
   2 drops garlic juice
and simmer until coated. Add:
   1 sprig of chopped fresh
      fennel
   1 small pinch thyme
   ¹/₄ teaspoon salt
Mix with the crumbs:
   Freshly ground pepper


## APPLE DRESSING

### About 4 Cups

Pare and slice:
   6 cups tart cooking apples
Combine them with:
   1 cup currants or raisins
   (2 tablespoons lemon juice)
You may steam the currants or raisins
in 2 tablespoons of water in the top
of a double boiler 15 minutes before
combining them with the apples.


## APPLE AND PRUNE DRESSING

### About 4¹/₂ Cups

Combine lightly:
   3 cups diced crustless bread
   ¹/₂ cup melted butter or
      drippings
   1 cup diced apples
   ³/₄ cup drained chopped
      cooked prunes
   ¹/₂ cup chopped nutmeats
   1 teaspoon salt
   ¹/₂ teaspoon paprika
   1 tablespoon lemon juice


## APPLE AND ONION DRESSING

### About 12 Cups

Place in boiling water for 5 minutes:
   1 cup raisins
Drain well. Add them to:
   7 cups soft bread crumbs
Melt:
   ³/₄ cup butter
Sauté in it 3 minutes:
   1 cup chopped onions
   1 chopped clove garlic
   1 cup chopped celery
Add these ingredients to the bread
crumbs with:
   3 cups diced tart apple
   ¹/₄ cup finely chopped parsley
   1¹/₂ teaspoons salt
   ¹/₄ teaspoon paprika

## HAM DRESSING FOR TURKEY

### About 7 Cups

Combine:

    1 to 1½ cups ground cooked
      ham

    4 cups soft bread crumbs,
      (II, 218)

    1 cup crushed pineapple

    1 cup plumped golden raisins

    1 cup chopped walnuts

    ¼ to ½ cup honey

## LIVER DRESSING

### About 4 Cups

Chop:

    ½ lb. calf or baby beef liver

Sauté it lightly in:

    1½ tablespoons butter

    (1 tablespoon grated onion)

Combine these ingredients with:

    2 cups soft bread crumbs,
      (II, 218)

    ¾ cup chopped nutmeats

    2 beaten eggs

    ½ cup cream or cream and
      stock

    1 teaspoon salt

    ½ teaspoon paprika

    1½ tablespoons mixed minced
      chives and parsley

    1 teaspoon chopped fresh
      tarragon

    ½ teaspoon lemon juice

    (2 tablespoons dry sherry)

## RICE DRESSING

### About 5 Cups

Mince:

    6 slices bacon

Sauté lightly 5 minutes with:

    3 tablespoons chopped onion

Pour off all but 2 tablespoons of the
fat. Combine the contents of the skillet with:

    4 cups Boiled Rice, 189

    1 cup dry bread crumbs,
      (II, 218)

    1 cup chopped celery

    ¾ teaspoon salt

    ¼ teaspoon pepper

    ⅛ teaspoon sage or nutmeg

    ½ cup milk

    ½ cup cream

    (¼ cup grated cheese)

## WILD RICE DRESSING FOR GAME

### About 3 Cups

Chop:

    Giblets

Bring to the boiling point:

    4 cups water, stock or tomato
      juice

    1 teaspoon salt

Drop the giblets into the water and
simmer about 15 minutes. Remove
giblets from the water and bring it to
a rolling boil. Stir into it:

    1 cup wild rice, 198

▶ Simmer until nearly tender, about
30 minutes.

Melt in a skillet:

    ¼ cup butter

Sauté in it about 3 minutes:

    2 tablespoons chopped
      shallots

    1 tablespoon chopped green
      pepper

    ¼ cup chopped celery

Add the hot drained rice and the
chopped giblets. You may also use
one or two of the following ingredients, but remember that the quantity
of dressing will be increased:

    (1 cup sautéed mushrooms)

    (½ cup chopped ripe or green
      olives)

    (¼ cup tomato paste)

    (½ cup chopped nuts)

    (½ cup sliced water chestnuts)

## RICE DRESSING FOR CORNISH HEN OR PIGEON

**About 4¹/₂ Cups**

Soak 10 minutes:

**¹/₂ cup golden raisins**

in:

**¹/₄ cup cognac**

Drain, reserving cognac, and sauté them in:

**6 tablespoons butter**

Add:

**¹/₄ cup chopped shallots**

Combine with the above and toss lightly:

**¹/₂ teaspoon salt**
**1¹/₂ cups Boiled Rice, 189**
**¹/₄ cup chopped pistachio or pine nuts**
**Grating of fresh nutmeg**

Moisten until just softened:

**2 cups soft bread crumbs**

in:

**1¹/₂ to 2 cups milk**

Add the bread crumbs to this mixture with the drained cognac.


## TANGERINE OR PINEAPPLE RICE DRESSING COCKAIGNE

**2 Cups**

Try this for chicken or squab.
Combine:

**6 chopped ribs pascal celery with leaves**
**¹/₄ cup chopped parsley**
**1 cup dry cooked rice, lightly sautéed in chicken fat or butter**
**Sections and julienned strips of 1 tangerine and some of its rind, or 1 cup drained crushed pineapple**
**¹/₃ cup lightly sautéed shallots**
**¹/₃ cup lightly sautéed mushrooms**

**(¹/₃ cup pine nuts)**
**(2 tablespoons brandy)**


## APRICOT OR PRUNE DRESSING

**About 5 Cups**

Cut into strips:

**1¹/₂ cups cooked apricots or seeded prunes**

Combine with:

**4 cups dry bread crumbs or 3 cups Boiled Rice, 189**
**¹/₄ cup melted butter**
**¹/₂ teaspoon salt**
**¹/₈ teaspoon pepper**
**¹/₂ cup chopped green pepper or celery**

Moisten lightly with:

**Stock or apricot or prune water**


## SWEET POTATO AND SAUSAGE STUFFING

**About 7 Cups**

Sufficient for a 10-pound turkey.
Prepare:

**4 cups Mashed Sweet Potatoes or Yams, 355**

Sauté until thoroughly cooked:

**¹/₂ lb. sausage meat: 1 cup**

Break it up with a fork. Remove it from the pan.
Add to the pan and sauté 3 minutes:

**3 tablespoons chopped onion**
**1 cup chopped celery**

Add the sausage meat, the sweet potatoes and:

**2 cups dry bread crumbs, (II, 218)**
**(3 tablespoons chopped parsley)**
**Season to taste**

Mix these ingredients well.

## SWEET POTATO AND APPLE DRESSING

### About 5 Cups

Prepare:

**Sweet Potatoes and
Fruit, 356**

using apples and replacing the apple
water with light or dark stock.

## CHICKEN FARCE OR FORCEMEAT

**Enough for 3 Six-Pound Chickens**

A gala stuffing for boned chicken or
galantines.

Grind 3 times:

About 3½ lb. raw chicken
meat

3 cups mushrooms

Add to this mixture:

2 cups pistachio nuts

1⅓ cups dry sherry

¼ cup sliced truffles

1 teaspoon grated onion

8 or 9 slightly beaten eggs

1⅓ cups butter, cut in small
dice

1½ tablespoons salt

¼ teaspoon freshly ground
pepper

½ cup canned or Sautéed
Mushrooms, 328

2 tablespoons chopped
parsley

## SAUERKRAUT DRESSING FOR GAME

Mix:

1 quart chopped drained
sauerkraut

with:

1 clove garlic

¼ cup chopped onion

1 tart pared and chopped
apple

(2 tablespoons brown
sugar)

(¼ cup dried currants)

(1 cup chopped water
chestnuts)

(⅛ teaspoon thyme)

Season to taste

# SHELLFISH

Connoisseurs used to dispute as to which stretches of the world's seacoasts provided the best breeding grounds for shellfish and were ready to do battle over the relative merits of oysters and mussels versus lobsters and crabs. Today they worry that the too-efficient factory methods of capture, plus mounting pollution of the oceans, will increasingly deprive them of these high-protein delicacies. We must sidestep most of these controversies in the pages that follow, but hope to clarify the distinctions among lobster, 454, langouste, 455, and langoustine, 455, and between crevettes, 461, and scampi, 455—sneaking in freshwater relatives like crayfish or écrevisses, as well as the snapping turtle and the land-based snail. And we will put our chief emphasis on how to cook so as to retain a just-caught flavor. Details for handling are given in each category.

For ways to serve seafood that exploit their decorative qualities, consider colorful pink and white shrimp impaled against the purplish soft glaze of an eggplant, shown at rear in the chapter heading. Next, to the right, is a large shell heaped with iced stone crab claws; and varied dips in small shells or in glass bowls are shown nearby. Heat scallops or seafood mixtures in beautiful large scallop shells, 449, seen in the center foreground. Alternated in a snail dish on the left are two ways of serving snails: tucked into the shell or nestled in mushroom caps.

If sea treats are to be served raw, they should be properly chilled. For a great variety of delectable small shellfish that may be gathered live along the seashore and eaten on the spot, see About Seaside Tidbits, (II, 98). Keep in mind that commercial shellfish collection is permitted only in areas where waters are unpolluted.

♦ If you collect on your own, be sure the water in the area is safe.

Recipes for mussels, oysters and clams are fairly interchangeable, and exciting dishes may be created by combining mollusks and crustaceans. Seafood is often seasoned with wine. For every 6 servings, allow 2 tablespoons dry sherry, 4 tablespoons white wine or 1 tablespoon brandy. Incidentally, what looks like bits of glass in canned seafoods usually turns out to be "struvite," a harmless crystal. If in doubt, test in a little vinegar; struvite will melt; glass will not.

## SHELLFISH COCKTAILS

Serve these well chilled, preferably in glasses embedded in ice. If serving individually, allow about 1/3 cup seafood per person, with about 1/4 cup sauce. You may pour the sauce over the seafood, present it separately for dipping, or toss the seafood in the sauce and serve it on lettuce, endive or cress. For appropriate sauces, see:

> **Russian Dressing, 420, or**
> **seafood dips and sauces,**
> **(II, 103) and 403**

Serve with these cocktails:

> **Oyster crackers**
> **Cheese crackers**
> **Matzos**
> **Crackers: rye, rice,**
> **seaweed or soy**
> **Garlic bread toast**

## ADDED COLOR AND FLAVOR IN SEAFOOD DISHES

To 3 well-crushed lobster shells and 2 pounds shrimp shells, add 1/2 bottle dry white wine. Reduce by boiling, 380, to half or one-third. A bright red sauce results which, when tepid, can be added with puréed shrimp or lob-

ster to Hollandaise sauce. A few tablespoons of purée of pimiento may also be used to add color.

## ABOUT OYSTERS

These shellfish, edible at any time, are best in flavor when they are not spawning. As southern oysters spawn all during the year, they do not have the fine flavor of northern types and are therefore often served highly condimented. These bivalves have one shallow and one deep shell, and it is in the deeper shell that they are served raw or baked. Some canny diners have been known to ask for them in restaurants on the shallow shell, in the hope of getting them absolutely freshly opened. Oysters in the shell should be alive. If they gape and do not close quickly in handling, discard them, as well as those with broken shells.

"He was a bold man," declared Dean Swift, "that first eat an oyster." In our own prejudiced opinion, once opened, this bivalve must have been found quite irresistible; only the shucking needed hardihood. ♦ To open oysters, provide yourself first with a strainer and a bowl in which to catch the juices. Later you may pour the strained liquor over the oyster before serving it on the bottom half shell—bedded down in coarse salt if served hot or on cracked ice if cold. When preparing oysters in a sauce, add the oyster liquor to it. Now back to the actual opening of the shells. Hold a well-scrubbed oyster, deep shell down, in a folded napkin in the palm of one hand, working over a strainer with a bowl beneath it. Insert the edge of an oyster knife into the hinge of the shells. Turn the knife to pry and lift the upper shell enough to cut through the hinge muscle.

Then run the knife between the shells to open.

Until you develop a knack, shucking is not easy. Should you grow slightly desperate, you may be willing to sacrifice some flavor for convenience. If so, place the oysters in a 400° oven for 5 to 7 minutes, depending on size, drop them briefly into ice water and drain. They should open easily.

However you open an oyster, complete the release of the flesh from the shell by using a knife, and examine each oyster with your fingers to be sure no bit of shell is adhering to it. If you are using the oysters off the shell, drop them into a strainer, reserving the rest of the juice. If the oysters are sandy, you may rinse them in a separate bowl, allowing ½ cup cold water to each quart of shucked oysters. Pour it over the oysters and reserve the water. Before using the oyster liquor and the water mixture in sauces, be sure to strain it through fine muslin to free it from grit. ◗ Before using oysters in any fried or creamed dish, dry them carefully in an absorbent towel.

If oysters have been bought in bulk, already opened, be sure, again, to free them of bits of shell. They should be plump and creamy in color; the liquor clear, not cloudy,

and free from sour or unpleasant odor. If oysters burst during cooking, they have been previously soaked in fresh water to plump them, and their flavor as well as their texture has been ruined. ◗ Allow 1 quart undrained, shucked oysters for 6 servings. It is hard to estimate amounts for oysters on the shell, as they vary in size—6 moderate-sized eastern oysters would equal about 20 of the tiny Olympia West Coast oysters.

◗ To store oysters in the shell, refrigerate at 39°, not directly on ice. Keep dry. Store shucked oysters at the same temperature, covered by their liquor, in a closed container. The container may be set in crushed ice, up to about three-fourths its height. If you received them fresh, oysters may be stored in this way up to 3 days.

For other oyster suggestions, see Hors d'Oeuvre, (II, 100), and Canapés, (II, 78 and 79). For cooked oyster suggestions and oyster cakes, see Lunch Dishes, 264. Champagne is a fine accompaniment.

## OYSTERS ON THE HALF SHELL

**Allow 5 to 6 Oysters per Serving**
◗ Please read About Oysters, 439.
Scrub well, chill and ◗ open just before serving:

**Oysters**
Arrange them in cracked ice on serving plates. You may place in the center a small glass of:

**Cocktail Sauce, 401, or**
**Lorenzo Dressing, 415**
or serve them with:

**Lemon wedges and ground,**
**flavored horseradish**
and:

**Buttered brown bread**

## BROILED OYSTERS

**Allow 6 Oysters per Serving**
◗ Please read About Oysters, 439.
Preheat broiler.
Shuck, drain and dry in a towel:

**Oysters**

Place them on a well-buttered baking sheet. Broil about 3 minutes, until lightly browned, turning once. Serve with:

**Lemon wedges, parsley or Lemon Butter, 397**

## ▤ GRILLED OYSTERS

**Allow 6 Oysters per Serving**
You may grill western oysters—except Olympias—right on the coals without toughening them, but if you have eastern oysters, put them on a piece of foil in which you have punched holes, before placing them on your grill over a bed of coals.

**I.** Put on the foil:

**Scrubbed, unopened oysters in their shells**

Grill until the shells pop. Season and serve with:

**Lemon wedges**
**Melted butter**

**II.** Open:

**Scrubbed oysters**

Sprinkle them with a:

**Gremolata, (II, 253)**

Heat for a few minutes on the grill over moderate coals.

## DEEP-FAT-FRIED OYSTERS

**2 Servings**
◗ Please read About Deep-Fat Frying, 94.
Drain:

**12 large shucked oysters**

Dry them well between towels. Beat together:

**1 egg**
**2 tablespoons water**

Inserting a fork in the tough muscle of the oysters, dip them in the egg, then in:

**Seasoned bread crumbs**

once more in the egg and again in the crumbs. Let them dry on a rack for 30 minutes. Fry them about 4 minutes in deep fat heated to 375°. Serve with:

**Andalouse Sauce, 421,**
**Tartare Sauce, 421, or**
**Sauce Indienne, 388**

## SAUTÉED OYSTERS

**2 Servings**
Bread, as at left for Deep-Fat-Fried Oysters:

**12 large shucked oysters**

When they are dry, sauté them until golden in a combination of:

**3 tablespoons vegetable oil**
**2 tablespoons butter**

Serve at once with:

**Watercress Sauce, 422, or**
**Aurore Sauce, 387**

## BAKED OYSTERS ON THE HALF SHELL

**Allow 6 Oysters per Serving**
Preheat oven to 475°.
Have ready:

**Oysters on the half shell**

Cover each with:

**1 tablespoon sauce as prepared for Creamed Oysters, 442**

Sprinkle them with:

**Bread crumbs**

Bake about 10 minutes or until golden.

## SCALLOPED OYSTERS

### I.

**6 Servings**

Preheat oven to 350°.
Have ready:

> **1 quart shucked oysters in
> their liquor**

and a deep buttered casserole. Mix
together:

> **2 cups coarsely crushed soda
> cracker crumbs**
> **1 cup dry bread crumbs,
> (II, 218)**
> **³/₄ cup melted butter**

Place in the bottom of the casserole a
thin layer of the crumb mixture.
Cover it with half of the oysters. Pour
over the oyster layer half of the following mixture:

> **1 cup cream**

seasoned lightly with:

> **Nutmeg or mace**
> **Salt and pepper**
> **(Celery salt)**

Follow with three-fourths of the remaining crumbs and the rest of the
oysters. Pour the other half of the seasoned cream over the oysters and
cover with the remaining bread
crumbs. Bake 20 to 25 minutes.

### II.

**6 Servings**

Preheat broiler.
Drain and dry, reserving the liquor:

> **1 pint shucked small oysters:
> 2 cups**

Combine:

> **1 cup dry bread or cracker
> crumbs**
> **3 tablespoons melted butter**
> **¹/₄ teaspoon salt**
> **1 teaspoon minced parsley**

Heat to the boiling point:

> **1 cup cream of celery,
> mushroom or chicken soup**

> **The oyster liquor or ¹/₄ cup
> clam juice or water**

or replace 1 tablespoon of the liquor
with:

> **(Catsup)**

Add the oysters. Heat until the edges
begin to curl. Place half the buttered
crumbs in a hot casserole; add the
oyster and soup mixture. Top with
the remaining crumbs. Place the dish
under a broiler until the top is golden
brown.

## CREAMED OYSTERS

**4 Servings**

◗ Please read About Oysters, 439.
Drain and dry:

> **1 pint shucked oysters**

Reserve the liquor. Melt in a saucepan:

> **2 tablespoons butter**

Add and stir until blended:

> **2 tablespoons flour**

Stir in slowly:

> **1 cup oyster liquor, or oyster
> liquor and cream, milk or
> chicken stock**

Add:

> **¹/₂ teaspoon salt**
> **¹/₈ teaspoon paprika or
> cayenne**
> **(¹/₂ to 1 teaspoon curry
> powder)**

When the sauce is smooth and hot,
add the drained oysters. Heat them
to the boiling point, but not above
it. When the oysters are thoroughly
heated, season with:

> **1 teaspoon lemon juice or
> ¹/₂ teaspoon Worcestershire
> sauce**

Serve them at once in:

> **Bread Cases, 236, or patty
> shells, or on hot buttered
> toast**

Sprinkle generously with:

> **Chopped parsley**

## OYSTERS CREAMED WITH CELERY

**4 Servings**

Preheat oven to 350°.
Prepare:

**Creamed Oysters, 442**

Before adding the oysters, thicken the sauce with:

**2 egg yolks**

Place in a baking dish:

**¾ cup peeled, diced white celery**

Cover with the creamed oysters and dust with:

**Parmesan cheese**

Bake until golden, about 15 minutes.

## BAKED CREAMED OYSTERS AND SEAFOOD

**6 Servings**

Do not take these proportions too literally. Change them, add or subtract to suit yourself. It's a grand basic dish with which to work.
Preheat oven to 375°.
Prepare:

**Creamed Oysters, 442**

seasoned with:

**1 tablespoon chopped fresh marjoram**

Add:

**1 cup chopped cooked shrimp, lobster, crab meat, tuna, scallops or leftover fish**

Cover with:

**Au Gratin II or III, (II, 221)**

Bake about 10 minutes.

## OYSTERS IN MUSHROOMS AU GRATIN

### I.

**4 Servings**

Preheat oven to 375°.
Sauté:

**20 large mushroom caps, 329**

in:

**3 tablespoons butter**

Place the mushrooms, cavity side up, in a greased baking dish. Fill them with:

**20 drained shucked medium-sized oysters**

and cover them with:

**1 cup hot White Sauce I, 383**

seasoned with:

**Dry sherry**

Sprinkle the top with:

**Grated Parmesan cheese**

Place the dish in the oven until the top is browned.

### II.

Or proceed as above, omitting the cream sauce and dotting each oyster in its mushroom cap with:

**¼ teaspoon butter**
**A few drops lemon juice**

Bake about 10 minutes, until the oysters are plump. Serve on:

**Creamed Spinach, 359**

## OYSTER RAREBIT

**4 Servings**

Cook in their liquor until plump:

**2 cups shucked oysters:**
**1 pint**

Drain. Keep them warm and reserve the liquor. Cook in a double boiler ▶ over—not in—boiling water, and stir until smooth:

**2 tablespoons butter**
**¼ lb. diced Swiss or Gruyère cheese**
**½ teaspoon salt**
**A few grains cayenne**

Add:

**The oyster liquor: about ¾ cup**

and enough:

**Milk to make 1 cup of liquid**

and:

    **2 beaten egg yolks**

Continue to cook and beat until the sauce thickens. Add the warm oysters and season with:

    **Salt**
    **1 teaspoon Worcestershire sauce**

Serve on:

    **Toast**

Garnish with a sprinkling of:

    **Paprika**


## OYSTERS ROCKEFELLER

        **6 Servings**

Best with oysters in the shell. The dish may also be approximated using bulk oysters in clean shells previously set aside for the purpose.

**I.**

Preheat oven to 475°.

Have ready:

    **36 medium-sized oysters on the half shell**

Put through a food grinder a mixture of:

    **2 cups cooked spinach**
    **1/4 cup chopped onion**
    **1/2 cup dry bread crumbs**
    **2 tablespoons chopped cooked bacon**
    **1 tablespoon parsley**
    **1 teaspoon salt**
    **6 drops hot pepper sauce**

Stir into this mixture:

    **6 tablespoons melted butter**
    **2 teaspoons anisette**

Spread the mixture over the oysters. Embed the filled shells in pans of rock salt to steady them and to protect the seafood from too high heat. Bake about 10 minutes, or until plump; run under broiler to brown. Serve at once.

**II.** A simpler version.

Half-fill a shell with:

    **Creamed Spinach, 359**

Place on spinach:

    **1 large shucked oyster**

Cover with:

    **1 teaspoon chopped parsley**
    **A few drops lemon juice and Worcestershire sauce**
    **A square inch of partly cooked bacon**

Bake as in I.


**III.** Fill half the shell, as above, with:

    **Creamed Spinach, 359**

Place the oyster on the spinach and cover with:

    **1 teaspoon well-seasoned White Sauce I, 383**
    **1 teaspoon grated Parmesan cheese**

Bake as above.


## OYSTERS CASINO

        **4 Servings**

▶ Please read About Oysters, 439.

Preheat oven to 450°.

Prepare:

    **24 oysters on the half shell**

Embed them in pans of rock salt. Cream together:

    **1/2 cup sweet butter**
    **1/3 cup finely chopped shallots**
    **1/4 cup finely chopped parsley**
    **1/4 cup finely chopped green pepper**
    **1/4 cup finely chopped white celery**
    **Juice of 1 lemon**

Put a piece of the butter mixture on each oyster, plus:

    **1/2 teaspoon chopped pimiento**
    **A small square partly cooked bacon**

Bake until the bacon is browned, from 5 to 8 minutes.

## ABOUT MUSSELS

Mussels are sometimes called "the oysters of the poor," which goes to show that poverty can be not only dignified, as some people claim, but for brief periods even endurable. These delicious mollusks do, however, deteriorate rapidly and, if uncooked, may be the cause of infections.

◗ To test mussels for freshness, try to slide the two halves of the shell across each other. If they budge, the shell is probably filled with mud, not mussel. Discard any mussels with broken shells or shells that will not close after placement in the freezer a minute or two. Mussels are distinguished by a beard which is usually clipped off with a scissors just before cooking.

Wash mussels in a colander under running water. Scrub them with a stiff brush and prepare as for clams, right: both fresh and canned mussels may be sandy. Mussels may be steamed, removed from the shell, debearded and served much like oysters or clams; or served with a sauce, shell and all. It is permissible—no doubt because it is necessary—to separate the shells by hand. Gourmets suggest that a half shell be used to spoon up the liquor to the last drop. ◗ For 4 servings allow about 1 quart undrained shucked or 3 quarts unshucked mussels. **Cockles,** (II, 98), and **periwinkles,** (II, 99), may also be cooked as for mussels.

## STEAMED MUSSELS OR MOULES MARINIÈRE

**3 to 4 Servings**

◗ Please read About Mussels, above.
Sauté until golden in:
   **¼ cup butter**
   **6 chopped shallots**

   **1 clove garlic**
Cook in a deep, heavy skillet about 2 minutes:
   **¼ cup dry white wine**
   **⅓ bay leaf**
Add the sautéed shallots and:
   **3 quarts scrubbed, bearded unshucked mussels**
Cook ◗ closely covered over high heat 6 to 8 minutes. Agitate the pan sufficiently during this time to cook the mussels evenly, but ◗ remove from heat the moment the shells open. Pour the mussels, shells and all, into heated bowls. Then pour in the sauce, as is or thickened with:
   **(2 tablespoons fresh bread crumbs or Rémoulade Sauce, 420)**
Serve garnished with:
   **¼ cup chopped parsley**

## BAKED BUTTERED MUSSELS

Preheat oven to 450°.
Place in a large pan:
   **Well-cleaned mussels**
   **2 tablespoons olive oil**
Heat in the oven until the shells open. Do not overcook. Remove the upper shell and beard or fringe. Reserve the liquor. If any has escaped to the pan, strain and add it to the reserved liquor from the shell. Serve the mussels on the lower shell with:
   **Melted butter or melted Garlic Butter, 399**
and the liquor in small cups or glasses. See Steamed Clams, 448.

## ABOUT CLAMS

All clams are sandy, especially surf clams. Before shucking, they should be scrubbed and washed in several waters, then soaked in a cold brine of ⅓ cup salt to 1 gallon of water; and it may even be necessary later to put the cooked clams under cold running water to rid them completely of sand. Clams are sold in the shell or shucked. If in the shell ◗ test to see that they are tightly closed, or, if slightly open, that they close tightly at once upon being touched. ◗ Discard any that float or have broken shells.

◗ Eight quarts of clams in the shell will yield about 1 quart shucked. ◗ Allow about 1 quart of unshucked clams per person for steamed clams, 6 to 8 medium-sized clams if served shucked.

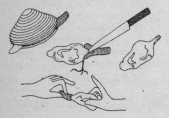

### SOFT-SHELL OR LONGNECK CLAMS

Found mostly north of Cape Cod, these are the preferred East Coast type for eating raw or steamed whole. They are easily opened by running a short sharp knife along the edge of the top shell. Work over a bowl, as for oysters, illustrated on 440, so as to trap the juices. Cut the meat from the bottom shell. Slit the skin of the neck, or siphon, as sketched, and pull off the neck skin. This skin is too tough to eat as it is, but may be chopped or ground and used in chowders or creamed dishes with other clam meat.

### HARD-SHELL CLAMS

These include **butter clams** and **quahogs,** which in turn are called **cherrystones** or **littlenecks.** The **Pacific butter clam** is distinguished from its Atlantic counterpart by its small size—even when adult—and its rarity, but makes up for both in succulence. Two other choice West Coast varieties are the aptly named **razor clam** and the **Pismo.**

The large, strongly flavored hardshells are preferred for chowders, the smaller sizes for eating on the half shell. If in the shell, you may wash them in several waters, then cover with a cold brine of 1/3 cup salt for each gallon of water and sprinkle on the top 1/4 cup cornmeal to every quart clams. Leave them in this bath 3 to—preferably—12 hours. This whitens them, rids them of sand, and causes them to eject the black material in their stomachs. After soaking, wash again in clear water.

Quahogs are difficult to open, but if they are covered 5 minutes with water and then gently picked up, you may be able to insert a knife quickly in the opening. Or, if you are using them in a cooked dish and do not mind a small loss in flavor, you may place them in a pan in a moderate oven until they open. After opening, cut through the muscle holding the shells together. If they have not had a cornmeal bath, open the stomachs with sharp shears and scrape out and discard the contents. Large hardshelled clams have a tough upper portion which may be separated from the tender portion, chopped or ground and used in various dishes, creamed, scalloped, in fritters, chowders, etc., following any of the recipes for oysters, or any of the following clam recipes.

### SURF CLAMS

These may be used in chowders, broth or cocktails, but their sweetness should be counteracted with salt. They are the sandiest of all clams.

For other recipes, see Soups and Chowders, 156–163, or Lunch Dishes, 264.

## ABOUT CLAMBAKES

Whatever the size of your bake, dig your clams the day before. Scrub them well to remove sand. Give them the cornmeal treatment as for hard-shell clams, 446. Leave the clams in a ◖ cool place. Rinse and drain them just before using. A big bake is described in I; a smaller one, often more practical, in II, with amounts proportionately cut.

### ▤ CLAMBAKE

#### I.

20 Servings

Allow:

**200 soft-shell clams
(50 hard-shell clams)**

Start preparations at least 4 hours before you plan to serve. Dig a sand pit about 1 foot deep and 3½ feet across. Line it with smooth round rocks. Have ready a wet tarpaulin larger than the pit area by 1 foot all around, and a few stones to weight the edges. Build a fire over the rock lining using hardwood, and keep feeding it for the next 2½ to 3 hours while the rocks are heating. Gather and wash about 4 bushels of wet rock seaweed. In fact, it is wise to soak the seaweed for at least 45 minutes before use. Have a pail of sea water at hand. Partially husk about:

**4 dozen ears sweet corn**

Do not pull them quite clean but leave on the last layer or two of husks. Rip these back far enough to remove the silk. Then replace them, so the kernels are fully protected. Reserve the pulled husks. Quarter:

**5 broiling chickens**

Have ready:

**10 sweet potatoes
(20 frankfurters)**

You may wrap the chicken pieces in cheesecloth or divide the food into 20 individual cheesecloth-wrapped servings, so that each person's food can later be removed as one unit. Scrub:

**Twenty 1½-lb. lobsters or
5 pecks soft-shell crabs**

Now you are ready to arrange for the "bake." Rake the embers free of the hot stones, remove them from the pit and line it with the wet seaweed. The lining should be about 6 inches deep. Put over it, if you wish, a piece of chicken wire. If you haven't wrapped the individual servings in cheese-cloth, now pack the pit in layers. For added flavor, put down first a layer of hard-shell clams, then the frankfurters, if you use them, and after that, in succession, the sweet potatoes, the lobsters or crabs, the chicken, the corn and the soft-shell clams. You may also put seaweed between the layers. Cover the layered food with the reserved corn husks and sprinkle the whole with the bucket of sea water. Quickly cover with the wet tarp. ◖ Weight the tarp down well with rocks. The whole should steam ◖ covered, about 1 hour. During the steaming, the tarp will puff up, which is a sign of a satisfactory "bake." To test, lift the tarp carefully at one corner ◖ so as not to get sand into the pit, and see if the clams have opened. If so, the whole feast should be cooked just to the right point. Have handy plenty of towels and:

**Melted butter**

Serve with the bake:

**Beer or ale**

and afterward:

**Watermelon
Coffee**

## II.

**8 Servings**

A more domesticated bake in a new wash boiler or lard can on a stove or outdoor grill.

Soak for 45 minutes and remove sand from seaweed in several rinsings. Line the bottom of the boiler with a 4-inch layer of the seaweed. Add about:

> 1 quart water

When water boils, add:

> 8 foil-wrapped potatoes
> 2 cut-up broiler chickens
>   wrapped in cheesecloth

◗ Cover boiler and cook gently 30 minutes. Add:

> 8 well-scrubbed 1½-lb.
>   lobsters

Cover and cook 8 minutes more, then place on top of the lobsters:

> 8 shucked foil-wrapped ears
>   of corn

Cook 10 minutes, still covered, and add:

> 48 well-scrubbed soft-shell
>   clams

Cover and steam until the clams open, from 5 to 10 minutes longer. In serving, use:

> Melted butter

## STEAMED SOFT-SHELL CLAMS WITH BROTH

**Allow 7 to 9 Medium-Sized Unshucked Clams per Serving**

Scrub thoroughly with a brush and wash in several waters:

> Soft-shell clams

Place them close together in the top of a steamer, as sketched on 281, or on a rack in a stock pot with a spigot, as shown on (II, 169). Place in the bottom of the steamer or stock pot:

> ½ inch water

Cover the kettle closely. Steam the clams over moderate heat until they

open, but no longer—5 to 10 minutes. Overcooking makes clams tough. Place them in individual soup bowls. Serve each bowl garnished with:

> Lemon wedges

and accompanied by a small dish of:

> Melted butter

The broth is served in cups along with the clams or used for clam juice cocktail later. ◗ To eat clams, pick them up from the shell by the neck with the fingers, dip into broth to remove possible sand, then into butter. All of the clam except the neck sheath is edible. The broth is delicious to drink, but, to avoid any residue of sand, don't entirely drain the cup. To prepare clam broth separately, see 157.

## BAKED SOFT-SHELL CLAMS

**4 Servings**

Preheat oven to 425°.

Scrub with a brush and wash in several waters:

> 36 soft-shell clams

To keep them steady, place them in a pan on a bed of rock salt or crumpled foil. Bake about 15 minutes until the shells open. Remove the top shell carefully to avoid spilling the juices. Serve on individual plates with:

> A Seasoned Butter, 396, or
>   Sour Cream Horseradish
>   Dressing, 408

and garnish with:

> Lemon wedges

## CLAMS BROILED ON THE HALF SHELL

**Allow 6 to 8 Medium-Sized Clams per Person**

Preheat broiler.

Place on an ovenproof dish in which foil has been crumpled to keep shells steady:

**Cherrystone clams on the
half shell**

Cover each clam with:

**A dash of Worcestershire
sauce**

**A square of bacon**

Broil the clams until the bacon is done.

## FRIED CLAMS

**Allow 6 to 8 Medium-Sized Clams
per Person**

◗ Please read About Clams, 445.

Shuck and wash well in a colander
under running water:

**Soft-shell clams**

Dry them between towels. Cut away
the black skin of the neck or siphon.
Dip the clams in a:

**Bound Breading, (II, 220)**

Sauté until golden in a combination of:

**3  parts vegetable oil**

**2  parts butter**

Serve with:

**Tartare Sauce, 421, Curry
Sauce, 390, or Hot Mustard
Sauce, 390**

## ABOUT SCALLOPS

These beautiful mollusks known on
menus as Coquilles St. Jacques are
emblematic of the pilgrims who visited the shrine of St. James of Com-
postella. They ate the mollusks as
penance—surely not a rigorous one—
and afterward fastened the cockle
shells to their hats. Scallops are also
responsible for the cooking term
"scalloped," which originally meant
seafood creamed, heated and served
in a shell. Scallops available at market are almost never the whole mollusk but are instead the edible sections
of its adductor muscle, which controls its very spectacular movement.

If you do get scallops in the shell,
wash and scrub them thoroughly.
Place in a 300° oven, deep shell
down, until they open. Remove, trim
and wash the hinge muscle. In Europe, both the handsome beanlike
coral and the beard are used, as well
as the meat. The former is treated as
for any roe; the latter is cut up,
sautéed briefly, and then simmered
◗ covered, in white wine 30 minutes.
Many people prefer the small, tender,
creamy pink or tan **bay scallops,**
shown below on the right, to the
larger, firmer, whiter, but also quite
delicious **sea scallops,** shown on the
left. If only the large ones are available, slice them—after cooking—into
3 parts, against the grain, for use in
salads and creamed dishes or sauces.

◗ To test scallops for freshness, see
that they have a sweetish odor. If in
bulk, they should be free of liquid.
For sautéing or broiling, allow about
1/3 pound of sea scallops or 1/4 pound
of bay scallops per serving. Cooked
scallops may be used in any recipe
for fish salads or creamed fish, or
they may be skewered and grilled,
see Kebabs, 450. The blandness of
scallops suggests combining them in
sauced dishes with more robustly flavored shellfish like shrimp and crab.
See also seafood suggestions in
Lunch Dishes, 259.

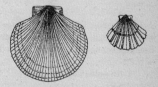

## POACHED SCALLOPS

**6 to 8 Servings**

Poach, 3 to 5 minutes:

**4  cups bay or sea scallops**

in a mixture of enough:

**Water and white wine or
light stock**

to cover, adding to the liquid:

**A bay leaf
3 sprigs parsley**

After poaching, remove herbs, drain
the liquid and reduce it to serve, further seasoned to taste, as a sauce.

## SCALLOPS MEUNIÈRE

**4 Servings**

Dry between towels:

**1 lb. shucked, drained bay or
sea scallops**

Dip them in a:

**Bound Breading, (II, 220)**

Let them dry on a rack about 15 minutes. Sauté one layer deep, using a
large heavy skillet, in:

**2 tablespoons butter
2 tablespoons vegetable oil**

◗ agitating frequently; about 5 minutes for bay scallops, 8 minutes for
sea scallops. Just before cooking time
is over, sprinkle with:

**Lemon juice
Finely chopped parsley**

Serve with:

**Tomatoes Provençale, 367**

## BAY SCALLOPS FONDU BOURGUIGNONNE

**4 Servings**

◗ Please read about Boeuf Fondu
Bourguignonne, 570, using instead
of beef:

**1 lb. poached bay scallops,
449**

Serve as sauces:

**Sweet-Sour Orange Sauce,
406, replacing game stock
with clam broth; or Aurore
Sauce, 387; or Quick
Creole Sauce, 401**

## ☷ SCALLOP KEBABS

**Allow ¼ Pound Bay or ⅓ Pound
Sea Scallops per Person**

Preheat broiler or grill.

If shucked scallops are large or old,
drop into boiling water and allow
them to stay immersed, but removed
from heat, 1 minute. Drain and dry. If
tender, simply brush:

**Shucked scallops**

with:

**Vegetable oil**

Dip in:

**Fine bread crumbs**

Skewer alternately with:

**1-inch squares of bacon**

Grill over moderate heat 10 minutes
or until golden brown, or broil 4 inches
from the source of heat, turning several times during the cooking period.
Serve with:

**Sauce Dijonnaise, 385, or
Curry Sauce, 390**

and garnish with:

**Lemon wedges
Fried Parsley, 338**

## DEEP-FAT-FRIED SCALLOPS

**6 to 8 Servings**

Wash and pick over:

**1 quart shucked scallops:
about 2 lb.**

Drain. Dry between towels. Season with:

**White pepper
Celery salt**

Dip them in a:

**Bound Breading, (II, 220)**

Fry 2 minutes in deep fat heated
to 385°. Drain on paper toweling.
Serve with:

**Tartare Sauce, 421,
Mousseline Sauce, 412, or a
tomato sauce, 400**

## SCALLOPS IN WINE

**6 to 8 Servings**

Wash well:

**2 lb. shucked scallops**

▶ Simmer them until tender, about 5 minutes, in:

**2 cups dry white wine**

Drain and reserve the liquid. Melt:

**¼ cup butter**

Sauté:

**4 finely chopped shallots**
**24 finely sliced mushroom caps**
**2 tablespoons minced parsley**

Stir in, until blended:

**2 tablespoons flour**

Add the reserved liquid and:

**2 to 4 tablespoons whipping cream**

Add the scallops to the hot ▶ but not boiling sauce. Place in a shallow casserole. Cover with:

**Au Gratin II, (II, 221)**

and run under a broiler until golden brown. For an unusual variation which stretches this recipe to 10 or more servings, add:

**2 cups minced cooked ham**

to the above mixture.

## SCALLOPED SCALLOPS OR SCALLOPS MORNAY

**6 Servings**

Scallops served in the shell are called **St. Jacques,** even when—as might happen in the recipe below—you substitute Creole Sauce, 394, for Mornay. Preheat broiler.

Prepare:

**Mornay Sauce, 384**

Poach:

**3 cups shucked scallops**

in:

**1½ cups dry white wine or Light Stock, (II, 171–172), or Fumet, (II, 173)**

Drain and slice the scallops. Coat each of the deep halves of 12 scallop shells with 1 tablespoon of the Mornay Sauce. You may edge the shell, using a pastry tube or bag, with a decorative rim of:

**(Duchess Potatoes, 353)**

Almost fill the shell with the sliced scallops. Coat each shell, staying within the rim of the potatoes, with:

**Mornay Sauce**

Dust the sauce coating with:

**Grated Parmesan or Gruyère cheese**

Run under a broiler until the sauce is lightly browned. Serve at once.

## ABOUT ABALONE

The foot of this delicious shellfish—contraband if shipped from California—comes to our markets canned or frozen from Mexico and Japan, shelled, pounded and ready to cook. If you get it in the shell, remove the edible portion by running a knife between the shell and the meat. Trim off the dark portion. Abalone, like inkfish, needs prodigious pounding to tenderize it, if it has died in a state of tension. Leave it whole or cut it in ¼-inch strips for pounding with an even, not too hard, motion. The meat is ready to cook when it looks like Dali's limp watch. ▶ For steaks, slice against the grain. Bread it if you like in dry crumbs or in a Bound Breading, (II, 220), and sauté. Or you may "boil," 479, as for any fish. Beat and chop abalone for chowder or for Fritters, (II, 152). Allow 1 pound for 2 to 3 servings.

## SAUTÉED ABALONE

**2 to 3 Servings**

Cut into ⅜-inch-thick steaks across the grain and pound:

**1 lb. abalone**

Dip in a:

**Bound Breading, (II, 220)**

Melt in a heavy skillet:

**2 tablespoons vegetable oil or clarified butter**

When the fat reaches the point of fragrance, sauté the abalone steaks, allowing 1½ to 2 minutes to each side.

## ABOUT CRABS

Recipes for cooking crab meat apply to almost all species of edible crab, but either the type of crab or the part of the crab from which the meat is taken may make a difference in color, taste and texture. ◗ Crabs must be both alive and lively when cooked. If mucky or slimy, they should be scrubbed. ◗ Freshly cooked crab meat in partially aerated cans must be under constant refrigeration until used. It should have no ammonialike odor. The completely sealed canned crab meats, Japanese and Korean, are all nonperishable until the cans are opened. ◗ For crab dishes made with cooked or canned crab, see 261–262. In using canned meat, be sure to pick it over for small bits of shell and bone.

To prepare crab shells for restuffing, select large, perfect shells and scrub them well with a brush until clean. Place them in a large kettle and cover with hot water. Add one teaspoon baking soda. Cover the kettle closely. Bring to a boil and simmer 20 minutes. Drain, wash and dry. The shells are now ready for refilling.

### BLUE CRABS

These denizens of the Atlantic furnish most of the fresh crab meat in the market. Lump or back-fin meat, taken from the body, is white in color and choice for looks. Flake meat, while less shapely, is also white. Claw meat is brownish, but very choice.

If taken live, blue crabs fall into two classifications: hard-shell and soft-shell, which are prepared and eaten quite differently.

**I.   Hard-shell** crabs designate those caught between their periodic sheddings of carapace, or "lid," when the carapace has hardened. To cook and eat them, see Poached Hard-Shell Crabs, 454. To prepare them for crab meat, first place them upside down in a large bowl and cover with very hot water until no air bubbles rise. Remove large claws at body. Turn the crab on its back and lift the pointed apron at the base away from the body. Shown right, 453, is a female with a wider fringed apron than the male on the left. With a firm hold at the wide end, slowly twist and pull so as to remove the apron and the intestinal vein simultaneously. Discard both. Scrub the crab under cold running water, using a vegetable brush. Grasping the legs in your fist, pull the entire chest section free of the hard carapace. Cut out and discard the feathery lung sections which lie as shown on the soft-shell crab, top. Next to the lungs lies the soft tomalley or liver. Remove the liver from the carapace with a small spoon and put it into a sieve to drain as for oysters, 440, reserving the strained liquid and the tomalley for later use as directed in crab recipes.

With a wooden mallet, lightly crack the crab shells, being careful not to pound any shell bits into the meat. Remove easily accessible meat with a curve-bladed knife, 288. Take each removed leg at the ends and bend it to break at the joint, while pulling the cartilage from the upper leg meat. Cut the lower section of the legs into small pieces and reserve them for a shellfish butter, 399.

**II.** Soft-shell crabs are those freshly molted whose carapace is still tender and flexible. Molting, incidentally, occurs often in a crab's career, but the carapace remains pliable only a few days. Since almost every part of a soft-shell crab is edible, it is usually broiled, breaded and sautéed, or deep-fat-fried, as in the specific recipes, 454.

▶ To prepare soft-shell crabs for cooking, wash them in several waters. Place live crab face-down on a board. Make an incision just back of the eyes and cut out the face. Lift the tapering points on each side of the back shell to remove sandbag and spongy gills, as shown in sketch. Turn crab on its back and with a pointed knife remove the small pointed apron at the lower part of the shell, pulling it, as described on 452 in Hard-Shell Crabs, to release the intestinal vein.

### DUNGENESS AND ROCK CRABS

Both packaged in one grade, combining body and claw meat. The rock crab flesh is brownish. Dungeness is native to the West Coast and is best in $2^1/2$- to 3-pound size.

### KING CRABS

Mostly from Alaskan waters, pinkish in tone, and consisting mainly of leg meat. Slit the underside of the leg shell with a cross-shaped cut before broiling.

### STONE CRABS

From Florida, with pale flesh, and very delicate in texture and flavor. Stone crabs have become so rare that the authorities now insist that when one is caught only one claw may be removed, and the crab must be returned to its habitat, where, hopefully, it will see fit to grow another claw—as crabs are quite capable of doing.

### OYSTER CRABS AND HERMIT CRABS

There are two edible types of miniature crabs. Oyster crabs are crispy $1/2$-inch pinkish "boarders" found living right in the shell with live oysters; they may be eaten raw, sautéed or deep-fat-fried. When deep-fat-fried, several dozen may be served with several dozen fried whitebait, 503, as one portion. Tiny hermit crabs are found in vacated univalve shells and respond to deep-fat frying and sautéing. They should not be eaten raw.

To deep-fat-fry either of these crabs or whitebait, keep them on ice until the last minute. Wash and dry carefully and put into a bag to dust with flour, (II, 219), then in a sieve to bounce off as much flour as possible. Place a few at a time in a frying basket in deep fat heated to 390° and cook only 2 to 3 seconds until crisp.

## DEEP-FAT-FRIED SOFT-SHELL CRABS

**Allow 2 to 3 per Serving**
▶ Please read About Deep-Fat Frying, 94.
Dry between towels:
**Cleaned soft-shell crabs**
Dip them in a:
**Bound Breading, (II, 220)**
Fry 3 to 5 minutes or until golden brown in deep fat heated to 375°. Turn once while frying. Drain on paper toweling. Sprinkle well with:
**Salt and pepper**
Serve at once with:
**Tartare Sauce, 421, or Rémoulade Sauce, 420, with parsley**

## BROILED SOFT-SHELL CRABS

**Allow 2 or 3 per Serving**
Preheat broiler.
Prepare for cooking:
**Soft-shell crabs**
Combine:
**1/4 cup butter**
**2 tablespoons lemon juice**
**A few grains cayenne**
**A small grating of white pepper**
Roll the crabs in the butter mixture, then lightly in:
**Flour**
Place them on the broiling rack 2 inches from the heat. Broil about 10 minutes. Turn once.

## SAUTÉED SOFT-SHELL CRABS

**Allow 2 to 3 per Serving**
To prepare the crabs for cooking, follow the above recipe for:
**Broiled Soft-Shell Crabs**
Sauté in butter or vegetable oil over moderate heat. Place on a platter. Serve with:
**Fried Parsley, 338**

## POACHED OR "BOILED" HARD-SHELL CRABS

Have ready a large pot of:
**Boiling salted water**
Allow for each quart of water:
**1 tablespoon salt**
Handling with a tongs, slide, one at a time, into the water so as not to disturb the boiling:
**Washed hard-shell crabs**
▶ Reduce heat at once to a simmer and cook about 25 minutes more.

To eat hard-shell crabs, open the tail flap on the bellyside and pull it against the carapace, removing both. Sometimes a sharp knife will be necessary to complete this job. Take out and discard the spongy substance under the shell and split the bodies to pick out the meat, discarding the gills, intestines and sandbags. Claw meat can be released with a nutcracker. ▶ From a 5-ounce hard-shell crab you can expect about 1 1/2 ounces of meat. The preparation recommended above is basic. Relax and serve the crabs whole, with a side dish of melted butter and lemon juice. Or choose one of the many recipes using cooked crab meat in Lunch Dishes, 259, and Salads, 65, or indexed under Seafood.

## ABOUT LOBSTERS

The **American** or **Northern lobster,** with its great delicious claw meat, is sketched on 454. It is caught from Maine to the Carolinas. Very similar, but somewhat smaller, is the **European lobster,** which is also found not infrequently along our own more southerly American coasts.

Called crayfish in Australia and New Zealand, this **spiny rock lobster,** or **langouste,** is shipped from Florida, California, Australia, South Africa and the Mediterranean. It has extra-long antennae but no claws; and most of the meat is in the heavy tail, as you can also see on 454.

The Americans and Europeans, when caught, are a mottled dark blue-green, most delicious we think, served hot. The spinys, which usually reach us frozen, may be tough, especially if they weigh over 10 ounces. They vary in color from tan through reddish orange to maroon, with lighter spotting and variable spininess. If fresh they are often preferred in cold dishes.

Still a third kind of lobster, more rarely encountered on this side of the Atlantic because exclusively native to European waters, is the **Norwegian,** a relative of the spinys, known in France as **langoustine,** and famous in Italy as **scampo.**

Of whatever kind, lobsters require about the same cooking time and may be cut and cleaned as shown on 456–457. But as lobster ritual is more complicated in the American type, we will discuss it in further detail, 456.

Among connoisseurs the female lobster is considered finer in flavor. Look for the soft, leathery, finlike appendages on the underside, just where the body and tail meet. In the male, these appendages are bony. In opening the female lobster, you may find a delicious roe or **coral** that reddens in cooking. Use it as a garnish or to color a sauce. The flesh of the male stays firmer when boiled. The greenish substance in both of them is the liver or **tomalley.**

◗ Allow 1/2 large lobster or 1 small lobster per serving. Buy active live lobsters weighing from 1 1/4 to 2 1/2 pounds. Lobsters weighing 3 pounds and over are apt to be coarse and tough. A 2 1/2-pound lobster will yield about 2 cups of cooked meat.

◗ To store live lobsters until ready to use, place them in the refrigerator, but not directly on ice. The claws should be plugged with a small piece of wood and held together with rubber bands. Before cooking, test to make sure your lobsters are active and that the tail snaps back if it is stretched out flat when you pick up the lobster. Make sure, too, that your crustacean is clean. Grasp it firmly at the back and rinse claws, body and back under a faucet.

## POACHED OR "BOILED" LOBSTER

**I.** To poach lobster for hot family-type table service, place in a large heavy cook-pot enough:

　　**Water**

so the lobster will be completely covered when you plunge it in. Allow for each quart of water:

　　**1 tablespoon salt**

Bring water to a rolling boil. Because of splashing, carefully immerse head first:

　　**Lobster**

and allow the water to return to a boil. ◗ Reduce the heat at once and simmer the lobster about 5 minutes for the first pound and about 3 minutes for each additional pound, slightly less time if the lobsters have recently shed and the shells are soft.

Drain. Serve with small bowls filled with a mixture of:

**The juices from the pot or melted butter**
**Lemon wedges**

And provide each person with a finger bowl, a bib and an abundance of napkins. The uninitiated are sometimes balked by the intractable appearance of a lobster at table. They may take comfort from the little cannibal who, threading his way through the jungle one day at his mother's side, saw a strange object flying overhead. "Ma, what's that?" he quavered. "Don't worry, sonny," said Ma. "It's an airplane. Airplanes are pretty much like lobsters. There's an awful lot you have to throw away, but the insides are delicious."

When a whole lobster is served, it lies on the plate with head and tail intact, arched shell up. The claws, detached before serving, rest cracked beside it, drained of excess moisture. Shielded by your lobster bib, you are ready to take the offensive. Pick up the lobster in your fingers, turn it soft side up and arch it until the tailpiece separates from the body, as shown in the upper part of the drawing below. Remove the tail flippers by bending them back until they too crack off.

Now lift the tailpiece downside up, insert the lobster fork at the point where the flippers broke off, and push the meat out through the open end, as shown at the right.

Having freed the tail meat, grasp the chest portion in both hands to release the contents as shown, left. Edible are the small quantity of meat, the greenish tomalley or liver, and the coral or roe, if there is any. Before turning your attention to the finger bowl, break off the legs one at a time, insert the broken end in your mouth and suck out the contents—quietly.

**II.** To cook lobster for salads, hors d'oeuvre or sauced dishes, prepare as for I, using:

**A 2½- to 3-lb. lobster**

Larger ones are apt to be tough. After the cooking period, drain and plunge into cold water to arrest further cooking. When cool, ▶ to remove the meat from the shell, place the lobster on its back. With sharp scissors cut a lengthwise gash in the soft underside as sketched on 459. Draw out the tail meat in one piece. Remove and discard the lady, or sandbag, and the intestinal vein, as well as the spongy lungs, which, while harmless, are tough. Add the red coral, if any, and the green liver, or tomalley, to the lobster meat or reserve it for use in sauces.

If you buy preboiled lobster in the shell, see that the color is bright red and that it has a fresh seashore aroma. ▶ Most important of all—as with the uncooked lobster—the tail, when pulled, should roll back into place under the body. This means the lobster was alive, as it should have been, when cooked.

To remove lobster meat from the large claws, crack them with a nutcracker or a mallet. If you want them in a single piece for garnish, break off the claw at the first joint. Place it on a flat surface, the lighter underside up. Using a mallet, hit the shell at the inner hump. This will crack it so that the meat in the entire larger pincer claw is released. Crack off the small pincer shell, and its meat will slide out. For attractive service, you may want to keep the lobster shell to refill with the seasoned sauced meat or use it to make Lobster Butter, 399.

For recipes which make use of lobster meat already cooked, see Lunch Dishes, 259 and the Index.

## ▤ BROILED LOBSTER

**1 Serving**

Preheat broiler.
Prepare for broiling: .

**A 1¼-lb. live lobster**

severing the vein at the base of the neck. Place the lobster on his back. Hold him with your left hand firmly over his head. Be sure to protect your hand with a towel. Draw the knife from the head down through the base of the abdomen, as shown below, so the lobster will lie flat, with the meat evenly exposed to the heat. All the lobster meat is edible, except for the stomach, or lady—a hard sac near the head—and the intestinal vein that

runs through the middle of the underside of the tail meat. Remove and discard these inedible parts. The spongy substance to either side of the body—the lungs—is harmless. It may or may not be removed when the lobster

is cooked in the half shell. Beyond a doubt edible are the delicious black roe, which turns into the so-called red coral in cooking, and the greenish-brown liver or tomalley. You may prepare a stuffing by removing and mixing together:

> **The coral**
> **The tomalley**
> **1 tablespoon toasted bread crumbs**
> **1 teaspoon lemon juice or dry sherry**

Replace in the cavity and brush it and the exposed lobster meat with:

> **Melted butter**

▶ If broiling stuffed, place shell side down on the oven grill and broil about 16 minutes. If broiling unstuffed or grilling over charcoal, place shell side toward heat 7 to 8 minutes; then turn and broil, flesh side to heat, about 8 minutes more. In either case, serve with:

> **Lemon wedges and melted butter**

▶ To eat broiled lobster served to you on the half shell, begin with the tail meat first, using the sharp-pronged small lobster or oyster fork, see sketches below. You may twist off bite-sized pieces with the fork. This needs some skill, and when dining out, we often wish for a good European fish knife. Dip the pieces in the

sauce. You may also squeeze lemon juice from the garnish wedges over the lobster meat. Twist off a large claw with the fingers and, if necessary, also use the cracker which should always be provided. Crack the claw, as shown, to release the delicate rich meat. You may then pull off the

small side claws, one by one, with the fingers, and suck out the meat. As you empty the shells, place them on the bone tray or extra plate, and make use of the finger bowl when needed. Continue to eat the contents of the shell: it is good to the last shred. Some people even suck the knuckle after releasing it from the gray gristle.

## LOBSTER AMERICAINE OR ARMORICAINE

**2 Servings**

Who really cares how it's spelled? This method of cooking lobster is good enough to credit regional inventiveness on both sides of the Atlantic. Have ready:

   **¹/2 cup Fish Stock or Fumet, (II, 173)**

Place on a flat pan, so as to be able to reserve any juice that results from cutting:

   **2 live 1¹/2-lb. hen lobsters**

With a sharp knife, sever the vein at the base of the neck. Cut off the claws. Divide the body at the tail and cut the tail into 3 or 4 pieces at the segmentations. Divide the shell in half, lengthwise. Remove and discard the sac. Reserve the coral, if any, and

the tomalley for the sauce. Have ready two heavy skillets. In one, sauté:

   **3 tablespoons butter**
   **1 cup Mirepoix, (II, 254)**
   **¹/2 cup chopped shallots**

Heat in the other, to the point of fragrance:

   **¹/2 cup olive oil**
   **1 clove garlic**

Sauté in the oil about 4 minutes ▶ still in the shell, the cut-up lobster. Keep the pan moving. When the lobster shell is red and the flesh firm, add it to the mirepoix in the first skillet. Flambé, 108, the lobster mixture in:

   **1 oz. brandy**

Place in the second skillet and simmer about 5 minutes:

   **¹/2 cup tomato purée**
   **1 cup white wine**
   **3 skinned, seeded, chopped tomatoes**

In winter use the small Italian-type canned tomatoes. Add the sautéed lobster pieces still in the shell, the fumet and:

   **1 teaspoon chopped fresh tarragon**
   **The juice or "blood" of the lobster**
   **The coral and tomalley**

to the tomato mixture. Simmer about 15 minutes.

   **Season to taste**

Thicken the sauce slightly with:

   **(Beurre Manié, 381)**

Serve the lobster with the hot sauce poured over it, garnished with:

   **Chopped parsley**

## ▤ GRILLED LOBSTER TAILS

**4 Servings**

Marinate several hours:

   **4 spiny lobster tails**

in a mixture of:

   **¹/4 cup lemon or lime juice**

¼ **cup vegetable oil**
1 **teaspoon each salt and
paprika**
¼ **cup minced shallots**

Preheat broiler or grill.

Remove with scissors the soft under-
cover of the lobster tails, as sketched,
below. Slightly crack the hard upper
shell with a cleaver so that the tails
will lie flat, and grease the meat
lightly. Broil about 4 inches from
coals or heating source about 5 min-

utes to a side, basting well with the
marinade. These make an attractive
plate served with:

**Asparagus spears**

placed to either side and:

**Meunière or Lemon
Butter, 397, or
Béarnaise Sauce, 412**


## BAKED STUFFED LOBSTER

**2 Servings**

Split in half, as for Broiled Lobster, 457:

**A freshly Boiled Lobster,
455: about 2½ lb.**

Remove the meat. Chop it. Melt:

¾ **tablespoon butter**

Stir in until blended:

¾ **tablespoon flour**

Stir in slowly:

½ **cup Chicken or Fish Stock,
(II, 172, 173)**

Season the sauce with:

1¼ **teaspoons dry mustard**
1 **teaspoon chopped onion
Salt**

**Paprika**

Melt in a separate saucepan:

2 **tablespoons butter**

Sauté the lobster meat in the butter
only until it is heated through. Add
the boiling sauce. Simmer these ingredients about 2 minutes. Remove
from the heat.

Preheat broiler.

Beat, then stir into the above:

1 **tablespoon cream**
2 **egg yolks**

Add:

(½ **cup chopped Sautéed
Mushrooms, 328)**

Fill the lobster shells with the mixture. Cover them with:

**Au Gratin I or II, (II, 221)**

Broil the lobster until the crumbs are
brown. Season it, as it is removed
from the oven, by pouring over it:

(2 **tablespoons sherry)**


## LOBSTER THERMIDOR

**2 Servings**

Prepare:

2 **Poached Lobsters, 455,
about 1 or 1½ lb. each**

Remove and crack claws; extract
meat. Remove entire tail portion,
body meat, tomalley and coral, if
present, keeping tail shell intact, and
discarding lower membrane: see
illustration for Spiny Lobster, 456.
Cut tail and claw meat into ½-inch
chunks. Have ready:

**Mornay Sauce, 384**

omitting cheese, and adding:

1 **teaspoon prepared mustard
The sieved tomalley and
coral**
(1 **to 2 tablespoons sherry)**

Fill tail shells with one-third of the
sauce, add meat and cover it with the
rest of the sauce. You may sprinkle
the tops with a mixture of:

**(Grated Parmesan cheese
and melted butter)**
Run the lobsters under a broiler until
the sauce is golden brown. Serve
with:

**Wilted Cucumbers, 58**


## LOBSTER OR SEAFOOD NEWBURG

**4 Servings**

**I.**
Melt in a double boiler ♦ over—not
in—boiling water:

**4 tablespoons butter**
Add, stir and cook 3 minutes:

**2 cups boiled diced lobster
meat**
Add:

**¼ cup dry sherry or Madeira**
Cook gently about 2 minutes more.
Add:

**½ teaspoon paprika**
**(⅓ teaspoon nutmeg)**
Beat and add:

**3 egg yolks**
**1 cup cream**
Cook and stir these ingredients until
they thicken.

**Season to taste**
Serve the lobster at once on:

**Hot buttered toast**


**II.** Heat in a double boiler:

**2 cups Newburg Sauce, 413**
Add, stir and cook for 3 minutes:

**2 cups boiled diced lobster
meat or 2 cups cooked
seafood**
You may add:

**(1 lb. sliced Sautéed
Mushrooms, 328)**
**Season to taste**
Serve at once on:

**Hot buttered toast or
Boiled Rice, 189**


## LOBSTER OR SEAFOOD CURRY

**4 Servings**
Heat in a double boiler ♦ over—not
in—boiling water:

**2 cups Curry Sauce, 390**
Add, stir and cook about 3 minutes:

**2 cups boiled diced lobster
meat or 2 cups cooked
seafood**
You may add:

**(3 sautéed chopped ribs
celery)**
**(½ sautéed chopped green
pepper, seeds and
membrane removed)**
**(1 teaspoon grated sautéed
onion)**
**Season to taste**
Cook until well heated. May be
served at once with:

**Boiled Rice, 189, Chutney,
(II, 685) or slivered almonds**


## ⅄ LOBSTER PARFAIT

**6 Servings**
This is an exceedingly elegant way
of presenting cold lobster. Consider
serving it with iced champagne.
Purée in the ⅄ blender:

**The meat of 1 freshly killed
and cooked 2½-lb. lobster,
or 2 cups cooked meat from
frozen lobster tails**
with:

**3 tablespoons tomato purée**
**2 tablespoons lemon juice**
**1 tablespoon dry sherry**
**2 teaspoons brandy**
**½ cup water**
Mix in:

**1 minced clove garlic**
**1 finely chopped shallot**
Cook the mixture over low heat until
reduced by one-third. Cool, then add:

**1½ tablespoons whipping
cream**

2  cups mayonnaise
1/2  teaspoon paprika
1  teaspoon salt

Chill 1 1/2 hours. Arrange an additional chilled:

4  oz. lobster meat per serving

in 6 parfait glasses. Cover the meat with the above sauce, letting it trickle down in parfait style. Garnish with:

**Chilled whipped cream**
**Watercress**

Serve at once.

## HOT LOBSTER RING

**5 Servings**

Preheat oven to 325°.
Melt:

2  tablespoons butter

Stir in, until blended:

3  tablespoons flour

Stir in gradually:

2  cups chicken bouillon or
1 cup bouillon and 1 cup
cream

Add:

1  tablespoon minced parsley
1/2  cup grated bread crumbs—
not toasted
4  beaten egg yolks
2  cups cooked diced lobster
meat
Salt and white pepper to
taste

Whip until stiff ◖ but not dry:

4  egg whites

Fold lightly into the other ingredients. Bake the lobster mixture in a well-oiled 9-inch ring mold until firm, about 20 minutes. Unmold and serve with:

**White Wine Sauce for**
**Fish, 385**

## ABOUT SHRIMP

Formerly our southern shrimp or **crevette** was the only one available

in most of our markets. Today we can buy many members of this family. So let us remind you of the miniature ones from our West Coast and from Scandinavia—now widely used as hors d'oeuvre; and those jumbo-sized varieties often called **prawns**— shrimp so large that two or three suffice for a serving. In spite of slight differences in flavor and texture, all may be substituted for one another if size is taken into consideration for serving amounts and cooking time.

◖ To test shrimp for freshness, see that they are dry and firm. For 3 servings allow about 1 pound of shrimp in the shell—these are called "green" shrimp—or 1/2 pound of cooked shrimp without shells. In buying, remember that 2 to 2 1/2 pounds of shrimp in the shell gives only about 1 pound cooked, shelled shrimp, or 2 cups. While shrimp may be cooked in the shell or unshelled, the shells add considerable flavor. To prevent curling and toughening, ◖ drain them at once after cooking. Shucking is easy, either before or after cooking. A slight tug releases the body shell from the tail.

Devein before or after cooking, using a small pointed knife or the end of a pick, as sketched at the top of page 461. This is essential. Large shrimp may be made more decorative by slicing them lengthwise after cleaning.

▶ To butterfly shrimp, before cooking peel the shrimp down to the tail, leaving the tail on. Devein. Holding so the underside is up, slice down its length, almost to the vein. Spread and flatten to form the butterfly shape. To butterfly after cooking, it is wise to begin by running a toothpick or small skewer the length of the inner curve to keep the shrimp from curling, see the illustration on the foot of page 461. After cooking, peel and devein them and cut along the inner curve, as shown in the center, being careful to cut only about three-fourths of the way through so as to retain the butterfly shape.

If using canned shrimp, you may rinse briefly in cold water to remove excess salt. To cook frozen shrimp, peeled and deveined, and also the "green" types, start from the frozen state, drop into boiling stock or water, and begin counting the time when the stock comes up to a simmer.

For other shrimp recipes, see the chapters on Hors d'Oeuvre, Salads, and Lunch Dishes.

## POACHED SHRIMP

**6 Servings**

We prefer this basic procedure to "boiling" shrimp.
Simmer about 5 minutes:

        8 cups water
        1/4 cup sliced onion
        1 clove garlic
        1 bay leaf
        2 celery ribs with leaves
        1 1/2 tablespoons salt

Wash, drain and add:

        2 lb. green shrimp

Slice and add:

        1/2 lemon

Simmer the shrimp about 5 minutes or until pink but not tightly curled. Drain immediately and chill. Serve the shrimp very cold in their shells—if they are to be shucked at table—with a bowl of:

        Russian Dressing, 420, or
        Rémoulade Sauce, 420

or shell them, removing the intestinal vein, and use the shrimp in a hot dish as desired.

## POTTED SHRIMP OR LOBSTER

This terrine can be used as a luncheon or hors d'oeuvre spread. Cook:

        Raw shrimp or lobster, see
        461

Drain and remove meat from shells. Chop coarsely. Reserve shells. Allow for every cup of seafood:

        2 to 3 tablespoons butter

To half of the butter, add the reserved shells to make:

        Shrimp or
        Lobster Butter, 399

Season to taste with:

        1/8 teaspoon mustard or mace
        A few grains cayenne

Stir the seafood into the heated shrimp or lobster butter until well coated. Place in a small jar. Clarify the remaining butter. ▶ Do not let it color. Pour it while hot over the seafood, making sure the food is well covered. Refrigerate lidded.

## MOLDED SHRIMP

Put through a coarse food chopper:

        1 1/2 lb. cooked cleaned shrimp
        2 tablespoons capers
        Juice of 1 very small onion

Combine the above ingredients in a mixing bowl with:

¼ lb. soft butter
¼ cup whipping cream
Season with:

Salt
Hot pepper sauce
Tarragon
Chopped parsley

Mix well until mixture has the consistency of whipped cream. Pack in a pretty mold which has been rinsed in cold water, and refrigerate covered 3 or 4 hours. Unmold and garnish with:

Cherry tomatoes, parsley or fennel

## ▤ SHRIMP TERIYAKI

**3 Servings**

Marinate:

1 lb. shelled, deveined raw shrimp

about 15 minutes in:

½ cup pineapple juice
2 to 4 tablespoons soy sauce
½ cup bland vegetable oil

Drain and broil or grill 3 or 4 minutes on each side, 4 inches from heat. Serve with:

Boiled Rice, 189, or
Curried Rice, 191

## NEW ORLEANS SHRIMP

**4 to 6 Servings**

Poach, see 462:

2 lb. raw shrimp

Shell and devein them. Rub a bowl with:

Garlic

Mix together in the bowl:

½ cup finely chopped celery
1 green onion, finely chopped
1 tablespoon chopped chives
6 tablespoons olive oil
3 tablespoons lemon juice
¼ cup hot pepper sauce
5 tablespoons horseradish

2 tablespoons prepared mustard
¼ teaspoon paprika
¾ teaspoon salt
½ teaspoon white pepper

You may marinate the shrimp in this sauce up to 12 hours. Keep refrigerated until ready to serve on:

Lettuce

## SHRIMP NEWBURG

**3 to 4 Servings**

Prepare:

1 lb. Poached Shrimp, 462

Serve with:

Newburg Sauce, 413

using 1 to 1½ cups of sauce, in a:

Rice Ring, 189

or over:

Baked Green Rice, 191

## SHRIMP CASSEROLE WITH SNAIL BUTTER

**4 Servings**

Prepare:

1½ lb. Poached Shrimp, 462

Have ready in refrigerator:

Colbert or Snail Butter, 398

Preheat oven to 400°.
Put a ¼-inch layer of the butter in the bottom of a shallow casserole. Lay shrimp in rows and press into the butter. Cover the shrimp with the remaining butter and bake about 10 minutes. Broil a few minutes to let top brown. Serve at once.

## DEEP-FAT-FRIED SHRIMP

**3 Servings**

▶ Please read About Deep-Fat Frying, 94.

Shell:

1 lb. raw shrimp

Remove the intestinal vein. Combine:

⅔ cup milk

⅛ teaspoon paprika
¼ teaspoon salt

Soak the shrimp in the milk 30 minutes. Drain the shrimp well. Sprinkle with:

**Lemon juice
Salt**

Roll in:

**Cornmeal**

Let them dry on a rack for 15 minutes before frying in deep fat heated to 375° until golden brown. Drain on paper toweling. Serve hot with:

**Lemon juice or
Mayonnaise, 419, seasoned
with puréed chutney**

## DEEP-FAT-FRIED STUFFED SHRIMP

**14 Large Shrimp**

Shell and devein:

**10 jumbo-sized raw shrimp**

Chop them into a pulp and add:

**6 water chestnuts**

which have been smashed with a cleaver and finely chopped. Now shell, leaving the tails intact, and devein:

**14 jumbo-sized raw shrimp**

Split lengthwise along the deveined edge ♦ but not far enough to separate. Spread the shrimp flat and lay along each crevice:

**A thin julienne of
prosciutto or Westphalian
ham**

Spread the shrimp and chestnut mixture in the crevices over the ham and mold it into a rounded smooth surface when you partially reclose the shrimp for breading. Dip each shrimp into:

**Beaten egg**

then into:

**Flour**

Allow to dry on a rack 15 to 20 minutes.

♦ Please read About Deep-Fat Frying, 94.

Heat deep fat to 370°. Lift the shrimp by the tails and slide them gently into the heated fat. Fry about 5 minutes or until golden. Drain on paper toweling. Serve at once with:

**Oriental Sweet-Sour
Sauce, 405**

adding some:

**Plum jam**

## BUTTERFLY SHRIMP

♦ Please read About Deep-Fat Frying, 94. To cut for butterfly shape, see About Shrimp, 461.

Don't flour or crumb the tails, but do coat the body of the shrimp with:

**Bread crumbs or grated
coconut, or flour or egg or
both; or in a Fritter Batter
for Fish, (II, 155)**

Fry in deep fat heated to 370° for 8 to 10 minutes or until golden. Drain on paper toweling. Serve at once with:

**Soy sauce, Tartare Sauce,
421, or Oriental Sweet-
Sour Sauce, 405**

## SHRIMP TEMPURA

♦ Please read About Deep-Fat Frying, 94.

Prepare:

**Butterfly Shrimp, above**

Dip them in:

**Fritter Batter for Fish,
(II, 155)**

Fry in deep fat heated to 350° until golden. Serve with:

**Hot Mustard Sauce, 390,
Oriental Sweet-Sour
Sauce, 405, or Sauce
Dijonnaise, 385**

## SHRIMP FRIED IN BATTER

◗ Please read About Deep-Fat Frying, 94.
Shell and clean, 461:

   **1 lb. raw shrimp**

You may leave the tails on. Prepare:

   **Fritter Batter for Fish,
   (II, 155)**

Dip a few shrimp at a time in the batter, holding them by the tail. ◗ Do not cover the tail with batter. Fry in deep fat heated to 370° until golden brown. Drain on paper toweling. Serve with:

   **Lemon wedges or
   Mayonnaise, 419, seasoned
   with catsup and mustard**

## ABOUT CRAYFISH, CRAWFISH, OR ÉCREVISSES

   ◗ **Allow About One Dozen per
   Serving**

One of the thrills of our grandparents was to find in Missouri streams the crayfish they had so relished in Europe. These crustaceans, looking like miniature lobsters, were brought to the table in great steaming crimson mounds, garnished with dill or swimming in their own juices; that is, *à la nage.* By the way, a single Australian "crayfish" suffices for one serving!
To cook, wash well in several waters:

   **Crayfish**

If they have been kept in fresh running water for several days, they need not be eviscerated. If they have not, clean them while still alive. Grasp the middle tail fin, as sketched; give a long firm twist, and pull to remove the stomach and intestinal vein. Have ready a large pot of:

   **Boiling water**

seasoned with:

   **A leek—white part only
   Parsley**

   **1 chopped carrot
   (3 tablespoons vinegar)**

Drop the crayfish one by one into the boiling water at a rate that will not disturb the boiling. Cook not longer than 5 to 7 minutes. Serve in the shell. Have on the side plenty of:

   **Melted butter**

seasoned with:

   **Fresh dill**

Crayfish are eaten with the fingers. Separate tail from body. Crack open tail by holding between thumb and finger of both hands and force it back against the curve of the shell. Be sure to serve with finger bowls. If you are preparing these crustaceans for hors d'oeuvre, cook only until the water is boiling well, after they are all immersed. Then remove from heat. Let them cool in the liquid. Shelled, they lend themselves to all kinds of combinations and sauces, but the connoisseur usually wants them for themselves alone.

## ABOUT SNAILS

The Romans, who were addicted to snails, grew them on ranches where they were fed special foods like bay, wine and spicy soups as preseasoning.

Before they hibernate, snails contract into their shells and tightly close their opercula. It is usually at this phase that snails are available in markets. When they feed in late spring and summer, they may indulge in some foliage inimical to humans and, if used during this period, must be placed in a covered basket in a cool place and starved for 48 hours. For the next ten days to two weeks, feed them on lettuce leaves, removing the old leaves and furnishing new ones every few days. Then, in any season, scrub until all slime is removed. Cut out the opercula and put the snails into a large stainless steel or enamel pot. To prepare enough acidulated water to cover about 50 snails, mix:

**Water**
**¼ cup vinegar**
**½ cup salt**

Rinse them and repeat this entire process two more times or until the acidulated water is clear. Discard any snails whose heads have not by this time popped out of their shells. Drain. Cover with boiling water and cook for 5 minutes. Drain, cool and remove the snails from shells with an oyster fork. Hold the upper part of the snail with the thumb and forefinger and score the lower part of the body to pull out the swollen intestinal tube. Discard it. Reserve shells. Simmer the snails in a court bouillon of:

**½ water or light stock and**
**½ white wine**

about 3 hours or until they are tender, adding during the last half hour of cooking:

**A Bouquet Garni, (II, 253)**
**2 cloves garlic**

Allow them to cool in the court bouillon. Drain.

## I.

**Allow 6 to 9 Snails per Serving**

Prepare snails and shells as described above. Dry the snails and shells with a cloth. Place in each shell a dab of:

**Snail Butter, 398**

Replace the snails. Pack them firmly in the shell, so generously covered that only the lovely green herbed butter is visible at the opening. You may chill the snails for later use, or bake them at once on a pan lightly sprinkled with water in a 425° oven just long enough to get them piping hot—a matter of a few minutes only. Have ready heated, grooved snail dishes as shown in the chapter heading. Also shown is the snail shell holder which has a spring handle to adjust its vise-like grip to the size of the snail. The long, closely tined fork is used with a slight twist to remove the meat.

## II.

For canned snails, the following effects a small miracle of resuscitation.

Prepare enough to fill 48 snail shells:

**Snail Butter, 398**

Reduce to 1 cup over high heat:

**1 cup canned condensed consommé**
**1 cup dry white wine**

cooked with:

**½ bay leaf**
**1 clove garlic**

Put in a colander:

**48 canned snails**

Pour over them:

**1 quart warm water**

Drain well. Simmer the snails briefly in the hot reduced consommé and wine. Wash the snail shells well and drain. Pack as described above with:

**Snail Butter, 398**

Heat and serve as for I.

## III.

Or, replace the shells with:

**Sautéed Mushroom Caps, 328**

Fill the mushrooms with one or more snails, depending on size. Coat the snails with:

**Snail Butter, 398**

and run under a broiler briefly until heated.

## ABOUT TURTLES AND TERRAPIN

**Sea** or **green turtles** are peaceable and sagacious. Their habits are nowhere more fascinatingly described than in *The Windward Road* by Archie Carr. Handling and cooking these monsters, some of which weigh over 300 pounds, is not a usual household procedure. Therefore most of us are content to enjoy their highly prized, highly priced gelatinous meat ready-diced and in cans. The greenish meat from the top shell is considered the best—that taken from the bottom is whitish.

While sea turtles are tropical in habitat, those most frequently caught and consumed in temperate North America are freshwater types, such as **snapping turtles,** which abound in streams and lakes from North Dakota to Florida. As to disposition, they are again a quite different kettle of fish: short-tempered and capable of inflicting nasty bites.

Choicest of all turtle meat is furnished by the **terrapin,** which inhabits salt-marshes along the East Coast. But this holds good only for the female of the species—the males being unacceptably tough—and to those weighing not much more than 3 pounds.

Regardless of the turtle's size, sectioning it for cooking is an irksome job, even if you overcome the worst of the opposition—as old hands are wont to do when dealing with snappers—by instantly chopping off the head.

Before preparation, however, it is advisable to rid turtles of wastes and pollutants. Put them in a deep open box, with well-secured screening on top; give them a dish of water; and feed them for a week or so on 3 or 4 small handouts of ground meat.

♦ To cook, place in a pan of cold water:

**A 7-inch turtle**

Bring water slowly to a boil and parblanch at least 10 minutes. Drain. Plunge into cold water and leave until cool enough to handle. Scrub well. Place the turtle in rapidly boiling water and add:

(**A Bouquet Garni, II, 253**)
(**An onion stuck with cloves**)
(**3 stalks celery**)

♦ Reduce the heat at once and simmer 35 to 45 minutes or until the claws can be removed by pulling. Drain, reserving the stock. Allow the turtle to cool on its back in order to trap the juices as it cools. When cool, pry the fat plastron free from the curved carapace—easier said than done. Near the head you will find the liver. ♦ Free it carefully from the gall. Discard the gall. Slice the liver thin and reserve it, as well as the eggs, if any. You may or may not want to reserve the small intestines, which may be chopped and added to the meat or sauce. Remove the meat from both the carapace and the skinned legs. When ready to serve, you may toss the meat, including the ground liver and intestines, in:

**6 tablespoons hot melted butter**

Garnish with:

**Parsley**

Serve with:

**Sherry, as a drink**

Or you may heat the meat briefly over very low heat or in the top of a double boiler ♦ over—not in—boiling water in a sauce made by combining:

**1 cup Brown Sauce, 391**

The chopped, cooked eggs, if any

1 teaspoon mixed herbs: including basil, sweet marjoram and thyme, with a touch of rosemary, bay and sage

3 tablespoons Madeira or dry sherry

Garnish with:
Watercress

# FISH

## ABOUT FISH

One of the ill winds ruffling late-twentieth-century waters is the belated discovery that many of our lakes and ocean estuaries have become nearly incapable of supporting life. But in compensation, this bad news has blown us a host of scientists determined to reverse the situation, to systematically create new spawning beds for the fish and crustaceans we already know, and to launch research into the possibility of reaping even the tiny, fantastically numerous and exotic creatures we call plankton after the Greek word for "wanderer."

Fish of all kinds provide high-grade protein, most of it considerably less fatty than most meats. For those concerned with lean and fat fish, the following are considered in the not-so-lean category: albacore, bloaters, butterfish, bluefish, chub, eel, herring, mackerel, pompano, salmon, sardine, shad, smelt, sprat, tuna, trout and whitefish—the fat content ranging from 15% to about 30% with eel.

▶ If you háve ány reason to believe that the fish you are using harbors objectionable amounts of DDT or other chemicals, filleting is the safest approach. Chemical residues tend to be concentrated in the fatty tissues, namely the belly flesh and the dark areas at the sides. These areas may all be cut away during the filleting process, see 472–473.

Now, a few more general comments. Fish of many kinds respond favorably to deep-fat frying or sautéing. Those with naturally dry flesh—pike, pickerel and muskellunge are freshwater examples—often profit by baking and by preliminary marination, marination being also a corrective for too strong a flavor; while fish of moister texture are better suited for broiling. And there are fish that steam or poach well: cod, buffalo fish, hake, haddock, sheepshead, red snapper, grouper, pollock, halibut and salmon. Some very oily fish may be smoked or may be bought smoked. Some others are available fresh or salted. For fish timbales and soufflés, see 229.

Many fish are seasonal delicacies. Available all year round are rock bass, carp, cod, eel, flounder, grouper, haddock, hake, halibut, herring, mullet, red snapper, salmon, sole and tuna.

If you are adventuring with eel, herring, some types of sole, or an officious stranger like octopus, consult the Index to see if we have some extra-special suggestions for preparing, cooking or seasoning them; and also look at the individual recipes for ways to use the cooking and serving equipment shown in chapter heading on the preceding page.

SEA FISH

These include: albacore, amberjack, sea bass, bluefish, bonito, butterfish, chub, cod, croaker, cusk, the small dolphin, flounder, grouper, haddock, hake, halibut, Atlantic herring, Pacific herring, kingfish, lingcod, mackerel, mullet, pilchard, plaice, pollock, pompano, porgy, red snapper, rosefish, sailfish, sand dab, sardines, smelt, the soles, sprat, swordfish, tuna, turbot, weakfish, whitebait and whiting.

FRESHWATER FISH

These include: bass, buffalo, carp, catfish, crappie, lake herring, mullet, muskellunge, perch, pickerel, pike, sheepshead, sucker, sunfish, brook trout, lake trout and whitefish.

Either sea or freshwater fish— depending on age and season—are eel, elver and shad. Some fish are changelings, as witness the recent effortless conversion of certain types of salmon, like the Coho, and of seatrout, notably the steelhead, from a lifecycle requiring freshwater infancy and saltwater adulthood to a cycle entirely accomplished in the Great Lakes and their tributaries.

## TESTING FOR AND MAINTAINING FRESHNESS OF FISH

With America gone fishing-crazy, no housewife knows when she will answer a knock at the kitchen door and be suddenly faced with a neighbor's surplus catch in all its chill, scaly impersonality. This need not be a moment of consternation. If it happens to you, judge the gift—after, of course, enthusiastically thanking the donor—as critically as you would judge a fish offered at market. To test its freshness ◗ make sure that its eyes are bulging and its gills are reddish, that the scales are adhering firmly to the skin, and that the flesh, when you press it, is firm to the touch. The scales should have a high sheen. Also be certain that the fish has no offensive odor—especially around the gills or the belly. If it is very fresh, and you cannot use it at once but plan to do so in a day or two, store it at 39°, preferably lidded, so that its penetrating odor does not permeate other foods in the refrigerator. Fish may be kept directly on ice if drainage is provided to prevent it from soaking up water. Length of fish storage depends largely on the condition in which it reaches you. The sooner it can be used the better, for its fragile gelatinous substances break down and dry out quickly as the fish ages, destroying flavor as they dry.

If you must hold fish for a longer period, see directions for freezing fish and for cooking frozen fish, (II, 654). When buying fish, remember that a whitish surface indicates excessive dehydration, and that in some stores ♦ thawed frozen fish is sold with no sign or comment to indicate the important fact that it should be used at once and never refrozen. If you are in doubt about the freshness of a fish, place it in cold water. A newly caught fish will float.

## PREPARING FISH FOR COOKING

The most important factor in fish cookery is to have or keep fish fresh. Whether your fish is large or small, choose the cooking method best suited to retain its juiciness, and no matter what its size or type ♦ never overcook it.

### SMALL FISH

To clean fish like smelts, sardines or sprats, spread open the outer gills, take hold of the inner gills with the forefinger and pull gently. The parts unfit for food are all attached to these inner gills and come out together, leaving the fish ready to cook after rinsing. These respond to deep-fat frying and pan-frying.

Small fish may be **butterfly-filleted**. In this technique, head and tail are removed, after which the flesh is cut cleanly away on both sides of the backbone and the dorsal fin; the ventral or belly fin is removed by slot-cutting around it. The meat is then cut off in a single piece, freeing it from the backbone, and flattened out ready for rinsing, drying and cooking.

### LARGE FISH

If fish are two pounds or over, bake, steam, poach or "steak" them as described on 472. Fish of this size and somewhat smaller ones both may be filleted.

You will sometimes see suggestions for slashing the skin of large fish before cooking. This expedient is adopted chiefly for firm-fleshed fish, to hasten heat-penetration; or when, as with a whole turbot, the skin area is extensive and might otherwise burst.

To prepare a fish which is to be cooked in one piece, begin by spreading on a firm work surface several layers of newsprint covered with 3 thicknesses of brown paper. If the fish needs scaling, cut off the fins with scissors so they will not nick you while you are working. Wash the fish briefly in cold water—scales are more easily removed from a wet fish. Grasp the fish firmly near the base of the tail as shown below. If it is very slippery, you may want to hold it in a cloth. Begin at the tail, pressing a

rigid sharp knife blade or scaler at a slight angle from the vertical position to raise the scales as you strip them off. Work against the "nap"—up toward the head. Be sure to remove the scales around the base of the head and the fins. After scaling, discard the first layer of brown paper with the scales on it.

Next, draw the fish. Cut the entire length of the belly from the vent to the head as shown on the next page, and remove the entrails. They are all contained in a pouchlike integument which is easily freed from the flesh, so evisceration need not be a messy job.

Now, cut around the pelvic and ventral fins on the lower side and remove them. If you are removing the head, cut above the collarbone and break through the backbone by snapping it off on the edge of the work surface as shown below. The pectoral fins, if they were not previously cut off,

should come off with the head. Then remove the tail by slicing right through the body just above it. Wrap and discard the entrails, keeping the choicer trimmings for making fish stock, (II, 173).

If the fish has been scaled and you are preparing it for stuffing, you can remove the dorsal fin in such a way

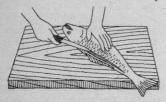

as to release unwanted bones. Cut first down to either side of it for its full length. Then give a quick pull forward toward the head end to release it, and with it the bones that are attached to it, as sketched at the top of the next column.

Wash the fish in cold running water, removing any blood, bits of viscera or membrane. ♦ Be sure the blood line under the backbone has been removed. Dry the fish well. It is then ready for cooking stuffed or unstuffed.

FISH STEAKS OR DARNES

To cut a fish into steaks, or darnes, begin at the head end and cut evenly, as shown, into cross sections at least one inch thick.

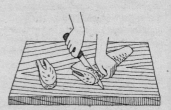

FILLETING FISH

To prepare skinned fillets, you need not scale the fish, remove its fins, or draw it.

Place on the work surface several thicknesses of newsprint covered by brown paper. Cut the fish, as shown on the top of page 473, first all around the base of the head and just above the tail, then all along the back ridge. Now slice down at a slight angle behind the collarbone beyond the gill, until you feel the backbone against the knife. Turn the knife flat,

with the cutting edge toward the tail and the point toward the cut edge of the backbone. Keep the blade flat and in the same plane with the backbone. Now, cut with a sliding motion along the backbone until you have freed the fillet all the way to the tail, see below. It should come off in one piece.

To skin, place the fillet skin side down. Hold the tail firmly with your free hand as shown. Cut through the flesh of the fillet about ½ inch above the tail. Flatten the knife against the skin with the blade pointing toward the top of the fillet. Work the knife forward, keeping in the same plane and close against the skin while your left hand continues to hold the skin taut.

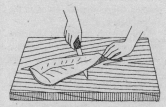

An exception to the above procedure must be made with a certain group of very flat fish, some of which, rather disconcertingly, have both eyes on their upper surface. All of them are skinned and filleted in a special way; and all of them, including turbot, which is less flat than most, may be cooked by recipes for sole or flounder.

The true English or Dover sole, whose eyes are situated normally, has

the most delicate flavor and texture of them all. But fillets of flounder, plaice, dab, and lemon or gray sole are often palmed off on the unsuspecting purchaser as the genuine article.

◗ To fillet these flat varieties, first skin the fish by cutting a gash through the skin above the tail. Peel back the skin for about ¾ inch. Grasp the released skin firmly in the right hand as shown below. Hold the tail flat in the left hand while pulling steadily toward the head with the right. When skinned, a flat fish reveals a lengthwise indentation down the center which separates a set of fillets—two on the dark-skinned side and two on the light side. Cut through the flesh on either side of the spine. Slip the knife under the fillet, close to the bone, and cut the fillet loose from the backbone toward the outside edge of the fish. Having freed the fillets, refrigerate them, discarding all the unusable entrails. You may keep the bone structure, skin, heads and tails for fish stock, (II, 173), unless the fish is a strong-flavored or oily one.

## COOKING FISH

Most of our fish recipes call for cooking in ovenproof dishes. Service is simplified if such dishes are attractive enough to appear at table. This way, fish—which is fragile—undergoes less handling, and you have fewer "fishy" dishes to clean up later.

◗ Allow per serving 1 pound whole small fish, ¾ pound if entrails, head, tail and fins are removed; $1/2$ pound fish steaks; or $1/3$ pound fish fillets.

♦ To test a fish for doneness, you may insert a thermometer at an angle into the thickest portion of the flesh. Fish is edible when the internal heat reaches 140°. At 150° its tissues begin to break down, allowing both juices and flavors to escape. Remove the fish from the heat, surely by 145°.

♦ Remember that because fish needs so little heat to cook, it will continue to do so on a hot platter.

If you have no thermometer, stick a wooden pick into the thickest part of the fish; if it meets little resistance and comes away clean, it is in all likelihood done. A "rule of finger" for doneness in a soft-fleshed fish is to press it as you would a cake to see if the flesh returns to its original shape. Another more reliable yardstick is the disappearance of translucency: a fish is done when its flesh flakes readily. A good cook knows through experience how long to cook her fish; but even she will watch the proceedings with a vigilant eye to guard against overdoneness.

Many fish are bland in flavor and profit by a sauce. If, on the contrary, the fish is strong in flavor, many expert cooks ♦ discard the butter or cooking oil in which it has been cooked. Otherwise, deglaze the pan, 381.

♦ To keep a whole fish warm, put it on a heated serving platter in a very low oven. Leave the door ajar. For fillets, treat as for a whole fish, but cover them with a damp warm paper towel or cloth. ♦ Be sure that any sauce served on the fish is very hot.

♦ To keep a sauced fish warm, use an uncovered double boiler, or place the baking dish in which you plan to serve the fish in a pan of boiling water and hold uncovered.

♦ If cooked fish is to be served cold, keep refrigerated until the very last minute. If served buffet-style, place it over cracked ice.

♦ To minimize fish tastes and odors, use lemon, wine, vinegar, ginger, spring onions, or garlic in the marinating or cooking. To remove the odor of fish from utensils and dishcloths, use a solution of 1 teaspoon baking soda to 1 quart water. Pans may be washed in hot suds, rinsed and dried, and then scalded with a little vinegar. To remove the odor of fish from the hands, rub them with lemon juice, vinegar or salt before washing.

To prepare fish dishes based on cooked fish and shellfish, see Brunch, Lunch and Supper Dishes, 236–276; Hors d'Oeuvre, (II, 81); and Canapés, (II, 63). To prepare Fish Stews and Soups, see 156–163. To cure and smoke fish, see (II, 637). A great variety of sauces suitable for fish are coupled with individual recipes in this chapter. Others may be found in the Sauce chapter, 374.

There are any number of attractive ways to serve and garnish fish. Handsome foundations for cold dishes are salmon, lake trout, chicken halibut, turbot, filleted Dover sole, walleyed pike and carp.

A tasty way to prepare a hot fish in summer is to ▤ broil it on a fish grill, as shown in the chapter heading, upper left, on 469. Then flambé it several seconds before serving over a dry bed of fennel stalks. Another addition to fish is Fried Parsley, 338, both delicious and decorative.

FROZEN FISH

Frozen fish should be thawed, refrigerated, before cooking, or cooked while still frozen, unless stuffed or rolled. Also, fish sticks or individual portions should not be thawed before cooking. ◗ Use thawed fish immediately, and do not refreeze; it may be cooked in the same way as its fresh counterpart. ◗ If cooked frozen, it is best baked, broiled, or cooked *en papillote* or in aluminum foil. Double the cooking time given for fresh fish, and in foil cooking add another 15 minutes to allow the heat to penetrate the foil. Freezing processes for fish have improved greatly in the last few years, bringing us varieties hitherto not available. But we still think that frozen fish cannot compare with fresh fish for flavor and texture. As the gelatins lose their delicate quality, it is apt to be dry and thus needs a well-flavored sauce or a good deal of moisture or fat in the cooking process. ◗ If you are buying frozen fish from frozen food cabinets, buy only solidly frozen packages. They should not be torn or misshapen or show evidence of refreezing. Follow the processor's directions. ◗ Skin frozen fish before cooking it.

Following below are the descriptions of cooking procedures especially appropriate for fish, such as sautéing, baking, steaming, poaching, braising and broiling, each followed by some typical recipes. Recipes devised for specific kinds of fish arranged in alphabetical order complete the chapter. We include those for octopus—really a mollusk—and for frogs—i.e., frogs legs—even though these agile amphibians have a disconcerting habit in cookbooks of leaping back and forth between the fish and the shellfish sections. Cooking times in individual recipes apply to fresh fish—including thawed fish—at 70°, but no warmer.

## BAKING FISH

Baking is a highly recommended way of cooking fish: it preserves nearly intact the subtle, distinctive and delicate fresh flavor of a soft-fleshed fish. Temperature in the preheated oven should reach 350°—no more. The unskinned and lightly greased fish is set in an amply large baking dish on an oiled rack high enough to clear not only the juices the fish itself may yield, but also those which may accumulate if it is basted; and the dish is placed a little higher than the oven center. Firmer-fleshed fish will, of course, require longer baking, as will stuffed fish. Try to turn your fish only once, if at all, and if necessary with two spatulas, to minimize the risk of its breaking apart. To test for doneness, see Cooking Fish, 473.

## BAKED UNSTUFFED FISH

**Allow ¹/₂ Pound per Person**
Preheat oven to 325°.
Scale, remove the entrails and clean:
**A 3-lb. fish**
A larger fish may be used, but it will require longer, but not proportionately longer, baking, see testing for doneness, 473. If the fish has a tough skin, slash it in several places. Place it on a greased rack in an ovenproof baking dish. Rub generously with:
**Clarified Butter, 396**
If the fish is lean, you may bard it, 511. If it is not barded, baste it frequently with:
**Clarified butter**
Bake about 30 minutes or until done. Serve on a hot platter garnished with:
**Slices of lemon**
**Sprigs of parsley or basil**
**Hot Stuffed Tomatoes, 369**
Suitable sauces are:
**Almond Garnish, (II, 221),**

**Shrimp Sauce, 385, or
Hot Mustard Sauce, 390**

and, for very bland fish:

**Lorenzo Dressing, 415, or
Salsa Verde, 415**

♦ To carve an unstuffed fish; remove the skin and cut a line down the middle of the exposed side from head to tail. To either side of this line, cut pieces 2 1/2 to 3 inches wide. Lift them off above the bone structure and serve. Pry up the backbone, beginning at the tail, letting it break at the neck, and lift it to one side. The exposed lower fillet will then be ready to carve just as the upper one was.

## BAKED STUFFED FISH

**6 Servings**

Stuffing for fish should not be so bold in seasoning as to destroy the naturally delicate fish flavor. Scandinavians would object to this counsel; they make lavish use of fennel in preparing many of their traditional seafood dishes.

♦ If you bone a fish before stuffing, be sure to leave the skin intact.
Scale, eviscerate and clean:

**A 3-lb. fish**

Preheat oven to 325°.
Stuff fish with:

**1 1/2 cups Oyster Bread
Dressing, 432, Bread
Dressing for Fish, 432,
Green Dressing, 432, or
Fennel Dressing, 434**

or with a combination of:

**Pressed cucumbers, bread
crumbs and almonds**

Bake about 40 minutes or until done.
Serve with:

**Soubise Sauce, 387,
Suprême Sauce, 388, or
Colbert Butter, 398**

and:

**Lime wedges**

## PLANKED FISH

**6 servings**

♦ Please read about Planking, 107.
Preheat oven to 350°.
Scale, clean, wash in running water and dry:

**A 3- to 4-lb. fish**

Brush with:

**Clarified Butter, 396, or
vegetable oil**

Place the fish on a well-greased ovenproof or metal platter, about 18 x 13 inches. A seasoned plank may be used ♦ but, if used, should in the future be reserved solely for fish. Bake the fish 40 to 60 minutes; ♦ if stuffed, about 10 minutes longer.
Preheat boiler.
Garnish the platter with a decorative edging of:

**Duchess Potatoes, 353**

Broil 6 to 8 minutes, 8 inches from the source of heat, or until the potato garnish is delicately browned. Further garnish the plank with:

**A stuffed vegetable
Parsley, fennel or
watercress**

and serve.

## FISH BAKED IN A COVERED DISH

**4 Servings**

This is a simple way to bring out the flavor of a delicate fish.
Preheat oven to 350°.
Combine:

**2 tablespoons Clarified
Butter, 396**

**1/8 teaspoon pepper or paprika
A fresh grating of nutmeg**

Rub the mixture over:

**2 lb. fish, preferably in 1
chunky piece**

Place the fish in an ovenproof dish. Cover with a closely fitting lid. Bake

20 to 25 minutes, or until done. The time depends largely on the shape of the fish. You may add while cooking:

**(2 tablespoons dry white wine)**

Place the fish on a hot platter. Melt:

**3 tablespoons butter**

Add:

**2 tablespoons capers**
**1 teaspoon chopped parsley**
**1 teaspoon chopped chives**
**2 teaspoons lemon juice**
**Season to taste**

Pour sauce over the fish.

## ▤ FISH BAKED IN FOIL

### Individual Serving

Please read about Foil Cookery, 104. Preheat oven to 350°.

Scale and clean a small fish. Rub with:

**Seasoned Butter, 396**

Place on a piece of buttered aluminum foil large enough to make a generous fold at the edges. Do not include more than 1 pound in each packet. Bake 35 to 40 minutes to the pound.

## FISH BAKED IN CLAY

Scoop out of the ground a hole about twice as big as the fish you are going to cook. Either wet and tamp the ground or line the area with stones, see 109–110. Prepare a bed of coals in the pit, and lay some flat stones on top of it to heat for 1 to 2 hours. After cleaning the fish and removing its gills, season the cavity with onions or herbs, or wipe with lemon. Close openings so that mud cannot get inside. Have ready a batch of "mudpie" clay, preferably blue clay, with which to coat the fish. Continue to lay on layers of mud until the covering is

1½ to 2 inches thick. Now clear away the top rocks and the coals from the pit. Place the "clay" fish on the hot lining stones and cover with earth and the rest of the hot stones you have set aside. Rebuild the fire over all and cook 1 to 3 hours, depending on size of fish. A 2½- to 3-pound fish will take about 2 hours. When it is done, uncover and crack open the clay mold. Skin and scales, head and tail will come off with the mold, revealing a delicious result. Needless to say, serve at once with corn roasted in the husks, 316.

## BAKED FISH FILLETS SPENCER

### 4 Servings

This method produces a tender crust outside and a tender and moist interior. Preheat oven to 550°.

Have ready:

**4 skinned fillets of carp or other fish**

and a plate of:

**Dry bread crumbs**

Fill a shallow pan with:

**½ cup warm milk**
**½ teaspoon salt**

Dip the fillets into the milk and crumbs, in that order, making sure they are well coated. Place them in a well-greased ovenproof pan and gently pour over them:

**3 tablespoons melted butter or bacon fat**

Place pan on top shelf of oven and bake 10 to 12 minutes, transferring at once to a hot platter garnished with parsley and lemon wedges. You may serve with:

**Tartare Sauce, 421,**
**Florentine Sauce, 384, or**
**Sauce Dijonnaise, 385**

## BAKED FILLETS OF FISH

**4 Servings**

Preheat oven to 350°
Place in a greased ovenproof dish:

**1½ lb. skinned fillets of sole or
    other fish**

If the fillets are large they may be cut
in half. Pour over them:

**1  cup dry white wine
(2  tablespoons dry sherry)**

Bake until just done, see 475. Serve
covered with the liquid from the dish,
which you may reduce slightly. Garnish with:

**Lemon wedges
Sautéed mushroom caps**

Or, you may omit the wine, baste
with a fish stock, (II, 173), or a small
quantity of canned clam juice, and
serve under:

**Curry Sauce, 390,
Champagne Sauce, 388, or
Aurore Sauce, 387**

## BAKED FISH WITH SOUR CREAM

**8 Servings**

Preheat oven to 350°.
Scale, clean, split and remove the
bones from:

**A 4-lb. whitefish or other
    fish**

Flatten it out. Rub inside and out with:

**Paprika and butter**

Place on an ovenproof dish. Cover
with:

**2  cups cultured sour
    cream**

Cover the dish. Bake about 45 minutes, or until done, see 475. Before
serving, sprinkle with:

**Chopped parsley**

## BAKED SMALL FISH FILLETS OR STICKS AU GRATIN

**Allow About ⅓ Pound per Serving**

Prepare for cooking:

**Small drawn, boned,
    skinned fish, pieces of fish
    or fish fillets**

Dip them in:

**¼  cup whole milk or cream**

then in:

**Seasoned bread crumbs or
    crushed cornflakes**

Let the fish dry on a rack for at least
20 minutes. Preheat oven to 350°.
Bake in an ovenproof dish until firm
and golden. Baste twice during the
cooking period with:

**Melted butter**

## QUICK BAKED FILLETS OF FISH

**3 Servings**

Preheat oven to 350°.
Place in a small ovenproof dish:

**1  lb. small, skinned fish fillets**

Stir and heat until smooth:

**⅔  cup condensed cream soup:
    tomato, celery, mushroom
    or asparagus**
**2  tablespoons milk or light
    stock**

Add:

**A few grains cayenne
(3  tablespoons finely chopped
    ham or prosciutto)**

Pour the sauce over the fish. Bake
♦ uncovered 10 minutes. Serve with:

**Boiled Rice, 189**

## FISH STEAKS OR FILLETS MARGUÉRY

**6 Servings**

Place in a mixture of boiling water
and wine and simmer until nearly
tender:

**6  skinned fillets or 3 steaks**

This will be a quick process if the pieces are thin. Drain the fish. Place in a greased baking dish. Keep them where they will remain warm. Melt:

**¼ cup butter**

Stir and sauté in it until done:

**½ lb. sliced mushrooms**

Stir in:

**¼ cup all-purpose flour**

Stir in gradually:

**1 cup milk**
**¾ cup cream**

Simmer in their liquor until plump:

**½ pint oysters: 1 cup**

Strain and reserve the liquor. Dry in a towel and add the oysters to the hot cream sauce. Stir in:

**¼ lb. cooked shelled deveined shrimp, split lengthwise**

Remove the sauce from the heat. Add the oyster liquor.

**Season to taste**

Pour the sauce over the fillets. Run under a boiler until the sauce colors.

## FILLETS OF FISH FLORENTINE WITH SHRIMP AND MUSHROOMS

**3 Servings**

Cook, 358, drain and chop:

**1 lb. spinach**

Poach, see right:

**1 lb. skinned fish fillets**

Cook, then shell and devein, 461–462:

**½ lb. shrimp cut lengthwise**

Sauté:

**½ lb. sliced mushrooms**

Place the spinach on a buttered oven-proof dish, with the fillets on top. Pour over them:

**White Wine Sauce, 389, Aurore Sauce, 387, or Mousseline Sauce, 412**

Surround them with the mushrooms and shrimp. Place the dish in a pre-heated 400° oven just long enough to heat.

## MOLDED FILLED FILLETS OF FISH, OR PAUPIETTES

**4 Servings**

Preheat oven to 350°.
Have ready:

**8 skinned fillets of Dover sole or bluefish, or other very thin fillets**

Butter 4 individual molds. Line each mold with 2 fillets crisscrossing at the bottom and extending up the sides, making sure that the fillets are long enough, when doubled back, to overlap at the top. Fill the center with the farce below, or with a fish quenelle mixture, 187, and fold the ends of the fillets to make a casing. With a fork, combine and stir a farce made of:

**¼ cup melted butter**
**1½ cups soft bread crumbs**
**¼ cup chopped celery**
**1 teaspoon grated onion**
**1 tablespoon chopped parsley**
**(⅛ teaspoon dried burnet or basil)**
**¼ teaspoon salt**

Fill the cases with this filling. Place the molds in a pan of hot water. Bake about 30 minutes. Unmold on a hot platter. Garnish with:

**Lemon wedges**
**Parsley or watercress**

Serve with:

**Lemon Butter, 397, Oyster Sauce, 386, or Anchovy Sauce, 386**

## STEAMING, POACHING OR BRAISING FISH

Steaming is one of the better ways to treat a delicate lean fish if you want to retain flavor; although—unlike meat—fish will lose more weight processed in this way than in poaching. Poaching—sometimes also called braising in fish cookery—runs steaming a close second.

A steamer has a perforated tray designed to hold the fish above the water level. Shown in the chapter heading is a poacher—the tray is not elevated and allows the fish to be immersed in the liquid. ❧ A poaching tray is always greased before the fish is placed on it. Fish may be poached in Fumets, (II, 173), in Court Bouillons, (II, 175), in Light Stocks, (II, 171–172), or à blanc, 555—depending on the flavor you wish to impart or the degree of whiteness you desire. If you are chiefly concerned with preserving the true flavor of the fish, salted water may be all you care to use. Allow 1 tablespoon of salt for every 2 quarts of water. For details, see individual recipes.

If fumet or light stock is used for the steaming or poaching liquid, you may want to use some of it either as is, or reduced, in the fish sauce. ❧ Court bouillons are not used in this way, nor are à blanc liquids, because they are both apt to contain too much vinegar and salt.

❧ Please read the general principles of Poaching, 101, which apply here. Small fish or cut pieces are started in a boiling liquid, large pieces in cold liquid—especially important— because ❧ immersing a fish of any considerable size in boiling water causes the skin to shrink and burst. In either case, when the liquid reaches the boiling point ❧ reduce it immediately to a simmer for the remainder of the cooking period, allowing 5 to 8 minutes per pound, depending on the size of the fish.

Without a poacher, there is the problem of keeping the top of the fish constantly bathed in liquid or steam. This problem can be solved by the use of a poaching paper, 101, or by tying the fish loosely in muslin. The latter procedure is a great help, after cooking, in lifting fish out of the pan without breaking them.

If a large pan is not available, cut the fish in two and place it in a smaller pan, with the halves dovetailed. The fish can be reassembled on a platter later. If served hot or cold, it can be masked with a sauce without anyone's being the wiser for your subterfuge. Whatever pan you are using, put into it several onion and lemon slices, a chopped carrot and a few ribs of celery. Fill the pan with Court Bouillon, (II, 175), to within an inch of the top. If you have used a cloth wrap, baste the fish with the court bouillon in which the fish is cooking as it simmers on the stove or in the oven. ❧ See that the cloth is always completely soaked. The top of the fish will then cook as quickly as the bottom.

After the cooking period the fish is sometimes allowed to cool in the water. We do not recommend this practice, as it leads to overcooking and waterlogging. ❧ If the fish is to be served cold, it is easier to remove the skin and trim the fish while it is still warm.

Another "hot-water" procedure— cooking au bleu—is fully described later in this chapter under the heading Blue Trout, 502.

## POACHED FISH STEAKS

**3 Servings**

Cut into pieces suitable for individual servings:

**1½ lb. halibut or other fish steak**

Place them in a skillet. Cover with:

**Boiling water**

Season with:

**4 whole peppercorns**

1/2 bay leaf
2 teaspoons lemon juice

Simmer about 10 minutes, or until tender. Remove to a hot platter. Strain the stock and use it to make the sauce. Try:

> Sauce Indienne, 388,
> Allemande Sauce, 390, or
> Anchovy Sauce, 386

## FISH FILLETS BONNE FEMME

**4 servings**

The tag **Bonne Femme** suggests the simple and straightforward flavor of this pleasing dish.

Cut, wipe with a damp cloth and dry:

> 4 skinned flat fish fillets, 472

Place in a buttered heavy skillet. Cover with:

> 3/4 cup finely sliced
>    mushrooms
> 1 minced shallot
> 1 teaspoon chopped parsley

Pour gently into the dish:

> 2/3 cup dry white wine

Cover with a poaching paper, 101, and ▶ simmer 10 to 15 minutes. Remove the fish onto a hot shallow ovenproof serving dish. Reduce the wine mixture by half. Stir into it gradually until well blended:

> 2/3 cup Velouté Sauce, 387

using fish stock. You may swirl in:

> 2 tablespoons butter

Pour the sauce over the fillets and run them under a broiler until sauce is lightly browned. Serve with:

> Boiled New Potatoes, 344

## FISH IN ASPIC COCKAIGNE

**About 5 Servings**

Scale and clean, leaving head and tail on, then cut into 4 or 5 pieces:

> A fish weighing about
>    2 1/2 lb.

Bring to the boiling point:

5 cups water
3 or 4 ribs celery with leaves
1 small sliced onion
4 or 5 sprigs parsley
3 tablespoons lemon juice
1 inch lemon rind
3 peppercorns
1/2 teaspoon dried herbs:
   tarragon, basil, etc.
1/2 teaspoon paprika
1 teaspoon salt

Drop the fish into the boiling stock. ▶ Simmer until tender. Do not let it boil again at any time. This is a quick process, requiring only 12 to 15 minutes or so. To test for doneness, see 474. Remove the fish from the stock. Strain the stock. There should be about 3 1/2 cups. If there is not, add water or chicken stock to make up the difference. Soak:

> 2 tablespoons gelatin

in:

> 1/4 cup cold fish stock

Dissolve it in the hot stock. Add:

> 2 tablespoons or more capers
> 2 or 3 tablespoons lemon
>    juice or dry white wine
>    Season to taste

Chill until stock begins to thicken. Remove the head, tail, skin and bone from the fish. Divide it into large flakes or pieces. Place a layer of aspic, (II, 234), in a wet mold, cover it with flaked fish and repeat this process, winding up with aspic on top. Chill. Serve the aspic very cold with:

> Mayonnaise, 419, or
> cultured sour cream

to either of which you may add:

> 1 to 2 tablespoons chopped
>    herbs: chives, tarragon or
>    parsley
>    Diced cucumbers

or with:

> Andalouse Sauce, 421, or
> Cold Mustard Sauce, 409

Decorate the platter with watercress

or shredded lettuce, and surround it with deviled eggs, radishes and olives. Serve with:

> **Brioche Loaf Cockaigne, (II, 306), or Garlic Bread, (II, 354)**

## GEFILTE FISH

**10 Servings**

In times gone by, this homely favorite was everywhere prepared in orthodox fashion, just as the name indicates: that is, a fish skin was stuffed with a mixture of ground-up raw fish, vegetables, eggs and spices, then cooked until tender in a rich fish broth. These days many of the good Jewish cooks we know dispense with this nerve-wracking ritual, and we follow suit. Clean thoroughly, bone and skin:

> **3 lb. mixed lean and fat fish, 469–470: whitefish, bluefish, jack salmon, pike, carp or buffalo**

Prepare a stock using the head, skin and bones, covered with a small amount of water. Simmer, covered, 30 to 40 minutes with:

> **1 medium-sized sliced onion**
> **3 chopped ribs celery, with leaves**
> **3 sliced carrots**
> **1 teaspoon salt**
> **1/4 teaspoon pepper**

If the broth cooks down too much, add more water. While the stock is cooking, grind the fish, using a medium blade, with:

> **1 small onion**
> **1 rib celery**
> **1/4 cup chopped parsley**

Put the fish mixture in a bowl and stir into it until fluffy:

> **2 beaten eggs**
> **1/4 cup matzo meal or crushed crackers**
> **1/2 teaspoon salt**

> **1/4 teaspoon pepper**
> **3/4 to 1 cup chilled water**

Cover the fish mixture and refrigerate until the stock has cooked. Dip hands in chilled water and shape fish into 1-inch balls. Strain fish stock and bring to a boil, adding more water if necessary to float the balls. Gently drop the balls into the stock: there should be enough room for them to puff up. Cover and barely simmer 2 hours; then simmer uncovered 30 minutes longer. Remove balls with slotted spoon. Thoroughly chill balls and stock. Chop the jellied stock as for aspic, 77, and serve as a garnish with:

> **Grated horseradish**

## PICKLED FISH OR ESCABÈCHE

**Allow 1/2 Pound per Serving**

For a similar raw fish, see Seviche, (II, 99).

▶ Please read About Deep-Fat Frying, 94. Use smelts, fresh anchovies, sardines, whitings or mullets not over 1/2 inch thick.

Clean, wash, dry and flour:

> **1 lb. small whole fish**

Plunge them into:

> **Hot cooking oil**

heated to 375°, for 5 to 10 seconds, according to size. Remove them, drain, and arrange in a shallow ovenproof glass or earthenware dish. Using 3 tablespoons of the oil, sauté until the onion is translucent:

> **2 tablespoons finely minced carrot**
> **1 small finely minced onion**
> **4 whole cloves garlic**

Add:

> **2/3 cup wine vinegar**
> **1/4 cup water**
> **A small bay leaf**
> **A sprig of thyme**
> **Salt**
> **2 small red hot peppers**

Simmer 10 minutes, then pour sauce over the fish. When cooled, refrigerate 24 hours. Serve the fish in the same dish in which it was marinated.

## ☰ BROILING FISH

"Ruling a large kingdom," observed Lao-tzu, "is like cooking a small fish." What he meant was that both should be discreetly handled, and the treatment never overdone. We have usually respected the old philosopher's advice. But in broiling fish, we have discovered that they taste even better when they can be subjected to quite high and intense, rather than gentle, heat. The following cooking procedure, for instance, is most effective.

For a 2½-pound fish, cleaned, scaled but unskinned, broil in the bottom of a preheated broiler at 400° for 5 minutes, then move to a top broiler for 5 minutes more at a preheated 800°. The 800° is not a misprint. But it requires coil or burner capacity that most household ranges are simply not equipped to supply, see 114. The closest practical home approach is to use a pair of vertical charcoal grills—set as sketched—which produce what is known in France as a *rôti* rather than a grill. Most of us, however, must be content with our range broilers preheated to 550°. ◗ It helps to warm up the broiling rack in advance, thus transferring some heat at once to the fish; but be sure to ◗ grease the rack after preheating so the fish will not stick. If the fish is to be turned, the double wire rack which fits into the vertical grill, as sketched, may also be conveniently used in the oven broiler pan. Grease it with cooking oil, and the fish with clarified butter. A lean fish may be floured before dotting with butter.

Fillets, flat and split fish are usually placed about 2 inches from the source of heat. If unskinned, place them skin side down. It is not necessary to turn them, but it is advisable to baste several times during the cooking period.

If thick fish steaks or large fish are being broiled, place the rack about 6 inches from the source of heat. They may take as long to cook as 5 or 6 minutes to a side.

Types of fish good for broiling include: halibut or salmon steaks, sole, and its cousins, split herring, mackerel and sea trout. For swordfish steaks, be sure to baste with plenty of butter, as they tend to become dry. Melted butter, lemon wedges and parsley adequately garnish broiled fish. If the fish is fat, try a spicy tomato sauce, 401–402, Cold Mustard, 409, Tartare, 421, or Allemande Sauce with capers, 390; if lean, Hollandaise, 410, Béarnaise, 412, or one of the seasoned butters. You will find specific sauce suggestions following some individual recipes.

## ☰ FISH BROILED ON SKEWERS, OR FISH KEBABS

**6 Servings**

Prepare:

**2 lb. skinned firm-fleshed fish: swordfish, halibut, cod or haddock**

Cut into 1-inch cubes. Place in a glass, enamel or stainless steel pan and marinate 30 minutes in:

½ cup cooking oil
½ cup lemon juice
¼ teaspoon powdered bay leaf
4 drops soy sauce

Stir once or twice to coat fish thoroughly.

Preheat broiler.

Thread on skewers, alternating with thick slices of:

2 marinated cucumbers II,
58, and stuffed olives

Broil or grill 10 minutes, turning frequently and basting with the marinade.

## SAUTÉED OR PAN-FRIED AND DEEP-FAT-FRIED FISH

In pan-frying sizable fish, it is important to use Clarified Butter, 396, but equally important to ◗ combine it about half and half with cooking oil, since the butter may otherwise burn. To keep the fat from spattering your hands, you may cover the pan with an inverted colander. The fish is placed in the pan when the fat mixture begins to sizzle. Reduce the heat slightly. When the bottom side is completely cooked, turn the fish and cook until the second side is done. Quite large fish may be sautéed on both sides until seared, then placed in a preheated 375° oven about 10 minutes for finishing.

To prepare deep-fat-fried fish, please read About Deep-Fat Frying, 94, and then follow the recipes below with care.

## SAUTÉED OR PAN-FRIED FISH

I. Scale, if necessary, and clean, 471:

A large fish or several small
pan fish: crappie, brook
trout, sunfish, perch, etc.

Cut the large fish into steaks or darnes before rolling them or the smaller fish in:

Seasoned flour or cornmeal
or Bound Breading, (II, 220)

Melt in a skillet to the depth of ⅛ inch:

Clarified Butter, 396, and
cooking oil

When the fat is hot, place the fish in the pan. Reduce the heat slightly and cook until done, from 3 to 5 minutes.

II.
2 Servings

Scale if necessary and clean, 471–472:

A small fish—1 lb. or less:
trout, sunfish, bream,
crappie, perch, etc.

Dip it into a mixture of:

½ cup milk
1 teaspoon salt

Sauté until flaky, turning once, in:

2 tablespoons Clarified
Butter, 396, and 2
tablespoons bacon fat, or
use 1 tablespoon each
butter and olive oil

Transfer fish to a hot plate and pour over it the pan drippings, seasoned with:

A little dry white wine or
light stock
Chopped dill or tarragon
(A few minced capers)

Garnish with sprigs of parsley.

## SAUTÉED FILLETS OF FISH AMANDINE

Allow ⅓ Pound per Serving

Dip:

Skinned fillets of sole,
perch, brook trout,
haddock, etc.

in:

Milk

Dust with:

Flour

Melt in a skillet:

Butter

Use enough to cover the bottom well. Sauté the fillets in the pan. Turn once. Place on a hot platter. Melt additional:

**Butter**

Brown in it lightly:

**Shredded blanched almonds**

Pour them over the fillets. Garnish the dish with:

**Lemon and parsley**

## SAUTÉED FISH FILLETS PALM BEACH

**2 Servings**

Bread if you like:

**2 small skinned fish fillets**

Sauté until golden brown in:

**2 tablespoons Clarified Butter, 396**

Serve with 3 or 4 alternate sections of:

**Grapefruit and orange**

on each fillet. Pour the pan gravy over the garnished fillets and serve at once.

## DEEP-FAT-FRIED FISH

**Allow About ¹/₃ Pound per Serving**

♦ Please read About Deep-Fat Frying, 94. Have fish at 70°. Clean and prepare for cooking:

**Small fish or 1-inch pieces of fish**

Dip them in:

**Fritter Batter for Fish, (II, 155), or Bound Breading, (II, 220)**

Fry in deep fat heated to 370° for 5 to 8 minutes, or until a golden brown. The fish will rise to the surface when done. Drain on absorbent paper. Serve very hot with:

**Lemon Butter Sauce, 397, Tartare Sauce, 421, or Sour Cream Horseradish Dressing, 408**

## MARINATED DEEP-FAT-FRIED FISH

**3 Servings**

♦ Please read About Deep-Fat Frying, 94. Skin and cut into pieces:

**1¹/₂ lb. fish steaks: cod, halibut, catfish, whitefish, etc.**

Marinate 30 minutes in:

**6 tablespoons dry white wine or 2 tablespoons lemon juice**

Drain dry and dip each piece separately in:

**6 tablespoons cream**

then in:

**Flour**

Fry the fish in deep fat heated to 370° about 7 minutes. Serve with:

**Tartare Sauce, 421**

## FISH AND CHIPS

**4 Servings**

♦ Please read About Deep-Fat Frying, 94.

Cut into uniform serving pieces:

**1¹/₂ lb. skinned fillet of flounder**

Coat with:

**Fritter Batter for Fish, (II, 155)**

Cut into thick uniform strips slightly larger than for French fries:

**1¹/₂ lb. mature baking potatoes**

Soak in cold water for ¹/₂ hour. Drain and dry thoroughly. Fry in deep fat heated to 375° until golden brown. Remove, drain and keep warm. Deep-fry the breaded fish until golden brown. Arrange potatoes and fish on a platter and serve on the side as a dip:

**Hot cider vinegar**

or serve with:

**Ravigote Sauce, 389**

## SOUTHERN-FRIED CATFISH

Clean and skin:

**A catfish**

Dredge with:

**Seasoned white cornmeal**

Fry in deep fat heated to 370° until golden brown.

Serve with:

**Hush Puppies, (II, 344)**
**Sliced Tomatoes, 64**

and:

**Sauce Dijonnaise, 385, or**
**Allemande Sauce with**
**capers, 390**

## ABOUT CARP

These great, languid soft-finned fish whose portraits we admire on Chinese scrolls can be admirable eating too. But be sure to hold them alive for several days in clear running water to rid them of the muddiness they acquire in their native haunts. To enjoy carp at their best, kill them just before cooking. If you cannot appoint a Lord High Executioner and must perform the act yourself, we recommend a preliminary perusal of the chapter called "Murder in the Kitchen" in Alice B. Toklas's weird and wonderful *Cookbook*.

Carp lend themselves to cooking Au Bleu, 502; are delicious baked, stuffed or braised; in red wine, (II, 176); and may be eaten hot or cold. If cold, try Sauce Gribiche, 422, or Aioli Sauce, 423. Serve hot with new potatoes and Celeriac, 313.

## ABOUT COD

Fabulous were the early voyagers' tales about the plenitude of cod, which gave its name to America's most curiously shaped and best-known cape. Because it was the mainstay of the colonists' diet, cod assumed many variations which persist today. **Scrod** is a term for cod weighing 2 pounds or under but may refer to pollock and haddock.

**Salt cod,** often very tough, is pounded before desalting. To freshen salt cod, leave it under running water for 6 hours; or soak it up to 48 hours in several changes of water in a glass, enamel or stainless steel pan. Salt cod is most often used flaked. To prepare for flaking, put the desalted fish in cold unsalted Court Bouillon, (II, 175), to cover, then bring it to a boil and ◗ simmer 20 to 30 minutes. Drain, skin, bone and flake it. One pound dried salt cod will yield about 2 cups cooked flaked fish.

## SCALLOPED COD

**4 Servings**

Preheat oven to 375°.

◗ Please read about Salt Cod, above.

Cook and flake:

**1 lb. dried salt cod**

Combine:

**1 tablespoon flour**
**2 cups milk**
**1 well-beaten egg**

Cook and stir these ingredients until they are thick, in the top of a double boiler ◗ over—not in—boiling water.

**Season to taste**

Prepare:

**1½ cups bread crumbs**
**1½ cups finely chopped celery**

Grease a baking dish. Place in it half the fish and a layer of one-third the crumbs and celery. Cover with half the sauce and repeat the process. Sprinkle the remaining crumbs on the top. Dot with:

**Buttered or grated cheese**

Bake about 20 minutes, or until the crumbs are golden brown.

## CODFISH BALLS OR CAKES

**4 Servings**

▶ Please read about Salt Cod, 486.
Prepare:

**1 cup desalted, flaked salt
cod**

Rice or mash:

**6 medium-sized boiled
potatoes, or half potatoes
and half parsnips**

Combine the fish and vegetables.
Beat in one at a time:

**2 eggs**

Beat in until fluffy:

**2 tablespoons cream
(1 teaspoon grated onion)
(1 teaspoon dry mustard)
(1 teaspoon Worcestershire
sauce)
Season to taste**

Shape the mixture into balls or patties, and use one of the following
cooking methods.


**I.** Form the mixture into 2-inch
cakes, dip in flour and sauté in butter
until brown. Serve at once.


**II.** Form into 1-inch balls, dip in
milk, roll in flour. Fry until golden
brown in deep fat heated to 375°.


**III.** Preheat oven to 375°.
Form into patties and bake in a
greased pan about 30 minutes. Dot
with butter and serve.


With all of the above versions you
may enjoy:

**Hot Mustard Sauce, 390,
Anchovy Sauce, 386, or
Aurore Sauce, 387**

## FRESH COD À LA PORTUGAISE

**4 Servings**

Season:

**4 thick cod fillets**

with:

**Pepper**

Place the fish in a heavy saucepan.
Add:

**1 finely chopped onion
1 crushed clove garlic
1/4 cup coarsely chopped
parsley
A sprig of thyme
3 peeled, seeded and coarsely
chopped tomatoes
1/2 cup dry white wine**

Bring to boiling point, ▶ reduce the
heat and simmer gently, covered,
about 10 minutes. Remove the fish
carefully. Arrange it on a hot serving
dish and keep warm. Reduce the
cooking liquid by one-third.

**Season to taste**

and finish with a:

**Butter Swirl, 380**

Pour the sauce over the fish and serve
at once.


## ⚒ BRANDADE DE MORUE

**10 Servings**

Suitable for serving hot as a main
dish or cold as an hors d'oeuvre, a
brandade is in either case beaten to a
mousselinelike consistency.
▶ Please read about Salt Cod, 486.
Prepare for flaking and poach about
30 minutes in water to cover:

**1 1/2 lb. freshened salt cod**

Have ready:

**2 cups freshly boiled, riced
potatoes**

Drain and flake the fish and combine
it with:

**1/3 cup warm olive oil**

in which you have sautéed, then
removed:

**2  cloves garlic**

Have ready:

**1  cup warm milk or cream**

Put the fish and oil mixture into a blender alternately with the potatoes and the warm milk, and blend at moderate speed until it is smooth and fluffy. Serve it hot on a platter garnished with:

**Grilled Tomatoes, 367, and**
**Buttered Croutons, (II, 219)**

or chilled, garnished with:

**Parsley and black olives**

## COD SOUNDS AND TONGUES

**Allow About ¼ Pound per Serving**

Sounds—or cod cheeks—and tongues, really the meat at the base of the tongue, may come fresh or salted. If salted, they must be soaked overnight, drained, simmered 5 minutes in water started cold, then drained again.

To poach, cover with boiling water, reduce the heat and simmer about 5 minutes. Drain. You may serve them with:

**Mornay Sauce, 384, or**
**Allemande Sauce, 390**

Or you may bread, (II, 219), and sauté them until golden brown and serve with:

**Maître d'Hôtel Butter, 398**

## FRESH COD BOULANGÈRE

**4 Servings**

Preheat oven to 350°.

Parboil in separate pans:

**16  small peeled potatoes**
**12  small white onions**

Place in a buttered shallow ovenproof dish:

**A center cut of cod or a**
**whole small cleaned cod**

Arrange the onions and potatoes around it and sprinkle with:

**A pinch of thyme**
**Season to taste**

Brush frequently during the baking process with:

**Melted butter**

Bake about ½ hour. Serve in the same dish garnished with:

**Chopped parsley**
**Slices of lemon**

## BROILED FRESH SCROD

**Allow ½ Pound per Serving**

Split, then remove the bones from:

**A young codfish**

Leave it whole, flatten it out, or cut it in pieces. Broil as described on 483.

## ABOUT EEL

The eel is a fish that believes in long journeys. It is spawned in the Sargasso Sea in the western Atlantic, and from there will travel back to its freshwater haunts in this country or in Europe to feed and grow up in the rivers and streams frequented by its parents. The young eel or elver is still only 2 or 3 inches long after its immense journey, and is transparent and yellowish. Little eels can be cooked and larger ones smoked or pickled to make a delicious addition to hors d'oeuvre or Antipasto, (II, 84).

As with cats, there is more than one way to skin a fresh eel. We prefer the following. Keep the eel alive until ready to skin. Kill it with a sharp blow to the head. Slip a noose around the eel's head and hang the other end of the cord on a hook, high on the wall. Cut the eel skin about 3 inches below the head all around, so as not to penetrate the gallbladder, which lies close to the head. Peel the skin back, pulling down hard—if necessary with a pair of pliers—until the whole skin comes off like a glove.

Clean the fish by slitting the white belly and removing the gut, which lies close to the thin belly skin.

Eel may be sautéed as for:

**Trout Meunière, 502**

poached 9 to 10 minutes and then served with a:

**Velouté Sauce, 387**

or one of its variations, made from the eel stock.

Skinned, cleaned, boned and cut into 3-inch pieces and dried, eel may be dipped in:

**Batter, (II, 155), or Bound
Breading, (II, 220)**

and deep-fried until golden brown. Serve this way with:

**Fried Parsley, 338, and
lemon wedges, or Tartare
Sauce, 421, or a tomato
sauce**

Eel may also be broiled as for any fat fish, 483.

## MARINATED FLOUNDER FILLETS

**6 Servings**

Marinate 10 minutes:

**2 lb. flounder fillets**

in:

**1 cup tarragon vinegar**

Drain, and coat with a mixture of:

**1/2 cup yellow cornmeal
1/2 cup flour
1/4 teaspoon salt
1/8 teaspoon freshly ground
pepper**

Sauté the fillets in:

**1/4 cup butter**

until golden brown, about 4 minutes on each side. Serve with:

**Ravigote Sauce, 389, or
Nantua Sauce, 385**

## ABOUT HADDOCK

Fresh haddock may be prepared as in any recipe for cod, flounder or other lean white fish. It may be baked plain or stuffed, its fillets fried, sautéed, or poached. Smoked haddock—or **finnan haddie**—may be broiled, well basted in butter, or baked, as in the recipes below.

## BAKED FILLETS OF FRESH HADDOCK IN CHEESE SAUCE

**4 Servings**

Preheat oven to 350°.

Place on an ovenproof dish:

**4 haddock or other lean fish
fillets**

Prepare:

**2 cups Mornay Sauce, 384**

Season the sauce well, adding:

**1 teaspoon Worcestershire
sauce, or 1/2 teaspoon dry
mustard, or 1 teaspoon
fennel, dill or celery seed**

Pour it over the fillets. Bake the fish until done, see 475. You may sprinkle over the top:

**(1 cup or more freshly cooked
or canned shrimp or crab
meat)**

Place the dish under a broiler until thoroughly warmed. Garnish with:

**Chopped parsley**

## BAKED FILLETS OF FRESH HADDOCK WITH MUSHROOMS AND TOMATOES

**6 Servings**

Preheat oven to 375°.

Using a large saucepan, sauté about 5 minutes:

**1/2 cup chopped onion
1/4 cup chopped celery
1/2 cup chopped fresh
mushrooms**

in:

**3 tablespoons butter**

Stir into the sautéed vegetables:

**2 cups soft bread crumbs**
**1 teaspoon salt**
**1/8 teaspoon pepper**
**A pinch of dried tarragon**
**(A pinch of dried rosemary)**

Arrange in a layer on a large shallow greased baking dish:

**2 lb. haddock fillets**

Sprinkle the fish with:

**Lemon juice**

and spread the dressing over it. Cover with:

**3 or 4 skinned sliced**
**tomatoes**

Bake uncovered 35 to 40 minutes. Serve with:

**Boiled Potatoes, 343**

## BAKED FINNAN HADDIE

**6 Servings**

Preheat oven to 350°.
Prepare for cooking:

**2 lb. smoked haddock**

by soaking it in warm water for 30 minutes, skin side down. Pour off the water. Put the fish on a greased oven-proof pan and cover with:

**1 cup cream**

Dot generously with:

**Butter**

Sprinkle with:

**1/4 cup chopped onions**
**Paprika**

Bake about 40 minutes. If cream evaporates, use additional cream. The dish may be served with:

**Florentine Sauce, 384, or a**
**tomato sauce, 400**

## CREAMED FINNAN HADDIE

Barely cover:

**Smoked haddock**

with:

**Milk**

Soak 1 hour. Bring slowly to the boiling point. Simmer 20 minutes. Drain. Flake and remove the skin and bones. Place the fish in very hot:

**White Sauce I, 383**

Use about two-thirds as much sauce as you have fish. Add for each cup of flaked fish:

**1 chopped hard-cooked egg**
**1 teaspoon chopped green**
**pepper, seeds and**
**membrane removed**
**1 teaspoon chopped pimiento**

Serve fish on:

**Rounds of toast**

sprinkled with:

**Lemon juice**
**Chopped chives or parsley**

## CURED FISH

You may smoke your own fresh fish, (II, 637), if you like, in which case they must be cooked before serving. Some commercially cured fish—smoked, dried, salted or pickled—come both preserved and prepared for serving. Haddock and several kinds of herring are usually Cold-Smoked, (II, 634). They have been salted and smoked over a smoldering fire to the dry stage, but have not been cooked. Whitefish, chub and salmon are usually Hot-Smoked, (II, 634), so that they cook in the heat of the smoking fire, and so can be used without further cooking. Haddock, when smoked, becomes **finnan haddie**. A smoked herring is known as a **kipper**—actually, a general term for any smoked fish. ♦ Store all smoked fish refrigerated in covered containers to lengthen their keeping period.

Cod, mackerel and herring are often salted and air-dried, and before cooking should be soaked in water for several hours—skin side down. If soaking in fresh running water is not practical, change the water frequently during the soaking period. For ways to cook, see salt cod, 486. Fish was often pickled in the days before refrigeration, and in eighteenth-century English and American cookbooks you will find recipes for "caveaching" fish in spices, oil and vinegar. We imagine there is a relationship between the French *escabèche,* and its Spanish variant, **seviche,** in word derivation and method. Nowadays, herring and mackerel are usually reserved for pickling, although Escabèche, 482, can be used for small fish, like fresh anchovies, sardines, young mullet and whiting.

## ABOUT HERRING

Herring is one of the least expensive, most nutritious and readily obtainable fish one can buy. It is very fat, with a calcium content twice that of milk. "Kippering" originally referred to the reddening of certain types of salmon when salted and smoked at spawning time. Reddish color induced in other kinds of similarly processed fish is due to artificial coloring. Split, salted and smoked, a herring of any hue today is known as a **kipper;** smoke-cured without salt, as a **bloater.** Bloaters are very perishable and should be eaten right after curing. Perhaps the reason herring is not more popular is that it has innumerable tiny, fine bones. If you split a herring down the center of the back with a sharp knife, lever up the backbone and carefully pull it out, most of these small bones will come with it. After cleaning, 471, you may then cook the herring in one piece or split it in two.

Marinated herring comes in various disguises. **Rollmops,** (II, 100), are fresh herring fillets seasoned and rolled—like Paupiettes, 479,—around a pickle or cucumber. **Bismarck herring** is the flat fillet in a sour marinade; **matjes** or virgin herring can be sour or salted. Commercially available, too, are female herring containing the "hard" roe, or egg-cluster, and male herring caught before the dispersal of their fertilizing fluid, or **milt**—sometimes also referred to as "soft" roe. Usually, when processed, both of these roes are extracted, thinned, and mixed with sour cream or a vinegar-based additive as the sauce in which the herring is packed. For more roe information, see 497.

## BAKED HERRING AND POTATOES

**4 Servings**

**I.** Preheat oven to 375°.
To prepare salt herring, soak overnight in water or milk to cover:

  **2  large salt herring**

Drain and split them. Remove and discard skin and bones. Cut fillets into 1-inch-wide pieces. Pare and slice very thinly:

  **6  raw potatoes**
  **2  medium-sized onions**

Butter a baking dish. Place in it alternate layers of potatoes, onions and herring, beginning and ending with potatoes. Cover the top with:

  **Au Gratin II, (II, 221)**

Bake 45 minutes or more.

**II.** A Yorkshire version substitutes:

  **Sour apples**

for the onions, and uses:

  **Fresh herring**

In this case, prepare as above, but season with:

  **Salt and pepper**

after each layer of herring.

## MARINATED HERRING

**12 Servings**

Soak for 3 hours in water to cover:

**24 milter herring**

Change the water twice. Cut off the heads and tails. Split the herring. Remove the milt, see 491. Reserve it. Remove the bones as described, 491. Discard them. Cut the fillets into pieces about 3 inches long. Place in a crock in alternate layers with the herring:

**½ the milt**
**2 very thinly sliced lemons**
**2 skinned and thinly sliced onions**
**⅓ cup mixed pickle spices**
**1 tablespoon sugar**

Cover these ingredients with:

**Malt or other vinegar**

Soften with a fork and add:

**The remaining milt**

Dilute the vinegar with a little water if it is very strong. ◗ Cover the crock and keep refrigerated. The herring will be ready to serve after one week.

## SWEET AND SOUR HERRING

**Allow 1 Herring per Serving**

Prepare as for Marinated Herring, above:

**6 milter herring**

using only 1 lemon, 1 onion, 2½ tablespoons mixed spices and ¼ cup vinegar. Add:

**1 cup cultured sour cream**

Keep in a cool place. Serve after 48 hours.

## SCOTCH FRIED HERRING

**Allow 1 Herring per Serving**

This dish must be made with:

**Fresh-caught herring**

You may fry them whole, but they are better split down the backbone and boned, as described, 491. Cut off head, tail and fins. Roll in:

**Medium-ground seasoned Scotch oatmeal**

pressing a little to make it stick. Fry the herring on both sides in:

**Bacon fat or olive oil**

Serve with:

**Lemon wedges**
**A pat of butter**

or with:

**Hot Mustard Sauce, 390**

Garnish with:

**Parsley**

## GRILLED OR BAKED KIPPERS OR BLOATERS

**Allow ½ Pound per Serving**

An excellent breakfast dish with scrambled eggs. Do not try to grill canned kippers; they are too wet. Preheat broiler.

Place:

**Kippers or bloaters**

skin side down on a hot oiled grill. Dot with:

**Butter**

Grill 5 to 7 minutes. Serve very hot. You may also bake them in a 350° oven 10 minutes, or En Papillote, 105, 15 minutes at the same temperature. Season with:

**A little lemon juice**
**Pepper**

## ABOUT OCTOPUS AND SQUID

Both of these **inkfish** belong emphatically to the large category of horrendous-looking sea creatures that must be eaten to be appreciated. These mollusks are not dissimilar in shape and taste, having long edible arms, a tail portion that can be formed into a natural sack for stuffing if desired, as well as an ink-expelling sac which furnishes the pigment known as sepia. The latter is used in recipes just as blood is used, 380, to color, flavor and give body to sauces, often seasoned with nutmeg and garlic. When the ink is not available, it is sometimes faked by the use of chocolate, as in the sauce for Turkey Casserole Mole, 524.

Octopus, which has eight arms, grows to enormous size but is apt to be very tough if over 2 to 2½ pounds in weight. These and squid that are longer than 8 inches after cleaning need tenderizing. Pound them mercilessly on a solid surface. To prepare fresh octopus for cooking, make sure

first that your victim is dead—by striking it a conclusive blow on the head. Remove the beaklike mouth, the anal portion and the eyes, taking care in doing so not to pierce the ink sac, which lies close by. Reserve this for later use. If the inkfish is small, these operations may be performed with a pair of scissors; if larger, you will need a knife to penetrate far enough to slip the creature inside out and remove and discard the yellowish pouch and the attached membranes. With octopus the very ends of the tentacles are also discarded. Cut out all cartilage and wash the fish well in running water to remove gelatinous portions.

Preparation procedure for fresh squid differs somewhat. After the same advance precautions—squid bite, too—grasp the head section firmly at a point just below the eyes. You can then pull free from the rest of the body the outer portion of the tail and fin section. Also revealed will be the grayish ink sac. Remove it carefully to a sieve. Next, cut the tentacles free just above the eye section. Discard the eye section along with the innards and a small roundish cartilage at the base of the tentacles which can be popped out with the fingers. Discard also the icicle-shaped pen or cuttlebone inside the tail. This slim bone, when dried, becomes the bone one sees in bird cages. You will also encounter a red membrane which covers much of the squid. This should be as nearly removed as possible by rubbing, or by parblanching briefly 1 to 2 minutes. Arrest further cooking by plunging into cold water. When plunging octopus into boiling water, drop it in with a sliding motion head first so its tentacles won't spread out. Remaining then, as edible, are the tentacles and the peeled tail section and fins, as well as the ink sac fluid, which, like that of the octopus, makes a flavorsome seasoning for a sauce.

With both types of inkfish, arms and tentacles are cut crosswise in 1- to 1¼-inch rounds, and to equalize the cooking time, the white portions of the body meat are often cut into squares or diamond shapes of about the same size. Octopus need long, slow cooking. Even after marinating, the simmering time may run close to 3 hours, unless the specimens are very young, when about 50 minutes should suffice. For squid cooking times, see individual recipes.

Squid is available in cans ready to use and is sometimes found frozen or dried. ◗ To use dried squid, marinate in a combination of water, gin and ginger for 45 minutes, and then use in recipes as for the fresh meat.

♦ Allow about ½ pound of fresh squid or octopus per person.

## CASSEROLED OCTOPUS OR SQUID

**Allow ½ Pound per Person**

Clean, pound, and cut up as described on 493 and place in a flameproof casserole:

**6 small octopus or squid**
**½ cup olive oil**
**⅓ cup vinegar or ½ cup dry wine**
**2 cups julienned mushrooms**
**1 cup chopped onions**
**1 pressed clove garlic**
**1 tablespoon each fresh chopped parsley, chervil and basil**
**⅓ bay leaf**

Cover and bring just to a boil. ♦ Reduce the heat at once and simmer, very tightly covered, 2½ to 3 hours. You may add the ink to the pan drippings just before serving. ♦ Do not boil. Serve with:

**Creamed Spinach, 359**

## FRIED SQUID

**Allow ½ Pound per Person**

Clean and wash as described on 493. Leave whole or cut into 1- to 1½-inch pieces:

**Small squid**

Some sophisticates discard the tentacles. Clean the pouch well, removing the cuttlebone in the flesh at the back and using only the remaining flesh, cut into narrow strips. Dry well and dust with:

**Flour**

Deep-fry at 365° until golden brown. Serve at once sprinkled with:

**Salt, white pepper and lemon juice**

## STUFFED SQUID

**Allow 2 per Person**

Choose:

**Twelve 5-inch squid**

Cut below the eyes and discard the head and tentacles. Without splitting, clean the pouch thoroughly, removing the bone. Cut out the fins and pull off the black skin.

Preheat oven to 325°.

Prepare half of the recipe for:

**Rice Dressing for Cornish Hen, 435**

and stuff each squid and tie each pouch at the top. Place them in a single layer in an ovenproof baking dish and cover with a mixture of:

**¼ cup olive oil**
**¼ cup tomato sauce**
**½ cup white wine**
**½ cup water**
**¼ cup finely chopped parsley**

Sprinkle this sauce with a heavy coating of:

**Dry bread crumbs**

Bake about 1 hour and 15 minutes or until the squid is tender. Serve hot or cold.

## SQUID IN INK SAUCE

**4 Servings**

♦ Please read About Squid, 492.

Clean and cut up:

**2 lb. squid**

Place the ink sacs in a sieve and press the ink into a bowl beneath it. To extract more ink, pour over the ink sacks while continuing to press:

**1 cup water**

Add to the ink mixture and beat until smooth:

**1½ tablespoons flour**
**A grating of nutmeg**

and reserve this mixture. Heat in a heavy skillet:

**¾ cup olive oil**

When hot, sauté until translucent:

**¾ cup chopped onions**
**1 pressed clove garlic**

Then add the cut-up squid. Reduce heat at once. Simmer covered about 20 minutes. Add the ink mixture. Stir constantly over low heat at least 5 minutes until the sauce thickens.
◗ Do not allow the sauce to boil.

**Season to taste**

and serve at once over:

**Pasta, 199, or**
**Boiled Rice, 189**

## BROILED FRESH MACKEREL

Preheat broiler.
Split and bone, see 471:

**A fresh mackerel**

Place it skin side down in a greased pan. Sprinkle with:

**Paprika**

Brush with:

**Melted butter or olive oil**

Broil slowly on one side only until firm, about 20 minutes. Baste with the drippings while cooking. Remove to a hot platter. Spread with:

**Anchovy Butter, 397**

Garnish with:

**Parsley and lemon slices**

## BOILED SALT MACKEREL

**Allow ⅓ to ½ Pound per Serving**

Soak overnight, skin side up, well covered with cold water:

**Salt mackerel**

Drain, place in a shallow pan, cover with water and simmer until tender, about 12 minutes. Drain well. Place on a hot platter. Pour over the fish:

**Melted butter**

to which add:

**Chopped chives or parsley,**
**lemon juice or**
**Worcestershire sauce**

## BROILED SALT MACKEREL

**Allow ⅓ to ½ Pound per Serving**

Soak as in the preceding recipe:

**Salt mackerel**

Drain, then wipe dry.
Preheat broiler.
Brush with:

**Melted butter**

Broil, skin side down, about 20 minutes. Baste twice with melted butter while cooking. Remove to a hot platter. Pour over the fish:

**½ cup Bercy Butter, 398**

Garnish with:

**Watercress**

## POMPANO EN PAPILLOTE

**Individual Serving**

Preheat oven to 450°.
Place on heart-shaped parchment paper, 101:

**2 medium-sized skinned**
**pompano fillets**

Cover with:

**Shrimp Sauce, 385**

Close the parchment paper, fold the edge and bake about 15 minutes until the paper is browned and puffed. Serve immediately. For a party, make individual packets ahead of time, refrigerate and, before baking, allow them to reach about 60°. Preheat oven and bake as above.

## ABOUT SALMON

Atlantic salmon, pink and prized, comes to our markets mainly fresh, pink—and prized. In England it wasn't always so. Indentured apprentices petitioned that they should not be forced to eat fresh salmon more than twice a week!

Pacific salmon reaches us in many forms. These include the choice King or Chinook from Alaska and the Columbia River areas. They may be pink or white-fleshed and are about 17% fat. Included also are the red-fleshed sockeye, the pinkish silver Coho and the yellowish-fleshed, almost fat-free dog salmon. ◗ All smoked salmon, including the delicious **lox,** is highly perishable and should be kept refrigerated. For other salmon dishes, see Brunch, Lunch and Supper Dishes, 262–265.

## BROILED SALMON STEAKS OR DARNES

**Allow ¹/₂ Pound per Serving**
Preheat broiler.
To cut steaks or darnes, see 472.
Brush preheated broiler rack and:

> **³/₄- inch-thick salmon steaks**

well with:

> **Clarified Butter, 396**

Place rack 6 inches from the source of heat. Broil 5 minutes. Baste, turn, baste again and continue to broil 5 to 8 minutes. To test for doneness, see if you can lift out the central bone without bringing any of the flesh with it. Serve with:

> **Freshly grated horseradish**

The steak shape lends itself to attractive service, as the hollow may be filled with:

> **A stuffed tomato, or a**
> **mound of vegetables, or**
> **potatoes garnished with**
> **parsley**

More elaborate dressings for this dish are:

> **(Sour Cream Horseradish**
> **Dressing, 408, or Hot**
> **Mustard Sauce, 390)**

## COLD GLAZED SALMON

**Allow ¹/₂ Pound per Serving**
This method of preparation applies to any fish you wish to glaze and serve cold.
Poach, 101, leaving head and tail on:

> **1  large cleaned salmon**

Remove from the poaching water when done. Leaving the head and tail, and working with the grain, skin and trim the rest of the fish, removing the fins and the gray, fatty portions until just the pink flesh is left. Place on a large serving platter and refrigerate. If time is limited, the fish may be eaten just this way with mayonnaise. But to glaze—and build up to a culinary event—read on. ◗ Work quickly to prevent the glaze from darkening, and keep chilling between processes. Coat the visible pink portion of the fish evenly and smoothly with:

> **Mayonnaise Collée, 427, or**
> **Sauce Chaud-Froid, 428**

Rechill until this sauce has set. Decorate as described in the Sauce Chaud-Froid recipe. Chill again. Coat the whole surface, head and tail too, with:

> **Aspic Glaze, 427**

Chill and continue coating and chilling until you have built up an even clear ¹/₄ inch of aspic. Clean the platter by removing aspic dribbles. Save any leftover aspic and chill it in sheet form. Chop it fine and surround the fish with an edging of little sparkling tidbits. Serve the fish with:

> **Andalouse Sauce, 421, or**
> **Green Mayonnaise, 420**

The classic garnish is:

> **Tiny tomatoes stuffed with**
> **Russian Salad, 54**

We suggest also:

> **Cold leeks marinated, 325**

## ABOUT SARDINES

Sardines were to us something that came out of a can on laundry day—until one summer we entertained a Breton guest. Her family had for centuries lived an amicably divided life in seaside castles on opposite sides of a river inlet. Her uncle's fleets dredged seaweed from which chemicals were produced. Her father's fleet sailed from Maine to Spain—following those Atlantic sardines which were fit even for the Czar of Russia himself, to whom they were purveyed. But fish, like people, may change habits suddenly. For three years the fleet failed to find the sardine runs. Sonar might have changed Odette's fate, but Brittany's loss was our vivacious and warm-hearted gain.

True sardines are types of herring, and those caught in the Pacific are much larger—up to 10 or 12 inches long—than those taken in Atlantic or Mediterranean waters, which are known in Britain and the Dominions as **pilchard. Anchovies** and **sprats** are closely related. Treat fresh sardines as for smelts, 499.

If you want to present canned sardines in an interesting way, skin and bone:

**12 canned sardines**

Mash 6 of them with:

**1 teaspoon minced onion**
**2 teaspoons butter**
**½ teaspoon prepared mustard**
**1 teaspoon lemon juice**

Spread:

**6 narrow toast strips**

with this mixture. Place a whole sardine on each toast and run under the broiler. Before serving, garnish with:

**Finely chopped fennel**
**A grating of black pepper**

## ABOUT SEA SQUAB OR BLOWFISH

These puffers are related to the sought-after Japanese fugu. As the ovaries and liver are very poisonous, be sure to discard all but the back flesh before cooking. Prepare as for any delicate fish.

## ABOUT ROE AND MILT

The eggs of the female fish are known as **roe** or hard roe; the male fish's sperm is known as **milt** or soft roe, as its texture is creamy rather than grainy. Both types are used in cooking, and the roe of certain fish is more valued than the fish itself, see Caviar, (II, 97).

Shad roe is considered choice. You may serve the roe or milt of other fish such as herring, mackerel, flounder, salmon, carp, or cod as in the following recipes for shad roe. The milt of salmon must have the vein removed.

Hard roe, to be cooked and served alone, should be pricked with a needle to prevent the membrane from bursting and splattering the little eggs. Cook roe gently with very slow heat. Overcooked, it is hard, dry and tasteless. If pepper is used in seasoning, use only white pepper. Roe may be served as a luncheon dish; as a savory; as stuffing or garnish for the fish from which it comes. Or it may be used raw, as in Marinated Herring, 492, or as an hors d'oeuvre. Also see canned roe dishes, 266.

◗ Allow 6 oz. per serving.

## PARBOILED SHAD ROE

◗ Please read About Roe, above.
Prick with a needle in several places and cover with boiling water:

**Shad roe**

Add to it:

  **2 tablespoons lemon juice or
  3 tablespoons dry white
  wine**

Simmer from 3 to 12 minutes, according to size. Drain and cool. Remove the membrane. Add salt if needed. The roe is now ready to be sautéed, sauced, or used in a garnish or hors d'oeuvre.

## BAKED SHAD ROE

Preheat oven to 375°.
Parboil, see above:

  **Shad roe**

Place in a buttered pan. Cover with:

  **Creole Sauce, 394
  Mushroom Wine Sauce, 392**

Bake 15 or 20 minutes, basting every 5 minutes.

## SAUTÉED SHAD ROE

Heat until light brown:

  **2 tablespoons Clarified
  Butter, 396**

Sauté in this until delicately browned on both sides:

  **Parboiled Shad Roe,
  497
  Season to taste**

Remove to a hot platter. Add to the drippings and heat:

  **2 teaspoons lemon juice
  1/2 teaspoon chopped chives
  1/2 teaspoon chopped parsley
  1 minced shallot
  1/2 teaspoon dried tarragon,
  chervil or basil**

Pour the sauce over the roe. Sautéed roe may also be served with:

  **(Mornay Sauce, 384, or
  Suprême Sauce, 388, or
  Brown Butter, 397)**

sprinkled with:

  **(Lemon juice and chopped
  parsley)**

and surrounded by:

  **(Peeled orange sections)**

## BROILED SHAD ROE

Preheat broiler.
Parboil, see 497, wipe dry and place on a greased rack:

  **Shad roe**

Sprinkle with:

  **Lemon juice**

Bard, 511, with:

  **Bacon**

Broil from 5 to 7 minutes. If the roe is large, you may have to turn it, baste with drippings and cook until firm. Serve on toast garnished with:

  **Maître d'Hôtel Butter, 398
  Parsley**

## ABOUT BONING AND CARVING SHAD

These are painstaking procedures. Sometimes the fishmonger can be inveigled into boning: an ounce of expertise in this difficult area is worth a pound of private initiative. Otherwise boning is a catch-as-catch-can affair: even tweezers may be necessary, since every effort must be made to remove as many bones as possible before cooking. When carving time comes, the fish is sliced completely through its entire thickness in about 4-inch parallel widths. Any exposed bones may again be removed with tweezers before the cut pieces are put on the individual plates.

## BAKED SHAD WITH CREAMED ROE

                                **6 to 8 Servings**
Preheat oven to 350°.
Bone, see above:

  **A 3- or 4-lb. shad**

Place it skin side down on a well-greased broiler rack or a flat pan. Brush with:

**Melted butter**

Bake, allowing about 8 minutes per pound. While the shad is baking, parboil, see 497:

**Shad roe**

◗ Simmer 15 minutes. Drain. Remove the outside membrane. Mash the roe. Melt in a saucepan:

**2 tablespoons butter**

You may add and sauté about 3 minutes:

**(1 tablespoon grated onion)**

Add the roe and stir in:

**2 tablespoons flour**
**1/2 cup cream**

When these ingredients begin to boil, remove from heat. Stir in:

**2 egg yolks**

Season the roe mixture well with:

**2 tablespoons lemon juice**

Spread the creamed roe over the baked fish and cover with:

**Au Gratin II, (II, 221)**

Return to the broiler and brown evenly. Serve at once garnished with:

**Lemon slices**
**Parsley or watercress**
**Pickled beets or cucumbers**

## ABOUT SHARK

If you are an adventurer—or adventuress—you will find that shark meat that is close to and along the backbone responds to recipes for Fish Fillets, 477–479, or to Poaching, 479–481. The belly sections need long simmering.

## SMELTS

**2 Servings**

Clean, 471, rinse thoroughly and wipe dry:

**12 smelts**

Leave whole. Season with:

**Lemon juice**

Let them stand covered for 15 minutes. Roll the smelts in:

**Cream**

Dip in:

**Flour or cornmeal**

and cook by one of the following methods:

**I.** Melt:

**1/4 cup butter**

Sauté the smelts gently in the butter until done.

**II.** Bake smelts in a buttered pan in a 450° oven about 8 to 10 minutes. Place them on a hot platter. Add to the butter in the pan:

**Juice of 1 lemon**
**2 tablespoons chopped**
**parsley or chives**

Pour the sauce over the smelts.

**III.** ◗ Please read About Deep-Fat Frying, 94. Smelts may be dipped in crumbs or in egg and crumbs and fried about 3 minutes in deep fat heated to 370°. Serve with:

**Tartare Sauce, 421**

BAKED RED SNAPPER WITH SAVORY TOMATO SAUCE

**4 to 6 Servings**

Preheat oven to 350°.

Prepare for cooking:

**A 3-lb. red snapper or**
**other large fish**

Dredge it inside and out with:

**Seasoned flour**

Place in a baking pan. Melt:

**6 tablespoons butter**

Add and simmer 15 minutes:

**1/2 cup chopped onion**
**2 cups chopped celery**
**1/4 cup chopped green pepper,**
**seeds and membrane**
**removed**

Add and simmer until the celery is tender:

   3  **cups drained canned tomatoes**
   1  **tablespoon Worcestershire sauce**
   1  **tablespoon catsup**
   1  **teaspoon chili powder**
   1/2  **finely sliced lemon**
   2  **bay leaves**
   1  **minced clove garlic**
   1  **teaspoon salt**
     **A few grains red pepper**

Press these ingredients through a potato ricer or food mill. Pour the sauce around the fish. Bake about 45 minutes, basting frequently with the sauce. To test for doneness, see 474.

## ABOUT FILLETS OF SOLE

The recipes which follow call for fillets of English or lemon sole—European flat fish flown fresh into better markets or available frozen. ▶ If frozen, the fish must be thawed completely before proceeding. These recipes are often prepared from more easily available fillets of flounder, freshwater trout, bluefish, brill or other fish that flake readily. For this reason the fish is usually served sauced in the baking dish in which it was cooked. ▶ Do not overcook. For other recipes for fish fillets, see 477–479.

## SOLE VÉRONIQUE

**4 Servings**

Marinate for about 1 hour in:

   1  **cup dry white wine**
   1 1/2  **cups skinned seedless grapes**

Drain grapes, reserving the wine. Preheat oven to 350°.
In a large skillet, place:

   2  **lb. skinned fillets of sole**

which have been carefully dried between paper towels. Heat the reserved wine and add to the fillets. Cover with a buttered poaching paper, 101, and simmer about 10 minutes or until fillets are opaque. Then, keeping the fish warm, place them in an ovenproof baking dish. If necessary reduce the fish stock to 1 cup for use in preparing:

     **White Wine Sauce, 389**

Fold into the sauce the marinated grapes and:

   1/2  **cup whipping cream**
   (1  **tablespoon curaçao)**

Coat the fish with this mixture and run the dish under a preheated broiler until the sauce colors. Serve at once, garnished with crescents and diamonds of egg-glazed:

     **Puff Paste, (II, 365)**

## SOLE AMBASSADEUR

     **Allow 1/2 Pound per Person**

Prepare for poaching:

   10  **skinned fillets of sole—lemon or English—trout or halibut**

Place in a buttered heatproof dish or skillet and sprinkle with:

   1  **tablespoon finely chopped shallot or onion**
     **Salt and pepper**

Add:

   1/2  **cup dry white wine**
     **Juice of 1 lemon**

Cover with a buttered poaching paper, 101, and simmer until the fillets are done, see 474. While they are cooking, melt in a heavy saucepan:

   1  **tablespoon butter**

Sauté in the butter:

   1  **cup finely chopped mushrooms**
     **Juice of 1/2 lemon**
     **Salt and pepper**

Cook over high heat about 3 minutes,

until the juices disappear. Reduce heat. Add:

**¹/₂ cup whipping cream**
♦ Simmer until reduced by a third. Remove from the heat and beat in:

**1 egg yolk**
Drain and save the stock from the fish. Spread the mushroom mixture on a heatproof serving platter and arrange the fillets over it. Heat the fish stock and add:

**Kneaded Butter, 381**
Beat in well until thickened. Add:

**¹/₂ cup whipping cream**
Heat to the boiling point. ♦ Remove from the heat and add:

**3 egg yolks**
Strain the sauce and pour it over the fish fillets. Glaze under the broiler until brown. Serve at once.

## SOLE DUGLÉRÉ

**4 Servings**

Preheat oven to 350°.
Prepare and dry well between paper towels:

**2 lb. skinned fillets of sole**
Sprinkle with:

**2 tablespoons lemon juice**
Sauté in a skillet:

**¹/₄ cup finely chopped shallots**
**¹/₄ cup finely chopped
   mushrooms**
**2 tablespoons very finely
   chopped parsley**
in:

**3 tablespoons butter**
Add the fish and:

**1 cup dry white wine**
Bring to a boil. Reduce heat at once and cover pan with a buttered poaching paper, 101. Remove pan to oven and bake about 10 minutes or until fish is opaque. Prepare, meanwhile, a fresh tomato purée by skinning and dicing:

**1 lb. tomatoes**
from which you have scraped out the seeds, 366. Place the fish in a buttered ovenproof baking dish, reserving the stock. If necessary reduce the stock to about 1 cup and use it in preparing:

**White Wine Sauce, 389**
to replace the stock and wine in that recipe. When the sauce thickens, add the puréed tomatoes. Pour the sauce over the fish. Sprinkle the top generously with:

**Grated Parmesan cheese**
mixed with:

**A dash of paprika**
Run under a boiler until the sauce colors.

## FILLETS OF SOLE FLORENTINE

**6 Servings**

Poach, 479:

**6 fillets of sole or other fish**
In the bottom of an ovenproof platter, put a layer of:

**1¹/₂ cups Creamed Spinach, 359**
Arrange the poached, drained fillets on top. Cover with:

**1 cup seasoned
   White Sauce II, 383**
Sprinkle over it:

**Au Gratin III, (II, 221)**
Run under the broiler to heat through until the sauce is glazed.
To prepare **Sole Marguéry,** see Fish Steaks Marguéry, 478.

## SWORDFISH STEAKS

Prepare as for:

**Salmon Steaks, 496**
This fish dries out even when in prime condition; be sure to use plenty of butter in the cooking.

## BROOK TROUT MEUNIÈRE

### 4 Servings

Clean and wash:

**4 brook trout: 8 inches each**

Cut off the fins. Leave the heads and
tails on. Dip in:

**Seasoned flour**

Melt:

**¼ cup Clarified Butter, 396**

Sauté the trout until they are firm and
nicely browned. Remove to a hot
platter. Add to the drippings in the
pan:

**3 tablespoons clarified butter**

Let it brown. Cover the fish with:

**Chopped parsley**

Pour the browned butter over the fish.
Garnish with:

**Lemon wedges**

## BROILED LAKE TROUT OR WHITEFISH

### Allow About ½ Pound per Serving

Preheat boiler.
Bone, 471–473:

**A large lake trout or
whitefish**

Flatten it out or cut it into pieces. Rub
a saucer with:

**Garlic**

Mix in it:

**1 or 2 tablespoons olive oil
¼ teaspoon white pepper**

Rub the fish on both sides with these
ingredients. Place it in a greased shallow pan. Broil until brown, turning
once. Spread with:

**Maître d'Hôtel Butter, 398
or Lemon Butter, 397**

Garnish with:

**Parsley
Wilted Cucumbers, 58**

## BLUE TROUT OR TRUITE AU BLEU

### Allow One 4- to 6½-Ounce Trout or Other Freshwater Fish per Person

It is only the skin that turns so brilliant a blue under this procedure,
not—of course—the whole fish. But
this startling achievement is only
possible if your fish is alive when
brought to the kitchen and if, in
cleaning, it is handled so carefully
that its natural coating of slime is left
undisturbed. We ate these first in the
Black Forest at an inn bordering a
stream, but we think of them always
in connection with Joseph Wechsberg's zestful book, *Blue Trout and
Black Truffles*.

Have ready and boiling:

**Court Bouillon for Fish,
(II, 175), using vinegar
rather than wine**

Kill the fish with one sharp blow on
the head. Split and clean it with a single stroke if possible. Plunge it at
once into the boiling water. Let the
water come to a boil again, then remove the pan from the heat and cover
it, allowing it to stand about 5 minutes, although the larger-sized fish
may need another 2 or 3 minutes. The
white eyeballs pop out when the fish
is done. Remove the fish and drain
well. Serve, if hot, with a flourish and
a garnish of:

**Parsley**

and:

**Boiled or steamed potatoes
and sweet butter balls, or
melted butter**

You may also serve other fancy butters or:

**(Hollandaise Sauce, 410)**

If you serve the fish cold, pass:

**Sauce Gribiche, 422, or
Watercress Sauce, 422**

## ABOUT TUNA

Very widely distributed and of widely differing characteristics, tuna range in size from the **bluefin** or **tunny**—a magnificent game fish which may weigh up to 1500 pounds—to the much smaller **albacore**, which furnishes the whitest and choicest meat. Most of us come by our tuna in prosaic tins. The label on the can must now show whether the fish is "white," "light," or "dark"—the darker grades being of inferior flavor; and designate the nature of the packing medium: olive oil, vegetable oil or water. It must also indicate whether the contents are "solid pack," that is, mostly in one piece; "chunk," or made up of irregular pieces; "flake," of less desirable irregular pieces; or "grated," pieces cut to small uniform size. Smoked canned tuna must also be so identified. To find additional recipes for canned tuna, see Index.

## FRESH TUNA OR BONITO

**Allow ½ Pound per Serving**
Clean:
**A fresh tuna or bonito**
Braise or roast as for veal, or brush the delicate stomach sections with:
**Vegetable oil**
and broil.

## POACHED TURBOT

**Allow ½ Pound per Serving**
This firm-fleshed, very white flat fish may be skinned and filleted, 472–473, and poached in Court Bouillon, (II, 175), with part wine—or part milk to reinforce its whiteness—and cooked as for any recipe for Sole, 500–501. As both the skin and the gelatinous areas near the fins are considered delicacies, turbot is often cooked and served unskinned. To keep it from curling or bursting, cut a long gash down the center of the brown underside before poaching.
To cook in the skin, place the fish in a greased pan; float it in a cool:
**Court Bouillon, (II, 175)**
Cover with a poaching paper, 101. Bring the liquid to a boil. ♦ Reduce the heat at once. Barely simmer about 30 minutes, basting several times during the cooking. Be sure to seal the paper after each basting. Serve with:
**Soubise Sauce, 387, or**
**Champagne Sauce, 388**

## WHITEBAIT OR BLANCHAILLE

Whitebait are really minnows, or the small fry of fresh or saltwater fish. Pick over, and wash only if necessary:
**Whitebait**
Roll them in:
**Seasoned Flour I, (II, 220)**
Fry 2 to 3 minutes, depending on size, in deep fat heated to 375°. Garnish with:
**Lemon slices**

## ABOUT FROG LEGS

Frog legs resemble chicken in texture and flavor. They are usually bought skinned and ready to use. Allow 2 large or 6 small frog legs per person. If the frogs are not prepared, cut off and discard the feet; then cut off the hind legs—the only part of the frog used—close to the body. Separate and wash the legs in cold water. Begin at the top and strip off the skin like a glove. Through an experiment with a twitching frog leg, Galvani discovered the electric current that bears his name. Should you prefer keeping your kitchen and your scientific activities separate and distinct, chill the frog legs before skinning.

## BRAISED FROG LEGS

**4 Servings**

Clean:

**8 large frog legs**

Roll them in:

**Seasoned flour**

Melt in a skillet:

**6 tablespoons Clarified Butter, 396**

Add to it:

**½ cup chopped onions**

Brown the frog legs in the butter. Reduce the heat and add:

**¾ cup boiling Light Stock, (II, 171–172)**

Cover skillet closely and cook the frog legs until tender, about 10 minutes. Melt:

**6 tablespoons butter**

Sauté in the butter:

**1¼ cups seasoned bread crumbs**

**(¾ cup finely chopped hazelnuts)**

Add:

**1 teaspoon lemon juice**

Roll the frog legs in the bread crumbs and serve them garnished with:

**Fennel**

or, if you have used the hazelnuts, with:

**Parsley**

## DEEP-FAT-FRIED FROG LEGS

◗ Please read About Deep-Fat Frying, 94.

Clean:

**Frog legs**

Dip them in:

**A Bound Breading, (II, 220)**

Let dry for 1 hour. Fry the frog legs in deep fat heated to 375° until golden. Drain. Serve with:

**Tartare Sauce, 421**

## FROG LEGS IN MUSHROOM SAUCE

**3 Servings**

Clean:

**6 large frog legs**

Cut the meat from each leg into 3 or 4 pieces. Place the meat in a saucepan. Cover with:

**Boiling water or Light Stock, (II, 171–172)**

Add:

**2 thin slices lemon**

**⅛ teaspoon white pepper (Celery, parsley, onion or vegetables suitable for soup)**

Simmer the frog meat, covered, until tender. Drain well. Melt in a saucepan:

**3 tablespoons butter**

Add to it and sauté until light brown:

**1 cup sliced mushrooms**

Stir in:

**1½ tablespoons flour**

Stir in slowly:

**1½ cups chicken stock or stock in which the frog legs were cooked**

**Season to taste**

When the sauce is hot, add the frog meat. Reduce the heat to low. Beat well:

**3 egg yolks**

**3 tablespoons rich cream**

Stir these ingredients into the sauce. Let the entire mixture thicken off the heat. Serve the meat at once, covered with the sauce.

## FROG LEGS FORESTIÈRE

**Allow 5 per Serving**

Sprinkle:

**Small frog legs**

with:

**Brandy**

Let stand about 2 hours refrigerated and wipe dry.

Sauté them in:

**Clarified Butter, 396**

During the last few minutes of cooking, when the frog legs become firm to the touch, sauté with the meat for each portion:

2 thinly sliced mushrooms

1 tablespoon chopped parsley
1 teaspoon lemon juice
(1 tablespoon very finely sliced fresh sweet red pepper)
Season to taste

# POULTRY AND WILDFOWL

The chicken is a world citizen; duck, turkey and geese cosmopolites. Along with a number of the game birds that migrate from continent to continent, they are international favorites. And each nation has learned to cook them in a manner distinctively its own. The worldly wise cook will not be content with chicken and dumplings, roast turkey, or quail served on a crouton, but instead will welcome into the kitchen some of the specialties that have enlivened a global cuisine: from Italy, chicken cacciatore, illustrated above left; pressed duck from France, for which the equipment is shown at the rear; from Mexico, turkey mole; from Germany, Gänseklein. The principles of cooking poultry and game birds are just sufficiently different to warrant separate treatment, wildfowl having its own peculiarities in handling even before cooking. There is the need to keep wild birds aired after shooting, and to the hunter interested in bringing home his booty in prime condition, a carrying strap such as that shown in the center foreground above is as important a piece of equipment as the wooden decoy shown behind it. Then there are determinations to be made as to the age of the bird and how long it should be hung—the results of which establish the specific method of cooking.

Whether you shoot your bird or buy it, you will always have to assess its quality and potential, sizing it up for the application of the cooking techniques that will be suitable and rewarding. ◗ See, for example, under the Dry Heat processes, 92, ways to cook young birds. For birds of questionable age, consult the Moist Heat processes, 98, or cook them in milk, or marinate them to tenderize them.

The preliminary steps are similar for all fowl, whether barnyard variety or rara avis.

## ABOUT POULTRY

That poultry served immediately after slaughtering is not a delicacy was brought home to me early when my father and I would go down to check Grandfather's holdings at Brickeys on the Mississippi. As the local landlady at whose abode my grandfather kept quarters saw us get off the train—for everyone looked out for newcomers and talked to the engineer while the engine was "watered"—she would dash to the yard behind her house, grab for the axe and behead the nearest chicken. The less said about lunch the better. So we learned early that quick cooling and hanging in a cool place from 8 to 24 hours will avoid stringiness and develop flavor. Cut-up poultry is more perishable than whole birds, and turkey and duck more perishable than chicken. All poultry is difficult to keep well in home refrigerators. When you buy poultry in an airtight wrapping, loosen the wrapping before refrigerating. Dressed poultry should be washed in running water before cooking. If you have to hold it more than a day or two, cook it, then reheat it in a sauce before serving.

Poultry must be cooked thoroughly at one time—never partially cooked and then stored for finishing later. Cooked poultry, stuffing and broth should be used within 2 days. ♦ Always remove the stuffing and store it in a separate container before refrigerating the loosely wrapped cooked meat.

For amounts of bird to allow per serving, see individual recipes; but if a large number of people are to be fed, turkey meat is the least expensive and turkey breast yields the greatest amount of protein per pound. The net amount of edible meat, minus fat or skin, is about 46% for turkeys, 41% for chicken and 22% for duckling.

A federal inspection stamp for dressed poultry sold in interstate commerce is mandatory, but as the stamp is placed on the carton rather than the bird, the consumer has no way of knowing whether he is purchasing inspected poultry.

## ABOUT FROZEN POULTRY

We are less than one hundred percent advocates of frozen poultry. Sometimes the fowl have been watered before freezing, and the weight loss on thawing may make them more expensive as well as less flavorful. Watch too for "freezer burn"—brownish skin areas that are telltale evidence of dehydration or improper storage. We do not advocate purchasing ready-stuffed frozen fowl, but if you should buy one ♦ never thaw it before cooking, but transfer it directly from freezer to hot oven. And ♦ read packer's directions carefully. Also available frozen are the so-called self-basting turkeys, in which butter or oil has been inserted into the breast meat before freezing. The fat bubbles out during the roasting process to baste the skin.

♦ Unstuffed frozen birds should be thawed before cooking. Thawing a large bird in the refrigerator may take several days, so buy your fowl well in advance. Leave the bird in its original bag, place it on a tray in the refrigerator and thaw 1 to 2 days for a bird weighing 4 to 12 pounds; 2 to 3 days for 12 to 20 pounds; 3 to 4 days for 20 to 24 pounds. A faster way to thaw is to leave poultry well sealed in original bag and place in cold water for 2 to 7 hours, depending on size. Change the water frequently. When the flesh is pliable, the bird is ready to cook. ♦ Thawed poultry must be cooked at once.

## PLUCKING AND SINGEING POULTRY

Poultry is usually plucked and drawn when purchased. Buy dry-picked poultry whenever possible. If, not already done, pluck it at once—except for those game birds which must hang and are easier to pluck later. It is much easier to pluck and draw a bird that is thoroughly chilled. After plucking the bird, remove all pinfeathers. Use a pair of tweezers, or grasp each pinfeather between forefinger and the tip of a knife, then pull.

After removing the coarser feathers, if those remaining are downy or small, you may use the paraffin method. Make up a mixture of 3/8 pound melted paraffin and 7 quarts boiling water. Brush enough of this mixture over the bird to cover. Allow it to harden. Pull off the paraffined coating, and it will carry the feathers with it.

♦ To singe a bird, hold it by the legs and singe the pinfeathers over a gas flame or a candle. Turn it so that all parts of the skin are exposed to the heat. ♦ But do not singe a bird that is to be frozen until you are just ready to use it, because the heat of singeing breaks down the fat and hastens rancidity.

## DRAWING AND DRESSING A BIRD

Cut off the head so that the neck is as long as possible, and at once catch hold of and bind the 2 tubes attached to the crop, to prevent contamination. Draw down the neck skin. Cut or twist off the neck, close to the body, ♦ being careful not to tear or cut through the tubes or the neck skin. The skin should then be loose enough to allow you to reach in at the base of the neck and draw out the bound tubes and the crop.

In large domestic fowl and in game birds the leg tendons are apt to be tough and should be removed. Most butchers use a clever gadget that breaks the foot, holds the carcass securely and draws the tendons as the foot separates from the body. Amateurs have a somewhat harder time. It is easier to get the tendons out if the feet have not been cut off. Cut through the skin 1 1/2 inches above the knee joint. Be careful not to cut the tendons. Lay the fowl down on its back, with the cut in the skin just at the edge of a table or board and the rest of the leg projecting beyond it. Press the foot and ankle down, sharply, to snap the bone at the knee joint. Pull steadily. The tendons should all come away with the foot and lower leg bone as seen in the foreground below. If they do not, remove those that are left by forcing a skewer crosswise under each and pulling them out one by one. If the

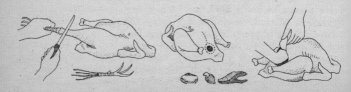

bird is young, there is no need to remove the tendons. Simply cut off the feet as shown below.

♦ Taking great care not to pierce the innards, make a shallow incision through the skin from the tip of the breastbone to and around the vent as shown in the center drawing on 508. Insert the hand, palm down, into the cavity between the organs and the breastbone. Feel for the gizzard, which is firm and roundish, and pull it out steadily. It will bring with it most of the other entrails except the kidneys. These lie in the hollows near the base of the backbone. To either side of the spine between the ribs you will find the spongy red lungs. Take them out. Explore carefully to ensure the removal of every bit of the viscera from the cavity, as well as surplus fat, which may prove to be too strong in flavor. ♦ Among the edible viscera of a fowl are the valuable giblets: heart, liver and gizzard. Remove veins, arteries, thin membrane and blood from around the heart and discard them. Cut the green sac or gallbladder away from the liver very carefully and discard it. It is better to leave a small piece of liver attached

to the sac than to cut the sac so close to the liver as to risk puncturing it, for the bitterness of its fluid will ruin whatever it touches. Cut away any portion of the liver that may be discolored. ♦ Discard the liver of a fryer if it is yellow; however, it may be normal to find a yellow liver in a stewer. Sever the intestines from the gizzard and remove membrane and fat from it. Then cut a shallow slit along the indented curve of the gizzard, being careful not to cut so deeply as to pierce the lining of the inner sac. Push against the outside of the opened gizzard with the thumbs to force out the sac. Discard it. Wash and dry giblets. Seen in the foreground, 508, are the gizzard, heart and liver. Keep them well refrigerated, and use or cook them as soon as possible. See Variety Meats, 638, Stuffings, 430, and Sauces, 375–413, for the many ways to use giblets. If the chicken is a hen, you may find some egg yolks in varying sizes which can be simmered in water and used in sauces and dressings.

Turn the chicken over and cut out and discard the oil sac at the base of the tail, as shown on the left above, by scooping out an oyster shape

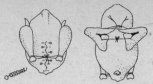

above the heart-shaped area called the croupion or—by the irreverent—the pope's nose.

◗ Do not soak the bird in water at any time. Wipe it well with a damp cloth after drawing. Should it be necessary to wash the bird, hold it briefly under running water to cleanse the inside, and ◗ dry it well with a cloth. It is then ready for stuffing or for cutting up for sautéeing or for a fricassee.

## CUTTING UP A DRAWN BIRD

Grasp the drawn bird by a wing, letting its weight tug against the skin at the wing joint, as shown in the sketch at the top of 509. Clip through the skin, flesh and joint, severing the wing from the body. Use the same method to sever the second wing. For easier eating, you may want to transform the wings into mock legs. Just cut off the wing tips and straighten the two remaining sections with the hands. You may have to cut through the skin to do this. Pull them into a straight line to look like a small double leg. Silly, but the wings seem to taste better this way.

To cut off the legs, force them outward and down, as shown at the top of 509. Where the leg joins the body, insert a knife to release the ligaments. When the leg has loosened, cut a long gash and continue to cut toward the back, allowing as much skin as possible to remain on the leg. Cutting off the neck is described previously on 508.

With the neck, wings and legs severed, you are ready to cut up the carcass. To cut the body apart, place the carcass flat on its back. Make a diagonal cut as shown on the bottom of 509.

With a young chicken, it is possible to pry the body apart by cracking the backbone, as shown on the right on the bottom of 509. Leave the breast in one piece, or cut it in two to four pieces with poultry shears, shown in the chapter heading. The back has little meat except for two choice "oysters" that lie above the croupion. Save the rest of the back and the neck for stock.

## STUFFING AND TRUSSING A BIRD

◗ Always wait to stuff a bird until just before roasting. This may not be convenient, but it is the only safe procedure. Contamination is frequent in prestuffed fowl, for even when the dressing is refrigerated, the cold may not fully penetrate it.

◗ Fill the bird only three-fourths full, as the dressing will expand. Stuff it loosely, as sketched above. Your task will be easier if you place the bird in a large pan. The crop cavity may be stuffed, too. You may also loosen the breast skin with a spoon and fill out the breast between the skin and the flesh. Close the openings with small skewers and a crisscrossed string. Or use a spiral skewer as shown in the center drawing on page 510. Fasten the legs close to the body by tying the ends of the drumsticks together, as shown in the center on page 510. Tie a piece of string around the skin of the neck. Leave two long ends. Turn the wings back, as shown on the right, and pass the string around them and secure it.

## BARDING FOWL

Guinea hen as well as partridge— very lean birds of any description— and birds from which the skin has been removed greatly benefit by barding before roasting; that is, by covering completely with a ¼-inch layer of salt pork or bacon, as shown on the left, below. Use pieces about 3 or 3½ inches square. As you truss the fowl, slip 2 pieces into place on either side between the legs and breast, as shown at center right. Cover the bird—legs and all—with other pieces, and tie securely, as shown at left below, making certain that all exposed surfaces are blanketed. After cooking, discard the barding. This procedure may be used also for pieces cut from larger fowl. Also see Larding, 550.

## BONING FOWL

Let's begin with boning up on chicken breasts, because that's the

only boning maneuver most of us will ever need. Once you start, you'll find it's a lot easier than you may have thought. First, place the breast skin side down; cut through the gristle and keel bone at the top center of the breast. This allows you to flatten the breast and remove the keel bone. Cut the meat free from the long rib-cage bone on both sides of the breast and then cut around the upper edge of the breast, up to and through the joint. Scrape the rest of the meat away from the bones. Loosen the tendons and pull them out. You may also remove the skin if desired. This gives you a butterflied whole breast. It is easier to bone the breasts singly by cutting free one side at a time.

As for the major boning operation on a whole bird that is to be restuffed and shaped into an impressive facsimile of its original self for a special occasion, the trick is again much less difficult than you might suspect. But do not attempt this plastic surgery on a dressed bird, because the previously cut openings, usually carelessly done, make success impossible. The bird to be boned, then, is neither dressed nor drawn. At the very end of the operation, you will be able to remove everything intact—innards, skeleton and all. ◖ During the entire boning job, be careful not to pierce the skin except for the initial incision. An unpierced skin will act as protection, encasement and insulation all through the cooking period. ◖ Always keep the tip of the knife toward the skeleton and close to the bone. When all the bones are out and you hold up the result, it looks—glory be!—like a small romper with wings. Pull the legs and sleeves into the lining.

Begin the boning by placing the bird breast down on the board. Make an incision the entire length of the spine, through both skin and flesh. Using a sharp-pointed short boning knife, follow as close to the frame as you can cut, pushing the skin and flesh back as you cut. Work the skin of the neck down so that the neck protrudes as much as possible. Chop the neck off short, protecting the skin and being careful ▶ not to cut through the crop tubes. Work first toward the ball-and-socket joint of the shoulder, cutting it free and boning the shoulder blade. Pull the wing bone through from the inside, bringing the skin with it. Bone the meat from the wing and reserve it. Then strike for the ball-and-socket joint of the leg and pull the bone through. Reserve the meat. After you have freed and reserved the meat from both wings and legs, continue to work the meat free, first from one side of the body, then from the other, until the center front of the breastbone is reached. ▶ Here great care is needed to free the skin without piercing it, as it is very thin at this point. You should now be able to get the whole skeleton out with its contents all in one mass. Leave the severing of the opening into the intestine until the last. Then, with the innards removed, wash the skin and flesh in cold running water and pat with a towel ▶ until very dry. For a farce for boned chicken, see 437.

## ROASTING FOWL

There are differences of opinion as to whether to salt poultry before roasting. We prefer to salt after the browning—if at all—and never salt the interior. For small birds, see Barding, 511. For larger birds, rub them well with melted unsalted shortening and place on a greased rack in an ▶ uncovered roasting pan. Cover the entire top surface of the fowl with a coarsely woven cloth that has been soaked in melted unsalted butter or vegetable oil. This procedure, we have learned by experience, is the best method of solving the problem built into the roasting of every bird—and especially of turkeys: that is, how to cook to moist tenderness two kinds of meat at the same time—the softer meat of the breast and the tougher, fatter leg meat. Basting is done both over and under the cloth. If necessary for browning, the cloth may be removed during the last half hour of cooking.

Directly upon removal from the refrigerator, place the bird in a preheated 450° oven. Reduce the heat immediately to 350°, or to 325° for large turkeys. After the first half hour of cooking, for birds of all sizes, ▶ baste frequently with pan drippings or additional fat—about every 10 minutes.

Timing involves many factors: the age of the bird and its fat content, its size, and whether it was frozen. If using a thermometer, insert it into the center of the inner thigh muscle, taking care that the tip is not in contact with the bone. Cook to an internal temperature of 180° to 185°. The center of the stuffing should reach at least 165°. If not using a thermometer, allow 20 to 25 minutes per pound for birds up to 6 pounds. For larger birds, allow 15 to 20 minutes per pound. For turkeys weighing over 16 pounds, allow 13 to 15 minutes per pound. In any case, add about 5 minutes to the pound if the bird you are cooking is stuffed. Other popular tests for doneness are to prick the skin of the thigh to see if the juice runs clear or to jiggle the drumstick to see if the hip joint is loose. This latter response, we find, usually means that the bird is not only done but overdone. Sometimes with a young bird the meat close to the bone remains reddish brown even after adequate cooking. The bone marrow in immature fowls has not yet fully hardened, and the red blood cells frequently seep into the adjacent meat.

Some people like to use an even, slow heat throughout the cooking period, placing the bird in a preheated 325° oven and not basting at all. This method has gained popularity because it is carefree and has been rumored to entail much less shrinkage. We have found the flavor remarkably superior when the meat is sealed by high temperature at the outset—and the difference in shrinkage is negligible.

## CARVING FOWL

After removing a chicken from the oven, allow it to rest about 10 minutes, a turkey about 20 minutes, to make slicing easier. If the bird is to be carved at table, be sure the heated serving platter is large enough, and garnish it lightly with parsley or watercress. There is a subtle art to carving. Keeping the knife keen-edged and using with it a 2-tined handle-guarded fork are fundamentals in mastering it.

Place the bird, breast side up, on a platter. Insert the fork firmly into the knee joint, as sketched below, pulling the leg away from the body of the bird. Slice the thigh flesh away from

the body until the ball-and-socket hip joint is exposed. To sever the thigh-joint, make a twisting movement with the knife and continue to hold the knee joint down firmly with the fork. Cut the joint between the thigh and drumstick, as shown. Repeat the above, cutting off the other leg. Arrange pieces attractively on the serving platter.

If a large bird is being carved, some slices of meat may be cut from the thigh and the drumstick at this point. Proceed to remove the wings in a similar manner and, if the bird is large, divide the wings at the second joint. To slice the breast, begin at the area nearest the neck and slice thinly across the grain, the entire length of the breast. With a large bird such as a turkey, carve only one side unless more is needed at the first serving.

In carving a duck, you will find the leg joint more difficult to sever because it is attached much farther under the bird and is somewhat recessed at the joint. Here, as in general, for the inexperienced carver or the impatient one, poultry shears are an inspired addition to his weaponry.

## ABOUT CHICKEN

Young chickens of either sex are called **broilers** if they weigh about 2½ pounds and **fryers** if they weigh 2½ to 3½ pounds. **Roasters**, also of either sex, are under 8 months old

and weigh 3¹/₂ to 5 pounds. Roasters are an appropriate choice for rotisseries or for Suprêmes, 521. **Stewing chickens**, usually over 10 months, are pretty much what their name implies. **Capons**, or castrated males, weigh 6 to 8 pounds. Their loss is the epicure's gain, capon flesh being exceptionally tender. Fowl is a broadly polite *nom de plume* for hens aged 10 months or more and **stag** and **cock** for males that are too old to roast but make well-flavored adjuncts for the stock pot.

To size up a chicken, look for moist skin, soft legs and feet, bright eyes, a red comb, a wing tip that yields readily if pressed back and, most importantly ◗ a flexible breastbone. If the tip of the bone bends easily, the bird is young; if it is stiff, the bird is past its prime. ◗ Beware of skin that is dry, hard, purplish, broken, bruised or scaly, or that has long hairs sprouting from it.

## ROAST CHICKEN

**6 Servings**

◗ Please read about Roasting Fowl, 512.
Preheat oven to 450°.
◗ Draw, singe, stuff and truss, 508–510:

> **A 4- to 5-lb. chicken or capon**

Use for the stuffing one-half the recipe for:

> **Rice Dressing, 435, Bread Dressing with Oysters, Nuts or Giblets, 431, or Chestnut Dressing, 433**

or make:

> **2 cups Dry Dressing, 431**

replacing the onion with:

> **¹/₂ cup chopped leeks—white part only**

and using:

> **French bread**

Put the bird on a rack, uncovered, in the oven and ◗ reduce the heat at once to 350°. Roast about 20 minutes per pound. Chicken without stuffing may take slightly less time. Baste frequently with pan drippings. Serve with:

> **Gravy or any Velouté Sauce variation, 387–390, or White Wine Sauce, 389, or Quick Mushroom Sauce, 395**

## ABOUT TURKEY

Benjamin Franklin wrote in a letter to his daughter: "I wish the bald eagle had not been chosen as the representative of our country. . . . The turkey is a much more respectable character and, withal, a true original native of America." Presumably Ben would have been delighted at the turkey's subsequent success story: its domestication, its genetic adaptability, its supplanting even the goose as the mainstay of Christmas dinner. Indeed, the turkey has taken first place in the feasts of his countrymen. Hens and toms are about equal in tenderness, although the butcher charges more per pound for the female. Look for plump white birds, well-rounded over the breastbone, and fresh rather than frozen. ◗ For turkeys less than 12 pounds, allow ³/₄ to 1 pound per serving, and ¹/₂ to ³/₄ pound per serving for those weighing over 12 pounds. With modern feeding methods, turkeys up to 25 pounds need not be older than 6 months. Certain white turkey types bred for heavy breasts and small bone structure cook more rapidly, if bought unfrozen, than the dark-feathered types. Boned, rolled turkey is sometimes a good buy economically, but the flavor developed with long, slow roasting may be lacking here. Ground turkey, too, is available. Prepare as for Chicken Patties, 620.

## ROAST TURKEY

**12 Servings**

◗ Please read about Roasting Fowl, 512.

Preheat oven to 450°.

◗ Draw, singe, and truss, 508–510:

> **A turkey**

If you stuff the turkey, 5 cups of one of the following stuffings should fill a 10-pound bird:

> **Dry Dressing, 431, Apple and Onion Dressing, 434, or Chestnut Dressing, 433**

Or you may want to use two kinds of dressing: in the crop a richer one like:

> **Sausage Dressing, 433**

and in the cavity:

> **Bread Dressing, 431, Ham Dressing for Turkey, 435, or Oyster Bread Dressing, 432**

Put the bird on a rack in an uncovered roasting pan and follow the directions under Roasting Fowl, 512. Make:

> **Poultry Pan Gravy, 383**

adding:

> **Sautéed Mushrooms, 328**

Or flavor the gravy with the finely chopped giblets if they were not used in the stuffing.

## CHICKEN OR TURKEY BAKED IN FOIL

Please read about Foil Cookery, 104. Today, "roasting" in aluminum foil has become popular because no basting is needed. So, if you decide, despite our Cassandra warnings about this method, that you'd rather clean the attic, improve your serve, or write Chapter IX of the Great American Novel than to baby-sit a bird, go ahead with the foil and take the consequences—which will be steamed rather than roasted. Roasting can go on only under ventilation. Remember that foil insulates against heat, so your oven will have to be hotter. And any attempt to brown your bird by removing the foil during the last half hour of cooking will just dry out the meat—although you can compensate somewhat by repeated bastings with pan drippings after taking off the foil. Preheat oven to 450°.

Season the fowl well, and add a little butter and fresh herbs, such as tarragon or rosemary. Or use one of the barbecue sauces on 404. Wrap the fowl in heavy-duty or double foil. Bake a 5-pound stuffed chicken about 2½ hours at 350°; parts or halves, 1¾ to 2 hours. A 10- to 12-pound stuffed turkey will take 3¼ to 3¾ hours, and a 14- to 18-pound stuffed turkey will need 3¾ to 4 hours. A 3- to 4-pound turkey quarter will take 2 to 2½ hours.

## ROASTED TURKEY BREAST

**Allow ⅓ Pound per Serving**

When the family prefers all white meat, serve whole turkey breasts, ranging in size from 3½ to 7 pounds. Preheat oven to 450°.

Rinse and dry:

> **A turkey breast**

You may stuff the cavity with any suitable:

> **(Dressing, 431–437)**

If possible, skewer the skin flaps together to hold the dressing; or cover the filled cavity with foil. Place the breast on a rack in a shallow pan and brush with:

> **Butter or margarine**

Reduce the heat to 325° and roast

uncovered, basting frequently, about 20 minutes per pound.

## BROILED CHICKEN

**Allow ³/₄ Pound per Person**

Broiling or barbecueing chicken should be a slow process—keeping meat at least 5 to 6 inches from the heat source. Preheat broiler.

Clean and cut into halves or quarters:
**Broilers, 513**
Rub on both sides with:
**Butter or vegetable oil**
Place them in a pan, skin side down. Broil the chickens until brown, 15 to 20 minutes for each side, basting with more fat as you turn the pieces. For excellent flavor we suggest basting with a mixture of:

2 **tablespoons butter**
1 **tablespoon lemon juice**
   **A grind of fresh pepper**
   **(Fresh or dry herbs)**

Or, for an accent on beautiful color:

2 **tablespoons butter**
¼ **teaspoon paprika**

Allow these amounts for each half broiler. Or, when the broilers are ready, flambé them, 108, with:

1 **oz. warmed brandy**

for each broiler. Or make:
   **A thickened Poultry Pan**
   **Gravy, 383, using tarragon;**
   **or an unthickened one,**
   **deglazing with dry white**
   **wine**

## ⊟ BARBECUED CHICKEN

Follow directions for:
**Broiled Chicken, above**
but place broilers cavity side down on the grill over moderate heat. Cook from 15 to 25 minutes per side or until fork-tender. Brush the birds with:
**A Barbecue Sauce, 404**
during the last 10 minutes.

## ⊟ CURRIED BARBECUE CHICKEN

**About 6 Servings**

Disjoint:
2 **broilers, 513**
Marinate chicken pieces overnight in refrigerator in a mixture of:

1½ **cups plain yogurt**
 ½ **cup lime juice**
  1 **teaspoon grated lime peel**
  1 **to 2 crushed cloves garlic**
  2 **teaspoons finely chopped**
    **ginger**
1½ **teaspoons paprika**
  2 **teaspoons ground**
    **coriander**
  1 **teaspoon ground cayenne**
  1 **teaspoon ground curry**
  1 **teaspoon salt**

Preheat broiler or grill and follow directions in:
**Broiled Chicken, left**
basting frequently with the strained marinade.

## ⊟ BROILED MARINATED CHICKEN

**I. With Tarragon and Wine**
**4 Servings**

Disjoint:
2 **broilers, 513**
Marinate the pieces at least 1 hour in:
¼ **cup fresh or 2 tablespoons**
   **dried tarragon leaves**
4 **finely minced shallots**
1 **cup dry white wine**
Preheat broiler or grill. Follow the directions for:
**Broiled Chicken, left**
basting with:
**Melted butter**
and the heated strained marinade. If oven broiling, save some of the marinade to deglaze the broiler pan.
**Season to taste**
and serve the chicken on a hot platter

with some of the marinade poured over it.

## II. Teriyaki
Follow recipe I, 516, using:
**Teriyaki Marinade, (II, 183)**

## III.
Follow directions under:
**Marinade for Chicken,
(II, 182)**

## PAN-FRIED OR SAUTÉED CHICKEN

**Allow ¾ Pound per Person**
Please read About Sautéing, 97.
Clean and cut into pieces:
**Young chickens**
You may dredge them lightly with:
**(Seasoned flour or
cornmeal)**
Melt in a skillet:
**A mixture of butter and
vegetable oil**
allowing for each half chicken 2 or more tablespoons of fat. When the fat has reached the point of fragrance, add the chicken. Cook and turn it in the hot fat until brown. Reduce the heat and continue cooking uncovered, turning the chicken frequently until done, from 25 to 40 minutes, according to size. ◗ Cook only until tender, as further cooking will dry and toughen the meat. Remove the chicken from the pan and make:
**Poultry Pan Gravy, 383**
**Season to taste**
Serve at once, garnished with:
**Parsley**

## OVEN-FRIED CHICKEN

### I.
**2 servings**
Preheat oven to 350°.
Disjoint:
**A broiler, 513**

Wipe dry. Dredge it in:
**Seasoned flour**
Heat to the point of fragrance in a heavy skillet:
**¼ cup butter**
Sauté the chicken lightly. Remove from the skillet to a rack in a shallow baking pan. Baste with the skillet pan drippings. Bake uncovered until tender, 30 to 40 minutes, basting with added fat if necessary and turning occasionally. Serve with:
**Poultry Pan Gravy, 383, or
Sauce Périgueux, 393, or
Quick Canned Soup
Sauce I, 394**

### II.
**2 Servings**
A simpler version but not quite so tasty.
Preheat oven to 400°.
Prepare as for I, above:
**A broiler, 513**
In a shallow 9 x 12-inch baking pan, melt in the preheated oven:
**¼ cup butter**
Remove the butter from the oven when melted and hot. Place the dredged chicken in it ◗ skin side down. Baste the upper surface with melted butter from the pan. Bake the chicken uncovered 25 minutes. Turn it skin side up. ◗ Reduce the heat to 350° and bake until tender, 30 to 35 minutes, basting often with the pan drippings. ◗ Do not overcook. White meat portions may be removed and kept warm while dark meat is cooked slightly longer. Serve at once. For gravy and other sauces, see I, left.

## OVEN-FRIED CHICKEN WITH FRUIT, OR CHICKEN TAHITI
**6 Servings**
Prepare and cook as for Oven-Fried Chicken I, left:

**2 frying chickens**

Meanwhile combine in a saucepan, stirring constantly:

**1 cup orange juice**

**2 tablespoons lemon juice**

**1/2 cup brown sugar**

**2 tablespoons soy sauce**

**1 tablespoon cornstarch**

Bring the mixture to a boil. When thickened and clear, add:

**1 fresh pineapple cut into cubes**

**1 fresh papaya cut into cubes**

Pour the sauce over the baked chicken. Place it in the oven and bake 10 minutes longer. Serve with:

**Boiled Rice, 189, and Green Peas, 338**

For more glamor, serve the chicken and fruit in warmed scooped-out pineapple halves cut lengthwise, see 69.

## MARYLAND CHICKEN

**4 to 5 servings**

Cut into pieces for serving:

**A frying chicken, about 3 1/2 lb.**

Bread it by dipping each piece into:

**Milk**

and rolling it in:

**Flour**

Let dry for 1 hour. Heat in a heavy skillet until it reaches the point of fragrance:

**1/2 to 1 inch combination of cooking oil and bacon drippings**

Add the chicken. Brown it on all sides.

Preheat oven to 375°.

Place the browned chicken in a fresh pan and bake, covered, until steamed through, about 1/2 hour. This Border dish is usually served with a cream gravy made from the drippings to which flour and milk are added, see

Poultry Pan Gravy, 383. You may further enrich the gravy with:

**(Egg Yolks, 380)**

Serve with:

**Corn and Ham Fritters, (II, 156)**

## CHICKEN IN BATTER

**4 Servings**

◗ Please read About Deep-Fat Frying, 94.

Cut into pieces:

**A 3-lb. roasting chicken**

Dip into:

**Fritter Batter for Meat, (II, 155)**

Place the dipped pieces on a rack and let them dry 15 to 30 minutes. Immerse a few pieces at a time in deep fat heated to 365° and cook 10 to 15 minutes. Drain on paper towels. Serve hot or cold.

## BRAISED CHICKEN WITH FRUIT

**Allow 3/4 Pound per Person**

Preheat oven to 350°.

Clean and quarter:

**Frying chickens**

Heat in a skillet:

**Butter**

Add chicken pieces and sauté until brown. Dip the browned chicken into a sauce of:

**1 cup orange juice**

**1/4 cup honey**

**2 tablespoons lemon juice**

**1/2 teaspoon ground curry powder**

**1 teaspoon salt**

Arrange the chicken in a baking dish, skin side down, cover with the sauce and bake uncovered 20 minutes. Turn the chicken over and add one of the following or in combination:

**Whole preserved kumquats, peaches, pears,**

or plumped prunes,
apricots or raisins
Strips of orange rind

Baste the fruit with the sauce and
bake 30 minutes longer or until the
chicken is tender.

## CHICKEN BRAISED IN WINE OR COQ AU VIN

**4 Servings**

We are often asked why this recipe
turns out a rich medium brown rather
than the very dark brown sometimes
served in restaurants. Abroad, in
country places where chickens are locally butchered, the blood is often
kept and added to the gravy at the last
minute as a thickener, see 380. After
this addition, the sauce is not allowed
to boil. Here in America, this effect is
imitated by adding caramel coloring,
(II, 232–233).

Disjoint, wash and dry:

A broiler or roasting
chicken

Use the back and neck for the
stock pot.

Melt in a large heavy skillet:

3 tablespoons butter or olive
oil

Add and brown lightly:

1/4 lb. minced salt pork
3/4 cup chopped mild onions or
1/2 cup peeled pearl onions
1 sliced carrot
3 minced shallots or scallions
1 peeled, finely chopped
garlic clove

Push the vegetables aside. Brown the
chicken in the fat. Add and stir:

2 tablespoons flour
2 tablespoons minced parsley
1 tablespoon fresh chervil or
marjoram
1/2 bay leaf
1/2 teaspoon thyme
1 teaspoon salt

1/8 teaspoon freshly ground
pepper
(1 tablespoon brandy)

Stir in:

2 cups dry red wine

Simmer the chicken covered over low
heat until done, about 1 hour. Add for
the last 5 minutes of cooking:

1/2 lb. sliced mushrooms

Skim off excess fat.

Season to taste

Serve the chicken on a hot platter,
with the sauce and vegetables poured
over it.

## CHICKEN PAPRIKA

**3 Servings**

Disjoint:

A frying chicken: about
2 1/2 lb.

Melt in a heavy pot:

1 1/2 tablespoons butter
1 1/2 tablespoons vegetable oil

Add and simmer until glossy and red:

1 cup finely chopped onions
2 teaspoons to 2 tablespoons
sweet Hungarian paprika

Add:

1/2 teaspoon salt
2 cups well-seasoned chicken
stock

As soon as these ingredients have
reached boiling point, add the chicken.
◗ Simmer covered until tender, about
1 hour. Stir:

2 teaspoons flour

into:

1 cup cultured sour cream

Stir it slowly into the pot and simmer
until thickened and smooth, about
5 minutes, but ◗ do not boil. Serve at
once. Good with noodles or rice.

## SMOTHERED CHICKEN

**6 to 7 Servings**

Preheat oven to 350°.

Prepare for cooking:

**A 4-lb. roasting chicken**

Disjoint it. Place the chicken in a paper bag with:

**¼ cup Seasoned Flour, (II, 220)**

Close the bag and shake vigorously. Brown the chicken in:

**¼ cup olive or vegetable oil**

Place it in a casserole. Cook in the fat for 10 minutes:

**1 small sliced onion**
**1 sliced clove garlic**
**3 or 4 chopped celery ribs**
**1 medium-sized carrot**

Put the vegetables in the casserole. Pour over the mixture:

**1½ cups hot chicken stock**

Bake ♦ covered about 1½ hours or until tender. Add to the dish 5 minutes before it is done:

**(1  cup sliced Sautéed**
    **Mushrooms, 328)**
**(12  sliced stuffed olives)**


## PERSIAN CHICKEN

**4 Servings**

Disjoint and cut into pieces:

**A broiler or roasting**
**chicken**

Sauté the chicken until brown and almost done in:

**Butter or vegetable oil**

Heat in a large saucepan or casserole:

**2 tablespoons butter**

Sauté until soft and golden:

**1 finely chopped onion**

Add and stir well:

**1 cup ground walnuts**

Add:

**½ cup fresh pomegranate**
    **juice or the juice of**
    **2 lemons**
**2¼ cups chicken stock**

Stir while sauce heats and thickens somewhat.

**Season to taste**

and, if necessary, add:

**1 to 2 teaspoons sugar**

Add the chicken pieces and simmer gently, covered, 30 minutes. Serve with:

**Boiled Rice, 189**


## CHICKEN OR TURKEY STEW OR FRICASSEE

A fricassee is a simmered meat, usually chicken, veal or rabbit. Whether this meat is to be simmered in stock or in water; whether it is to be sautéed first in butter or put directly into boiling liquid; whether it is to be simmered first and browned afterward; what the additions are to be; whether or not a thickening of flour is to be used; whether the stock is to be thickened at the last with cream and eggs—these are all matters of tradition, personal taste and convenience. Typical fricassees are the following.

### I.

**5 Servings**

Clean and cut into pieces:

**A 5-lb. stewing chicken or**
    **pieces of turkey**

Place the chicken in a stewing pan and bring to the boiling point with:

**3 cups water**
**1 sliced carrot**
**2 ribs celery with leaves**
**1 small sliced onion**

Reduce heat and simmer the fowl about 15 minutes and remove scum. Continue to ♦ simmer covered until the meat is tender, 2 hours or more ♦ Do not boil at any time. At the end of the first hour of cooking, add:

**3 or 4 peppercorns**

Remove the meat and strain the stock. If a very concentrated gravy is desired, boil the stock before thickening until reduced to 1½ cups. Thicken with:

**Flour, see Poultry Pan**
    **Gravy, 383**

Pour the gravy over the chicken. Garnish with:

**Parsley**

Serve with:

**Noodles, 200, Dumplings, 182, or Boiled Rice, 189**

## II.

4 to 5 Servings

Cook à Blanc, 555, until tender, and reserve:

**1 dozen mushrooms**
**1 dozen small onions**

Cut into pieces:

**A 5-lb. stewing chicken or pieces of turkey**

reserving the neck and back for stock. Dust the meat with:

**Flour**

Melt in a heavy pan:

**2 tablespoons butter**

When the butter reaches the point of fragrance, add the floured chicken. Cook until the flour crusts but does not color. Add just enough to cover:

**Water or**
**Chicken Stock, (II, 172)**
**An onion stuck with**
**3 cloves**
**1 teaspoon salt**

Bring the liquid to a boil. ◗ Reduce heat at once. ◗ Simmer, uncovered, about 45 minutes. Remove the meat and the clove-studded onion from the liquid. Discard the onion. Keep the meat warm. Melt in the top of a double boiler over direct heat:

**3 tablespoons butter**

Add:

**3 tablespoons all-purpose flour**

Make a sauce by adding to this roux the liquid from the meat. Simmer, stirring, about 5 minutes. Have everything else ready to serve, because the sauce does not hold well once the eggs are added. Stir some of the sauce into:

**3 beaten egg yolks**

**³/4 cup cream or milk**

Pour the egg sauce into the rest of the sauce and place ◗ over—not in—boiling water, stirring until the eggs thicken. Add the reserved mushrooms and onions. Place the chicken on a hot platter, inside a:

**Rice Ring, 189**

Pour the garnished sauce over the meat. You may decorate the platter with small bunches of:

**Cooked carrots**
**Parsley**

so arranged as to look like fresh carrots with tops.

## FRENCH CASSEROLE CHICKEN

5 Servings

Whenever we see one of our contemporaries trying to regain her youthful allure with gaudy sartorial trappings, we think of a dish we found in a collection of college alumnae recipes, called: "Suprême of Old Hen." We all know that "suprême," in chef's parlance, simply means a breast of fowl. But in this case it really lives up to its billing and makes such a good dish out of a poorish bird that the old girl is still an acceptable morsel.

Disjoint:

**A 5-lb. stewing chicken**

Sear the pieces in:

**¹/4 cup butter**

Add:

**¹/4 cup dry white wine**

Remove the chicken from the pot. Place in the pot:

**2 pared, cored, sliced tart apples**
**6 chopped celery ribs with leaves**
**1 minced or grated onion**
**3 sprigs parsley**
**¹/2 teaspoon salt**
**¹/4 teaspoon paprika**

Cover and cook these ingredients gently until tender. Stir in:

> 2½ tablespoons flour
> 2 cups Stock, (II, 171–172)

Cook and stir the sauce until it boils. Add the chicken. Cover and simmer until tender, 1 hour or more. Remove the chicken to a hot ovenproof serving dish. Strain the sauce. Reheat it in the top of a double broiler ▶ over—not in—boiling water and add to the strained sauce:

> ⅓ cup sweet or cultured sour cream
> Season to taste

Add:

> 1 tablespoon fresh tarragon or basil

Pour the sauce over the chicken. Sprinkle it generously with:

> Grated Parmesan cheese

Place the dish under a broiler until the cheese is melted.


## BRUNSWICK STEW

**8 Servings**

This southern specialty has many variations: combinations of chicken and pork, in equal amounts, or squirrel and pork. Chili peppers and mustard are optional seasonings.
Disjoint for cooking:

> A 5-lb. chicken

Sauté it slowly until light brown in:

> ¼ cup shortening

Remove from the pan. Brown in the fat:

> ½ cup chopped onions

Place in a large stewing pan the chicken, onions and:

> 1½ to 2 cups skinned, seeded, quartered tomatoes
> 3 cups fresh lima beans
> 1 cup boiling water
> A few grains cayenne
> (2 cloves)

▶ Simmer these ingredients, covered, until the chicken is nearly tender. Add:

> 3 cups corn, cut from the cob

Simmer the chicken and vegetable mixture covered until tender.

> **Season to taste**

Add:

> 2 teaspoons Worcestershire sauce

Stir in:

> (1 cup toasted bread crumbs)


## CHICKEN CACCIATORE OR HUNTER'S CHICKEN

**4 Servings**

Hunters who cook always seem to have tomatoes and mushrooms handy. Cut into individual pieces:

> A 4-lb. chicken

Dredge with:

> 2 to 3 tablespoons flour

Sauté until golden brown in:

> ¼ cup olive oil

with:

> 2 tablespoons chopped shallots
> (1 minced clove garlic)

Add:

> ¼ cup Italian tomato paste
> ½ cup dry white wine
> 1 teaspoon salt
> ¼ teaspoon white pepper
> ¾ cup Chicken Stock, (II, 172)
> ½ bay leaf
> ⅛ teaspoon thyme
> ½ teaspoon basil
> ⅛ teaspoon sweet marjoram
> ½ to 1 cup sliced mushrooms
> (2 tablespoons brandy or ¼ cup Muscatel)

Simmer the chicken covered for 1 hour or until tender. Serve with:

> Boiled Pasta, 200, or Tiny New Potatoes, Sautéed, 344

# CHICKEN MARENGO

**8 Servings**

This was the dish served to Napoleon after he had fasted through his victory at Marengo. Composed of findings from the nearby countryside, the dish was such a success that from there on in, Napoleon's chef had to prepare it after every battle. It is a good buffet casserole which profits by a day's aging, refrigerated.

Cut into quarters:

**2 frying chickens**

Sauté until delicately colored:

**1 thinly sliced onion**

in:

**½ cup olive oil**

then remove. Add the chicken pieces and brown on all sides. Add:

**½ cup dry white wine**
**2 crushed garlic cloves**
**½ teaspoon thyme**
**1 bay leaf**
**Sprigs of parsley**
**1 cup Chicken Stock, (II, 172)**
**2 cups Italian-style tomatoes**

Cover the pot and simmer about 1 hour, until tender. When meat is done, remove it to a platter. Strain the sauce and reduce it about 5 minutes and:

**Season to taste**

Sauté:

**16 to 20 small white onions**
**1 lb. sliced mushrooms**

in:

**¼ cup butter**
**Juice of 1 lemon**

Arrange chicken quarters, mushrooms, onions and:

**1 cup pitted black olives**

in a deep earthenware casserole. Sprinkle over all:

**1 jigger brandy**

Add the sauce and reheat in a 350° oven. Garnish with:

**Chopped parsley**

Serve with:

**Boiled Rice, 189, or Wild Rice, 198**

# COUNTRY CAPTAIN OR EAST INDIA CHICKEN CURRY

**4 Servings**

This dish has become a favorite in America, although it probably got its name not from the sea captain who brought the recipe back to our shores, but from the Indian officer who first made him acquainted with it. So says Cecily Brownstone, a great friend; this is her time-tested formula. For still another oriental chicken curry, see Rijsttafel, 197.

Preheat oven to 350°.

Cut into pieces:

**A fryer**

Coat them with:

**Seasoned Flour, (II, 220)**

Brown the chicken in:

**¼ cup butter**

Remove, drain and place in a casserole. Simmer gently in the pan drippings until golden:

**¼ cup finely diced onions**
**½ cup finely diced green pepper, seeds and membrane removed**
**1 minced garlic clove**
**1½ to 3 teaspoons curry powder**
**½ teaspoon thyme**

Add:

**2 cups stewed or canned tomatoes**

and simmer until the pan is deglazed. Pour this sauce over the chicken and bake uncovered about 40 minutes or until the chicken is tender. During the last 5 minutes of cooking add:

**3 tablespoons currants**

Serve with:

**Boiled Rice, 189**

garnished with:

**Toasted slivered almonds**


## CHICKEN OR TURKEY À LA CAMPAGNE

**10 to 12 Servings**

Roast, uncovered, 2 hours at 350°:

**A 5-lb. chicken**

Remove meat from bones. Use bones and skin in your stock pot. Sauté, 328:

**1 lb. small button mushrooms**

Have ready:

**1 cup cooked green peas**
**(3 cups canned artichoke hearts)**

Prepare à la Parisienne, 280:

**1 cup each cooked carrots and white turnips**

Arrange these ingredients in a 3-quart casserole, alternating layers of chicken and vegetables until all are used, with chicken on the top layer. Make the sauce by melting in a saucepan:

**½ cup butter**

Add and stir until smooth over low heat:

**½ cup flour**

Continue to stir over low heat and add:

**2 cups strong Chicken Stock, (II, 172)**
**1½ cups dry white wine**
**1 cup cream**
**½ cup chopped parsley**

Season to taste with:

**Salt**
**Freshly ground white pepper**

Continue to cook over low heat 10 minutes. Pour sauce over the food in the casserole. Shake the dish well, so the sauce penetrates all layers. You may cover the top with:

**(Au Gratin I, II, 221)**

and heat about 30 minutes in a 350° oven.


## TURKEY CASSEROLE MOLE

This Mexican recipe combines the native bird with chocolate and a few varieties of native peppers.

◗ Please read About Deep-Fat Frying, 94.

Cut up:

**A 12- to 14-lb. turkey**

Dip the pieces first in:

**Milk**

then in:

**Flour**

and put them on a rack to dry, about 15 minutes. Prepare by removing seeds and membrane of:

**6 Chimayo peppers**
**6 broad bell peppers**
**3 chili peppers**

If the chilis are dry, drop them into hot water about 10 minutes before removing seeds and veins. Deep-fry the peppers about 5 minutes in fat heated to 370°. Drain and reserve them.

Preheat oven to 325°.

Slide the turkey pieces gently into the 370° pepper-flavored fat and deep-fry about 5 minutes. Drain the pieces and put them into a large casserole. Cover with:

**Turkey or Game Stock, (II, 172)**

Cover the casserole and bake the turkey about 1 hour. Toast in a dry pan, over gentle heat:

**1 tablespoon sesame seeds**
**½ cup pine nuts**
**½ cup blanched almonds**

Grind together with the fried peppers:

**2 tortillas**

Cook:

**3 minced garlic cloves**

in:

**2 tablespoons vegetable oil or lard**

Add:

**2 cups skinned, seeded tomatoes**

1 bay leaf
1/2 teaspoon coriander
3 cloves
1 teaspoon cinnamon
(2 tablespoons vinegar)

Combine the above ingredients with the nuts and pepper mixture and simmer 15 minutes. Pour this thick sauce with about:

2 cups turkey stock

over the cut-up turkey and simmer, covered, about 2 1/2 hours more. This dish may be made a day or two before serving, but its most characteristic ingredient is reserved for the very last. Just before serving, add to the heated sauce:

1 to 2 oz. grated unsweetened chocolate
(A pinch of sugar)

## BREAST OF CHICKEN COCKAIGNE

**Allow a Whole Breast per Serving**

This delicate recipe does not work with frozen chicken.
Skin, bone, divide in halves, see 511:

Chicken breasts

Cook up a flavorful stock from the skin and bones of the chicken. When ready to cook, dust the chicken breasts, which should be 70°, lightly with:

Flour

For each breast, heat in a heavy skillet to the point of fragrance:

1/2 tablespoon butter
1/2 tablespoon vegetable oil

Put the floured pieces of chicken into the hot oil. Shake the pan constantly so the flour crusts but does not color. Cover and poach in the butter over very low heat 10 to 15 minutes, depending on the thickness of the meat. Turn the meat occasionally. Remove pan from heat and allow to stand covered about 10 minutes more. This rather unorthodox procedure makes breasts puff up and keeps the meat both tender and moist. Remove chicken from pan and keep warm. Prepare a gravy of the pan drippings and the stock made from the bones and skins, see:

**Poultry Pan Gravy, 383**

## STUFFED CHICKEN BREASTS

**Individual Serving**

These are quickly prepared in a chafing dish or electric skillet.
Have ready:

A boned, skinned breast of chicken

beaten with a cleaver until very thin, 550. Heat to the point of fragrance:

1 1/2 to 2 tablespoons butter

Quickly move the chicken about in this hot fat until it is no longer pink, ◗ about 2 to 3 minutes in all. Fold this thin piece over once to hold:

1 thin slice Virginia ham
1 very thin small piece Swiss cheese
(1 preserved kumquat or cooked apricot, sliced nearly in half)

Remove chicken from pan and keep warm. Sauté in pan drippings:

1 tablespoon finely minced shallots
3 mushroom caps

When mushrooms have cooked about 3 minutes, add:

1/4 cup dry white wine
2 tablespoons freshly skinned, chopped, seeded tomato

Simmer about 3 minutes again. Add to this sauce:

2 tablespoons cream

Heat the chicken breasts in the sauce slowly, but ◗ do not let them boil. Turn once or twice. When heated through, add:

1 tablespoon chopped parsley

**Season to taste**
Serve at once, over:
**Boiled Rice, 189, with saffron, or Buttered Noodles, 200**

## CHICKEN BREASTS IN QUANTITY FOR CREAMING OR SALAD

This recipe is particularly useful in preparing large quantities of chicken meat for such dishes as Chicken à la King, 257, or Chicken Pot Pies, 239. Many knowledgeable cooks consider poaching an ideal approach, but we would like to suggest the following method, which we find more flavorful. After the chicken is baked, save the pan juices and make a stock of the skin and bones. Combine these two defatted by-products in making sauce if the chicken is to be served hot or in an aspic. Or use the juices and defatted stock for broth or other cooking if the chicken is served as salad.
Preheat oven to 300°.
Place on a rack in a large shallow pan, skin side up:
**Chicken breasts**
Brush them, allowing for each whole breast:
**1 1/2 tablespoons butter**
Bake about 40 minutes, basting frequently. When slightly cooled, remove the skins and bone the breasts. Cover and refrigerate the meat until ready to use.

## CHICKEN KIEV

**4 Servings**
Bone, skin, cut in halves and pound, 511, to a 1/4-inch thickness:
**4 chicken breasts**
Form into 8 rolls about 2 inches long and 1/2 inch in diameter:
**Butter**

Roll butter lightly in a mixture of:
**2 tablespoons chopped chives**
**2 tablespoons chopped parsley or tarragon**
**(1 minced clove garlic)**
**1/2 teaspoon salt**
**1/4 teaspoon white pepper**
Place one of the seasoned butter pieces in the center of each half breast and roll so that the butter is completely enclosed. Secure with a wooden pick, if necessary. Dust with:
**Flour**
Brush with:
**Beaten egg**
Roll in:
**Dry bread crumbs**
Fry in deep fat heated to 360° until golden brown. Drain on paper toweling before serving.

## BRANDIED CHICKEN BREASTS

**4 Servings**
Skin, bone and divide into halves:
**4 chicken breasts**
Rub with:
**Brandy**
Let them stand about 10 minutes. Season with:
**Salt, pepper and marjoram**
Heat to the point of fragrance:
**6 tablespoons sweet butter**
Sauté the breasts over medium heat, 6 to 8 minutes on each side. Remove to a heated ovenproof platter and keep warm. To the remaining butter in the pan, add:
**1/2 cup dry sherry**
Simmer over ♦ low heat until the liquid is reduced to half. Add, stirring constantly:
**2 cups cream**
beaten with:
**4 egg yolks**
Season with:
**Salt and pepper**
**(Nutmeg)**

Stir and cook until slightly thickened. Pour the sauce over the chicken breasts. Sprinkle with:

**Shredded Swiss cheese**

mixed with equal parts of:

**Fine buttered crumbs**

Glaze under the broiler.

## CHICKEN AND SWEETBREADS

**8 Servings**

♦ Please read About Sweetbreads, 642. Blanch, firm, dry, trim and poach 25 minutes:

**2 pairs calf sweetbreads**

In the meantime, prepare and cook:

**Brandied Chicken Breasts, 526**

coarsely chopping the chicken after it is sautéed.

When the sweetbreads are cooked, coarsely chop and add them to the chicken and sauce with:

**1 cup blanched button mushroom caps, 328**

Instead of garnishing with Swiss cheese, use:

**Chopped parsley**

and served in coquille dishes or warmed patty shells, (II, 369).

## QUICK CREAMED CHICKEN BREASTS

**6 Servings**

Preheat oven to 350°.

Place in a shallow baking dish:

**6 boned whole chicken breasts**

Combine and pour over the chicken:

**1 cup canned cream of mushroom soup**

**1 cup cultured sour cream**

**(1/2 cup chopped mushrooms)**

**1/4 cup chopped parsley**

Sprinkle with:

**Paprika**

and bake, uncovered, about 1 hour.

## CHICKEN BREASTS CHAUD-FROID

**6 Servings**

Prepare and cook in advance as for Chicken Stew, 520:

**3 large split chicken breasts**

Simmer only 30 minutes or until tender, then refrigerate. Make certain to have on hand at least 2 cups well-seasoned chicken stock to make:

**Sauce Chaud-Froid, 428**

Coat the chicken as directed on 427. After decorating, serve with:

**Rice Salad, 62**

## STIR-FRIED CHICKEN BREASTS

**6 Servings**

♦ Please read about Stir-Frying, 98. If you plan serving this dish with fluffy rice, cook:

**Boiled Rice, 189**

while preparing the following. Skin and bone, see 511:

**3 whole chicken breasts**

Cut the meat into strips 1 1/2 to 2 inches long and 1/8 inch wide. Simmer the bones and skin of the chicken in a little water to make a stock. Mix the chicken strips thoroughly with:

**1 teaspoon salt**

**2 teaspoons cornstarch**

**1 tablespoon dry sherry or Chinese rice wine**

**1 lightly beaten egg white**

Have ready:

**1/2 cup sliced onions**

**1 cup shredded green or red sweet pepper, seeds and membrane removed**

**1/2 cup diced water chestnuts**

**1/2 cup diagonally sliced celery**

Pour into a wok or a large skillet over medium-high heat:

2 **tablespoons peanut or
vegetable oil**

When hot, add half the chicken and
briskly stir about 1 minute. The meat
will turn white when done. Push to
one side and cook the rest of the
chicken, adding more oil if necessary.
Add the vegetables and:

¹/₂ **cup chicken stock**

Cover and steam about 2 minutes.
Combine in a bowl:

2 **tablespoons soy sauce**
2 **tablespoons cornstarch**
³/₄ **cup chicken stock**

and stir into chicken and vegetable
mixture. Heat and stir about 1 minute
or until sauce is slightly thickened.
Serve over the rice.

## ▤ CHICKEN KEBABS

### I. Yakitori

6 Servings

Cut into bite-sized pieces:

3 **whole boned and skinned
chicken breasts, 511**
1 **lb. chicken livers**

Marinate the pieces about 1 hour in:

**Teriyaki Marinade, (II, 183)**

Preheat broiler or grill.
Cut into 1-inch pieces:

5 **leeks, white part only**

Alternate on skewers the chicken,
leeks and livers. Grill 5 minutes; turn
and grill 5 minutes more, basting
with the marinade. When done, serve
immediately, sprinkled with:

**Cayenne pepper**

### II. A good kebab combination is:

**Pieces of chicken or
chicken breasts**

marinated in:

**Marinade for Chicken,
(II, 182)**

wrapped in:

**Bacon**

and grilled on skewers with:

**Cherry tomatoes**

Broil each side about 3 minutes.

## ★ STUFFED BONED CHICKEN

See about Boning Fowl, 511.
This recipe, which we enjoyed on
many holiday occasions with our
friend Clara Kupferschmid, is one
she brought close to perfection over
the years.
Choose a very fresh, dry-picked,
undressed:

**6-lb. chicken**

Be sure the skin is intact. Bone it. Allow for the filling ¹/₃ of the recipe for:

**Chicken Farce, 437**

Before stuffing the chicken "romper,"
tie it off securely at the neck, wing
ends and legs. Sew shut the vent under the tail. Be sure not to pack the
farce or fill the skin too tightly or it
may burst during the cooking as the
stuffing swells. In filling, "make like"
a taxidermist or a sculptor, shaping
the stuffing so that, when you have
sewn the seam down the back, the
bird will resemble its former self.
Preheat oven to 450°.
Brush the bird generously all over with:

**Clarified Butter, 396**

For this and for subsequent basting,
allow about ¹/₂ pound of butter. Prick
the chicken all over with a darning
needle and repeat this operation after
every basting. Place the bird on a
rack in a pan in the hot oven and ♦ reduce the heat at once to 350°. After
40 minutes of cooking, baste it at
10-minute intervals and continue until done, about 2 hours in all. Boned
stuffed chickens may be served hot
but are unusually delicious when
served cold. Chill at least 24 hours to
allow the seasonings to develop. To
serve, slice very thin with a hot serrated knife.

## GALANTINE OF TURKEY

**If Served Hot, 15 Servings**
**If Served as an Hors d'Oeuvre, 30**

A galantine of fowl is a white-tie-and-tails production that begins with the boning process. The skin of the bird eventually becomes the covering of an oversized sausage that contains the meat of the bird combined with eggs, spices and other meats. When a galantine finally appears in all its glazed and truffled splendor, no one could suspect how it began, for in no way does it resemble any avifauna. For this reason, it is possible to start with a ready-dressed bird—but if you do, be sure to choose one with the smallest possible precut opening. For either dressed or undressed turkey, follow the boning instructions on 511. After making the first slit down the spine ♦ it is vital to keep the rest of the skin intact. Any cuts must be patched by sewing.

Bone:

**A 12- to 15-lb. turkey**

Reserve the meat, including that cut from the drumsticks and the breast. Make a Stock, (II, 171), of the bones. Reserve half the breast meat for filling and cut it into 1/2-inch strips. Grind 3 times and put into a large bowl:

**1 lb. lean white veal**
**1 lb. lean pork**

as well as the turkey meat, except the reserved strips. Season the mixture with:

**1/4 cup brandy, dry sherry or Madeira**
**1 teaspoon freshly grated nutmeg**
**Ground black pepper**
**2 teaspoons Worcestershire sauce**
**1 tablespoon salt**
**A dash hot pepper sauce**

Add:

**8 eggs**
**1/2 cup finely chopped parsley**

Mix these ingredients into a smooth paste. Spread a large piece of clean linen or cheesecloth on the table. Place in the center of the cloth the turkey skin, outer side down, as shown in the center, below. Pat the meat mixture onto it in an even rectangular shape, extending it all the way to the edges of the skin. Arrange in neat alternating rows down the center, as shown:

**Strips of cooked ham or tongue**

and the reserved strips of turkey breast. Arrange a center row of:

**Small whole truffles, 332, or seeded black olives**

Over the whole, sprinkle:

**3/4 cup pistachio nuts**
**1/4 cup finely chopped parsley**

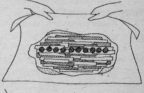

Starting at the long side farthest away from you, pull the cloth toward you gently—rolling the filled turkey skin into a sausagelike shape. You do not want the cloth to be inside the turkey roll, but keep manipulating it until it forms an outside casing. You may need an extra helping hand. Tie the cloth securely at both ends. The roll should be smooth and even. Also tie it lengthwise, as sketched. Place it on a rack, seam side down, in a large poaching kettle over:

**Mirepoix, (II, 254)**

and in:

**Enough turkey or poultry stock to cover, (II, 172)**

Cover the kettle and bring to a boil, then ▶ reduce the heat and simmer very gently 1½ to 2 hours until the roll is firm to the touch. Carefully remove it from the broth. You may serve it—unwrapped—hot, sliced, with buttered toast. Or let it cool—wrapped—on a large platter. You may weight it if you wish. When it has cooled to at least 70°—not before—remove the outside wrapping and refrigerate the galantine thoroughly. To decorate, either use:

**Sauce Chaud-Froid, 428**

or cover with a savory:

**Aspic Glaze, 427**

made from the poaching broth. Serve thinly sliced with:

**Buttered toast**

as an hors d'oeuvre or an entrée.

## ABOUT DUCK

As it happens these days, we ordinarily dine not on duck but on **duckling**, if we dine on the domesticated bird. Most such ducks, like the members of other prominent American families, grow up on Long Island. Unlike their human counterparts, however, the ducks exhibit very uniform characteristics. When we make their acquaintance at market, dressed for the occasion, they are commonly 7 to 8 weeks old and weigh 3 to 5 pounds. As duck has both a heavy frame and a high fat content, we allow about 1⅓ to 1½ pounds per serving. The only trouble with these otherwise su-

perlative young birds is that one is too little for two persons, and two are too much. A practice followed by some prudent ménagères is to serve a whole duckling to each person anyway, but to remove the legs beforehand for subsequent mincing. For a far more attractive presentation, serve duck as a Salmi, 537. In purchasing, look for a white skin and a plump body. Remember to save the carcasses for conversion to stock. Duck livers furnish excellent material for pâtés, 629.

## ROASTING DUCK OR GOOSE

▶ Please read About Duck, left. Pluck, singe, draw and truss as described on 508. Remove the oil sac at the base of the tail, see 509. Since these birds are so fat, we often prefer to prepare a separate stuffing in a baking dish, so that the dressing will not be overpowered by the flavor and slickness of the fat. These birds ▶ must be pricked frequently, but lightly, all over to allow excess fat to escape. If they are not stuffed, you may rub the cavity with lemon juice, or place a cored and peeled apple, a carrot, an onion, celery ribs or a potato in the body cavity to attract off-flavors. Discard these vegetables before serving. You may also hasten the cooking with the old Chinese trick of placing several heated metal forks in the cavity to intensify the heat at that point. Place the bird in a 450° preheated oven, lower the heat to 350° and proceed as for chicken, allowing about 20 minutes to the pound for an unstuffed duck, 25 minutes per pound for a gosling. Larger geese take about 15 minutes per pound. Add 20 to 30 minutes if the duck or goose is stuffed.

## ROAST DUCKLING

**3 Servings**

◗ Please read About Duck and Roasting Duck, 530.

Preheat oven to 450°.

Pick, clean and singe, if necessary:

**A 4¹/₂- to 5¹/₂-lb. duckling**

Dry with paper toweling and rub with:

**(Garlic)**

or sprinkle evenly with:

**(Paprika)**

Place it on a rack in a roasting pan. If stuffing is used, try:

**Sausage Dressing with apples, 433, or**
**Apple and Prune Dressing, 434, or**
**Sauerkraut Dressing for Game, 437**

Put the bird, uncovered, into the oven and ◗ reduce the heat at once to 350°. Cook until tender allowing about 20 minutes to the pound for an unstuffed bird, longer for a stuffed one, see 530. Make:

**Poultry Pan Gravy, 383**

Serve with:

**Polenta, 180**

or, if the duck has not been stuffed, with:

**Crushed pineapple, Sweet-Sour Orange Sauce, 406, or Cranberry Glaze for Fowl, 427, or Fruit and Honey Glaze, see below**

## FRUIT- AND HONEY-GLAZED DUCKLING

**3 Servings**

For those who like sweet with meat.

Preheat oven to 450°.

Prepare and cook:

**Roast Duckling, above**

Remove from oven just before done. Make a thick glaze to pour over the duck. Combine and mix well:

**1  cup apricot, cherry or peach preserves**
**¹/₂  cup clover honey**
**1  tablespoon brandy**
**1  tablespoon Grand Marnier or other orange-flavored liqueur**

Coat the duck with this glaze and return it to the oven 10 to 15 minutes until the glaze caramelizes.

## ROAST DUCK BIGARADE OR À L'ORANGE

This famous recipe depends for its flavor on the Seville or bitter orange, (II, 126), which gives the dish its name.

Prepare:

**An unstuffed Roast Duckling, left**

When it is done, remove it from the roasting pan and keep warm. Prepare:

**Sweet-Sour Orange Sauce, 406**

using Seville or bitter oranges and omitting the lemon. Degrease the pan juices and deglaze the pan as described on 381.

## DUCKLING ROUENNAISE

**4 to 5 Servings**

Unless you choke your duck, pluck the down on its breast immediately afterward and cook it within 24 hours, you cannot lay claim to having produced an authentic Rouen duck. The first two steps assure the dark red flesh and the special flavor of this dish. If, as is likely, duck-strangling will bring you into local disrepute, you may waive the sturdy peasant preliminaries and serve a modified version, garnished with quotation marks. First of all ◗ please read About Salmi of Wildfowl, 537.

Clean:

**A 5-lb. duckling**

reserving the liver. Free it from the

gall. Tuck the liver into the body cavity. Use a spit or rotisserie to roast the duck, only 20 to 22 minutes in all. Only the breast and legs, if tender, are reserved and kept warm. The rest of the carcass and skin is pressed as described on 537.

Meanwhile melt:

> 2 tablespoons butter

When the fat reaches the point of fragrance, add and simmer:

> 1 finely minced small onion
> 3/4 cup Burgundy

When the duckling is done, remove and crush the liver and add it to the reduced wine mixture. Poach it gently in the wine with the drippings from the pressed carcass. Add several tablespoons of:

> (Pâté de Foie de
> Volaille, 631)
> Season to taste

Slice the breast lengthwise into about 20 thin strips and put them in a chafing dish. Should you want to serve the legs, they must at this point be removed and grilled, as they are too raw without further cooking. We prefer to utilize them later in some other dish.

◗ Cover the sliced meat quickly with the hot liver sauce and serve ◗ immediately from the chafing dish at table.


DUCK PILAF

**4 Servings**

Remove the meat from:

> **Roast Duckling, 531**

There should be about 2 cups. Break the carcass apart. Add to it:

> 4 cups water
> 1 chopped onion
> Some celery leaves

Simmer this stock covered for 1 hour. Strain. Bring to boiling point. Stir in slowly, not disturbing the boiling:

> 2/3 cup rice

Cook the rice until it is tender, about 1/2 hour. Strain it. Reserve the liquor. Melt:

> 2 tablespoons butter

Add and sauté covered for 5 minutes:

> 3/4 cup finely chopped celery
> 1 teaspoon grated onion

Add the duck meat, the rice and:

> 1 cup liquid: leftover gravy,
> duck liquor or cream

Mix these ingredients well with a fork. Season them, if needed, with:

> Salt and paprika

Serve the pilaf hot with:

> **Stewed plums or apricots**


ABOUT GOOSE

Among the reasons for the decline in the popularity of goose are its high fat content and the toughness of a fully matured bird. The first drawback is being constantly reduced by breeders; the second may be lessened by buying no goose weighing over 12 to 14 pounds, dressed. Braise rather than roast any bird larger than this or one you suspect is older than 6 months. All goose meat is dark. Goose fat should be rendered and saved as a flavoring. It is especially good with braised cabbage or sauerkraut. Allow approximately 1 pound for each individual serving.


★ ROAST GOSLING OR GOOSE

**Allow 1 Pound for Each Serving**

Since goose is roasted like duck, ◗ please read about Roasting Duck or Goose, 530.

Preheat oven to 450°.

Pick, clean, and singe, if necessary:

> **An 8-lb. gosling or a 10- to
> 14-lb. goose**

Fill the cavities or a separate baking dish with:

**Apple, Prune, Chestnut or Sauerkraut Dressing for Game, 433–437**

Allow 1 cup dressing to each pound of bird. If not stuffing the bird, try filling the cavity with:

**(Quartered oranges, pricked to release juices)**

Place the goose on a rack in an uncovered pan, allowing 25 minutes to the pound for a gosling and about 15 minutes to the pound for larger birds. Reduce the heat at once to 350° and pour off the fat as it accumulates. Make:

**Poultry Pan Gravy, 383**

Season it with:

**Pearl onions**
**Ginger**

Or, if unstuffed, serve with:

**Prunes in Wine, (II, 135),**
**Gooseberry Preserves,**
**(II, 672), Red Cabbage, 307,**
**Curried Fruit, (II, 113), or**
**Boiled Chestnuts I, 313**

## BRAISED TRIMMINGS OF GOOSE OR GÄNSEKLEIN

Rub with garlic:

**Goose back, neck, gizzard, wings and heart**

Place in a heavy pot. Add:

**Mirepoix, (II, 254)**

Half cover with boiling water. Simmer ◗ closely covered, until nearly tender, about 1½ hours.

**Season to taste**

and add:

**(A pinch of ginger)**

Cover and simmer the meat until tender, about ½ hour longer. Remove from the pot. Strain the stock, removing the grease. Make:

**Poultry Pan Gravy, 383**

Pour it over the meat. Garnish with:

**Chopped parsley**

Serve with:

**Apples Stuffed with Sauerkraut, (II, 118), or Dumplings, 182, and applesauce**

## POTTED GOOSE OR CONFIT D'OIE

Draw, pluck, singe, 508, and cut up:

**A 10-lb. goose**

Cut off, reserve and refrigerate the heavy fat. Salt the pieces of goose well on all sides. Place in an earthenware crock and weight with a nonresinous hardwood board. Cover and leave in a cool, dry place, not over 40°, 6 to 8 days. When ready to cook, place the refrigerated fat in the bottom of a large heavy pan.

Put on top of it:

**A Bouquet Garni, (II, 253)**

Wipe the salt from the meat and put the pieces on the fat layer. Simmer slowly 2 to 4 hours. ◗ Be sure, as the fat melts, that there is enough to cover the meat completely. If not, add, as needed:

**Lard**

Use at once or store in a cool place, again making sure that the meat is ◗ well covered with the fat. This dish will keep for months and can be served cold or reheated in the fat. If hot, a good accompaniment is:

**Franconia Potatoes, 348**

which are cooked in the goose fat. Or use in:

**Cassoulet, 599**

## ABOUT ROCK CORNISH HENS, GUINEA FOWL, AND SQUABS

Like iced tea and peanut butter, **Rock Cornish hens** are, so to speak, an American invention, and a surprisingly recent one, the result of patient crossbreeding of Cornish gamecocks and Plymouth Rock hens. They are plump little birds with all white meat and an attractive gamy flavor, due partly to their ancestry and partly to a diet that usually includes acorns and cranberries. Choose young birds, 5 to 7 weeks old, weighing about 2 pounds dressed.

**Guinea fowl** came originally from Africa—hence their name. The hens are much tenderer than the cocks. Because their meat is naturally very dry, it is of prime importance ◑ to bard them, 511, and not to overcook.

**Squabs,** originally wildfowl, are now raised on farms, like chickens. When young—about ¾ pound—they are called **doves;** when grown up—1¼ pounds or so—**pigeons.** No one in the least hungry has ever been satisfied with fewer than two doves.

## ROAST CORNISH HENS, GUINEA FOWL AND SQUABS

**Allow 1 Small Bird per Person**
◑ Please read about these birds, above.
Preheat oven to 450°.
Pick and draw:

> **Small guinea fowl, squabs or Cornish hens**

Either bard, 511, or brush with:

> **Melted butter**

and dredge with flour. They may be loosely stuffed with:

> **Wild Rice Dressing for Game, 435, or Rice Dressing for Cornish Hen, 435, or a fruited dressing, 436, adding some green grapes**

Place the birds breast side up, with legs tied, uncovered, in the oven. ◑ Reduce the heat at once to 350° and roast until tender: 1 hour or more if stuffed, about 45 minutes if not. They may be basted while cooking. If

barded, remove the salt pork and allow them to brown. Make:

> **Poultry Pan Gravy, 383, with mushrooms**

or serve with:

> **Bar-le-Duc Preserves, (II, 672)**

## BREASTS OF GUINEA HEN

**Allow 1 Breast per Person**
Preheat oven to 425°.
Bard, 511, each:

> **Breast of guinea hen**

Put into the oven and ◑ reduce the heat at once to 350°. Baste the breasts frequently. Cook about 45 minutes or until they are tender. Serve *sous cloche,* a fancy way to say under a glass bell, with:

> **Colbert Butter, 398**

Or serve with:

> **White Wine Sauce, 389, or Champagne Sauce, 388**

and:

> **Sautéed Mushrooms, 328**

## BRAISED SQUABS

**4 Servings**
◑ Please read about Squabs, left.
Preheat oven to 350°.
Cut into pieces or leave whole:

> **4 pigeons or 8 doves**

Dredge them with:

> **Seasoned Flour, (II, 220)**

Melt:

> **¼ cup butter**

Sauté the birds slowly in the butter until they are just seared. Place them in a casserole. Add to the fat in the pan:

> **¼ cup chopped onion**
> **1 diced carrot**
> **¼ cup chopped celery**

Stir these ingredients about 3 minutes. Add:

> **1 cup boiling Chicken Stock, (II, 172)**

Pour this over the birds. Cover closely. Bake about 45 minutes or until tender. You may add for the last 1/2 hour:

**1 cup sliced mushrooms:**

Do not let birds become dry. If they do, add more stock. Make:

**Poultry Pan Gravy, 383**

to which you may add:

**Cultured sour or
sweet cream
(Chopped olives)**

Serve the squabs within a ring of:

**Boiled Rice, 189**

Sprinkle them with:

**Chopped parsley or chives**

### BROILED SQUABS

Preheat broiler.
Pick, draw and clean:

**Squabs**

Split down the back and flatten them. You may cut out the backbone with shears. Put them on a greased broiler, skin side up. Brush well with:

**Melted butter**

Place the birds 4 inches from the heat. Broil 15 to 30 minutes, turning once. Season with:

**Salt and paprika**

Serve on:

**Buttered toast**

Pour the drippings over them. Garnish with:

**Chopped parsley**

Serve with:

**Cranberry Jelly or
Sauce, (II, 123)
Crusty Soft-Center Spoon
Bread, (II, 343)**

### ABOUT WILDFOWL

The opening of the season for grouse—that very British bird which dwells in and feeds on heather—stirs up a degree of knowledgeable excite-

ment equaled only by a *vendage* in the Côte d'Or. All over Southern Europe, each autumn, small birds, spicy with berries, are netted by the hundreds. And along the shores of Chesapeake Bay, the canvasback duck—which in October feeds on the wild celery of the shoreline—is preferred above all others.

We lived for years under one of the major flyways of the world and looked forward to the days when the males in our family sought out the bird-blinds in the surrounding marshes and rich fields. On their return, dinner parties were held in profusion. The children usually clamored for the plump little quail, leaving the rare, well-hung ducks to their more sophisticated elders.

To a large extent, proper care immediately after shooting determines the ultimate excellence of flavor in wild birds. While the bird is still warm, the neck is split and the carcass bled. To keep the blood for use in sauces, see 380. Check the neck for any undigested food and remove it.

Some birds—snipe, woodcock and plover—are cooked with the trail still inside, see 543. Although quail and a few other smaller birds should be plucked, drawn and cooked within 24 hours of killing, it is important in general not to pluck or draw any wildfowl until you are ready to cook it, since the added surface exposure of the carcass to air will induce spoilage before tenderization can be accomplished.

To tenderize and improve flavor, it is advisable to hang many wild birds, specifically partridge, prairie fowl, ducks, plover, grouse and hazel hen. How long to hang depends first on age. Old birds can be held longer than young ones. A second consideration is the weather. In muggy periods, ripening is accelerated. The third—and perhaps the most important—is personal preference. Some hunters go to extremes, holding a bird until the legs stiffen, even until head and body part company. A more moderate and acceptable state of maturity is reached when the feathers just above the tail can be drawn out easily or when a slight bluish-green tinge appears on the thin skin of the abdomen. However long birds are to be hung, suspend them, undrawn, by the feet ♦ in a cool, dry, airy place. If the weather is very warm, dust the feathers with charcoal. In any season, the birds should be protected with cheesecloth or screening.

♦ Dry-pluck all fowl. This is easier to do if the bird is chilled. Scalding or soaking preparatory to plucking breaks down the fatty tissues in the skin too rapidly if they are subsequently to be held for even a short time or are to be frozen.

Before cooking, look the birds over carefully and remove any shot with a pointed utensil. Do not use any livers or gizzards that have been penetrated by shot. Cut out meat that has discolored near the shot or any dog-damaged areas. Remove the oil sac at the base of the tail. After plucking, wildfowl should never be washed before cooking, merely wiped with a damp cloth. Safe exceptions are fish-feeding ducks which, if they must be used, should be parblanched for 1/2 hour before cooking.

♦ Singe all fowl just before cooking, including those which have been frozen. The interior of the bird may first be salted or rinsed with 2 tablespoons of brandy or sherry. Should it be necessary to counteract a too gamy taste, we suggest cooking with sauerkraut or using a marinade. Never try

to soak out the taste with water. If the bird is to be cooked unstuffed, placing in it an apple, an onion, a carrot, parsley, a few celery ribs or some juniper berries helps attract off-flavors. These fillers are, of course, discarded before serving.

♦ Age determines how wildfowl should be cooked. If you are at all doubtful that a bird is young or prime, do not hesitate ♦ to use a moist-heat method of cooking, 98, or roasting in foil, 515. Very old birds are fit only for the stock or soup pot or for making hash, forcemeat and sauces.

On many occasions only the breasts of wildfowl are served, as the legs are often tough and full of tendons. If you use the legs, remove the tendons, see 508. Otherwise, simmer the legs with the wings, necks and giblets for game stock, (II, 172). This is most useful, for in no cooking is less gravy naturally produced than in that of game. Therefore, it is doubly important to increase the stock of the game you are cooking, in order to bring up the flavor of a sauce or aspic. If game stock is not available, veal stock is the most sympathetic substitute.

Before roasting or marinating wildfowl, break down the breastbone by a blow with the flat side of a cleaver. This not only makes carving easier, but reduces the amount of marinade needed. To prepare a wildfowl for broiling, split the back and spread the breasts flat, using poultry shears for small birds.

Whether roasted or broiled, wild birds are, without exception, leaner than domestic varieties and for this reason should be cooked for shorter periods. Barding, 511, is usually advisable. Sometimes a flour and butter paste is used to coat them before barding. The barding may be removed halfway through the cooking process, but, if so, basting with butter or pan drippings should continue until the bird is taken from the heat. If a paste has not been applied you may, after the removal of the barding, want to dust the bird with flour to hasten its browning.

Most light-fleshed wildfowl is cooked well done and most dark fowl is cooked *vert-cuit* or *saignant*, that is, roasted brown on the outside under high heat, but still rare and running with juice and blood within. With these differences in mind, you can prepare most larger wildfowl by the recipes suggested for chicken, 514–528.

With smaller birds the situation is more complex. Ideally, the criterion for doneness should be internal temperature; but the flesh of such birds is shallow, and the usual meat thermometers are too bulky for practical use. Instead, the cook is advised to choose a time somewhere within the suggested limits we recommend and, if necessary, cut into the meat carefully toward the end of the period to determine how much more time it requires.

Suggestions are given in individual wildfowl recipes for those combinations of foods which are classic with game. Let us also recommend, as compatible accompaniments, a dressing of chestnuts or wild rice; a salad of chicory or cress; a dish of gooseberry or quince conserve; and a sour cream or wine sauce, not too powerfully seasoned.

## ABOUT SALMI OF WILDFOWL

A true salmi has two major characteristics. The meat is roasted—barely so, if the game is dark. And the meat from the breasts and the legs, if choice, is sliced and put to one side and kept warm. Preparation is concluded at table, much as in Duckling Rouennaise, 531, where the skin and the chopped carcass are put through a duck press, shown in the chapter heading. If the game is a water bird, the skin may be too oily to use. The pressed juices are combined with the flambéed livers, the sauce enhanced with a mirepoix and then reduced and strained. It is then reinforced by a Demi-Glaze Sauce, 391, or Sauce Espagnole, 391, based on the same kind of game as that being served. Salmis may also be enriched with mushrooms or truffles. The meat is just heated through at table in a chafing dish with this very rich sauce, given a swirl of butter, 380, and served at once.

Obviously, a classic salmi, fully accoutered, is only for the skilled cook whose husband is a Nimrod and has presented her with more than a single bird. If she is less well endowed, she will have to base her sauce on the backs, wings and necks of the bird that is being presented and eke out her Espagñole Sauce with veal stock. Needless to say, the dish is rarely presented in its original form. And the salmis that appear on menus are usually made from reheated meat, with sauces which have been previously confected. They can still be delicious, especially if care is taken ♦ not to boil the sauce and thereby toughen the meat. Another simpler way to serve precooked game is to make up a mixture similar to Pheasant in Game Sauce, 541, which lends itself even to ❄ freezing.

## MARINATED WILDFOWL

**Serves 2**

♦ Please read About Wildfowl, 535.
Clean and disjoint a:

**Pheasant, partridge or
grouse**

Place in a casserole and cover with a
marinade of:

**1 small quartered onion
1 small bay leaf
1 clove garlic
2 cups port wine
1½ teaspoons salt
½ teaspoon pepper**

Be sure the wine covers the pieces.
Let stand refrigerated 24 hours. Remove the meat from the marinade,
and dry with a towel. Reserve the
marinade.
Preheat oven to 375°.
Put into a heatproof casserole:

**2 tablespoons butter**

Add the cut-up pieces of bird and
bake, uncovered, about 45 minutes,
turning several times. Strain the marinade and pour it over the pieces. Return to the oven for another 30 minutes
or until tender. Take the pieces from
the casserole. Keep them warm. Reduce the sauce and:

**Season to taste**

Serve with:

**Wild Rice, 198, Kasha, 181,
or Noodles, 200**

## ABOUT WILD DUCKS

Flavor depends so much on the
way ducks have been feeding. The
shallow-water types may have been
feasting in nearby grain fields and
may be very succulent. These include
**mallard, black duck, pintail, bald-
pate, gadwall, teal, widgeon, shov-
eler** and **wood duck.** The deep-water
or diving ducks thrive on aquatic
vegetation. They include **canvasback,**

**redhead, ruddy, bufflehead, golden
eye, scaup** and **ring-neck.** Sometimes these varieties feed on fish or
shellfish, a diet which alters their
flavor. The red and American mer-
gansers or other habitual fish eaters
should be used only in emergencies.

Wild ducks are usually not stuffed,
but their interiors may be greased to
help retain juices. If gamy, they may
be rubbed with ginger or lemon. Celery, grapes or sliced apples in the
cavity also help minimize a too pronounced taste. Discard these additions before serving.

Cooking times vary with types.
They may be as long as 20 minutes
for canvasback and mallard or just
12 minutes for teal. The livers of
most ducks, as well as those of coot,
see under Small Game Birds, 543,
are especially choice and make delectable pâtés, 631–632.

## ROAST WILD DUCK

**4 Servings**

To draw, pluck, singe and truss
♦ please read About Wildfowl, 535,
and About Wild Ducks, above. This
cooking method seems to be the
hunter's ideal. The juices are red and
flow freely when the duck is carved.
Preheat oven to 500°.
Prepare:

**2  wild ducks**

Have them at room temperature. Dry
thoroughly inside and out. Rub the
insides with:

**Butter**

Fill cavities loosely with:

**A few skinned onions or
peeled, cored and chopped
apples, or drained
sauerkraut**

Bard, 511. Place the ducks on a rack in
a roasting pan. ♦ Reduce heat to 350°

and roast, uncovered, 18 to 20 minutes. Degrease the drippings and add:

**Wine and stock**

Reduce, then remove from heat and add:

**Cultured sour cream**

Reheat, but ♦ do not boil. Serve the ducks at once with the sauce and:

**Braised Celery, 312**

## ▤ BROILED OR BARBECUED WILD DUCK

A good way to cook wild duck and an easy way to serve it.
Preheat broiler.
Split down the back, clean well and wipe until dry:

**A wild duck**

Rub it with:

**(Garlic)**

Spread with:

**Unsalted butter**

seasoned with:

**Paprika**

Broil about 4 inches under the broiler or 4 inches above charcoal. Baste frequently with:

**An unsalted fat or oil and wine**

Cook until tender. Remove to a hot platter.

**Season to taste**

Make a sauce with the drippings, (II, 204). Serve with:

**Oranges in Syrup, (II, 126), or Kumquat Compote, (II, 127)**

Fried hominy is a well-known accompaniment to wild ducks. So are grilled sweet potatoes, or apples stuffed with sweet potatoes.

## BRAISED WILD DUCK

Draw, pluck, singe and truss:

**A wild duck**

Melt in a heavy flame-proof casserole:

**4 tablespoons butter**

When it reaches the point of fragrance, put in the duck and brown on all sides. Add, when browned:

**1 leek—white part only—or 6 button onions**
**4 tender turnips**
**1 Bouquet Garni, (II, 253)**

♦ Simmer, covered, 25 to 35 minutes or until the duck is tender. Degrease the drippings and garnish the casserole with:

**Green Peas, 338**

Serve at once with:

**Citrus Fruit Salad II, 72**

## WILD GOOSE AND WILD TURKEY

**1 Pound per Person**

These birds are only table-worthy if under a year old—preferably between 6 and 9 months. Whatever the age, both types of birds should be hung, from 24 hours to a week, and cooked with moist heat, 98. Weights fluctuate, depending on variety and age, from about 4 to 9 pounds. ♦ To draw, pluck, singe and truss, see 508–510. For wild goose and wild turkey proceed as for turkey, 515, or cut into pieces:

**A 5- to 6-lb. wild goose**

In a heavy casserole, heat to the point of fragrance:

**1/3 cup butter**
**1 1/2 cups small white whole onions**

Add:

**1/4 lb. finely diced salt pork**

and continue to cook until onions are golden. Lift out onions and pork and discard. In the remaining fat, brown the cut-up bird. Add:

**Juice of 1/2 lemon**
**1/2 teaspoon allspice**
**(A few slivers gingerroot)**

♦ Simmer, covered, about 30 minutes. Stir if necessary. Add:

**2 cups dry red wine**

♦ Simmer, covered, about 45 minutes longer or until tender. Thicken the pan gravy slightly with:

**Toasted dry bread crumbs**

Serve with:

**Noodles, 200**
**Spiced apricots or crab apples**

## POTTED WILDFOWL

**Allow 1 Pound per Person**

A good way to preserve any extra wildfowl.

♦ Please read about Wild Goose, 539. Draw, pluck, singe and cut into pieces:

**A young wild goose or other wildfowl**

Prepare as for:

**Potted Goose, 533**

Serve either hot or cold.

## HAZEL HEN

**Allow 1 Pound per Person**

Please read About Wildfowl, 535. Since this bird is apt to be resinous, it is best to poach it first in milk for 15 minutes. Bone, and grill about 12 minutes in all.

## ABOUT PHEASANT

♦ Please read About Wildfowl, 535. We hope your pheasant is young, with a flexible breastbone, gray legs and a large pointed terminal feather in its wings. If it is a cock, it should have rounded, not sharp or long, spurs. Then you may roast or broil it even without hanging. With pheasant, barding is usually advisable. These young birds can be used as in any recipe for chicken.

Otherwise, to give the bird both flavor and tenderness, about a 3-day hanging period is advised, during which the color of the breast will change somewhat and there will be a slight odor.

An old bird should be barded and either braised or used in another moist heat recipe.

## ROAST PHEASANT

**3 Servings**

♦ Please read About Wildfowl, 535, and About Pheasant, left.

Preheat oven to 400°.

Bard, 511:

**A young pheasant**

You may stuff it with:

**Chestnut Dressing, 433, or**
**Sausage Dressing, 433**

Place in oven. ♦ Reduce heat at once to 350°. Cook about 25 minutes per pound or until tender. If unstuffed, serve with:

**Fried Croutons, (II, 219),**
**or Bread Sauce, 387,**
**currant jelly and Braised**
**Celery, 312; or Rice Pilaf,**
**194, and Gooseberry**
**Preserves, (II, 672)**

or, classically, with:

**Smitane Sauce, 389**

## BRAISED PHEASANT

**3 Servings**

This recipe comes from a hunting fan.

♦ Please read About Wildfowl, 535, and About Pheasant, left.

Preheat oven to 400°.

Prepare:

**A 3½- to 4-lb. pheasant**

Pound:

**A thin slice salt pork**

Separate the skin from the breast flesh of the pheasant and insert the salt pork. Place in the body cavity the pheasant liver and:

**A small peeled tangerine**

Lace the opening tightly. Truss the pheasant, 510. Melt in a heavy pan:

**¼ cup lard**

Brown the bird, turning it and basting until it is golden all over. Place in a casserole. Add and turn in the fat:

**12 sliced mushroom caps**

Pour these over the pheasant. Melt in a saucepan:

**¼ cup butter**

Stir in, cook, but do not let brown:

**3 shallots or 1 small
  minced onion**

**2 tablespoons flour**

Stir in gradually:

**¼ to ⅓ cup Marsala or
  Madeira**

**½ teaspoon salt and freshly
  ground pepper**

Pour this into the casserole. Our correspondent adds a sprig of fresh fennel and 2 crushed juniper berries. ♦ Cover the casserole and bake the pheasant about ½ hour. Serve it from the casserole with:

**Hominy, 179, and currant
  jelly
A green salad**

❈ PHEASANT IN GAME SAUCE

**10 to 12 Servings**

♦ Please read About Wildfowl, 535.
Preheat oven to 400°.
Prepare for roasting:

**5 or 6 pheasants**

Bard, 511, with:

**Bacon or salt pork**

Fill the cavity, if you wish to reduce the gamy taste, with:

**Apple or onion slices**

Discard them after birds are roasted. Roast at 400° for 20 minutes. Remove meat from bones and reserve, keeping the meat in as large pieces as possible. Cook for 2 hours, or until reduced about a third, a stock made

from the bones, skins, drippings and barding, using:

**2 large chopped onions**

**2 cloves garlic**

**2 bay leaves**

**1 tablespoon black
  peppercorns**

**1 teaspoon thyme**

**1 small pinch rosemary**

**1 cup chopped parsley**

**(6 juniper berries)**

**¼ lb. ham trimmings**

**1 quart dry red wine**

**2 quarts water or Chicken
  Stock, (II, 172)**

**Stems from 2 lb. of
  mushrooms**

**3 fresh tomatoes**

Strain the stock and add it to:

**¾ cup White Sauce I, 383**

Add to this sauce:

**Caps of 2 lb. of mushrooms**

**¾ cup red wine**

Simmer about 25 minutes.

**Season to taste**

Reduce by one-third, strain and add:

**¼ cup brandy**

Simmer another 10 minutes. Arrange meat in a 3-quart casserole. You may put it on a bed of:

**(Cooked wild rice)**

Pour sauce over it. To serve, reheat, uncovered, in a 350° oven 45 to 55 minutes. If frozen, thaw and bring to room temperature before reheating.

PHEASANT SMITANE

**3 Servings**

Bard, 511:

**A 3½- to 4-lb. pheasant**

with:

**Sliced salt pork or bacon**

Brown the pheasant in:

**Butter**

in a heavy pan. Then place it in a deep casserole with the drippings. Cover tightly and let simmer over low heat until tender, about 45 minutes. Add:

**4 cups diced tart apples
2 tablespoons brandy or Calvados
2 cups cultured sour cream
Season to taste**

and cook over low heat until the apples are tender. ◗ Do not boil. Serve with:

**Wild Rice, 198, or
Gnocchi, 185–186**

## ABOUT PARTRIDGE

French restaurant menus list young partridge as *perdreau*—masculine; older ones, invariably and ungraciously, as *perdrix*—feminine. Hang an old bird the better part of a week. Marinate it before cooking, preferably by braising. An old partridge in full feather may be recognized by the conspicuous red ring on the eye circle, its yellow beak and its dark legs. If a partridge is under six months old, it still has its pointed first-flight feather, and its legs will be plump. The red-legged French partridges are larger and not considered so delicate as the English. There is some confusion in America about the very name of partridge. No true partridge is native, but the name is given in the north to the ruffed grouse and in the south to quail.

If the bird is fresh, it has a rigid vent. ◗ A true partridge can be cooked by any recipe for chicken if larded; or, if barded, as for pheasant. But, if it is old, a longer cooking period will be necessary. It may be served in a Salmi, 537, as for duck. Some people like it braised with Sauerkraut, 308, allowing 2 pounds of the sauerkraut to three 3-pound birds. Add the sauerkraut the last ½ hour of cooking. Others shudder at so strongly flavored an accompaniment. A more delicate one

is Braised Endive, 312. Or wrap the partridge in grape leaves, simmer it in wine and stock for 35 minutes; then roast it in a 350° oven 25 minutes. Allow 1 pound per person. Make Poultry Pan Gravy, 383, and serve the partridge with Boiled New Potatoes, 344, and watercress.

## GROUSE, PTARMIGAN OR PRAIRIE CHICKEN

**Allow 1 Pound per Person**

Young grouse which feeds on the tender shoots of the heather is one of the most coveted of all game. To test for youth, hold the bird aloft by the lower mandible. If this breaks, failing to support the weight of the bird, you have a young specimen. Roast or broil if young. Braise if old. The same treatments apply to **Canadian Grouse** or **Black Game**, also known as **Black Grouse** or **Coq de Bruyère.** Resinous in flavor, this species is not quite so delicious as true grouse. Both must be dry-plucked, because of the birds' soft feathers and tender skin. We do not recommend broiling grouse, as the meat is too dry. Preheat oven to 300°.

Prepare for cooking as you would a chicken:

**Young grouse**

You may lard the breast, 550, with thin strips of:

**Salt pork**

or bard it, 511. Or you may stuff it with:

**A small apple, a skinned onion or ribs of celery**

Grouse is served rare, cooked to a pale pink tone. Allow 30 to 45 minutes' cooking in all. Baste frequently with:

**Melted butter or drippings**

Remove the bacon. Brush the bird with:

**Butter**

Dredge it lightly with:

**Flour**

Place it in a hot 500° oven until brown. Make:

**Poultry Pan Gravy, 383**

Serve with:

**Rowanberries or
cranberry sauce**

## ABOUT SMALL GAME BIRDS

Birds here discussed are of many kinds: **quail, woodcock, ortolans, figpeckers, coots or mudhens, wild doves, snipe, rails, curlews, plover, larks, reed birds, thrushes, moorhens** and **gallinules.** They are bracketed on the basis of similar treatment, although coots should be skinned rather than plucked, and the fact that they are served one or more to a person. Small birds are usually used as fresh as possible, although they remain edible as long as the legs are flexible. Quail, which is about the largest discussed here, should not be hung longer than 24 hours. ◗ All small birds, except coots, should be dry-plucked. You may clean as for chicken. In fact, some, like snipe, plover, ring doves and woodcock, may be cooked undrawn, although the eyes and crop are discarded before roasting. To use the entrails after cooking, sieve or chop the intestines and flambé them, 108, briefly in brandy. Mix with pan drippings and spread on a crouton or over the bird as a glaze before serving. Or, if you draw the bird before cooking, reserve the intestines, chop them, sauté them briefly in butter, then proceed as above.

Small birds should be barded, 511, or you may wrap them first in fig or grape leaves. All lend themselves to roasting and skewering or broiling

from 3 to 10 minutes. Blackbirds and crows, if eaten as a matter of necessity, must be parblanched 10 to 15 minutes first, 106.

Small birds produce very little pan drippings. Pour what there is on a crouton, or on a piece of crisp scrapple. Or combine the drippings with a Demi-Glaze Sauce, 391, and wine or lemon, or use them to make Smitane Sauce, 389, Hunter's Sauce, 392, Bread Sauce, 387, or White Wine Sauce, 389; or use any recipe for braised chicken—allowing in the timing for difference in size. Any special peculiarities or classic combinations are listed in individual recipes.

## ROASTED SMALL GAME BIRDS

◗ Please read About Small Game Birds, left.

Preheat oven to 450°.

Bard, 511:

**6 small game birds**

It is not necessary to stuff them, although a few peeled grapes or bits of celery or parsley may be tucked inside and discarded later. Place in the pan with the birds:

**1 tablespoon butter**

Bake the birds about 5 minutes, ◗ reduce the heat to 350° and bake them 5 to 15 minutes longer, according to their size. Timing in general varies from woodcock, 8 to 10 minutes, to quail, unstuffed, 10 to 15 minutes; to stuffed, 15 to 18 minutes.

## BROILED SMALL GAME BIRDS

◗ See About Small Game Birds, left.

Preheat broiler.

Bard, 511:

**6 small game birds**

Place them on a broiler. Cook from 12 to 20 minutes, according to size. Turn frequently. The barding may be removed toward the end of the cooking period and the birds browned briefly by further broiling. Add the juice of:

**1 lemon**

to:

**Stock or wine**

if there is an insufficient amount of drippings.

**Season to taste**

Serve the birds on:

**Croutons, (II, 219)**

Pour the gravy over them. Garnish with:

**Parsley**

## BRAISED SMALL GAME BIRDS

◗ Please read About Small Game Birds, 543.
Preheat oven to 350°.
Prepare for cooking:

**6 small game birds**

Melt in a saucepan:

**2 tablespoons butter**

Add the birds and sauté them until lightly browned. Add:

**½ cup boiling stock or wine**
**A Mirepoix, (II, 254)**

Cover the birds with a poaching paper, 101, and bake 15 to 20 minutes. Make:

**Poultry Pan Gravy, 383**

Add to the gravy:

**(2 tablespoons lemon juice or cultured sour cream or brandy)**

Serve on:

**Croutons, (II, 219)**

Garnish with:

**Parsley**

## ☰ SKEWERED SMALL BIRDS

◗ See About Small Game Birds, 543.
Wrap in buttered grape or fig leaves:

**Small birds**

or bard them, 511, with very thin slices of:

**Salt pork**

Roast skewered over coals 10 to 15 minutes. To finish for serving, you may remove the barding, roll the birds in bread crumbs, baste with drippings and heat in a moderate oven 5 minutes longer.

## DOVES OR WOOD PIGEONS

**1 to 2 per Person**

◗ Please read About Small Game Birds, 543.
A dark meat with a fine flavor. Dove is usually tenderer than pigeon. Unless the birds are very young, prepare as for:

**Braised Small Game Birds, left**

Serve the sauce garnished with:

**Almond-stuffed olives**

or with a compote of:

**Red Sour Cherries, (II, 124)**

## QUAIL

**1 per Person**

Somtimes called partridge in our deep South. ◗ Please read About Small Game Birds, 543. Quail has a delicious white meat. If the fat of the bird is hard rather than firm before cooking, the flesh will be tough and must be prepared by a moist heat method. If the bird is young, roast or broil. ◗ Never overcook. Serve with:

**Quince preserves and curried rice, or watercress and lemon wedges**

or with:

**Smitane Sauce, 389, and green grapes; or a baked pear, the center stuffed with a pimiento**

If you have broiled the quail, brush it with:

(Anchovy Butter, 397)

SNIPE OR WOODCOCK

**Allow 1 to 2 Birds per Person**
These fowl are highly prized by some epicures in the autumn when they are fat and meaty. At other seasons the more critical connoisseurs claim that the only part worth bothering with is the cooked entrail, au jus, on a few croutons.

♦ Please read About Small Game Birds, 543.

Prepare and cook as for:

**Small Game Birds**

or use the recipe for Grouse, 542. You may use the trail, see 543. Skin the head, but leave it on. Remove the eyes and crop. Bring the long, curved beak down to pierce and hold the legs in place. Bard, 511, and roast 10 to 15 minutes.

# MEAT

## ABOUT MEATS

A reappraisal of meat and its role is due in this protein-hungry world. With milk, eggs and fish, meat is still the source of our most complete protein, and, coming at the end of the food chain, it provides as well a richness of minerals and trace elements, many of which are increasingly recognized as essential to our physical development. In this period of world inflation, however, many see meat as a wasteful commodity whose production costs far exceed those of grains, which, if skillfully combined and supplemented, can furnish us with adequate nourishment. For many, too, meat eating provokes ethical considerations. For whatever reasons vegetarianism may be adopted, see page 2 for a discussion of its potential nutritional pitfalls.

With these factors in mind, our meat shopping is done with a greater awareness than ever of the need for intelligence in the use of this valuable element in menu building, whether we serve hamburger or splurge with a Crown Roast of Lamb, 593–594, or a Suckling Pig, 602, or blend meat and innards in a pâté, 629, all illustrated above.

A novice approaching the meat counter may also approach a state of panic. The friendly, informative butcher of a good while back has often been succeeded by a presence that mysteriously slices, grinds and wraps behind a glass partition; or, more recently, by binfuls of boxed meat-cuts straight from the processing plant, where new procedures of boning and packaging save transportation costs and safeguard sanitation. Whatever the merits of prepackaging—and skillful aging is not likely to be one of them—the cuts look bafflingly similar, but often react to cooking in totally unexpected ways. If you are a rank amateur, we hope that this chapter will give you the skill of an expert in choosing the right cut for the type of dish in mind. Note, too, that meat recipes are grouped consistently, first for tender and then for tougher cuts.

Tender cuts generally, you will see on the diagram, 561, lie in those sections of the animal where the least movement and stress occur, and respond to ♦ dry-heat processes: roasting, broiling, pan-broiling, sautéing and stir-frying. For further details, see the chapter on Heat, 91, for these processes and those for the tougher cuts. The latter, with more connective tissue, demand long, slow cooking with moisture or with ♦ moist-heat processes: braising, stewing, fricasseeing, pot-roasting, poaching and deep-fat frying. In all but the last named, the temperature of the cooking liquid ♦ should never go above 180°. For this reason, we do not recommend the pressure cooking of meats, although expediency sometimes overcomes our better judgment. But if you should pressure-cook meat, follow the directions given by the manufacturer of your equipment.

For ways to counteract toughness, see about Cooking Tough Meats, 549; about Marinating, 552; about Grinding and Pounding, 550; and About Larding, 550. For a discussion of microwave cooking of meat, see 116.

But there is more about meat than cuts, grades and cooking methods that must be learned the hard way. How the animal was fed—whether on grass or corn; how long the meat has been held and at what temperatures; whether it is watered or treated with preservatives; when it was packaged—all are factors for which you must rely partly on your experience but mostly on the integrity of the butcher.

# ABOUT MEAT GRADES AND BUYING

Most American consumers benefit from two forms of protection offered in the meat market by the U.S. Department of Agriculture. First, all meats sold in interstate commerce are subject to government inspection for wholesomeness and cleanliness; but do be cautious in purchasing ♦ locally butchered meats not subject to these rigid federal sanitation regulations. Second, meats sold by the wholesale packing companies are graded and stamped by government-employed "graders" according to nationally uniform federal standards of quality for tenderness, juiciness and flavor. We are especially concerned here with grading, for the quality of the meat is as important in our choice of cooking method as is the cut—or where the meat lies on the animal's body. U.S. grading falls into six main classes, as follows—although **Choice** and **Good** are the two grades of major interest to most consumers:

### PRIME

A scarce grade generally commandeered by hotels and clubs and rarely available in neighborhood markets. From young, specially fed cattle, Prime is abundantly marbled or flecked with fat; it is tender, well-flavored, fine-textured and usually aged; the encasing fat is white.

### CHOICE

Meat of high quality but with somewhat less marbling than prime. There are now five subcategories of the Choice grade, of increasing degrees of leanness; the tenderer cuts may be dry-roasted or broiled.

GOOD

Still a relatively tender grade, but with a higher ratio of lean. The encasing layer of fat may be thin; there is less juiciness and flavor. Oven-roasting by the constant-heat method may be satisfactory for tenderer sections, but moist-heat cooking should usually prevail.

STANDARD

From low-quality young animals, with a very thin fat covering and virtually no marbling. The youth of the animals gives this grade a bland flavor, but tenderness cannot be counted on; there may also be a tendency toward dryness. Use moist-heat cooking methods only.

COMMERCIAL AND UTILITY

Meat from old animals. By reason of maturity and fat content, these meats have better flavor than Standard grade, but are tough and coarse in texture—even when carefully cooked—because of their great proportion of connective tissue.

Although we are always being assured that ⬧ the protein value of meat from older animals is comparable to that from the younger, more tender ones, we know that they rarely match in eating quality. Definite exceptions apply to meats for stocks, (II, 171), and for soups, 126. Both have more flavor if made from the meat of more mature animals.

Sometimes you will see a further USDA inspection stamp—K for **Kosher** or "clean" meat. This is meat from which the jugular vein has been removed to facilitate the drainage of blood at the time of slaughtering. The Kosher stamp should also guarantee freshness, as ritual demands consumption within 72 hours of slaughter.

Besides being graded, meats are sometimes marked with a second USDA stamp, a **Yield** number, which indicates in increasing proportion from 1 to 5 the amount of excess fat content or waste. The usual yield number available in most markets is Yield 2. In purchasing meat, bear in mind that cuts with the smallest percentage of bone and fat make the best buys, and that while price per pound may go down for bonier cuts with more fat, the amount you need per serving goes up. It may surprise you to know that the cost of sirloin steak is comparable per portion to unboned chuck, that center-cut pork chops are cheaper per serving than loin or rib chops, and that spareribs can be twice as expensive per serving as center-cut pork chops.

In buying trimmed meats, allow for boneless cuts $1/4$ to $1/3$ pound per serving. This category includes ground beef, lamb and veal, boneless stew, boned roasts and steaks, flank, tenderloin and most variety meats. ⬧ In buying meat with some bone, allow $1/3$ to $1/2$ pound per serving. These cuts include rib roasts, unboned steaks, chops and ham. ⬧ For bony cuts, allow $3/4$ to 1 pound per serving. In this bracket are short ribs, spareribs, lamb shanks, shoulder, breast and plate cuts, brisket and hock. The diagram on 561 will give you an additional appraisal of the proportion of bone as a cost factor in various meat cuts.

## STORING MEAT BEFORE COOKING

Raw meat should be stored at once at 35° to 40°, loosely wrapped; or, if encased in fat, uncovered. You will see a typical butcher wrap illustrated on (II, 644). If you will simply pull out the ends of the paper and loosen them, adequate protection and proper ventilation are usually ensured. As a general rule, the larger the piece of meat, the longer it will store.

Ground meat, fresh sausage and variety meats are among the most perishable kinds, both as to flavor-retention and safety. Cook them within 24 hours of purchase; and, if the ground meat is to be stored in amounts over a pound, make sure it is loosely covered and so placed in a container that it is no more than 2 inches thick, thereby allowing the chill of the refrigerator to penetrate it quickly. Uncooked diced and cubed meats should be used within 48 hours or so. Roasts will hold 3 to 5 days; steaks 2 to 4.

Pork, lamb and veal are slightly less stable than beef. Prepackaged cured or smoked meat and sausages may be stored refrigerated for a week in the original wrapper. Once meat is opened, exposed surfaces should be protected. In checking for spoilage, be sure meat is not slimy to the touch; that there is no off-odor on the surface of beef, or in pork where the bone meets the flesh. To freeze meat for storage, see (II, 652).

## SEASONING MEAT

If you add salt to meat, it is best to do so at or toward the end of cooking, whether by dry- or moist-heat methods, because salting before browning draws the juices, with their considerable natural salt content, out of the meat and into the pan. There are other ways to accent flavor. In dry-heat methods, meat may be rubbed with garlic, onion, herbs or spices about a half hour before cooking; or slivers of garlic or onion may be inserted near the bone of a roast. Any

bits of garlic remaining on the surface of the meat should be discarded before cooking, as its scorched flavor is objectionable. In moist-heat methods, the addition of herbs or wine to the stock will lessen the need for salt. For flavoring meat by marination, see 552. Delicacy of flavor may be preserved in meat heavy with fat by pouring off excess grease after the first half hour of cooking.

## COOKING TOUGH MEATS

Tenderness in raw meats depends not only on the comparative youth of the animal, but on the strain of cattle to which it belongs and the way it was fed. Toughness is due both to the presence of connective tissues and to a lack of fat in the muscle. Larding, 550, and Barding, 511, can help to make up somewhat for lack of fat. But the best way to convert stringy to tenderer tissue is by very long and very slow covered cooking in the presence of moisture. See Pot-Roasting, Stewing and Braising, 554. Grinding and mincing, too, make chewing easier. The texture of the meat, however, if basically tough, remains so, and it should never be used in luxury dishes like galantines or, for that matter, even in those so commonplace as hamburger.

Any meat can be made more palatable by seasonings and by added fats or dressings. Pounding and scoring are a help in cuts that are normally treated by dry-heat methods, like sautéing and pan-frying. Another favorite technique is marination, 552.

Chemical tenderizing is a modern development. One controversial innovation of this type is beyond the control of the consumer. The live animal is given an injection of vegetable enzyme, the effects of which are carried throughout the body before butchering. Special aging and storing techniques must accompany this method. The enzyme is reactivated at 130° and reduces cooking time. Unfortunately all meat tissues—those which need it and those which do not—are affected by enzyme injection. As a result, the tender portions may become flabby and somewhat tasteless, and the meat generally has a jellied consistency which we find unpleasant.

Nor can we say much for the home method of sprinkling the meat with papain, a derivative of papaya, which also tenderizes but adversely affects the flavor. If you care to try out a papain derivative of the household type, sprinkle it on both sides of the meat, allowing 1 teaspoon of tenderizer per pound. Prick the meat all over with a fork after applying the tenderizer. Recent studies seem to indicate that papain enzymes function as meat warms up to between 140° and 176°, so the tenderizer may be applied just before the meat is put on to cook.

## MINCING, GRINDING, POUNDING AND MACERATING MEAT

The effects of the first two processes are quite different. Particles of minced meat remain separate in further preparation; but ground meat, especially if ground 2 or 3 times, tends to pack. ♦ Always handle ground meat lightly to avoid a dense finished texture.

Pounding, which breaks down the tough fibers of meat, may be done with a wooden or rubber mallet or the flat side of a cleaver. If you are inexperienced, hold the cleaver in both hands and ♦ be sure the handle projects beyond the board or table surface—so that you don't bang your

fingers. Or use a macerating mallet such as shown in the foreground.

If you slightly moisten the cleaver or mallet, and strike with a glancing motion, the meat is not so apt to stick. In pounding something delicate, like a capon breast, put it first into a fold of oiled parchment paper. These precautions will keep the meat intact, even when pounded paper-thin. A chef friend has suggested that if you find a very thin piece of meat too measly-looking, it can be pounded and then folded over for the cooking to make it more presentable when served.

♦ All working surfaces in these procedures—especially those of wood—should be carefully cleansed with hot water and detergent afterward and carefully dried, since *salmonella* and other dangerous bacteria thrive in equipment not properly sanitized.

## ABOUT LARDING

Larding, or the insertion of strips of pork fat into lean cuts, helps give meat juiciness and flavor. This process has become more useful now that the trend in meat production is toward less marbled meat. To prepare lardoons, see directions on 551. Use short ones inserted near the surface, and put them in across the grain of the meat or fowl. Cut long ones so they protrude slightly at either end of a chunk of meat, and force them in parallel to the grain so they show up when the meat is sliced. It is important for attractiveness to cut all lardoons in uniform square-cut thicknesses varying from 1/8 to 1/2 inch. Larding needles are of two types. Those used in surface larding are very thin pinpointed models with a flexible top which can easily be pried open to insert the lardoon and then pressed tightly against the lardoon to hold it as the needle is drawn completely through the meat at a shallow angle as shown below. Sometimes these shallow lardoons are so placed that their ends form decorative rosettes. Allow about 2 to 3 ounces of pork fat for one pound of meat.

For internal larding, use the handled lardoire. Its blade is like a pen point, the base of which elongates the entire length of the shaft and remains open all along the top. Use this type to make, as well as insert, the lardoon. To fill, run it along the top of a long piece of salt pork. Then insert the point of the lardoire into the meat.

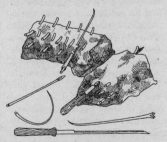

With a slow motion, push the lardoire through the meat, turning it continuously in one direction until at least 1/2 inch of the lardoon projects at either

end of the meat. With the still-filled lardoire at rest, release the exposed lardoon from the lardoire, both top and bottom, with the tip of a knife. With the thumb of one hand, hold the released top portion of pork fat firmly against the top of the meat so as to keep the lardoon from coming out of the meat as you withdraw the lardoire with the other hand. Pull the lardoire gently, twisting it from side to side, so the lardoon releases along its entire length. Allow about one lardoon for every inch of the diameter of the meat.

For another method of preventing the drying out of meat, see Barding, 511.

## LARDOONS

**Enough for 2 1/2 Pounds of Meat**

Please read About Larding, 550. Lardoons may be blanched briefly to release salt; then dried. They may also be frozen just long enough to stiffen them before insertion into meat, or you may proceed as follows.

**I.** Rub:

  1/4 **lb. pork back fat, salt pork or bacon**

with a cut:

  **(Clove of garlic)**

Cut into small uniform strips varying in cross section from 1/8- to 1/2-inch squares. Dip into:

  **Freshly ground pepper**
  **Ground cloves**

**II.** Marinate:

  1/4 **lb. salt pork lardoons**

in:

  **A few tablespoons of brandy**

Just before using, sprinkle with:

  **Nutmeg**
  **Chopped parsley or chives**

## MARINATING MEAT

This is a process which enhances tenderness and flavor in meat by soaking it in a liquid containing some form of seasoning and almost always an acid, such as vinegar, wine, lemon juice, buttermilk or yogurt. Using this process involves nutritive losses unless the marinade is subsequently used to sauce the meat. Because marination is also used for foods other than meat, it is discussed fully in Ingredients, (II, 180).

## SAUTÉING OR PAN-FRYING MEAT

Since this process is often used for foods other than meat, a full description will be found on 97. It is a popular and quick method of cooking thin or breaded cuts of meat.

## PAN-BROILING MEAT

This method of broiling may be convenient for cooking steaks or chops about an inch or less in thickness or for hamburgers. Slowly heat a heavy—preferably iron—skillet until the edge of a steak lightly touched to the skillet will sizzle briskly—not hiss sharply. Greasing the pan is unnecessary for meats that are marbled or for hamburger with normal fat content; for lean meat you may rub the skillet with a very small amount of fat. Let meat cook uncovered, sizzling briskly, for about 5 minutes. When the meat is seared and brown on the bottom, turn at once and sear for a few minutes on the other side. Avoid long cooking, which toughens the meat. ◆ Pour off any fat that may accumulate, or the meat will wind up fried or sautéed rather than pan-broiled. We do not recommend the old technique of pan-broiling on a salt base, which extracts meat juices. Fat-free broiling may be done in a coated skillet or on a soapstone griddle; in either case, follow manufacturer's instructions.

## BROILING MEAT

Please read about Broiling, 93, and about spit-cooking and outdoor grilling, 108. Choose tender cuts, see diagram, 561, such as beef steak or lamb chops. London Broil, or Flank steak, 570, is also broiled, but must be cooked rare. The broiling of veal and fresh pork is not recommended; instead, sauté or pan-fry such cuts. Kebabs are frequently marinated before broiling. For broiling frozen meats, see (II, 653).

Consult your range manufacturer's instructions as to whether preheating is required and whether or not the oven door is to be left ajar. Remove meat from refrigerator about an hour before cooking. Cut off excess fat and score the remaining fat about every 2 inches around the edge, to keep the meat from curling. Center the meat on the grid—which should be cold to prevent sticking—and adjust the broiler rack so that the top surface of the meat is 3 to 5 inches from the heat source. If grid is hot, grease it or the meat. Without seasoning the meat, broil the top side until well browned; then turn and broil until the second side is browned. Only one turning is required for a 1-inch steak or chop. For 2-inch thickness lower the rack so the surface of the meat is 4 inches from the heat source and turn more frequently. Broiling time depends on thickness, fat content, whether the meat was aged, and the degree of doneness desired. Approximate timings for various meats are given under the individual broiling recipes.

## ROASTING MEAT

Please see the diagram on 561, and About Meat Grades and Buying, 547, for types of meat appropriate for dry-heat roasting. In choosing meat for this process and deciding what variation of the procedure to follow, the important factors are the tenderness of the cut and the amount of marbling. Temperatures and timings are given in the individual recipes. Please read about Timing and Doneness, 555. For gravy-making methods, please read about Sauces Made by Degreasing and Deglazing, 381, or about Meat Pan Gravy, 382.

In all cases, the meat should be removed from the refrigerator about 2 hours before cooking. For Prime and Choice grades, place roast—not less than about 3 ribs in thickness—on a rack, fat side up, in an open shallow greased pan in a preheated oven. As soon as you close the oven door, reduce the heat and time the cooking from that point, depending on the size of the roast and degree of doneness wanted. For Prime meats, the fat content makes basting unnecessary. Choice-grade meats are subdivided into five categories, depending on the amount of marbling, but ▶ all Choice-grade cuts profit by basting, see right; and the last two categories—which are quite lean—may benefit from larding, 550, or barding, 511.

If you are dealing with the next lower grade, U.S. Good, be fore-warned that you may be taking a chance if you dry-roast rather than pot-roast meat of this type, and that dry-roasting is not recommended for pieces weighing less than 4 pounds. For Good-grade, use the following constant-heat, dry-roasting method as an alternative to the initial high-heat procedure used in **Joy** recipes. Place meat in a preheated oven—350° for pork, 325° for beef and lamb—and keep temperature steady during the entire roasting process. Larding, barding and basting may prove helpful. In short, everything possible should be done to accentuate whatever tenderness the leaner grades may have. One of the tricks is never to roast the less tender cuts more than medium rare—except for pork, which must be cooked until all pink color disappears—and to carve the meat in very thin slices, diagonally, across the grain.

Another constant-heat roasting method for meats other than pork, left, uses lower heat for a longer period. The oven should remain ▶ at least 275° at all times, for unwanted organisms may not otherwise be destroyed, no matter how long the cooking. Dry-roasting is not recommended for meat lower than Good-grade. These tougher meats should be prepared by long, slow moist-heat cooking. See Pot-Roasting, Stewing and Braising, 554.

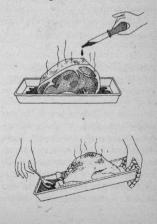

## BASTING

Basting is a method of retaining the juiciness of meat by moistening its surface with melted fat from time to time during the roasting process. Since roasting, like broiling, is a dry-heat process, the meat remains uncovered and no water or stock is used, for these liquids form steam and change the process to moist-heat cooking. No basting is necessary for well-marbled meats with a high intrinsic fat content. But all the less marbled cuts profit by basting. ◗ Before roasting brush the pan with a small bit of fat to prevent charring the drippings, which results in a bitter taste in the juices used later for gravy. Basting should begin after about the first half hour of cooking and should be repeated as often as necessary to prevent drying—at intervals of 10 minutes or more, depending on the size of the roast, its leanness, the oven temperature, and the stage of the roasting process. The best utensil for basting is a bulb-type baster, illustrated in the sketch on 553, that suctions pan drippings, to which other melted fat may be added if necessary. Or a spoon may be used as shown in the sketch. Very lean meats profit by larding, 550; and barding, 511, produces an effective form of self-basting.

## ABOUT POT-ROASTING, STEWING AND BRAISING MEAT

All three procedures benefit the less tender cuts such as chuck, shoulder, bottom round and brisket. These moist-heat methods cook by simmering meat in varying amounts of liquid in a closed pot or casserole for relatively long periods. Pot-roasting may be used for pieces up to 4 or 5 pounds, and stewing for meat in smaller chunks. Cuts of various sizes may be braised, using less liquid than for a stew, and a somewhat longer simmering period. Braising is invariably preceded by browning. The ideal type of container for all three methods is a heavy pan like a Dutch oven, with a tight-fitting cover.

For moist-heat cooking in general, and especially on an electric range, we recommend the following procedure. Before it is browned, the meat may simply be wiped dry, or it may be dredged with flour, (II, 219), or it may be marinated, 552. For browning, we prefer rendered fat from the meat itself—or fat that complements its flavor—and only enough to cover the bottom of the pan and to prevent charring, which imparts a bitter taste to gravy. In a heavy skillet or Dutch oven, heat the fat slowly until a piece of meat sizzles briskly when it touches the pan. Turn the meat frequently so that it browns slowly. It is important not to crowd the pan—which lowers the heat, causes steam to form, and results in graying rather than browning. For flavoring, diced vegetables such as onions, celery and carrots may be added to the fat when the meat is partially colored. Or, to control the heat more easily, the vegetables may be sautéed separately until they have a translucent quality and then combined with the meat. Separately sautéed onions may be sprinkled with a very small amount of sugar; the caramelizing that results adds attractive color to a stew.

After browning meat, pour off excess fat. You may leave 1 or 2 tablespoons of fat in the pan and set the meat on a bed of Mirepoix, (II, 254). Or, for pot-roasting, place the meat on a rack or on a piece of pork rind. Then add boiling stock. For a stew, the liquid should barely cover the meat. In pot-roasting and braising, add liquid in the bottom of the pan to a depth of $1/4$ to $1/2$ inch. As soon as the liquid reaches a boil, reduce the heat at once to maintain a simmer ▶ and cover the pan tightly. If necessary, replenish the liquid from time to time, adding boiling stock or water. Turn the meat occasionally to keep it moist. After browning, you may place the pan in a preheated slow oven for the remainder of the cooking, ▶ keeping the temperature constant throughout. The temperament of your oven and the degree of heat retention of your pan will determine the correct temperature—300° to 325°—for long, slow, steady cooking.

If cooking is done on top of the stove, the vegetables you will serve with the meat may be added to the casserole during the last 45 minutes of cooking—about $1/4$ pound of vegetables to $3/4$ pound of meat. Very mature vegetables may profit by a brief blanching beforehand. For oven stews, it is preferable to cook the vegetables separately on top of the stove and add them to the casserole toward the very end of the cooking period.

You can, of course, short-cut the entire process above by ✪ pressure cooking, but the necessarily high heat produces a less desirable result.

There is a method known as cooking **à blanc**—sometimes used for veal, pork or poultry in stews and pot roasts—in which raw meat is placed directly in boiling water and the heat reduced ▶ almost at once to a simmer as the meat changes color. Also cooked without browning are the **Chinese red stews**, but because the liquid used is half soy sauce and half water, the meat is colored during the

cooking. In red-stewing, season with ginger, scallions and sherry.

Gravy served with a stew should not be thick but should have good body—what the French call *du corps*. Always allow a stew or pot roast to stand at least 5 minutes off the heat so that the fat will rise and can be skimmed off before serving. If the stew is made some hours in advance, the meat may be drained and the gravy cooled and defatted more easily. You may thicken the gravy with a small amount of flour paste, 379. To reheat leftover stews, see 558.

## TIMING AND DONENESS

Timings and temperatures for varying degrees of doneness are given in the individual meat recipes. But, at best, meat timings are approximate, for there are many factors that make precision impossible—the temperature of the meat at the outset of cooking, its shape and thickness, the fat and bone content, the matter of aging. We recommend, therefore, the use of a meat thermometer for more accurate results. Insert the thermometer into the center of the meat, away from fat or bone, with the top of the thermometer as far as possible from the heat source.

If you have no thermometer, there are a couple of time-honored tests for doneness. Press the surface of the roast with your finger; if the meat is soft yet resilient, if it dents easily and at once resumes its shape, it is cooked to medium rare. If it remains firm under finger pressure, it is well done. Another test is to prick or cut into roasted or broiled meats, though you thus lose valuable juice. Rare meat produces red juice; medium-rare, pink; well-done, colorless juice. ▶ Because of the danger of trichinosis, it is vital that pork, see 601, be cooked thoroughly, to the stage when juices run clear. Most other meats—with the exception of white meat of fowl—will be overdone at this stage.

The following are some general rules related to the timing of meats. Ovens must be preheated for roasting; in broiling, consult range manufacturer's instructions. Take roasts from the refrigerator about 2 hours before cooking; steaks or chops about 1 hour. To ensure internal temperatures high enough to destroy bacteria, 275° is the minimum oven heat for roasting meats, except for pork, see 601, no matter how long the meat is cooked—even up to 12 hours of roasting. For comparative periods of moist-heat cooking, a simmering temperature of 180° suffices because of the more penetrating quality of the heat.

If a household product for tenderizing is used the papain derivative, see 550, greatly shortens the cooking period. The insertion of metal pins in roasting conserves energy to the extent that cooking time is shortened while juiciness is retained; but the meat will not be quite so tender. We recommend the ♀ pressure cooking of meats only if saving time is important; but tests show that the flavor is better retained at 10 pounds pressure; in any case, consult manufacturer's instructions. ▲ In high altitudes, roasting meat needs no time adjustment up to 7000 feet; after that, a longer cooking period may be needed. For the thawing and cooking of frozen meats, please see (II, 653).

## COOKING MEAT EN CROÛTE

Meat in a crust, or en croûte, lends itself particularly to buffet service: hot, it remains in good serving condition for half an hour; and, hot or cold, it is a conversation piece. There are two ways to proceed. Roasted meat—which may be beef, lamb, fowl or ham—may be precooked to within 30 to 45 minutes of doneness and cooled somewhat before the encasing dough is applied; the wrapped meat is then baked only long enough to brown the pastry and conclude the cooking of the meat, see Beef Wellington, 566. An alternate method applies the dough to uncooked meat, and the whole encased roast or ground-meat pâté is baked long enough to cook the meat thoroughly while the crust browns; see Pâté en Croûte, 629. For meats not precooked, it is essential that the dough covering be vented in several places when applied, to allow the escape of steam and to prevent buckling of the crust.

Following the French tradition, the tough croûte or dough covering is not eaten, but serves merely as a medium to preserve aroma and juices. If you prefer a latter-day American variety of edible crust, you may use a Pâte Brisée, (II, 362); a Brioche Dough, (II, 320); a Puff Paste, (II, 365); or a stiff bread dough—which will need to be punched down once before rolling out. The recipe given here is for the traditional nonedible croûte—heavy in egg to lend the tensile strength necessary to cover big pieces of meat securely.

### I. For Partially Cooked Meats

Preroast meat to within 30 or 45 minutes of doneness. Remove meat from oven and let it cool to room temperature. Make a covering of one of the doughs mentioned above, or the following:

Have all the ingredients at 70°. Mix together, to the consistency of coarse cornmeal:

**4  cups all-purpose flour**
**1  cup shortening**
**1½  teaspoons salt**

Make a well, (II, 366), of these ingredients and work in, one at a time:

**3  to 4 eggs**

and:

**½  cup water**

Knead the dough until well bound. Roll into a ball and rest covered for several hours at 70°. Preheat the oven to 450°. Roll the dough into a large sheet about 3/16 inch thick. Place the meat on the dough, top surface down. Then fold the dough over it neatly, pressing it to take the form of the meat. Be careful to keep the covering intact. Bring the edges of the dough together and seal the seam with egg white. Then turn the covered meat right side up. Brush any excess flour off the dough with a dry brush.

Now the fun begins. From the pastry scraps that remain, cut rounds, flowers and leaves, or any decorations that suit your mood. If you like, score them with a fork to give their surfaces a variation that will show up markedly after baking. You may even use Puff Paste, (II, 365), for such trimmings. Space them on the dough up to three thicknesses by applying French Egg Wash, (II, 503), to each as a glue. When you are satisfied with your design—and don't make it too cluttered—brush the surfaces with egg wash again. Put the meat in a preheated 450° oven. Reduce the heat at once to 350°. Allow the crust to bake until it is delicately browned. For an even effect, repeat the egg glazing at the end of the baking. You may also brush the crust with butter on removal from the oven.

**II.  For Uncooked Meats**

Prepare the dough as in I above; or use one of the previously mentioned doughs. Coat the meat to be covered with Egg Wash, (II, 503). Fold the pastry around the meat and decorate as described in I above. ◗ Cut a series of decorative gashes—steam vents—in the dough casing, as for a covered pie. Bake the meat in a preheated 300° oven 2 to 3 hours, depending on size. Hams and legs of lamb may be boned and stuffed before wrapping. ◗ Precook any stuffing you may use, as the heat may not penetrate it sufficiently to cook it through.

## ABOUT MEAT PASTRIES AND MEAT PIE TOPPINGS

How we'd relish judging an international competition of housewives turning out their native meat pastries! The doughs would range from the resilient to the flaky, with fillings running a full gamut of flavor. They would include: Won Ton, Ravioli, Kreplach, Piroshki, Rissoles, Enchiladas, Pot Pies. It is in such homely functional dishes, varied according to the season and by the individual cook, that the true cuisine of a country dwells. Many of the small-sized specialties call for precooked fillings which, already encased, need only a brief cooking of the dough and reheating of the filler, either by simmering in a broth, deep-fat frying, sautéing or baking. Pastry-covered meats can fit into the menu in many ways, depending on their size—from hors d'oeuvre or soup garnishes to a one-dish meal. The prize for the heartiest would go to the English with their Steak-and-Kidney Pie, 583. Usually the one most common on American tables is the Pot Pie, 239—pre-stewed meat heated in gravy, sometimes with vegetables, covered in various fashions with a dough topping.

One method is to place unbaked biscuits or dumplings on top of a stew, spacing them widely enough to allow steam to escape. The two essentials in making a meat pie are: first, to have enough tastily seasoned gravy to almost cover the cooked meat, and, second, to ensure that steam does not produce a soggy crust. One surefire procedure to prevent sogginess is the following.

**I.** Use:

**Any unsweetened Pie
Dough, (II, 360)**

and prebake separately on a baking tin dough cut to cover the casserole or smaller individual dishes in which you will serve the meat pie. Since pie dough shrinks in baking, you must cut it slightly larger than the dish and prick the dough with a fork. Bake the pastry separately at 425° for 15 or 20 minutes, until golden brown. Remember that this separate baking means you will have to cover your casserole in some other way as the stew itself heats—with a piece of foil placed lightly on top, or with a loose-fitting lid. Just before serving, when the casserole has been heated through, place the prebaked crust on top and serve at once.

**II.** If you prefer to put an unbaked dough topping on the stew and heat the meat mixture and the dough at the same time, proceed as follows:
Preheat oven to 350°.
Fill baking dish with cooked stew and gravy to one inch from the top. Place over it a generous round of dough to allow for shrinkage, brushing the undersurface with white of egg to help make it impervious to steam. ◗ Be sure to slash vents in the dough covering. Heat the dish 45 minutes to 1 hour, when the stew

should be thoroughly heated and the crust golden. You may brush the crust with butter before serving.

## STORING COOKED MEAT

It is wise to promptly cover meat that is left over and to refrigerate it, covered, as soon as it has cooled slightly.

Do not store ◗ meat in hot gravy in quantities larger than 3 cups. Drain off the gravy and allow it to cool separately if the amounts are larger. If meats are ◗ stuffed, unstuff them and store the stuffing separately.

## REHEATING MEAT

For convenience one is sometimes obliged to prepare roasted meat in advance, to be reheated just before serving. Although this procedure is not always satisfactory because of the tendency of meat—especially large roasts—to become dry on reheating, it can be done if there is no other solution to your problem of time. Simply bring the preroasted meat to room temperature and warm through in a ◗ preheated moderate oven.

Reheat sliced or sauced meats or hash by first heating the sauce separately, just to the point of boiling. Add the meat. ◗ Reduce heat to low at once. When the meat is thoroughly heated, serve immediately. Another method for warming sliced roasted meat is suggested on 119.

## SHARPENING KNIVES FOR CARVING

A dull knife is a lazy servant that requires you to do more than your share of the work. But a sharp knife allows you to make neater, less ragged slices; it permits greater precision; it requires less cutting pres-

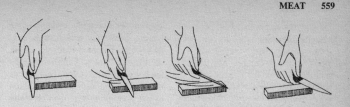

sure, and therefore you are less likely to slice yourself. We recommend two implements for sharpening knives. One is a 6- to 10-inch sharpening stone with coarse and fine sides. Place this stone in front of you lengthwise on a countertop. Lay the knife against the stone first on the coarse side at about a 15° to 20° angle and draw it in a curved sweeping motion toward you, as shown in the first three drawings above, ten times for each side. Then turn the stone over to the fine side, increase the angle of the blade very slightly, as shown on the right of the sketch, and repeat. Be sure to clean from the blade the excess grit which you will have removed from the stone.

If you are sharpening your knife with a steel, you should do so before each carving period. The steel, which must be kept magnetized, realigns the molecular structure of the blade.

❱ To true the blade, hold the steel firmly in the left hand, thumb on top of the handle. Hold the knife in the right hand, point upward, the blade away from you, and the hand slightly away from the body. Place the heel of the blade against the far side of the base of the steel and begin to draw it along the length of the blade as illustrated in the first two sketches below. The steel and blade should meet at about a 15° to 20° angle. ❱ Draw the blade across the steel, bringing it up from the left hand, with a quick swinging motion of the right wrist. ❱ The entire blade should pass lightly over the steel.

To start the second stroke, shown below right, bring the knife into the same position as in the first, but this time the blade should lie in front of the steel, away from you. About twelve strokes are enough to true the edge.

If you will get into the habit of sharpening your knife at frequent intervals, you will find that chopping, slicing and carving chores will go incredibly faster, and you will have a truly useful, extremely snappy servant at your command.

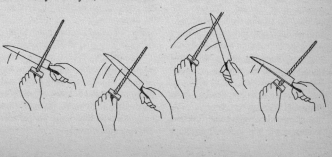

## TO MAKE A FRILL FOR A SHANK BONE

To make a frill for a shank ham, a lamb bone or drumsticks, fold in half dinner-sized stiff paper napkins, about 12 x 8 inches. Cut through the fold at ½-inch intervals to within 1 inch of the open edge. Reverse the fold, bringing the open edges together. Begin to roll the uncut portion of the newly folded paper, leaving an opening at the folded open edge big enough to slip over the bone. Fasten this roll with scotch tape and slide the frill over the bone.

## ABOUT MEAT CUTS

If you are doing your own butchering, you need to know intimately every bone in the body of the animal. We show, 561, the skeleton of a beef, which is very similar to that of other quadrupeds, except for proportion of bone to meat.

With all quadrupeds, the areas along the central spine portion which more or less hangs between the shoulder blade and the hip socket—areas with the least active musculature—are the tenderest. They can be counted on to cook by the dry-heat methods: roasting, broiling and pan-frying. Those areas just contiguous sometimes respond to dry heat by the constant-heat method, 92, but, like all the rest of the meat up through the shoulder and foreshank in front and from the rump to the hind shank, where muscles are active, they will need slow, moist cooking to break down the connective tissues. This is particularly true as you descend from Prime to Utility grades, 547.

If you buy your meat ready cut and prepackaged, you need a different kind of knowledge of these same bones—what they look like as they lie cut and trimmed ready to use in see-through wraps. Familiarity with the bone structure is your best clue as to whether the meat should be cooked by a dry- or moist-heat method. While there are slight variations of shape among beef, veal, lamb and pork, you can roast, broil, pan-broil or pan-fry all cuts with the following shapes.

Reading from left to right are the T-bone, the rib bone and three types of the wedge bone. The first of the wedge bones is the pin bone near the short loin; in the front of this group is the flat bone which is in the center cut, and above that is the wedge bone near the round. With veal, pork and lamb you may also cook by dry-heat methods if they show a round bone such as that seen last on the right above. If it is not ground, beef with this type of bone should be prepared by a moist-heat method, as should any cut having a blade bone or a brisket bone, grouped left and right in the foreground.

There are, of course, other differences in cuts and major differences in cooking procedures, all carefully noted in the meat recipes and in the Abouts on beef, veal, pork, lamb and venison. Taste and flavor preferences are highly individual, depending in large part on the sophistication of one's palate.

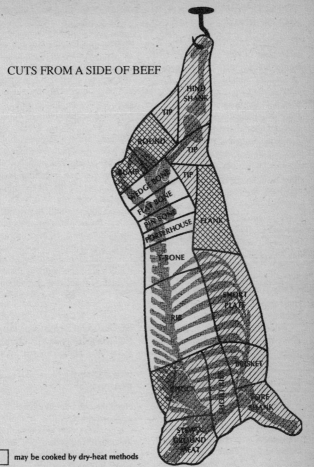

CUTS FROM A SIDE OF BEEF

may be cooked by dry-heat methods

must be cooked by moist-heat methods,
except for ground meats

in Prime or Good grade, may be cooked by either of the above

## GUIDE TO APPROXIMATE YIELD OR CUTS FROM 250-POUND SIDE OF BEEF, CUT FROM AN 800-POUND STEER

Please see diagram, 561, for location of alternate choices immediately below; and read About Fillet of Beef, 565, and Steaks, 567. As an example, from 26 pounds of short loin you will have a choice of club, sirloin and porterhouse steaks—which are a combination of T-bone, sirloin and fillet. But, if you want 5 pounds of fillet from the short loin, you must forgo the porterhouse steaks, which will leave you 21 pounds of short loin for sirloin steaks, T-bone and club steaks. If you choose to have the fillet, see the illustration, 565, to utilize it to the best advantage.

| FROM | CHOICE OF |
|---|---|
| 21 lb. loin end | Butt steaks and roasts |
| 2 lb. flank steak | Ground beef—flank steak |
| 45 lb. boneless round | Top and bottom, Swiss steak, pot roasts, hamburger, cubed steak |
| 23 lb. rib | 7-rib roast, rolled roast, rib steaks |
| 42 lb. boneless chuck | Ground beef, stew, pot roast |
| 10 lb. boneless brisket | For braising, stewing, ground, corned beef |
| 17 lb. plate | Ground beef, stew |
| 10 lb. shank | Soup meat, marrowbones |

Usable also will be the tripe, tongue, liver, heart, sweetbreads, brains, kidneys, oxtail and head. But you will have 49 pounds of unusable fat, bone and waste, and about 5 pounds will be lost in trimming.

## ABOUT ECONOMICAL USE OF LARGE CUTS OF MEAT

If you are shopping for a household of two, there are times when you may look longingly at the "weekly special" on meat. How tempting the standing rib roast of beef, the rump of beef, the leg of spring lamb, the loin of pork, the round of veal or the half or whole ham! But unless you are planning to have guests, it looks like far more meat than you care to buy. But by taking advantage of special sale prices and planning ahead to freeze a part of the cut for future use, it is an economy to buy the larger piece. You can still have your delicious small roast—or steaks from the ham or veal, chops from lamb or pork, short ribs from beef. Then the remainder of the roast may be used in many interesting leftover dishes, see Brunch, Lunch and Supper Dishes, 236.

## SUGGESTIONS FOR THE ECONOMICAL USE OF LARGE CUTS

### 6 RIBS OF BEEF—18 TO 20 POUNDS

Have the butcher cut a roast of 6 ribs as shown on 563.

The **short ribs** are on the right of the dotted line. Baked, 581, or barbecued, these ribs will serve two persons. If you then look at the roast from the top, you will see two long, rather coarse-grained pieces of meat called **lifters.** They are shown above the roast and sliced, although they extend for the full depth of the roast. These are best cooked by moist heat in a beef stew, 573–574, and will serve four to five persons.

The **eye of the rib** removed next is

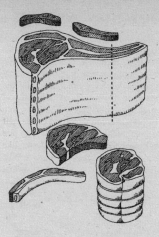

## RUMP OF BEEF—4 TO 5 POUNDS

Have butcher cut off a piece about 2 inches thick and dice it into 1-inch cubes for:

Or use it in 1 piece for:

Use the leftovers as:

or hot as hash, or in:

## LOIN OF PORK—9 TO 10 POUNDS

Have butcher cut off 4 chops from center of loin for:

Use one end for:

Freeze the other end for:

Use leftovers in:

tied into a roast which will produce about 24 slices; or, sliced horizontally, about ten 1-inch Delmonico or Spencer steaks; and the six bones will serve two persons.

## 2 RIBS OF BEEF—5 POUNDS

Have butcher cut off:

The leftover beef can be reheated in a Cumberland Sauce, 407–408.

Or use it in:

## LEG OF LAMB, VEAL, FRESH PORK OR HAM

The bone structure of the leg in veal, lamb and pork is similar to that of beef shown on the diagram, 561. In all these leg cuts, the center can be sliced separately for lamb steaks, veal cutlets or ham slices. The veal and lamb center cuts can be sautéed, as can pork, if smoked. Legs of lamb can be roasted. Similar veal and pork cuts demand moist-heat cooking. To cut or carve, see illustrations on 592 and 612, and the suggestions below.

## LEG OF LAMB—5 TO 6 POUNDS

## ROUND OF VEAL

## HALF HAM—4 TO 7 POUNDS

## ABOUT BEEF

Beef, far and away the most popular American meat, is from mature cattle usually older than 9 months. There are other beef terms, such as **bullock beef**, which denotes meat from male cattle under 24 months; **calf**, usually between 3 and 8 months; and **veal**, see 585. Please read the general remarks About Meats, 546; and, to identify the various beef cuts, see the beef illustrations, 563, 565, 567, and 568; for Economical Use of Large Cuts, see 562. The recipes that immediately follow are those involving ▶ dry-heat first, then moist-heat methods. For ground beef recipes, see 617–627; for cooked and leftover beef recipes, see Brunch, Lunch and Supper Dishes, 236.

## ROAST BEEF

### 2 to 3 Servings to the Pound

These directions are for the large, tender cuts we think of as Sunday dinner roast beef. The most tender are the standing rib roast and rolled rib roast. The sirloin-tip roast, eye of round or rolled rump may be cooked the same way if they are of Prime or Choice grade. If you choose a standing rib roast, have your butcher remove spinal cord, shoulder bone and chine, and have him tie the chine back on to keep the contour of the meat and to protect the eye of the roast during cooking.

Preheat oven to 550°.

Having removed the roast from the refrigerator about 2 hours before, place meat fat side up on a rack in a shallow greased roasting pan. Do not cover. Add no liquid. Insert meat thermometer, 555, so that the tip is in the center of the thickest part and not touching fat or bone. ◗ Immediately reduce heat to 350° and roast 18 to 20 minutes to the pound for medium-rare. A rolled roast will require 5 to 10 minutes longer to the pound. Thermometer reading should be between 140° rare and 170° well-done.

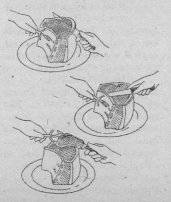

To make gravy, see Sauces Made by Degreasing and Deglazing, 381, or About Meat Pan Gravy, 382. Serve the roast with:

**Baked Macaroni, 205, or
Yorkshire Pudding, 188, or
Tomato Pudding
Cockaigne, 368**

To carve, see left below.

## ROAST STRIP SIRLOIN

### 24 to 30 Servings

Preheat oven to 550°.

Having removed meat from refrigeration about 2 hours before, trim excess top fat from:

**An 18- to 22-lb. eye of the
strip sirloin**

Place fat side up on a rack in a greased shallow pan in the oven. ◗ Reduce heat at once to 350°. Roast uncovered, about 1 hour for rare meat, or until thermometer registers between 130° and 140°.

## ABOUT FILLET OF BEEF

This choicest, most tender cut can be utilized in many ways. First trim off fat and sinew. Loosen fat at the small or tail end and tear this off, as well as the clods of fat near the thicker end. With a sharp pointed knife, remove the thin, tough, bluish sinew underneath. To cook the fillet whole, tuck the thin end under to equalize thickness; or you may simply cut off about 6 inches of the tail end and save it for Beef Stroganoff, 571; Sukiyaki, 571; Beef Kebabs, 573; or Steak Tartare, (II, 95). There is some dissension about classic fillet cuts for steaks.

Perhaps the drawing on 565 will help clarify the situation. Beginning and extending not quite halfway through the heavy end of an entire fillet is the head, or tenderloin butt. In the second half of the heavy end lies the **Chateaubriand** section, usually cut thick enough for a double or triple portion. If you divide the remainder of the fillet into four sections, as shown, you have first the **fillet steaks**, next the **tournedos**, then the **filet mignons**, or small fillets, and finally a tip section that is usually cubed for Beef Stroganoff, 571, or brochettes or Beef Kebabs, 573. The cuts vary from 2 to 3 inches in thickness for Chateaubriand, 1½ to 2 inches for fillets, and 1 inch for tournedos. Cooking times, therefore, vary proportionately.

## FILLET OR TENDERLOIN OF BEEF

**Allow ⅓ Pound per Serving**
Remove meat from refrigerator about 1 hour before.
Preheat oven to 500°.
Remove the surplus fat and skin from:
**A fillet of beef, at least 5 lb.**
You may lard, 550, with narrow strips of:
**(Salt pork or bacon)**
Fold over the thin end of the fillet and secure with string. If not larded, spread the meat generously with butter or tie strips of bacon over it. Place on a rack in a greased roasting pan in the oven. Do not cover or baste it.
▶ Reduce the heat immediately to 400° and bake 30 minutes in all. A fillet is usually cooked rare when the internal temperature reaches 130°. Season when done. You may surround the fillet with:
**Broiled Mushrooms, 329**
Garnish the platter with:

**Sprigs of parsley**
**Soufflé Potatoes, 350**
Serve with:
**Marchand de Vin Sauce, 392**
**Bordelaise Sauce, 392**
**Béarnaise Sauce, 412**

## BEEF WELLINGTON OR FILET DE BOEUF EN CROÛTE

**About 12 Servings**
If time is no object and your aim is to out-Jones the Joneses, you can serve this twice-roasted but rare beef encased in puff paste—but don't quote us as devotees.
Double the recipe for:
**Puff Paste, (II, 365)**
which can be prepared the day before and reserved in the refrigerator.
Preheat oven to 425°.
Rub with butter:
**A 5-lb. fillet of beef**
Roast on a rack 25 minutes or until thermometer reads 120°—very rare. On taking meat from oven, you may flambé with:
**(⅓ cup brandy)**
▶ Let meat cool to room temperature. You may then thinly coat with:
**(Pâté de foie gras or de volaille, 631)**
Now roll out part of the puff paste into a rectangle about 1½ inches larger in width and length than the fillet. Spread the rectangle with:
**Duxelles, (II, 255)**
that have been well cooled. Preheat oven again to 425°. Center the fillet on the rolled-out dough. Roll out remaining dough and shape it over the entire fillet. Secure top and bottom pieces together, finger-pinching all around after brushing edges with:
**White of egg**
Use any excess dough for decora-

tions, which you can stick to the surface with more of the egg white. Brush exposed surfaces with:

**French Egg Wash, (II, 503)**

Place the covered fillet on a greased baking sheet. Bake 10 minutes. ▶ Reduce heat to 375° and bake until crust is golden, about 20 minutes more. Allow to stand 15 minutes before serving on a garnished platter. Carve with a very sharp knife into slices about ¾ inch thick. Serve with:

**Sauce Périgueux, 393, or Bordelaise Sauce, 392**

## ABOUT BEEF STEAK CUTS

As the growth of steak houses has shown, no meat is more popular, and at home when celebrating, the cry is usually, "Let's have steak." This word covers many cuts, the most desirable in the white section of the diagram, 561. Coming from the sirloin section are the **wedge bone**, the **flat bone**, and the **pin** or **hip bone**, illustrated below. The pin bone, closest to the short loin, has a large tenderloin

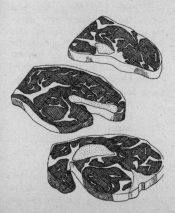

or fillet portion. The **sirloins** coming from the end near the hip are leaner than the porterhouse and T-bones that lie in the short loin section described next. Again see the diagram, 561.

From the short-loin section comes the **porterhouse**, see sketch on 568, which has a larger section of tenderloin and a longer tail than the **T-bone** below it. Still another cut in this area, shown last, 568, is the **club** or **minute** or, when trimmed, **Delmonico** steak, which has no tenderloin.

When steaks from the loin section are cut whole or in individual servings with the tenderloin removed, they are called **strip** or **shell** steaks. When cooked in individual portions they are broiled; in one piece they may be roasted, 566. For the sectioning of a whole **tenderloin** or **fillet** into steaks, see 566. For **Spencer** or **rib eye** or **rib** steaks from the rib section shown next on the diagram, 561, please see illustrations in Economical Use of Large Cuts of Meat, 562.

By courtesy and custom the term steak is applied to the following beef cuts. Some, like **Salisbury** steak and **hamburger**, 616; **cube**, if macerated; and **flank** when prepared as for London Broil, 570; are treated by dry-heat methods. Hamburger patties made of ground meat, and Salisbury steak patties made of minced meat, are from trimmings of round or chuck and sometimes from the **hanging tender**. For scraped fillet of tender beef called **Steak Tartare**, which is eaten raw, see (II, 95).

To avoid toughness, it is best to cook the so-called steaks mentioned below by moist-heat procedures. They are **flank, cube, tip of the round,** the **round** itself, with its characteristic bone, the **blade chuck, Swiss** and **rump steaks**.

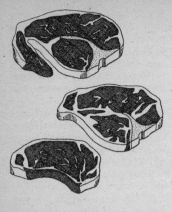

## COOKING STEAKS

A roving friend of ours who dropped into a tavern in upstate New York not long ago tells us that the management had chosen to preface a rather limited menu list with the proud claim: "All steaks broiled to your likeness." Few cooks anywhere would attempt such feats of portraiture, but steak—from charcoal grilled to planked Château-briand, 566—does duty for so many different occasions that we think it worthwhile to discuss steak varieties below. Unless special directions are given, all types of steak · may be broiled, see following, or pan-broiled, 569. The meat should be removed from refrigeration about an hour before cooking. The grid should be cold; or, if it is hot, either grid or meat should be oiled to prevent sticking. The broiling compartment should be preheated and the oven door left slightly ajar if the range manufacturer so recommends. Season steak at the end of cooking, not before. Hot or cold, steak is sometimes enhanced by a sauce such as one of the following:

> Garlic Butter, 399
> Maitre d'Hôtel Butter, 398
> Colbert Butter, 398
> Mushroom Wine Sauce, 392
> Béarnaise Sauce, 412
> Bordelaise Sauce, 392
> Sour Cream Horseradish
> Dressing, 408

## BROILED STEAK

❧ Please read About Beef Steak Cuts, 567. Remove meat from refrigeration about an hour before cooking.
Preheat broiling compartment.
Prepare for cooking:

> Sirloin, T-bone, strip or
> porterhouse steak, 1½ to
> 2 inches thick

You may rub the steak with:

> (A cut clove of garlic)

Or, an hour before cooking, spread it with:

> (Olive oil)

Put steak on a cold grid—or on a greased hot grid—over a shallow greased pan, the top surface of the meat 3 inches from the heat source for a 1½-inch-thick steak. Brown the meat on one side, then turn once and brown the other side, allowing about 7 minutes per side for rare and about 8 minutes for medium. For a 2-inch steak, place meat 4 inches from heat source; turn more frequently, allowing in all about 9 minutes per side for rare and about 10 minutes for medium. When done, spread with butter or degreased pan drippings. Add:

> Chopped parsley or chives

Serve the steak garnished with:

> Sautéed Mushrooms, 328
> French Fried Onion
> Rings, 336

## BROILED FILLET STEAK

For fillet steak cuts, please see About Fillet of Beef, 565. The thickness of the steak varies, and therefore the cooking times vary proportionately. These steaks are usually served quite rare.

Flatten slightly:

> **Fillet steaks: 1 to 2 inches thick**

Or have the butcher shape and surround them with a strip of bacon secured by a wooden pick.

Spread with:

> **Butter**

Broil as for:

> **Broiled Steak, 568**

When done, remove the bacon. Serve steak on:

> **A toasted crouton, (II, 219)**

with:

> **Béarnaise Sauce, 412**
> **Lemon and parsley**
> **Broiled Mushrooms, 329**
> **Potatoes Anna, 348, or**
> **Duchess Potatoes, 353**

## PLANKED STEAK

It seems to us a regrettable state of affairs that this way of serving broiled steak in high style has become "dated." If you can come by one of those special hardwood planks incised with well-and-tree design to catch the juices, you're in. ◗ Follow directions for seasoning a plank, 107, if it's new. Prepare:

> **Duchess Potatoes, 353**

Brush the plank with:

> **Vegetable oil**

and preheat it. Broil, 568, ◗ to rare only:

> **A 1½- to 2-inch steak**

Brush the steak with:

> **Melted butter**

and season with:

> **Salt and pepper**

Place steak in center of plank. Using a fluted pastry tube, ruffle a border of potatoes around the edge of the plank. Now place the filled plank briefly under the broiling element, just long enough for the potatoes to color. Remove from oven and garnish with several of the following, arranged between the steak and potatoes:

> **Green Peas, 338**
> **Grilled Tomatoes, 367**
> **Broiled Mushrooms, 329**
> **Young Carrots in Bunches, 310**
> **Parsley or watercress**

## PAN-BROILED STEAK

Please read About Beef Steak Cuts, 567, and about Pan-Broiling, 552. This method is not recommended for steaks more than about 1 inch thick. Prepare for cooking:

> **A beef steak**

Heat a heavy frying pan over lively heat until meat sizzles briskly as it touches the pan. If the meat is very lean, rub the pan lightly with:

> **A bit of beef fat**

Put the steak into the pan and sear uncovered about 5 minutes. Turn and sear the other side. Reduce heat and continue cooking until done, about 8 or 10 minutes in all. Pour off any fat that may have accumulated in the pan, for, if it is allowed to remain, the steak will be "fried," not "broiled." Season with:

> **Salt and freshly ground pepper**

Make with the drippings:

> **Meat Pan Gravy, 382**

or use:

> **Maitre d' Hôtel Butter, 398**

For suggestions for steak sauces, see 568. Serve with:

> **Franconia Potatoes, 348**

## PAN-BROILED FILLET STEAK

Pan-broil, 569:

**Four 1-inch fillet steaks**

using, to prevent sticking, a small amount of:

**Butter**

When meat is done—not more than 3 minutes to a side—deglaze pan, 381, with:

**¼ cup dry red wine**
**2 tablespoons beef stock**
**1 teaspoon Meat Glaze, 427**

Serve with:

**Artichoke hearts, stuffed with Creamed Spinach, 359**

## STEAK AU POIVRE OR PEPPERED STEAK

Use:

**Trimmed 1-inch-thick strip sirloin, club or filet mignon steaks**

Crush ◗ don't grind:

**Peppercorns**

coarsely on a board with a pressing, rolling movement, using the bottom of a pan. Press the steaks into the crushed pepper and work it into both sides of the meat with the heel of your palm or with the flat side of a cleaver. Sprinkle the bottom of a 9-inch skillet with:

**2 teaspoons salt**

When it begins to brown, put the steaks into the pan and brown ◗ uncovered over high heat.

◗ Reduce to medium heat, turn steaks and cook to desired degree of rareness. In a separate pan, prepare:

**¼ cup butter**
**1 teaspoon Worcestershire sauce**
**2 tablespoons lemon juice**

Remove steaks from the pan in which they have been cooked and discard the pan drippings. If you wish to flambé the steaks, 108, do so with:

**(2 oz. brandy)**

Serve the butter mixture separately.

## LONDON BROIL OR FLANK STEAK

**4 Servings**

Have the butcher score the meat crosswise on both sides. It may be rubbed before cooking with a mixture of:

**(1 tablespoon vegetable oil)**
**(1 finely chopped shallot)**
**(1 clove garlic, crushed)**

Preheat broiler.

Place on greased broiler rack:

**A 2- to 3-lb. flank steak**

Broil within 2 to 3 inches of heat—the hotter the better—about 5 minutes on one side and 4 minutes on the other, ◗ making sure meat is kept rare. If flank steak is cooked medium or well done, it becomes extremely tough. ◗ Carve in ¼-inch slices and cut diagonally across the grain.

Serve with:

**Béarnaise Sauce, 412**
**Bordelaise Sauce, 392**

## BOEUF FONDU BOURGUIGNONNE

**6 Servings**

This dish is cooked at table in a special deep metal pot which narrows at the top to keep the butter from spattering. It can also be cooked in an electric skillet ◗ if the butter is sweet and clarified, which keeps it from popping. We love this dish inordinately. It gives the hostess an easy time, both from the cooking angle and from the entertaining one—as the guests quickly reveal their individual characteristics. They are all there—hoarder, cooperator, kibitzer, boss. ◗ Don't try to get more than 5 or 6 guests around one heat source.

Allow for each person $1/3$ to $1/2$ pound fillet of beef.

Cut into 1-inch dice and bring to the table on a platter garnished with parsley:

**About 3 lb. fillet of beef**

Have ready at room temperature or slightly warmed several of the following accompaniments:

> **Mustard with capers**
> **Sour Cream Horseradish**
> **Dressing, 408**
> **Andalouse Sauce, 421**
> **Herb or Curry**
> **Mayonnaise, 420, 422**
> **Watercress Dressing, 414**
> **Chutney Dressing, 416**
> **Orange Marmalade,**
> **(II, 673)**
> **Marchand de Vin**
> **Sauce, 392**

Melt in an electric skillet or in a fondu pot:

**1 cup clarified butter or**
**peanut oil**

When the butter is brownish, announce the rules of the game. Ask each guest to limit himself to two pieces of meat at a time, so as not to crowd the pot and lower the cooking temperature. If a skillet is used, each person impales the cubes on his fork, releases the meat into the pan and worries it around in the hot fat until it's done to his liking; if he prefers rare, the time is very short. If a deep fondu pot is used, the meat must stay on the fork during the cooking, or it will be irretrievably lost—but, according to an old Swiss custom, the loser gets a consolation prize: the right to kiss the Swiss miss on his left! Meantime, each guest has arranged on his plate an assortment of sauces—like oils on an artist's palette—into which he dips the hot browned meat. Serve with crusty French bread or rolls and a tossed salad with green grapes or avocado slices.

## BEEF STROGANOFF

**4 Servings**

This dish ❀ freezes well and can be made with fillet ends, shown on 565. Cut into $1/2$-inch slices across the grain:

**$1^1/2$ lb. fillet of beef**

Pound them until thin. Cut into strips about 1 inch wide. Melt in a pan:

**1 tablespoon butter**

Sauté in the butter about 2 minutes:

**$3/4$ tablespoon grated onion**

Sauté beef quickly in the butter about 5 minutes, until browned evenly. Remove and keep hot. Add to the pan:

**2 tablespoons butter**

Stir and sauté in the butter:

**$3/4$ lb. sliced mushrooms**

Drain and add the beef. Season with:

**Salt and pepper**
**A grating of nutmeg**
**($1/2$ teaspoon basil)**

Add and heat briefly:

**$1/4$ cup dry white wine**

Then add:

**1 cup warm whipping cream**
**or cultured sour cream**

Serve with:

**Green Noodles, 199**

## SUKIYAKI

**6 Servings**

Japan's famous "friendship dish" is winning more and more Stateside friends. It's a one-plate meal prepared ceremoniously at table in an electric skillet—or, less festively, in the kitchen in a heavy skillet or wok. The orderly cooking ritual lasts about 15 minutes, as one after another the uniformly sliced ingredients are taken from a beautifully arranged platter and sautéed. Have ready on the platter:

**2 lb. beef: sirloin tip, eye of round or fillet, sliced 1/8 inch thick**

The meat is easy to slice if put in the freezer for 20 minutes. Cut against the grain. But meat and all other ingredients should be ▶ at room temperature for cooking. Have ready:

**2 strips beef suet, about 1 oz. each, or 3 tablespoons vegetable oil**

Also arrange attractively on the platter, in diagonally cut uniform slices:

**1/2 cup thinly sliced onions
6 scallions with 2 inches of green
Canned bamboo shoots
2 cups thinly sliced mushrooms
1/2 cup Chinese cabbage or watercress, or
1/4 cup Chinese chrysanthemum leaves
1/2 cup 3/4-inch cubes soybean curd, (II, 192)**

If a single skillet is used, it is best to cook only half the amount on the platter at one time, sharing that batch and then cooking the "seconds" later. Put the suet or oil into the hot skillet over medium heat. When the point of fragrance is reached, remove unmelted bits—if you have used suet—and add the thin beef slices. Sauté ▶ without browning, turning frequently, about 3 minutes. Push the meat to one side and sauté in sequence the onions, scallions, mushrooms and Chinese cabbage. The sautéing of the onions to almost golden, followed by the gradual addition of the other vegetables, should take about 7 minutes in all. As the other vegetables are being added, pour in, a little at a time, a mixture of:

**1/4 cup soy sauce
1/2 cup stock
1 teaspoon sugar**

This procedure produces a fast-rising steam but not enough moisture to waterlog the vegetables. Push the meat into the center of the skillet, add the bamboo shoots and bean curd and stir about 4 minutes more. The vegetables should retain crispness and color.

**Season to taste**

Serve this mixture at once over:

**Boiled Rice, 189**

As an authentic detail, you may have at room temperature in individual dishes:

**(Raw eggs)**

to coat the bits of the Sukiyaki as the food is dipped into it with chopsticks.

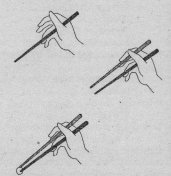

To eat with chopsticks, hold them by the upper square portion. Although the two are alike in shape, the functions of the chopsticks differ in that the lower stick remains stationary; the upper one, which is pressed against the lower, moves up and down to complete a tonglike action in grasping the food. First place the lower stick in the crease of the thumb as shown upper left, with the lower end of the chopstick braced firmly against the soft inner surface of the last joint of the ring finger as shown. Then position the upper stick much as you would hold a pencil but with the point of the stick protruding about one-third of its entire length and approximately equalized with the lower stick when pressed together at the point. For westerners these tools at first automatically bring on a leisured pace of consumption, and it is a comfort to know that in eating rice and noodles it is not bad form to bring the bowl up just under the chin—a maneuver which facilitates matters greatly for the uninitiated.

## ☰ BEEF KEBABS

**4 Servings**

◗ Please read about Skewer Cooking, 94, and About Marinades, (II, 180).
Cut into 1½-inch cubes:

    **1½ lb. good-quality round, flank or chuck**

Marinate and cook as for:

    **Lamb Kebabs, 595**

using one of the marinades listed in that recipe; or use:

    **Teriyaki Marinade, (II, 183), or Beer Marinade, (II, 182)**

## BEEF POT ROAST

**6 Servings**

◗ Please read About Pot-Roasting, 554.
Prepare for cooking one of the following in this general order of preference:

    **3 to 4 lb. chuck, shoulder, top or bottom round, brisket, blade or rump**

If the meat is lean, you may lard it, 550. Rub meat with:

    **(Garlic)**

Dredge in:

    **(Flour)**

Heat in a heavy pan:

    **2 tablespoons rendered suet or vegetable oil**

Brown the meat on all sides in the fat.
◗ Do not let it scorch. Add to pot when the meat is half browned:

    **1 chopped carrot**
    **1 diced rib celery**
    **(1 diced small white turnip)**
    **(¼ cup chopped green pepper, seeds and membrane removed)**

When the meat is browned, spoon off excess fat. Add:

    **1 small onion stuck with 3 cloves**
    **2 cups boiling meat or vegetable stock or part stock and part dry red wine**
    **1 bay leaf**

Cover and bake 3 to 4 hours in a 300°–325° oven, or simmer on top of the stove. During this time turn the meat several times and, if necessary, add additional:

    **Hot stock**
    **Season to taste**

When the meat is tender, spoon off excess fat, remove bay leaf and serve with the pot liquor as it is or slightly thickened with:

    **Kneaded Butter, 381, or**
    **¾ cup cultured sour cream**

You may, if you wish, add to the pot roast drained boiled vegetables. Serve with:

    **Potato Pancakes, 349;**
    **Kasha, 181; or**
    **Green Noodles, 199, sprinkled with poppyseed**

and:

    **Blue Plum or Cherry Compote, (II, 111)**

## BEEF STEW GASTON

**4 to 6 Servings**

This one-dish meal seems to taste better when cooked a day ahead.
Cut into small pieces and, if very salty, parblanch, 106, briefly:

¹/₂ **lb. salt pork**
Dry and sauté the pork slowly in a large skillet. Cut into pieces:

**2 lb. boneless stewing beef**
Brown the beef in the hot drippings over high heat. Spoon off most of the accumulated fat. Sprinkle the meat with:

**Seasoned Flour, (II, 220)**
Combine and heat until boiling:

1¹/₂ **cloves garlic, chopped**
1 **large chopped onion**
1 **cup bouillon**
1 **cup canned tomato sauce**
12 **peppercorns**
3 **whole cloves**
¹/₄ **cup chopped parsley**
¹/₃ **bay leaf**

Place the meat in a heavy saucepan. Pour above ingredients over it. Simmer covered 2 to 3 hours or until meat can be easily pierced with a fork. During the last hour of cooking, add:

¹/₂ **cup dry white wine**
Cook separately until nearly tender:

6 **medium-sized pared quartered potatoes**
6 **pared quartered carrots**
1 **rib celery, chopped**

Add these vegetables to the stew for the last 15 minutes of cooking.

## BEEF STEW WITH WINE OR BOEUF BOURGUIGNONNE

**4 to 6 Servings**
For added bouquet, the meat may be marinated and refrigerated overnight in dry red wine. Drain and reserve wine for use in cooking the stew. Preheat oven to 300°.
Try out, (II, 204):

¹/₂ **lb. thinly sliced blanched salt pork**
You may substitute 3 tablespoons butter for the pork, but don't expect the same subtle flavor. Peel, add and sauté lightly:

12 **small onions or 4 shallots**
Remove pork and onions from pan and reserve. Cut into 1-inch dice and sauté in the hot fat until light brown:

**2 lb. lean boneless stewing beef**
Sprinkle meat with:

(1¹/₂ **tablespoons flour)**
Place it in an ovenproof dish with:

1 **teaspoon salt**
4 **peppercorns**
¹/₂ **bay leaf**
1 **or 2 cloves garlic, minced**
(¹/₂ **teaspoon thyme or sweet marjoram)**

Using the reserved wine if you marinated the meat, bring to the boiling point enough dry red wine and water to cover the meat:

³/₄ **wine to ¹/₄ water**
Simmer ▶ covered in a 300° oven for 2 hours. Place pork and onions on top of the meat and continue to simmer covered another hour or until beef is tender. For the last 10 minutes of cooking you may add:

(1 **cup sautéed mushrooms)**
**Season to taste**
Serve the stew sprinkled with:

**Chopped parsley**
You may flambé, 108, at the last minute with:

(¹/₄ **cup brandy)**
Serve with:

**French Bread, (II, 306), or**
**Noodles, 200, or**
**Mashed Potatoes, 344**

## SAUERBRATEN

**6 Servings**
Prepare for cooking:

3 **lb. beef shoulder, chuck, rump or round**
If the meat does not appear to have much fat, lard it, 550, with:

(18 **seasoned Lardoons, 551, ¹/₄ inch thick)**

Rub into the meat thoroughly:

**Pepper**
**(Garlic)**

Place the meat in a deep crock or glass bowl. Heat together ◖ but do not boil:

**2 cups mild vinegar or wine**
**vinegar**
**2 cups water**
**½ cup sliced onions**
**2 bay leaves**
**1 teaspoon peppercorns**
**(2 teaspoons caraway seeds)**
**¼ cup sugar**

Pour the hot marinade over beef; more than half should be covered. Cover with a lid and refrigerate 2 to 4 days, turning occasionally. The longer you leave it, the sourer the meat. When ready to cook, drain the meat, saving the marinade. Heat in a heavy pan:

**2 tablespoons vegetable oil or**
**other fat**

Brown the meat on all sides and cook as for:

**Pot Roast, 573**

using the heated marinade in place of stock. When the meat is tender, sprinkle it with:

**¼ cup brown sugar**

and roast 5 to 10 minutes more or until sugar is dissolved. Remove meat from the pot. Thicken stock with:

**Flour, see Pan Gravy, 382**

Add:

**1 cup sweet cream or**
**cultured sour cream**

We like the gravy "straight." Some cooks add:

**(Raisins, catsup and**
**ground gingersnaps)**

Serve roast with:

**Potato Dumplings, 184, or**
**Potato Pancakes, 349**

and you will have a treat. ◖ This dish does not freeze successfully.

## BOEUF À LA MODE

**6 Servings**

A pot roast de luxe, because so elegantly presented. The meat is sliced very thin and even, covered with a sauce, and the platter garnished with beautifully arranged vegetables.
Prepare the beef as for:

**Sauerbraten, 574**

larding it but marinating for only 4 to 5 hours in a mixture of:

**1½ to 2 cups dry red wine**
**¼ cup brandy**

When ready to cook, add:

**2 boned blanched calves' feet**

Use Blanch II, 106, simmering 10 minutes. ◖ Then simmer covered 3½ to 4 hours. Toward the last hour of cooking, add to the degreased sauce and cook with the meat:

**1 cup sliced carrots**
**1 cup sliced onions**

Just before serving, heat with the dish:

**1 cup sautéed mushrooms**

Cut the meat as described above and serve garnished with the vegetables and with the calves' feet cut into one-inch squares.

## GLAZED BOEUF À LA MODE OR DAUBE GLACÉ

Showy on a buffet table.
Prepare:

**Boeuf à la Mode, above**

◖ So as to get a clear stock, do not add the vegetables. When the beef is tender, drain the liquid through a cloth. Degrease it as much as possible. Allow it to cool until it starts to jell. Meanwhile, cut the meat from the calves' feet into 1-inch squares, and cut the beef into thin, even slices. Arrange the slices in an overlapping pattern on a platter, surrounded by the cubed calf meat. When the stock begins to congeal, pour it over the meat. Refrigerate covered. When the stock has completely jellied, serve the glazed beef surrounded with cooked vegetables at room temperature:

**Artichokes à la Grecque, 285**
**Marinated Raw Carrots, (II, 92)**

and garnished with:

**Parsley or watercress**

## BOILED BEEF OR BOEUF BOUILLI

**6 to 8 Servings**

Joseph Wechsberg reminds us in *Blue Trout and Black Truffles* of the Viennese enthusiasm for boiled beef—in no less than 24 local variations. Its superiority there can be credited in large part to the beef itself—from cattle bred selectively and fed a diet of sugar beets—comparable in quality to the Kobe beef of Japan and the Charolais of France.

Bring to a boil in a heavy pot:

**6 cups water**

Put in:

**3 lb. lean stewing beef in one piece**

Bring to a boil and skim the pot. Add:

**1 onion stuck with 3 cloves**
**1 bay leaf**
**1/2 cup sliced carrots**
**1/2 cup sliced celery with leaves**
**1 teaspoon salt**
**(1 sliced turnip)**

Cover and simmer the meat until tender, 3 to 4 hours. Drain and reserve the stock. Melt:

**1/4 cup butter**

Brown lightly in the butter:

**1/4 cup chopped onions**

Stir in until blended:

**2 tablespoons flour**

Stir in slowly 2 cups of the degreased stock. Season the sauce with:

**2 tablespoons horseradish**
**Salt**
**(Sugar)**
**(Vinegar or lemon juice)**

If using prepared horseradish, use less vinegar or lemon juice, and:

**Season to taste**

Cut the meat into thin slices against the grain and reheat ♦ very briefly in the hot gravy. Garnish with:

**Chopped parsley**

Serve with:

**Spätzle, 186, or**
**Boiled New Potatoes in their jackets, 344**
**Sauerkraut, 308**

## BEEF BRISKET WITH SAUERKRAUT

**6 Servings**

Tie into a compact shape:

**3 lb. beef brisket or other boneless stewing beef**

Melt in a deep kettle:

**3 tablespoons bacon fat or other fat**

Add and brown lightly:

**(1/4 cup chopped onions)**

Add the meat and place over it:

**2 lb. sauerkraut**
**(1 large apple, cored and quartered)**
**2 cups boiling water or beef stock**

Simmer the meat covered about 2 1/2 hours or until tender. Season with:

**Salt and pepper**
**(Caraway seed)**

Serve with:

**Boiled Potatoes, 343**

garnished with:

**Cultured sour cream**
**Chopped parsley or chives**

## BELGIAN BEEF STEW OR CARBONNADE FLAMANDE

**4 to 6 Servings**

Cut into 1½-inch cubes and coat in seasoned flour, (II, 220):

**2 lb. boneless stewing beef**

Sauté lightly in:

**1 tablespoon butter**
**¼ cup thinly sliced onions**

Reserve the onions. Add:

**1 tablespoon butter**

and brown the floured meat. Drain off any excess fat. Combine and bring to a boil:

**1 cup flat beer**
**1 clove garlic, pressed**
**½ teaspoon sugar**
**½ teaspoon salt**

Pour this over the meat and add the onions. Cover and simmer 2 to 2½ hours. After straining the sauce, you may add:

**½ teaspoon vinegar**

Serve meat with:

**Boiled New Potatoes, 344, garnished with parsley or dill**

Use sauce as gravy.

## WEST AFRICAN BEEF STEW

**8 Servings**

Cut into cubes:

**2 lb. boneless stewing beef**

Brown it in:

**4 tablespoons hot butter or other fat**

Remove meat from pan and add:

**1 cup chopped onions**

When golden in color, add:

**2 tablespoons flour**
**2 to 3 tablespoons curry powder**
**¼ cup peanut butter**

Slowly add to the above mixture and stir until thickened:

**2 cups beef stock, or 1 cup**

**water and 1 cup coconut milk, (II, 244)**

Add the meat and simmer covered about 2 hours or until tender. Twenty minutes before end of cooking time, add:

**½ lb. trimmed whole okra**

Serve over:

**Boiled Rice, 189**

Garnish with:

**4 quartered hard-cooked eggs**

Have ready to pass in small individual dishes:

**Grated toasted coconut, preferably fresh**
**Chutney**
**Fresh or broiled banana and pineapple chunks**
**Fresh orange, mango or melon slices**
**Fresh or broiled tomato slices**
**Fried onion rings**
**Roasted peanuts**
**Croutons**

## CHINESE FIREPOT

A participatory complete-meal simmered dish for which equipment can be improvised if the conventional firepot shown to the left rear in the chapter heading, 91, is not available. But there are caveats. If the heat source is charcoal, it is mandatory ▶ to enjoy this ritual out-of-doors. It is also necessary to have the broth or water in which the food is to be simmered ▶ piping hot and in the firepot before the charcoal, ▶ heated to grayness in advance, is tucked into the firepot base just before the diners assemble. This precaution keeps the soldered seams of the pot from melting. There should be enough charcoal in the pot to provide heat for the entire process.

Allow at least ¹/₂ pound of food and 1 to 1¹/₂ cups of liquid per person. All food to be simmered by the guests is previously cut and trimmed. Some stalk vegetables need to be parblanched; noodles and the dried mushrooms require soaking in advance. Sometimes the raw food is lightly marinated. Condiment containers at hand should include soy sauce, vinegar, tomato paste, hot pepper oil, Chinese mustard, sugar, salt and pepper, and herb leaves such as coriander, (II, 268), gingerroot and various onions, (II, 272). The food is grouped on platters. You may use meat or fish and shellfish, or a combination with the white meat of poultry. Allow about 2 minutes' cooking time for meat cut into thin strips—diagonally against the grain—except for pork, which, after cutting, needs to be cooked until it is no longer pink. Shellfish cook in a minute or less. Fish fillets are cut into cubes or strips thicker than the meat to prevent their disintegrating. Have ready at each diner's place a plate; 2 sets of chopsticks—one for cooking, the other for eating; or one set of chopsticks for eating and a small strainer for cooking; a bowl for the broth; and a small sauce bowl for each diner's choice of condiments in which to make his own flavorful sauce. The order of cooking is meat or fish first, then noodles and vegetables. Broth is the only liquid served with the meal. Should the broth run low, add more preheated broth to the firepot. If it should go above simmering, guests are asked to simultaneously immerse a vegetable for cooking to reduce the heat somewhat. The broth may be ladled out early but is usually reserved for the end as the customary finish for a Chinese meal.

**9 to 10 Servings**

Allow for:

**2¹/₂ quarts chicken broth**

at least three of the following:

**1 lb. sliced beef tenderloin**
**1 lb. shelled deveined shrimp**
**1 lb. bite-sized chicken breasts**
**1 lb. fish fillets in thick strips**
**¹/₂ lb. chicken livers or oysters**

and two of the following vegetables:

**1 lb. washed spinach with stalks removed**
**¹/₂ lb. watercress**
**1 lb. celery cabbage sliced into stalks and blanched, 106, briefly**

Add also:

**¹/₄ cup scallions or other green onion types, (II, 273–276), cut into 1-inch pieces**
**9 dried mushroom caps, soaked 1 hour in warm water, drained and cut into 1-inch cubes**
**3 cakes tofu cut into 1-inch cubes**
**¹/₂ cup canned Chinese chestnuts or**
**¹/₂ cup bamboo shoots**

and:

**2 oz. Chinese noodles**

soaked for 30 minutes, then drained and cut into 4-inch lengths.

## CASSEROLED BEEF WITH FRUIT

**6 Servings**

A complete meal with a Middle Eastern flavor.

Soak until soft:

**2 cups chopped mixed dried fruit: apricots, pears, prunes**

in:

**2 cups water**
**Juice and rind of 1 lemon**

Cut into small cubes:

**2 lb. lean stewing beef**
Preheat oven to 300°.
Melt in a heavy skillet:

> **3 tablespoons butter**
> **2 tablespoons vegetable oil**

When the fat is fragrant, add the diced meat. When well browned, stir in the fruit mixture and:

> **(1 tablespoon cinnamon or**
> **2 teaspoons curry)**

Put this mixture into a covered casserole and bake about 1 1/2 hours. Add:

> **2 lb. shredded spinach**

Cover and bake 1/2 hour longer or until the meat is tender. Serve over:

> **Boiled Rice, 189**

## SOUP MEAT

Even though many of a meat's nutrients are dissolved into the stock in soup making, the meat may be served as a separate dish—with an assertive sauce as a fillip for its bland flavor. Remove meat from soup kettle before the vegetables are added, and serve the meat with:

> **Horseradish Sauce, 386;**
> **Cold Mustard Sauce, 409;**
> **Thickened Tomato**
> **Sauce, 400; or Brown**
> **Onion Sauce, 391**

## SPICED BEEF

**8 to 10 Servings**

Good served hot. Fine for a cold meat platter.
Place in a large bowl:

> **4 to 5 lb. chuck, shoulder or**
> **round roast**

Cover with:

> **Dry red wine or cider**
> **2 sliced onions**
> **1/2 bay leaf**
> **1 teaspoon each cinnamon**
> **and allspice**
> **1/2 teaspoon cloves**

> **1 1/2 teaspoons salt**
> **1 teaspoon pepper**

Cover bowl and refrigerate in this marinade 12 hours or more. Drain and reserve the marinade.
Preheat oven to 275°.
Place the meat in a roasting pan. Heat to the boiling point and pour over it half the marinade and:

> **1 cup boiling water**

Cover and ♦ simmer about 3 hours. Mince and sauté in butter:

> **2 onions**
> **4 large carrots**
> **1 medium-sized yellow**
> **turnip**
> **1 rib celery**

Add these ingredients to the roast for the last half hour of cooking.

> **Season to taste**

You may thicken the sauce with:

> **(Flour, see Gravy, 382)**

or reduce it, 380. Add to the stock at the very end:

> **6 to 8 preserved kumquats**

sliced into 1/4-inch pieces.

## CHUCK ROAST IN FOIL

**12 Servings**

Foil-cooked meats often have a pasty look about them, but the use in this recipe of dehydrated onion soup gives great vigor of color and flavor, in spite of the fact that the meat is not browned first. Try this for informal company.
Preheat oven to 300°.
Place:

> **A 7-lb. chuck roast**

on a double thickness of heavy-duty foil large enough to envelop it. Sprinkle the meat with:

> **1/2 to 1 package dehydrated**
> **onion soup**

Turn the meat over and sprinkle the other side with:

½ **to 1 package dehydrated**
    **onion soup**

Now wrap the roast carefully with
the foil, seaming so that no juices can
escape. Place the package in a pan
and bake 3½ to 4 hours. If your company is informal, do not cut the foil
until you are at table and ready to
carve. The sudden burst of fragrance
adds to the anticipation. Serve with:

**Spätzle, 186, or with a Rice**
    **Ring, 189, filled with fresh**
    **peas**

## SWISS STEAK

**6 Servings**

Preheat oven to 300°.
Trim the edges of a ¾-inch thick:
    **2-lb. bottom round steak**
Rub with:
    **½ clove garlic**
Pound, 550, into both sides of the
steak with a mallet:
    **As much seasoned flour as**
        **the steak will hold**
Cut into serving pieces or leave
whole. If left whole, gash the edges
to prevent curling. Heat in a large
heavy casserole:
    **¼ cup bacon drippings or**
        **ham drippings**
Sear steak on one side until brown.
Turn it over and add:
    **½ cup finely chopped onions**
    **1 cup finely mixed chopped**
        **carrots, peppers and celery**
Do not allow vegetables to brown.
    **Season to taste**
Add:
    **1 cup hot stock**
    **(½ cup hot tomato sauce)**
Cover casserole and place in the oven
1½ to 2 hours or more. Remove
steak to a hot platter. Strain and de-
grease drippings. Make:
    **Pan Gravy, 382**

Pour gravy over the steak and
serve with:
    **Mashed Potatoes, 344**

## STEAK AND GREEN PEPPERS

**8 Servings**

Cut into ½-inch strips:
    **2 lb. round steak, ½ inch**
        **thick**
Combine:
    **¼ cup soy sauce**
    **1 cup beef bouillon**
    **2 cloves garlic, mashed**
    **½ teaspoon ginger**
Pour this marinade over the meat
and refrigerate covered 2 to 12 hours.
Drain meat, discarding the garlic
and reserving ½ cup marinade. Dry
meat strips on paper toweling. In a
large skillet sauté meat until light
brown in:
    **3 tablespoons vegetable oil**
Add heated reserved marinade and:
    **1 cup boiling water**
◗ Cover skillet and simmer meat
about 45 minutes. Add:
    **3 large green peppers, cut**
        **into ½-inch strips, seeds**
        **and membrane removed**
        **(1 cup sliced water**
        **chestnuts)**
Simmer 15 minutes more or until
meat is tender.
Mix until smooth:
    **3 tablespoons cornstarch**
    **¼ cup water**
and gradually stir this mixture into
the skillet until gravy has thickened
slightly. Serve with:
    **Boiled Rice, 189**

## FLANK STEAK WITH DRESSING

**4 to 6 Servings**

The sharper the seasonings, the more
"deviled" the total effect.
Have ready:

A 2- to 3-lb. flank or round
steak, 567

Trim the edges. Season with and
pound in:

1 teaspoon salt
1/8 teaspoon paprika
1/4 teaspoon mustard
(1/8 teaspoon ginger)
(1 teaspoon Worcestershire
sauce)

Melt:

1/4 cup butter or bacon
drippings

Add and sauté until golden:

2 tablespoons chopped onion

Add:

1 cup rye or white bread
crumbs
1/4 teaspoon salt
A few grains paprika
2 tablespoons chopped
parsley
3 tablespoons chopped celery
1 slightly beaten egg

Spread this dressing over the steak,
roll loosely and tie it. For variety, try
Sausage Dressing with apples, 433.
Preheat oven to 300°.
Heat in a skillet:

3 tablespoons vegetable oil

Sear the rolled steak on all sides in
the hot oil. Place it in a casserole. Stir
into the oil in the skillet:

2 tablespoons flour

Add:

1 cup water or stock
1 cup tomato juice or dry red
wine
1/4 teaspoon salt

When thickened, pour this mixture
over the steak. Bake covered about
1 1/2 hours. Add seasoning if required.

SHORT RIBS OF BEEF

**2 to 3 Servings**

This is a two-step recipe. Tenderizing
the meat may be done ahead of time,

and the oven crisping just before
serving.
Cut into about 3-inch pieces:

2 lb. lean short ribs of beef

Place in a heavy pot with a lid:

5 cups water
1 small sliced onion
1 small sliced carrot
4 or more ribs celery with
leaves

Bring these ingredients to the boiling
point. Add the meat. Simmer covered
until ▶ nearly tender, about 2 hours.
Take out meat. Strain and degrease
the stock. Make about 3 cups of thin
gravy, 382, using:

1/4 cup fat
1/4 cup flour
3 cups stock
Season to taste

Preheat oven to 325°.
Heat in a heavy skillet:

1/4 cup fat

Slice, add and stir until golden:

1 small onion

Brown the meat in the hot fat. Pour
over it half the gravy. Bake ▶ uncovered about 45 minutes until brown and
crisp. You may baste occasionally
with the drippings. Reheat remaining
gravy. Add to it:

1 teaspoon marjoram,
preferably fresh
Season to taste

Place the meat on a hot platter. Garnish with:

Mashed Potatoes, 344

Serve piping hot with gravy.

## ABOUT GOULASH, GULYAS OR PÖRKÖLT

This Hungarian specialty is a thick
stew that may be cooked in many
ways; it is always highly spiced—
usually, but not always, seasoned
with sweet paprika. Some epicures
insist that only the imported Rosen

paprika will do, while others use freshly ground black pepper instead. In Beef Goulash, the meat is always browned before simmering. A knowing friend claims that shinbone meat with its high gelatin content makes a glorious goulash. But variations using veal, pork or lamb alone or in combination, on 598 and 607, may be cooked à blanc—that is, without browning. Versions containing lamb or pork may be called Pörkölt. The liquid is sometimes water, sometimes stock or dry red wine. Vegetables may be added for the last hour of cooking.

BEEF GOULASH

**6 Servings**

Cut into 1-inch cubes:

**2 lb. stewing beef, or 1 lb. beef and 1 lb. lean veal**

Melt in a heavy pot:

**1/4 cup butter, vegetable oil or bacon drippings**

Brown meat on both sides in the hot oil. Add and sauté until transparent:

**1 1/2 cups chopped onions**

Add:

**1 cup boiling Stock, (II, 171–172), or tomato juice**

**1 diced green pepper, seeds and membrane removed**

**1 teaspoon salt**

**1 teaspoon to 1 tablespoon paprika**

Use just enough stock to keep the meat from scorching, adding more gradually during cooking, if necessary. Cover the pot and simmer the meat for 1 1/2 hours. Six small peeled potatoes may be added for the last half hour of cooking, but they soak up the gravy, which is apt to be the best part of the goulash. Remove the meat from the pot and thicken the stock for:

**Pan Gravy, 382**

It may be necessary to add more stock or tomato juice.

**Season to taste**

If potatoes have not been included, serve the goulash with:

**Polenta, 180, or**

**Noodles, 200**

# ABOUT BEEF ROLLS, ROULADES OR PAUPIETTES

Thin strips of pounded meat or poultry or fish rolled around vegetables or other fillings are known also as roulades or paupiettes. They may be further wrapped in salt pork or bacon. To make them with bacon, use:

**Thin strips of pounded round or flank steak, 3 x 4 inches**

Season with:

**Salt and pepper**

Place on each strip about 2 tablespoons of one of the following fillings:

**I. Well-seasoned smoked or cooked sausage with chopped parsley or dill pickle**

**II. Minced ham, julienned carrot and celery**

**III. Seasoned cooked rice, chopped stuffed olives, or seedless green grapes with lemon zest**

Roll meat and tie with string near both ends, or wrap as for cabbage leaves, shown on 103. Dredge in:

**Flour**

Brown in bacon drippings or rendered salt pork. Place in a casserole and use for every 6 rolls:

**1 1/2 cups stock or dry wine**

**1 1/2 to 2 tablespoons tomato paste**

Cover and cook slowly in a preheated

300° oven, or simmer on direct heat about 1 hour and 15 minutes.

## STEAK-AND-KIDNEY PIE

**4 Servings**

Classic recipes for this old English favorite often call for beef kidneys. If they are used, they must be blanched, 106, and cooking time must be increased to assure tenderness. Rather than encasing the stew in dough, we recommend a topping only.
Preheat oven to 350°.
Cut into half-inch-thick slices:

**1½ lb. round or other beefsteak**
Wash, skin and slice thin:

**¾ lb. veal or lamb kidneys**
Melt in a skillet:

**3 tablespoons butter or beef fat**
Sauté the kidneys over high heat for 1 to 2 minutes. Shake constantly. Add and sauté lightly:

**⅓ cup onions**
Shake the beef in a bag of:

**Seasoned Flour, (II, 220)**
Lightly grease an ovenproof baker. Place in it a layer of meat, then a layer of kidneys and onions. Or you may reserve the kidneys and add them the last 15 minutes before placing the pastry cover.
Add:

**2 cups Brown Stock, (II, 171)**
**1 cup dry red wine or beer**
Cover the dish and bake 1 to 1½ hours. Cool slightly. Increase oven heat to 425°. Cover the meat, see 558, with:

**Pâte Brisée, (II, 362)**
Bake 12 to 15 minutes.

## ☰ KENTUCKY BURGOO

**10 to 12 Servings**

The accent is on the first syllable. This thick, long-simmered potpourri, a catch-as-catch-can mixture of meats, fowl and garden gleanings—with squirrel thrown in, in some authentic local versions—has an assortment of Old World forebears as numerous and far-flung as the Gypsies. In Spain it is known as **Olla Podrida;** in Ireland it surfaces as **Mulligan Stew.** But in Kentucky it came into its own as the local solution to feeding the multitudes; it used to be made, in amounts to serve several hundreds, in a huge hog-butchering kettle over an outdoor fire, providing an occasion for great socializing, a "stirring" overnight vigil. This simplified version can be varied according to your preference or to what meat is available—lamb or veal may be used as well. It makes good sense, too, to freeze this seasonal dish in meal-sized packages.
Place in a heavy, lidded kettle:

**¾ lb. lean stewing beef, cubed**
**¾ lb. pork shoulder, cubed**
**3½ quarts water or stock**
Bring slowly to a boil. ◗ Reduce heat at once and simmer about 1½ hours.
Add to the pot:

**One 3½-lb. chicken, disjointed**
Bring ingredients again to a boil, ◗ reduce heat and simmer about 1 hour more or until meat falls from the bones. Cool the mixture enough to remove bones from meat. Return meat to the pot and bring to a boil.
Add:

**2½ cups quartered, skinned ripe tomatoes**
**1 cup fresh lima beans**
**½ diced hot red pepper**
**2 diced green peppers, seeds and membrane removed**
**¾ cup diced onions**
**1 cup diced carrots**
**½ cup diced celery**
**2 cups diced potatoes**

1 cup diced okra
1 bay leaf
1 tablespoon Worcestershire
  sauce

Stirring frequently as it thickens,
◆ simmer the whole mixture 45 minutes or more over very low heat before adding:

2 cups corn, freshly cut from
  the cob

Simmer about 15 minutes more or
until all vegetables are soft.

Season to taste

Garnish with:

Fresh parsley

Serve hot in deep bowls with
squares of:

Salt-Rising Bread, (II, 308),
or Corn Bread, (II, 341)

CORNED BEEF

I. Wash under running water to remove surface brine:

Corned Beef, (II, 633)

Cover with boiling water and simmer, allowing about 1 hour per pound,
or until a fork can penetrate to center. Always slice corned beef very
thin, diagonally across the grain. A
classic accompaniment of corned beef
served hot is:

Cabbage wedges

simmered with the beef the last
15 minutes of cooking. Serve hot with:

Horseradish Sauce, 386
Boiled Potatoes, 343, or
Gnocchi with Farina, 185

Serve corned beef cold with:

Horseradish

◆ To press for slicing, cool the meat
and force it into a deep pan; cover
and refrigerate weighted. The moisture pressed from the meat should
form a jellied coating.

II. After cooking corned beef as in I,
above, you may coat it with the fol-

lowing glaze and bake in a preheated
350° oven 15 minutes or until the
topping is set.

Combine and mix well:

1 tablespoon brown sugar
1 tablespoon water
1 teaspoon soy sauce
2 teaspoons paprika
1/2 teaspoon ginger

III. Tenderized corned beef can now
be bought for oven roasting; follow
manufacturer's directions.

CORNED BEEF AND CABBAGE
OR NEW ENGLAND BOILED
DINNER

10 to 12 Servings

This is a delectable dinner if composed only of beef, onions and cabbage. But for authenticity, additional
vegetables are included.

Cook until tender:

Corned Beef I, left

Meantime, cook separately until tender, then skin and reserve:

10 to 12 medium-sized
beets, 300

Some devotees of this dish add about:

(1/2 lb. salt pork)

to the corned beef for the last 2 hours
of cooking. When done, remove the
beef from the pot and cook in the
simmering stock 30 minutes:

3 peeled, quartered small
  parsnips
6 peeled, quartered large
  carrots
3 peeled, quartered large
  yellow turnips

Skin and add:

10 small onions

Pare, quarter and simmer in the stock
15 minutes longer:

6 medium-sized potatoes

Cut into wedges, add and simmer until tender, about 10 to 15 minutes:

**A head of cabbage**

Reheat the meat in the stock. Serve it on a large platter, surrounded by the vegetables, including the beets. Garnish with:

**Parsley**

If there is enough of this dish left over, use for Red Flannel Hash, below.

## RED FLANNEL HASH

New Englanders say that this hash, to be properly made, must be concocted from the leftovers of:

**New England Boiled Dinner, 584**

Chop the leftover beets, cabbage, turnips, corned beef, etc., and brown the mixture in a skillet in:

**2 tablespoons vegetable oil**

until a brown crust forms.

## ABOUT VEAL

A friend of ours at boarding school reports that one of the specialties served there with notorious frequency has been dubbed "Dreaded Veal Cutlet." Veal—young beef 3 to 8 months of age—enjoys much more esteem in Europe than in America. This, we are convinced, is a pity; partly because veal has a superbly delicate and distinctive flavor, and partly because a number of classic dishes cannot be confected using a substitute. Occasionally still to be found is milk-fed veal—the very best; but in any case, top-quality veal should be tender and succulent and have a white or very pale pink color. The redder the meat, the older and tougher the veal. Veal over 225 pounds is known as calf. To improve older veal, blanch briefly, starting in cold water; or soak refrigerated in milk overnight; or marinate in lemon juice for 1 hour.

Veal needs a careful cooking approach, as it is lacking in fat and may toughen quickly. Since it also has a higher proportion of connective tissue, veal should not be broiled; ▶ long, slow, covered cooking is best. Large cuts of veal need some moisture, and the meat should be covered at least part of the cooking time. Abroad, certain dishes like Veal à la Meunière or à la Crême are served both rosy and juicy, but here veal is generally served well done or after reaching an internal temperature of 170°. For the Economical Use of Large Cuts, see 562. Also, see About Veal Scallops and Cutlets, 586.

## VEAL ROAST

Remove the meat from the refrigerator at least 1 hour before cooking. Veal roasts, both rolled and unrolled, need to be rubbed well with butter or oil. Or they may be barded, 511, with thin slices of salt pork or bacon which have been blanched to remove some of the salt.

Preheat oven to 425°. Season well:

**A leg, shoulder, loin, saddle or rack of veal**

with a choice of your favorite:

**Herbs: garlic, dill, tarragon, chervil or thyme**
**Salt and pepper**

or you may sprinkle the roast with:

**(Lemon juice)**

Place the oiled and seasoned meat on a rack in a greased shallow roasting pan. Add to the pan a:

**Mirepoix, (II, 254)**

Bake ▶ uncovered about 30 minutes. ▶ Reduce the heat to 325°, cover the roast loosely with foil or parchment, and continue cooking until the internal temperature reaches 170°, or approximately 15 to 20 minutes per pound. Baste occasionally with pan juices. If necessary, supplement these with a little:

> **Melted butter and white wine**

You may add parboiled vegetables—potatoes, carrots, etc.—for the last half hour or so of cooking. Or you may spread over the roast for this last half hour a combination of:

> **(1 cup cultured sour cream)**
> **(1 tablespoon flour)**

Serve with:

> **Dumplings, 182, or**
> **Spätzen, 186**
> **Pickled Prunes, (II, 136)**

## VEAL ROAST STUFFED OR FARCI

The meat may be rubbed first with garlic, or gashes may be cut in a shoulder roast, in which fine slivers of garlic, marjoram, peppercorns, anchovies or anchovy paste may be inserted. Remove the meat from the refrigerator at least 1 hour before cooking.

Preheat oven to 450°.

Cut a pocket in:

> **A breast or shoulder of veal**

Rub with:

> **Garlic**

Dust pocket lightly with:

> **Ginger**

before filling with:

> **3 cups Dry Dressing, 431, plus 1 tablespoon chopped costmary (II, 268); or Bread Dressing, 431, with 2 slices chopped salt pork added; or Oyster Dressing, 432; or Baked Green Rice, 191, the cheese omitted**

Sew up the pocket with a coarse needle and thread. Rub the meat with:

> **Butter**

Dredge with:

> **Seasoned Flour, (II, 220)**

Place in oven on a rack in a greased roasting pan and ♦ reduce the heat to 325°. Bake ♦ uncovered 25 to 30 minutes to the pound until done. Baste occasionally, or you may place on the roast several strips of:

> **(Blanched bacon, 106)**

From the drippings left in the pan, make:

> **Pan Gravy, 382**

When the gravy is done, you may remove it from the heat and add:

> **(1/4 cup cultured sour cream)**

Heat the gravy but ♦ do not let it boil.

## ABOUT VEAL SCALLOPS AND CUTLETS

The most prized meat for scallops comes from the long round muscle of the leg freed from its membrane and tough connective tissue; it is sliced thinly across the grain and pounded, 550, to 1/8- to 1/4-inch thickness. Cutlets, cut from the round of the leg, are usually cut 1/2 to 3/4 inch thick, with the small round bone intact. They are often pounded, especially if used in recipes calling for rolling or stuffing when the bone is removed. Sometimes veal from the rib section is treated in similar fashion. Whether you call them scallops, cutlets or **Schnitzels,** they may be sautéed with or without breading. Trim off any fat, and if any membrane adheres, slash in a number of places so the meat will not curl up during cooking. Do not crowd the pan or you will get a steamed effect.

## VEAL CUTLET OR SCALLOPINI

**3 to 4 Servings**

Please read About Veal Cutlets, above. Dredge lightly with flour on one side only:

1½ lb. pounded thin veal
    cutlets
Sauté them, floured side first, in:
    ¼ cup butter
heated until fragrant. In about 3 minutes, when juices begin to emerge on
the upper side, turn the meat and continue to sauté about 3 minutes more.
Shake the skillet vigorously from
time to time until the meat is done.
Remove from skillet and keep warm.
Deglaze the pan juices with:
    ½ cup veal or chicken stock,
        or ¼ cup stock and ¼ cup
        Marsala or Madeira
    Season to taste
You may swirl in at the end:
    (1 tablespoon butter)
or add:
    (½ lb. Sautéed Mushrooms, 328)
If you do not use the wine, you may
add:
    (1 tablespoon lemon juice)
Pour the sauce over the cutlets and
serve.

## VEAL SCALLOPINI WITH TOMATOES

### 3 to 4 Servings

Please read About Veal Cutlets, 586.
Preheat oven to 325°.
Cut into 1-inch squares:
    1½ lb. veal cutlet cut thin,
        trimmed, boned and
        pounded
Dredge with:
    Flour
Brown in a mixture of:
    1 tablespoon butter
    1 tablespoon olive oil
Add:
    ½ lb. thinly sliced mushrooms
    ½ to 1 clove garlic, pressed
    2 tablespoons chopped
        parsley
    2 tablespoons chopped fresh
        basil

½ cup skinned, seeded, diced
    fresh tomatoes
½ cup Marsala
2 tablespoons grated
    Parmesan cheese
Cover and bake about 45 minutes.

## WIENER SCHNITZEL OR BREADED VEAL CUTLET

### 3 to 4 Servings

Viennese friends insist that the true
Wiener Schnitzel is deep-fat-fried;
others contend it is sautéed. But most
typical Viennese recipes put up to
¾ cup of butter in the sauté pan,
which virtually gives a deep-fat
rather than a sautéed result anyway.
Although there are many variations,
we suggest the following. ♦ Please
read About Veal Cutlets, 586. Before
cooking, pound to about ¼ inch thick:
    1½ lb. veal cutlet
Coat with:
    Bound Breading, (II, 220)
Let cutlets stand at least 15 minutes.
Sauté them over low heat 2 minutes
on one side in:
    ½ to ¾ cup butter
Turn and cook 2 minutes on the other
side. Turn again and cook until done,
not more than 10 minutes in all. Garnish with:
    Lemon slices and rolled
        anchovies
If you cap the garnished cutlet with a
fried egg, you may call it Holstein.

## VEAL PARMIGIANA

### 3 to 4 Servings

Cut into 2 x 2-inch slices:
    1½ lb. veal cutlets, ¼ inch
        thick
Pound thin until they reach about
3 x 3 inches.
Dip into a:
    Bound Breading, (II, 220)

Add to bread crumbs an equal amount of:

**Grated Parmesan cheese**

Allow the pieces to stand at least 15 minutes, then sauté them until crisp in:

**Clarified Butter, 396**

about 2 minutes on each side. Serve with:

**Quick Tomato Sauce, 400**

## PAPRIKA SCHNITZEL OR CUTLET

**3 or 4 Servings**

Trim edges and remove bone from:

**A 1/4- to 1/2-inch-thick veal cutlet, 1 1/2 lb.**

Dredge one side only in:

**Seasoned Flour, (II, 220)**

Heat in a skillet:

**1/4 cup butter or shortening**

Sauté lightly in the fat:

**(1/2 cup or more sliced onions)**

Remove and reserve the onions and sauté the meat, first on the seasoned side, in the hot fat, until lightly browned. Turn, then add until the fat becomes red:

**Paprika**

Remove pan from heat and add:

**1 cup boiling vegetable or chicken stock**

and the reserved onions. Cover and simmer the veal ◗ over very low heat until almost tender, about 15 minutes. Add:

**1/2 cup cultured sour cream**
**Season to taste**

Garnish with:

**Parsley, capers, or anchovies**

Serve with:

**Applesauce, (II, 118)**
**Creamed Spinach, 359**

## VEAL SCALLOP OR ESCALOPE DE VEAU ORLOFF

**3 to 4 Servings**

Please read About Veal Cutlets, 586.
Preheat oven to 350°.
Cut into 2 x 2-inch slices:

**1 1/2 lb. scallops, 1/4 inch thick**

Pound until about 3 x 3 inches each. Sauté until barely frizzled on both sides in:

**Clarified Butter, 396**

Remove from pan and drain on paper toweling. To make a **Soubise,** mix and grind in a food chopper:

**1/2 cup cooked rice**
**1/2 cup white onions**
**1/2 cup mushrooms**

Season with:

**Salt and pepper**

Cover each scallop of veal with:

**1 tablespoon liver paste**

Then press firmly over each scallop the onion-rice mixture. Sprinkle over each:

**1 teaspoon brandy or dry sherry**

Dust generously with:

**Grated Parmesan cheese**

Place the meat on an ovenproof serving platter and bake about 15 minutes until the cheese is golden.

## VEAL SCALLOPS WITH HAM

**6 Servings**

This recipe, also called **Cordon Bleu,** is good made with chicken breasts too.
Pound:

**2 large veal cutlets**

and slice into about 12 three-inch squares. Sauté until barely frizzled on both sides in:

**Clarified Butter, 396**

Remove from pan and drain on paper toweling.
Cut into 6 thin slices:

**Prosciutto or smoked ham**

Place the ham on 6 slices of veal. Top with a similar sized slice of:

> **Swiss cheese**

Cover the pieces with the remaining veal slices.

Gently pat the meat in:

> **Bound Breading, (II, 220)**

Let stand 15 minutes. Sauté in:

> **Clarified Butter, 396**

until golden on each side, about 3 minutes. Or after breading you may bake the meat on an ovenproof platter in a 350° oven about 15 minutes, turning once.


## BRAISED VEAL CHOPS

**4 Servings**

Veal chops may be cooked the same way as veal cutlets; or simply browned, then simmered slowly, covered, on top of the stove until done, about 15 to 20 minutes.

Preheat oven to 325°.

Brown on both sides in a large skillet:

> **4  veal chops, ³/₄ inch thick**

in:

> **Butter and vegetable oil**

Arrange the chops in an overlapping pattern in a casserole. Sauté in the hot fat until limp:

> **2  tablespoons chopped green onions or shallots**

Add:

> **¹/₃  cup dry white wine**
> **1  teaspoon each basil and tarragon**
> **Salt and pepper**

Pour the pan juices over the chops, cover and bake about 20 minutes, basting occasionally. Serve with a choice of:

> **Quick Tomato Sauce, 400, Mushroom Wine Sauce, 392, or Madeira Sauce, 391**


## VEAL BIRDS OR PAUPIETTES

Prepare:

> **Slices of veal from the round, ¹/₃ inch thick**

as for:

> **Beef Rolls or Paupiettes, 582**

Since veal is leaner than beef, you may prefer to bard or wrap the pounded paupiettes in blanched salt pork, 107. We suggest using Filling III. Cook about 45 minutes.


## MOCK CHICKEN DRUMSTICKS OR CITY CHICKEN

**6 Servings**

Still popular, though the veal is now more costly than the chicken it used to mock.

Preheat oven to 325°.

Cut into 1 x 1¹/₂-inch pieces:

> **1  lb. veal**
> **1  lb. pork**

Arrange veal and pork cubes alternately on 6 skewers. Press pieces close together into the shape of a drumstick. Roll the meat in:

> **Seasoned Flour, (II, 220)**

Beat:

> **1  egg**
> **2  tablespoons water**

Dip sticks in the diluted egg, then roll in:

> **Bread crumbs**

Melt in a skillet:

> **¹/₄  cup butter**

Brown meat partially in the fat. Add:

> **1  tablespoon grated onion**

Continue to brown meat. Cover bottom of skillet with:

> **boiling stock, (II, 171)**

Cover skillet and bake in oven about 50 minutes or until meat is tender. Make:

> **Pan Gravy, 382**

## VEAL STEW MÉNAGÈRE

**4 Servings**

Cut into 1 1/2-inch cubes:

**1 1/2 lb. veal with little bone or
2 lb. neck or shanks**

Melt in a heavy pot:

**3 tablespoons butter or
shortening**

Brown the meat in the hot fat with:

**12 very small peeled onions**

Remove meat and onions from the pan. Pour off all but 1 tablespoon of fat. Stir in:

**1 tablespoon flour**

Add and stir until smooth:

**1 1/2 cups consommé or stock
(1/2 cup dry red wine)**

Add the meat and onions. Simmer covered until very tender, 1 1/2 to 2 hours. Season and serve with:

**Crusty Soft-Center Spoon
Bread, (II, 343), or Farina
Balls, 184**

or serve it in:

**A Noodle Ring, 201**

Veal stew is also good with a baked top crust. See About Meat Pies, 557.

## BLANQUETTE DE VEAU

**6 Servings**

"Serenely full, the epicure may say, 'Fate cannot harm me: I have dined today,' " As the name suggests, this stew is cooked à blanc and enhanced with an egg sauce.

Cut into 1-inch pieces:

**1 1/2 lb. boneless veal shoulder
1 1/2 lb. boneless veal breast**

Parblanch, 106, the pieces of veal about 2 minutes in salted water. Drain and wash well under cold running water, removing all scum. Put meat in a heavy pan and add:

**5 cups chicken or veal stock
1 large onion studded with
1 clove**

**1 peeled carrot
1 rib white celery, chopped
A Bouquet Garni, (II, 253)**

Simmer uncovered 1 1/4 to 1 1/2 hours, until veal is tender and can be pierced with a fork. Now skim out the vegetables and the bouquet. Add:

**24 small white onions
2 cups fresh button
mushroom caps**

Simmer about 10 minutes. Combine:

**1/4 cup flour
1/4 cup butter**

Add this thickener to the stock and simmer another 10 minutes. Remove pan from heat. Mix together:

**3 beaten egg yolks
1/2 cup warm whipping cream**

Stir about 2 tablespoons of the hot veal stock into the eggs and cream; then return mixture to the pan. Add:

**2 to 3 tablespoons lemon
juice
Season to taste**

Serve with:

**Noodles or rice**

garnished with:

**Chopped parsley**

## VEAL AND PORK PIE

**4 Servings**

▶ Please read About Meat Pies, 557.

Cut into 1-inch pieces:

**1/2 lb. veal
1/2 lb. lean pork**

Stir and brown the meat lightly in:

**2 tablespoons butter or
vegetable oil**

Add:

**3 cups boiling water
1 teaspoon salt
1/2 teaspoon paprika
1/2 bay leaf
2 whole cloves**

Simmer covered about 15 minutes. Remove bay leaf and cloves. Add:

¼ **cup diced carrots**
¾ **cup diced celery**
1 **cup diced potatoes**
12 **small onions**

Bring the stew to the boiling point
◗ then reduce heat and simmer covered until meat is tender, about 30 minutes longer.

**Season to taste**

Make:

**Pan Gravy, 382**

Preheat oven to 425°.
Place stew in a baking dish. Cool slightly. Top it with a vented:

**Pie Crust, 558**

Brush with the white of egg and bake 15 to 20 minutes.

## MEXICAN VEAL STEAK WITH NOODLES

**5 or 6 Servings**

Cut into small sections:

1 **lb. thin veal steak**

Dredge with:

¼ **cup flour**

Heat:

3 **teaspoons butter or olive oil**

Sauté meat quickly on both sides until brown.
◗ Reduce heat. Cover meat with:

1½ **cups sliced onions**
6 **tablespoons chili sauce**
1¼ **cups boiling stock**

Simmer covered about ½ hour.
Meanwhile, cook and drain:

2 **cups Noodles, 200**

Toss them in:

¾ **cup canned condensed cream of chicken soup**

Serve noodles mounded, covered with:

¼ **cup buttered crumbs**
2 **tablespoons grated Parmesan cheese**

Surround noodles with the veal. Garnish with:

**(Parsley)**

## CASSEROLED VEAL WITH SOUR CREAM

**4 Servings**

This dish can be produced in quantity for large gatherings.
Preheat oven to 300°.
Cut into cubes:

1½ **lb. boneless veal**

Brown lightly in:

1½ **tablespoons butter**

Remove meat to an ovenproof baking dish. Add to butter, stir and sauté lightly:

1 **tablespoon chopped onion**
½ **lb. sliced mushrooms**

Remove from heat. Stir in slowly:

1 **tablespoon flour**
⅔ **cup stock**
½ **teaspoon salt**
⅛ **teaspoon pepper**

Pour sauce over meat. Cover and bake about 45 minutes. Degrease, 381, if necessary. Stir in:

½ **cup warm cultured sour cream**

Heat thoroughly before serving.

## BAKED MARROWBONES OR OSSO BUCO

**3 Servings**

Preheat oven to 300°.
◗ To make this dish really delectable, the animal should be not more than 2 months old. Saw into 2-inch pieces:

2 **lb. shin bone or knuckle of veal**

Dip the bones first in:

**Olive oil**

then in:

**Seasoned Flour, (II, 220)**

Brown the bones very slowly for about 15 minutes in:

¼ **cup olive oil or half oil and half butter**

Place the bones upright as close together as possible in a heavy pan just large enough to hold them. Cook until golden in the fat:

**¹/₄ cup chopped onions**

Add them to the bones. Heat and pour over bones:

**¹/₂ cup white wine**
**¹/₂ cup skinned, diced, seeded fresh tomatoes**
**Seasoned stock—enough to cover the lower third of the bones**

Cover and bake 1 to 1¹/₂ hours until any meat on the bones is tender. Before serving, sprinkle the tops of the bones with:

**Gremolata, (II, 253)**

Serve garnished with:

**Fried Chipolata sausage and Boiled Chestnuts, 313, or Risotto alla Milanese, 193**

and scoop the delicious marrow from the bones with marrow spoons.

## ABOUT LAMB, MUTTON, KID AND GOAT MEAT

Since lamb is now shipped from various climates, young lamb is no longer referred to as spring lamb. When 3 to 5 months old, it is called baby or milk finished lamb. From 5 months to a year, it is simply called lamb, and from there on out—mutton. Mutton, with its stronger flavor and tougher meat, may be substituted for lamb, but cooking time is usually increased from 5 to 10 minutes to the pound. Both lamb and mutton are covered with a papery whitish membrane called the fell, which is often removed before cooking, as it tends to make the flavor strong. Almost any cut of lamb may be cooked by dry-heat methods—including skewer cooking—for which recipes immediately follow; and many cuts are adaptable to the covered,

moist-heat methods in the second group. To identify dry- and moist-heat cuts, please see diagram, 561. For the Economical Use of Large Cuts, see 562. For ground lamb recipes, see 619, and for the use of leftover lamb, see Brunch, Lunch and Supper Dishes, 236. To carve, see below.

The meat of young goat, or kid, has an agreeable flavor that has long been appreciated in Southern Europe. It is sometimes available in U.S. markets, labeled chevon by government ruling. It may be cooked as for mutton—provided the animal is young, for it is always tougher than mutton; and the meat of a male goat must be eaten when the animal is very young indeed, not older than 4 months.

## ROAST LEG OF LAMB OR MUTTON

**About 8 Servings**

◗ Please see Economical Use of Large Cuts, 562.

Remove from the refrigerator about 1 hour before cooking:

**A 5-lb. leg of lamb or mutton**

Preheat oven to 450°.

Remove the fell or papery outer covering. Rub the meat with:

(Cut garlic or lemon and
rosemary)

Insert under the skin, using a pointed
knife:

(Slivers of garlic or herbs)

or place on it as it goes into the oven:

(Lemon slices)

Place meat, fat side up, on a rack in
an uncovered greased pan. Immediately ♦ reduce the heat to 325°. Roast
it 30 minutes to the pound, or until
the internal temperature reaches 175°
to 180°, for meat well done. Most
Europeans like lamb slightly rare
or at an internal temperature of 160°
to 165°.

♦ Do not cover or baste. Make:

**Pan Gravy, 382, using
cultured sour cream or
milk**

Or serve the roast with:

**Deglazed drippings, 381**

and:

**Mint Sauce, 406**

Instead of mint sauce you may prefer:

**Cumberland Sauce, 407**

To carve a lamb roast, see illustration, 592.

## ▤ BARBECUED BUTTERFLY LEG OF LAMB

Please read about grilling and spit-cooking in Outdoor Cooking, 108.

**I.** Have butcher bone and flatten:

**A leg of lamb**

At least 2 hours before cooking,
cover the leg with:

**Fresh mint**

Rub with:

**Dry mustard
Pepper
Onion juice**

Preheat grill or prepare coals. While
charcoal is burning down to embers, cook gently about 5 minutes a
sauce of:

¹/₄ **cup butter**
¹/₂ **clove garlic, crushed**
1 **tablespoon grated onion**

Remove garlic and add:

¹/₂ **cup chopped fresh mint
leaves**

Place lamb on grill. During cooking,
brush often with the warm sauce. After about 20 minutes, turn the meat,
and continue to turn at intervals unless it is on a spit. If you like lamb
pink, it should be ready in 35 to
45 minutes, depending on the heat of
the coals. Well-done lamb will require 15 minutes more.

**II.** Marinate a boned, flattened leg of
lamb refrigerated overnight in:

**Lamb or
Game Marinade, (II, 181)**

Wipe dry before grilling as in I,
above.

## RACK OF LAMB

**3 Servings**

This is the rib end of the saddle or
double loin, and has about six chops.
Preheat oven to 400°.

Remove the fell and excess fat from:

**A rack of young lamb**

If you French the rib bones as described in a Crown Roast, below,
cover the ends with foil. Coat the
rack with:

**A cut garlic clove
Butter
Salt and pepper**

Place it on a metal rack in a shallow
pan and roast about 25 minutes or until the internal temperature reaches
145°. Carve into chops and serve.

## CROWN ROAST OF LAMB

**Allow 2 Ribs per Person**

Preheat oven to 450°.
Wipe with a cloth:

### A crown roast of lamb

French the ends of the bones by scraping clean from the end of the chops almost to the eye of the meat. Protect ends of bones by covering with aluminum foil. Proceed as directed for Roast Leg of Lamb, 592, but remove meat from oven before the last hour of cooking and fill center with:

> 3 cups Bread Dressing, 431,
> or Dressing for Cornish
> Hen, 436

Return to oven and complete cooking. Remove covering from bones. Cover each with a paper frill, a slice of pickle or a stuffed olive. Top the dressing with a bunch of parsley or a pineapple crown, as in the illustration on 546. To carve into chops, see 602. Make:

> Pan Gravy, 382

Serve with the gravy and:

> Mint Sauce, 406, or currant
> jelly

An unfilled crown roast may be cooked upside down. Omit covering the bones. When done, fill the hollow of the roast with:

> Green Peas, 338

or with:

> Baked Chestnuts, 314, or
> Brussels Sprouts, 303

Garnish with:

> Parsley

## LAMB SHOULDER ROAST

**About 8 Servings**

Preheat oven to 450°.
Prepare:

> A 4- to 5-lb. cushion
> shoulder of lamb

by cutting a pocket in one side for inserting dressing. Rub meat with:

> A cut clove of garlic

Fill cavity with:

> Bread Dressing, 431,

> Tangerine Rice
> Dressing, 436, or
> Apricot Dressing, 436

Sew or skewer open side. Place roast uncovered on a rack in a greased pan in the oven. ◗ Reduce heat immediately to 325° and cook about 30 minutes to the pound. Serve with:

> Pan Gravy, 382

## ABOUT LAMB CHOPS

There are several kinds of lamb chops; those from the loin and rib are the tenderest and most costly; they are cooked by broiling. Large leg chops of varying shapes—sometimes called lamb steaks—often have a fine flavor and are also cooked by dry heat. Shoulder chops are the least tender, but they can be broiled and are excellent breaded or braised.

### BROILED LAMB CHOPS

**2 Chops per Person**

Trim the outer skin or fell from:

> Loin or rib chops

**I.  Oven-broiled**

Follow directions for:

> Broiled Steak, 568

allowing a shorter time for cooking, according to thickness.

**II.  Pan-broiled**

For chops an inch or less in thickness. Sear chops in a hot skillet which has been rubbed lightly with a small piece of lamb fat. Turn chops several times during cooking. Allow for well-done chops about 15 minutes in all. Pour off fat as it accumulates in the pan. Season with:

> Salt and freshly ground
> pepper

Serve very hot, garnished with:

> Parsley

## BRAISED LAMB CHOPS

Shoulder chops, arm or blade, may be braised as for:

**Pork Chops, 605**

but reduce cooking time to about 40 minutes.

## GARNISHED ENGLISH MIXED GRILL

**1 to 2 Servings**

While this is the classic serving for one, it does very well for two in our family.

Preheat broiling compartment.

Place on cold grid or greased hot grid:

- **2 lamb chops**
- **2 small link sausages**
- **2 chicken livers**
- **1/2 blanched veal kidney**
- **2 thin slices bacon**
- **1 halved small tomato seasoned with salt, pepper and butter**
- **1/2 cup mushroom caps dipped in butter**
- **4 small whole blanched onions**

Position broiler rack so that meat surface is about 3 inches from heat source. During cooking process, turn meats and mushrooms. Baste if necessary with Clarified Butter, 396. The chops may require a longer cooking than the other ingredients. Arrange on hot plates and serve with:

**Béarnaise Sauce, 412**

## ☰ ABOUT KEBABS

Please read about Skewer Cooking, 94, and see example of a brazier for kebabs, 91, and the hibachi, 110. Kebabs lend themselves perfectly to picnics; the meat cubes, presoaked in a savory marinade, can be grilled over an open fire and served straight from the skewer onto a piece of Flatbread, (II, 313). The grilled cubes may be slipped off the skewers onto a bed of rice, kasha or bulgur, or served on parsley, watercress or shredded lettuce.

Though various kinds of meat and seafood can be used for kebabs, with a wide international choice of marinades, our own meat preference for tenderness and taste is lamb, which is traditional in the Middle East— whence comes the term **shish kebab.** For any meat kebabs, the meat is cut into 1 1/2-inch cubes, which are marinated refrigerated 2 to 3 hours, then wiped dry and threaded on skewers— close together if the meat is to be rare—widely spaced for well-done; bits of lamb fat or bacon or bay leaf may be inserted between the pieces of meat to add flavor. Kebabs are grilled or broiled about 3 inches from the heat source, the meat brushed frequently with melted butter or olive oil and turned to brown evenly; about 8 to 12 minutes according to taste.

The meat cubes may be alternated on skewers with an assortment of vegetables such as tomato chunks, green pepper slices, mushrooms and onions, or with pineapple slices or stuffed olives. But differences in cooking time require that firm vegetables such as onions and green peppers be parboiled; or, as we prefer, that the vegetables be skewered separately and cooked at the side of the grill where heat is less intense. For a dramatic effect, you may serve kebabs flambéed, see 108.

## ☰ LAMB KEBABS

Follow procedure described in About Kebabs, left, using one of these marinades:

Yogurt or Buttermilk
Marinade, (II, 181)
Apricot or Sassaties
Marinade, (II, 181)
Lamb or
Game Marinade, (II, 181)
Fish or Lamb Marinade
I, II or III, (II, 181)

## BRAISED SHOULDER OF LAMB

6 Servings

Melt in a heavy pot:
1/4 cup vegetable oil or butter
Sear on all sides in the hot fat:
A rolled shoulder of lamb
Remove it from the pot. Sauté slowly
in the fat 10 minutes:
1/2 cup chopped onions
1/4 cup chopped carrots
1/4 cup chopped turnips
1/2 cup chopped celery with
leaves
(1 sliced clove garlic)
Return the meat to the pot. Add:
1/2 bay leaf
4 whole peppercorns
1 teaspoon salt
4 cups boiling vegetable stock
or 3 cups stock and 1 cup
tomato pulp
Cover the pot and simmer meat until
tender, about 2 hours. When the meat
is done, degrease and thicken stock
slightly with:
Kneaded Butter, 381

## BRAISED STUFFED SHOULDER OR FARCE OF LAMB

6 Servings

Rub:
A boned shoulder of lamb
with:
(Garlic)
or insert slivers of garlic under the
skin. Prepare about:
3 cups Bread Dressing, 431

Spread it on the meat. Roll like a jelly
roll. Secure with string, or fasten
with spiral skewers, 510. Brown in:
3 tablespoons vegetable oil or
butter
Place in a roasting pan:
1 cup hot Vegetable
Stock, (II, 174)
Put the browned roast in it and bake
covered at 300°. Allow about 40 minutes to the pound. For added flavor
you may put some of the bones in the
pan. Meanwhile, prepare for cooking:
3 cups diced vegetables:
celery, carrots, onions,
potatoes
After the meat has cooked about
45 minutes, place the vegetables in
the roasting pan with:
An additional cup
vegetable stock
Cover and continue to cook meat
about 1 hour after adding vegetables,
or until the internal temperature of
the meat is 175° to 180°. Pour off and
reserve most of the liquid, and allow
meat and vegetables to glaze by baking them ▶ uncovered about 10 minutes longer. Meanwhile, make the
sauce. Degrease reserved liquid and
reduce it somewhat.
Season to taste

## LAMB FORESTIÈRE OR MOCK VENISON

About 8 Servings

Wipe with damp cloth:
A 5-lb. leg of lamb or
mutton
Marinate refrigerated 24 hours or
more in:
Buttermilk or Yogurt
Marinade, (II, 181)
turning occasionally.
Preheat oven to 450°.
Drain, wipe dry and lard meat,
550, with:

**Blanched salt pork or
bacon**

Put roast on a rack in a pan in the
oven and bake for 15 minutes. Add:

> 1/2 cup hot Vegetable
>   Stock, (II, 174)
> 1 bay leaf
> 2 small whole peeled onions

Cover. ♦ Reduce heat at once to 325°
and allow 35 minutes to the pound.
When roast is nearly done, degrease,
381. Pour over roast:

> 1 cup Sautéed
>   Mushrooms, 328
> 1 cup warm cultured sour
>   cream

Cook ♦ uncovered 10 minutes. Make:

> **Pan Gravy, 382**

Serve roast surrounded by:

> **Browned Potatoes, 348, or
>   Puréed Turnips, 284**

Garnish with:

> **Parsley**

## BRAISED LAMB SHANKS AND TROTTERS

**4 Servings**

Use shanks for stews also. Cooked as
for shanks, trotters or feet are not ap-
proved by the U.S. Government but
are still served abroad.
Rub:

> **4 lamb shanks: 3 1/2 to 4 lb.**

with:

> **Garlic**

Roll in:

> **Seasoned Flour, (II, 220)**

Melt until fragrant:

> **2 tablespoons vegetable oil**

Partially sear shanks and add:

> **2 tablespoons diced onions**

Continue to cook meat until browned
on all sides. Pour off fat. Place meat
on a rack in a lidded pan. Add:

> 1 1/2 cups boiling stock
> (1/2 cup lemon juice)
> 1/3 teaspoon pepper

> 1 1/2 teaspoons salt
> 1/2 bay leaf

Cover. ♦ Simmer meat or bake covered in a 325° oven about 1 1/2 hours
or until tender. You may add for the
last 1/2 hour of cooking:

> 3 cups diced vegetables
> 1/2 cup boiling stock or water

The vegetables may be onions, carrots, celery, green peppers, turnips,
tomatoes and potatoes—a matter of
choice and expediency. Strain, degrease and reduce stock. Serve as it is
or make:

> **Pan Gravy, 382**

If you have not added the vegetables,
you may serve the shanks with:

> **Creole Sauce, 394**

## LAMB STEW OR NAVARIN PRINTANIÈRE

**8 Servings**

This stew is called **printanière** because of its "springlike" host of
ornately cut vegetables. Cut into
1 1/2-inch pieces:

> 1 lb. boned shoulder of lamb
> 1 lb. boned breast of lamb

Brown the meat in a heavy skillet in:

> **2 tablespoons vegetable oil**

Remove meat to a Dutch oven. Pour
off fat and deglaze pan with:

> **2 cups light stock**

to which you may add:

> **2 tablespoons tomato paste**

Bring to a boil and pour over meat.
Simmer covered. Meanwhile, peel
and shape into ovals about 1 1/2 inches
long and reserve:

> 2 cups new potatoes
> 6 carrots
> 3 white turnips

Add:

> **18 small onions**

After lamb has cooked about 1 hour,
skim off fat, add vegetables to the pot
and simmer covered about 1 hour

longer or until vegetables are tender. Have ready to add:

> 1 cup cooked fresh peas
> 1 cup cooked sliced fresh
>   green beans

When lamb and vegetables are tender, skim off any fat and gently fold in cooked peas and beans. Serve at once, sprinkled with 1/2 cup finely chopped parsley.

## LAMB OR PORK GOULASH À BLANC

**6 Servings**

Please read About Goulash, 581. Sauté:

> 1 1/2 to 2 cups chopped onions

in:

> 1/2 cup butter or vegetable oil

Mash in a mortar and add:

> 1 teaspoon caraway
> 2 teaspoons marjoram
>   A grating of lemon rind
> 1 clove garlic
> 1 tablespoon sweet paprika

Add and bring to a boil:

> 1 cup water or stock

Add:

> 2 lb. lamb or pork, cut into
>   1 1/2-inch cubes

Simmer covered 1 1/2 hours. Garnish with:

> Slivered red or green
>   peppers

## IRISH STEW

**4 to 6 Servings**

This famous stew is not browned. Cut into 1 1/2-inch cubes:

> 1 1/2 lb. lamb or mutton

Peel and slice to 1/8-inch thickness:

> 3/4 cup onions
> 2 1/2 lb. potatoes

Put in the bottom of a heavy pan a layer of potatoes, a layer of meat, and a few slices of onion. Repeat this twice, ending with potatoes on top. Season each layer with:

> Salt and pepper

Add to the pot:

> 1 bay leaf

Pour over the layers:

> 2 cups boiling stock or water
> 2 tablespoons finely chopped
>   parsley

Bring to a boil. Cover and simmer gently about 2 1/2 hours or until the meat is tender. Shake pot periodically to keep the potatoes from sticking. When done, all the moisture should have been absorbed by the potatoes.

## CURRY OF LAMB WITH RICE

**4 Servings**

Remove gristle and fat from:

> A 2-lb. lamb shoulder

Cut meat into 1-inch cubes. Heat:

> 3 tablespoons fat or vegetable
>   oil

Brown meat in the hot fat with:

> 1 tablespoon chopped onion
> 1 tablespoon curry powder

Add:

> 1 cup Light Stock,
>   (II, 171–172)
> 1/4 cup or more chopped celery
> 2 tablespoons chopped parsley
> (1 tablespoon chopped
>   pimiento)
> (1/4 cup peeled, seeded, diced
>   cucumbers)

Cover meat and simmer until tender, about 1/2 hour. Stir frequently.

> **Season to taste**

Make:

> **Pan Gravy, 382**

Place on a platter a mound of:

> **Boiled Rice, 189**

Arrange meat and gravy around it. Garnish platter with:

> **Parsley**

CASSOULET

**About 15 Servings**

With a thicker texture than a Pot-au-Feu, 131, this controversial dish from the South of France has one solid pivot—white beans. They are cooked usually with fresh pork and sausage, but often with mutton and duck, partridge or potted goose, 533. Goose fat is a frequent component; also an onion stuck with cloves. Vegetables vary seasonally. Garlic is essential. For this recipe you almost need a routing sheet. If, however, you follow directions, you may proceed with the self-confidence of the bullfighter who put mustard on his sword. The beans soak overnight and are cooked the next day with meat and other trimmings. The pork roasts for a while before the lamb joins it. Then the meats that have been cooking with the beans are taken from the bone and sliced before being returned to the beans. This way the flavors unite in a single casserole and make a final triumphant appearance under a crust of golden crumbs.

Soak overnight in cold water:

**1 lb. dried marrowfat, broad
or Great Northern beans**

Roast in a preheated 350° oven about 2½ hours or until tender:

**3 lb. boned Loin of Pork, 601**

After the pork has been roasting for about 1 hour, brown in a heavy skillet:

**3 lb. rolled lamb shoulder
and the cut-out bones
1 tablespoon butter**

Drain off any excess fat. Roast the lamb and the lamb bones about 1½ hours longer in the same pan with the pork roast. Meanwhile, blanch, 106, by placing in cold water and bringing just to a boil:

**1 ham shank**

**1 lb. salt pork**

Drain beans. Heat the water in which they were soaked, adding:

**Enough water to make
4 quarts**

Bring to a boil and skim the pot. Add drained, blanched ham shank, salt pork and:

**A Bouquet Garni, (II, 253)
3 cloves garlic**

Simmer covered about 1½ hours. Add:

**6 small white onions
½ lb. hard Italian sausage,
like Salcisetta**

Simmer about 1 hour longer, until the beans are tender but still intact. Remove the lamb bones and, leaving the pork and lamb roasts in the same pan, reduce heat to 300°. Pour over the meat:

**Thickened Tomato
Sauce, 400**

and bake covered about ½ hour more. Drain off and reserve sauce and drippings. Remove and slice the meat of both the lamb and the pork roast. Drain beans, adding the juice to the drained tomato sauce. Trim and slice the ham, the sausage and the salt pork in bite-sized pieces. Layer all these meats with the beans in a casserole and skim excess fat from the combined tomato and bean juices before adding them to the other ingredients. Top with:

**1 cup buttered dry bread
crumbs**

Bake about 1 hour longer in the oven, when the crumbs should have turned a golden color.

COUSCOUS

**6 Servings**

Because this dish can be varied according to what ingredients are available and extended to serve any number, it is the classic main meal in

North Africa, where the hospitality of the Arab people is legendary. The one constant ingredient is the cereal—fine-grained semolina—cooked so that each grain is separate and the mass light and fluffy. For perfect results, the cooking vessel should be a "couscoussier" of pottery or—a modern version—of stainless steel, shown below with its removable perforated top and its deep stewpot. A muslin-lined colander over a heavy double-boiler bottom makes a fair substitute, provided the two parts of the cooker may be fitted so closely that vapor can escape only through the colander perforations, and the colander does not touch the liquid below. Since the cereal, after steaming, has a very bland, delicate flavor, the meat and

vegetable mixture is frequently sharpened with additional seasonings like cayenne or chili pepper; or a portion of the sauce is reserved, fired up and passed around for the stimulation of the more able-bodied guests. And every Arab is able-bodied when it comes to consuming hot sauce!

Soak overnight, drain and reserve:

> 1/3 **cup dried chick-peas**
> 1/2 **lb. dried fava beans**

Cut into a dozen or so good-sized chunks:

> 2 **lb. lamb; or 1 lb. lamb,**
> 1/2 **lb. beef, 1/2 chicken**

Place in the bottom element of the couscoussier the meat, beans and:

> 2 **cups sliced turnips, 372**
> 1 1/2 **cups sliced carrots**
> 3/4 **cup chopped onions**
> 1/4 **teaspoon black pepper**
> 1/2 **tablespoon salt**
> (1/4 **teaspoon saffron)**
> (1/2 **teaspoon turmeric)**
> (1/4 **teaspoon ginger)**
> 2 **to 3 cups stock, to cover**

Bring this mixture to a boil, ♦ reduce the heat, and simmer 40 minutes. Add:

> 2 **cups sliced zucchini or**
>    **yellow squash**
> 2 **quartered tomatoes or**
>    1/2 **cup tomato paste**
> 1 **small cabbage, quartered**
> (1 **stalk finocchio, quartered)**
> (3 **or 4 minced sweet peppers)**
> (1/4 **to** 1/2 **cup raisins)**
> 1/4 **cup chopped parsley**

and simmer 20 minutes longer. Ten minutes before the end of the above procedure, have ready in a large dish:

> 1 **lb. semolina**

Moisten the semolina slightly with a little cold water, working it with the fingers to keep it cohesive but not lumpy. The grains will swell. Place the cereal in the top or strainer element of the couscoussier and steam it, uncovered, over the simmering meat and vegetable mixture 30 minutes more.

Remove the couscoussier from the heat. Remove strainer and turn cereal into a large dish. Sprinkle it with cold water to enlarge the grains further, stirring with a wooden spoon to break up any lumps. Return cereal to strainer, and strainer to pot, ♦ fitting it on tightly. Simmer an additional 30 minutes. Remove the cereal to a large heated platter, mixing with it 2 tablespoons of fat scooped from the top of the stew. You may at this point remove one cupful of the stew liquid and "inflame" it with:

(¹/₄ **teaspoon cayenne, or red or
    chili pepper**)
(¹/₄ **teaspoon ginger**)
(¹/₂ **teaspoon harissa, or
    concentrate of red
    pimiento**)

Arrange the meat and vegetable mixture around the cereal, and serve the dish with the fiery sauce in one pitcher and the remaining sauce—partially defatted—in another.

## ABOUT PORK

Someone has observed that a pig resembles a saint in that he is more honored after death than during his lifetime. High-grade pork is fine-grained and firm, the shoulder cuts marbled, the fat white. Formerly, because of its heavy fat content, all parts of pork could be cooked by dry-heat methods, and the meat was virtually self-basting. Today, hogs are bred leaner, and some pork may require supplementary basting, or cooking by moist heat.

◖ An important word of caution. Incredible as it may seem at the end of the twentieth century, our government still has no requirement for the systematic microscopic inspection of pork. As long as this is true, the pork we buy as well as that from animals we raise ourselves may, under certain conditions, harbor the dangerous parasite that is passed on to man in the insidious disease called trichinosis. The only way to be certain that the parasite is destroyed is ◖ to cook pork thoroughly. The internal temperature must reach at least 137°. Judged by the eye, the meat must be white or grayish throughout, without a trace of pink, even in the very center of a large roast; the juices will run clear. Finally, ◖ never taste even a tiny bit of raw pork in any form, including bacon and sausage; and after handling it, carefully cleanse your hands and any knife, utensil or surface the pork may have touched. Slow cooking of pork is desirable, 30 to 45 minutes to the pound. Rolled and stuffed roasts require the longer cooking time. If you use a meat thermometer, the roasts of varying degrees of choiceness which come from the loin section—center cut, rib cut, loin end and blade or shoulder end—should be cooked to an internal temperature of 170°. The thicker roasts, which include leg of pork—known somewhat confusingly as fresh ham—and the shoulder, known as the picnic, are cooked to an internal temperature of 185°. Fresh ham may also be braised or pot-roasted. To identify those portions which cook by dry- or moist-heat methods, see diagram, 561. Generally, the recipes for each cut of meat calling for dry-heat methods are given first, followed by the recipes for moist-heat methods. For Economical Use of Large Cuts, see 562. For uses of cooked pork, see Brunch, Lunch and Supper Dishes, 236. For hams, see 610.

## PORK ROAST

Remove meat from refrigerator about 1 hour before cooking, and read About Pork, left.
Preheat oven to 450°.
Use a fine, juicy roast:

> **Loin or shoulder of pork**

If boned or rolled, the roast will take 5 to 10 minutes more per pound than the timing given below. Rub the roast well with:

> **A cut clove of garlic, fresh
> sage, dried rosemary,
> tarragon or thyme**

Dredge with:

> **Seasoned Flour, (II, 220)**

Place fat side up on a rack in a shallow greased pan in the oven. ♦ Reduce the heat at once to 325°. Cook ♦ uncovered 25 to 35 minutes to the pound, depending on cut and thickness of meat. The internal temperature should be 170° for a loin cut and 185° for a shoulder cut. Remove roast from oven and let rest 10 to 15 minutes before carving. In the meantime, make:

> **Pan Gravy, 382**

You may roast alongside the meat for the last 35 minutes of cooking:

> **Peeled and parboiled sweet potatoes or parsnips**

or on top of the roast:

> **Prunes and apricots or Orange Marmalade, (II, 673)**

or serve the roast with:

> **Applesauce, (II, 118), seasoned with 2 tablespoons horseradish and a grating of nutmeg**
> **Sweet Potatoes and Fruit, 356**
> **Apples with Sauerkraut, (II, 118), or other sauerkraut variations**
> **Onion and Apple Casserole, 337**

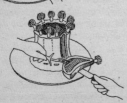

> **Turnips and apples**
> **Puréed Green Beans, Peas or Limas, 284**

## CROWN ROAST OF PORK

> **Allow 2 Ribs per Person**

Remove meat from refrigerator about 1 hour before cooking.
Preheat oven to 450°.
Wipe with a cloth:

> **A crown roast of pork**

Protect the ends of the bones by covering with aluminum foil. Immediately after putting the roast in the oven ♦ reduce the heat to 325°, allowing 25 to 30 minutes to the pound. If the crown is not to be filled with dressing, omit covering the bones and cook the roast upside down. Serve filled with a cooked vegetable; or, if the roast is to be stuffed, remove it 1 hour before it is done and fill the center with:

> **Stuffing for Crown Roast of Pork, 433, or Sausage Dressing, 433, or Apple and Onion Dressing, 434, or Chestnut Dressing, 433**

Return the roast to the oven and complete cooking. Make:

> **Pan Gravy, 382**

Serve with:

> **Glazed Onions, 335**
> **Apples Cockaigne, (II, 118)**
> **Watercress or broiled canned apricots and crystallized ginger slices**

To carve, see sketch, left.

## ROAST SUCKLING PIG

> **10 Servings**

We never think of suckling pig without recalling our friend Amy, an American, long a resident of Mexico but determined to reconstruct in alien surroundings the traditional Christmas dinners of her youth. Describing the preparation of roast pig to her skilled Indian cook, she wound up with the announcement, "The pig is brought to table on plenty of greenery, with an apple in the mouth." The cook looked first baffled, then resentful, and finally burst out with a succession of "no's." Her employer persisted patiently with helpful gestures and increasing firmness. When the pig was served, she discovered that her cook could effect an entrée which surpassed her wildest expectations. There was plenty of greenery and a distinct air of martyrdom; but the apple was clenched, not in the pig's mouth, but in that of the desperate cook!

Preheat oven to 450°.

Dress, by drawing, scraping as for Opossum, 664, and cleaning as for Rabbit, 661:

**A suckling pig**

Remove eyeballs and lower the lids. The dressed pig should weigh about 12 pounds. Fill it with:

**Onion Dressing, 433, or Stuffing for Crown Roast of Pork, 433**

It takes 2½ quarts of dressing to stuff a pig this size. Multiply all your ingredients, but not the seasonings. Use these sparingly until dressing is combined, then taste it and add what is lacking. Sew up the pig. Put a block of wood in its mouth to hold it open. Skewer legs into position, pulling forelegs forward and bending hindlegs into a crouching stance. Rub the pig with:

**Oil or soft butter**
**(A cut clove of garlic)**

Dredge it with:

**Flour**

Cover ears and tail with aluminum foil. Place the pig in a pan ◗ uncovered, in the oven for 15 minutes.

◗ Reduce heat to 325° and roast until tender, allowing 20 minutes to the pound. Baste every 15 minutes with:

**Pan drippings or additional vegetable oil if necessary**

Remove foil from ears and tail. Rest 30 minutes before carving. Place pig on a platter. Remove wood from mouth. Replace with:

**A small apple, lemon or carrot**

Place in the eyes:

**Raisins or cranberries**

Drape around the neck a wreath of:

**Small green leaves**

or garnish the platter or board with:

**Watercress**

The pig may be surrounded with:

**Apples Cockaigne, (II, 118), Sweet Potatoes and Fruit, 356, Apples Stuffed with Mincemeat, (II, 630), or Tomatoes Florentine, 384**

Make:

**Pan Gravy, 382**

To carve, place head to left of carver. Remove forelegs and hams. Divide meat down center of back. Separate ribs. Serve a section of crackling skin to each person.

## ROAST FRESH HAM OR LEG OF PORK

You may place a fresh leg of pork called:

**A fresh ham**

in a marinade, (II, 180), and refrigerate covered for 24 to 48 hours. Preheat oven to 450°. Wipe the meat before roasting. Marinated or not, cook the ham as for:

**Pork Loin Roast, 601**

basting every half hour with part of the marinade or with the traditional:

**(Beer)**

When done, the internal temperature should be 185°. Make:

**Pan Gravy, 382**

Serve with any of the accompaniments suggested in Pork Roast, 601. Leftover cold pork is a luxury to be used in many dishes, see Index.

## PORK ROAST STUFFED WITH SAUERKRAUT

Preheat oven to 450°.
Have butcher remove bones from:

**A pork shoulder**

Also have one side left open for inserting:

**Drained sauerkraut**

Dredge with:

**Flour**

Close opening by sewing or skewering. Place the roast in the oven uncovered on a rack in a greased pan. ◗ Immediately reduce heat to 325° and bake about 40 minutes to the pound.

## PORK TENDERLOIN

Preheat oven to 350°.
Split lengthwise:

**A pork tenderloin**

Flatten it with a cleaver, 550. Rub lightly with:

**Butter**
**(Garlic)**

Spread with:

**Bread Dressing, 431, using**
**¼ the amount; or with**
**Sweet Potato and Apple**
**Dressing, 437, using about**
**⅓ the amount; or with**
**stewed drained apricots or**
**pitted prunes**

Roll and tie it up. Dredge with:

**Seasoned Flour, (II, 220)**

or brush with unsalted fat. Place tenderloin on rack in greased pan.

Bake 30 to 35 minutes to the pound. Make:

**Pan Gravy, 382**

You may add to the gravy:

**(Cultured sour cream and**
**cooked mushrooms, or**
**sweet cream and currant**
**jelly)**

## FRENCHED PORK TENDERLOIN

Cut crosswise into ¾-inch slices:

**Pork tenderloin**

Flatten slices slightly with a cleaver, as shown on 550. Dredge with:

**Seasoned Flour, (II, 220)**

Sauté as for:

**Pork Chops, 605**

Add to the pan juices or the gravy:

**½ teaspoon grated lemon rind**

## PORK TENDERLOIN WITH MUSHROOMS AND OLIVES

**4 Servings**

Cut into 1-inch crosswise slices and pound:

**1 lb. or more pork tenderloin**

Roll in:

**Seasoned Flour, (II, 220)**

Sauté until golden in:

**2 tablespoons butter**

with:

**A sliced onion**

Bring just to the boiling point:

**½ cup dry white wine**

Pour over the meat. Add at this time:

**½ lb. sliced mushrooms**
**(⅛ teaspoon fresh rosemary, or**
**¼ teaspoon crushed**
**coriander seed)**

Cover the skillet closely. ◗ Simmer the rounds until done, about 45 minutes. Add:

**6 sliced green olives, stuffed**
**with almonds**
**(2 tablespoons lemon juice)**

Serve garnished with:

2 **tablespoons chopped**
  **parsley**

## PORK CHOPS

### I. Sautéed

Brown in a hot pan in just enough
vegetable oil or rendered pork fat to
keep them from sticking:

  **Pork chops, 1 inch thick or**
  **less**

Before searing, they may be rubbed
with:

  **(Garlic or powdered**
  **rosemary)**

After searing ♦ reduce heat. Cook the
chops slowly, covered or uncovered,
until done. Pour off excess grease as
they cook. Season with:

  **Salt and pepper**

Make:

  **Pan Gravy, 382**

### II. Baked

Recommended for thick chops.
Preheat oven to 350°.
After searing them as above, bake
covered about 1 hour:

  4 **pork chops**

During the last half hour, you may
add for seasoning:

  (3 **tablespoons minced green**
   **pepper and celery)**
  (1 **clove garlic)**
  (1 **piece gingerroot mashed in**
   **1 tablespoon vinegar)**
  (3 **slices orange)**
  (¹/₂ **cup orange juice)**

## BREADED PORK CHOPS

  **4 Servings**

Rub with garlic:

  4 **half-inch thick pork chops**

Bread them, (II, 220). Using a heavy
hot pan, brown lightly in:

  2 **to 3 tablespoons rendered**
  **pork fat or vegetable oil**

Reduce heat. Cook uncovered about
20 minutes longer or until tender.
Make:

  **Pan Gravy, 382**

## BRAISED PORK CHOPS WITH FRUIT

  **Allow 1 Chop per Person**

Preheat oven to 325°.
Sear in a lightly greased hot skillet:

  **Trimmed pork chops,**
  ³/₄ **inch thick or more**

Season lightly with:

  **Salt and pepper**
  (¹/₈ **teaspoon curry powder)**

Place on the chops, skin side down:

  **Halved cored apples,**
  **pineapple slices or pitted**
  **apricots or prunes**

Fill the centers of the fruit with:

  **Brown sugar**

Cover the bottom of the skillet to
¹/₂ inch with:

  **Chicken stock and/or some**
  **of the fruit juice**

Cover the pan closely. Bake about
1 hour. Remove the chops from the
pan carefully, so as not to disturb the
fruit. Keep warm. Partially degrease
and add to the pan juices:

  ³/₄ **to 1 cup sweet cream or**
  **cultured sour cream**

Serve this sauce with the chops and
fruit.

## BRAISED STUFFED PORK CHOPS COCKAIGNE

  **6 Servings**

Preheat oven to 350°.
Cut from the bone:

  6 **rib pork chops about 1 inch**
  **thick**

Trim off excess fat and cut a large
gash or pocket in the side of each
chop. Prepare a dressing of:

  1 **cup bread crumbs**

¼ cup chopped celery
¼ cup chopped onions
2 tablespoons chopped
   parsley
Milk to moisten the
   dressing
¼ teaspoon salt
⅛ teaspoon paprika

These proportions and ingredients may be varied. Fill the pockets with the dressing. Skewer them. Sear the chops in a hot skillet and place in a lidded ovenproof dish with:

Milk or stock, about
¼ inch deep

Cover and bake about 1 hour and 15 minutes or until tender. Make:

Pan Gravy, 382

or serve with:

Cranberry Sauce, (II, 123)

## BRAISED PORK CHOPS WITH SAUERKRAUT

**6 Servings**

Preheat oven to 350°.
Have ready:

6 slices diced Sautéed
   Bacon, 615

Mix it in a casserole with:

2 lb. drained sauerkraut
2 cups Applesauce, (II, 118)
1 tablespoon brown sugar
¼ cup dry white wine
½ tablespoon dry mustard
¼ teaspoon freshly ground
   pepper

Sauté gently on both sides:

6 loin pork chops, 1 inch
   thick

Place them on top of the mixture. Cover and bake about 1 hour.

## BRAISED PORK CHOPS CREOLE

**6 Servings**

Preheat oven to 350°.
Dredge:

6 pork chops, ½ inch thick or
   more

with:

Seasoned Flour, (II, 220)

Gently sauté them in:

Hot fat or vegetable oil

Place them in a baking dish. Combine, heat and pour around them:

1 can condensed tomato
   soup: 10½ oz.
½ can water or stock
½ cup chopped celery
1 chopped green pepper,
   seeds and membrane
   removed
¾ cup minced onions
½ teaspoon salt
¼ teaspoon paprika

Bake covered about 1 hour. Cook another 15 minutes ▶ uncovered and topped with:

Crushed cornflakes

## BRAISED DEVILED PORK CHOPS

**4 Servings**

Using:

Pork Marinade, (II, 182)

marinate 3 to 6 hours, covered and refrigerated:

4 pork chops, 1 inch thick

Preheat oven 325°.
Drain the chops, reserving the marinade. Wipe them dry. Brown them in a hot greased skillet. Heat the marinade and:

½ cup water or stock

Pour around the chops. Bake covered about 1 hour or until tender.

## PORK BIRDS

**6 Servings**

Pound to the thickness of ¼ inch:

2 lb. pork steaks cut from the
   shoulder

Cut them into 6 oblong pieces. Spread them with half the recipe for:

**Apricot or**
**Prune Dressing, 436**

Roll them. Secure the rolls with string or wooden picks. Dredge in:

**2 tablespoons flour**

Brown in:

**2 tablespoons fat**

Add:

**1 cup boiling water or stock**

Simmer covered about 50 minutes or until tender. Serve with the degreased and reduced pan juices, or thicken to make:

**Pan Gravy, 382**

## SWEET AND SOUR PORK

**6 Servings**

**I.** Cut into 1/2-inch strips, 2 inches long:

**2 lb. lean boneless pork loin**
**or shoulder**

In a wok or skillet, brown the meat in:

**2 tablespoons hot vegetable**
**oil**

Drain the meat on paper toweling. Cook the following sauce until slightly thickened and clear:

**1 cup pineapple juice**
**1/2 cup water or chicken stock**
**1/3 cup vinegar**
**1/4 cup packed brown sugar**
**2 tablespoons cornstarch**
**2 tablespoons soy sauce**
**2 teaspoons Worcestershire**
**sauce**

Add the meat and simmer, covered, about 1 hour or until tender. Add:

**1 1/2 cups pineapple chunks**
**1 small sliced green pepper,**
**seeds and membrane**
**removed**
**(1/4 cup onion slices)**

Cook uncovered about 10 minutes. Serve over:

**Boiled Rice, 189**

## II. Stir-Fried

This quick version is best used with very thinly sliced raw pork or larger pieces of cooked pork. Prepare:

**Oriental Sweet-Sour**
**Sauce II, 405**

Cut into strips 1/4 inch thick and about 1/2 inch wide:

**2 lb. lean boneless pork**

Dust pieces with:

**Seasoned Flour, (II, 220)**

Sauté meat, a little at a time, in a wok or skillet in:

**2 to 3 tablespoons vegetable**
**oil**

Return all the meat to the skillet and add the above sauce. Cover and simmer about 5 to 8 minutes. A good addition at this time would be:

**(Cooked Podded Peas, 339)**

Serve over:

**Boiled Rice, 189**

## PORK AND VEAL GOULASH WITH SAUERKRAUT

**4 Servings**

Sauté until translucent:

**6 tablespoons chopped**
**onions**

in:

**2 tablespoons butter or**
**vegetable oil**

Add and sauté:

**1/2 lb. 1-inch lean pork cube~**
**1/2 lb. 1-inch veal cubes**

Heat and add:

**1 lb. drained sauerkraut**
**1 teaspoon caraway seed**

Simmer covered about 1 hour. Heat and add:

**1 cup cultured sour cream**
**A generous grating of**
**freshly ground pepper**

Serve at once.

## ABOUT SPARERIBS

There is much bone and little meat to spareribs—we love the self-explanatory name. ◗ Allow at least 1 pound per person. Country-style back ribs, also sold as spareribs, are meatier. Try using spareribs in some of the recipes calling for pork chops. These gloriously messy old favorites can simply be baked in a 325° oven about 1¹/₂ hours, but there are a good many more lively things to do with them. Before both baking and barbecuing, we recommend parboiling, 106, 2 to 4 minutes, which not only removes unwanted fat but makes the end result more palatable.

Comparatively little known but quite delicious are lamb spareribs. They need not be parboiled but in other respects may be prepared as for pork spareribs, except that cooking time should be reduced about one-third. For Glazed Cocktail Ribs, see (II, 95).

## BAKED SPARERIBS WITH APPLE-ONION DRESSING

**4 Servings**

Preheat oven to 500°.
Parboil 2 minutes:

**4 lb. spareribs**

Cut into 2 pieces. Spread 1 piece with:

**Apple and
Onion Dressing, 434**

using only 4 cups of dressing. Cover the dressing with the other piece of meat. Tie the 2 pieces together. Rub the outside of the meat with:

**2 tablespoons flour**
**¹/₈ teaspoon salt**
**A few grains pepper**

Place on a rack in an uncovered roasting pan and ◗ reduce the heat at once to 325°. Bake about 1¹/₂ hours or until tender. Baste every 10 minutes with the fat in the pan.

## SWEET-SOUR SPARERIBS

**4 Servings**

Preheat oven to 350°.
Have a butcher cut into 2-inch pieces:

**4 lb. spareribs**

Parboil, 106, 3 to 4 minutes. Drain and dry. Brush with:

**Soy sauce**

Bake uncovered on a rack in a pan in the oven 1 hour. Have ready the following sauce. Boil briefly:

**1 cup vinegar**
**1 cup sugar**
**¹/₂ cup sherry**
**2 tablespoons soy sauce**
**2 teaspoons grated fresh
ginger**

Mix together and add:

**4 teaspoons cornstarch**
**2 tablespoons water**

Cook until cornstarch is transparent. Pour the sauce over the cooked spareribs and serve at once with:

**Baked Green Rice, 191**

## ▤ BARBECUED SPARERIBS

### I. Indoors

Bake spareribs in a 450° oven 15 minutes, covered with aluminum foil—do not seal. ◗ Reduce heat to 350° and pour a barbecue sauce over the meat. Bake 1 hour longer, basting frequently. Try one of the following sauces:

**Barbecue Sauce I or II, 404**
**Oriental Sweet-Sour
Sauce, 405**
**Ferocious Barbecue
Sauce, 404**
**Mexican Tomato Sauce, 401**
**Plum Sauce, 406**

### II. Outdoors

Please read About Outdoor Cooking, 108, and also note illustration of ribs woven on a spit, 113.

Season:

**2 sides spareribs**

with:

**Salt and pepper**

Grill very slowly 30 minutes, then brush with one of the sauces, 608, and continue to cook about 1 hour longer. Turn occasionally and brush with more sauce, until done.

## BOILED SPARERIBS

Place:

**Spareribs**

in:

**Boiling water to cover**

Add:

**Salt and pepper**
**Chopped onion, celery, parsley and carrots**
**(1 teaspoon caraway seed)**

▶ Simmer the meat covered until tender, 1½ to 2 hours. If you care to crisp the ribs, drain well and just before serving sauté them in butter. Or simply drain and serve on a mound of hot:

**Sauerkraut or Red Cabbage, 308**

surrounded by:

**Mashed Potatoes, 344, or Purée of Lentils, 295**

## STEWED PORK NECK BONES

Partly cover with seasoned boiling water:

**Pork neck bones**

Simmer covered until tender, about 1½ hours. Vegetables may be added to the stew for the last ½ hour of cooking.

## STEWED PORK HOCKS

Cover with seasoned boiling water:

**Pork hocks**

Simmer covered 1½ to 3 hours. You may add potatoes for the last ½ hour of cooking, or greens or cabbage for the last 20 minutes. Or marinate the cooled cooked hocks 2 hours or more in:

**Herbed French Dressing, 414**

and serve cold with a salad.

## SALT PORK IN MILK GRAVY

**4 Servings**

Dip thin slices of:

**1 lb. salt pork**

in:

**Boiling water**

Drain and dip in:

**Cornmeal**

Brown slowly in a skillet, turning frequently until cooked through. Remove salt pork and all but 2 tablespoons drippings. Add and sauté until golden:

**1 to 2 tablespoons chopped onion**

Thicken drippings with:

**2 tablespoons flour, see Pan Gravy, 382**

Blend in slowly:

**1 cup milk**

Serve with:

**Corn Bread, (II, 341), and Greens, 324**

## ABOUT DESALTING HAM AND OTHER CURED MEAT

Because of the prevalence of refrigeration, ham and Canadian bacon, tongue, corned beef, pastrami and salt pork are today subjected to much weaker brining than formerly. But all of these salted meats, while relished for their pungent flavors, are, like brined vegetables, less valuable nutritionally than when they are fresh. If the meats have been heavily pickled, (II, 633), or aged—like "old" or country hams, 613—be sure to soak 12 hours, allowing 1 quart of water to 1 pound of cured meat. Or ♦ parblanch, 106, before cooking. After blanching, put the meat into rapidly boiling water, bring to a boil again and ♦ at once reduce heat to a simmer. Salted meats are always simmered à blanc, 555. Cook ♦ uncovered until tender. Time indications are noted in the individual recipes.

## ABOUT HAMS

Someone defined eternity as a ham and two people. The definition probably dates from the days when the term applied only to the small mountain of meat we now call a whole ham—the cured and smoked hind of a hog. Now that there is a wide variety of cuts and sizes available, eternity has somewhat shortened. To identify cuts and use them economically, see 561 and 562.

Pork becomes ham after undergoing a thorough processing which includes curing with salt, smoking and sometimes aging. Years ago these processes were necessary to preserve the meat. Nowadays it is taste and convenience that govern processing, and often the packer keeps his method a well-guarded secret. Curing, a process that uses salt to retard the growth of bacteria, may be done by one or a combination of three methods: dry-curing—in which salt and spices are rubbed directly into the meat—the method recommended for home processing, (II, 632); immersion of the pork in a brine and spice solution; or injection of a brine solution into the meat itself—the curing method usually used in commercial packing today.

The second step in processing—smoking—is what adds flavor, color and character to a ham. Smoking—often skipped for mild-tasting precooked hams—is done in a hot, airtight smokehouse, and flavor depends on the wood used, hickory being an old favorite. The U.S. Department of Agriculture requires that ham labeled "ready-to-eat" prior to being sold must have been exposed to an internal temperature of 140° for half an hour to destroy the dangerous trichina parasite. Light smoking accomplishes this, and produces a mildly flavored, juicy ham. Heavy and long smoking is used for such specialty hams as the domestic Smithfield and the European prosciutto and Westphalian, which are dryer and of a deeper color and richer flavor, having undergone, besides curing and smoking, a long and painstaking aging process—up to a year. These steps cause these "old" hams to shrink in size and to go up in price.

What pigs are fed produces nuances of flavor in hams from one area to another. Eighty percent of American hogs are corn-fed, but the mainstay of a porker's menu can also be acorns or peaches or peanuts—the last being the diet of the famous Smithfield hogs of Virginia and North Carolina. German pigs that produce the aged Westphalian hams thrive on a diet of sugar beets, while Italian pigs whose meat will in time become the delicacy called prosciutto are fed chestnuts or—in the Parma region—whey from the local cheese. These European hams are succulent and translucent and need no further preparation after their long aging; when sliced paper-thin they have a flavor and texture reminiscent of smoked salmon.

**Fresh ham** is a misnomer; it is in reality simply a pork roast—the hind leg which has not been cured or smoked. Today there are many cuts of ham with a confusing variety of names. Ham is usually labeled one of two ways: "Cook Before Eating" or "Ready to Eat." Whatever cut you buy, ♦ follow scrupulously the packer's instructions on the label. "Cook before eating" hams need roasting to an internal temperature of 160°. "Ready to eat" hams—also called "fully cooked" or "ready to serve"—may be eaten cold, as is, with no further preparation; but they will taste and look better if heated thoroughly, to an internal temperature of 140°, and glazed, 426, during the latter part of cooking.

Less frequently prepared in this instant-everything age is a third type of ham, the old-time **country ham,** or Virginia, Kentucky or Tennessee ham. The prototype of the country types is the Smithfield ham; all country hams are dry-cured and heavily salted and require soaking followed by long simmering, see Country Hams, 613. The flavor and aroma of these hams are worth the extra time and effort.

The wide assortment of **canned hams** now available offers the instant convenience one needs when the house is suddenly flooded with unexpected guests. When you buy canned ham, ♦ check the label for perishability and need of refrigeration. Most of the larger canned hams, including the superior qualities imported from Denmark, Holland and Poland, must be kept under refrigeration before opening, and can be stored thus for a few months. Some of the smaller canned hams can be stored without refrigeration. These hams have been sterilized in the canning process, but texture and taste are the losers in this overcooking process. Canned hams are usually sold under a manufac-

turer's label, and only by sampling various brands will you eventually reach the stage where purchasing one is not buying a pig in a poke.

A few basic cuts of ham to be found under various names in the market are described here with suggestions as to yield and uses. The whole ham, a 10- to 15-pound hind leg of pork, with bone intact, is the most flavorful and least wasteful cut. It will serve 20 to 30 people generously, probably with leftovers. A short plump shape, with a stubby rather than elongated shank or pointed end, is the better choice. For average families, it is more usual to buy a cut section of the whole ham, either the rounded part called the butt portion—the upper thigh of the animal—or the lower shank end. The butt half is somewhat more meaty but more difficult to carve. A 5- to 7-pound shank end will serve 10 to 12 people. From the flat cut end of either butt or shank, several slices or individual ham steaks may be removed for separate cooking.

Ham is available in many boneless forms—whole, in halves or in chunks of various sizes. After boning, the meat may be shaped by the packer or rolled and packaged in airtight wrappers or cans. These forms may lack the flavor of ham with the bone intact and are more expensive. ♦ Allow one-third pound per serving.

The smoked shoulder of pork, also known as picnic or Calais—"cally"— is a less expensive cut, but because it contains more fat, bone and skin in proportion to lean meat, you must figure ♦ almost a pound of roast shoulder per serving.

The smoked shoulder butt is a boneless cut from the neck and shoulder of the hog and may have several aliases: Boston butt, cottage ham or daisy ham. Though tender and tasty, it may be very fatty. A long narrow piece is usually preferable to a short plump selection, and ◗ will serve 3 or 4 people. Cut into slices, it makes a delicious alternative to bacon. It may be broiled, sautéed, roasted or simmered.

Ham should be served warm or cool, but never chilled. If a rainbow iridescence appears on sliced ham, it is merely due to light refraction on the fat film. To store ham, the rule is that all hams must be kept refrigerated, with two exceptions: small unopened canned ham not labeled perishable, and dry-cured ham—the country or Smithfield type—which can be kept in a cool, dry, dark place—or in the refrigerator. For best results, uncanned whole hams should not be stored longer than a week in the refrigerator before cooking; smaller portions not longer than 3 to 5 days. Sliced ham is best used within 2 days. Freezing any ham is not recommended because of rapid deterioration in quality and flavor, and canned ham is especially vulnerable because of its high water content.

## BAKED HAM

◗ Please read About Hams, 610, to determine the type of ham and the number of servings.

### I. Ham labeled "Cook Before Eating"

Preheat oven to 325°.

Place ham on a rack, uncovered, in a shallow pan. For a whole 10- to 15-pound ham, allow 18 to 20 minutes per pound; for a half—5 to 7 pounds—about 20 minutes per pound. For a shank or butt portion weighing 3 to 4 pounds, bake about 35 minutes to the pound. Or, in all

cases, cook until internal temperature reaches 160°. Remove rind and excess fat and serve with:

> **Raisin Sauce, 407; Sour Cream Horseradish Dressing, 408; Barbecue Sauce, 404; Hot Cumberland Sauce I, 407; or Sauce Dijonnaise, 385**

Or, if you prefer an attractive, quick finish, use:

> **Spirit Glaze for Ham, 427**

Suggested accompaniments are:

> **Scalloped Potatoes, 345; or a barquette of Puréed Chestnuts, 284**

To decorate and carve a whole ham, see sketches above. To carve the butt end, see below.

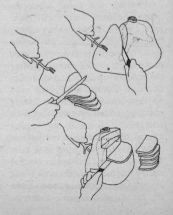

## II. Ham labeled "Fully Cooked" or "Ready to Eat"

Preheat oven to 325°.

To heat the ham, place it on a rack, uncovered, in a shallow pan. For a whole ham, allow 15 to 18 minutes to the pound; for a half, 18 to 24 minutes per pound. The ham will be ready when internal temperature reaches 140°.

Remove ham from the oven about 1/2 hour before it is done. While preparing it for glazing, increase oven heat to 425°. Remove rind, all but a collar around the shank bone. Cut diagonal gashes across the fat top side of the ham, in diamond shapes, and cover this surface with:

> 1 1/3 cups brown sugar
> 2 teaspoons dry mustard
> 1/3 cup fine bread crumbs

moistened with:

> 3 tablespoons cider vinegar, prune juice, wine, or ham drippings

Stud fat at intersections of each diamond with:

> Whole cloves

Or decorate as shown on 612 with:

> Alternating 1/2 pineapple rings studded with cranberries and stars cut from preserved orange peels

♦ Reduce oven heat again to 325° and return ham to oven about 30 minutes. Place on platter. Garnish with:

> Jellied cranberry slices topped with thin orange or pineapple slices

or with already cooked:

> Sweet Potatoes and Apples, 356

## COUNTRY HAMS: VIRGINIA, SMITHFIELD, KENTUCKY, ETC.

Please read about country hams, 611. To prepare a country ham, soak it in cold water to cover 24 to 36 hours. Then scrub it well, using a brush and yellow soap, if necessary, to remove the mold. Rinse thoroughly and place in a kettle of simmering well-seasoned water to cover. Simmer 20 minutes to the pound or until the meat reaches an internal temperature of 150°. Add to the water before the last quarter of cooking time:

> 1 quart cider
> 1/4 cup brown sugar

Drain when cooking time has elapsed. Remove skin while ham is still warm, being careful not to tear fat. Trim fat partially. Dust the ham with a mixture of:

> Freshly ground black pepper
> Cornmeal
> Brown sugar

Place ham in a preheated 425° oven long enough to glaze. Serve warm or cold. Be sure to slice ♦ very, very thin.

## BROILED HAM

> Allow 1/3 Pound per Person

Preheat broiler.

Slash in several places the fat edge of:

> A piece of ham, about 1 inch thick

Place it on a broiler rack, 3 inches below heating unit. Broil 8 to 12 minutes to a side. After cooking it on one side and turning, you may brush it, toward the end of cooking, with a mixture of:

> 1 teaspoon dry mustard
> 1 tablespoon lemon juice
> 1/4 cup grape jelly

If you do not use the glaze, a traditional accompaniment is:

## SAUTÉED HAM AND EGGS

Trim the edges of:

**A thin slice of smoked ham**

Rub a skillet with ham fat. Heat it. Brown ham lightly on one side, then the other. Remove to a hot platter. ♦ Reduce the heat. Sauté gently in the tried-out ham fat:

**Eggs, 212**

## CASSEROLED HAM SLICES

**2 to 3 Servings**

Appetizing dishes variously flavored are easily made from raw ham slices. Preheat oven to 350°.

Place in a casserole:

**A slice of smoked ham, about 1 inch thick**

Pour over ham:

**Barbecue Sauce I or II, 404, or Hot Cumberland Sauce I, 407**

Bake covered until tender, about 1 hour.

## HAM SLICE WITH FRUIT

**2 to 3 Servings**

Ham and fruit truly complement each other. You may arrange the fruit either between layers and on top of several ham slices or just on top of a single slice.

Preheat oven to 325°.

If the ham is not fatty, grease the bottom of a casserole lightly. Place in it:

**A slice of ham, about 1 inch thick**

sparingly seasoned with:

**(Prepared mustard)**

Cover ham with fruit seasoned to taste:

**Cranberries, sliced apples or oranges**

sprinkled with:

**Brown sugar or honey**

Or cover with drained:

**Slices of canned pineapple, apricots, peaches, red plums, prunes, cherries or raisins**

These may be sprinkled with:

**Cinnamon, cloves or curry powder**

Cover casserole. Baste several times with the pot juices or additional:

**Fruit juice, sherry or cider**

Bake about 45 minutes or until tender. Uncover for the last 10 minutes of cooking. Serve with:

**Mashed Sweet Potatoes, 355**

## HAM BAKED WITH TOMATOES AND CHEESE

**2 to 3 Servings**

Preheat oven to 350°.

Place in a baking dish:

**A slice of ham, about 1 inch thick**

Pour over it:

**1 cup seeded, chopped, drained canned tomatoes**

Cover the dish. Bake the ham until tender, about 45 minutes. For the last 15 minutes of cooking, uncover the dish and sprinkle over ham:

**¼ cup grated Parmesan cheese**

## HAM BUTT, SHANK OR PICNIC HAM

Use these comparatively small cuts of ham as a substitute for the corned beef in:

**New England Boiled Dinner, 584**

Cook ham until nearly tender or until

the internal temperature reaches 160°. Add vegetables the last half hour of cooking.

## SMOKED SHOULDER BUTT OR COTTAGE HAM

This cut may be boned. You may cut slices from this piece for broiling or sautéing, or roast or "boil" it.

## HAM HOCKS WITH SAUERKRAUT

A tasty dish rather heavy in fat.
Rinse and put in a pot half filled with cold water:

> 4 smoked pork hocks

Add:

> 1 sliced onion
> 1 bay leaf

Cover the pot and ♦ simmer about 1½ hours. Turn the hocks several times during this period. Drain. Return the hocks to the pot with one cup of the drained, degreased liquid and:

> 1½ to 2 lb. drained sauerkraut
> 2 large cored sliced apples
> 1 teaspoon celery seed

Cover and simmer about 30 minutes more, stirring with a fork several times during this period. Serve with:

> **Mashed Potatoes, 344**

## ABOUT BACON

Thinly sliced bacon with a good proportion of lean striping, cured without excessive salt, is not easy to come by; the new packaging may help. But no matter how packaged, bacon remains flavorful for only about a week, even if refrigerated. It is a sobering fact that unless you use the rendered grease, you are eating only one-fifth of what you buy.

In separating raw bacon slices, sticking may be avoided if two or three slices are removed at a time and then subdivided into singles. ♦ Allow about 2 slices per person. To oven-broil bacon, begin with a cold grid; or, if you are sautéing it, place it in a cold skillet. We have found these methods prevent curling and work better than weighted covers or specialized gadgets. Keep heat low and check constantly: bacon burns in seconds, and old bacon twice as fast as fresh.

The usual bacon is the cured smoked sliced abdominal wall of pork; **Canadian bacon,** on the contrary, is the eye of the loin—which accounts for its leanness, its lack of layering and its high cost. It should be treated like ham. In England a side of bacon is called a **gammon,** and a slice or a portion is a **rasher.**

## BAKED BACON

The preferred method for bacon in quantity.
Preheat oven to 350°.
Place on a cold grid over a drip pan:

> **Strips of bacon**

If they are hard to separate, place in a slightly warm pan the entire block of strips you will need, and as they heat, slide them apart. Bake until crisp, 10 to 15 minutes. No turning is necessary. Drain on paper toweling.

## SAUTÉED BACON

Place in a cold skillet:

> **Strips of bacon**

Sauté slowly until done. You may spoon off the drippings while cooking. Turn frequently. Place between paper towels to drain.

CANADIAN BACON

**I.** Place in boiling water to cover:

**1 lb. or more Canadian bacon**

Simmer until tender, about 1 hour.

**8 Servings**

**II.** Preheat oven to 325°.

Bake uncovered 1 hour:

**2-lb. piece of Canadian bacon**

Baste every 15 minutes with:

**¹/₂ cup pineapple or other acid fruit juice, dry sherry, cider or ginger ale**

Combine:

**¹/₂ cup brown sugar**
**¹/₂ teaspoon dry mustard**
**2 tablespoons fine bread crumbs**
**1 tablespoon cider vinegar**

Spread the mixture over the bacon. Bake about 15 minutes more or until sugar has glazed.

**III.** Place in a heavy skillet:

**¹/₈- to ¹/₄-inch slices Canadian bacon**

Cook them over low heat for 3 to 5 minutes. Turn frequently. When done, the lean part is a red brown and the fat a light golden brown. Serve with:

**Hot Cumberland Sauce I, 407, or Raisin Sauce, 407**

## ABOUT GROUND MEAT AND HAMBURGER

Merchants of the German port of Hamburg, through centuries of trade with Estonians, Latvians and Finns, had acquired the Baltic taste for scraped raw beef; but it was not until the St. Louis World's Fair in 1904 that broiled, bunned beef was introduced to the rest of the world by the Germans of South St. Louis as hamburger. Americans quickly latched on to the hamburger as their all-time favorite; for a bustling people it offered a combination of convenience, economy and tasty nourishment that seemed just what the doctor ordered. As a matter of fact, it was. Its more glamorous hotel-menu name, Salisbury steak, harks back to the end-of-the-century London physician, Dr. J. H. Salisbury, who invented a regimen based on broiled lean minced beef three times a day. Nowadays, alas, some American children are unconsciously such fans of Dr. Salisbury's diet that they will eat nothing else; one desperate mother we know has dubbed it "the daily grind."

According to federal ruling, ground beef sold as "hamburger" must contain no more than 30% fat, though most markets sell several grades labeled according to the degree of leanness, the leanest and most expensive grade containing perhaps 15% fat. This is an important consideration in buying hamburger, for the range reflects a drop in calories of more than a third. It may also affect your choice of cooking method. Federal statute further forbids the use of sodium sulfite, an additive which keeps the meat rosy. Recent surveys, however, indicate that the practice is far from dead. Should you find the color of ground meat too persistently red, expose a sample to bright sunlight. Untreated meat will darken.

◗ Do not store any uncooked ground meat longer than 24 hours. ◗ Be sure the mass is not more than 2 inches thick, so the cold can penetrate it quickly and thoroughly. ❄ To freeze beef for hamburger, see (II, 652).

If you want very lean beef ground for hamburgers, use chuck, flank, shank, neck, heel, round or hanging tenderloin. ◗ Twice-ground meat will compact more than once-ground. You may be surprised at the apparently large amount of fat you didn't see go into the grinder. Grinders are so constructed that often as much as a fourth of every pound of meat that goes in stays in; the unexpected fat may come from the grinding of the previous order.

Good quality beef, freshly ground and used at once, needs only ◗ light shaping. You may want to incorporate into it some onion juice or finely chopped chives. ◗ If the beef has to be kept ground for 12 to 18 hours, it profits by having worked into it with a fork about 2 tablespoons beef stock for each pound of meat. This is done before shaping.

If beef is to be "stretched," see Additions to Hamburger, below. ◗ Incorporate these ingredients into the meat lightly with a fork and, with a light touch, shape the mixture into patties. Always decide before you put the meat into the pan how thick you want the finished hamburger. ◗ Never compact it in the pan by pressing down on it with a spatula.

## ADDITIONS TO HAMBURGER AND MEAT LOAF

### I. To Stretch

◗ The addition of root vegetables or cereals may require more seasonings. To one pound of ground meat, you may mix in lightly with a fork any one of the following:

> 1/2 cup soft bread crumbs, (II, 218)

soaked briefly in:

> 1/3 to 1/2 cup milk or stock

or add:

> 1/2 cup finely grated raw carrots or potatoes or chopped raw mushrooms or bean sprouts

or add:

> 1/4 cup ground nuts, dry cereals, wheat germ, ground sunflower seeds, presoaked cracked bulgur, or textured vegetable protein, up to 20%, (II, 193)

moistened with:

> 2 tablespoons beef stock, cream, tomato paste or lemon juice

Also, some of the piquant sauces found in the Sauce chapter, 374, will help stretch your main dish.

### II. To Enrich

To one pound of ground meat, add one or more of the following:

> 1 egg
> 1/4 cup dry milk solids
> 1 teaspoon dolomite or bone meal
> 1 tablespoon brewer's yeast

The above may need additional liquid.

### III. To Flavor

About 1/2 hour before cooking, mix into one pound of ground meat one of the following combinations:

> 2 teaspoons chili sauce
> 1 teaspoon ground anchovy or anchovy paste
> 3 tablespoons sautéed mushrooms
> 1 tablespoon finely diced stuffed olives or 1 teaspoon capers

or:

> 1/4 teaspoon thyme
> 1 garlic clove, pressed
> 1 teaspoon Worcestershire sauce

or:

> 2 tablespoons each chopped fresh parsley and chives, or 1 tablespoon grated

chopped onions and
1 tablespoon coffee cream

or:

¼ cup crumbled Roquefort
cheese or cultured sour
cream
2 tablespoons chopped chives
or green onion tops
A sprinkling of hot pepper
sauce
¼ teaspoon dry mustard

olives or sautéed onions or
mushrooms

Or spread over them:

Herb butters, (II, 70–71),
or mustard

You may garnish with:

Very thin raw or sautéed
slices of sweet onion
A slice of tomato or
cucumber

## SAUTÉED HAMBURGERS

**4 Servings**

◗ Please read About Hamburger, 616.
Shape lightly into patties, allowing
2 for each serving:

1 lb. ground beef

Preheat an ungreased heavy skillet
slowly, to the point where the meat
when added will sizzle, not hiss
sharply. If you use very lean beef,
you will need to add to the pan:

1 tablespoon butter, beef fat
or oil

Sauté over medium heat ◗ uncovered,
for 3 or 4 minutes. During this time
sufficient fat should come from the
patty itself to permit the hamburger
to be turned without sticking. Turn
and cook on the other side another
3 minutes or even longer, depending
on the thickness of the patty and the
whims of your diners. Remove meat
from the pan and season with:

Salt
Freshly ground pepper

Defat the pan drippings. Deglaze
them with:

Stock

Reduce the juices slightly and pour
them over the patties before serving.
Or mix with the pan juices a little:

Barbecue or chili sauce,
tomato catsup, red wine,
horseradish, a few chopped

## BROILED HAMBURGERS

**4 Servings**

Preheat broiler.
◗ Please read About Hamburger, 616.
Shape lightly into ¾-inch-thick
patties:

1 lb. ground beef

Place them on a broiler pan, 4 inches
from source of heat, or place them so
they cover the untoasted side of:

A piece of bread toasted on
one side only

If on bread, broil about 12 minutes. If
not, broil 6 minutes on one side, turn
and broil about 4 minutes on the
other. If the meat is very lean, you
may brush it during broiling with:

Butter

## ▤ GRILLED HAMBURGERS

We have watched with agony as good
juices fed the flames and the guests
were dealt dry chips. If you must grill
ground meat, please see 112. To
make the meat adhere well during
handling and grilling, you may add to
each pound:

(1 beaten egg)

Shape lightly into 1-inch-thick patties:

Hamburger

Grill each side 5 to 6 minutes for
a medium-rare to medium-cooked
hamburger.

## CHEESEBURGERS

Although it is traditional to top hamburger with a piece of cheese, and broil until the cheese melts, we find the following method tastier.

Mix together with a fork:

    1 lb. ground beef
    1/2 cup shredded cheddar or
        Gruyère cheese
    2 teaspoons Worcestershire
        sauce
    1/2 teaspoon salt
    (1 clove garlic, pressed)

Sauté or broil as directed in above recipes.

## ▤ FILLED BEEF OR LAMBURGERS

                        6 Servings

◗ Please read About Hamburger, 616.
Preheat broiler or grill.
Divide into 12 portions and shape into flat patties:

    1 1/2 lb. ground beef or lamb

Sauté lightly:

    (6 slices bacon)

Use one of the following fillings which you may vary with the addition of chopped avocados, celery, pickles, radishes, chili sauce, bread dressing or chopped leftover vegetables:

### I.

    6 tablespoons chopped
        nutmeats
    3 tablespoons chopped
        parsley
    2 tablespoons grated onion

### II.

    A mashed anchovy and a
    few capers for each patty

### III.

    Roquefort or cheddar
    cheese or braunschweiger
    Prepared mustard

Spread the filling on 6 of the patties. Top them with those remaining. Bind the edges with the partially sautéed bacon strips and fasten with a wooden pick. Broil 10 to 15 minutes, turning once.

## BEEF OR BIFF À LA LINDSTRÖM

                        4 to 5 Servings

Almost a meal in one dish.
Sauté until limp and transparent:

    2 tablespoons finely chopped
        onions

in:

    2 teaspoons butter

In a large bowl mix with a fork the onions and:

    1 lb. lean ground beef:
        ground twice
    2 egg yolks
    1 to 2 tablespoons finely
        chopped capers
    1 teaspoon salt
    1/4 teaspoon pepper
    1/2 cup cream

Stir in:

    1/4 cup finely diced pickled
        beets
    (1 cup diced boiled potatoes)

Form the mixture into round patties about 1 inch thick. Heat in a large skillet:

    3 to 4 tablespoons butter and
        oil combined

Brown the meat quickly, turning only once. The patties should be pink inside and deep brown on the outside. In Sweden these hamburgers would be served garnished with:

    (A fried egg)

but we prefer the pan juices instead.

## CHICKEN, VEAL OR LAMB PATTIES

The French make many attractive dishes by grinding uncooked meat or fish, shaping it with other ingredients into patties, and poaching, broiling or sautéing them.

### I.
About 15 Servings

Preheat broiler.
Cut the meat from:

A 4¹/2-lb. chicken, or use
3¹/2 lb. veal or lamb

Pick over the carcass for all edible bits of meat. Put the meat through a grinder, using a coarse blade. Save the juices, if any. Combine the ground meat, the juices and:

³/4 cup whipping cream
1¹/2 cups soft bread crumbs
1 teaspoon salt
1 teaspoon dried basil or 1 tablespoon chopped parsley
A grating of lemon rind
¹/4 teaspoon paprika
A grating of nutmeg

Shape the mixture into 15 large patties. Roll them in a:

Bound Breading, (II, 220)

and let rest for 15 minutes. Place them in a ♦ shallow greased pan. Broil under moderate heat about 10 minutes to a side or until lightly browned. The patties may be left unbreaded and poached in a pan in the oven in a small amount of milk or stock, enough to cover the bottom of the skillet, until done. This means very low heat. Serve with:

Béarnaise Sauce, 412, or Soubise Sauce, 387

### II.
8 Servings

Mix together:

2 lb. ground chicken, veal or lamb
¹/2 cup soft bread crumbs
1 egg
¹/2 cup chopped onions
1¹/2 teaspoons grated lemon rind
1 teaspoon salt
1 teaspoon each ground coriander, nutmeg and curry powder
¹/2 teaspoon pepper

Shape and broil as described in I, left.
Serve with:

Curried Rice, 191, and mint

## BAKED LIVER PATTIES
6 Servings

Preheat oven to 350°.
Combine:

1 lb. ground beef liver
¹/2 cup dry bread crumbs
¹/4 cup evaporated milk or cream
¹/2 teaspoon salt
¹/8 teaspoon pepper
2 teaspoons grated onion
2 tablespoons chopped parsley

Shape these ingredients into 6 flat patties. Wrap around them:

6 slices bacon

Secure the bacon with wooden picks. Place the patties in a lightly greased pan. Bake until well browned, about 6 minutes. Turn to ensure even baking.

## GERMAN MEATBALLS OR KÖNIGSBERGER KLOPS

### About Ten 2-Inch Balls

A good buffet dish if shaped into 1-inch balls.

Soak in water, milk or stock to cover:

**1 slice of bread, 1 inch thick**

Put through a meat grinder twice:

**1½ lb. meat: ½ lb. beef, ½ lb. veal, ½ lb. pork or liver**

Beat well and add to the meat:

**2 eggs**

Melt:

**1 tablespoon butter**

Sauté until golden:

**¼ cup finely chopped onions**

Add to the meat. Wring the liquid from the bread. Add bread to the meat and:

**3 tablespoons chopped parsley**

**1¼ teaspoons salt**

**¼ teaspoon paprika**

**½ teaspoon grated lemon rind**

**1 teaspoon lemon juice**

**1 teaspoon Worcestershire sauce or a grating of nutmeg**

A few minced anchovies or one-fourth herring may be added at this time to the mixture or later to the gravy. Combine these ingredients well. Do this lightly with the hands rather than with a fork or spoon. Shape lightly into 2-inch balls. Drop into:

**5 cups boiling Vegetable Stock, (II, 174)**

Simmer covered about 15 minutes. Remove from the stock. Measure the stock. Make gravy of it, 382, by using for every cup of stock:

**2 tablespoons butter**

**2 tablespoons flour**

**Season to taste**

Cook and stir until smooth. Add:

**2 tablespoons capers, or**

**2 tablespoons chopped pickles, lemon juice or cultured sour cream**

**2 tablespoons chopped parsley**

Reheat the meatballs in the gravy. Serve with a platter of:

**Boiled Noodles, 200, or Spätzle, 186**

Cover generously with:

**Buttered Crumbs, (II, 219)**

## ITALIAN MEATBALLS

Preheat oven to 350°.

Follow the recipe for:

**German Meatballs, left**

but omit the Worcestershire sauce. Add to the meat mixture:

**½ chopped clove garlic**

**3 tablespoons grated Parmesan cheese**

**¼ teaspoon oregano**

Mix and form into balls. Brown lightly in:

**2 tablespoons butter**

Place in a casserole. Half cover with:

**Unthickened Tomato Sauce, 400, or Marinara Sauce, 403**

Bake covered about 30 minutes. Serve with:

**Pasta, 199**

## SWEDISH MEATBALLS

### About Eighteen 1½-Inch Balls

There are many recipes for this dish, all similar to, but in our opinion none superior to:

**German Meatballs, left**

Omit the Worcestershire sauce and add:

**¼ teaspoon nutmeg**

**⅛ teaspoon allspice**

Shape the meat into 1½-inch balls. Brown in:

**2 tablespoons butter or drippings**

Simmer closely covered until done, about 15 minutes, in:

**2 cups consommé or other stock**

Make:

**Pan Gravy, 382**

Season it with:

**Sherry or 1 to 2 teaspoons finely minced fresh dill**

Reheat the meat in the gravy. This is attractive served in a chafing dish, garnished with:

**Small Potato Dumplings, 184**


## CHINESE MEATBALLS

**6 Servings**

◗ Please read About Deep-Fat Frying, 94.

Shape into 18 balls:

**1½ lb. ground beef**

Season with:

**1½ teaspoons salt**
**2 teaspoons soy sauce**
**¼ teaspoon dry mustard**
**1 tablespoon finely chopped parsley**

Coat the balls with:

**Fritter Batter for Meat, (II, 155)**

Let them dry on a rack 30 minutes. Deep-fry in fat heated to 365° until golden brown. Serve at once covered with:

**Oriental Sweet-Sour Sauce II, 405**


## HAWAIIAN MEATBALLS

**6 Servings**

Combine in a large bowl:

**1 lb. lean ground beef**
**½ cup soft bread crumbs moistened with milk**
**1 beaten egg**
**1 clove garlic, pressed**
**½ teaspoon dry mustard**

**¼ teaspoon ginger**
**½ teaspoon salt**
**1 tablespoon soy sauce**

Form meat into 1-inch balls and sauté until brown in:

**2 tablespoons vegetable or peanut oil**

Pour over all:

**Oriental Sweet-Sour Sauce II, 405**

garnished with:

**(Bean sprouts, 294)**

Serve over:

**Boiled Rice, 189**


## PORK BALLS IN TOMATO SAUCE

**4 Servings**

Soak in water to cover:

**A slice of bread, 1½ inches thick**

Wring the water from it. Add to the bread:

**1 lb. ground pork**
**⅓ cup chopped onions**
**1 beaten egg**
**¾ teaspoon salt**
**¼ teaspoon paprika**

Combine these ingredients lightly until well blended. Shape into 2-inch balls. Bring to a boil in a large pan:

**1 can condensed tomato soup: 10½ oz.**
**An equal amount of water**

Drop the balls into it. ◗ Reduce the heat at once. Cover the pan and simmer about 45 minutes.


## SAUERKRAUT BALLS

**4 Dozen 1¼-Inch Balls**

◗ Please read About Deep-Fat Frying, 94.

Grind with a medium blade:

**½ lb. each ham, corned beef and lean pork**

Sauté the meat in:

3 **tablespoons butter or fat**
with:
1/3 **cup finely chopped onions**
To the above, add:
2 **cups flour**
1/2 **to 1 teaspoon dry mustard**
1 **teaspoon salt**
2 **cups milk**
Simmer the mixture until thickened,
♦ stirring constantly. Combine it
with:
2 **lb. cooked drained**
**sauerkraut**
Then regrind the entire mixture. Form
into 1 1/4-inch balls. Roll them in:
**Bound Breading, (II, 220)**
Let stand about 15 minutes before
deep-frying in fat heated to 365° until
golden brown. Drain on paper toweling and serve at once.

## PORCUPINES

**6 Servings**

Far too formidable a name for a dish
without either pork or spines.
Combine:
1 **lb. ground beef**
1/2 **cup bread crumbs**
1 **egg**
3/4 **teaspoon salt**
1/4 **teaspoon paprika**
(2 **tablespoons chopped green**
**peppers)**
Roll these ingredients ♦ lightly into
balls. Press into flat cakes. Roll in:
1/4 **cup uncooked rice**
Heat in a heavy pot:
**Thickened Tomato**
**Sauce, 400**
Add:
(1 **teaspoon chili powder)**
Add the meat cakes. Cover and simmer about 45 minutes.
**Season to taste**

## ☰ SLOPPY JOES

**8 Sandwiches**

Heat in a skillet:
2 **tablespoons butter**
Add and sauté:
1/2 **cup minced onions**
1/2 **cup chopped celery**
1/2 **cup chopped green pepper,**
**seeds and membrane**
**removed**
When these are limp, add:
1 1/2 **lb. ground beef**
Cook and stir until meat is lightly
browned. Add:
1/2 **cup chopped mushrooms**
4 **tablespoons chili sauce**
1/2 **cup water**
**Season to taste**
Simmer uncovered over low heat
about 15 minutes until thickened
enough to spoon onto:
8 **slightly toasted sandwich**
**buns**

## CHILI CON CARNE

**8 to 12 Servings**

Melt:
2 **to 3 tablespoons bacon**
**drippings or butter**
Sauté in the fat:
1/2 **cup chopped onion and/or**
1/2 **clove garlic, chopped**
Add:
1 **to 2 lb. ground beef or**
**lamb**
Stir and sauté the meat until well
done. Add:
1 1/4 **cups canned tomatoes**
3 **to 4 cups canned kidney**
**beans**
3/4 **teaspoon or more salt**
1/2 **bay leaf**
1 **teaspoon sugar**
(1/4 **cup dry red wine)**
2 **teaspoons to 2 tablespoons**
**chili powder**

depending on your taste and the strength of the chili powder. Cover and simmer about 1 hour or longer. The longer it cooks, the thicker it becomes and the better it tastes. Or make it a day ahead and reheat. Serve with:

> **Tortillas or crackers**

or over:

> **Cooked spaghetti**

garnished with:

> (Chopped onions)
> (Shredded cheese)

## SPANISH CASSEROLE WITH RICE

**6 Servings**

A one-dish meal.
Steam:

> ²/₃ **cup rice, 189**

Prepare:

> 1 **cup chopped celery**
> ¼ **cup chopped green pepper, seeds and membrane removed**

Melt in a saucepan:

> 2 **tablespoons butter or other fat**

Sauté in the butter until golden:

> 1 **chopped medium-sized onion**

Add and sear:

> 1 **lb. ground round steak or lean beef**

Season with:

> ¾ **teaspoon salt**
> ¼ **teaspoon paprika**

Preheat oven to 350°.
Place in a greased baking dish one-third of the rice and half of the meat. Sprinkle over it half of the celery and pepper. Repeat this process. Place the last of the rice on top. Pour over all:

> 1 **can condensed tomato soup: 10½ oz.**
> **Season to taste**

Cover the dish and bake about ½ hour.

## LAMB AND EGGPLANT CASSEROLE

**4 Servings**

Preheat oven to 350°.
Pare and chop until fine:

> 1 **medium-sized eggplant**

Combine with:

> 2 **cups ground lamb: 1 lb.**
> ½ **cup chopped onions**
> 3 **tablespoons chopped parsley**
> 1 **teaspoon salt**
> ¼ **teaspoon paprika**
> (½ **teaspoon curry powder or** ¼ **teaspoon oregano**)
> 1 **cup chopped drained tomatoes**

Pour the mixture into a buttered casserole. Bake covered about 45 minutes. Remove the cover and let the top brown.

## MOUSSAKA OR EGGPLANT CASSEROLE

**8 to 10 Servings**

For a large party, the quantity may be doubled or tripled to fill two or three casseroles.
Cut into lengthwise slices ¼ to ½ inch thick:

> 3 **peeled medium-sized eggplants**

Salt the slices generously and let drain in a colander at least 45 minutes. Meanwhile, sauté until golden in:

> 1 **cup finely chopped onions**
> ¼ **cup olive oil or butter**

Add and brown slowly:

> 2 **lb. lean ground lamb**

Add:

> 1 **cup well-drained canned or fresh tomatoes or**
> 3 **tablespoons tomato paste**
> ⅓ **cup chopped parsley**

1 cup white wine or stock
¼ teaspoon nutmeg
**A grating of black pepper**

Simmer the above gently about 45 minutes. In the meantime, quickly sauté the drained eggplant slices until lightly browned on all sides in:

½ cup olive oil or butter

using only a little oil at a time, since eggplant soaks it up. Drain on paper toweling. Now, ▶ beat until stiff, but not dry:

3 egg whites

Fold the beaten whites into the cooked and cooled meat mixture with:

½ cup fine bread crumbs

Prepare a double portion of:

**White Sauce II, 383**

When hot, pour a small amount of the sauce into:

3 beaten egg yolks
**A grating of nutmeg**

Pour the yolk mixture into the sauce. Preheat oven to 350°.

Assemble the ingredients in a 9 x 13-inch or larger baking dish, placing first a layer of eggplant, then the meat mixture, and ending with an egg-plant layer. Cover the whole with the sauce. Sprinkle the top generously with:

**Grated Parmesan cheese**

Bake the casserole until thoroughly heated through, but do not allow the mixture to reach the boiling point.

The moussaka can be cut into squares if you will allow it to stand about 20 minutes before serving. This is the way moussaka is served all through Greece. The classic version omits the sauce, and the egg-plant skins are used to line the dish and to protect the ingredients while cooking. The skins must be well oiled if they are to be used in this way.

## STUFFED CABBAGE OR GEFÜLLTER KRAUTKOPF

**6 Servings**

▶ Please read about Leaf-Wrappings, 103, and how to prepare and cook the leaves from:

**A head of cabbage**

Use one of the following meat fillings:

**I.** Soak in water for 2 minutes:

1 slice of bread, 1 inch thick

Press the water from it. Combine the bread with:

½ lb. ground pork
½ lb. ground beef
½ lb. ground veal
3 beaten eggs
¾ teaspoon salt
¼ teaspoon paprika

**II.** Or use a filling of:

1 lb. fresh pork sausage meat
3 slices of bread, ½ inch thick
1 beaten egg

**III.** Or cook until tender:

½ cup dried peas, 294

Drain the peas and combine with:

1 lb. ground lamb or beef
½ cup chopped onions
¼ cup chopped parsley
1 teaspoon grated lemon rind
½ teaspoon cinnamon
1 teaspoon salt
½ teaspoon pepper

You may make and simmer individual packets as described on 104, or line a bowl with a large napkin or cloth and fill it with alternate layers of the leaves and the meat dressing. Cover the top with 1 or 2 large leaves, gather up the cloth and tie it with a string. Place the bag in boiling water—the water in which the cabbage was boiled and as much fresh boiling water as needed to cover well.

♦ Simmer the cabbage gently for 2 hours if you are old-fashioned, but 45 minutes should be ample time. Drain it in a colander, untie the bag and place the cabbage in a hot serving dish. Serve with the following onion sauce. Brown in the top of a double boiler:

>1/4 cup butter

Add and stir until brown:

>2 tablespoons flour

Have ready:

>2 cups Stock, (II, 171–172), or cabbage water

Stir 1/2 cup of this into the butter mixture. Add:

>1/2 cup or more chopped onions

If required:

>Season to taste

Cook the onions covered ♦ over—not in—boiling water, until very tender. Add the remainder of the stock gradually. The gravy is best when it is thick with onions.

## BAKED STUFFED CABBAGE LEAVES

**4 Servings**

Preheat oven to 375°.

♦ Please read about Leaf-Wrappings, 103, and how to wash and parblanch:

>8 large cabbage leaves

Drain and dry them on a towel. Combine:

>1 lb. ground beef or a mixture of beef, veal, pork and liver
>3 tablespoons finely chopped onions
>2 tablespoons finely chopped parsley
>3/4 teaspoon salt
>1/2 teaspoon thyme
>1/2 clove garlic, pressed
>A few grains cayenne

If you want a sweet-sour effect, add:

>2 tablespoons vinegar
>3 tablespoons brown sugar
>1 teaspoon capers

Divide the meat mixture into 8 parts. Put one part on each cabbage leaf. Roll the leaves as directed on 103. Tie or secure them with wooden picks. Place them seam side down and close together in a buttered baking dish. Dot each roll with:

>1/2 teaspoon butter

Pour into the dish:

>1/2 cup boiling stock

or you may use:

>1/2 cup water, tomato juice or cultured sour cream and paprika

Bake the rolls covered about 50 minutes.

## STUFFED GRAPE LEAVES OR DOLMAS

**30 Dolmas**

♦ Please read about Leaf-Wrappings, 103, and prepare for stuffing:

>30 fresh or canned grape leaves

Fill each one with a generous tablespoon of the following mixture:

>2 cups finely chopped onions
>1/2 cup uncooked rice
>1/3 cup olive oil
>2 tablespoons finely chopped parsley
>2 tablespoons finely chopped dill
>1/4 cup pine nuts
>1/4 cup currants
>(1 cup finely minced lamb)

Do not roll the leaves too tightly, as the rice will swell. Cook as for Cabbage Leaves I, 104, weighted with a plate, over low heat about 1 1/2 hours. Serve chilled.

## ABOUT MEAT LOAF

Although proportions of beef, veal and pork are specified in the following recipes, they may be varied, provided the total amount of meat remains the same. Be sure to ♦ cook thoroughly if pork is used. Handle ingredients for meat loaf ♦ lightly, mixing with a two-tined fork. Do not overcook; it should be firm but not dry. To stretch, see Additions to Hamburger, 617.

Meat loaf may be mounded on a flat greased pan or put into a greased ring mold or loaf pan. It may also be baked in 2 layers with a stuffing between. Individual meat loaves take only about 20 to 30 minutes and—for attractive service—may be baked in greased muffin tins and glazed. You may pour about ¹/₂ cup of catsup in the bottom of the pan before filling it with the meat; or you may pour about 2 tablespoons of chili sauce over the meat loaf when it is half baked. This gives it a good flavor and a light crust. You may cover the loaf with a piece of foil, but remove it the last quarter hour of baking.

If baked in a ring mold, it may be served hot, filled with green peas or some other vegetable and surrounded by browned potatoes. Or serve it cold, filled with potato or some other vegetable salad. Don't neglect to use it for sandwiches and for picnics.

## MEAT LOAF

**4 servings**

**I.** Preheat oven to 350°.
Combine and shape into a loaf:

>    1 **lb. ground beef:** ¹/₄ this
>      amount may be pork
>   (1 **egg yolk**)
>    2 **tablespoons chopped**
>      **parsley**

>    1 **tablespoon soft butter**
>    1 **tablespoon bread crumbs**
>    1 **teaspoon lemon juice**
>    1 **teaspoon salt**
>   ¹/₄ **teaspoon pepper**
>   ¹/₂ **teaspoon onion juice**

Place the loaf in a lightly greased pan. Baste at intervals with the following sauce:

>   ¹/₂ **cup stock or ¹/₂ cup boiling**
>      **water plus ¹/₄ package**
>      **dried soup mix**

Bake about 45 minutes.
Serve the loaf with:

>   **Sweet Potato Puffs, 356**

## II.

**4 Servings**

Preheat oven to 350°.
Place in a bowl:

>    1 **lb. ground round steak**
>    1 **to 2 tablespoons**
>      **horseradish**
>    2 **tablespoons catsup or chili**
>      **sauce**
>    1 **teaspoon salt**
>   ¹/₄ **teaspoon pepper**
>   ¹/₂ **cup cream**

Grind in a food chopper, then add:

>    6 **slices bacon**
>    2 **medium-sized onions**
>    1 **cup broken crackers**

Mix with a fork. Mold into a loaf.
Roll in:

>   ¹/₄ **cup cracker crumbs**

Place the loaf in a shallow baking pan. Pour into the pan:

>   ¹/₂ **cup stock**

Bake the loaf about 50 minutes. Baste occasionally, adding more liquid if necessary. Make:

>   **Pan Gravy, 382**

## MEAT LOAF COCKAIGNE

**6 Servings**

A favorite luncheon dish sliced and served cold.

Preheat oven to 350°.
Mix lightly:

1½ lb. lean ground beef—be
     sure beef has been ground
     only once
  1 can condensed cream of
     chicken or mushroom
     soup: 10½ oz.
 ¾ cup dry bread crumbs
 ¼ cup mixed fresh tarragon,
     parsley, basil or chives
  1 teaspoon salt
  1 clove garlic, pressed
 10 or more chopped stuffed
     olives or ¼ cup chopped
     water chestnuts
 (½ cup chopped nuts)

Bake in a 4 x 8 x 4-inch pan, about
45 minutes.
You may serve hot with:

   (Thickened Tomato
    Sauce, 400)


## VEAL LOAF

                    8 to 10 Servings
Preheat oven to 350°.
Grind:

  2 lb. veal
  1 lb. smoked ham or sausage

Add and ♦ mix very lightly:

  1 tablespoon minced onion
 ¼ cup chopped green pepper,
     seeds and membrane
     removed
  2 beaten eggs
 ½ teaspoon salt
 ⅛ teaspoon paprika
 ¾ cup dry bread crumbs
  1 cup condensed mushroom
     soup

Place half of this mixture in a 4 x 8 x
4-inch loaf pan. You may then press
whole mushrooms or hard-cooked
eggs, stuffed olives or pistachio nuts
into the meat in a pattern. Cover
with the remaining meat. Bake about
45 minutes. Serve hot or cold.


## LIVER LOAF

                       6 to 8 Servings
This makes a most appetizing every-
day liver spread.
Preheat oven to 350°.
Boil for 5 minutes:

  1 cup water
  1 medium-sized chopped
     onion
  3 chopped ribs celery with
     leaves

Prepare for cooking, 639, slice, add
and simmer for 2 minutes:

  1 lb. liver: beef, lamb or pork

Drain, reserving liquid. Put liver
and vegetables through a meat chopper with:

  2 slices bacon or a 1½-inch
     cube salt pork

Add to mixture and blend well:

  1 or 2 beaten eggs
 ¾ teaspoon salt
 ⅛ teaspoon pepper
  1 cup cracker or dry bread
     crumbs
 ½ teaspoon dried marjoram
     or thyme
  1 cup liquid: reserved liver
     stock, milk, tomato juice,
     etc.

Pour into a greased loaf pan:

 (½ cup catsup)

Place the meat in the pan. Bake about
40 minutes.


## RAW SMOKED HAM LOAF

                       4 to 6 Servings
You may dress this up or down.
Preheat oven to 350°.
Try using:

 (½ cup crushed pineapple)
 (½ teaspoon dry mustard)

in the bottom of the pan. Grind:

  1 lb. raw smoked ham
 ½ lb. lean pork
 ¼ cup chopped onion

Add and mix lightly with a fork:

**2  well-beaten eggs**
**1/2  to 1 cup cracker or dry bread crumbs**
**An equal amount of milk**
**1/8  teaspoon pepper**
**3  tablespoons mixed fresh herbs**

Shape the above ingredients and place in a greased loaf pan. Bake about 2 hours, basting frequently with:

**Honey Glaze, 427, or Spirit Glaze for Ham, 427**

## ABOUT PÂTÉS AND TERRINES

Pâtés are the rich relatives of the meat loaf clan, and though they sometimes arrive at table dressed to the nines in their formal jacket of glazed pastry or glistening aspic, they are basically no harder to make than a meat loaf. What distinguishes them is the luxury quality of their ingredients, which may include some or all of the following: ground meat—veal, pork, liver; poultry or pork, often marinated in wine or brandy; diced fresh pork fat; sliced or cubed tongue, chicken, ham or game; cream, eggs, spices; perhaps pistachios, or, for the *ne plus ultra* touch, truffles. Endless combinations are possible to tempt you to eventually develop a pâté maison of your own. The texture may be smooth if all the meat is fine-ground, or patterned if the more colorful ingredients are diced or sliced to show decoratively when the loaf is cut as in a Galantine, 529. The less formal terrine is baked in an enamel or earthenware dish, shown on 630, and is never enclosed in a crust.

Although many European countries have produced characteristic pâtés, the unrivaled queen of the traditional mixtures is France's now astronomically costly **pâté de foie gras,** made of goose liver marinated in cognac and flavored with truffles. The chief component of the genuine article is the liver of geese force-fed by hand until the liver has grown to one-fourth of the bird's total weight. American law forbids force-feeding, and chicken livers are a more than acceptable substitute. Recipes that follow give a few versions of chicken liver pâté. To serve a pâté coated with aspic, follow directions for the gelatin covering in Souffléed Liver Pâté Cockaigne, 632.

## ABOUT PÂTÉ EN CROÛTE

A pâté presented in a pastry covering is called pâté en croûte—in a crust. Decorated and golden brown, the case does full justice to the pâté it encloses; sliced, it is even lovelier, revealing the smooth or patterned texture of the meat inside, with a clear gelatin top under the crust, see illustration on 630. The novice sometimes does not realize that the crust—in the traditional version—is not meant to be eaten but serves to protect the flavor and juices of the meat mixture. The late Chef Pierre Adrian, our good friend, worried so about his American diners' insistence on consuming the crust that he usually used Pâte Brisée, (II, 362), a more appetizing if harder to handle pastry. He also warned us that the conventional hinged pâté molds, illustrated on 546, nearly always leak, and if the crust breaks in any way, the delicious juices will run into the oven. If, instead, a 9 x 4½ x 4½-inch loaf pan is used, the juices as well as the characteristic shape are retained.

Pâte versus pâté: let's clarify once and for all the spelling that for most of us remains a "bafflement." With the "e" accented, we have seen that the word means a combination of meats and spices forming a kind of loaf; pâte with an unaccented "e" simply means dough—in this instance, the pastry used for the crust. The recipe that follows is for the traditional tough dough covering ♦ that is not to be eaten.

## CRUST OR PÂTE FOR PÂTÉ

Work together with your fingers until you have achieved the consistency of coarse cornmeal:

> **6 cups sifted all-purpose flour**
> **2 teaspoons salt**
> **1½ cups lard or shortening**

Make a well, (II, 366), of these ingredients and break into the center, one at a time:

> **2 eggs**

working them into the flour mixture from the inside and adding gradually:

> **About 3 cups water**

You may need a little more water to make a dough that can be worked into a smooth mass and rolled into a ball. The dough is easier to handle if allowed to rest covered at about 70° for several hours. Then form about three-fourths of the dough into a thick oval approximately the size of the base of the mold or pan, and line the bottom. With the sides of the hands, in chopping motions, gradually work the dough from the base so that it thins out and creeps up the sides. Then, with the fingers patting it thin, form the rest of the crust. Let the excess hang over the sides, see opposite. Do not stretch or tear the dough. Next, line the mold with thin strips of blanched fat bacon in parallel U shapes, as sketched. Let the strips rest temporarily over the sides. Place the meat mixture in the mold; if

you are aiming at a patterned texture, the diced or sliced ingredients are placed in alternate layers with the ground meat, to show a pattern in cross section when cut, as shown below. When the mold pan has been filled with the meat and the bacon strips folded over the meat filling, crimp the dough at the edges of the mold and cut off the excess. From the remaining fourth of dough, roll a 3/16-inch-thick piece for the lid. Apply the lid by pinching the dough into the already crimped edges of the pastry case, brushing the edges with Egg Wash, (II, 503), as glue. Leave the dough lax enough so that it will not

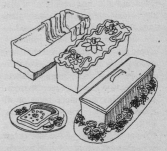

crack or distort in baking; trim edges. Cut from the scraps small geometric or floral shapes to ornament the top. Work your pattern around 2 or 3 circles which can hold pastry vents, as shown in the drawing. These will later form openings for inserting the funnels when the aspic is carefully poured between the pâté and the upper crust. Apply the ornaments with egg wash and brush the top with it before baking. Vent the top crust with a few fancy cuts, as you would for a pie.

Preheat the oven to 400°.

To avoid too rapid browning of the crust, you may have ready a piece of foil to put loosely over the top. This will protect it in the early stages of baking. As soon as you put the pâté in the oven ◗ lower the heat to 325°. Pâtés are usually cooked 1¹/₂ to 2 hours. Test for doneness as for cake, (II, 400).

Allow the pâté, still in the pan, to cool on a rack. Fill the space which will have formed at the top between filling and crust by pouring through the vents enough flavorful aspic that—when it solidifies—it will support the crust. Use a firm gelatin, allowing 1 tablespoon for each cup of meat stock. Hold a funnel in one of the vents and pour the mixture—being careful not to moisten the crust on the outside. Allow the pâté to remain in the pan refrigerated until the aspic is set. To unmold the pâté, proceed as for unmolding a gelatin, (II, 235). Use a rack, however, on which to reverse it—to facilitate turning the pâté right side up onto a serving platter.

Pâtés should, of course, be stored refrigerated, and most pâtés profit by ◗ resting refrigerated for at least 48 hours before serving—so that the flavors blend and the contents are firm enough for even slicing. The whole pâté may be garnished with a border of chopped aspic jelly, parsley and lemon wedges. When serving, cut with a warm knife. An individual serving should be at least ³/₈ to ¹/₂ inch thick and garnished with parsley and a lemon wedge, as shown on 630. For smaller servings, cut each slice in half on the diagonal.

## CHICKEN LIVER PÂTÉ OR PÂTÉ DE FOIE DE VOLAILLE

Either of the following recipes may or may not be baked en croûte; please read about Pâtés and About Pâté en Croûte, 629.

### ♪ I.
#### About Twenty ¹/₂-Inch Slices
Divide into 3 parts:

**1¹/₂ lb. chicken livers**

In a blender, mix one part with:

**2 eggs**

Blend the second part ◗ briefly with:

**¹/₄ cup whipping cream**

Blend the third part with:

**4 slices chopped bacon, blanched**
**1 egg**
**3 tablespoons brandy**
**2 tablespoons port wine**
**¹/₄ cup flour**

Mix these three blends together ◗ very lightly with:

**1 teaspoon ginger**
**2 teaspoons salt**
**¹/₂ teaspoon freshly ground black pepper**
**1 teaspoon allspice or nutmeg**
**(¹/₄ cup pistachio nuts or 1 to 2 minced truffles)**

If you want to serve as pâté en croûte, follow directions on 629. If not, place mixture in a greased loaf pan and top with:

**Thin-sliced blanched salt pork**

Cover ◗ tightly with heavy foil and place baking pan up to about half its depth in a larger pan of boiling water. Bake at 325° about 1¹/₂ to 2 hours, or to an internal temperature of 180°. Serve cold, after removing some of the fat from the top surface if necessary. To store leftover pâté, be sure it is well covered with a layer of fat or clarified butter.

### II.
#### About Forty ¹/₂-Inch Slices
Should the veal be reddish, marinate it refrigerated overnight covered with milk.
Pound:

**1 lb. white veal**

Add and ◗ grind 3 times with the veal:

**1½ lb. chicken livers**
**¼ lb. blanched salt pork**
**2 anchovy fillets**

Mix in lightly until very smooth:

**4 beaten eggs**
**½ cup whipping cream**
**3 tablespoons grated onions**
**2 tablespoons chopped**
**parsley or chervil**
**⅛ teaspoon freshly ground**
**black pepper**
**¼ cup brandy**
**1 tablespoon Madeira**
**(2 tablespoons chopped**
**truffles)**

If not served en croûte, top the pâté
with blanched salt pork and bake and
serve as described in I, 631.

## SOUFFLÉED LIVER PÂTÉ
COCKAIGNE

Preheat oven to 350°.
Have ready two identical 9-inch
bread pans. Prepare one of them as
for a soufflé dish, 225. Grind:

**1 lb. raw chicken livers**

Beat in:

**2 eggs**
**2 egg yolks**
**2 teaspoons onion juice**
**2 tablespoons chopped**
**parsley**
**2 cups whipping cream**

◗ You may use a 🔨 blender and
◗ very briefly blend liver and the
above ingredients. Fold in:

**2 stiffly beaten egg whites**

Place the mixture in the prepared
baking pan in a larger pan of boiling
water and bake about 1 hour or until
set. Refrigerate overnight.

To coat the soufflé with aspic, proceed as follows. Soak 3 minutes:

**1 tablespoon gelatin**

in:

**¼ cup cold water**

Bring to a boil:

**2 cups well-seasoned**
**Consommé, 130**

and combine with the soaked gelatin,
stirring until dissolved. Rinse the second 9-inch pan with cold water and
pour in ½ inch of the gelatin mixture.
Refrigerate until almost set. Reverse
the chilled loaf onto the gelatin layer.
Pour the remaining gelatin on the exposed surface, allowing it to coat the
sides of the loaf as well. When the
gelatin coating is well set, reverse
the mold onto a platter and serve the
gelatin-covered loaf garnished with:

**Thinly sliced limes or**
**stuffed olives and parsley**

## ❋ TERRINE OF VEAL WITH
CHICKEN, HAM OR PORK

The essential ingredient here is the
fresh veal, which is responsible for
jelling the whole as it cools. Please
read About Terrines, 629.
Preheat oven to 300°.
Line the bottom and sides of an
earthenware dish or a loaf pan with:

**Strips of blanched bacon**

overlapping the strips slightly and
draping them as shown on 630—
without the crust.
Sprinkle with:

**1 tablespoon chopped parsley**
**1 tablespoon chopped onion**

Pound, 550, very thin:

**2 lb. veal scallops, cut ¼ inch**
**thick**

Have ready:

**2 lb. finely sliced chicken,**
**ham or pork or a**
**combination of these**

Overlay the bacon lining with a layer
of the thin-pounded veal seasoned
with:

**Pepper**
**Thyme**
**Powdered bay leaf**

Place a layer of chicken, ham or pork slices over the veal. Then continue to build up layers to the top of the casserole, alternating a layer of seasoned veal, parsley and onions with a layer of chicken, ham or pork. Pour:

**1 cup dry white wine**

**1 to 2 teaspoons brandy**

over the meat layers until all the crevices are filled with liquid. Fold the bacon strips over the top. Cover and set the pan in a larger pan of boiling water. Bake about 2 hours or until done. As soon as you remove the meat from the oven, cover with heavy aluminum foil and weight as in Cheese Making, (II, 194). When the meat has cooled, a fatty jelly will have formed, which keeps the meat in prime condition. To serve, slice very thin. Store leftovers refrigerated and covered with:

**Clarified Butter**

## ABOUT SAUSAGE

One of our early European memories is that of the rapt stance of the citizenry as they gazed at window displays of German sausage. It made us aware for the first time of the wealth of choice. Sausage is one of the oldest of processed foods; 3000 years ago, grinding meat into sausage was an old Mediterranean custom. Around the world it has proliferated over the centuries into some 200 varieties from Alesandri to Kielbasa to Weiswurst. And any farm-bred American remembers early-winter butchering seasons when every family round about made its very own combination of the scrappier meat parts flavored with herbs.

Types of sausage fall into three main classes. First there is freshly ground sausage meat or so-called **country sausage,** which is very perishable and must be cooked and used at once; among these are Blood Sausage, or Boudin Noir, and Boudin Blanc, see 635. Added sometimes to this fragile category are spiced meats and innards such as liver loaf or braunschweiger, cooked ham and veal loaves—all of which need constant refrigeration. Next are the **lightly cured sausages,** often smoked precooked types such as frankfurters, wieners, vienna sausage, bologna, salami and mettwurst, all of which may be eaten as bought—unless the label reads to the contrary; but in all cases heating before serving improves taste. Federal regulation now requires that commercially available sausages be precooked before sale, to the point of safety for eating as is; or, if not precooked, they must be ◗ marked "fresh," which requires cooking them thoroughly before serving. They may be simmered, baked, or broiled, or cooked with beans or other vegetables or in pasta dishes. In broiling or pan-frying cased sausages, add a small amount of water to the pan. Puncture the sausages with a fork to keep the skins from bursting and to permit the fat to escape.

A third type, the partially dry or **dry sausage,** is delicious in sandwiches or as hors d'oeuvre or used to flavor bland dishes. These kinds are somewhat confusingly known as **summer sausage** because, though made in the winter, they keep through spring and summer without refrigeration, provided the casing is intact—which explains the traditional popularity of this highly seasoned meat in Southern European countries. Dry sausages include cervelat, salami, saucisson de Lyon, mortadella, pepperoni, chorizo and thuringer.

If you make your own sausage,

you can be assured of lean, good quality meat. As for the commercial types, their contents can be a mystery wrapped in an enigma—despite government labeling regulations. The label must show the ingredients but not the exact proportions; they are listed in descending order, the largest content first. USDA limitations permit up to 30% fat, 10% added water, 20% corn syrup, and 3 1/2% cereal or dry-milk fillers. If sausage is marked "all meat," its meat component must be muscle meat with its natural fat content only and no fillers. But beware! A label reading "all meat" and listing the ingredients as "beef, water, pork, seasonings," in that order, means that you are buying more water than pork. Chemical additives are usually responsible for bright pink or red color; choose the more muted tones. For a discussion of casings, see (II, 630).

◗ Never taste raw or "fresh" sausage whether bought or homemade, because of the danger of trichinosis. After handling raw sausage, always carefully wash your hands and any knife, utensil, or surface you have used. ◗ For 4 servings, allow about 1 pound of freshly ground sausage meat, slightly less for the more aged and drier types. Once the sausage casing is cut open, smoked or cooked sausage can be stored refrigerated about 1 week; semidry and dry types, 2 weeks or more.

## COUNTRY SAUSAGE

◗ Please read About Sausage, 633.
At butchering time in our valley, the popular man is the one who knows how to flavor the sausage—not too much pepper or sage and just enough coriander. This process has to be played by ear, for ◗ uncooked meat cannot be tasted to correct the seasoning, and the strength of spices is so variable. The best way to learn is to mix a small batch and cook up a sample for the always hungry helpers to test.

**I.** Chill, then grind together:
　　**2 parts lean ground pork**
　　**1 part firm diced lard**
Season with a mixture of:
　　**Thyme**
　　**Coriander**
　　**Summer savory**
　　**Sweet marjoram**
　　**Pulverized bay leaf**
　　**Freshly ground pepper**
To sauté fresh sausage patties, start them in a ◗ cold ungreased pan over moderate heat, draining the fat as it accumulates in the pan. Cook until well done and medium brown on both sides.

**II.**
　　　　　　　**6 Medium Patties**
A convenient small-scale recipe. Grind ◗ twice with the finest blade:
　　1/2 **lb. lean pork**
　　1/2 **lb. pork fat**
　　1/2 **lb. lean veal**
Mix in a large bowl:
　　**1 cup bread crumbs**
　　**Grated rind of 1 lemon**
　　1/4 **teaspoon each sage, sweet**
　　　　**marjoram and thyme**
　　1/8 **teaspoon summer savory**
　　1/2 **teaspoon freshly ground**
　　　　**black pepper**
　　**2 teaspoons salt**
　　**A grating of fresh nutmeg**
Add the ground meat and form this mixture into a 1 1/2-inch layer. Store overnight refrigerated and covered to

blend the seasoning. ◗ To cook, see
I, 634.

## BLOOD SAUSAGE OR BLACK PUDDING

In France, known as **boudin noir;** in
Germany, as **Blutwurst.**
◗ Please read About Sausage, 633.
Have ready:

> **Sausage casings, 1 inch
> wide, (II, 630)**

Cook gently without browning:

> **³/₄ cup finely chopped onions**

in:

> **2 tablespoons lard**

Cool slightly and mix in a bowl
with:

> **¹/₃ cup whipping cream**
> **¹/₄ cup bread crumbs**
> **2 beaten eggs**
> **A grind of fresh pepper**
> **¹/₈ teaspoon fresh thyme**
> **¹/₂ bay leaf, pulverized**
> **1 teaspoon salt**

Add:

> **¹/₂ lb. leaf lard, (II, 203), diced
> into ¹/₂-inch cubes**
> **2 cups fresh pork blood**

Fill casings only three-fourths full;
the mixture will swell during the
poaching period. Without overcrowding, put the sealed casings into a wire
basket. Bring to a boil a large pan
half full of water or half milk and
half water. ◗ Remove pan from heat
and plunge the basket into the water.
Now return pan to very low heat—
about 180°—for 15 minutes. Test for
doneness by piercing sausage with a
fork; if blood comes out, continue to
cook about 5 minutes more or until
barely firm. Should any of the sausages rise to the surface of the simmering liquid, prick them to release
the air that might burst the skins.
To prepare, split and grill them very
gently.

## WHITE SAUSAGE OR BOUDIN BLANC

Delicate, perishable and the most
costly of all.
Please read About Sausage, 633.
Have ready and tied at one end:

> **Sausage casings, 1 inch
> wide, (II, 630)**

Mince:

> **¹/₄ lb. leaf lard or hard back
> fat**

Grind once with the finest blade:

> **¹/₂ lb. pork loin**
> **¹/₂ lb. chicken or rabbit
> breast**

Combine meat with the minced fat.
Add:

> **2 teaspoons salt**
> **1 teaspoon freshly ground
> white pepper**
> **¹/₈ teaspoon each cloves,
> nutmeg and ginger**
> **¹/₄ teaspoon cinnamon**

Regrind with:

> **2 cups chopped
> onions**

Soak in:

> **¹/₄ cup warm cream**
> **¹/₂ cup bread crumbs**

Add to crumbs:

> **3 beaten eggs**

and the meat mixture.
Fill casings only about three-fourths
full, twisting and tying with white
string at 6-inch intervals. Without
overcrowding, put the sealed casings
into a wire basket and plunge them
into boiling water. ◗ Reduce heat at
once to 190°, and continue to cook at
this temperature about 20 minutes.
Should any sausages rise to the surface of the liquid, puncture them to
release air and prevent bursting.
Cool. Brush with:

> **Melted butter**

and grill until golden brown.

## SAUTÉED SAUSAGE MEAT PATTIES

**4 Servings**

▶ Please read About Sausage, 633.
Combine:

**1 lb. sausage meat**
**2 tablespoons flour**
**(¼ cup drained crushed
     pineapple or grated fresh
     apple)**

Shape the meat into patties ½ inch
thick. Sprinkle with:

**Flour**

Rub a skillet with melted suet or butter, and heat. Brown the patties
quickly on both sides. Cover. ▶ Reduce the heat and cook about 10 minutes on one side. Pour off excess fat.
Turn and cook 10 minutes on the
other side until well done. Serve
with:

**Sautéed Onions, 335, or on
Apple Rings, (II, 116)**

garnished with:

**(Parsley)**

## ▤ PAN-BROILED SAUSAGE

**4 Servings**

▶ Please read About Sausage, 633.
Cut apart and place in a skillet:

**8 sausages**

Add:

**½ cup boiling water**

Cover pan. Simmer gently, not over
190°, for 8 to 10 minutes or until almost done. Pour off liquid. Return
sausages to the pan. Cook over low
heat, shaking the pan constantly until
they are an even brown. Drain. Serve
with:

**Prepared mustard**

## TOAD-IN-THE-HOLE

What's in a name? Don't let the toad
in this one deter you! Prepare for
baking:

**Yorkshire Pudding
Cockaigne, 188**

Pan-broil, see left:

**12 small pork sausage links**

Preheat oven to 400°.
Melt in a 2-quart oblong ovenproof
pan:

**5 tablespoons beef drippings
or butter**

Pour pudding batter into pan and
bake about 20 minutes. ▶ Reduce
heat to 350°. Arrange the drained
sausage links on top of batter. Continue to bake 10 to 15 minutes longer.
Serve at once, with:

**Honey Apples, (II, 116)**

## BAKED SAUSAGE MEAT RING

**6 Servings**

▶ Please read About Sausage, 633.
Preheat oven to 350°.
Grease lightly a 7-inch ring mold.
Cover bottom with:

**3 tablespoons cornflakes**

Combine well:

**1 lb. sausage meat**
**1 tablespoon minced onion**
**¾ cup fine bread crumbs**
**2 tablespoons chopped
     parsley**
**1 beaten egg**

Place these ingredients in the mold.
Bake the ring 15 minutes. Drain the
fat and bake 15 minutes longer until
well done. Invert the ring onto a hot
platter and fill the center with:

**8 Scambled Eggs, 215**

Garnish the top with:

**Chopped parsley or
paprika**

## SAUSAGE MEAT, SWEET POTATO AND FRUIT CASSEROLE

**4 Servings**

Doubled, this recipe makes a fine dish for an informal group.

◗ Please read About Sausage, 633.

Preheat oven to 350°.

Peel and cut into thin slices:

**4 large boiled sweet potatoes, 355**

Grease a baking dish. Cover the bottom with half the sweet potatoes. Shape into 4 flat cakes and brown lightly in a skillet:

**1 lb. sausage meat**

to which you may add:

**(1 tablespoon minced bacon)**

Pare and cut into thick slices:

**4 large apples**

or use:

**(Canned pineapple slices)**

Place the drained meat cakes on the sweet potatoes and cover with the bacon bits and fruit. Sprinkle lightly with:

**Salt and brown sugar**

Place the remaining sweet potatoes over the fruit. Brush with:

**Milk**

and sprinkle with:

**Brown sugar**

Bake about 45 minutes.

## APPLE-STUFFED SAUSAGE ROLL

**Serves 8 to 10**

Try this nourishing dish doubled and serve it sliced for a teen-aged group on a winter evening.

◗ Please read About Sausage, 633.

Preheat oven to 350°.

Pat into an oblong about ½ inch thick:

**2 lb. bulk pork sausage**

Combine as a stuffing and mix well:

**2 cups finely chopped apples**
**⅓ cup finely chopped onions**
**1 cup soft bread crumbs**
**1 cup wheat germ**
**2 tablespoons brown sugar**

Spread apple mixture on sausage and roll up like a jelly roll. Bake in a shallow pan about 1 hour.

## FRANKFURTER-SAUERKRAUT CASSEROLE

**6 Servings**

◗ Please read About Sausage, 633.

Preheat oven to 375°.

Toss lightly together and place in a 1½-quart baking dish:

**1 lb. drained sauerkraut**
**½ cup flat beer**
**¼ teaspoon caraway seeds**

Cover and bake about 10 minutes. Top with:

**6 frankfurters**

Return to oven and bake about 20 minutes longer.

## BOILED SAUSAGE

◗ Please read About Sausage, 633.

Place in a kettle:

**Smoked sausage**

Cover with:

**Boiling water**

Simmer about 10 minutes. Drain, skin, slice and serve with:

**Sauerkraut, 308**

## PORK SCRAPPLE OR GOETTA

**About 6 Servings**

◗ Please read About Sausage, 633.

If you use cornmeal, call it scrapple. If you use oats, call it goetta.

Place in a pan:

**2 lb. pork neck bones or other bony pieces**

Add:

**1½ quarts boiling water**
**1 sliced onion**
**6 peppercorns**
**(1 small bay leaf)**

Simmer the pork until the meat falls from the bones. Strain, ▶ reserving the liquor. There should be about 4 cups. Add water or light stock if necessary to make this amount. Using this liquid in place of boiling water, prepare:

**Cornmeal Mush, 180**

You may substitute 1 cup oatmeal for the cornmeal, in which case, reduce liquid by one cup. Remove all meat from the pork bones and chop or grind it fine. Add it to the cooked mush. Season with:

**Salt to taste**
**1 teaspoon or more grated onion**
**(½ teaspoon dried thyme or sage)**
**A grating of fresh nutmeg**
**A little cayenne**

Pour the scrapple into a bread pan that has been rinsed with cold water. Let it stand until cold and firm. Slice it. To serve, sauté slowly in:

**Melted butter or drippings**

## ABOUT VARIETY MEATS

Variety, we know, is the spice of life. And variety meats provide welcome relief from the weekly round of beef, pork, veal, chicken and fish. They include organ meats like sweetbreads, brains, lamb kidney, calf and chicken liver, shown from left to right in the upper row, below; muscle meats like heart, tongue and tripe; and very bony-structured meats like oxtails and knucklebones and their delicious marrow centers, seen again from left to right in the lower row. Time was when most of these tidbits were ours almost for the asking simply because most Americans had built-in prejudices against them. But in recent years, the American passion for travel has developed more cosmopolitan tastes in food, and more of us have learned to appreciate the odds and ends from which European cooks prepare some of their most celebrated dishes. There are practical reasons, too, to serve these delectable oddments: with the exception of calf liver and sweetbreads, now in the higher-priced bracket, they are still gentle to a fragile budget; and last but not least, they contribute significantly to our well-being; although some of

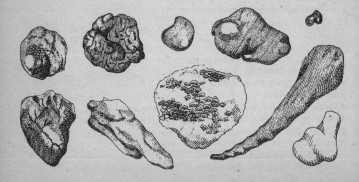

those formerly used, like lungs, are now outlawed. But even the muzzle of beef can be prepared as for tongue, 650. ♦ It is essential that variety meats be fresh. They are highly perishable; use them at once.

## ABOUT LIVER

Chicken and calf livers are the tenderest and most desirable unless, of course, you can secure extra-fat goose livers—the kind which in Europe almost invariably find their way into Pâtés, 629. Baby beef liver comes next for quality. Lamb liver is also tender but less flavorful. Sheep, pork and older beef livers have a strong, distinctive flavor and should be soaked several hours in a spicy marinade or in milk, after which time the liquid is discarded. Pork liver is quite rich in vitamins and minerals and well worth the added effort of trimming out the tough fibers. Since it is pork, ♦ cook it until no pink shows, but try not to overcook.

Most recipes call for ¼-inch-thick sliced liver; however, thick slices over 1 inch may be successfully broiled as for steak.

♦ To prepare any liver for cooking, wipe it first with a damp cloth, then remove the thin outer skin and veining. The outer skin may be easily peeled from fresh liver. Except for the timing noted in individual recipes, the cooking method for liver generally is the same. ♦ Never toughen it by cooking too long or over excessive heat. ♦ Never cook beyond the point of tenderness. Sometimes the drippings in which liver has been cooked are bitter. Test them by tasting before you use them as sauce. Some good sauces to serve with liver are Béarnaise Sauce, 412, Barbecue Sauces, 404, Lyonnaise Sauce, 392,

and Seasoned Butters, 396. ♦ Allow 1 pound liver for 4 servings.

## SAUTÉED CALF OR CHICKEN LIVER OR LIVER LYONNAISE

**2 Servings**

♦ Please read About Liver, left.
Have sliced to a ¼-inch even thickness:

**½ lb. calf liver, or halved chicken livers**

Coat lightly on both sides with:

**Flour**

In a skillet brown the slices quickly over moderate heat, about 1 minute to each side, in:

**1 tablespoon butter**

Add to taste:

**Salt and pepper**

In a separate skillet heat:

**2 tablespoons butter**

Add and sauté until golden:

**¼ cup sliced onions**
**(¼ cup sliced mushrooms)**

Put the liver on a hot plate, cover with the onions and serve with:

**Chopped parsley**
**(Sautéed Bacon, 615)**

The chicken livers may be served on toast.

## ▤ BROILED LIVER

♦ Please read About Liver, left.
Some epicures prefer liver "pure and simple," prepared the following way. We acknowledge its sterling qualities. Place on a broiling rack, about 3 inches from the source of heat:

**Slices of calf liver, ⅓ inch thick**

You may brush them with:

**(Butter or vegetable oil)**

Broil the liver exactly 1 minute on each side.

**Season to taste**

and serve as is, or with:

Mushroom Wine Sauce,
392, or
Madeira Sauce, 391

Or serve with:

Sautéed Bacon, 615
Sautéed Bermuda Onion
Slices, 335

garnished with:

Parsley
A lemon cut into quarters

## BRAISED LIVER WITH VEGETABLES

**6 Servings**

◗ Please read About Liver, 639.

Cut into 1-inch slices:

1½ lb. calf or beef liver

If you use beef liver, you may lard it, 550. Dredge with:

Seasoned Flour, (II, 220)

Brown the liver in:

¼ cup hot bacon drippings

Combine and heap on the slices:

2 diced carrots
2 chopped green peppers,
seeds and membrane
removed
6 small onions
1 cup sliced celery

Add to the pan:

1 cup boiling water or stock

Cover and simmer until the liver is tender. If necessary, add more boiling stock. Calf liver will be tender in about 15 minutes, beef liver in about 30.

## BRAISED LIVER COCKAIGNE WITH WINE

**8 Servings**

◗ Please read About Liver, 639.

Place:

2½ lb. calf or baby beef liver in
1 piece

in the following marinade refrigerated for 1 hour or more:

⅓ cup vegetable oil
1½ tablespoons lemon juice
¼ teaspoon salt
⅛ teaspoon paprika
¼ bay leaf

Turn it from time to time.

Preheat oven to 325°.

Melt in an ovenproof baking dish:

3 tablespoons butter

Add and stir about until lightly cooked:

1 small chopped onion or leek
1 diced carrot
2 or 3 diced ribs celery
2 or 3 minced sprigs parsley
1 tablespoon fresh basil or
tarragon

Place the liver, marinade and all, in the ovenproof dish. Cover closely and bake until nearly tender, about 40 minutes. Baste from time to time. If you wish to serve the liver without further additions, continue cooking it until very tender.

The following ingredients are optional, but they complement the dish. While the liver is cooking, place in a heavy skillet and sauté over very slow heat:

4 slices diced bacon

Cook until the bacon is clear. Add and stir until well glazed:

18 small peeled shallots or
onions
6 large or 8 small sliced
carrots
3 ribs celery, sliced

Add:

1 cup Stock, (II, 171–172), or
canned consommé

Cover the skillet and cook the vegetables and bacon over direct low heat 15 minutes. Add them to the liver in the baking dish, cover and cook 15 minutes longer. Drain the contents of the baking dish, reserving the liquor. Place the liver on a hot platter. Add to the liquor:

½ **cup dry white wine, or**
   ¼ **cup dry sherry**
Cook and stir the sauce over low heat until hot. Pour the sauce over the liver. Serve with:

   **Boiled New Potatoes, 344,**
   **browned in butter**
garnished with:

   **Parsley**

## BEEF LIVER CREOLE

**4 Servings**

▶ Please read About Liver, 639.
Cut into thin slices:

   **1 lb. beef liver**
Dust lightly with:

   **Flour**
Brown the liver in:

   **3 tablespoons hot butter or**
   **drippings**
Add:

   **1¼ cups sliced onions**
   **1½ cups canned tomatoes**
   **½ cup diced celery**
   **1 thinly sliced green pepper,**
   **seeds and membrane**
   **removed**
   **½ teaspoon salt**
   **A few grains cayenne**
Cover the pan and simmer these ingredients about 20 minutes. Drain, reserving the liquid. Thicken with:

   **Flour, see Pan Gravy, 382**
Add the liver and vegetables. Simmer 2 minutes longer. Serve with:

   **Boiled Rice, 189, or**
   **Noodles, 200**

## ▤ LIVER, PEPPER, ONIONS AND OLIVES ON SKEWERS

**4 Servings**

▶ Please read About Liver, 639.
Also see Hot Skewered Tidbits, (II, 87).
Simmer covered in a little boiling water until nearly tender:

   **¾ lb. calf liver in 1 piece**
Drain the liver. Cut it into 1-inch cubes. Peel and quarter:

   **4 medium-sized onions**
Cut into 1-inch pieces:

   **6 strips bacon**
   **2 green peppers, seeds and**
   **membrane removed**
Alternate on skewers pieces of liver, onion, green pepper, bacon and:

   **Stuffed olives**
Place them under a broiler or over heated coals until the bacon is crisp and the liver tender.

## SKEWERED CHICKEN LIVERS

The Hors d'Oeuvre chapter has numerous suggestions for cooking chicken and goose livers en brochette, see About Chicken and Goose Livers as Hors d'Oeuvre, (II, 97); Rumaki, (II, 88); and Hot Skewered Tidbits, (II, 87).

## CHICKEN LIVERS À LA KING

Prepare:

   **1 cup or more Sautéed**
   **Chicken Livers, 639**
Combine with:

   **1 cup Quick à la King**
   **Sauce, 395**
Serve on rounds of toasted whole wheat bread.

## CHICKEN LIVERS IN BATTER

Wipe with a cloth:

   **Chicken livers**
Season them lightly with:

   **Salt and pepper**
Dip them into:

   **Fritter Batter for Meat,**
   **(II, 155)**
Fry them in deep fat, heated to 365° until well browned. Serve with:

   **An omelet, 221**

or as a garnish for a hot vegetable plate.

## CHICKEN LIVERS IN SOUR CREAM SAUCE

**6 Servings**

Cut into halves:

**1 lb. chicken livers**

Sauté until lightly browned in:

**2 tablespoons butter**

**2 tablespoons vegetable oil**

Remove the meat, add to the pan and sauté about 5 minutes:

**¼ cup finely minced green pepper**

**½ cup minced onions**

**1 cup sliced mushrooms**

Sprinkle over the vegetables and stir well:

**2 tablespoons flour**

Add:

**1 cup cultured sour cream**

**¼ cup chicken stock**

Stir and cook gently until mixture thickens. Add the livers and:

**2 tablespoons chopped parsley**

**Season to taste**

When thoroughly heated, serve over:

**Boiled Rice, 189**

or over small rounds of toast.

## GOOSE LIVER

Remove the gallbladder, if attached. Soak in cold salted water for 2 hours:

**A goose liver**

Dry it with a cloth. Sprinkle it with:

**⅛ teaspoon paprika**

**½ teaspoon sugar**

**⅛ teaspoon ginger**

Sauté it in hot goose fat until tender. It is excellent served with sautéed onions and apples and with a little dry sherry.

## ABOUT SWEETBREADS

To paraphrase Puck: "What foods these morsels be!" Veal sweetbreads are those most favored. But beef sweetbreads are sometimes incorporated into mixtures like meat pies, pâtés and terrines. Sweetbreads, properly so-called, are the rounded, more desirable "heart" or "kernel" types, the pancreas. The thinner "throat" type is the thymus.

♦ Like all organ meats, sweetbreads are highly perishable and should be prepared for use as soon as purchased. First soak them at least 1 hour in a large quantity of cold water to release any blood, changing the water 2 or 3 times. Next they must be blanched: cover them with cold acidulated water, 661. Bring slowly to a boil and simmer uncovered from 2 to 5 minutes, depending on size. Drain. Firm them by plunging them at once into cold water. When cool, drain again and trim by removing cartilage, tubes, connective tissue and tougher membrane. Weight them refrigerated for several hours if you plan using them whole. If not, break them into smaller sections with your hands, being careful not to disturb the very fine membrane that surrounds the smaller units.

After these preliminary processes, ♦ to which all sweetbreads must be subjected, you may poach, braise, broil or cream or sauce them. ♦ Allow 1 pair for 2 servings.

## SAUCED POACHED SWEETBREADS

**2 Servings**

♦ Please read About Sweetbreads, above.

Soak, blanch, firm, drain and trim:

**1 pair veal sweetbreads**

Bring to the boiling point:

**Enough water to cover**
**1/4 cup chopped onions**
**3 ribs celery with yellow**
**leaves**
**2 peppercorns**

Drop the sweetbreads into the liquid and ▶ lower the heat at once. Simmer covered with parchment paper, 101, 15 to 20 minutes, depending on size. ▶ Do not overcook. Serve in a delicate sauce such as:

**Béchamel Sauce, 383, or**
**Poulette Sauce, 390**

made with some of the sweetbread liquor as stock, plus:

**1 tablespoon dry sherry,**
**Madeira, brandy or lemon**
**juice**

or use:

**White Wine Sauce, 389**

to any of which you may add:

**(Chopped English walnuts**
**or almonds)**

Sauced sweetbreads are often served on:

**A thin slice of Virginia ham**
**or prosciutto or Canadian**
**bacon**

or in:

**Patty shells, (II, 369), or**
**Bread Cases, 237**

or with a:

**Spinach Timbale, 230; a**
**Vegetable Soufflé, 227; or**
**Wild Rice, 198**

## SAUTÉED SWEETBREADS

**2 Servings**

▶ Please read About Sweetbreads, 642. Blanch, firm, dry, trim and poach about 25 minutes:

**1 pair veal sweetbreads**

Bread with a:

**Seasoned Bound**
**Breading, (II, 220)**

Sauté them in:

**Hot butter**

until they are a rich brown. Serve with one of the sauces in Poached Sweetbreads, 642. Serve with:

**Boiled New Potatoes, 344,**
**and green peas**

garnished with:

**Watercress**

## BROILED SWEETBREADS

**2 Servings**

▶ Please read About Sweetbreads, 642. Soak, blanch, firm, drain, trim and poach about 25 minutes:

**1 pair calf sweetbreads**

Preheat broiler.

Place the broiling rack about 6 inches from the heat source. Break the sweetbreads into large pieces. Roll them in:

**Seasoned Flour, (II, 220)**

Surround them with:

**Strips of bacon**

Secure them with wooden picks. While broiling them, baste frequently with the juices that drip, and if they are rather dry, use additional:

**Butter**

Add to the drippings a small amount of:

**(Sherry or lemon juice)**

Serve with:

**Madeira Sauce, 391,**
**Poulette Sauce, 390, or**
**broiled tomatoes**

or on a bed of:

**Creamed Spinach, 359**

## ▤ SWEETBREADS ON SKEWERS

**2 Servings**

▶ Please read About Sweetbreads, 642.

Soak, blanch about 10 minutes, firm and trim:

**1 pair calf sweetbreads**

Break them into 1-inch chunks. Wrap the pieces with partially cooked:

**Lean bacon, thinly sliced**

Spread:

**Mushroom caps**

lightly with:

**Butter**

Place the wrapped sweetbreads and the mushrooms alternately on skewers. Grill over charcoal until the bacon is crisp. Or you may rest skewers on the edges of an ovenproof pan and bake at 400° about 10 minutes. Serve with:

**Soufflé Potatoes, 350, or
Tomatoes Provençale, 367**


## GLAZED SWEETBREADS

**2 Servings**

◗ Please read About Sweetbreads, 642. Soak, blanch, firm, drain and trim:

**1 pair calf sweetbreads**

Melt in a heavy pan and sauté about 10 minutes or until the onions are translucent:

**3 tablespoons butter**
**2 tablespoons finely julienned carrots**
**2 tablespoons finely chopped shallots or onions**

Add the sweetbreads and stir with the vegetables. Add:

**1½ cups veal stock**

Simmer covered about 20 minutes. ◗ Make sure that the vegetables do not brown. Add more stock, if necessary. When the sweetbreads are cooked, transfer them to an ovenproof serving dish. Keep them warm. Deglaze the pan by the addition of:

**½ cup dry white wine**
**Season to taste**

Preheat oven to 400° for glazing. Reduce pan liquors to about ½ cup. Ladle 2 tablespoons of this glaze over each sweetbread and place the dish in

the oven about 10 minutes, basting often. Meanwhile, melt in a skillet:

**2 tablespoons butter**

Sauté in it:

**½ cup sliced mushrooms**
**¾ cup chopped cooked chestnuts**

Serve the sweetbreads at once on:

**Rounds of toast**

garnished with:

**Finely chopped chervil or parsley**

and surrounded with the mushroom and chestnut mixture.


## RAGOÛT FIN

**4 Servings**

A delicate and far-reaching dish.
◗ Please read About Sweetbreads, 642. Prepare and drain:

**2 pairs poached sweetbreads, 642**

Drain:

**2 cups halved cooked asparagus tips**

Reserve the asparagus liquor. Melt in a heavy skillet:

**¼ cup butter**

Sauté in the butter about 3 minutes:

**½ lb. mushrooms**
**(¼ cup chopped shallots)**

Remove them from the skillet. Add to the fat in it:

**6 tablespoons butter**

Add and stir until blended:

**6 tablespoons flour**

Stir in slowly:

**3 cups liquid: milk or cream, asparagus liquor or stock**

When the sauce is smooth and boiling, gradually add the asparagus tips, the mushrooms and the sweetbreads. ◗ Reduce the heat. Put a small amount of sauce in a separate pan and beat in:

**2 egg yolks**

Add the egg mixture to the sauced sweetbreads and ◗ without letting it boil, stir for about 1 minute very gently, to avoid mashing the asparagus. Season with:

> **Salt and paprika**
> **Freshly grated nutmeg**

Just before serving, you may add:

> **(2 tablespoons dry sherry or 1 teaspoon Worcestershire sauce)**

Serve the ragoût at once in:

> **Hot Patty Shells, (II, 369); on hot buttered toast; in Bread Cases, 236; in a baked Noodle Ring, 201; or on hot Waffles, (II, 150)**

## ABOUT BRAINS

Calf, sheep, lamb, pork and beef brains are listed in order of preference. Brains may be used in all recipes calling for sweetbreads, but, as with sweetbreads, they must be very fresh. ◗ Keep refrigerated, for they are very perishable.

To prepare, give them a preliminary soaking of 1½ to 2 hours in cold acidulated water, 661. After skinning, soak them in several changes of cold water for 1 hour to free them from all traces of blood. Then, as they are rather mushy in texture, firm them by simmering in acidulated water to cover, about 20 minutes for calf brains, 25 for the others. ◗ Be sure the water does not boil. Let the brains cool in the cooking liquid about 20 minutes before draining. If not using immediately, refrigerate the drained brains. Brains are often combined with eggs or with sweetbreads in ragoût and soufflés. Because they are bland, be sure to give the dish in which they are used a piquant flavoring, as suggested, right. ◗ Allow

1 pound of brains for 4 servings or 1 set for 2 servings.

## SAUTÉED BRAINS

> **4 Servings**

◗ Please read About Brains, left.
Prepare by soaking, skinning and blanching:

> **2 sets brains**

Cut in two, lengthwise. Dry them between towels. Season with:

> **Salt and paprika**

Roll them in:

> **Cornmeal or flour**

Melt in a skillet rubbed with:

> **Garlic**
> **⅓ cup butter or bacon drippings**

When the fat reaches the point of fragrance, sauté the brains on each side about 2 minutes. Cover, reduce heat and complete the cooking, about 10 minutes in all. Serve with:

> **Lemon wedges**
> **Thickened Tomato Sauce, 400, or Worcestershire sauce; or Brown Butter, 397, or Black Butter, 397**

## BAKED BRAINS

> **3 Servings**

◗ Please read About Brains, left.
Preheat oven to 400°.
Prepare by soaking, skinning and blanching:

> **1 set brains**

Chop coarsely and combine them with:

> **½ cup bread crumbs**
> **2 chopped hard-cooked eggs**
> **6 tablespoons cream**
> **1 tablespoon catsup**
> **2 peeled chopped green chilis**
> **½ tablespoon lemon juice**
> **Season to taste**

Place in a greased baking dish or in individual dishes. Sprinkle the top with:

**Au Gratin II, (II, 221)**

Bake about 15 minutes.

## BAKED BRAINS AND EGGS

**4 Servings**

♦ Please read About Brains, 645.
Preheat oven to 350°.
Prepare by soaking, skinning and blanching:

**2 sets brains**

Cut into 1-inch dice and place them in 4 small greased casseroles. Skin, seed and dice:

**4 tomatoes**

Combine them with:

**1½ tablespoons hot olive oil**
**1 teaspoon chopped parsley**
**1 teaspoon chopped onion or chives**
**Salt and paprika**
**1 teaspoon brown sugar**

Pour these ingredients into the casseroles. Break into each one:

**1 egg**

Bake about 8 minutes, or until the eggs are firm. Melt and brown lightly:

**¼ cup butter**

Add:

**2 teaspoons lemon juice**

Pour this mixture over the eggs. Garnish with:

**Parsley**

Serve at once.

## BROILED BRAINS

♦ Please read About Brains, 645.
Prepare by soaking, skinning and blanching:

**Brains**

Preheat broiler.
Brush brains with:

**Vegetable oil or melted butter**

Sprinkle with:

**Paprika**

Place broiler about 6 inches from heat source and broil the brains about 8 minutes on each side or until done. Baste with oil or butter. Serve piping hot with:

**Sautéed Bacon, 615**
**Chopped parsley and lemon wedges**

or:

**Grilled Tomato Slices, 367, and watercress**

## ABOUT KIDNEYS

Veal kidneys are the tenderest and most delicious. Those of lamb are somewhat soft and flat in flavor, but especially suitable for grilling. They should not be washed or soaked in water, as they absorb it. Simply split and remove the cores. Large beef kidneys tend to be hard and strong in flavor and need soaking first for 2 hours in cold salted water. Off-flavors may be withdrawn by blanching II, 106, in acidulated water, 661, for 20 minutes; or, after soaking and drying, the kidneys may be sautéed briefly over brisk heat and allowed to cool partially before further cooking.

The white membrane should be snipped from all kidneys before they are washed. Curved scissors are convenient for this. Removal of membranes is easier if you first sauté the kidneys in fat about 1 minute. Discard the fat.

♦ To prepare for broiling, almost halve the kidneys. Keep them from curling during cooking by skewering them open. Expose the cut side to the heat first.

Veal and lamb kidneys should be cooked as short a time as possible over medium heat. ♦ Do not overcook. The center should be slightly pink. The veal kidney may be left surrounded by its delicious delicate fat, or you can use it for seasoning or render it for deep-fat frying, 94. If kidneys are to be flambéed, never flame for more than 1 minute. Longer exposure to such high heat will toughen them. If kidneys are of the best quality, pan juices may be used. If not, discard the juices and use freshly melted butter or a wine sauce. In any case, ◗ never allow kidneys to boil in a sauce, as this only hardens them. Pour the hot sauce over them or toss them in it for a moment or two.

Beef, mutton and pork kidneys are most often used in terrines, braises and stews, and need the slow, moist cooking that is described in some of the following recipes.

◗ Allow 1 medium-sized veal kidney, 2 or 3 lamb kidneys, 1 1/2 to 2 mutton, 1/2 beef or 1 small pork kidney per person.

## BAKED VEAL KIDNEYS

Note for the lone householder: 1 veal kidney makes a fine little roast for 1 person.
◗ Please read About Kidneys, 646.
Preheat oven to 300°.
Prepare, leaving the fat on, and place in a pan, fat side up:

**Veal kidneys**
Bake uncovered until tender, about 1 hour. Serve with:

**Quick Mushroom Sauce, 395, or Quick Brown Sauce, 394, or Marchand de Vin Sauce, 392**

## KIDNEY NUGGETS

**2 Servings**
◗ Please read About Kidneys, 646.
Preheat oven to 375°.
Prepare for cooking and slice in half:

**4 lamb kidneys or 2 veal kidneys**
Prepare:

**Dressing for Braised Stuffed Pork Chops Cockaigne, 605**
adding:

**1 beaten egg**
Spread the dressing on:

**8 slices of thin lean bacon**
Wrap the spread bacon around the kidney halves and fasten with a wooden pick. Bake about 20 minutes.

## SAUTÉED KIDNEYS OR KIDNEYS BERCY

**3 Servings**
◗ Please read About Kidneys, 646.
Remove some of the fat from:

**3 veal kidneys**
Cut them crosswise into slices, removing all the white tissue. Rub a pan with:

**(Garlic)**
Melt in it:

**1/4 cup butter**
Sauté in the butter until golden:

**1/2 cup sliced onions or shallots**
Remove onions and keep hot. Sauté the kidneys in the hot fat, a quick process, about 5 minutes. Add the onions and season with:

**Salt and paprika**
**1 tablespoon lemon juice or 1/4 cup dry white wine**
You may serve this flambé, 108, with:

**Mushrooms on toast**

## SAUTÉED KIDNEYS WITH CELERY AND MUSHROOMS

**4 Servings**
◗ Please read About Kidneys, 646.
Prepare:

**8 lamb kidneys**
Skin and quarter them. Sprinkle with:

**Lemon juice**

Heat in a skillet:

**3 tablespoons butter or
drippings**

Sauté lightly in the fat:

**1 cup chopped celery
¹/₄ cup chopped onions**

Add the kidneys. Simmer covered
about 5 minutes. Stir in:

**1 tablespoon flour
1 cup hot stock**

When these ingredients are blended,
add:

**¹/₂ lb. chopped mushrooms**

Season the kidneys lightly with:

**Paprika
Worcestershire sauce**

Simmer covered about 15 minutes.
Add and allow to just boil up:

**2 tablespoons dry sherry or
Madeira**

**1 tablespoon chopped parsley
Season to taste**

Serve in a:

**Rice Ring, 189**

or you may cut the caps off:

**(4 Brioches, II, 320)**

Scoop them out, warm in a 350°
oven, insert the hot kidney mixture,
cover with the caps and serve at once.

## ▤ BROILED KIDNEYS

**Allow 1 Kidney per Person**

◗ Please read About Kidneys, 646.
Preheat broiler.
Remove most of the fat from:

**Veal kidneys**

Cut them crosswise into slices. Place
3 to 4 inches from source of heat and
broil them about 5 minutes. Turn, and
baste with:

**Melted butter**

Broil about 5 minutes longer or until
done. Season with:

**Lemon juice
Salt and paprika or freshly
ground pepper**

Serve with:

**Chutney, (II, 685), or Cold
Mustard Sauce, 409**

## ▤ KIDNEYS EN BROCHETTE

**Individual Serving**

◗ Please read About Kidneys, 646. Prepare for cooking, allowing per serving:

**1 veal or 3 lamb kidneys**

Split the kidneys, remove the core
and blanch 2 to 3 minutes in:

**Milk or cold water and
lemon juice**

Dry. Cut in quarters. Wrap pieces in:

**Bacon**

Arrange on skewers and grill or broil
3 inches from heat source, about
3 minutes. Turn and broil 3 minutes
more. Serve at once.

## VARIETY MEAT PATTIES

**4 Servings**

◗ Please read About Kidneys, 646,
About Liver, 639, or About Brains,
645. Prepare one of the following for
cooking and then chop until fine:

**2 pairs blanched brains; 1 lb.
raw liver; or 1 beef, 2 pork
or veal or 5 lamb kidneys**

Sprinkle them with:

**1 tablespoon lemon juice**

Rub a skillet with:

**Garlic**

Heat in it:

**2 tablespoons butter**

Sauté in this lightly:

**1 chopped onion or leek
¹/₂ cup minced celery
2 tablespoons minced green
pepper, seeds and
membrane removed**

Remove from heat. Add the chopped
variety meat and:

**¹/₄ cup dry bread crumbs
¹/₄ cup milk
1 egg**

¼ teaspoon salt

¼ teaspoon freshly ground
pepper

4 drops Worcestershire sauce

(¼ teaspoon caraway or dill
seed)

Drop this mixture by the tablespoon
into a hot pan containing:

2 tablespoons hot bacon
drippings

Brown the patties lightly on both
sides. Serve with:

Quick Tomato Sauce, 400,
Coleslaw, 49, or Vegetables
à la Grecque, 285

## VEAL KIDNEY CASSEROLE

4 Servings

◗ Please read About Kidneys, 646.
Preheat oven to 350°.
Prepare:

4 veal kidneys

Heat them about 1 minute in:

2 tablespoons vegetable oil or
fat

Discard the fat. Skin and dice the kidneys and place them in a heated
ovenproof dish. Heat in a skillet:

1 tablespoon butter

Sauté in the butter:

¼ to ½ lb. sliced mushrooms

2 tablespoons minced onion
or ¼ clove garlic

1 tablespoon minced parsley

Stir and cook these ingredients about
2 minutes. Stir in:

3 tablespoons flour

Stir in:

1 cup boiling Veal or Light
Stock, (II, 171–172)

Bring to the boiling point and add:

¼ cup dry white wine or
½ cup orange juice
Season to taste

Pour these ingredients over the kidneys in the casserole. Cover closely.
Bake about 20 minutes or until ten-

der. You may remove the kidneys and
keep warm, reduce the sauce slightly
if necessary, and then pour the thickened hot gravy over the kidneys.
Have ready, by cutting into triangles:

4 thick slices bread

Sprinkle them with:

Grated cheese

Place bread on top of the kidneys.
Broil until cheese is melted.

## BEEF KIDNEY STEW

4 Servings

A favorite for Sunday breakfast,
brunch or supper.

◗ Please read About Kidneys, 646.
Soak, blanch and cut away all the
white tissue from:

2 small beef kidneys

Drain and cool them. For easier slicing, you may place them in a covered
dish in the refrigerator. When cold,
cut the meat into wafer-thin slices.
Dredge the slices with:

Seasoned Flour, (II, 220)

Melt:

1 or 2 tablespoons butter

Sauté the slices lightly in the hot butter. Remove and keep them warm.
Sauté in the drippings:

½ cup thinly sliced onions

Add the meat and:

1 cup stock or red wine, or
½ cup stock and
½ cup flat beer

Simmer about 15 minutes. If the
sauce is too thin, thicken with:

Beurre Manié, 381

Flavor by adding:

1 slice lemon or 2 tablespoons
tomato paste
Salt and paprika, as needed

Serve with:

Boiled Potatoes, 343, or
Noodles, 200; or on toast or
Bacon-Cornmeal Waffles,
(II, 151)

garnished with:

**Chopped parsley**

## ABOUT TONGUE

Lucky indeed is the cook with the gift of tongues! No matter from which source—beef, calf, lamb or pork—the smaller-sized tongues are usually preferable. The most commonly used and best flavored, whether fresh, smoked or pickled, is beef tongue. For prime texture, it should be under 3 pounds.

♦ Scrub the tongue well. If it is smoked or pickled, you may wish to blanch it first, 106, simmering it about 10 minutes. Immerse the tongue in cold water. After draining, cook as for Boiled Fresh Beef Tongue, below. If the tongue is to be served hot, drain, plunge it into cold water for a moment so you can handle it, skin it and trim it by removing the roots, small bones and gristle. Return it very briefly to the hot cooking water to reheat before serving.

If the tongue is to be served cold, allow it to cool just enough to handle comfortably. It skins easily at this point ♦ but not if you let it get cold. Trim and return it to the pot to cool completely in the cooking liquor. It is attractive served with Chaud-Froid Sauce, 428, or in Aspic, 651.

♦ To carve tongue, cut nearly through at the hump parallel to the base. But toward the tip, better-looking slices can be made if the cut is diagonal.

## BOILED FRESH BEEF TONGUE

**6 to 8 Servings**

♦ Please read About Tongue, above. Place in a kettle:

**A fresh beef or calf tongue, about 2 lb.**

Peel and add:

**2 medium-sized onions**
**1 large carrot**
**3 or more ribs celery with leaves**
**6 sprigs parsley**
**4 peppercorns**
**(4 whole cloves)**
**1 bay leaf**

Barely cover these ingredients with boiling water. Skim off any scum after first 5 minutes. Simmer the tongue uncovered until tender, about 50 minutes per pound. Drain and reserve liquid. Skin and trim the tongue. Reheat in the cooking water before serving with:

**Hot Mustard Sauce, 390;**
**Piquant Sauce, 393; or**
**Horseradish Sauce, 386**

or with:

**Harvard Beets, 300, or**
**capers or chopped pickle**

## BEEF TONGUE WITH RAISIN SAUCE

An undemanding dish to prepare while working on other things in the kitchen.

♦ Please read About Tongue, left.
Boil, as in previous recipe:

**A fresh beef tongue**

After it has been skinned and trimmed, place it where it will keep hot.
For the sauce, make:

**Raisin Sauce, 407**

to which you may add:

**½ cup blanched almonds, (II, 237)**
**¼ cup crushed gingersnaps**
**(2 teaspoons Caramelized Sugar II, (II, 232)**
**Season to taste**

Serve the tongue with:

**A Rice or Noodle Ring, 189, 201, filled with green peas**

## BOILED, SMOKED, CORNED OR PICKLED TONGUE

**6 to 8 Servings**

◗ Please read About Tongue, 650, and blanch as directed:

**A 2-lb. smoked, corned or pickled beef tongue**

Drain, then cover the tongue with:

**Fresh water**

Add:

**1 whole onion stuck with 3 cloves**
**1/2 cup chopped celery with leaves**
**3 bay leaves**
**6 peppercorns**

Simmer the tongue uncovered until tender, about 50 minutes per pound. Drain, skin and trim, as directed. Slice and serve hot with:

**Creamed Spinach, 359**
**Boiled Potatoes, 343**
**Horseradish Sauce, 386**

or cold with:

**Cold Mustard Sauce, 409, or Sauce Gribiche, 422, or Cream Horseradish Dressing, 408**

## TONGUE BAKED IN CREOLE SAUCE

**6 Servings**

◗ Please read About Tongue, 650.
Boil:

**A fresh or smoked beef tongue, about 1 1/2 lb., or 2 veal or 8 lamb tongues**

Skin and trim as directed.
Preheat oven to 375°.
Prepare:

**Creole Sauce, 394**

Place the drained tongue, sliced or unsliced, in a casserole. Pour the sauce over it. Bake covered 1/2 hour. Serve with:

**Chopped parsley**

## TONGUE IN ASPIC

**8 Servings**

A fine-looking dish.
Boil:

**A Smoked Beef Tongue, left**

Drain, skin and trim the tongue, then leave it in the stock until it is cool. Make the following aspic. Soak:

**1 1/2 tablespoons gelatin**

in:

**1/2 cup cold beef stock**

Dissolve this mixture in:

**2 1/2 cups boiling beef stock**
**1/2 cup dry white wine or the juice of 2 lemons**
**1 tablespoon sugar**
**Salt, if required**
**A few drops Caramelized Sugar II, (II, 232), or commercial coloring**
**1 teaspoon Worcestershire sauce**

Chill the aspic, and when it is about to set, add:

**1/2 cup chopped sweet-sour pickles**
**1 cup chopped celery**
**1/2 cup chopped green peppers, seeds and membrane removed**

Have ready a mold or bread pan moistened with cold water. Place a small amount of aspic in the bottom of the mold. If desired, add at this time small cooked carrots, beets, canned mushrooms, etc. Chill the aspic in the pan so it hardens somewhat. Then put the tongue into the mold and pour the remaining aspic around and over it. When well chilled, unmold the aspic onto a platter. Garnish it with:

**Lettuce leaves**
**Deviled eggs**
**Parsley**
**Slices of lemon**

Serve with:

Mayonnaise, 419, or
Mayonnaise Collée, 427

## ABOUT HEART

Heart, which is firm and rather dry, is
best prepared by slow cooking. It is
muscle, not organ meat, and so may
be used in many recipes calling for
ground meat. Before cooking, wash
it well, removing fat, arteries, veins
and blood, and dry carefully. ◗ A 4- to
5-pound beef heart will serve 6; a
veal heart will serve one.

## BAKED STUFFED HEART

**3 Servings**

◗ Please read About Heart, above.
Preheat oven to 325°.
Prepare:

**A small beef heart or 3 veal
hearts**

Tie with a string to hold its shape, if
necessary, and wrap in muslin or foil
and tie. Place on a rack in an ovenproof dish and pour over it:

**2 cups stock or diluted
tomato soup**

Place over the heart:

**4 slices bacon**

Cover the dish closely and bake until tender—if beef, a matter of 3 to
4 hours, depending on size; if veal,
about 2. Remove the heart to a plate
and cool slightly. Heat in a double
boiler, then fill the heart cavity with:

**Apple and
Onion Dressing, 434**

You will need about 1 cup for a veal
heart, about 3 for a beef heart. ◗ To
allow for expansion, do not pack the
dressing. Sprinkle the heart with:

**Paprika**

Return it to a 400° oven long enough
to heat quickly before serving. The
drippings may be thickened with:

**Flour, see Pan Gravy, 382**

## BRAISED HEART SLICES IN SOUR SAUCE

**6 Servings**

A homey treat.
◗ Please read About Heart, left.
Prepare:

**A 4- to 5-lb. beef heart or
6 veal hearts**

If veal, you may halve the heart;
if beef, cut it across the fiber into
1/4-inch slices. Pour into a large
saucepan or ovenproof dish to the
depth of 3/4 inch:

**Boiling water**

Add:

**1/4 cup diced carrots
1/4 cup chopped celery with
leaves
1/4 cup sliced onion
1/2 teaspoon salt
(1/4 cup diced green pepper)**

Place the heart slices on a rack in the
pan, well above the water. Cover
closely. Steam the meat until tender, about 1 1/2 hours for veal and
2 1/2 hours for beef. Strain and reserve the stock. Chill and degrease it.
Save the fat. Reserve the stock. Melt
in the pan:

**3 tablespoons butter or fat
from the stock**

Stir in:

**3 tablespoons flour**

Then add:

**1 1/2 cups stock**

When it reaches a boil, add the meat
and vegetables and ◗ reduce the heat.
Add:

**2 tablespoons lemon juice or
dry red wine
1/2 teaspoon sweet
marjoram or
2 tablespoons chopped
parsley or olives
Season to taste**

When heated through, serve with:

**Spoon Bread, (II, 343),**

**Boiled Rice, 189, or Potato Dumplings, 184**

## ABOUT TRIPE

Tripe is the muscular lining of the four stomachs of ruminants. It includes *plain* tripe from the paunch or belly of the first stomach, the rumen; *honeycomb,* the most available, along with the fatter, partially honeycombed *gras double* near the belly end of the second stomach, or reticulum; *feuillet* or *manyplies* from the third stomach, the omasum; and *reed* from the fourth stomach, the abomasum.

Honeycomb tripe is the most delicate variety and today comes either in refrigerated plastic pouches or in large sheets, and fresh tripe usually comes already blanched and parboiled. After cutting into pieces, wash thoroughly. It is now ready to season and cook. ♦ Since tripe is very perishable, it should be kept refrigerated and used as soon as possible.

If you start from scratch, cooking tripe is a long-drawn-out affair. Fresh whole tripe calls for a minimum of 12 hours of cooking, some time-honored recipes demanding as much as 24. To prepare fresh tripe, trim if necessary. ♦ Wash it thoroughly, soaking overnight, and blanch, 106, for ½ hour in salted water. Wash well again, drain and cut for cooking. When cooked, the texture of tripe should be like that of soft gristle. More often, alas, ♦ because the heat has not been kept low enough, it has the consistency of wet shoe leather.

Sometimes tripe is pickled after cooking and served hot or cold in a marinade. Pickled tripe may also be found in the market.

Trim, wash, soak, blanch, wash again, drain and cut into 1½-inch squares:

**3 lb. fresh tripe**

Wash and blanch about 5 minutes:

**2 calves' feet, split**

Peel and slice:

**2 lb. onions**

Dice:

**¼ lb. beef suet**

Line the bottom of the casserole with a layer of onions, then a layer of tripe and a sprinkling of the beef suet. Sprinkle each layer with:

**Salt and pepper**

Continue to build successive layers, topping with the split calves' feet and:

**An onion stuck with
3 cloves
A bay leaf
A Bouquet Garni, (II, 253)**

Pour over this:

**¼ cup brandy or Calvados or dry white wine**

and enough:

**Hard cider or cider**

to cover all the ingredients. Seal the casserole with a strip of pastry dough, or cover with a double thickness of foil and tie securely. Cover with a lid. No steam should escape. Bring to a boil and transfer at once to the oven. Put a drip pan under the casserole just in case! Bake in the oven at least 12 hours. When ready to serve, break the seal on the casserole, remove the bouquet garni, the bay leaf and the whole onion. Degrease the sauce and pick the meat from the calves' feet. Return the meat to the casserole to heat through and serve the tripe in individual hot covered casseroles with:

**Boiled Potatoes, 343**

garnished with:

**Chopped parsley and chives**

## FRIED TRIPE

◗ Please read About Tripe, 653.
Cut into squares or strips:

**Cooked Tripe, 653**

Or, you may use blanched and par-boiled tripe, but it will need about 2½ hours of simmering first in salted water.
Sprinkle with:

**Salt and paprika**

Dip it into:

**Fritter Batter for Meat, (II, 155)**

Fry in deep fat heated to 365°. Serve with:

**Tartare Sauce, 421**

## SPANISH TRIPE

**6 Servings**

◗ Please read About Tripe, 653.
Wash well, then cut into 1½-inch strips:

**2 lb. tripe, blanched and parboiled**

Boil the tripe, covered, about 2½ hours in:

**Salted water**

Drain. Heat in a skillet:

**2 tablespoons vegetable oil or olive oil**

Add and sauté until golden:

**½ cup chopped onions
1 clove garlic, pressed**

Add:

**1 cup tomato purée
1 small diced green pepper, seeds and membrane removed
½ teaspoon thyme, basil or oregano
1 bay leaf
½ teaspoon salt
Freshly ground pepper**

Cover and simmer about 15 minutes. Add the tripe and:

**(½ cup cooked minced ham)**

(½ **cup sliced mushrooms**)

Simmer 15 minutes more. If the sauce is too dry, add a small amount of:

**Red wine**

Good served with:

**Boiled Rice, 189**

## LAMB FRIES

Also known as animelles, frivolitées or "mountain oysters," these testicles of young lambs are a great delicacy.

To prepare, first cut into the loose outer skin for the entire length of the swelled surface. Remove this skin and again cut into the two inner skins in the same manner, disturbing the flesh as little as possible in peeling off these skins. An oval flesh form will remain. Soak the peeled fries in enough cold water to cover for about 3 hours, refrigerated, changing the water several times during this period. Drain. Cover fries with fresh cold water. Bring to a boil. ◗ Reduce heat at once and simmer about 6 minutes. Drain again and plunge into cold water until cool.

**I.**

**2 Servings**

Prepare as above and slice thinly crosswise:

**4 lamb fries**

Fry in deep fat heated to 365° until golden. Serve with:

**Lemon slices**

or combine with:

**Scrambled Eggs, 215**

**II.**

**2 Servings**

Prepare as above and slice across in ⅓-inch slices:

**4 lamb fries**

You may marinate them about 1 hour in:

(¼ **cup olive oil**)

(2 **tablespoons lemon juice**)

(1 **teaspoon tarragon**)

If you have marinated them, dry before rolling them in:

(**Bound Breading, (II, 220)**)

Or, simply sauté them briskly until golden in:

¼ **cup butter or butter and olive oil**

Garnish with:

**Deep-Fried Parsley, 338**

and serve with:

**Quick Tomato Sauce, 400**

## CALF OR LAMB HEAD

**4 Servings for a Calf Head—**
**2 Servings for Lamb**

It is always so easy to say, "Let the butcher prepare, etc." In this case, it is assumed that he has been more than duly accommodating: he has removed the eyes, and skinned the head, then split it the long way to facilitate removing the brains. These we prefer to cook separately, 645, as well as the tongue, 650. After scraping away blood clots, soak overnight refrigerated in salted cold water to cover:

**1 calf or lamb head**

Wash again in cold water. You may dry the head and brown it in butter or put in a large kettle and bring to a boil:

**Enough water to cover the head**

with:

**1 carrot**

**1 onion**

½ **sliced lemon**

**1 bay leaf**

**4 cloves**

**1 tablespoon salt**

¼ **teaspoon pepper**

You may also add, to keep the bones white:

(1/2 cup veal kidney fat or suet)

When this mixture reaches a boil, add the head. ◗ Reduce the heat at once and simmer uncovered until the meat is tender, about 1 hour for lamb, about 2 hours for calf. If you have included the tongue, it may take a little longer. When the meat is tender, drain and remove it from the bones and dice it. Keep the meat warm. Skin, trim and slice the tongue. Meanwhile prepare a double portion of:

**Rosemary Wine Sauce, 392**

using as stock the liquid in which the calf head was cooked.

**Season to taste**

You may wish to spice the sauce with:

**(Mild white wine vinegar, lemon juice, or dry white wine)**

Reheat the meat, the tongue and the cooked brains in the sauce. ◗ Do not boil. Serve this dish garnished with:

**Chopped parsley**

## HEAD CHEESE OR BRAWN

**4 Servings**

A well-liked old-fashioned dish of jellied meat. Have the butcher skin and quarter:

**A calf head**

Clean teeth with a stiff brush and remove ears, brains, eyes, snout and most of the fat. Soak the quarters about 6 hours in cold water to extract the blood. Wash them. Barely cover with fresh cold water, to which you may add:

**(2 onions)**

**(5 cut-up celery ribs)**

Simmer until the meat is ready to fall from the bones, about 2 to 3 hours. Drain but reserve stock. Chip the meat off the bones. Dice it. Reduce the stock by one-half. Cover the meat well with the stock. Reserve the brains. Now add:

**1 tablespoon salt**

**1 teaspoon pepper**

**1/8 teaspoon hot pepper sauce**

**1/2 teaspoon mace or sage**

Cook for 1/2 hour. Pour into a mold and cover with a cloth. Put a weight on top. Chill. Serve, cut into slices, with:

**French Dressing, 413**

to which you have added the diced cooked brains.

## BRAISED OXTAILS OR OXTAIL STEW

**6 Servings**

Preheat oven to 350°.

Melt in a large heavy pan:

**1/4 cup butter or beef drippings**

Brown in the fat:

**3 oxtails, joints separated**

Add:

**3 cups hot Brown Stock, (II, 171), or 1/2 stock and 1/2 tomato juice**

**1 teaspoon salt**

**2 peppercorns**

Bring these ingredients to a boil, then place them in a casserole, cover, and bake until oxtails are tender, 3 to 5 hours, adding more stock if needed. For the last 45 minutes or so of cooking add:

**8 small peeled onions**

**1/2 cup diced celery**

**1/4 cup peeled diced carrots**

Strain stock from the oxtails and skim off most of the fat. Thicken stock with:

**Flour, see Pan Gravy, 382**

**Season to taste**

Combine meat, vegetables and gravy. Serve with a platter of:

**Boiled Noodles, 200**

covered with:

**Au Gratin II, (II, 221)**

## JELLIED PIGS' OR CALVES' FEET

**6 Servings**

Wash, leave whole or split in halves:

**6 pigs' or calves' feet**

You may wrap and tie them in cheesecloth to retain their shape. Cover them with water. Add:

**1 large sliced onion**
**1 cut clove garlic**
**1 sliced lemon**
**2 bay leaves**
**3 or 4 whole black peppercorns**
**6 or 8 whole cloves**

Bring this mixture to the boiling point. ◗ Reduce the heat and ◗ simmer uncovered about 4 hours. Add boiling water, if needed. Strain the stock through a sieve and cook until reduced by one-third. Remove the skin and the bones from the pigs' feet. Place the meat in the stock. Season to taste with:

**White vinegar or dry white wine**

Chop and add:

**(1 pimiento, optional but decorative)**

Pour the pigs' feet or calves' feet into a mold and chill until the stock is firm. Slice and serve cold with:

**Rémoulade Sauce, 420**

## STEWED PIGS' FEET

**6 Servings**

Follow the recipe for:

**Jellied Pigs' Feet, above**

During the last 30 minutes of simmering, add:

**1½ to 2 lb. green beans, cabbage or sauerkraut**

Cook the vegetables with the pigs' feet until tender.

**Season to taste**

and serve hot.

## PIGS' KNUCKLES AND SAUERKRAUT

**8 Servings**

Combine in a large pot with a lid:

**2 lb. sauerkraut**
**4 cleaned pigs' knuckles**
**1 onion stuck with 2 cloves**
**1½ teaspoons caraway seeds**
**1 teaspoon pepper**
**2 cups beer, white wine or stock**

Cover and ◗ simmer gently until the meat is tender, about 3 hours. Serve with:

**Boiled Potatoes, 343, or Mashed Potatoes, 344**

## PIGTAILS

Wash and blanch II, 106, about 3 to 5 minutes:

**Pigtails**

Skim the scum off and simmer 1½ to 2 hours in a seasoned stock as suggested in:

**Jellied Pigs' Feet, left**

Drain. Cut into serving lengths and serve with:

**Turnip Greens, 323**

You may make a sauce from the reduced liquid in which the meat was cooked, adding a little:

**Lemon juice**

## PIGS' EARS

Singe and clean the insides well:

**Pigs' ears**

Cover with:

**Salted boiling water**

seasoned with:

**A Bouquet Garni, (II, 253)**
**An onion stuck with 3 cloves**

◗ Reduce the heat at once to a simmer and cook about 50 minutes. Skin the ears and cut into coarse julienne

strips, 310, or in halves. You may
bread them with:

**(A Bound Breading,
(II, 220))**

and deep-fry them at 365°, or pan-fry
them. Serve as a garnish for a pork
roast or as an entrée with:

**Mashed Potatoes, 344**

## CHITTERLINGS

**6 to 7 Servings**

We were well along in years before
we discovered that the name of this
dish had an "e," an "r," a "g"—and
3 syllables, and still farther along before we found these were the base for
the sausage, **Andouillette,** the French
set such store by. Just after slaughtering, empty the intestines of a young
pig while still warm, by turning them
inside out and scraping the mucous
covering off completely. Wash in
cold water, then soak 24 hours refrigerated in cold salted water to cover.
Then wash again in 5 or 6 waters. Remove excess fat, but leave some for
flavor.
Put in a large pot with enough water
to cover:

        10  lb. chitterlings cut into
            2-inch lengths
         1  garlic clove
         2  teaspoons salt
       1/2  teaspoon pepper
       1/2  teaspoon each thyme, clove,
            mace and allspice
         1  bay leaf
       1/4  cup sliced onions
        (3  red pepper pods)
         2  tablespoons fresh parsley
         2  tablespoons white wine
            vinegar

Bring slowly to a boil. Cover and
♦ reduce the heat at once and simmer 3 to 4 hours. Stir occasionally to
keep it from sticking. During the last
30 minutes of cooking, you may add:

        (1/4  cup tomato catsup)
            **Season to taste**

and serve with:

**Corn Bread, (II, 341), or
Black-Eyed Peas, 294**

## SAUTÉED CHITTERLINGS

Prepare previous recipe for:

**Chitterlings**

omitting the vinegar and catsup.
When tender, drain and dry well. Dip
them in:

**Seasoned Flour, (II, 220)**

Sauté gently in:

**Butter**

until a delicate brown.

## CHICKEN GIBLET STEW

Dice, put into boiling water or stock,
then ♦ reduce the heat at once and
simmer until tender, about 1 hour:

**Chicken giblets: gizzards
and hearts**

Add, for the last 15 minutes of
cooking:

**Chopped green pepper,
seeds and membrane
removed
Diced onion
Sliced carrot
Chopped celery**

Drain these ingredients, reserving the
stock. Make:

**Pan Gravy, 382**

using:

        2  tablespoons butter
        2  tablespoons flour to 1 cup
           stock, or stock and dry
           white wine
           **Season to taste**

Add the giblets and vegetables and
simmer ♦ but do not boil. Serve on:

**Toast**

or with:

**Rice or noodles**

## COCKSCOMBS

These have been used since the time of Apicius as a garnish for chicken dishes.

Blanch:

**Cockscombs**

Peel off the outer skin. ◗ Steam, covered, on a:

**Mirepoix, (II, 254)**

moistened with:

**1 cup Light Stock,
(II, 171–172)**

until tender, about 45 to 50 minutes. Drain well, cut an incision and stuff with:

**Duxelles, (II, 255), or
Chicken Farce, 437**

Dip in:

**Allemande Sauce, 390**

then in crumbs and fry in deep fat heated to 365° until the crumbs color.

## ABOUT MARROW

Spinal marrow may be substituted in any of the recipes for brains. Bone marrow may be removed from split large bones. ◗ It must not be overcooked, as it is very fat and simply disintegrates under too high heat. It may be cut into 1/2-inch slices and softened in the top of a double boiler over—not in—boiling water; or gently and briefly poached in a little stock 1 1/2 to 2 minutes. Serve on small toast rounds as an appetizer. It may also be gently poached in the bone in water barely to cover, or baked in a 300° oven about 1 hour. If you have used spinal marrow, remove the filament before serving. See also Marrow Balls, 174, and Osso Buco, 591.

# GAME

Through the ages every art lover has enjoyed vicariously the excitement of the chase. Those of us with sportsmen in the family have had more immediate gustatory pleasures. Venison has again become easily available to hunters in many sections of the country, and small creatures are still triumphantly pursued by the rural young. Friends from France have told us of stirring and fashionable boar hunts around Poitiers in their youth. Although we never expect to hear the hunting horn ourselves or to see the fierce tusks of this formidable foe on our own table, we have had the fun of the symbolic substitute, 667, during the holiday season. And with protein so sought after, we may all become more interested in having a colony of coneys nearby from which to make Hasenpfeffer in a handsome clay casserole, as shown above. May these recipes be a help.

## ABOUT SMALL GAME

Small game should be dressed as soon as possible, see Preparing Game, (II, 626). If you are a novice, the most important things to remember are the following: ◗ Never handle any wild meat without using gloves, because of the danger of tularemia infection. ◗ Always make sure the meat of wild animals is sufficiently cooked because any omnivorous warm-blooded animal may be harboring trichinosis. Be guided in your choice of recipe by the age of the animal, using a moist-heat process, 98, for older animals. Some of the most delicious game sauces use blood as a thickener. To trap and preserve the blood, see (II, 627). To incorporate it into a sauce, see 380.

Small game such as rabbit, squirrel and muskrat may be substituted in most recipes calling for chicken. Here are some classic, and some not so classic, recipes which take into account the special characteristics of these small animals.

## ABOUT RABBITS AND HARES

Rabbits weigh between 3 and 5 pounds, while hares may weigh up to 10 to 14 pounds. European hare is all dark meat, while American domestic hare is all white. When rabbit or hare is young and fresh, the cleft in the lip is narrow, the claws smooth and sharp. Test for the youth of the animal, also, by turning the claws sideways. If they crack, the animal is old. The ears should be soft and should bend easily. A young hare has a stumpy neck and long legs. To ensure tender meat, hang the animals by the feet from 1 to 4 days. They will be tender without hanging, however, if used before they have time to stiffen. Once stiffened, they are edible as long as the hind legs are rigid, but if the joint has become pliable, discard them.

◗ To dress rabbit or hare, don gloves to avoid possible tularemia infection. Sever the front legs at the joint as shown, 662, by the dotted line. Cut through the skin around the hind legs the same way. Tie the feet together securely. Hang the rabbit on a hook where tied. From the dotted line pull skin off the legs toward the hind feet, stripping it inside out like a glove. Then pull the remaining skin over the body and forelegs. Sever the head and discard it with the skin. Slit the rabbit down the front. Remove the entrails and discard them, except for the heart and liver. Wash the carcass inside and out with **acidulated water**—water to which 1 or 2 tablespoons of vinegar have been added. Rinse and dry carefully. Cook by any recipe calling for chicken, especially highly seasoned dishes like curries, or use any of the following recipes.

## SAUTÉED RABBIT

If rabbit is very young, prepare as for:
>    **Sautéed Chicken, 517**

Serve with:
>    **Elderberry preserves**

## ROAST RABBIT OR HARE

Preheat oven to 450°.
Skin and clean:
>    **A young rabbit or hare**

Stuff it with any recipe suitable for fowl, adding the rabbit's sautéed chopped liver. Truss it. Brush the rabbit all over with:
>    **Melted butter or vegetable oil**

Dredge with:
>    **Seasoned Flour, (II, 220)**

Place on a rack on its side in a roasting pan in the oven. ◗ Reduce the heat to 350°. Baste every 15 minutes with the drippings in the pan or, if necessary, with:
>    **(Additional butter)**

Turn the rabbit when cooking time is about half over. Cook until tender, about 1½ hours. Make:
>    **Pan Gravy, 382**

Serve with:
>    **Grated fresh horseradish and Boiled Potatoes, 343**

## FRICASSEE OF RABBIT OR HARE

Skin, clean and cut into pieces:
>    **A rabbit**

Dredge with:
>    **Seasoned Flour, (II, 220)**

Melt in a skillet:
>    **¼ cup butter**

or you may use:
>    **(¼ lb. diced, lightly rendered salt pork)**

Add:
>    **¼ cup chopped shallots or onions**
>    **(1 cup cut-up mushrooms)**

Remove the shallots and mushrooms before sautéing the meat in the drippings until lightly browned. Flambé the rabbit by pouring over it:
>    **(2 oz. brandy)**

Add:

**1½ cups stock or dry wine**

and, in a cloth bag:

**A piece of lemon rind**

**3 peppercorns**

**2 sprigs parsley**

**2 ribs celery with leaves**

Cover the pot closely. Simmer the meat until done, 1 hour or more, or put it in a 300° oven covered for about 2 hours—but ◗ do not let it boil at any time. Ten minutes before you remove the rabbit from the pot, take out the seasoning bag and add the mushrooms and shallots. Place the rabbit on a hot serving dish. Remove the sauce from the heat and thicken with:

**Beurre Manié, 381**

## BRAISED RABBIT OR HARE WITH ONIONS

Skin, clean and cut into pieces:

**A rabbit**

Dredge with:

**Seasoned Flour, (II, 220)**

Melt in a pot or skillet:

**3 tablespoons drippings or butter**

Sauté the rabbit in the drippings until browned. Cover thickly with:

**Sliced onions**

Pour over them:

**1 cup cultured sour cream**

Cover and simmer 1 hour, or place the pot in a 300° oven and bake the rabbit until tender, about 1½ hours.

## RABBIT À LA MODE OR JUGGED HARE

In Germany this marinated stew of either hare or rabbit is known as **Hasenpfeffer;** in France, jugged rabbit is **civet de lapin,** and jugged hare is **civet de lièvre.**

Skin:

**A rabbit**

Cut into pieces by severing the legs at the joints and cutting the back into 3 sections. Place the pieces in a crock or jar. Marinate refrigerated 24 to 48 hours in:

**Cooked Marinade for Game, (II, 182)**

Drain and reserve the marinade. Dry the pieces of rabbit. Dip them in:

**Flour**

Brown until golden in:

**3 tablespoons bacon drippings**

Remove the browned rabbit to an ovenproof casserole.

Preheat oven to 300°.

Sauté in the pan the rabbit was browned in:

**1 cup finely chopped onions**

**2 tablespoons butter**

Add the sauté to the casserole with the warmed marinade and bring to a boil on top of the stove. ◗ Remove at once, cover and place in the oven about 2 hours or until tender.

**Season to taste**

Place rabbit on a serving dish and pour sauce over it. Serve with:

**Noodles, 200**

## CASSEROLED RABBIT AND SAUSAGE

**4 Servings**

Skin, clean and cut into pieces:

**A rabbit**

Place pieces in a large skillet and add:

**1 lb. pork sausage or**
**3 smoked pork sausages**
**1 cup beer**
**¼ cup cider vinegar**
**1 cup consommé or stock**
**1 cup browned bread crumbs**
**or ¼ cup rice**
**1 teaspoon caraway seeds**
**1 teaspoon grated lemon peel**
**1 teaspoon brown sugar**
**Salt and pepper**

Bring to a boil, then ◗ reduce heat, cover and simmer gently 2 hours. Skim off fat before making:

**Pan Gravy, 382**

## RABBIT WITH CHILI BEANS

**4 Servings**

Skin, clean and cut into pieces:

**A rabbit**

Brown the pieces in a large skillet in:

**2 tablespoons olive oil**

with:

**1 clove garlic, pressed**

Add:

**1 cup hot water or light stock**
**½ teaspoon salt**
**½ teaspoon pepper**
**1 small can tomato paste:**
**6 oz.**
**1 teaspoon chili powder**
**2 cups kidney beans**

Cover and simmer gently about 2 hours. Before serving, sprinkle with:

**2 tablespoons grated cheese**

Place under broiler until the cheese is golden.

## SQUIRREL

◗ Please read About Small Game, 660. Gray squirrels are preferred to red squirrels, which are quite gamy in flavor.

◗ To skin, don gloves to avoid possible tularemia infection. Cut the tail bone through from beneath, but take care not to cut through the skin of the tail. Hold squirrel by the tail and then cut the skin the width of the back, as shown above. Turn the squirrel over on its back and step on the base of the tail. Hold the hind legs in one hand and pull steadily and slowly, as shown in the center sketch, until the skin has worked itself over the front legs and head. While holding the squirrel in the same position, pull the remaining skin from the hind legs. Proceed then as for Rabbit, 662, cutting off the head and the feet and removing the internal organs, plus two small glands found in the small of the

back and under each foreleg, between
the ribs and the shoulders.

Stuff and roast squirrels as for
Doves or Wood Pigeons, 544, barding
them, or as for Braised Chicken with
Fruit, 518, or use them in Brunswick
Stew, 522. Season the gravy with:

**Walnut Catsup, (II, 687)**

and serve with:

**Polenta, 180**

## OPOSSUM

Please read About Small Game, 660.
If possible, trap 'possum and feed it
on milk and cereals for 10 days before killing. Clean, but do not skin.
Treat as for pig by immersing the unskinned animal in water just below
the boiling point. Test frequently by
plucking at the hair. When it slips out
readily, remove the opossum from
the water and scrape. While scraping
repeatedly, pour cool water over the
surface of the animal. Remove small
red glands in small of the back and
under each foreleg between shoulder
and ribs. Parblanch, 106, about 20
minutes each, in two or three changes
of water, then roast as for pork, 601,
or use recipes for rabbit. Serve with:

**Turnip greens**

## PORCUPINE

◗ Please read About Small Game,
660. Skin by hanging back legs from
hooks. Remove several kernel-like
glands in small of back and under
forelegs. Hang in a cool dry place 48
hours. Soak overnight refrigerated in
salted water:

**A porcupine**

In the morning, bring this water to a
boil. Drain and immerse porcupine
again in cold water. Bring to a boil
and again drain. Place the meat in a
Dutch oven. Add:

3 cups water or light stock
1 rib celery, chopped
1 sliced medium-sized onion
1/4 teaspoon pepper
1 teaspoon salt

Simmer until tender, about 2 1/2 hours.

## RACCOON

◗ Please read About Small Game,
660. Skin and remove glands in small
of back and on either side of spine,
and one under each foreleg of:

1 raccoon

Remove all fat, inside and out. Soak
overnight refrigerated in:

**Salt water**

Blanch, 106, for 45 minutes. Add:

2 tablespoons baking soda

and continue to cook uncovered for
5 minutes. Drain and wash in warm
water. Put in cold water and bring to
a boil. ◗ Reduce heat and simmer 15
minutes.

Preheat oven to 350°.

Stuff the raccoon with:

**Sweet Potato and Apple
Dressing, 437**

Bake, covered, about 45 minutes.
◗ Uncover and bake 15 minutes longer
before serving.

## MUSKRAT

**4 Servings**

◗ Please read About Small Game, 660.
Skin and remove all fat from hams
and shoulders of:

1 muskrat

These are the only edible portions.
Remove musk glands under legs and
belly and white stringy tissue attached to musk glands. Poach, 101, in
salted water for 45 minutes. Drain.
Place cut-up meat in Dutch oven and
cover with:

**Bacon strips**

Add:

1 **cup water or light stock**
1 **small sliced onion**
1 **bay leaf**
3 **cloves**
½ **teaspoon thyme**

Cover and simmer until very tender. Serve with:

**Creamed Celery, 312**

## WOODCHUCK

♦ Please read About Small Game, 660. After field-dressing woodchuck and hanging it for 48 hours, skin as for rabbit, but watch for and remove 7 to 9 small kernel-like glands under the forelegs. Soak refrigerated overnight in salted water. Drain and wipe dry. Cook by any recipe for rabbit or chicken.

## BEAVER

♦ Please read About Small Game, 660. Use young animals only. Remove all surface fat when skinning, but avoid cutting musk glands, which must be removed from beneath the skin in front of the genital organs. Also remove kernels in small of back and under each foreleg. Hang in the cold for several days. Poach, 101, in salted water for 1 hour. Braise as for beef, 554, until tender.

## BEAVER TAIL

To Indians and settlers alike, this portion of the animal was considered the greatest. Hold over open flame until rough skin blisters. Remove from heat. When cool, peel off skin. Roast over coals or ♦ simmer until tender.

## ARMADILLO

Under its shell this small scaly creature has a light meat, porklike in flavor. Draw and cut free from the shell:

1 **armadillo**

Discard fat and all but the back meat. Wash thoroughly in cold water and soak overnight refrigerated in cold water. Drain and dry. To cook, cut into pieces. Brush well with:

**Butter or vegetable oil**

Broil until the meat is a rich brown.

**Season to taste**

and serve at once.

## ABOUT LARGE GAME

Today, when hunters are so aware of the need to treat their booty with care from the moment it is shot, joy can prevail. See About Preparing Game (II, 626). No matter what the method of handling, certain preparations are basic. Game shot in an unsuspecting moment is more tender and will also deteriorate less quickly than game that is chased. Avoid buying any trapped animals for food. Immediate and careful gutting, immediate removal of all hair near exposed flesh, and prompt skinning are essential. In dressing game, be careful not to cut into musk glands on lower belly.

♦ Care must be taken to remove all fat from any of these game animals, as it grows rancid quickly. ♦ Do not use it to grease pans or for sautéing or browning. The livers and heart, after cooling, are often eaten at the campsite. As with all game, the lushness of the season and the age of the animal contribute to the decision as to how to cook it. For Marinades for Game, see (II, 182). Buttermilk Marinade, (II, 181), will lessen the gamy flavor of the antlered animals.

For sauces for game, use a Cumberland Sauce, 407–408. Cabbage, turnips, chestnuts and mushrooms are often suggested as classic game accompaniments, as are brandied fruits.

## ABOUT VENISON

This romantic word can cover any of the edible animals taken in the chase, but we are discussing here only antlered types. A famous sportsman called venison a gift of joy to some, a matter of secret interment to others. ♦ Please read About Large Game, 665.

The choice cuts of very young deer and of fat old bucks can be roasted or broiled as for beef. Since venison is lean, it needs larding, 550, or barding, 511. Other cuts should be marinated and cooked as for any moist-processed beef, 554. Reindeer meat also is cooked as for beef.

Moose meat, which is relatively fat, calls for cooking like pork and can also have the same sweet and sweet-sour garnishes and sauces. Elk is close to beef in taste and texture. Cook elk calf as for veal, but watch it for spoilage, as it sours quickly.

**Mouffle,** the loose covering around the nose and lips of the moose or elk, is prized for stewing or roasting. Cook as for Fresh Tongue, 650.

## SADDLE OF DEER, MOOSE OR ELK

**8 Servings**

Preheat oven to 550°.
Lard, 550:

> **A 6- to 7-lb. saddle of venison**

Rub it with:

> **A cut clove of garlic**
> **Butter**

Place the roast, fat side up, uncovered on a rack in the oven. ♦ Reduce the heat to 350° and bake, allowing in all 20 minutes to the pound. Make:

> **Pan Gravy, 382**

Serve with:

> **Hot Cumberland Sauce, 407–408**
> **Wild Rice, 198**

## ROAST LEG OF VENISON

Bard, 511, the roast. Cook as for Roast Beef, 565.

## SAUTÉED VENISON STEAKS

**I.** Have ready:

> **Young venison steaks, 1/2 inch thick**

Before cooking, rub with:

> **Garlic**

To keep them crisp and brown on the outside, rare and juicy within, sauté them in:

> **1 tablespoon butter**
> **2 tablespoons vegetable oil**

5 to 6 minutes to the side. Serve with:

> **Hot Cumberland Sauce, 407–408**

or with:

> **Maître d'Hôtel Butter, 398**

or with:

> **Puréed celery with croutons and Sauce Poivrade, 393**

**II.** Soak for 24 hours refrigerated:

> **Venison steaks, 3/4 inch thick**

in:

> **Lamb or Game Marinade, (II, 181)**

Drain and dry. Sauté and serve as directed in I, above.

## BRAISED VENISON

For this process, use the less tender cuts of meat either in 1 large piece or cut into small ones, but be sure to remove all fat. Place the meat in a marinade, (II, 181–182), from 12 to 48 hours in the refrigerator. Turn it from time to time. Dry it. Prepare as for Pot Roast, 573. Use the marinade in the stock. Cook until tender; the length of time will depend on the age of the animal.

## VENISONBURGER

To make this lean meat more interesting in ground form, combine:

**2 parts ground venison**

with:

**1 part fresh sausage meat**

Cook as for Hamburger, 616, but allow extra time ▶ to be sure the meat is no longer pink.

## VENISON MEAT LOAF

Prepare:

**Meat Loaf I, 627**

using:

**3/4 lb. ground venison**
**1/4 lb. ground sausage**

## BEAR

▶ Please read About Large Game, 665.

Remove all fat and bone from bear meat. The fat turns rancid very quickly. If rendered at once, it is prized for cooking; if held, it is good only for boot grease. All bear is edible. Tough, strongly flavored bear may be improved by refrigerating at least 24 hours in an oil-based marinade before cooking. Cook, after marination, as for any recipe for Beef Pot Roast or Stew, 573. Bear cub will need about 2 1/2 hours' cooking; for an older animal, allow 3 1/2 to 4 hours. ▶ Bear, like pork, can carry trichinosis, so be sure the meat is always well cooked through.

## PECCARY

Immediately after killing, remove the musk glands in the middle of the back. This meat needs marinating before cooking. After this, you may prepare it as in any moist-heat pork recipe, 605–609.

## WILD BOAR

Use only very young animals, a year or under, and prepare as for:

**Suckling Pig, 603**

If older, prepare by a moist-heat process for:

**Pork, 605–609**

## ★ STUFFED BOAR'S HEAD

**30 Servings**

Among treasured Christmas traditions, like the gilded peacock, the boar's head ranks high, see illustration on 660. While this fierce creature may not be available, his domestic counterpart still subsists in Appalachia and can even be ordered in supermarkets throughout the U.S. during the holiday season. The separate ingredients for the stuffing can be prepared and refrigerated a day or two in advance, with the final mixing taking place immediately before stuffing and roasting the head.

After experiments with several different methods of preparing a boar's head, the following rather unconventional foil procedure was found to be most effective. It culminates in a gloriously glazed and garnished presentation. So gird up your loins for the fray and prepare to receive a hero's reward in gratitude from your assembled guests.

To loosen the head skin and to cook the head meat, place on a shallow rack in a large ham boiler:

**A 15- to 18-lb. head of a
young boar or pig**

with eyes, teeth and brains intact. Pour into the boiler:

**Water**

deep enough to cover 1 inch of the base of the head, and keep the water ▶ simmering at that depth while steaming, covered, 2 to 3 hours.

After removing the head from the boiler, refrigerate it to chill thoroughly. When ready to remove the skin all in one piece, let the head reach a temperature warm enough on the outside so the skin is pliable. Put the head on a large cutting board. With a short thin knife, make a lengthwise incision from the base of the snout to the base of the neck skin. Beginning at the end of the incision, ♦ gently and carefully, especially around the eyes, cut upward under the skin on both sides to loosen the skin as you go. Continue to release the skin, being careful not to puncture it. Some fat will adhere to the skin; leave it on, as it will render away during the roasting and will help give the final brown and shiny look you want in the finished product. Fold and keep the skin chilled in a plastic wrapping until ready to stuff it.

Now start to remove the head meat. If it proves not to be tender enough to cut easily into bite-sized pieces, return the skinned head to the pot and steam 1 hour longer. When cutting, discard as much of the fat as possible. If meat still seems undercooked, you may sauté the small pieces very slowly until gray throughout. Discard the overcooked brains and eyes. Also discard the skull, and refrigerate the head meat until ready to prepare the stuffing.

### STUFFING FOR BOAR'S HEAD

Have ready:

> A 2- to 3-lb. cooked Boston butt pork roast, cut into bite-sized pieces
> 2 lb. cooked ground pork sausage
> 7 cups Boiled long-grain Rice, 189

Heat in a very large pot:

> 5 tablespoons butter

Add and sauté until golden, then cover and simmer until tender:

> 2 cups chopped onions
> 1 cup chopped celery
> 1 tablespoon poultry seasoning or Four Spices, (II, 253)
> 1 to 1½ teaspoons sage
> ½ teaspoon salt

Gently stir in:

> 1 cup dry white wine
> 1 cup Chicken Stock, (II, 172)
> 1 lb. coarsely chopped walnuts or Boiled Chestnuts, 313

and the cut-up cooked pork, the cooked sausage and the head meat. If there is excess fat, remove it. Take the pot off the heat and add:

> 6 cups seasoned coarse dry bread crumbs or cubes

The stuffing should have a ♦ moist, not wet, quality, as fat rendered from the skin will give it added cohesion. If you feel it needs more moisture, you may add:

> (½ cup additional wine or stock)

Preheat oven to 325°.

Now to the stuffing of the skin, which needs two people. Have the skin at room temperature or warm enough so it is pliable. Prepare a large roasting pan with a rack. Cover the rack with heavy-duty foil, first lengthwise and then crosswise, allowing long enough pieces to eventually encompass the whole head and form a pyramid shape over the top. Neatly cut a lengthwise 5-inch gash through the center of the foil to allow excess fat to drain into the roaster. Place the skin "face up" in the middle of the foil, with the snout facing you. Should the skin have split at the bridge of the snout during the steaming, you can repair it with skewers or by sewing it with loose stitches, using a coarse thread and a meat or upholstery needle, 551. Do not tighten the stitches, as the stuffing will expand and damage the skin further. Or, you may even leave the split if you subsequently tighten the foil well when shaping up the head.

As one person lightly stuffs the hollow head, his helper carefully draws the foil up and around the head skin, letting it assume its own shape. You may have to lift the head slightly for it to shape up. When no more stuffing can be inserted without packing it, cover the open cavity with foil and crimp the foil tightly over the bridge of the snout and over eye openings, carefully pulling so it conforms to the head shape and also supports it. Protect the ears with additional foil so they will not burn.

Put any leftover stuffing in a separate ovenproof dish for the last hour of baking the head. Bake the head about 2 hours or until the skin is brown and lightly crisped. Serve on a large platter with the foil cut away. Surround with a lush bed of garnishes such as:

**Glazed Vegetables, 283**
**Colorful drained poached fruits, (II, 110–111), or greens**

Place in each eye:

**Halves of hard-cooked egg, 212**

and under the snout:

**An apple**

For tusks, use:

**Small scraped carrots**

and, traditionally, a small flag is waving from the top of the head when it is brought to the table with a fanfare! The boar's head may be served with your favorite Christmas roast.

# INDEX

"Knowledge," said Dr. Johnson, "is of two kinds. We know a subject as our own, or we know where we can find information on it." Below we put into your hands the second kind of knowledge—a kitchen-door key which will help to open up the first.

If you want information on a certain food, you will find that the initial listing is often an "About," giving characteristics, peculiarities of handling, tests for doneness, storage needs and serving quantities. The titles which follow usually indicate how that particular food may be cooked: Sweetbreads, braised, or Fish, broiled.

In using the Index look for a noun rather than an adjective: Cake, almond, not Almond Cake; unless the modifying term is a foreign one, in which case it will be listed and lead you to an explanation. Foreign terms are frequently translated in an alternate title, thus: Pickled Fish or Escabèche, revealing a process; or, as in Senegalese or Chicken Curry Soup, showing the ingredients mainly responsible for the term. Or the recipe itself will clear your doubts—"à la mode" used with a savory food like beef will describe a stew, whereas with a sweet one, like pie or cake, it will indicate the expected scoop of ice cream. Since cooking terms, both foreign and domestic, are dealt with at the point of use, as described above, we have dispensed with a separate glossary.

Remember, too, that the book as a whole divides into three sections—The Foods We Eat, The Foods We Heat and The Foods We Keep—with Know Your Ingredients at the center of things; and that many "convenience" recipes are grouped under Lunch, Brunch and Supper Dishes. Within chapters, too, initial text or recipes often cover basic methods of preparation, and are followed, as in Fruits, Fish and Vegetables, by alphabetical listings of varieties—from Acerola to Tamarind, Carp to Sea Squab, Artichoke to Zucchini. Under Meats you will find in the Index general comments and processes, with further references to Beef, Veal, Lamb, Pork, Ham, Ground and Variety Meats and Game. In this chapter a further differentiation is made between those cuts cooked by dry heat—often a quick process—and those cooked by moist heat, which, to be effective, is always slower. Note, too, that in the listings below, you can find the illustrations immediately by looking up the italic numerals.

As you familiarize yourself with the **Joy**, you will need the Index less and less and will become, in the fullest sense of Dr. Johnson's words, a know-it-all. Meanwhile, happy hunting!